The Law of the Sea is a fascinating area for a variety of stakeholders: from dedicated mariners working in the challenging and dangerous maritime environment, to maritime lawyers applying the rule of law, to politicians seeking to exercise their dominion and control over national waters and resources, to citizens and consumers trying to understand the implications of the Law of the Sea to their daily lives. "A Practical Guide to the Law of the Sea" seeks to introduce this robust topic, and to place it in context regardless of the reader's particular background.

A PRACTICAL GUIDE TO THE LAW OF THE SEA

James P. Benoit

Cover designed by James P. Benoit

Printed in the United States of America

First Printing: January 2021
Second Printing: July 2021

ISBN-13 978-1-6994950-7-0

To Alina, my love, my life, my muse, my wife,
but most importantly the loving mother
of our beautiful son Jayden,
who is the light of our lives.

CONTENTS

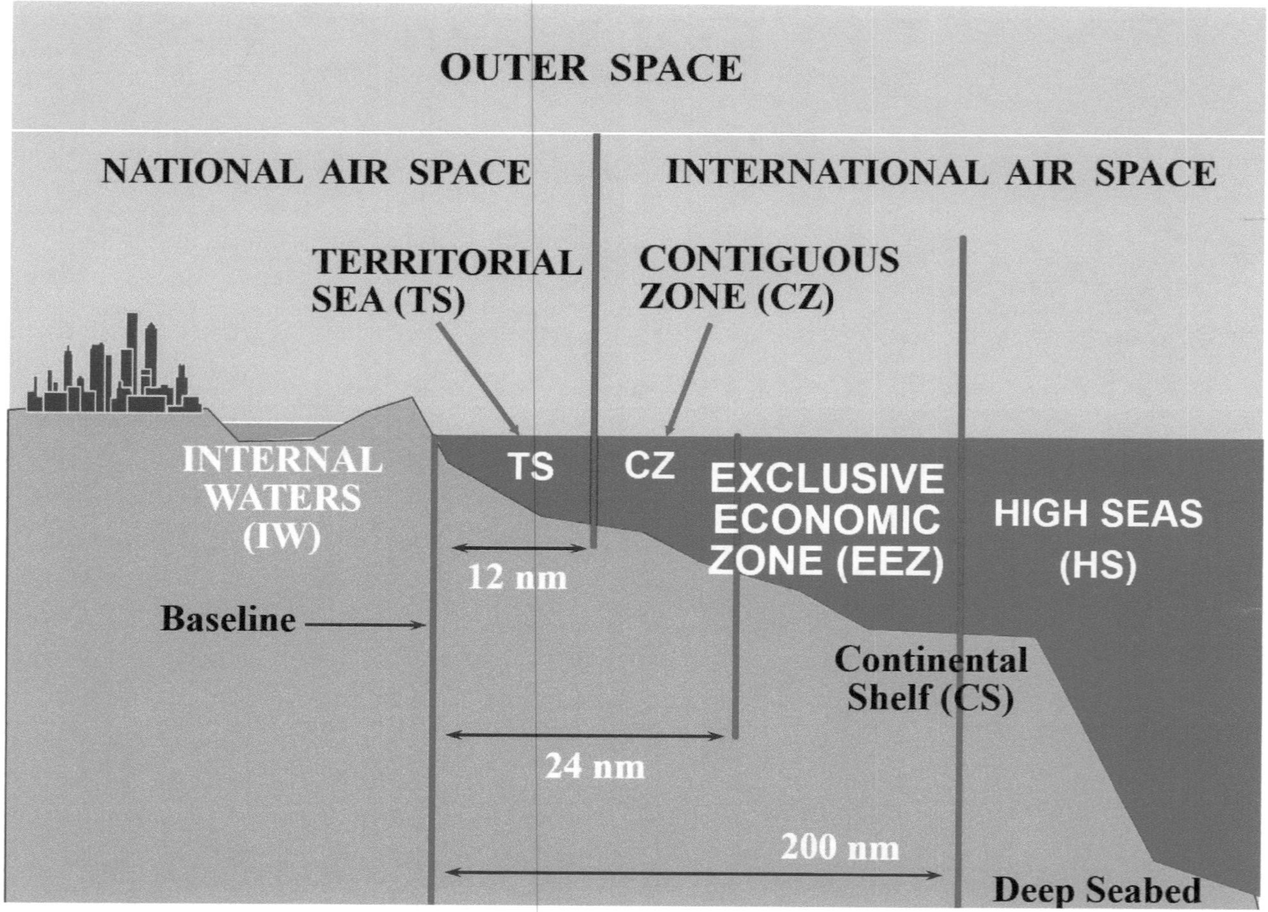

OUTER SPACE

NATIONAL AIR SPACE

INTERNATIONAL AIR SPACE

TERRITORIAL SEA (TS)

CONTIGUOUS ZONE (CZ)

EXCLUSIVE ECONOMIC ZONE (EEZ)

HIGH SEAS (HS)

Continental Shelf (CS)

Deep Seabed

INTERNAL WATERS (IW)

Baseline

TS

CZ

12 nm

24 nm

200 nm

CHAPTER 1: INTRODUCTION & OVERVIEW

"The oceans are in trouble. Our coasts are in trouble. Our marine resources are in trouble ... all perhaps in serious trouble."
— United States Commission on Ocean Policy

THE LAW OF THE SEA touches on a wide variety of subjects: from environmental law and fisheries, to international relations between States,[1] to international commercial law, to international crimes (such as piracy), to national security law, to the law of armed conflict. The paramount importance of the maritime environment cannot be overstated. Seventy-one percent of the earth's surface is covered by water. The overall economic value of the oceans has been estimated to be worth at least $24 Trillion.[2] There are extensive mineral and petroleum resources on the seafloor, both in areas controlled by States (on their Continental Shelves[3] below their Exclusive Economic Zones),[4] and beneath the High Seas[5] on the Deep Seabed. "Oceans produce half the oxygen we breathe and absorb 30% of carbon dioxide emissions."[6] Twenty percent of the protein consumed by humans originates in the oceans. Over eighty percent of the world's trade is carried by sea,[7] yet the maritime shipping industry remains largely insular and opaque.[8]

In terms of the marine environment, here's the bottom line up front (BLUF): we've taken the oceans for granted for centuries, and now we're seeing the negative effects of doing so. The world's population has increased dramatically since World War II, especially along the coasts.[9] This has led to increased ocean pollution from non-point sources,[10] such as farming, urban runoff, and air pollution, which wash pollutants such as fertilizers, pesticides, oil, chemicals, and litter (especially plastics)[11] into rivers and coastal waters. Globally, fish stocks are being increasingly depleted to the point of failure (i.e., extinction).[12] In short, it is difficult to balance the competing uses of the oceans with the need to maintain their ecological and economic value.

The maritime domain is also marked by a number of "hot spots," where geography, local politics, and international relations make for very interesting international dynamics. The Middle East has been described as "the poster child for instability."[13] Nothing typifies this statement more than the Strait of Hormuz (SOH), which connects the Arabian Sea with the Persian (aka Arabian) Gulf. Sixty percent of the world's oil reserves sit beneath the

Persian Gulf's shores, and seventeen million barrels of crude oil exports pass daily through the Strait of Hormuz. The Strait of Hormuz is patrolled by Iran's two Navies: the regular Iranian Navy, which is small and

professional but underfunded, and the Islamic Revolutionary Guard Corps Navy (IRGCN), which is controlled by Iran's religious leaders, appears to be much better funded, and has consistently been much more provocative, especially with its well-armed fast inshore attack craft.[14] "Sadly, harassment by the IGRC Navy is not a new phenomenon …. It is something that all our commanding officers and crews of our vessels are trained for, when serving in the Central Command area of responsibility, particularly in and around the [Persian] Gulf."[15]

The South China Sea (including the Spratly and Paracel Islands) has been a contentious area since at least 1968[16] when oil was discovered there; huge oil and gas reserves are believed to lie beneath its seabed.[17] Vietnam, Malaysia, Brunei, the Philippines and China all claim ownership

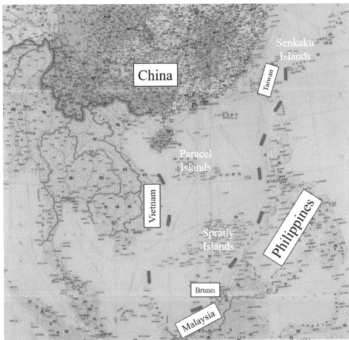

of the islands and sovereignty over some or all of the waters, which reveals the need for international dispute settlement.[18] The purchase of three of the Senkaku Islands by the Government of Japan, and China's subsequent submission of baseline coordinates around the islands to the United Nations, has escalated tensions between Japan and China,[19] as have nearby patrols and harassment by Chinese government ships.[20] The South China Sea is "one of the great contemporary pressure cookers of international relations",[21] and is a very timely, real-world example where Law of the Sea impacts on national and international security.

Another maritime hot spot is the Western (aka Yellow) Sea between North and South Korea. The 1953 Korean Armistice Agreement established a military demarcation line between North and South Korea on land, but did not delimit a maritime border in the Western Sea. United Nations (UN) forces (led by the United States) unilaterally set the "Northern Limit Line" north of the South Korean islands (blue line A below). In 1999 (forty-six years later), North Korea unilaterally asserted a maritime Military Demilitarization Line (red line B below), which provides South Korea with very narrow (3 nautical mile (nm)[22] wide) maritime "corridors" to reach its islands. Since 1999, North Korean vessels

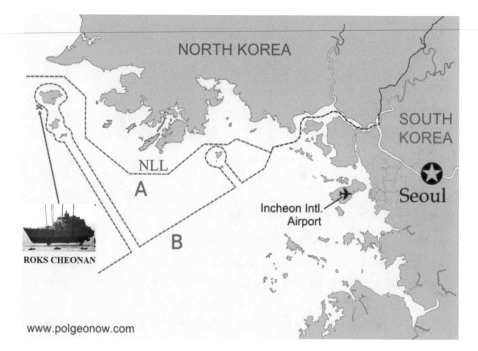

have crossed the Northern Limit Line, but usually return north when challenged by South Korean naval vessels. However, there have been collisions, occasional exchanges of naval weapons fire, and the South Korean Navy corvette ROKS CHEONAN was sunk in the Yellow Sea just south of the disputed Northern Limit Line.[23] The maritime border between North and South Korea would appear to be a prime candidate for mandatory dispute settlement under the United Nations Convention on the Law of the Sea (UNCLOS).[24] However, like the United States, North Korea is **not** party to UNCLOS. Moreover, in 2006, South Korea "opted out" of mandatory dispute settlement for delimitations of maritime borders.[25] Therefore, until international relations between North and South Korea "normalize" and they are able to negotiate an equitable settlement, the maritime border between North and South Korea is likely to remain in limbo.

The first half of this book lays out the various maritime zones and each of their "regimes" (i.e., set of rules). [NOTE: There is a diagram of the various maritime zones at the beginning of the Chapter.] The latter half of this book then delves into specific maritime issues that deal with the application of these rules (e.g., fisheries, regulation and enforcement, illegal maritime activities, excessive maritime claims, etc.). "Terms of art" within the Law of the Sea are capitalized (e.g., Territorial Seas), since they have specific meanings. The endnotes at the end of each Chapter (in a smaller font & highlighted in light grey) provide sources and references for further study if desired.

Because the Law of the Sea touches on such a wide variety of subjects, it is a fascinating area for a variety of stakeholders: from dedicated mariners working in the challenging and dangerous maritime environment, to maritime lawyers applying the rule of law, to politicians seeking to exercise their dominion and control over national waters and resources, to citizens and consumers trying to understand the implications of the Law of the Sea to their daily lives. This book seeks to introduce this robust topic, and to place it in context regardless of the reader's particular background.

---

[1] In international relations (and in international law), "State" refers to a sovereign nation or country, and shall be used accordingly in this book. For example, a "Coastal State" (aka a "littoral State") is a nation with a coastline.

[2] World Wildlife fund (WWF), Stories, *Ocean Assets Valued at $24 Trillion, but Dwindling Fast* (Kimberly Vosburgh, Apr. 22, 2015), https://www.worldwildlife.org/stories/ocean-assets-valued-at-24-trillion-but-dwindling-fast.

[3] Chapter 6 discusses the Continental Shelf and Deep Seabed.

[4] Chapter 4 discusses the Exclusive Economic Zone (EEZ).

[5] Chapter 5 discusses the High Seas and associated High Seas freedoms.

[6] WWF, Stories, *Ocean Assets Valued at $24 Trillion, but Dwindling Fast* (full cite above).

[7] United Nations Review of Maritime Transport, https://www.un-ilibrary.org/transportation-and-public-safety/review-of-maritime-transport_70fdea36-en. Ninety-five percent of American imports and exports are moved via maritime shipping. Real time maritime shipping maps are available online. Marine Traffic, Live Map http://www.marinetraffic.com/en/ais/home/centerx:25/centery:37/zoom:3.

[8] "Humans have sent goods by water for four thousand years," yet the largest container shipping company in the world (Maersk) is largely unknown to the public, except in Denmark where it is the largest company. Rose George, NINETY PERCENT OF EVERYTHING 4-8 (2013).

[9] Coastal areas comprise only seventeen percent of the United States, yet half of the American population lives there. Eighty-five percent of U.S. tourism revenues originate from the 180 million people who visit U.S. coastal areas every year. Twenty-five percent of U.S. domestic energy production is from offshore oil and gas facilities.

[10] Whereas a point source for pollution has a discrete source (e.g., an old automobile spewing exhaust), a non-point source of pollution has many, diffuse sources (e.g., more modern automobiles polluting just a bit each).

[11] Chapter 5 discusses the Environment, including the problem of plastic pollution in the oceans.

[12] Chapter 7 discusses fisheries and overfishing.

[13] Global Risks 2035: The Search for a New Normal, Atlantic Council Strategy Papers, Foreword by Lt. Gen. Brent Scowcroft, USAF (Ret.), Chairman, Int'l. Advisory Board, Atlantic Council (2016), *webcast available at* https://atlanticcouncil.org/event/global-risks-2035-search-for-a-new-normal/.

[14] For example, on January 6, 2008, five IRGCN patrol boats rapidly approached three United States Navy (USN) warships on a collision course in the Strait of Hormuz. The patrol boats refused to respond to hails on the radio from the USN ships, circled them, and dropped several packages into the water. The USN ships took the threats seriously, and maintained a defensive posture. American officials said the Iranians "harassed and provoked" the three USN vessels, coming within two hundred yards of one warship. *See also* Military.com, Military News, *US Navy*

Fires Warning Shots at Iranian Fast Attack Craft (Patricia Kime, Apr. 27, 2021), https://www.military.com/daily-news/2021/04/27/us-navy-fires-warning-shots-iranian-fast-attack-craft.html (describing how 2 U.S. patrol boats were harassed by armed IRGCN speed boats, and ultimately needed to fire warning shots to stop the harassment); Military.com, News, Headlines, *Swarm of Iranian Boats Harassed US Ships in Persian Gulf, Navy Says* (Gina Harkins, Apr. 15, 2020), https://www.military.com/daily-news/2020/04/15/swarm-iranian-boats-harassed-us-ships-persian-gulf-navy-says.html?ESRC=eb_200416.nl (providing details of a similar swarm of 11 IRGCN patrol boats that aggressively maneuvered within 10 yards of a U.S. Coast Guard Cutter, and harassed other U.S. naval vessels operating in the Northern Arabian/Persian Gulf for an hour on April 15, 2020); Military.com, News, Headlines, *Will Navy Ships Really Open Fire on Harassing Iranian Gunboats? It Depends, Officials Say* (Richard Sisk, Apr. 22, 2020), https://www.military.com/daily-news/2020/04/22/will-navy-ships-really-open-fire-harassing-iranian-gunboats-it-depends-officials-say.html?ESRC=navy-a_200429.nl (quoting the U.S. Vice Chairman of the Joint Chiefs of Staff as indicating that the Captain of the U.S. ship decides whether to respond with lethal force to harassing Iranian gunboats). Chapter 3 discusses international straits, including the Strait of Hormuz.

[15] Military.com, Military News, *Coast Guard Cutter Fires Warning Shots at Charging Iranian Speedboats* (Stephen Losey, May 10, 2021), https://www.military.com/daily-news/2021/05/10/coast-guard-cutter-fires-warning-shots-charging-iranian-speedboats.html. The terms "ship" and "vessel" are not defined in UNCLOS, but are considered to be synonymous. Letter Of Transmittal Forwarding The 1982 UN Law Of The Sea Convention To The United States Senate, DOS Commentary p. 93 (William J. Clinton, Oct. 7, 1994) (S. Treaty Doc. 103–39), https://www.foreign.senate.gov/imo/media/doc/treaty_103-39.pdf.

[16] Mark E. Rosen, *U.S. International Oceans Law and Policy Interests in the South China Sea Arbitration: Implications for the U.S. Administration in the South China Sea and Elsewhere*, 22 J. OF CHINESE POLIT. SCI. 251, online unnumbered p. 4 (2017), https://www.readcube.com/articles/10.1007/s11366-017-9468-9.

[17] Rosen, *South China Sea Arbitration*, p. 4 (full cite above); China claims the resources inside its "9-dash line" are worth $1 trillion.

[18] Chapter 12 discusses Mandatory Dispute Settlement, including the South China Sea and China's claimed "9-dash line."

[19] "The United States has repeatedly stated that the Senkakus, as a territory administered by Japan, are covered by Article V of the U.S.-Japan mutual defense treaty. A Chinese attack on the Senkakus, to include actions by the [Chinese coastal police agencies (CCG)], would trigger U.S. defense obligations under the treaty." Raul (Pete) Pedrozo, *Maritime Police Law of the People's Republic of China*, 97 INT'L. L. STUD. 465, 469 (2021), https://digital-commons.usnwc.edu/ils/vol97/iss1/24/.

[20] Raul (Pete) Pedrozo, *U.S. Recognition of Japanese Sovereignty Over the Senkaku Islands*, 97 INT'L. L. STUD. 652, 654-655 (2021), https://digital-commons.usnwc.edu/ils/vol97/iss1/30/ (noting that "[s]ince mid-April 2020, Chinese government ships have maintained a near continuous presence in the waters off the Senkakus," and arguing that by "[r]ecognizing Japanese sovereignty over the islands [the U.S.] would demonstrate strong support for our extremely important ally in the Pacific and would send a clear message to Beijing that the United States will stand up to Chinese aggression in the region and not abandon its allies and partners.").

[21] universitätbonn institute for public int'l. law, Bonn Research Papers on Public Int'l. Law, Paper No 14/2018, *The South China Sea Arbitration: Observations on the Award of 12 July 2016*, p. 99 (Stefan A. G. Talmon, May 17, 2018), https://papers.ssrn.com/sol3/papers.cfm?abstract_id=3180037.

[22] Chapter 2 explains what is a nautical mile (nm).

[23] In March 2010, the South Korean Navy corvette ROKS CHEONAN sank in the Yellow Sea (just south of the disputed Northern Limit Line near Baengnyeong Island) after an explosion in the ship's stern. Forty-six of the 104 South Korean sailors either died or remain missing. South Korea led a team of international experts (from South Korea, United States, United Kingdom, Canada, Australia, and Sweden) in conducting an official investigation, which concluded that the warship was sunk by a torpedo fired by a North Korean midget submarine. North Korea denied responsibility.

[24] United Nations Convention on the Law of the Sea (UNCLOS), Dec. 10, 1982, 1833 U.N.T.S. 397, https://www.un.org/Depts/los/convention_agreements/convention_overview_convention.htm.

[25] Chapter 12 discusses Mandatory Dispute Settlement, including the ability of a State to "opt out" of mandatory dispute settlement.

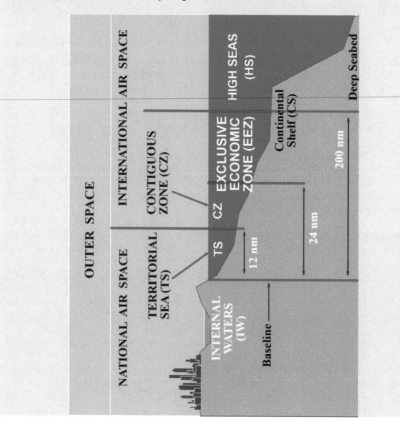

CHAPTER 2: HISTORICAL DEVELOPMENT & BASELINES

States drafting the United Nations Convention on the Law of the Sea (UNCLOS) sought to "establish[] ... a legal order for the seas and oceans which will facilitate international communication, and will promote the peaceful uses of the seas and oceans, the equitable and efficient utilization of their resources, the conservation of their living resources, and the study, protection and preservation of the marine environment".
—UNCLOS Preamble.[26]

"FROM THE TIME THE SEAS BEGAN TO BE USED FOR THE CONDUCT OF COMMERCE AND WAR, politicians, merchants, and scholars have debated who could use the sea and who could control it."[27] The modern law of the sea evolved in the 16th and 17th centuries, and was the foundation for modern public international law.[28] In particular, the catalyst for the Law of the Sea was the 17th Century debate over States'[29] rights to exercise "freedom of the seas," versus the extent to which States should be able to assert sovereignty over the ocean, particularly the seas immediately adjacent to their coastlines. This debate was dubbed the "Battle of the Books," with its primary authors being the young Dutch scholar Hugo Grotius and a number of other writers arguing the counter position, including the English jurist John Selden and the Scottish jurist William Welwood.[30]

Young master Grotius argued for the **inclusive** use of ocean space as a free and open trading highway for ships of all nations. Grotius contended that, by its nature, ocean space was not subject to occupation and therefore could not be claimed as property, but instead should be available for all to use.[31] He argued for the most important inclusive use of all, freedom of the High Seas for international trade.[32] Scottish Judge Welwood argued for Scotland's ability to limit Dutch fishing in Scottish coastal waters.[33] Twenty years later, English Judge Selden argued that a Coastal State[34] had a natural right to exercise **exclusive** control over the waters and resources off its coast, and to use appropriate force to ensure its exclusive use.[35] Nevertheless, Grotius' view of "freedom of the seas" prevailed, and formed the basis for modern international law—hence Grotius is viewed as the father of international law.

Under the "freedom of the seas" doctrine, oceans were broadly divided into two main areas: a Coastal State's Territorial Waters generally extending out to one marine league or three nautical miles (nm)[36] from the coastline, and the High Seas beyond.[37] Yet some European States continued to claim sovereignty over larger maritime areas:

As noted by J.L. Brierly, "[a]t the dawn of international law most maritime states claimed sovereignty over certain seas; Venice claimed the Adriatic, England the North Sea, the Channel, and large areas of the Atlantic, Sweden the Baltic, and Denmark-Norway all the northern seas." Similarly, C. John Colombos has noted that "[u]p to the end of the eighteenth century there was no part of the seas surrounding Europe free from the claims of proprietary rights by individual Powers, nor were there any seas over which such rights were not exercised in varying degrees." Throughout this era, the maritime regions were viewed as a web stretching across the world's oceans, porous in some areas, impermeable in others.[38]

Nevertheless, "freedom of the seas" remained the overarching principle of the Law of the Sea until shortly after World War II, when President Truman issued Proclamation 2667, unilaterally extending U.S. jurisdiction over the natural resources found on the

"the continental shelf [which] may be regarded as an extension of the land-mass of the coastal nation".[39] President Truman's proclamation became "instant" Customary International Law as other States quickly followed suit.[40]

Additional pressure was placed on freedom of the seas by States seeking to expand not only **ownership of resources on the seabed** (i.e., on their Continental Shelves), but to vastly expand their **sovereignty claims over the ocean itself**.[41] The bottom line is that after World War II, States began to encroach on the freedom of the seas that had existed for over 300 years. Potential encroachment on the resources of the Deep Seabed[42] concerned other States, particularly the smaller and newly independent States, who saw these resources as being the "common heritage of mankind,"[43] and therefore not subject to any one State's possession or control.[44] These concerns reveal the inherent diplomatic or political aspect of the Law of the Sea,[45] and led to the United Nations (UN) General Assembly adopting Resolution 2750 in 1970 to convene the Third UN Conference on the Law of the Sea.[46]

Before discussing the Third UN Conference on the Law of the Sea, which culminated in the 1982 UN Convention on the Law of the Sea (UNCLOS), we need to understand the two major types of international law. But to understand how international law is formed, we should begin by contrasting it with the formation of national law.

Most democratic States have a legislative branch that prepares legislation (i.e., laws), an executive branch that executes and enforces the laws, and a judicial branch that reviews the validity (e.g., constitutionality) of the laws.

In contrast, there is no international legislature that prepares "laws" applicable to all 195 States in the world.[47] Nor is there an international executive branch that executes or enforces international law.[48] "Inter-national" law is the law between nations (i.e., States), and thus is made by States.[49] "States comply with international law because it is in their interest to do so."[50]

To understand the sources of international law, one must look to a court which is tasked with applying international law. The International Court of Justice (ICJ) is one of the UN "organs" (i.e., bodies), and was created to resolve disputes between States by applying international law. As its founding document, the ICJ Statute directs the "World Court" to consider four sources of International Law:

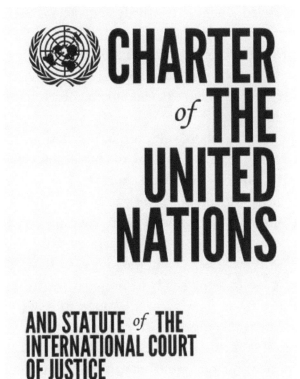

1) International conventions (aka Treaties);

2) Customary International Law (CIL);

3) General principles of law recognized by "civilized" States; and

4) Judicial decisions and teachings of scholars (who are more influential in Civil Law countries in Europe and Asia).[51]

Of these four sources of International Law, the first two are generally considered the most important and the most straight-forward to interpret and apply: Treaties and CIL.[52]

Treaties are akin to a written contract between States, and are only binding on those States who are "party" to the treaty (i.e., those States which have either ratified or acceded to the treaty, and become a "State Party" to the treaty).[53] Since treaties are in written form (although often in more than one official language, which can lead to ambiguity), the specific meaning of their articles (i.e., specific provisions) is somewhat more definitive and less ambiguous than other types of international law.

In contrast, Customary International Law (CIL) develops over time between States, based upon a relatively consistent State Practice done out of a sense of legal obligation.[54] Due to how CIL "crystallizes" into norms (or rules) of international law, CIL is relatively easy to claim but can be difficult to prove.[55] Unlike treaty language which is fairly well-defined, CIL can only be described,[56] and thus is inherently more ambiguous.[57] "Customary international law is the principal source of international law and is binding upon all States,"[58] except for those few States who continue to "persistently object" to the CIL norm.[59] The author likens CIL to a gauzy fabric swaying in the breeze of international relations, to which a more substantial and more definite treaty "patch" may be sewn by agreement between States—the less substantial CIL fabric still exists beneath the more substantial treaty patch, and continues to apply both to non-parties to the treaty, and to help fill in gaps (aka "interstices" or "lacunas/lacunae") in the treaty language.[60]

An example may help shed light on the difference between a CIL norm and mere international custom (which may be performed out of a sense of courtesy or "comity"). Although there is a custom of literally "rolling out the red carpet" for visiting diplomats as they disembark from their airplane, this does not represent CIL because there is no sense of legal obligation—it is done out a sense of courtesy. However, granting "Diplomatic Immunity" to visiting diplomats is done out of a sense of legal obligation: the United States grants Diplomatic Immunity to foreign diplomats stationed in the U.S. in order for U.S. diplomats to be extended similar diplomatic immunity when they are stationed abroad (i.e., to obtain reciprocal privileges). Thus, "Diplomatic Immunity" has been a matter of CIL for thousands of years. Only relatively recently was a treaty developed on the topic of Diplomatic Immunity: The 1961 Vienna Convention on Diplomatic Relations (VCDR).[61] The CIL norm of Diplomatic Immunity is binding as a matter of CIL on all States (even those three States which have yet to ratify the treaty), and as a matter of treaty law on the 192 State Parties to the VCDR.

Now that we've laid the groundwork, let's discuss the three United Nations (UN) Conferences on the Law of the Sea, which eventually culminated in the 1982 UN Convention on the Law of the Sea (UNCLOS). The bottom line up front (BLUF) is that it took twenty-four years and three attempts for the international community of States to fully define the Law of the Sea framework treaty, and another twelve years to amend the treaty in order to try to surmount U.S. objections to ratifying UNCLOS, which has yet to happen. Yet "[t]he U.S. likes UNCLOS because it provides a legal framework that generally advances U.S. interests and gives countries a framework for peacefully resolving maritime rights disputes."[62]

The UN General Assembly adopted Resolution 1105 in 1957 to convene the First UN Conference on the Law of the Sea.[63] After working feverishly for two months, the eighty-six State participants were able to draft four, relatively short treaties on the Law of the Sea, all of which went into effect within eight years: the 1958 Convention on the Territorial Sea and the Contiguous Zone[64]; the 1958 Convention on the High Seas[65]; the 1958 Convention on Fishing and Conservation of the Living Resources of the High Seas[66]; and the 1958 Convention on the Continental Shelf.[67] The 1958 Convention on the Territorial Sea and the Contiguous Zone laid out a "regime" (i.e., set of rules) regarding the Territorial Sea and the Contiguous Zone, including that a State's sovereignty "extends, beyond its land territory and its internal waters, to a belt of sea adjacent to its coast" (i.e., to the Territorial Sea).[68] The 1958 Convention on the Territorial Sea and the Contiguous Zone defined the width of the Contiguous Zone[69] as 12 nautical miles (nm),[70] yet it failed to define the width of the Territorial Sea![71] Similarly, the 1958 Convention on Fishing and Conservation of the Living Resources of the High Seas failed to define fishery limits,[72] and the 1958 Convention on the Continental Shelf failed to define the outer limits of the Continental Shelf![73] Nevertheless, these four 1958 law of the sea conventions form the foundation for the modern Law of the Sea.[74]

One year later (in 1958), the UN General Assembly adopted Resolution 1307 to convene the Second UN Conference on the Law of the Sea specifically to resolve "the breadth of the territorial sea and fishery limits".[75] Unfortunately, after meeting for only six weeks, the eighty-eight State participants in the Second Conference on the Law of the Sea were unable to resolve either question.[76]

Undeterred by this lack of progress, twelve years later (in 1970) the UN General Assembly adopted Resolution 2750 to convene the

Third UN Conference on the Law of the Sea. The General Assembly broadened the scope of the Third Conference on the Law of the Sea to not only consider the breadth of the Territorial Sea and fishery limits, but also the establishment of an "international regime" to equitably share the resources of the Deep Seabed as the "common heritage of mankind,"[77] as well as ownership of resources on the Continental Shelf, "the question of international straits," the Contiguous Zone, preservation of the marine environment including the prevention of pollution, and Marine Scientific Research (MSR).[78]

One hundred and sixty States met over the course of nine years (from 1973 to 1982)[79] in a variety of locales (e.g., Geneva, Caracas, New York, Jamaica) as part of the Third UN Conference on the Law of the Sea, which laid the framework for allocating reciprocal rights and responsibilities between States, carefully balancing the interest of Coastal States (aka "littoral States") in controlling activities off their coasts, with the interests of all States in protecting the freedom to use international waters without undue interference (e.g., freedom of navigation). The concept of a 200 nautical mile (nm)[80] Exclusive Economic Zone (EEZ) was presented for the first time at the Third Conference on the Law of the Sea,[81] with 97% of all known and estimated hydrocarbons and the most lucrative fishing grounds now falling within national jurisdiction as a result.[82]

The U.S strongly supported the initiative of the third Conference and played a leading role in its negotiation over the course of the Nixon, Ford and Carter administrations. U.S. negotiators focused on preserving principles of freedom of navigation and other vital security concerns, as well as protecting the right of the U.S. to conserve and exploit the resources of the continental shelf and the 200-nautical mile exclusive economic zone. The U.S. negotiators were successful in these efforts.[83]

The final vote of the Third UN Conference on the Law of the Sea was held in Montego Bay, Jamaica on April 30, 1982 and was overwhelmingly in support, with only 4 States in opposition.[84] "The 1982 LOS Convention was a monumental achievement in multilateral negotiations."[85] Besides establishing the new Exclusive Economic Zone (EEZ),[86] UNCLOS also defined regimes for Transit Passage through International Straits,[87] and special rules for States comprised entirely of a number of islands (aka Archipelagic States).[88] One of the longest multilateral treaties,[89] UNCLOS was seen as somewhat of a panacea, "package deal,"[90] or *quid pro quo* (solving many issues, and addressing the disparate requirements of a variety of States by providing tradeoffs or "something for everyone"), as well as an umbrella convention,[91] and the "Constitution of the oceans."[92] The 1982 UN Convention on the Law of the Sea (UNCLOS), entered into force on November 16, 1994. "UNCLOS has withstood the test of time. It now has 168 parties, including nearly all the major maritime powers except for the United States."[93]

UNCLOS balances Coastal States' rights to control activities off their coasts, with protecting other States' freedoms:

> *[A] central tenet of the law of the sea ... is the fair balancing of the desire by coastal States to protect their sovereign rights and to conserve and exploit natural resources of neighboring waters with the desire of maritime States to freely navigate the world's oceans in pursuit of their own economic and security interests. As a country with significant coastal resources and as the world's leading naval power, the U.S. has an abiding interest in both aspects of that balance.[94]*

Yet the United States is still not party to UNCLOS,[95] despite overwhelming support for accession[96] from a wide variety of interested American stakeholders (from federal agencies, including the U.S. Department of Defense (DoD), to maritime industries, to environmental groups).[97] "As far as the military is concerned, UNCLOS is gospel. The Navy treats it like law and even acts as an enforcer of the Convention by peacefully challenging what they see as excessive claims through what they call 'Freedom of Navigation' operations"[98] (discussed in Chapter 11).

President Reagan expressed American concerns about UNCLOS in a 1982 National Security Decision Directive, and again in 1983:[99]

> *[T]he United States will not sign the United Nations Law of the Sea Convention ... because several major problems in the Convention's deep seabed mining provisions are contrary to the interests and principles of industrialized nations and would not help attain the aspirations of developing countries.*
>
> * * *
>
> *However, the convention also contains provisions with respect to traditional uses of the oceans which generally confirm existing maritime law and practice and fairly balance the interests of all states.*
>
> * * *

First, the United States is prepared to accept and act in accordance with the balance of interests relating to traditional uses of the oceans – such as navigation and overflight. In this respect, the United States will recognize the rights of other states in the waters off their coasts, as reflected in the Convention, so long as the rights and freedoms of the United States and others under international law are recognized by such coastal states.

Second, the United States will exercise and assert its navigation and overflight rights and freedoms on a worldwide basis in a manner that is consistent with the balance of interests reflected in the convention. The United States will not, however, acquiesce in unilateral acts of other states designed to restrict the rights and freedoms of the international community in navigation and overflight and other related high seas uses.

Third, I am proclaiming today an Exclusive Economic Zone in which the United States will exercise sovereign rights in living and nonliving resources within 200 nautical miles of its coast.

Within this Zone all nations will continue to enjoy the high seas rights and freedoms that are not resource related, including the freedoms of navigation and overflight.[100]

President Reagan's statement that UNCLOS includes provisions *"which generally confirm existing maritime law and practice and fairly balance the interests of all states"* is generally viewed as a declaration that the U.S. views most UNCLOS provisions (especially its "navigational bill of rights")[101] as reflecting existing Customary International Law (CIL), with which the United States will comply.[102] Thus, even though the U.S. is not party to UNCLOS (and therefore is not bound by UNCLOS as a matter of treaty law), the U.S. follows UNCLOS navigational regimes (i.e., the rules of the various maritime zones) as a matter of CIL.[103]

The United Nations (UN) General Assembly addressed the U.S.' and other major industrialized States' concerns, and passed the

1994 Implementing Agreement (aka Part XI Agreement) to modify UNCLOS accordingly, in order to gain their accession to UNCLOS.[104] President Reagan's former Secretary of State George Shultz confirmed that the 1994 Implementing Agreement adequately addressed President Reagan's concerns.[105] Accordingly, U.S. Ambassador to the UN Madeleine Albright signed the 1994 Implementing Agreement, and President Clinton forwarded UNCLOS and its 1994 Implementing Agreement to the U.S. Senate for its advice and consent, outlining the benefits of UNCLOS to the U.S.[106]

As Law of the Sea expert John Norton Moore has so succinctly and eloquently stated:

> *President Ronald Reagan's conditions for U.S. acceptance eventually were met. After which, the United States strongly supported the Convention, and it was promptly submitted to the Senate for advice and consent. Subsequently, every U.S. President of both parties has supported U.S. adherence. Sadly, despite repeated favorable votes and recommendations from the Senate Foreign Relations Committee, for over two decades the Convention has languished in the Senate and has yet to come up for a vote in the full Senate. The reason is opposition from an isolationist faction endlessly repeating a patina of falsehoods about the Convention; a faction which at least has seemed to Senate leadership to have a blocking third in votes and has thus been able to prevent Senate advice and consent under Article II, section 2, of the United States Constitution requiring treaty concurrence by a two-thirds majority.*
>
> *The United States will at some point fully adhere to the Convention. Every oceans industry interest in the United States supports the Convention, from the oil majors to the environmentalists. Indeed, the only opposition is ideologically based, rather than interest based, and even then is senseless unless rooted in inaccuracies about the Convention. In the meantime, the United States accepts the normative provisions of the Convention as customary international law, and the United States Navy has one of the best records in the world in careful compliance.[107]*

Before transitioning from this Chapter's first sub-topic (the historical development of the Law of the Sea) to the second sub-topic (maritime baselines, from which all maritime zones are measured), it is important to understand the concept of a nautical mile. The BLUF is that a nautical mile is 1,852 meters, or 6,076 feet,[108] or about fifteen percent longer than a land-based (aka statute) mile.[109] Technically, one nautical mile (nm) represents one "minute" of Latitude at the Equator, with 60 minutes per degree of Latitude[110] (or 60 minutes/degree x 360 degrees = 21,600 nm circumference of the Earth). Mariners and pilots use nautical miles for navigation in order to read charts (aka maps) that use Latitude and Longitude (e.g., New Orleans is located at approximately 30° North Latitude and 90° West Longitude—see the diagram on the next page). A speed of one nautical mile per hour is expressed as 1 nm/hour or 1 "knot."[111] Thus, the average speed of a merchant ship is 15 knots,[112] which would equate to 15 x 1.15 = 17.25 miles per hour or 27.76 kilometers per hour on land. Although this generally would be considered a relatively slow speed on land for most vehicles, ships can maintain this pace for twenty-four hours per day, seven days per week, or 15 nm/hour x 24 hours/day x 7 days/week = 2,520 nm/week x 1.15 = 2,898 miles (4,664 kilometers), or slightly more than the width of the United States in one week, sailing continuously.[113]

Sailors have been using Latitude and Longitude to navigate for hundreds of years. Sailors are also known to be both superstitious and tradition-bound. Thus, it should come as no surprise that Sailors developed a tradition about crossing the Equator, known as "Crossing the Line." Crossing the Line ceremonies are traditionally held on both civilian and military vessels. Before Crossing the Line, a Sailor is considered a "Slimy Pollywog"; after crossing the equator (and undergoing any associated initiation), a Sailor is considered a "Trusty Shellback." "Shellback" ceremonies are

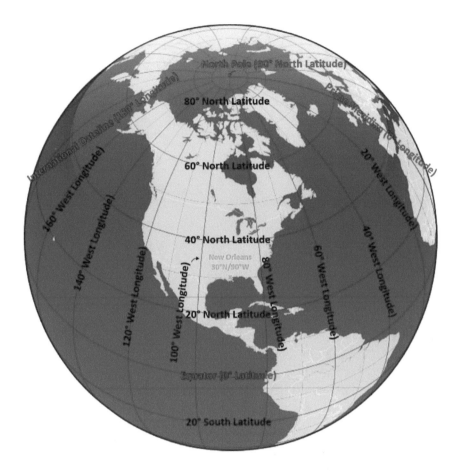

meant both to "toughen up" Sailors for the rigors of life at sea, and are considered good for morale during long sea voyages. "With the pollywog to shellback transition complete, a certificate was often awarded to the new shellback as a rite of passage."[114] The author underwent two Shellback ceremonies: the first on a cruise ship in 1997, and the second on a U.S. Navy warship in 1999 (photo of the author's U.S. Navy Shellback certificate below).

MARITIME BASELINES

This Chapter's second sub-topic is maritime baselines, from which all maritime zones are measured. [NOTE: There is a diagram of the various maritime zones at the beginning of the Chapter.] Since each of the various air and sea boundaries are measured from the baseline, States have an incentive to push their baselines out as far out from land as possible in order to maximize the extent of their maritime zones.

Each maritime zone has a different "regime" (i.e., set of rules) that govern the air, water and land (i.e., seabed) found within it. As a point of comparison, a State has exclusive (aka "complete") sovereignty over its land territory, and any waters inside the baseline, which are known as Internal Waters;[115] the related regime could be described as "complete sovereignty."[116] As discussed in Chapter 3, a State has "almost complete sovereignty" over its 12 nautical mile (nm) Territorial Sea (subject primarily to Innocent Passage), and the National Airspace above it. Chapter 4 discusses a State's "limited jurisdiction" to enforce laws in only four substantive areas (Fiscal, Immigration, Sanitation and Customs, or FISC) in its 24 nm Contiguous Zone. Chapter 4 also discusses a State's "ownership of all resources" within the water column of its 200 nm Exclusive Economic Zone (EEZ). Chapter 5 discusses the "freedoms" of the High Seas. Chapter 6 discusses a State's "ownership of all resources" on the Continental Shelf (i.e., the seabed beneath the EEZ). Chapter 6 also discusses the view expressed in UNCLOS that the resources of the Deep Seabed (beneath the High Seas) are the "common heritage of mankind."[117]

Thus, the two most important maritime boundary lines are the baseline (because all other maritime zones are measured from that), and the 12 nm Territorial Sea (because Territorial Seas are considered National Waters, and the airspace above is considered National Airspace, over which a Coastal State exercises almost complete sovereignty).[118] Outside the Territorial Seas are International Waters[119] and International Airspace,[120] over which the Coastal State exercises less and less sovereignty the further one gets from land.

From the absolute sovereignty that every State exercises over its land territory and superjacent airspace, the exclusive rights and control that the coastal State exercises over maritime areas off its coast diminish in stages as the distance from the coastal State increases. Conversely, the rights and freedoms of maritime States are at their maximum in regard to activities on the high seas and gradually diminish closer to the coastal State. The balance of interests between the coastal State and maritime States thus varies in each zone recognized by the Convention. [emphasis added][121]

"The regime for these zones was supported by a complex regime of baseline delineation, intended to ensure consistency and discourage excessive claims."[122] Article 5 defines the "normal baseline":

Article 5 / Normal baseline
Except where otherwise provided in this Convention, the normal baseline for measuring the breadth of the territorial sea is the low-water line along the coast as marked on large-scale charts officially recognized by the coastal State. [emphasis added][123]

Thus, the "normal baseline" is the low-water line which a Coastal State publishes on its own large-scale charts,[124] which generally equates to the lowest low tide ever recorded. This is fairly generous to Coastal States, and pushes out the baseline as far as is reasonably possible. Two initial observations: first, the lowest low tide has been used as a baseline for delimiting maritime borders since Roman law. Second, a Coastal state determines its own baselines by publishing official large-scale charts that show their baselines, and thus Coastal States are in control of interpreting the "reasonableness" of their own baseline claims. This Coastal State control, in combination with the incentive to maximize all maritime zones (particularly the 200 nm Exclusive Economic Zone (EEZ) and Continental Shelf claims which include ownership of all resources lying within), leads to egregious baseline claims. However, as we shall see, excessive maritime baseline claims are generally not due to excessive low-water lines, but to the misuse of the special exceptions enumerated in Article 7 that permit a Coastal State to draw "straight baselines":

Article 7 / Straight baselines

1. In localities where the coastline is deeply indented and cut into, or if there is a fringe of islands along the coast in its immediate vicinity, the method of straight baselines joining appropriate points may be employed in drawing the baseline from which the breadth of the territorial sea is measured.

2. Where because of the presence of a delta and other natural conditions the coastline is highly unstable, the appropriate points may be selected along the furthest seaward extent of the low-water line and, notwithstanding subsequent regression of the low-water line, the straight baselines shall remain effective until changed by the coastal State in accordance with this Convention.

3. The drawing of straight baselines must not depart to any appreciable extent from the general direction of the coast, and the sea areas lying within the lines must be sufficiently closely linked to the land domain to be subject to the regime of internal waters.

4. Straight baselines shall not be drawn to and from low-tide elevations, unless lighthouses or similar installations which are permanently above sea level have been built on them or except in instances where the drawing of baselines to and from such elevations has received general international recognition.

5. Where the method of straight baselines is applicable under paragraph 1, account may be taken, in determining particular baselines, of economic interests peculiar to the region concerned, the reality and the importance of which are clearly evidenced by long usage.

6. The system of straight baselines may not be applied by a State in such a manner as to cut off the territorial sea of another State from the high seas or an exclusive economic zone. [emphasis added][125]

"The purpose of authorizing the use of straight baselines is to allow the coastal State, at its discretion, to enclose those waters which, as a result of their close interrelationship with the land, have the character of internal waters. By using straight baselines, a State may also eliminate complex patterns".[126] Thus, a Coastal State may use "straight baselines" in order to reduce the complexity (i.e., to simplify) irregular coastlines:

> A deeply indented coastline;
> Fringing islands along the coastline;
> A highly unstable coastline; or
> A low-tide elevation (aka LTE, "drying rock" or "washing rock," mud flats, or sand bars)[127] within the Territorial Sea, but only if a structure (e.g., a lighthouse) has been built upon the LTE and the structure is always above sea level (ostensibly to warn mariners away from the dangers of the LTE).[128]

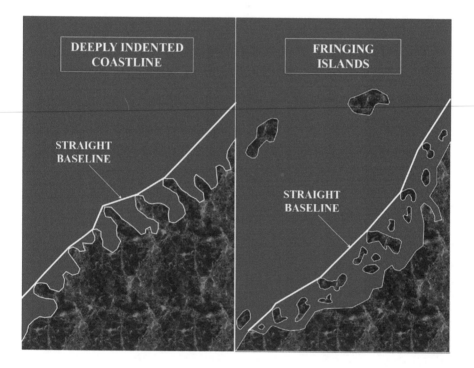

Thus, irregular coastlines tend to extend the baseline, and hence all of the maritime zones that are measured from it (although the intent of drawing straight baselines was to reduce complexity, not to unduly increase maritime zones).[129] Any waters inside straight baselines are considered Internal Waters, over which a Coastal State has "complete sovereignty."[130] We shall also see subsequently in this Chapter the use of straight baselines across the mouth of a bay, and in Chapter 4 by Archipelagic States.

Article 7 only mentions two caveats: one "mandatory" caveat in paragraph 3 (that the "straight baselines must not depart to any appreciable extent from the general direction of the coast"),[131] and one optional caveat in paragraph 5 (that the Coastal State "may" take into account regional "economic interests ... clearly evidenced by long usage"). A failure to abide by these caveats, or the misuse of straight baselines more generally, may only be challenged diplomatically by the international community (e.g., via another State's formal written diplomatic protest, aka a *démarche*),[132] or possibly via the mandatory dispute settlement provisions in UNCLOS Part XV (discussed in Chapter 12).

The criteria for drawing straight baselines in Article 7 are inherently subjective and left undefined by UNCLOS,[133] which provides considerable latitude (no pun intended) to Coastal States. How deeply indented does a Coastal State's coastline need to be  before it can justify drawing a straight baseline? How many islands constitute a "fringe of islands," and how close to the coast do they have to be to be "in the immediate vicinity"? Due to the inherent subjectivity, a significant number of States have claimed straight baselines (in geographical areas never intended by UNCLOS to constitute irregular coastlines) in order to "enclose[e] ocean space within internal waters"[134] and to extend their maritime claims further out to sea, creating larger ocean areas where they claim sovereign rights. "Given the subjective criteria which can be applied in many of the relevant provisions, it is perhaps not surprising that some coastal states have sought to interpret the baseline provisions of [UNCLOS] liberally."[135] In fact, "[a]rticle 7 [permitting straight baselines] is perhaps the most abused provision of the entire [UNCLOS]."[136] Anticipating the potential liberal application of inherently subjective straight baseline requirements, the UN published a detailed handbook (including a five-page flowchart) on drawing baselines in accordance with UNCLOS in 1989, five years before UNCLOS had even gone into effect![137]

Coastal State baseline claims (and their maritime zone claims more generally) may be found online in the U.S. Department of Defense (DoD) Maritime Claims Reference Manual, maintained by the U.S. Navy Judge Advocate General's (JAG) Corps' National Security Law (NSL) division (aka Code 10).[138]

The U.S. National Oceanic and Atmospheric Administration (NOAA) updates and publishes large scale nautical charts denoting the American "normal" baselines. [139] The United States strictly uses its low-water line to draw U.S. baselines (even though it could justify the use of straight baselines in certain areas),[140] and restrictively interprets the use of straight baselines by other States by applying the following criteria:[141]

In light of the modernization of the law of the sea in the Convention, it is reasonable to conclude that, as the Convention states, straight baselines are not normal baselines, straight baselines should be used sparingly, and, where they are used, they should be drawn conservatively to reflect the one rationale for their use that is consistent with the Convention, namely the simplification and rationalization of the measurement of the territorial sea and other maritime zones off highly irregular coasts.

    * * *

"Deeply indented and cut into" refers to a very distinctive coastal configuration. The United States has taken the position that such a configuration must fulfill all of the following characteristics:

    [*] ... there exist at least three deep indentations;

    [*] the deep indentations are in close proximity to one another; and

    [*] the depth of penetration of each deep indentation ... is, as a rule, greater than half the length of that baseline segment.[142]

    * * *

"Fringe of islands along the coast in the immediate vicinity of the coast" refers to a number of islands, within the meaning of article 121(1). The United States has taken the position that a such a fringe of islands must meet all of the following requirements:

    [*] the most landward point of each island lies no more than 24 miles from the mainland coastline;

    [*] each island to which a straight baseline is to be drawn is not more than 24 miles apart from the island from which the straight baseline is drawn; and

    [*] the islands, as a whole, mask at least 50% of the mainland coastline in any given locality.

    * * *

The United States has taken the position that, to be consistent with article 7(3), straight baseline segments must:

    [*] not depart to any appreciable extent from the general direction of the coastline, by reference to general direction lines which in each locality shall not exceed 60 miles in length;

    [*] not exceed 24 miles in length; and

    [*] result in sea areas situated landward of the straight baseline segments that are sufficiently closely linked to the land domain to be subject to the regime of internal waters. [emphasis added][143]

Although these criteria were not adopted by UNCLOS (e.g., limiting the maximum length of straight baselines), the U.S. view that the maximum length of each segment of a straight baseline cannot exceed 24 nm[144] basically applies the same criteria that is used to close the mouth of a juridical (i.e., legal) bay with a straight baseline, discussed subsequently in this Chapter.

The 1989 UN Baselines Handbook suggests that "[i]n determining whether the conditions apply which would permit the use of straight baselines it is necessary to **focus on the spirit as well as the letter** of the first paragraph of article 7" (regarding deeply indented coastlines and fringing islands—emphasis added).[145] The Baselines Handbook suggests that coastlines with several deep indentations that would satisfy the criteria for juridical (i.e., legal) bays (discussed below) would generally be considered as qualifying as deeply indented coastlines.[146] The Baselines Handbook also provides specific examples of situations that would qualify as fringing islands,[147] and agrees with the U.S. view that islands lying within 24 nm from the coastline would generally satisfy the test for fringing islands.[148] Norway's *skjaergaard* (pronounced "*shar-gor*") is a classic example of the legitimate use of straight baselines connecting the outermost points of the fringing islands, and enclosing sea areas closely linked to the land as internal waters.

Although "Article 7 [permitting straight baselines] is perhaps the most abused provision" of UNCLOS,[149] Article 10 (dealing with bays) has been the subject of the most written commentary.[150] UNCLOS permits a Coastal State to draw "a closing line" (i.e., a baseline) across the mouth of a bay, and thereby enclose the waters of the bay as internal waters.[151] Article 10 enumerates two types of bays—juridical (i.e., legal) bays and historic bays:

Article 10 / Bays

1. This article relates only to bays the coasts of which belong to a single State.

2. For the purposes of this Convention, a bay is a well-marked indentation whose penetration is in such proportion to the width of its mouth as to contain land-locked waters and constitute more than a mere curvature of the coast. An indentation shall not, however, be regarded as a bay unless its area is as large as, or larger than, that of the semi-circle whose diameter is a line drawn across the mouth of that indentation.

3. For the purpose of measurement, the area of an indentation is that lying between the low-water mark around the shore of the indentation and a line joining the low-water mark of its natural entrance points. Where, because of the presence of islands, an indentation has more than one mouth, the semi-circle shall be drawn on a line as long as the sum total of the lengths of the lines across the different mouths. Islands within an indentation shall be included as if they were part of the water area of the indentation.

4. *If the distance between the low-water marks of the natural entrance points of a bay does not exceed 24 nautical miles, a closing line may be drawn between these two low-water marks, and the waters enclosed thereby shall be considered as internal waters.*

5. Where the distance between the low-water marks of the natural entrance points of a bay exceeds 24 nautical miles, a straight baseline of 24 nautical miles shall be drawn within the bay in such a manner as to enclose the maximum area of water that is possible with a line of that length.

6. The foregoing provisions do not apply to so-called "historic" bays, or in any case where the system of straight baselines provided for in article 7 is applied. [*emphasis added*][152]

Although the test for a juridical (i.e., legal) bay is easy to understand, it is cumbersome to define (as evidenced by Article 10's overly confusing definition above). **UNCLOS established an objective, two-part test for a juridical bay: (1) the mouth of the juridical bay must not be wider than 24 nm,[153] and (2) the volume of water enclosed within the juridical bay must fill a semi-circle drawn across the mouth of the bay.**[154] In the diagram below, only indentation "b" would qualify as a juridical bay, because its mouth

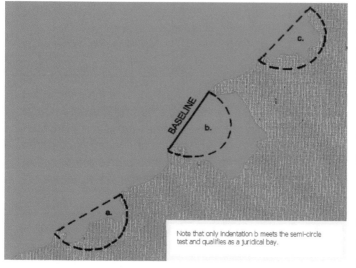

Note that only indentation b meets the semi-circle test and qualifies as a juridical bay.

is not too wide (i.e., less than 24 nm), and it contains enough water to fill a semi-circle drawn across the mouth of the bay.

If an indentation in the coastline qualifies as a juridical (i.e., legal) bay, then a Coastal State may draw "a closing line" (i.e., a baseline) across its mouth, and thereby enclose the waters of the bay as internal waters. Ports and harbors are similarly considered internal waters.[155] Coastal States have virtually complete sovereignty over internal waters, and Coastal State permission is required for ships to enter[156] (except possibly for vessels in distress).[157] For example, while in port, all ships are subject to local laws and regulations, including inspection (except sovereign immune vessels—discussed in Chapter 10). Since the Coastal State has complete sovereignty over internal waters, they may be likened to "mud," because they might as well be land (over which a State also has complete sovereignty).

"Historic" bays are exempt from the objective test required to qualify as a juridical (i.e., legal) bay, but are similarly considered as internal waters.[158] Although the adjective "historic" is undefined, significant bodies of water historically treated as internal waters of a particular State "for the purposes of sovereignty and jurisdiction"[159] would appear to qualify as historic bays (e.g., the 50 nm mouth to Canada's Hudson Bay would be too wide to qualify as a juridical (i.e., legal) bay, but the Hudson Bay has historically been treated as the internal waters of Canada, and thus would seem to qualify as a historic bay).[160] However, the U.S. does not recognize Canada's historic bay claim to Hudson Bay.[161] The U.S. view is that a Coastal State (aka a "littoral State") must have openly, effectively, and continuously exercised jurisdiction over a body of water as internal waters for a considerable period of time, coupled with acquiescence by other States in the exercise of such authority, in order to claim "Historic Bay" status.[162]

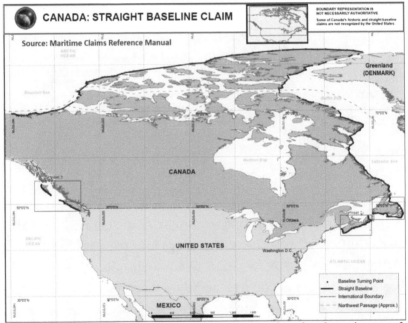

Drawing a closing line across the mouth of a bay is another example of simplifying a Coastal State's baseline—otherwise the baseline would dip into the bay, and all of the corresponding maritime zones measured from the baseline would have similar dips. Drawing a closing line across the mouth of the bay smooths out the baseline and smooths out each of the corresponding maritime zones, as can be seen in the following diagram.

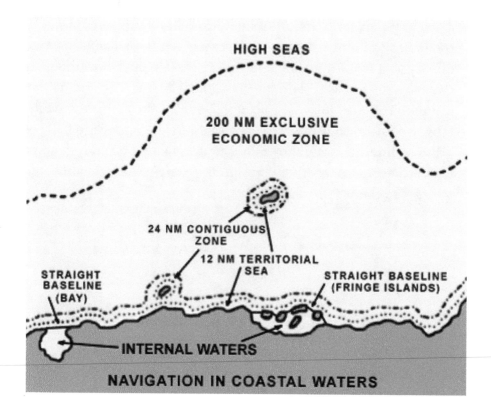

HIGH SEAS

200 NM EXCLUSIVE ECONOMIC ZONE

24 NM CONTIGUOUS ZONE

12 NM TERRITORIAL SEA

STRAIGHT BASELINE (BAY)

STRAIGHT BASELINE (FRINGE ISLANDS)

INTERNAL WATERS

NAVIGATION IN COASTAL WATERS

One of the most notorious examples of a historic bay claim is Libya's Gulf of Sidra.[163] The Gulf of Sidra fails to satisfy either prong of Article 10's objective, two-part test for a juridical (i.e., legal) bay: it has a closing line of 300 nm, and its waters would not fill a semi-circle drawn across its mouth (see chart below). However, the Libyan Arab Republic claimed the Gulf of Sidra as a historic bay in 1973, by submitting an informal *note verbale*[164] as a diplomatic announcement to the United Nations. Libya asserted that "[t]hrough history and without any dispute, the Libyan Arab Republic has exercised its sovereignty over the Gulf."[165] Libya's long-serving leader Muammar Gaddafi drew a "line of death" across the mouth of the Gulf of Sidra, and threatened military action against any foreign ships or aircraft that crossed it. The U.S. disputes Libya's historic bay claim to the Gulf of Sidra, and issued diplomatic protests in 1974, 1979 and 1985. Notwithstanding the threat against crossing the "line of death," the U.S. conducted at least nine Freedom of Navigation (FON) operations into the Gulf of Sidra between 1974 and 2013.[166] At least three of these operational challenges (in 1981, 1986 and 1989) involved the exchange of weapons fire between American and Libyan aircraft.[167]

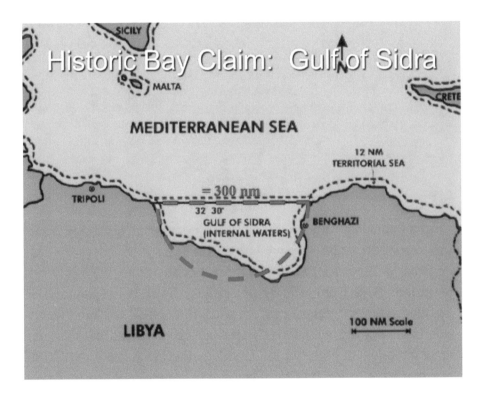

Since all maritime zones[168] are measured from a Coastal State's maritime baselines, it was important for States to agree on which land areas could generate (or influence) maritime baselines. Thus, UNCLOS distinguishes between Islands, Rocks, and Low Tide Elevations (LTEs).[169] The BLUF is that since naturally formed

Islands are above water at high tide and can sustain human habitation (i.e., life), they are entitled to the same maritime zones as continental land masses (i.e., the mainland).[170] This only makes sense when considering the maritime interests of island States such as Bahrain, Barbados, Cuba, Iceland, Jamaica, Singapore, Sri Lanka, United Kingdom, etc.[171] Article 121 sets out the regime of Islands:

Article 121 / Regime of islands

1. An island is a naturally formed area of land, surrounded by water, which is above water at high tide.

2. Except as provided for in paragraph 3, the territorial sea, the contiguous zone, the exclusive economic zone and the continental shelf of an island are determined in accordance with the provisions of this Convention applicable to other land territory.

3. Rocks which cannot sustain human habitation or economic life of their own shall have no exclusive economic zone or continental shelf. [emphasis added][172]

Thus, although Rocks are also above water at high tide, since they cannot sustain human habitation (i.e., life), they are only entitled to Territorial Seas and a Contiguous Zone.[173] "[L]ow tide elevations (which literally do not rise to the status of islands)"[174] are also called "drying rocks" because they only "dry out" at low tide (i.e., they are only above water or "elevated" at low tide, and are submerged at high tide). A Low Tide Elevation is not entitled to any maritime zones, but it can be used to "bump out" the maritime zones (i.e., as a point on a straight baseline) if it is found within the Territorial Seas, and the Coastal State has constructed a lighthouse upon it.[175]

Even a small naturally formed[176] Island has the potential to include vast oil, mineral and fishing resources within its 200 nm

Exclusive Economic Zone and underlying Continental Shelf (discussed in Chapters 4 and 6, respectively). Thus, Coastal States have an incentive to claim that an offshore land feature qualifies as an Island, and not merely as a Rock (which lacks both an Exclusive Economic Zone and an underlying Continental Shelf). Unfortunately, the difference between an Island and a Rock is whether or not it can "sustain human habitation," which is yet another subjective standard in UNCLOS that is subject to abuse.[177]

The historical development helps to put the modern Law of the Sea in context. Since all maritime zones are measured from the baseline, establishing proper baselines are also of paramount importance.

---

[26] United Nations Convention on the Law of the Sea (UNCLOS), Dec. 10, 1982, 1833 U.N.T.S. 397, https://www.un.org/Depts/los/convention_agreements/convention_overview_co nvention.htm.

[27] THE FLETCHER SCHOOL OF LAW AND DIPLOMACY—TUFTS UNIVERSITY, LAW OF THE SEA, A POLICY PRIMER 6 (2017), https://sites.tufts.edu/lawofthesea/introduction/.

[28] The Law of the Sea is part of public international law between States, and not private maritime law between stakeholders that is often taught and discussed under the rubric of "Admiralty Law" (e.g., carriage of goods, charter parties, salvage, towing, pilotage, collision, stranding, personal injury, ship mortgages, marine insurance, etc.) or the domestic/municipal law of any particular State. R. R. CHURCHILL & A. V. LOWE, THE LAW OF THE SEA 1 (1999).

[29] Once again, in international relations and in international law, "State" refers to a sovereign nation or country, and shall be used accordingly in this book.

[30] See generally William J. Aceves, The Freedom of Navigation Program: A Study of the Relationship between Law and Politics, 19 HASTINGS INT'L & COMP. L. REV. 259, 260-262 (1996), https://repository.uchastings.edu/hastings_international_comparative_law_revi ew/vol19/iss2/2/.

[31] HUGO GROTIUS, MARE LIBERUM [THE FREE SEA] (1609). See also DONALD R. ROTHWELL & TIM STEPHENS, THE INT'L. LAW OF THE SEA 3 (2nd ed. 2016).

[32] Grotius' position is understandable once we recognize that he had been commissioned by the Dutch East India Company, which was the first multinational corporation, and which wanted to break Portugal's monopoly over trade with Asia.

[33] WILLIAM WELWOOD, AN ABRIDGEMENT OF ALL THE SEA LAWES (1613); WILLIAM WELWOOD, DE DOMINIO MARIS (1615).

[34] A "Coastal State" (aka a "littoral State") is any nation with a coastline (i.e., that borders a sea or ocean).

[35] JOHN SELDEN, MARE CLAUSUM [THE CLOSED SEA] (1635). England was concerned about Europeans fishing in English coastal waters. *See also* DONALD R. ROTHWELL & TIM STEPHENS, THE INT'L. LAW OF THE SEA 3 (2nd ed. 2016).

[36] *See, e.g.*, Elliot L. Richardson, *Power, Mobility and the Law of the Sea*, J. FOREIGN AFF., 902, 903 (1980). Chapter 2 subsequently discusses the definition of a nautical mile (nm).

[37] American Society of Int'l. Law (ASIL), Resources, eResources - Insights and other E-Publications, Electronic Resource Guide (ERG), *Law of the Sea*, p. 4 (Barbara Bean, Apr. 27, 2015), https://www.asil.org/resources/electronic-resource-guide-erg.

[38] William J. Aceves, *The Freedom of Navigation Program: A Study of the Relationship between Law and Politics*, 19 HASTINGS INT'L & COMP. L. REV. 259, 259 (1996), https://repository.uchastings.edu/hastings_international_comparative_law_review/vol19/iss2/2/, quoting J.L. BRIERLY, THE LAW OF NATIONS 304 (Sir Humphrey Waldock ed., 6th ed. 1984) and C. JOHN COLOMBOS, THE INT'L. LAW OF THE SEA 48 (6th ed. 1967).

[39] Chapter 6 discusses the Continental Shelf and the Deep Seabed. *See also* Richardson, *Law of the Sea*, p. 903 (full cite above) (noting that "the Truman Proclamation constituted the first major breach in modern times of the classic principles of ocean law laid down by Hugo Grotius in 1609."); UNITED NATIONS OFFICE FOR OCEAN AFFAIRS AND THE LAW OF THE SEA, THE LAW OF THE SEA, BASELINES: AN EXAMINATION OF THE RELEVANT PROVISIONS OF THE UNITED NATIONS CONVENTION ON THE LAW OF THE SEA vii (1989), https://www.un.org/Depts/los/doalos_publications/publicationstexts/The%20Law%20of%20the%20Sea_Baselines.pdf (same); Michael W. Lodge (Secretary-General of the International Seabed Authority), Enclosure of the Oceans versus the Common Heritage of Mankind: The Inherent Tension between the Continental Shelf Beyond 200 Nautical Miles and the Area, 97 INT'L. L. STUD. 803, 831 (2021), https://digital-commons.usnwc.edu/cgi/viewcontent.cgi?article=2971&context=ils (noting that "[i]n many ways, the history of the law of the sea, starting with the unintended and ill-thought-out consequences of the Truman Declaration, has been one of an erosion of the doctrine of the freedom and commonality of the sea towards enclosure. This is perhaps ironic given that the original impetus for UNCLOS came from those nations interested in preserving freedom of navigation against the creeping jurisdiction of other States."); ROTHWELL & STEPHENS, LAW OF THE SEA, p. 5 (full cite above).

[40] ROTHWELL & STEPHENS, LAW OF THE SEA, pp. 105 & 114 (full cite above); Aceves, *The FON Program*, pp. 266-267 (full cite above).

[41] In 1952, Chile issued the Santiago Declaration, becoming the first State to unilaterally claim "sole sovereignty and jurisdiction" over the sea adjacent to its coast out to 200 nautical miles (nm—explained subsequently). This was followed by similar declarations by African and South American countries, and by Indonesia. After World War II, developing technology (such as large scale fisheries, off-shore oil production, and larger oil tankers) also created economic interests beyond the Territorial Sea, which led to competition for offshore resources. In addition, States established the United Nations in 1945 to maintain international peace and security, which had a major impact both on public international law and on State sovereignty. Chapter 9 discusses the United Nations Charter and its framework.

[42] Chapter 6 discusses the Continental Shelf and the Deep Seabed.

[43] United Nations Convention on the Law of the Sea (UNCLOS) Preamble unnumbered ¶ 7 & arts. 125(1), 136, 137(2), 140(1), 143(1), 149, 150(i), 153(1), 155(1)(a), 155(2), 246(3), 311(6) & 1994 Implementing Agreement Preamble ¶ 2, Dec. 10, 1982, 1833 U.N.T.S. 397, https://www.un.org/Depts/los/convention_agreements/convention_overview_convention.htm; THE FLETCHER SCHOOL OF LAW AND DIPLOMACY—TUFTS UNIVERSITY, LAW OF THE SEA, A POLICY PRIMER 8 (2017), https://sites.tufts.edu/lawofthesea/introduction/.

[44] Tullio Treves, *Introductory Note to the United Nations Convention on the Law of the Sea*, AUDIOVISUAL LIBRARY OF INT'L. LAW, http://legal.un.org/avl/ha/uncls/uncls.html. *See also* Richard Nixon, Statement About United States Oceans Policy (May 23, 1970), https://www.presidency.ucsb.edu/documents/statement-about-united-states-oceans-policy (making a similar argument).

[45] *See generally* UNCLOS, Introduction at p. 2 (full cite above) (noting that the genesis for UNCLOS negotiations originated in "the First Committee of the [UN] General Assembly, as the item was perceived from the very beginning as being of primarily political significance, and not limited to strictly legal or economic concern"); TUFTS, LAW OF THE SEA, p. 6 (full cite above) (noting that "[p]olitical, strategic, and economic issues are reflected in the historical tension between the exercise of state sovereignty over the sea and the idea of 'the free sea.'"); Aceves, *The FON Program*, p. 259 (full cite above) (noting that there is a "persistent interaction between law and politics" throughout the history of the development of the Law of the Sea, as exemplified by the U.S. FONOPs program); Military.com, News, Headlines, *'Elephant Walk' on Guam Serves as Timely US Airpower Demonstration, Defense Expert Says* (Seth Robson, Apr. 15, 2020), https://www.military.com/daily-news/2020/04/15/elephant-walk-guam-serves-timely-us-airpower-demonstration-defense-expert-says.html?ESRC=eb_200416.nl (reporting that in order to counter the perception that U.S. military projection power was degraded due to the sidelining of the aircraft carrier USS THEODORE ROOSEVELT (CVN 71) in Guam due to its crew being infected with Coronavirus 2019 (COVID-19), the U.S. Air Force conducted an "elephant walk" of 11 of its largest airplanes in Guam; this caught the attention of North Korea, which fired shore-based cruise missiles and air-to-surface missiles into the Sea of Japan off its eastern coast the following day in response).

[46] G.A. Res. 2750 (XXV), ¶ C.2, U.N. Doc A/AC.138/58 (Dec. 17, 1970), https://research.un.org/en/docs/ga/quick/regular/25. *See also* Richard Nixon, Statement About United States Oceans Policy (May 23, 1970), https://www.presidency.ucsb.edu/documents/statement-about-united-states-oceans-policy (similarly calling for a multilateral treaty on the law of the sea). The UN General Assembly debates and passes an annual omnibus resolution on oceans and the law of the sea. United Nations, Departments, Law of the Sea, Oceans and the Law of the Sea in the General Assembly of the United Nations, General Assembly resolutions and decisions, https://www.un.org/Depts/los/general_assembly/general_assembly_resolutions.htm.

[47] RESTATEMENT (THIRD) OF FOREIGN RELATIONS, pt. 1, introductory note (pp. 16-17) (1987). The European Parliament serves as the legislative body of the European Union, and its member States. European Parliament, https://www.europarl.europa.eu/portal/en. The role of the United Nations General Assembly is to "discuss any questions or any matters within the scope" of the UN

Charter, and to make recommendations for their resolution. United Nations, Charter of the United Nations, arts. 10-17, https://www.un.org/en/charter-united-nations/. There are generally considered to be 195 States in the World, although the inclusion of 2 States is disputed. *See, e.g.,* Independent States in the World Fact Sheet, U.S. Dept. of State Bureau of Intelligence and Research (March 27, 2019), https://www.state.gov/independent-states-in-the-world/ (including Kosovo but not Palestine, which has observer status at the UN similar to the Holy See); Frequently   Asked   Questions,   Worldometers, https://www.worldometers.info/geography/how-many-countries-are-there-in-the-world/ (including Palestine, but not Kosovo since China and Russia are blocking its membership in the UN).

[48] RESTATEMENT (THIRD) OF FOREIGN RELATIONS, pt. 1, introductory note (p. 17) (1987). The United Nations Security Council has "primary responsibility for the maintenance of international peace and security," but not to enforce the full spectrum of international law. UN Charter, art. 24(1) (full cite above); *see also* UN Charter arts. 25-26.

[49] RESTATEMENT (THIRD) OF FOREIGN RELATIONS § 101 & pt. 1, introductory note (p. 16) (1987); Dept. of Defense Law of War Manual § 1.10.1.3, pp. 37-38 (June 2015, updated Dec. 2016), https://www.hsdl.org/?view&did=797480; William J. Aceves, *The Freedom of Navigation Program: A Study of the Relationship between Law and Politics,* 19   HASTINGS   INT'L   &   COMP.   L.   REV.   259,   306   (1996), https://repository.uchastings.edu/hastings_international_comparative_law_revi ew/vol19/iss2/2/, (exploring origins of *opinio juris*).

[50] U.S. NAVY, MARINE CORPS & COAST GUARD, THE COMMANDER'S HANDBOOK ON THE LAW OF NAVAL OPERATIONS, NWP 1-14M/MCTP 11-10B/COMDTPUB P5800.7A, Preface (p.   17)   (2017), www.jag.navy.mil/distrib/instructions/CDRs_HB_on_Law_of_Naval_Operations_AUG17.pdf.

[51] Statute of the Int'l. Court of Justice (ICJ) art. 38(1), https://www.icj-cij.org/en/statute. The ICJ is not to be confused with the International Criminal Court (ICC), which is also based in The Hague, a medium-sized city in the Netherlands. *See generally* James Benoit, *The Evolution of Universal Jurisdiction Over War Crimes,*   53   NAVAL   L.   REV.   259   (2006), https://heinonline.org/HOL/LandingPage?handle=hein.journals/naval53&div=9&id =&page= (exploring the history of exercising jurisdiction over war crimes, and arguing that the U.S. should embrace the ICC rather than reject it). *See also* RESTATEMENT (THIRD) OF FOREIGN RELATIONS § 102(1) (1987) (listing the 4 sources of international law).

[52] RESTATEMENT (THIRD) OF FOREIGN RELATIONS, pt. 1, introductory note (p. 18) (1987).

[53] DoD Law of War Manual § 1.7, p. 27 (full cite above); COMMANDER'S HANDBOOK, ¶ 5.5.2 (p. 5-6) (full cite above).

[54] RESTATEMENT (THIRD) OF FOREIGN RELATIONS § 102(2) & cmt. C (1987); DoD Law of War Manual, § 1.8, pp. 29-30 (full cite above); COMMANDER'S HANDBOOK, ¶ 5.5.1 (p. 5-6) (full cite above). In Latin, this "sense of legal obligation" is known as "*opinio juris*" ("an opinion of law or necessity,' pronounced "*oh pin ee oh yur is*"). THE FLETCHER SCHOOL OF LAW AND DIPLOMACY—TUFTS UNIVERSITY, LAW OF THE SEA, A POLICY PRIMER 6 (2017), https://sites.tufts.edu/lawofthesea/introduction/. *See also* Aceves, *The FON Program,* pp. 316-318 (full cite above) (exploring the origins of *opinio juris*).

[55] RESTATEMENT (THIRD) OF FOREIGN RELATIONS § 102 cmt. c (1987). *See generally* James Benoit, *Mistreatment of The Wounded, Sick and Shipwrecked by The ICRC Study on Customary Int'l. Humanitarian Law*, *in* 11 YEARBOOK OF INT'L. HUMANITARIAN LAW 175 (2008), https://www.cambridge.org/core/journals/yearbook-of-international-humanitarian-law/article/abs/mistreatment-of-the-wounded-sick-and-shipwrecked-by-the-icrc-study-on-customary-international-humanitarian-law/FEC9385F35650A0B0E69212576C3AE63 (arguing that the ICRC Study articulates "rules" that are not sustainable under the traditional theory of customary international law formation, as evidenced by three seeming uncontroversial proposed rules for safeguarding the wounded, sick and shipwrecked).

[56] For example, the venerable San Remo Manual is a description (a "restatement") of the Customary International Law (CIL) of the Law of Armed Conflict at Sea. It represents good evidence of what the esteemed contributors believe to be CIL, but the San Remo Manual itself is not CIL. Unfortunately, the San Remo Manual also includes "some progressive development" of the law. Gros Espiell, Pres. Int'l. Inst. Of Humanitarian Law, *Foreword* to LOUISE DOSWALD-BECK, SAN REMO MANUAL ON INT'L. LAW APPLICABLE TO ARMED CONFLICTS AT SEA ix (1994). The San Remo Manual is thus aspirational as to how CIL should develop (i.e., not merely describing what the law is (*lex lata*) but also what the law could be (*lex ferenda*)). Unfortunately, the lack of a clear indication as to which paragraphs describe existing CIL and which paragraphs are aspirational detracts from the usefulness of the San Remo Manual as a description of CIL, although it remains a useful reference.

[57] TUFTS, LAW OF THE SEA, pp. 4, 6 (full cite above).

[58] DoD Law of War Manual § 1.8, pp. 29-30 (full cite above); COMMANDER'S HANDBOOK, Preface (p. 17) (full cite above).

[59] DoD Law of War Manual, § 1.10.1.2, p. 37 (full cite above). *See generally* Aceves, *The FON Program*, pp. 302-310 (full cite above) (providing detailed examples of how Customary International Law is formed).

[60] *See, e.g.,* United Nations Convention on the Law of the Sea (UNCLOS) Preamble unnumbered ¶ 9, Dec. 10, 1982, 1833 U.N.T.S. 397, https://www.un.org/Depts/los/convention_agreements/convention_overview_convention.htm ("*Affirming* that matters not regulated by this Convention continue to be governed by the rules and principles of general [i.e., customary] international law"). *See also* Int'l. Court of Justice (ICJ), *Military and Paramilitary Activities in and against Nicaragua* (Nicaragua v. United States of America), Judgment of June 27th, 1986, 1986 I.C.J. Reports 14, 96 (¶ 179), https://www.icj-cij.org/en/case/70/judgments (concluding that "[i]t will therefore be clear that customary international law continues to exist and to apply, separately from international treaty law, even where the two categories of law have an identical content.").

[61] United Nations Treaty Collection, Depositary, Status of Treaties, Chapter III Privileges and Immunities, Diplomatic and Consular Relations, etc., Vienna Convention on Diplomatic Relations (Vienna, Apr. 18, 1961) https://treaties.un.org/Pages/ViewDetails.aspx?src=TREATY&mtdsg_no=III-3&chapter=3&lang=en.

[62] Defense News, The Drift, A Quick-Reference Guide on UNCLOS for Gen. Hyten: The Drift, Vol. XLIII, (David B. Larter, Aug. 4, 2019), https://www.defensenews.com/naval/the-drift/2019/08/04/a-quick-reference-guide-on-unclos-for-gen-hyten-the-drift-vol-xliii/.

[63] G.A. Res. 1105 (XI), U.N. Doc A/CN.4/104 (Feb. 21, 1957), http://legal.un.org/diplomaticconferences/1958_los/.

[64] The 1958 Convention on the Territorial Sea and the Contiguous Zone entered into force on September 10, 1964. United Nations Convention on the Territorial Sea and the Contiguous Zone, Apr. 29, 1958, 516 U.N.T.S. 205, http://legal.un.org/diplomaticconferences/1958_los/. *See also* DONALD R. ROTHWELL & TIM STEPHENS, THE INT'L. LAW OF THE SEA 7 (2nd ed. 2016) (noting that "[t]he Convention on the Territorial Sea and Contiguous Zone was predominantly a codification of existing customary international law, and for the first time provided significant content in treaty law to the regime of the territorial sea.").

[65] The 1958 Convention on the High Seas entered into force on September 30, 1962. United Nations Convention on the High Seas, Apr. 29, 1958, 450 U.N.T.S. 11, http://legal.un.org/diplomaticconferences/1958_los/.

[66] The 1958 Convention on Fishing and Conservation of the Living Resources of the High Seas entered into force on March 20, 1966. United Nations Convention on Fishing and Conservation of the Living Resources of the High Seas, Apr. 29, 1958, 559 U.N.T.S. 285, http://legal.un.org/diplomaticconferences/1958_los/.

[67] The 1958 Convention on the Continental Shelf entered into force on June 10, 1964. United Nations Convention on the Continental Shelf, Apr. 29, 1958, 499 U.N.T.S. 311, http://legal.un.org/diplomaticconferences/1958_los/.

[68] United Nations Convention on the Territorial Sea and the Contiguous Zone, Apr. 29, 1958, 516 U.N.T.S. 205, http://legal.un.org/docs/?path=../ilc/texts/instruments/english/conventions/8_1_1958_territorial_sea.pdf&lang=EF.

[69] Chapter 4 discusses the Contiguous Zone (CZ).

[70] Chapter 2 subsequently explains what is a nautical mile (nm).

[71] William J. Aceves, *The Freedom of Navigation Program: A Study of the Relationship between Law and Politics*, 19 HASTINGS INT'L & COMP. L. REV. 259, 267 (1996), https://repository.uchastings.edu/hastings_international_comparative_law_review/vol19/iss2/2/. This left the Customary International Law (CIL) norm of a 3 nautical mile (nm—explained subsequently) Territorial Sea in place. ROTHWELL & STEPHENS, LAW OF THE SEA, p. 7 (full cite above). *See also* Richard Nixon, Statement About United States Oceans Policy (May 23, 1970), https://www.presidency.ucsb.edu/documents/statement-about-united-states-oceans-policy (calling for a multilateral treaty on the law of the sea, including a 12 nm Territorial Sea). *But see* John Norton Moore, *Navigational Freedom: The Most Critical Common Heritage*, 93 INT'L. L. STUD. 251, 253 (2017), https://digital-commons.usnwc.edu/ils/vol93/iss1/8/ (arguing that law of the sea negotiations had been preoccupied for 400 years "on a single line in the oceans focused on the breadth of the territorial sea.").

[72] United Nations Convention on Fishing and Conservation of the Living Resources of the High Seas, Apr. 29, 1958, 559 U.N.T.S. 285, http://legal.un.org/docs/?path=../ilc/texts/instruments/english/conventions/8_1_1958_fishing.pdf&lang=EF.

[73] ROTHWELL & STEPHENS, LAW OF THE SEA, p. 8 (full cite above).

[74] ROTHWELL & STEPHENS, LAW OF THE SEA, p. 9 (full cite above). However, States which are party to both the 1958 law of the sea conventions and the 1982 United Nations Convention on the Law of the Sea (UNCLOS) are bound by the latter. United Nations Convention on the Law of the Sea (UNCLOS) art. 311, Dec. 10, 1982, 1833 U.N.T.S. 397,

https://www.un.org/Depts/los/convention_agreements/convention_overview_convention.htm.

[75] G.A. Res. 1307 (XIII), ¶ 1, U.N. Doc A/PV.783 (Dec. 10, 1958), http://legal.un.org/docs/?path=../diplomaticconferences/1960_los/docs/english/vol_1/a_res_1307_xiii.pdf&lang=E.

[76] "[T]he principal proposal was a compromise put forward by the United States and Canada in which the limit of the territorial sea was proposed as being six nm beyond which a six nm fishing zone would exist. However, the so-called 'Six plus Six' proposal failed to achieve the necessary two thirds support by a single vote". ROTHWELL & STEPHENS, LAW OF THE SEA, p. 9 (full cite above). Had the South Korean delegate voted as instructed by Seoul, the 'Six plus Six' proposal would have passed, and very well might still be the rule to this day! Per a former international Law of the Sea student of the author, the South Korean delegate's father was a fisherman, and informed his son that the 'Six plus Six' proposal was too confusing to enforce. See generally Second United Nations Conference on the Law of the Sea, http://legal.un.org/diplomaticconferences/1960_los/. See also Moore, Navigational Freedom, pp. 253-254 (full cite above) (positing that the First and Second UN Conferences on the Law of the Sea could not resolve the breadth of the Territorial Sea because they "fail[ed] to functionally separate the issues of fishery management and navigation"); The New Yorker, A Reporter at Large, The Law of the Sea—I at 46 (William Wertenbaker, Jul. 25, 1983), https://www.newyorker.com/magazine/1983/08/01/i-the-law-of-the-sea (noting that Russia claimed a 6 nm Territorial Sea plus a 6 nm fishing zone as early as 1911).

[77] UNCLOS, Preamble unnumbered ¶ 7 & arts. 125(1), 136, 137(2), 140(1), 143(1), 149, 150(i), 153(1), 155(1)(a), 155(2), 246(3), 311(6) & 1994 Implementing Agreement Preamble ¶ 2 (full cite above); THE FLETCHER SCHOOL OF LAW AND DIPLOMACY—TUFTS UNIVERSITY, LAW OF THE SEA, A POLICY PRIMER 8 (2017), https://sites.tufts.edu/lawofthesea/introduction/.

[78] G.A. Res. 2750 (XXV), ¶ C.2, U.N. Doc A/AC.138/58 (Dec. 17, 1970), https://research.un.org/en/docs/ga/quick/regular/25. The UN General Assembly debates and passes an annual omnibus resolution on oceans and the law of the sea. United Nations, Departments, Law of the Sea, Oceans and the Law of the Sea in the General Assembly of the United Nations, General Assembly resolutions and decisions, https://www.un.org/Depts/los/general_assembly/general_assembly_resolutions.htm.

[79] One author noted that the negotiations at the Third UN Conference on the Law of the Sea were "protracted and extremely complicated." Helmut Türk, Questions Relating to the Continental Shelf Beyond 200 Nautical Miles: Delimitation, Delineation, and Revenue Sharing, 97 INT'L. L. STUD. 231, 236 (2021), https://digital-commons.usnwc.edu/ils/vol97/iss1/18/.

[80] The definition of a nautical mile (nm) is discussed subsequently in this Chapter.

[81] UNITED NATIONS OFFICE FOR OCEAN AFFAIRS AND THE LAW OF THE SEA, THE LAW OF THE SEA, BASELINES: AN EXAMINATION OF THE RELEVANT PROVISIONS OF THE UNITED NATIONS CONVENTION ON THE LAW OF THE SEA vii (1989), https://www.un.org/Depts/los/doalos_publications/publicationstexts/The%20Law%20of%20the%20Sea_Baselines.pdf.

[82] Türk, Questions Relating to the Continental Shelf Beyond 200 Nautical Miles, pp. 234, 237-238 (full cite above).

[83] TUFTS, LAW OF THE SEA, p. 8 (full cite above).

[84] The United States was concerned about the Deep Seabed mining provisions (including technology transfer and profit-sharing). Israel was concerned about sharing Deep Seabed mining profits with Palestine. Turkey was concerned over Territorial Sea boundaries with Greece, and Venezuela had a delimitation dispute with Colombia. In addition, seventeen States abstained from the final vote, including the United Kingdom, Russia and West Germany. *See* Ronald Reagan Presidential Library & Museum, Statement on United States Actions Concerning the Conference on the Law of the Sea (July 9, 1982), https://www.reaganlibrary.gov/research/speeches/70982b (noting that although the number of States in opposition "appear small in number [they] represent countries which produce more than 60 percent of the world's gross national product and provide more than 60 percent of the contributions to the United Nations). *See generally* United Nations Publications prepared by the Division for Ocean Affairs and the Law of the Sea, Office of Legal Affairs, https://www.un.org/Depts/los/doalos_publications/doalos_publications.htm (providing a number of Law of the Sea publications, including the negotiating history (aka legislative history or *travaux préparatoires*) for specific UNCLOS provisions).

[85] William J. Aceves, *The Freedom of Navigation Program: A Study of the Relationship between Law and Politics*, 19 HASTINGS INT'L & COMP. L. REV. 259, 268 (1996), https://repository.uchastings.edu/hastings_international_comparative_law_review/vol19/iss2/2/.

[86] Chapter 4 discusses the Exclusive Economic Zone (EEZ).

[87] Chapter 3 discusses Transit Passage through International Straits.

[88] Elliot L. Richardson, Power, Mobility and the Law of the Sea, J. FOREIGN AFF., 902, 904 (1980) (referencing the "archipelagic problem"). Chapter 4 discusses the special regime for Archipelagic States.

[89] Jiangyu Wang, *Legitimacy, Jurisdiction and Merits in the South China Sea Arbitration: Chinese Perspectives and International Law*, 22 J. OF CHINESE POLIT. SCI. 185, online p. 5 (2017), https://papers.ssrn.com/sol3/papers.cfm?abstract_id=2967254.

[90] United Nations Convention on the Law of the Sea (UNCLOS) Introduction at p. 2, Dec. 10, 1982, 1833 U.N.T.S. 397, https://www.un.org/Depts/los/convention_agreements/convention_overview_convention.htm (noting that the "package deal" concept became a *leitmotif* (accompanying melody) that permeates throughout UNCLOS); TUFTS, LAW OF THE SEA, p. 9 (full cite above); DONALD R. ROTHWELL & TIM STEPHENS, THE INT'L. LAW OF THE SEA 13, 79 (2nd ed. 2016); Türk, *Questions Relating to the Continental Shelf Beyond 200 Nautical Miles*, p. 239 (full cite above). *See also* G.A. Res. 2750 (XXV), ¶ C, U.N. Doc A/AC.138/58 (Dec. 17, 1970), https://research.un.org/en/docs/ga/quick/regular/25 (noting "that the problems of ocean space are closely interrelated and need to be considered as a whole" when the United Nations General Assembly convened the Third United Nations Conference on the Law of the Sea); Permanent Court of Arbitration, Cases, Past Cases, [2013-19] The South China Sea Arbitration (*The Republic of Philippines v. The People's Republic of China*), Documents, Award on Jurisdiction and Admissibility (Oct. 29, 2015) ¶¶ 107, 225 (pp. 37, 87-88), https://pcacases.com/web/sendAttach/2579. *But see* Michael W. Lodge (Secretary-General of the International Seabed Authority), *Enclosure of the Oceans versus the Common Heritage of Mankind: The Inherent Tension between the Continental Shelf Beyond 200 Nautical Miles and the Area*, 97 INT'L. L. STUD. 803, 808 (2021), https://digital-

commons.usnwc.edu/cgi/viewcontent.cgi?article=2971&context=ils (noting that "while UNCLOS as a whole represented a 'package deal,' several of the key aspects were negotiated in isolation of one another, only converging at the end of UNCLOS III, or even in the drafting committee. This is particularly true for the regime for the Area, in Part XI and Annex III of the Convention, which was dealt with in the First Committee at UNCLOS III, and the regime for the continental shelf, which was dealt with by the Second Committee and in specialized negotiating groups.").

[91] Rose George, NINETY PERCENT OF EVERYTHING 9 (2013).

[92] Tommy T.B. Koh, President of the Third United Nations Conference on the Law of the Sea, Remarks at the Final Session of the Conference at Montego Bay (December 6 & 11, 1982), https://www.un.org/Depts/los/convention_agreements/texts/koh_english.pdf. *See also* Tullio Treves, *Introductory Note to the United Nations Convention on the Law of the Sea*, AUDIOVISUAL LIBRARY OF INT'L. LAW, http://legal.un.org/avl/ha/uncls/uncls.html; THE FLETCHER SCHOOL OF LAW AND DIPLOMACY—TUFTS UNIVERSITY, LAW OF THE SEA, A POLICY PRIMER 8-9 (2017), https://sites.tufts.edu/lawofthesea/introduction/; DONALD R. ROTHWELL & TIM STEPHENS, THE INT'L. LAW OF THE SEA 1 (2nd ed. 2016). *But see* Shicun Wu, *A Legal Critique of the Award of the Arbitral Tribunal in the Matter of the South China Sea Arbitration, in* 24 ASIAN YEARBOOK OF INT'L. LAW 151, 167 (2020), https://brill.com/view/book/edcoll/9789004437784/BP000019.xml ("as opposed to a constitution or a formulation of general norms from which no derogation is permitted (*jus cogens*), [UNCLOS] is an ordinary multilateral treaty, however comprehensive and significant its provisions may be.").

[93] Lodge, *Enclosure of the Oceans*, p. 804 (full cite above). *See also* Int'l. Tribunal for the Law of the Sea, States Parties, https://www.itlos.org/the-tribunal/states-parties/. Most recently, Azerbaijan ratified UNCLOS on June 16, 2016. United Nations, Oceans & Law of the Sea, Division for Ocean Affairs and the Law of the Sea, Chronological lists of ratifications of, accessions and successions to the Convention and the related Agreements, http://www.un.org/Depts/los/reference_files/chronological_lists_of_ratifications.htm#The%20United%20Nations%20Convention%20on%20the%20Law%20of%20the%20Sea. There are generally considered to be 195 States in the World, although the inclusion of 2 States is disputed. *See, e.g.*, Independent States in the World Fact Sheet, U.S. Dept. of State Bureau of Intelligence and Research (March 27, 2019), https://www.state.gov/independent-states-in-the-world/ (including Kosovo but not Palestine, which has observer status at the UN similar to the Holy See); Frequently Asked Questions, Worldometers, https://www.worldometers.info/geography/how-many-countries-are-there-in-the-world/ (including Palestine, but not Kosovo since China and Russia are blocking its membership in the UN). Thus 168/195 or eighty-six percent of States are party to UNCLOS.

[94] TUFTS, LAW OF THE SEA, p. 2 (full cite above). *See also* U.S. Dept. of Defense, Under Secretary of Defense for Policy, OUSDP Offices, FON, DoD Annual Freedom of Navigation (FON) Reports, *Freedom of Navigation: FY 2020 Operational Assertions*, p. 2, https://policy.defense.gov/OUSDP-Offices/FON/ ("International law as reflected in the 1982 Law of the Sea Convention recognizes the rights and freedoms of all nations to engage in traditional uses of the sea. These rights and freedoms are deliberately balanced against coastal States' control over maritime activities. As a nation with both a vast coastline and a significant maritime presence, the United States is

committed to preserving this legal balance as an essential part of the stable, rules-based international order.").

⁹⁵ Although the U.S. is not yet party to UNCLOS, it routinely participates as an observer at meetings of UNCLOS State Parties. *See, e.g.*, CarrieLyn D. Guymon (editor), DIGEST OF UNITED STATES PRACTICE IN INTERNATIONAL LAW 419 (2019), https://www.state.gov/digest-of-united-states-practice-in-international-law-2019.

⁹⁶ United Nations, Dag HammarskJöld Library, What is the difference between signing, ratification and accession of UN treaties?, http://ask.un.org/faq/14594 (noting that "'Accession' is the act whereby a state accepts the offer or the opportunity to become a party to a treaty already negotiated and signed by other states. It has the same legal effect as ratification. Accession usually occurs after the treaty has entered into force.").

⁹⁷ U.S. Dept. of State, Key Topics, Office of Ocean and Polar Affairs, Law of the Sea Convention, https://www.state.gov/law-of-the-sea-convention/; Mark E. Rosen, *U.S. International Oceans Law and Policy Interests in the South China Sea Arbitration: Implications for the U.S. Administration in the South China Sea and Elsewhere*, 22 J. OF CHINESE POLIT. SCI. 251, online unnumbered p. 2 (2017), https://www.readcube.com/articles/10.1007/s11366-017-9468-9.

⁹⁸ Defense News, The Drift, *A Quick-Reference Guide on UNCLOS for Gen. Hyten: The Drift*, *Vol. XLIII*, (David B. Larter, Aug. 4, 2019), https://www.defensenews.com/naval/the-drift/2019/08/04/a-quick-reference-guide-on-unclos-for-gen-hyten-the-drift-vol-xliii/.

⁹⁹ Ronald Reagan Presidential Library & Museum, Statement on United States Actions Concerning the Conference on the Law of the Sea (July 9, 1982), https://www.reaganlibrary.gov/research/speeches/70982b (expressing similar concerns); William J. Aceves, *The Freedom of Navigation Program: A Study of the Relationship between Law and Politics*, 19 HASTINGS INT'L & COMP. L. REV. 259, 270 (1996), https://repository.uchastings.edu/hastings_international_comparative_law_review/vol19/iss2/2/.

¹⁰⁰ Ronald Reagan Presidential Library & Museum, Statement on United States Ocean Policy (Mar. 10, 1983), https://www.reaganlibrary.gov/research/speeches/31083c; U.S. NAVY, MARINE CORPS & COAST GUARD, THE COMMANDER'S HANDBOOK ON THE LAW OF NAVAL OPERATIONS, NWP 1-14M/MCTP 11-10B/COMDTPUB P5800.7A, ¶ 2.8 (p. 2–15) (2017), www.jag.navy.mil/distrib/instructions/CDRs_HB_on_Law_of_Naval_Operations_AUG17.pdf.

¹⁰¹ United States Senate Committee on Foreign Relations (SFRC), Chairman's Press, *"24 Star" Military Witnesses Voice Strong Support for Law of the Sea Treaty* (June 14, 2012), https://www.foreign.senate.gov/press/chair/release/24-star-military-witnesses-voice-strong-support-for-law-of-the-sea-treaty (quoting then SFRC-Chairman John Kerry as stating "There's a reason every living Chief of Naval Operations supports U.S. accession to the Law of the Sea.... They know the United States needs the Treaty's 'navigational bill of rights' for worldwide access to get our troops to the fight, to sustain them during the fight, and to get back home without the permission of other countries.").

¹⁰² Reagan, Statement on U.S. Actions Concerning UNCLOS (full cite above) (expressing similar concerns); COMMANDER'S HANDBOOK, ¶ 1.2 (p. 1–1) (full cite above); THE FLETCHER SCHOOL OF LAW AND DIPLOMACY—TUFTS UNIVERSITY, LAW OF THE

SEA, A POLICY PRIMER 2 (2017), https://sites.tufts.edu/lawofthesea/introduction/; William J. Aceves, *The Freedom of Navigation Program: A Study of the Relationship between Law and Politics*, 19 HASTINGS INT'L & COMP. L. REV. 259, 271-272 (1996), https://repository.uchastings.edu/hastings_international_comparative_law_revi ew/vol19/iss2/2/. *But see* Aceves, *The FON Program*, p. 285 (full cite above) (noting that "[w]hile the United States claimed that the navigational provisions in the Convention codified customary international law, a number of states challenged this assertion. The Group of 77 argued that the navigational provisions of the Convention did not codify customary international law but rather created new international law. Therefore, only signatories to the Convention could benefit from its provisions. Similarly, Ambassador Tommy Koh, the second President of UNCLOS Ill, argued that the Convention did not codify customary law or reflect existing international practice.").

[103] TUFTS, LAW OF THE SEA, p. 10 (full cite above). *See also* U.S. Dept. of Defense, Under Secretary of Defense for Policy, OUSDP Offices, FON, DoD Annual Freedom of Navigation (FON) Reports, *Freedom of Navigation: FY 2020 Operational Assertions*, p. 1, https://policy.defense.gov/OUSDP-Offices/FON/ (using the mantras "International law as reflected in the 1982 Law of the Sea Convention" and "customary international law as reflected in the Law of the Sea Convention"); CarrieLyn D. Guymon (editor), DIGEST OF UNITED STATES PRACTICE IN INTERNATIONAL LAW 419 (2019), https://www.state.gov/digest-of-united-states-practice-in-international-law-2019 (statement by counselor for legal affairs for the U.S. Mission to the United Nations that "[t]he United States underscores the central importance of international law as reflected in the Law of the Sea Convention"); Michael W. Lodge (Secretary-General of the International Seabed Authority), *Enclosure of the Oceans versus the Common Heritage of Mankind: The Inherent Tension between the Continental Shelf Beyond 200 Nautical Miles and the Area*, 97 INT'L. L. STUD. 803, 804 (2021), https://digital-commons.usnwc.edu/cgi/viewcontent.cgi?article=2971&context=ils (noting that "[t]here can be no doubt that the main substantive provisions of UNCLOS may now be regarded as customary international law."). However, there are repercussions to the U.S. not being Party to UNCLOS. For example, Chapter 12 discusses the South China Sea arbitration between China and the Philippines, whose proceedings were closed to the public. The other littoral States bordering the South China Sea (Indonesia, Japan, Malaysia, Singapore, Thailand and Vietnam) were permitted to observe the proceedings, as were Australia and the UK (which decided not to attend). However, the arbitral tribunal rejected the U.S. request to observe the hearings, since the U.S. is not Party to UNCLOS. Permanent Court of Arbitration, Cases, Past Cases, [2013-19] The South China Sea Arbitration (*The Republic of Philippines v. The People's Republic of China*), Documents, Award on Jurisdiction and Admissibility (Oct. 29, 2015) ¶¶ 15, 65-70, 84, 86-87 (pp. 5, 22-25, 27-29, 30), https://pcacases.com/web/sendAttach/2579.

[104] United Nations, Departments, Law of the Sea, Convention Agreements, Texts, UNCLOS, Agreement relating to the Implementation of Part XI of the United Nations Convention on the Law of the Sea of 10 December 1982, https://www.un.org/Depts/los/convention_agreements/texts/unclos/closindxAgre e.htm; Aceves, *The FON Program*, pp. 273-274 (full cite above). The UN General Assembly debates and passes an annual omnibus resolution on oceans and the law of the sea. United Nations, Departments, Law of the Sea, Oceans and the Law of the Sea in the General Assembly of the United Nations, General Assembly resolutions and   decisions,

https://www.un.org/Depts/los/general_assembly/general_assembly_resolutions.htm.

[105] *The Law of the Sea Convention (Treaty Doc. 103-39): Hearing Before the Comm. on Foreign Relations, U.S. Senate, 112th Cong.* 12 (May 23, 2012) (prepared statement of Sec. of State Hon. Hillary Rodham Clinton), https://www.govinfo.gov/content/pkg/CHRG-112shrg77375/html/CHRG-112shrg77375.htm (noting that "[t]he United States signed the Agreement on the deep seabed mining provisions in 1994. As George P. Shultz, Secretary of State to President Reagan, said in a letter to Senator Lugar in 2007: 'The treaty has been changed in such a way with respect to the deep sea-beds that it is now acceptable, in my judgment. Under these circumstances, and given the many desirable aspects of the treaty on other grounds, I believe it is time to proceed with ratification.' Indeed, every former Secretary of State since Secretary Shultz, Democrat and Republican alike, has called for the United States to secure and advance our national interests by joining the Convention."). President Reagan's specific concerns about the Deep Seabed mining regime included:
"– Provisions that would actually deter future development of deep seabed mineral resources, when such development should serve the interest of all countries.
– A decisionmaking process that would not give the United States or others a role that fairly reflects and protects their interests.
– Provisions that would allow amendments to enter into force for the United States without its approval. This is clearly incompatible with the United States approach to such treaties.
– Stipulations relating to mandatory transfer of private technology and the possibility of national liberation movements sharing in benefits.
– The absence of assured access for future qualified deep seabed miners to promote the development of these resources." Ronald Reagan Presidential Library & Museum, Statement on United States Actions Concerning the Conference on the Law of the Sea (July 9, 1982), https://www.reaganlibrary.gov/research/speeches/70982b.

[106] William J. Aceves, *The Freedom of Navigation Program: A Study of the Relationship between Law and Politics*, 19 HASTINGS INT'L & COMP. L. REV. 259, 275 (1996), https://repository.uchastings.edu/hastings_international_comparative_law_review/vol19/iss2/2/. "The primary benefits of the Convention to the United States include the following:
•   The Convention advances the interests of the United States as a global maritime power. It preserves the right of the U.S. military to use the world's oceans to meet national security requirements and of commercial vessels to carry sea-going cargoes. It achieves this, *inter alia*, by stabilizing the breadth of the territorial sea at 12 nautical miles; by setting forth navigation regimes of innocent passage in the territorial sea, transit passage in straits used for international navigation, and archipelagic sea lanes passage; and by reaffirming the traditional freedoms of navigation and overflight in the exclusive economic zone and the high seas beyond.
•   The Convention advances the interests of the United States as a coastal State. It achieves this, *inter alia*, by providing for an exclusive economic zone out to 200 nautical miles from shore and by securing our rights regarding resources and artificial islands, installations and structures for economic purposes over the full extent of the continental shelf. These provisions fully comport with

U.S. oil and gas leasing practices, domestic management of coastal fishery resources, and international fisheries agreements.

- As a far-reaching environmental accord addressing vessel source pollution, pollution from seabed activities, ocean dumping, and land-based sources of marine pollution, the Convention promotes continuing improvement in the health of the world's oceans.
- In light of the essential role of marine scientific research in understanding and managing the oceans, the Convention sets forth criteria and procedures to promote access to marine areas, including coastal waters, for research activities.
- The Convention facilitates solutions to the increasingly complex problems of the uses of the ocean—solutions that respect the essential balance between our interests as both a coastal and a maritime nation.
- Through its dispute settlement provisions, the Convention provides for mechanisms to enhance compliance by Parties with the Convention's provisions."

Letter Of Transmittal Forwarding The 1982 UN Law Of The Sea Convention To The United States Senate (William J. Clinton, Oct. 7, 1994) (S. Treaty Doc. 103–39), https://www.foreign.senate.gov/imo/media/doc/treaty_103-39.pdf.

[107] John Norton Moore, *Navigational Freedom: The Most Critical Common Heritage*, 93 INT'L. L. STUD. 251, 260 (2017), https://digital-commons.usnwc.edu/ils/vol93/iss1/8/. *See also* U.S. Dept. of State, Key Topics, Office of Ocean and Polar Affairs, Law of the Sea Convention, https://www.state.gov/law-of-the-sea-convention/ (providing a fairly detailed timeline of U.S. involvement in UNCLOS, and attempts at ratification/accession); THE FLETCHER SCHOOL OF LAW AND DIPLOMACY—TUFTS UNIVERSITY, LAW OF THE SEA, A POLICY PRIMER 82-87 (2017), https://sites.tufts.edu/lawofthesea/introduction/ (describing arguments for and against U.S. accession to UNCLOS); Brookings Institution, Center for East Asia Policy Studies, East Asia Policy Paper 9, The U.S. FON Program in the South China Sea—A lawful and necessary response to China's strategic ambiguity, p. 29 (Lynn Kuok, June 2016), https://www.brookings.edu/research/the-u-s-fon-program-in-the-south-china-sea/ (arguing that "[t]he United States' failure to accede to UNCLOS continues to hurt it as it leaves it open to repeated charges of hypocrisy."); Mark E. Rosen, *U.S. International Oceans Law and Policy Interests in the South China Sea Arbitration: Implications for the U.S. Administration in the South China Sea and Elsewhere*, 22 J. OF CHINESE POLIT. SCI. 251, online unnumbered pp. 2-3 (2017), https://www.readcube.com/articles/10.1007/s11366-017-9468-9 (making the same arguments for U.S. accession to UNCLOS); Defense News, The Drift, *A Quick-Reference Guide on UNCLOS for Gen. Hyten: The Drift, Vol. XLIII*, (David B. Larter, Aug. 4, 2019), https://www.defensenews.com/naval/the-drift/2019/08/04/a-quick-reference-guide-on-unclos-for-gen-hyten-the-drift-vol-xliii/ (noting that "[c]onservatives have long been suspicious of international legal bodies and the idea of ceding sovereignty to the international community and its whims.").

[108] Letter Of Transmittal Forwarding The 1982 UN Law Of The Sea Convention To The United States Senate, DOS Commentary p. 2 (William J. Clinton, Oct. 7, 1994) (S. Treaty Doc. 103–39), https://www.foreign.senate.gov/imo/media/doc/treaty_103-39.pdf.

[109] TUFTS, LAW OF THE SEA, p. 3 (full cite above). *See generally* National Geospatial-Intelligence Agency, Nautical Calculators, https://msi.nga.mil/Calc.

[110] Latitude measures the number of degrees North or South of the equator.

51

[111] "The term knot dates from the 17th century, when sailors measured the speed of their ship by using a device called a 'common log.' This device was a coil of rope with uniformly spaced knots, attached to a piece of wood shaped like a slice of pie. The piece of wood was lowered from the back of the ship and allowed to float behind it. The line was allowed to pay out freely from the coil as the piece of wood fell behind the ship for a specific amount of time. When the specified time had passed, the line was pulled in and the number of knots on the rope between the ship and the wood were counted. The speed of the ship was said to be the number of knots counted (Bowditch, 1984)." National Oceanic and Atmospheric Administration (NOAA), U.S. Dept. of Commerce, Ocean Facts, *What is the Difference Between a Nautical Mile and a Knot?*, https://oceanservice.noaa.gov/facts/nauticalmile_knot.html.

[112] World Ocean Review, Living with the oceans. A report on the state of the oceans (2010), https://worldoceanreview.com/en/wor-1/transport/global-shipping/2/.

[113] Globe graphic from Free clipart: http://www.clker.com/clipart-globe-with-longitude-and-latitude-lines.html (annotated by the author).

[114] Naval History and Heritage Command, Crossing the Line: Pollywogs to Shellbacks, https://www.history.navy.mil/browse-by-topic/heritage/customs-and-traditions0/crossing-line.html. A Royal Shellback is a Sailor who crossed the Equator at the Prime Meridian (southwest of Africa). A Golden Shellback is a Sailor who crossed the Equator at the 180th meridian/International Dateline (northeast of Fiji). *See also* America's Navy, Forged by the Sea, News, *USS Donald Cook Applies Lessons for Second Trip to Arctic* (Sarah Claudy & Teresa Meadows, May 14, 2020), https://www.navy.mil/submit/display.asp?story_id=112964&utm_source=phplist5723&utm_medium=email&utm_content=HTML&utm_campaign=Headlines (describing a "Blue Nose" ceremony for crossing the Arctic Circle).

[115] United Nations Convention on the Law of the Sea (UNCLOS) art. 8(1), Dec. 10, 1982, 1833 U.N.T.S. 397, https://www.un.org/Depts/los/convention_agreements/convention_overview_convention.htm. *See also* Dept. of Defense Law of War Manual § 13.2.2.1, p. 881 (June 2015, updated Dec. 2016), https://www.hsdl.org/?view&did=797480; U.S. Navy, Marine Corps & Coast Guard, The Commander's Handbook on the Law of Naval Operations, NWP 1-14M/MCTP 11-10B/COMDTPUB P5800.7A, ¶¶ 1.3.1, 1.5.1, 2.5.1 (pp. 1-2, 1-7, 2-5) (2017), www.jag.navy.mil/distrib/instructions/CDRs_HB_on_Law_of_Naval_Operations_AUG17.pdf; Letter Of Transmittal Forwarding The 1982 UN Law Of The Sea Convention To The United States Senate, DOS Commentary pp. 2-3 (William J. Clinton, Oct. 7, 1994) (S. Treaty Doc. 103–39), https://www.foreign.senate.gov/imo/media/doc/treaty_103-39.pdf.

[116] Commander's Handbook, ¶ 2.5.1 (p. 2-5) (full cite above); DOS Commentary, p. 14 (full cite above). The concept that each State has exclusive sovereignty over its (land) territory originates from the 1648 Treaties of Westphalia (aka the Peace of Westphalia). Encyclopædia Britannica, European History, *Peace of Westphalia*, https://www.britannica.com/event/Peace-of-Westphalia; Restatement (Third) Of Foreign Relations, pt. 1, introductory note (p. 17) (1987).

[117] UNCLOS, Preamble unnumbered ¶ 7 & arts. 125(1), 136, 137(2), 140(1), 143(1), 149, 150(i), 153(1), 155(1)(a), 155(2), 246(3), 311(6) & 1994 Implementing Agreement Preamble ¶ 2 (full cite above); Tufts, Law Of The Sea, p. 8 (full cite above).

[118] DoD Law of War Manual § 13.2.2, pp. 881-883 (full cite above); COMMANDER'S HANDBOOK, ¶ 2.7.1 (p. 2-13) (full cite above).

[119] COMMANDER'S HANDBOOK, ¶¶ 1.5, 1.6, 2.6.1 to 2.6.2 (pp. 1-7, 1-8, 2-9) (full cite above); TUFTS, LAW OF THE SEA, pp. 30-31 (full cite above).

[120] COMMANDER'S HANDBOOK, ¶¶ 1.1, 1.9, 2.7.2 (pp. 1-1, 1-10, 2-13) (full cite above); Raul (Pete) Pedrozo, *Military Activities in the Exclusive Economic Zone: East Asia Focus*, 90 INT'L. L. STUD. 514, 519-521 (2014), https://digital-commons.usnwc.edu/ils/vol90/iss1/15/; DOS Commentary, p. 7 (full cite above).

[121] DOS Commentary, p. 2 (full cite above).

[122] Michael W. Lodge (Secretary-General of the International Seabed Authority), *Enclosure of the Oceans versus the Common Heritage of Mankind: The Inherent Tension between the Continental Shelf Beyond 200 Nautical Miles and the Area*, 97 INT'L. L. STUD. 803, 807 (2021), https://digital-commons.usnwc.edu/cgi/viewcontent.cgi?article=2971&context=ils.

[123] UNCLOS, art. 5 (full cite above).

[124] COMMANDER'S HANDBOOK, ¶ 1.4.1 (p. 1-3) (full cite above).

[125] UNCLOS, art. 7 (full cite above).

[126] DOS Commentary, p. 8 (full cite above).

[127] DOS Commentary, p. 10 (full cite above).

[128] UNCLOS, arts. 7(4) & 13(1) (full cite above); UNITED NATIONS OFFICE FOR OCEAN AFFAIRS AND THE LAW OF THE SEA, THE LAW OF THE SEA, BASELINES: AN EXAMINATION OF THE RELEVANT PROVISIONS OF THE UNITED NATIONS CONVENTION ON THE LAW OF THE SEA 25 ¶ 52 (1989), https://www.un.org/Depts/los/doalos_publications/publicationstexts/The%20Law%20of%20the%20Sea_Baselines.pdf; COMMANDER'S HANDBOOK, ¶¶ 1.4.2, 1.4.2.2, 1.5.3 & Figures 1-2 & 1-6 (pp. 1-3, 1-4) (full cite above). This is known as the "Norway exception," which was accepted by the International Court of Justice (ICJ) in the 1951 Fisheries Case. Int'l. Court of Justice (ICJ), Fisheries (United Kingdom v. Norway), Judgement of Dec. 18, 1951 at p. 31, https://www.icj-cij.org/en/case/5.

[129] BASELINES, p. 21 ¶ 39 (full cite above).

[130] UNCLOS, art. 8(1) (full cite above). *See also* Law of War Manual § 13.2.2.1, p. 881 (full cite above); COMMANDER'S HANDBOOK, ¶¶ 1.3.1, 1.5.1, 2.5.1 (pp. 1-2, 1-7, 2-5) full cite above). *See also* Nilüfer Oral, Ukraine v. The Russian Federation: *Navigating Conflict over Sovereignty under UNCLOS*, 97 INT'L. L. STUD. 478, 499 (2021), https://digital-commons.usnwc.edu/ils/vol97/iss1/25/ (noting that "UNCLOS does not provide a regime of rights and obligations for internal waters as it does for other maritime zones.")

[131] BASELINES, p. 25 ¶ 54-55 (full cite above).

[132] U.S. Dept. of State Foreign Affairs Manual (FAM) and Handbook (FAH), 7 FAM 034, *"Demarches"* (2005), https://fam.state.gov/FAM/07FAM/07FAM0030.html. *See generally* U.S. Dept. of State FAM/FAH Search, https://fam.state.gov/search.

[133] The reader will note that UNCLOS has 320 provisions or "articles" (plus at least another 116 articles in its Annexes), and yet UNCLOS only includes six definitions in Article 1. This would seem to imply that the State Parties wanted some degree of ambiguity in the language of UNCLOS.

[134] DONALD R. ROTHWELL & TIM STEPHENS, THE INT'L. LAW OF THE SEA 45 (2nd ed. 2016).

[135] ROTHWELL & STEPHENS, LAW OF THE SEA, p. 51 (full cite above).

[136] JAMES KRASKA & RAUL PEDROZO, INT'L. MARITIME SECURITY LAW 246 (2013).

[137] BASELINES, p. 25 ¶ 52 (full cite above). *See generally* United Nations Publications prepared by the Division for Ocean Affairs and the Law of the Sea, Office of Legal Affairs, https://www.un.org/Depts/los/doalos_publications/doalos_publications.htm (providing a number of Law of the Sea publications, including the negotiating history (aka legislative history or *travaux préparatoires*) for specific UNCLOS provisions).

[138] Dept. of Defense Maritime Claims Reference Manual (MCRM), http://www.jag.navy.mil/organization/code_10_mcrm.htm. *See also* U.S. Dept. of State, Bureau of Oceans and Int'l. Environmental and Scientific Affairs, Policy Issues, The Ocean and Polar Affairs, Key Topics, Limits in the Seas, https://www.state.gov/limits-in-the-seas/. *See generally* U.S. Navy Judge Advocate General's Corps, About Us, Organization, National Security Law (Code 10), https://www.jag.navy.mil/organization/code_10.htm (explaining the mission, functions and references maintained by Code 10).

[139] National Oceanic and Atmospheric Administration (NOAA), U.S. Dept. of Commerce, Ocean Facts, *What is the Law of the Sea?*, https://oceanservice.noaa.gov/facts/lawofsea.html.

[140] National Oceanic and Atmospheric Administration (NOAA), U.S. Dept. of Commerce, Office of Coast Survey, Data, U.S. Maritime Limits & Boundaries, https://www.nauticalcharts.noaa.gov/data/us-maritime-limits-and-boundaries.html.

[141] U.S. NAVY, MARINE CORPS & COAST GUARD, THE COMMANDER'S HANDBOOK ON THE LAW OF NAVAL OPERATIONS, NWP 1-14M/MCTP 11-10B/COMDTPUB P5800.7A, ¶ 1.4.2 (p. 1-3) (2017), www.jag.navy.mil/distrib/instructions/CDRs_HB_on_Law_of_Naval_Operations_AUG17.pdf. *See also* Letter Of Transmittal Forwarding The 1982 UN Law Of The Sea Convention To The United States Senate, DOS Commentary p. 7 (William J. Clinton, Oct. 7, 1994) (S. Treaty Doc. 103–39), https://www.foreign.senate.gov/imo/media/doc/treaty_103-39.pdf ("Objective application of baseline rules contained in the Convention can help prevent excessive claims in the future and encourage governments to revise existing claims to conform to the relevant criteria.").

[142] This "depth of penetration" factor essentially applies the semi-circle test used for bays, discussed subsequently in this Chapter.

[143] DOS Commentary, pp. 8-9 (full cite above).

[144] *See* JAMES KRASKA & RAUL PEDROZO, INT'L. MARITIME SECURITY LAW 246-247 (2013) ("Although UNCLOS does not specify the maximum length of a straight baseline most experts would agree that a straight baseline should not exceed between 24 and 48 nm.").

[145] UNITED NATIONS OFFICE FOR OCEAN AFFAIRS AND THE LAW OF THE SEA, THE LAW OF THE SEA, BASELINES: AN EXAMINATION OF THE RELEVANT PROVISIONS OF THE UNITED NATIONS CONVENTION ON THE LAW OF THE SEA 18 ¶ 35 and 21 ¶ 42 (1989), https://www.un.org/Depts/los/doalos_publications/publicationstexts/The%20Law%20of%20the%20Sea_Baselines.pdf.

[146] BASELINES, p. 18 ¶ 36 (full cite above).

[147] BASELINES, pp. 21-22 ¶¶ 43-45 (full cite above).

[148] BASELINES, p. 22 ¶ 46 (full cite above).

[149] KRASKA & PEDROZO, MARITIME SECURITY LAW, p. 246 (full cite above).

[150] BASELINES, p. 28 ¶ 65 (full cite above).

[151] COMMANDER'S HANDBOOK, ¶ 1.4.3 & Figures 1-3 to 1-5 (pp. 1-5 to 1-6) (full cite above).

[152] United Nations Convention on the Law of the Sea (UNCLOS) art. 10, Dec. 10, 1982, 1833 U.N.T.S. 397, https://www.un.org/Depts/los/convention_agreements/convention_overview_convention.htm.

[153] UNCLOS, arts. 10(4) & (5) (full cite above).

[154] UNCLOS, art. 10(2) (full cite above).

[155] UNCLOS, art. 11 (full cite above).

[156] Thus, it should come as no surprise when another State's warships enter a foreign port. *See, e.g.*, The Straits Times, Asia, Australia/NZ, *Chinese warships cause surprise in Sydney Harbour* (June 3, 2019), https://www.straitstimes.com/asia/australianz/chinese-warships-cause-surprise-in-sydney-harbour.

[157] COMMANDER'S HANDBOOK, ¶ ¶ 3.2.2 (p. 3-2) (pp. 1-3, 1-4) (full cite above).

[158] UNCLOS, art. 10(6) (full cite above).

[159] DONALD R. ROTHWELL & TIM STEPHENS, THE INT'L. LAW OF THE SEA 49 (2nd ed. 2016).

[160] *See* ROTHWELL & STEPHENS, LAW OF THE SEA, p. 50 (full cite above) (listing Canada's Hudson Bay, the American Chesapeake and Delaware Bays, *inter alia* as identified by the "1957 study undertaken by the United Nations in preparation" for the First United Nations Conference on the Law of the Sea). *See also* Historic Bays: Memorandum by the Secretariat of the United Nations, at 6, U.N. Doc. A/CONF. 13/1 (Sep. 30, 1957), https://legal.un.org/diplomaticconferences/1958_los/docs/english/vol_1/a_conf13_1.pdf.

[161] DoD MCRM—Canada 2017 (full cite above).

[162] DOS Commentary, pp. 11-12 (full cite above). *See also* COMMANDER'S HANDBOOK, ¶ 1.4.3 (p. 1-5) (full cite above); ROTHWELL & STEPHENS, LAW OF THE SEA, p. 50 (full cite above). The concept of historic bays is similar to the Property Law concept of "acquisition by adverse possession" of property owned/titled to another: exclusive possession of property that is continuous, open and notorious.

[163] ROTHWELL & STEPHENS, LAW OF THE SEA, p. 51 (full cite above).

[164] U.S. Dept. of State Foreign Affairs Manual (FAM) and Handbook (FAH), 5 FAH-1 H-612.2-1, *"Note Verbale"* (2019), https://fam.state.gov/FAM/05FAH01/05FAH010610.html. *See generally* U.S. Dept. of State FAM/FAH Search, https://fam.state.gov/search.

[165] Libyan Foreign Ministry *Note Verbale* MQ/40/5/1/3345, www.un.org/Depts/los/LEGISLATIONANDTREATIES/PDFFILES/LBY_1973_Information.pdf.

[166] DoD MCRM— Libya 2014 (full cite above). Chapter 11 discusses Freedom of Navigation (FON) Programs in more depth.

[167] KRASKA & PEDROZO, MARITIME SECURITY LAW, pp. 247-252 (full cite above); William J. Aceves, *The Freedom of Navigation Program: A Study of the Relationship between Law and Politics*, 19 HASTINGS INT'L & COMP. L. REV. 259, 294-295 (1996), https://repository.uchastings.edu/hastings_international_comparative_law_review/vol19/iss2/2/.

[168] NOTE: There is a diagram of the various maritime zones at the beginning of the Chapter.

[169] United Nations, Legal, Audiovisual Library of Int'l. Law, Lecture Series, Law of the Sea, Regime of Islands (Sean D. Murphy), https://legal.un.org/avl/ls/Murphy_LS.html.

[170] COMMANDER'S HANDBOOK, ¶ 1.5.3 & Figure 1-6 (pp. 1-7 to 1-8) (full cite above).

[171] Chapter 4 discusses the special rules for nations comprised of a group of islands (i.e., archipelagoes or archipelagic nations).

[172] United Nations Convention on the Law of the Sea (UNCLOS) art. 121, Dec. 10, 1982, 1833 U.N.T.S. 397, https://www.un.org/Depts/los/convention_agreements/convention_overview_convention.htm.

[173] U.S. NAVY, MARINE CORPS & COAST GUARD, THE COMMANDER'S HANDBOOK ON THE LAW OF NAVAL OPERATIONS, NWP 1-14M/MCTP 11-10B/COMDTPUB P5800.7A, ¶ 1.5.3 (p. 1-7) (2017), www.jag.navy.mil/distrib/instructions/CDRs_HB_on_Law_of_Naval_Operations_AUG17.pdf. Rocks are still considered pieces of land that can be owned, and thus are entitled to a corresponding Territorial Seas and the limited enforcement provided for in the Contiguous Zone (discussed in Chapter 4). Rocks are defined by UNCLOS as being above water at high tide, but incapable of sustaining human habitation. Thus, a sandbar that remains above water at high tide but cannot sustain human life would qualify as a Rock. THE FLETCHER SCHOOL OF LAW AND DIPLOMACY—TUFTS UNIVERSITY, LAW OF THE SEA, A POLICY PRIMER 16 (2017), https://sites.tufts.edu/lawofthesea/introduction/; DONALD R. ROTHWELL & TIM STEPHENS, THE INT'L. LAW OF THE SEA 3 (2nd ed. 2016). *But see* universitätbonn institute for public int'l. law, Bonn Research Papers on Public Int'l. Law, Paper No 14/2018, *The South China Sea Arbitration: Observations on the Award of 12 July 2016*, pp. 80-81 (Stefan A. G. Talmon, May 17, 2018), https://papers.ssrn.com/sol3/papers.cfm?abstract_id=3180037 (positing that "there are three categories of islands:
(1) rocks that cannot sustain human habitation or economic life of their own;
(2) rocks that can sustain human habitation or economic life of their own; and
(3) all other islands.
Only the first category does not generate an EEZ or continental shelf.").

[174] Letter Of Transmittal Forwarding The 1982 UN Law Of The Sea Convention To The United States Senate, DOS Commentary p. 12 (William J. Clinton, Oct. 7, 1994) (S. Treaty Doc. 103–39), https://www.foreign.senate.gov/imo/media/doc/treaty_103-39.pdf.

[175] UNCLOS, arts. 7(4) & 13 (full cite above); COMMANDER'S HANDBOOK, ¶ 1.5.3 & Figure 1-6 (pp. 1-7 to 1-8) (full cite above). This is known as the "Norway exception," which was accepted by the International Court of Justice (ICJ) in the 1951 Fisheries Case. Int'l. Court of Justice (ICJ), Fisheries (United Kingdom v. Norway), Judgement of Dec. 18, 1951 at p. 31, https://www.icj-cij.org/en/case/5.

[176] Although artificial islands may be constructed in a Coastal State's Exclusive Economic Zone, they are not entitled to any maritime zones. UNCLOS, arts. 56, 60 & 121 (full cite above). *See also* Imogen Saunders, *Artificial Islands and Territory in Int'l. Law*, 52 VANDERBILT J. OF TRANSNATIONAL LAW 643 (2019); TUFTS, LAW OF THE SEA, p. 16 (full cite above). Chapter 12 discusses the requirements for claiming the status of an island in more depth in the context of the Permanent Court of Arbitration Tribunal's decision in the South China Sea arbitration.

[177] The Permanent Court of Arbitration held in the Philippines vs. China case that an Island must have "fresh water" meeting modern standards of potability (i.e., not

brackish), arable land capable of growing crops, and diverse vegetation permitting year-round human occupation, which is a fairly high standard for what constitutes an Island. Permanent Court of Arbitration, Cases, Past Cases, [2013-19] The South China Sea Arbitration (*The Republic of Philippines v. The People's Republic of China*), Documents, Award (July 12, 2016) ¶¶ 621-622 (p. 253), https://pcacases.com/web/sendAttach/2086 (discussed in more depth in Chapter 12).

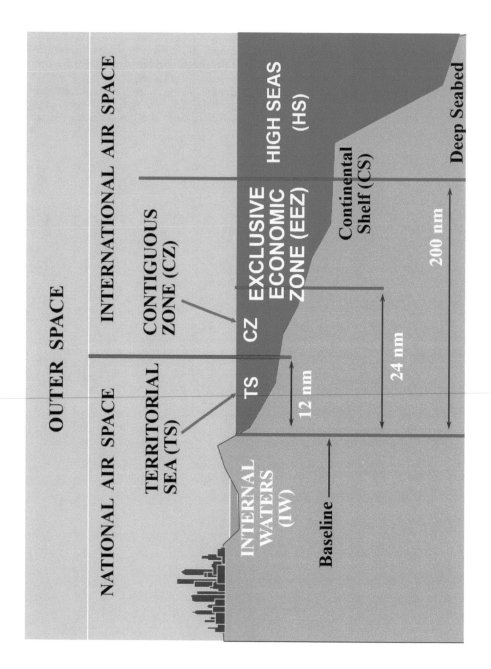

58

CHAPTER 3: TERRITORIAL SEAS & INTERNATIONAL STRAITS

"The first and most obvious light in which the sea presents itself from the political and social viewpoint is that of a great highway; or better, perhaps, of a wide common, over which all men may pass in all directions ...."
—*Alfred Thayer Mahan*

THE FIRST (AND PERHAPS PARAMOUNT) MARITIME ZONE measured from the baseline is the Territorial Sea. Bottom line up front (BLUF): the Territorial Sea is generally 12 nm wide,[178] and the Coastal State exercises almost complete sovereignty over its national waters/Territorial Seas, subject primarily to the right of all ships to conduct Innocent Passage. As discussed in Chapter 2, beyond 12 nm from the maritime baseline are International Waters[179] and International Airspace,[180] over which the Coastal State exercises less and less sovereignty and control the further one travels from land. [NOTE: There is a diagram of the various maritime zones at the beginning of the Chapter.] This Chapter discusses Innocent Passage through

Territorial Seas (which can be abbreviated IP-TS or TS/IP) and Transit Passage through International Straits (which can be abbreviated TP-IS or IS/TP), all of which are terms of art which should not be confused. One way to distinguish these terms of art, is that the acronyms for both regimes (i.e., set of rules) have the letters: T S I P or "tea sip" (albeit in different orders). [NOTE: If the reader conflates the wrong type of passage with the incorrect body of water, you won't be able to spell T S I P.]

UNCLOS' regimes for Innocent Passage through Territorial Seas and Transit Passage through International Straits are based upon the first case before the new, post-World War II International Court of Justice: The Corfu Channel case of 1949. The North Corfu Channel is a narrow, secondary strait located between the mainland border between Albania and Greece to the east and the Greek Island of Corfu to the west. The North Corfu Channel had long been used as a strait for international navigation, especially for coastal trading vessels between Greece and then-Yugoslavia. Due to the rocky seabed on the Corfu Island/western side and the fact that the channel is only 3 nm wide at its narrowest point, ships are required to navigate to within 1 nm of the Albanian coast.

During World War II, the Axis Powers extensively mined the Corfu Channel to prevent ships from transiting through it. After victory was declared in Europe on May 8, 1945, the British Royal Navy conducted mine clearance operations throughout the Corfu Channel. About one year later, two small British warships transited the Corfu Channel. But by then, relations between the Eastern and Western Blocs had begun to turn frosty. Albania was part of the Eastern Bloc led by the Soviet Union, and Greece (Albania's southern neighbor) was part of the Western Bloc (led by the U.S., and which became the North Atlantic Treaty Organization, NATO). Moreover, Albania had declared that "foreign warships should obtain previous authorization before passing through its territorial waters."[181]

The two British light cruisers came under fire from Albanian coastal batteries (i.e., anti-ship artillery). The United Kingdom issued a *démarche* (i.e., a formal diplomatic protest)[182] seeking an apology from the Albanian government. The Albanian government claimed the British ships had trespassed in Albania's territorial waters without prior authorization. Five months later, a four-ship Royal Navy squadron transited the Corfu Channel during daylight to test Albania's reaction to their "innocent" passage. The first destroyer struck a mine, which blew off its bow. A second destroyer was towing the damaged ship back into port when the second destroyer (HMS *Volage*—pictured below) hit a mine as well, and

blowing off its bow as well — over forty British sailors died, and another forty plus were injured. Fortunately, an Albanian naval vessel rendered assistance.[183] Three weeks later, the United Kingdom notified Albania before it conducted minesweeping operations without Albania's permission. The British minesweepers found 22 new German contact mines (see photo next page). Since Albania did not have any minelayer vessels, the United Kingdom surmised that the mines had probably been laid by Yugoslavian minelayers furnished by the Soviets.[184]

Albania denied laying the mines or having any knowledge of them, and complained about the British incursion into Albanian territorial waters. The United Kingdom enlisted the aid of the new United Nations Security Council (UNSC), but a proposed UNSC Resolution against Albania was vetoed by the Soviet Union (remember that Albania was part of the Eastern Bloc). However, the UNSC agreed to recommend that the two States submit their dispute to the new World Court—the International Court of Justice (ICJ).

The World Court held:

1) There is a generally recognized Customary International Law (CIL)[185] right for States to send their ships (including warships) through straits used for international navigation between two parts

COUR INTERNATIONALE DE JUSTICE

RECUEIL
DES ARRÊTS, AVIS CONSULTATIFS ET ORDONNANCES

AFFAIRE DU DÉTROIT
DE CORFOU
(FOND)

ARRÊT DU 9 AVRIL 1949

1949

INTERNATIONAL COURT OF JUSTICE

REPORTS
OF
JUDGMENTS, ADVISORY OPINIONS AND ORDERS

THE CORFU
CHANNEL CASE
(MERITS)

JUDGMENT OF APRIL 9th, 1949

LEYDE
SOCIÉTÉ D'ÉDITIONS
A. W. SIJTHOFF

LEYDEN
A. W. SIJTHOFF'S
PUBLISHING COMPANY

of the High Seas, without previous authorization of the Coastal States bordering the straits, so long as the passage is innocent.

2) There is no right for Coastal States bordering a strait to prohibit passage through the strait in time of peace.

3) Due to Albania's intensive monitoring of the North Corfu Channel/Strait, Albania must have known about the minefield and should have warned other States of the danger.[186]

4) However, the subsequent British minesweeping operations were inconsistent with innocent passage (i.e., minesweeping is a form of military use of force, which is inconsistent with "innocent" passage).

5) Albania was required to pay approximately £850,000 in compensation to the United Kingdom, which was worth about $2M at the time.[187]

The Corfu Channel case was decided thirty-three years before UNCLOS was adopted.[188] UNCLOS bifurcated the concepts of Innocent Passage through Territorial Seas and Transit Passage through International Straits. Yet the Corfu Channel case is viewed as the source of the definition of Innocent Passage through Territorial Seas in UNCLOS: passage is innocent so long as it does not prejudice the peace, good order or security of the Coastal State.

There are thirty-one articles in UNCLOS Part II dealing with the Territorial Sea, some of which were discussed previously (regarding baselines and bays),[189] and many of which can be summarized quite succinctly. A Coastal State's sovereignty "extends, beyond its land territory and internal waters ... to an adjacent belt of sea, described as the territorial sea," including the airspace above it and the seabed and subsoil beneath it,[190] out to 12 nautical miles from the baselines.[191] The Coastal State exercises almost complete sovereignty over its Territorial Seas (which are considered national waters), subject primarily to the right of all ships (including warships, **but not aircraft**)[192] to conduct Innocent Passage,[193] which shall be "shall be continuous and expeditious."[194]

Article 19 defines what constitutes Innocent Passage in general terms, and then lists prejudicial acts that are contrary to it:

Article 19 / Meaning of innocent passage
1. *Passage is innocent so long as it is not prejudicial to the peace, good order or security of the coastal State. Such passage shall take place in conformity with this Convention and with other rules of international law.*
2. *Passage of a foreign ship shall be considered to be prejudicial to the peace, good order or security of the coastal State if in the territorial sea it engages in any of the following activities:*
    (a) *any threat or use of force against the sovereignty, territorial integrity or political independence of the coastal State, or in any other*

manner in violation of the principles of international law embodied in the Charter of the United Nations;

(b) any exercise or practice with weapons of any kind;

(c) any act aimed at collecting information to the prejudice of the defence or security of the coastal State;

(d) any act of propaganda aimed at affecting the defence or security of the coastal State;

(e) the launching, landing or taking on board of any aircraft;

(f) the launching, landing or taking on board of any military device;

(g) the loading or unloading of any commodity, currency or person contrary to the customs, fiscal, immigration or sanitary laws and regulations of the coastal State;

(h) any act of wilful and serious pollution contrary to this Convention;

(i) any fishing activities;

(j) the carrying out of research or survey activities;

(k) any act aimed at interfering with any systems of communication or any other facilities or installations of the coastal State;

(l) any other activity not having a direct bearing on passage.
[emphasis added][195]

Thus, Article 19 defines Innocent Passage in the negative (i.e., by providing specific examples of what violates Innocent Passage by being prejudicial to the peace and security of the Coastal State).[196] Submarines have an additional requirement: in order for their passage to be innocent, **"submarines ... are required to navigate on the surface and to show their flag."**[197] There is no corresponding right for aircraft to engage in Innocent Passage—only ships and surfaced submarines. Thus, a good mnemonic for remembering the Territorial Sea/Innocent Passage (TS/IP) regime is that **passage must be on the surface of the ocean in order to remain innocent.**

The Coastal State has certain rights and responsibilities in conjunction with the Territorial Sea/Innocent Passage regime, including adopting and publicizing laws and regulations related to:

➢ the safety of navigation in the Territorial Sea;

➢ the regulation of maritime traffic in the Territorial Sea;

➢ protecting "navigational aids ... and other facilities or installations" within the Territorial Sea;

➢ protecting cables and pipelines lying on the seabed beneath the Territorial Sea;

➢ conserving living resources, including fisheries, in the Territorial Sea;

➢ preserving the environment in the Territorial Sea;

➢ preventing, reducing and controlling pollution in the Territorial Sea;

➢ Marine Scientific Research (MSR) and hydrographic surveys in the Territorial Sea;[198]

➢ preventing the infringement of fiscal, immigration, sanitation and customs (FISC) laws and regulations;

➢ limiting "the design, construction, manning or equipment of foreign ships" engaged in Innocent Passage through the Territorial Sea, but only if doing so gives "effect to generally accepted international rules or standards";[199]

➢ establishing sea lanes and traffic separation schemes to ensure the safety of navigation of foreign ships exercising Innocent Passage;[200]

➢ preventing non-innocent passage (i.e., violations of Innocent Passage);[201]

➢ setting conditions on entering port (aka port entry);[202]

➢ temporarily suspending Innocent Passage in specific areas of the Territorial Sea, when essential to protect its security, and after due publicity (e.g., when conducting weapons exercises);[203]

> levying charges against foreign ships for actual services rendered (e.g., pilotage, bunkering—providing fuel), but not for exercising their right of Innocent Passage;[204]

> only exercising criminal jurisdiction onboard foreign ships engaged in Innocent Passage "if the consequences of the crime extend to the coastal State," the crime disturbs the peace and good order of the Coastal State (e.g., murder), the ship's Master or Flag State has requested assistance, or to combat illicit drug trafficking;[205] and

> generally not imposing civil jurisdiction onboard foreign ships engaged in Innocent Passage.[206]

Several of the above provisions implicitly impose a **duty on the Coastal State not to hamper Innocent Passage** (e.g., only temporarily suspending innocent passage in specific areas, and only charging for actual services rendered). This duty of the Coastal State not to hamper Innocent Passage harkens back to the Corfu Channel case discussed earlier in this Chapter, and is also expressed explicitly in Article 24:

Article 24 / Duties of the coastal State

1. The coastal State shall not hamper the innocent passage of foreign ships through the territorial sea except in accordance with this Convention. In particular, in the application of this Convention or of any laws or regulations adopted in conformity with this Convention, the coastal State shall not:
(a) impose requirements on foreign ships which have the practical effect of denying or impairing the right of innocent passage; or

(b) discriminate in form or in fact against the ships of any State or against ships carrying cargoes to, from or on behalf of any State.

2. The coastal State shall give appropriate publicity to any danger to navigation, of which it has knowledge, within its territorial sea. [emphasis added][207]

The Coastal State's final right in conjunction with the Territorial Sea/Innocent Passage regime, is the ability to deal with noncompliant warships, which is expressed in Article 30:

Article 30 / Non-compliance by warships with the laws and regulations of the coastal State

If any warship does not comply with the laws and regulations of the coastal State concerning passage through the territorial sea and disregards any request for compliance therewith which is made to it, the coastal State may require it to leave the territorial sea immediately.[208]

Thus, **if a foreign warship violates Innocent Passage** (e.g., a submarine remains submerged instead of surfacing and flying her flag), **the Coastal State may use the minimum military force necessary to compel the foreign warship to depart the Territorial Sea**.[209] Article 30 confirms that the Coastal State's ability to prevent non-innocent passage (i.e., violations of Innocent Passage) applies to military warships as well as civilian ships.

Accompanying the right to engage in Innocent Passage through another Coastal State's Territorial Seas, foreign ships have the responsibility to "comply with all such [Coastal State] laws and regulations [mentioned above] and all generally accepted international regulations relating to the prevention of collisions at sea."[210] Although the U.S is not party to UNCLOS,[211] President Reagan issued a proclamation in 1988 (after the UNCLOS conference had concluded in 1982, but before UNCLOS went into effect in 1994), claiming a 12 nm Territorial Sea for the U.S., and recognizing both the right of Innocent Passage through Territorial Seas, and Transit Passage through International Straits:

The territorial sea of the United States henceforth extends to 12 nautical miles from the baselines of the United States determined in accordance with international law.

In accordance with international law, as reflected in the applicable provisions of the 1982 United Nations Convention on the Law of the Sea, within the territorial sea of the United States, the ships of all countries enjoy the right of innocent passage and the ships and aircraft of all countries enjoy the right of transit passage through international straits. [emphasis added][212]

INTERNATIONAL STRAITS

Part III of UNCLOS is titled "Straits Used for International Navigation," and contains twelve articles dealing with the new regime of Transit Passage through International Straits. Before UNCLOS, passage through straits was treated the same as passage through Territorial Seas (*see* the previous discussion of the Corfu Channel case). This made sense since straits are maritime chokepoints formed by touching/overlapping Territorial Seas. However, States recognized that "[i]f an exception did not exist for straits, with the extension of coastal state jurisdiction over the waters of the territorial sea, many straits would become subject to the navigational regimes imposed by the coastal state, possibly resulting in severe limitations on international maritime commerce and navigation by all vessels."[213] Thus, UNCLOS created a new regime of Transit Passage through International Straits, thereby distinguishing it from the historical concept of Innocent Passage through Territorial Seas.

With the expansion of the maximum permissible breadth of the territorial sea from 3 to 12 miles, it was necessary to develop stronger guarantees for navigation and overflight on, over, and under international straits. Such rules were critical to maintain the essential balance of interests between States bordering straits and other concerned States..

* * *

With the extension by coastal States of their territorial seas to 12 miles, over 100 straits, which previously had high seas corridors, became overlapped by such territorial seas. Without provision for transit passage, navigation and overflight rights in those straits would have been compromised.[214]

Article 37 defines International Straits that are subject to Transit Passage:

Article 37 / Scope of this section

This section applies to straits which are used for international navigation between one part of the high seas or an exclusive economic zone [i.e., international waters] and another part of the high seas or an exclusive economic zone [i.e., international waters].[215]

The new regime of Transit Passage through International Straits specifically does not apply:

> ➢ to a strait subject to a more specific treaty (e.g., the Turkish Straits into the Black Sea (aka the Bosporus and the Dardanelles), which are governed by the Montreux Convention);[216]

- if a route of similar convenience exists through International Waters (i.e., High Seas or Exclusive Economic Zone);[217] or
- if a strait lies between a Coastal State and its island, and a route of similar convenience exists seaward of the island through International Waters (i.e., High Seas or Exclusive Economic Zone—aka Strait of Messina exception; *see* chart on the next page).[218]

"Transit passage means the exercise ... of the freedom of navigation and overflight solely for the purpose of continuous and expeditious transit of the strait between one part of the high seas or an exclusive economic zone [i.e., International Waters] and another part of the high seas or an exclusive economic zone [i.e., International Waters]."[219] Thus, **UNCLOS established an objective, four-part test for an International Strait: (1) a maritime chokepoint which is formed by touching or overlapping Territorial Seas,**[220] **(2) which is used for international navigation (i.e., by ships and aircraft of more than one State) (3) between two bodies of International Waters,**[221] **and (4) is not subject to an exception.**[222]

Article 38 explains that "**all ships and aircraft** enjoy the right of transit passage" through International Straits. Since "all ships" enjoy the right of Transit Passage through International Straits, **this includes warships.**[223] **Aircraft also expressly have the right of Transit Passage through International Straits,**[224] **whereas aircraft do not enjoy the right of Innocent Passage through Territorial Seas.** Ships and aircraft enjoy the right of Transit Passage through International Straits in their "normal modes of continuous and expeditious transit."[225] "For example, submarines may transit submerged and military aircraft may overfly in combat formation and with normal equipment operation; surface warships may transit in a manner necessary for their security, including formation steaming and the launching and recovery of aircraft [e.g., helicopters, or fighter jets], where consistent with sound navigational practices."[226]

The navigational provisions of the Convention concerning international straits are fundamental to U.S. national security interests. Merchant ships and cargoes, civil aircraft, naval ships and task forces, military aircraft, and submarines must be able to transit international straits freely in their normal mode as a matter of right, and not at the sufferance of the States bordering straits.[227]

The U.S. view is that the right of Transit Passage through an International Strait applies "shoreline to shoreline."[228] In other words, ships and aircraft are not required to transit down the middle of the navigable channel, and can hug either coastline (i.e., navigate as close to the coast as safely possible). This may have been Japan's motivation to claim less than 12 nm Territorial Seas in five Japanese straits—in order to create High Seas corridors through them.[229] This encourages ships to navigate in the High Seas corridors down the middle of the straits instead of conducting Innocent Passage through the narrow Territorial Seas,[230] or Transit Passage shoreline to shoreline (if Japan had claimed full 12 nm Territorial Seas that would have touched or overlapped, thereby creating International Straits).[231]

Once again, Coastal States bordering International Straits have certain rights and responsibilities regarding Transit Passage, including adopting and publicizing laws and regulations related to:

> the safety of navigation in International Straits;[232]
> the regulation of maritime traffic in International Straits;[233]
> both foreign and Coastal States bordering International Straits are encouraged to cooperate in establishing and maintaining navigational and safety aids in International Straits;[234]
> preventing, reducing and controlling pollution in International Straits,[235] with both foreign and Coastal States bordering International Straits being encouraged to cooperate in doing so;[236]
> foreign ships engaged in Transit Passage through International Straits may not conduct either marine research or maritime surveys;[237]
> preventing fishing, including requiring fishing vessels to stow their fishing gear while engaged in Transit Passage through International Straits;[238]

- ➢ preventing the infringement of fiscal, immigration, sanitation and customs (FISC) laws and regulations;[239] and
- ➢ designating sea lanes and traffic separation schemes to ensure the safety of navigation.[240]

However, "[s]uch laws and regulations [adopted by Coastal States bordering International Straits regarding Transit Passage] shall not discriminate in form or in fact among foreign ships or in their application have the practical effect of denying, hampering or impairing the right of transit passage ...."[241] This duty of the Coastal State not to hamper Transit Passage harkens back to the Corfu Channel case discussed earlier in this Chapter, and is also expressed explicitly in Article 44:

Article 44 / Duties of States bordering straits

States bordering straits shall not hamper transit passage and shall give appropriate publicity to any danger to navigation or overflight within or over the strait of which they have knowledge. There shall be no suspension of transit passage. [emphasis added][242]

Thus, "[u]nder article 44, a State bordering an international strait may not suspend transit passage through international straits for any purpose, including military exercises."[243]

Under the Convention, the criteria in identifying an international strait is not the name, the size or length, the. presence or absence of islands or multiple routes, the history or volume of traffic flowing through the strait, or its relative importance to international navigation. Rather the decisive criterion is its geography: the fact that it is capable of

---

This last point, that the decisive criterion to constitute an international strait is the fact that it **CAN** be used for international navigation, not that it **HAS** been so used, lies at the heart of the dispute between the U.S. and Canada regarding the Northwest Passage. The Northwest Passage (the red line in this chart) through  the Canadian Arctic is melting, and provides a route[245] between the Atlantic and the Pacific Oceans that is 5,000 nm shorter than the Panama Canal route (dark blue line in this chart),[246] and is even more advantageous for supertankers that are too large to pass through the Panama Canal and must otherwise navigate around the tip of South America. In 1986 (i.e., after the UNCLOS conference had concluded in 1982, but before UNCLOS went into effect in 1994), Canada proclaimed straight baselines around the Canadian Arctic Islands as a historic archipelago,[247] even though it would not qualify under UNCLOS' objective, two-part test for an Archipelagic State (discussed subsequently in Chapter 4). Therefore, Canada views the "Canadian Northwest Passage" as strictly "historic internal waters" over which it exercises complete sovereignty.[248] Canada argues that even if the Northwest Passage *could* be viewed as a potential International Strait, the fact that it has *NOT* been so used (since the waters were previously frozen year-round) argues against considering it an International Strait.[249] The U.S. disputes this claim as inconsistent with UNCLOS, and the fact that the Northwest Passage *CAN* be used for international navigation. The U.S. has challenged this claim via Freedom of Navigation (FON) operations[250] (discussed subsequently in Chapter 11).

251

Accompanying the right to engage in Transit Passage through International Straits, foreign ships have the responsibility to comply with the Coastal States' laws and regulations [mentioned above],[252] and "with generally accepted international regulations, procedures and practices for safety at sea, including the International Regulations for Preventing Collisions at Sea."[253] Aircraft in Transit Passage shall comply with the safety measures established by the International Civil Aviation Organization (ICAO).[254]

As discussed in the first part of this Chapter, foreign ships engaged in Innocent Passage through Territorial Seas shall refrain from conduct that is "prejudicial to the peace, good order or security of the coastal State ... [including] any threat or use of force against the sovereignty, territorial integrity or political independence of the coastal State."[255] Similarly, foreign ships and aircraft conducting Transit Passage through International Straits shall "refrain from any threat or use of force against the sovereignty, territorial integrity or political independence of States bordering the strait."[256] Thus, warships cannot fire weapons or launch missiles while conducting Transit Passage through International Straits.

There are many similarities between the two regimes (of Transit Passage through International Straits and Innocent Passage through Territorial Seas). However, as the reader may have noticed, the International Straits/Transit Passage regime does not precisely mirror the Territorial Seas/Innocent Passage regime. Not only are some of the rights different (e.g., aircraft have the right to engage in Transit Passage through International Straits but not Innocent Passage through Territorial Seas), but UNCLOS is silent as to certain rights in the International Straits/Transit Passage regime. For example, in the Territorial Sea the Coastal State may use the minimum military force necessary to compel a noncompliant foreign warship to depart the Territorial Sea.[257] However, there is no corresponding right to forcibly eject a noncompliant foreign warship or aircraft from an International Strait. Instead, if a foreign warship or aircraft violates Transit Passage (e.g., by collecting intelligence), "[t]he flag State ... shall bear international responsibility for any loss or damage which results to States bordering straits."[258]

Similarly, there is no mention of exercising criminal or civil jurisdiction onboard foreign ships engaged in Transit Passage through International Straits, or levying charges for services. In international law, such gaps are called "lacunas" or "lacunae," and can be quite illuminating. **What is NOT said is often as important as what IS said.**

	Territorial Seas (TS)	International Straits
Type of Passage?	**Innocent (IP)**	**Transit (TP)**
For Whom?	All Ships & Submarines on Surface	All Ships, **Submerged Submarines & Aircraft**
How?	Navigation ("just cutting through")	**Normal Mode of Transit**
Meaning of Passage?	Continuous & Expeditious	Continuous & Expeditious
Limitations on Passage?	Refrain from Threat or Use of Force	Refrain from Threat or Use of Force
Coastal State MAY:	1) Have criminal jurisdiction 2) Impose charges for services 3) temporarily suspend IP if essential for security 4) Require noncompliant (war)ships to leave TS	LACUNA
Coastal State may NOT:	Hamper Innocent Passage	Hamper/Suspend TP

A broad contrast of the two regimes (of Transit Passage through International Straits and Innocent Passage through Territorial Seas) may also be illuminating. **Innocent Passage is a broad right of Customary International Law (CIL) that applies in Territorial Seas worldwide, but it only applies to ships** (and surfaced submarines), **and ships can only engage in "innocent" passage** (i.e., on the surface and non-threatening). **In contrast, Transit Passage is a new Treaty right under UNCLOS that only applies in about 200 International Straits throughout the world, but provides a few more "transit" freedoms (i.e., normal mode of transit) for ships, submerged submarines and aircraft.**[259] Besides saving time and money, transit passage also saves the need to obtain permission from other States to conduct military missions (versus flying over their land territory).

The U.S. view is that Transit Passage applies not only throughout International Straits, but also in their approaches.[260] If Transit Passage applied only within the portion of the International Strait where the Territorial Seas overlap, and not also to areas leading into/out of the International Strait, there would be no effective Transit Passage. For example, in entering the Strait of Hormuz, ships and aircraft would go from: (1) exercising High Seas freedoms of navigation and overflight in the Gulf of Oman; (2) possibly to Innocent Passage through Territorial Seas (and since there's none for aircraft, they would have to land, and submarines would have to surface); (3) to Transit Passage, and then reverse the process exiting the strait. The Strait of Hormuz (SOH) is of particular interest, both because it forms the entrance to the Persian (aka Arabian) Gulf which has strategic significance,[261] and because Iran is one of the Coastal States (aka "littoral States") bordering the International Strait.[262]

When States ratify a treaty, they often attach Reservations, Understandings and Declarations (aka RUDs). The U.S. Senate often attaches RUDs as part of providing their advice and consent to the President to ratify a treaty. A Reservation is a unilateral statement by one State that seeks to modify the effect of the treaty on that particular State.[263] However, this essentially "pokes holes" in the treaty fabric for individual States, and makes the treaty's application between States more complex.[264] UNCLOS Article 309 expressly prohibits "reservations or exceptions" to UNCLOS. States may also attach other statements to their ratification of a treaty with a variety of names (e.g., Understandings and Declarations). UNCLOS Article 310 expressly permits States to make "declarations or statements, however phrased or named, with a view, *inter alia* [i.e., among other things], to the harmonization of its laws and regulations with the provisions of this Convention, provided that such declarations or statements do not purport to exclude or to modify the legal effect of the provisions of this Convention in their application to that State."

Iran attached a five-part "Understanding" when it signed UNCLOS, including:

"1) ... that only states parties to the Law of the Sea Convention shall be entitled to benefit from the contractual rights created therein.... specifically (but not exclusively) to the following:

– The right of Transit passage through straits used for international navigation (Part III, Section 2, article 38). ...

2) ... the rights of the Coastal States to take measures to safeguard their security interests including the adoption of laws and regulations regarding, *inter alia*, the requirements of prior authorization for warships willing to exercise the right of innocent passage through the territorial sea."[265]

As discussed in Chapter 2, treaties are akin to a written contract between States, and are only binding on those States which are "party" to the treaty (i.e., those States which have ratified the treaty, and become a "State Party"). The U.S. has not yet ratified UNCLOS, and thus is not yet a State Party to UNCLOS.[266] **Under Iran's view, American ships and aircraft would NOT be entitled to the treaty right of Transit Passage through International Straits, including the Strait of Hormuz,** which is bordered by Iran, the United Arab Emirates (UAE), and Oman.[267] However, the U.S. view is that the UNCLOS regime of Transit Passage through International Straits has crystallized into a new norm (or rule) of Customary International Law (CIL),[268] which is binding on all States. Thus, American ships and aircraft WOULD be entitled to the CIL right of Transit Passage through International Straits, including the Strait of Hormuz, and their right to Transit Passage cannot be hampered or suspended.[269]

Due to these divergent views, and consistent Iranian challenges to American ships and aircraft transiting the Strait of Hormuz, U.S. Navy strike groups conduct detailed planning before conducting Transit Passage through the Strait of Hormuz. The bottom line is that American warships know that Iran will challenge them during their transit of the Strait of Hormuz, and they need to be prepared to respond to the full continuum of potential Iranian challenges and threats during their transit. On the chart of the Strait of Hormuz below, notice the designated sea lanes (marked as pink shipping lanes), as well as the traffic separation scheme between them (which is like the median strip or land buffer between opposing traffic on a highway).

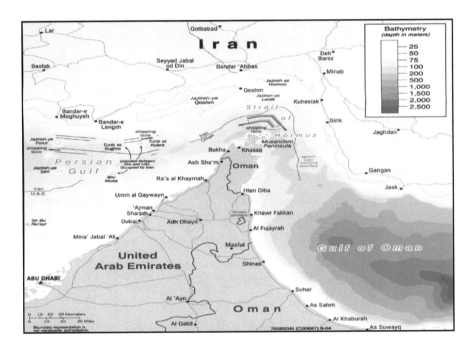

Iran has repeatedly used military force in the Strait of Hormuz in a manner inconsistent with UNCLOS,[270] which exposes how Iran's "Understanding" is similarly inconsistent with UNCLOS. [NOTE: as discussed earlier in this Chapter, Iran attached an Understanding to its signing of UNCLOS that: (1) only State Parties have the right of Transit Passage through the Strait of Hormuz; (2) since the U.S. has not ratified UNCLOS yet, American warships would thus only be entitled to the right of Innocent Passage through Iran's Territorial Seas that comprise the strait; and (3) Iran can safeguard its security interests in its Territorial Seas, such as by requiring prior authorization before warships can engage in Innocent Passage.]

On July 19, 2019, the Islamic Revolutionary Guard Corps Navy (IRGCN) radioed a British-flagged oil tanker "*Stena Impero*" (owned by Sweden) to "alter its course" for a "security inspection," but the oil tanker refused to comply. [NOTE: as discussed in Chapter 1, the Strait of Hormuz is patrolled by Iran's two Navies: the regular Iranian Navy, which is small and professional but underfunded, and the IRGCN, which is controlled by Iran's religious leaders,[271] is better funded, and has consistently been much more provocative, especially with its well-armed fast inshore attack craft.] A nearby British Royal Navy frigate "*HMS Montrose*" overheard the radio traffic and warned the IRGCN that the *Steno Impero*'s right of Transit Passage through an International Strait "must not be impaired" under international law (i.e., in accordance with Article 44 of UNCLOS). The IRGCN responded that they did not intend to challenge the *Stena Impero*, merely conduct a security inspection of the vessel (which, at the very least, would hamper the oil tanker's right of Transit Passage through an International Strait by unnecessarily delaying its transit for an unspecified period of time). When the *Stena Impero* refused to alter its course, the IRGCN seized the vessel at the end of the northern/inbound sea lane in the Strait of Hormuz (which lies entirely in Omani Territorial Seas) and redirected the tanker into Iranian Territorial Seas. The UK Department for Transport released the following chart of the incident. To muddy the waters further (pun intended), and perhaps realizing that its justification did not have a solid basis in international law, Iran subsequently claimed that the *Stena Impero* violated maritime rules by sailing into the Persian (aka Arabian) Gulf via the southern/outbound sea lane in the Strait of Hormuz (i.e., driving on the wrong side of the road, as they do in Britain).[272]

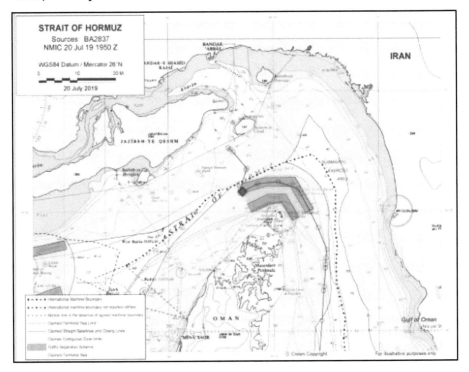

Although Iran's stated reason for seizing the British oil tanker *Stena Impero* was for failing to comply with a "security inspection," most international commentators consider it to be retaliation for Britain's seizure of the Iranian oil tanker "*Grace 1*" on July 4, 2019 (i.e., just over two weeks earlier) near Gibraltar because the *Grace 1* was transporting crude oil to Syria in violation of European Union (EU) sanctions against Syria.[273] A senior IRGC military officer had previously indicated that "[i]f Britain does not release the Iranian oil tanker, it is the [Iranian] authorities duty to seize a British oil tanker. Iran has never initiated hostilities, but it has also never hesitated in responding to bullies."[274]

Taking Iran's position at face value, is it permissible under UNCLOS to direct a merchant vessel to alter its course during Transit Passage through an International Strait in order to conduct a "security inspection"? Article 42 of UNCLOS provides:

Article 42 / Laws and regulations of States bordering straits relating to transit passage

1. Subject to the provisions of this section, States bordering straits may adopt laws and regulations relating to transit passage through straits, in respect of all or any of the following:

(a) the safety of navigation and the regulation of maritime traffic, as provided in article 41;

(b) the prevention, reduction and control of pollution, by giving effect to applicable international regulations regarding the discharge of oil, oily wastes and other noxious substances in the strait;

(c) with respect to fishing vessels, the prevention of fishing, including the stowage of fishing gear;

(d) the loading or unloading of any commodity, currency or person in contravention of the customs, fiscal, immigration or sanitary laws and regulations of States bordering straits.

2. Such laws and regulations shall not discriminate in form or in fact among foreign ships or in their application have the practical effect of denying, hampering or impairing the right of transit passage as defined in this section.

3. States bordering straits shall give due publicity to all such laws and regulations.

4. Foreign ships exercising the right of transit passage shall comply with such laws and regulations.

5. The flag State of a ship or the State of registry of an aircraft entitled to sovereign immunity which acts in a manner contrary to such laws and regulations or other provisions of this Part shall bear international responsibility for any loss or damage which results to States bordering straits. [emphasis added][275]

Article 42 makes no mention of a State bordering an International Strait being permitted to adopt laws related to protecting the State's security, let alone conducting security inspections. Moreover, Articles 42(2) and 44 provide that **"States bordering [international] straits shall not hamper transit passage."** At the very least, ordering a ship to alter its course in order to be subjected to a "security inspection," would delay the ship's transit for an unspecified period of time. This would seem to "have the practical effect of ... hampering or impairing the right of transit passage," in violation of Articles 42(2) and 44. Therefore, it would appear that Iran's actions violate their obligation as a signatory to UNCLOS. Although Iran is not one of the 168 State Parties to UNCLOS[276] (having signed but not yet ratified UNCLOS), Article 18 of the Vienna Convention on the Law of Treaties (VCLT) imposes a requirement on treaty signatories (even before ratification) to "refrain from acts which would defeat the object and purpose of a treaty."[277] Hampering the regime of Transit Passage through International Straits would arguably defeat one of the objects and purposes of UNCLOS.

Iran is also suspected of attacking an Omani oil tanker on June 13, 2019, and four other oil tankers (flying the flags of UAE and

Norway, and two flying Saudi Arabian flags)[278] previously on May 12, 2019 with naval mines (specifically limpet mines manually placed on the sides of the five oil tankers). Iran denied attacking the oil tankers, but the U.S. released a video that shows a darkened IRGCN boat surreptitiously removing an unexploded limpet mine on the hull of one of the oil tankers at night, presumably to recover evidence of Iran's participation.[279] Tensions have been rising in the Strait of Hormuz and Persian (aka Arabian) Gulf since then-President Trump withdrew from the nuclear deal with Iran in May 2018, and particularly since he designated the Islamic Revolutionary Guard Corps (IRGC) as a Foreign Terrorist Organization on April 8, 2019.[280] Iran responded by declaring "the United States as a terrorist sponsored government and ... all its affiliated [military] forces as terrorist groups."[281] Thus, due to sustained and rising tensions in the Arabian Gulf area, it would appear that the ships and aircraft of all States will need to conduct detailed planning before conducting Transit Passage through the Strait of Hormuz (discussed in more depth in Chapter 10).[282] Warships in particular will need to be prepared to respond to the full continuum of potential Iranian challenges and threats during their transit.

---

[178] Most States claim a 12 nm Territorial Sea, although Greece only claims a 6 nm Territorial Sea and purports to claim a 10 nm Territorial Sea for purposes of aviation (i.e., to keep aircraft at least 10 nm away from the coastline unless they have permission for a closer approach). Dept. of Defense Maritime Claims Reference Manual (MCRM)—Greece 2014, http://www.jag.navy.mil/organization/code_10_mcrm.htm; Emmanuella Doussis, *Marine Scientific Research: Taking Stock and Looking Ahead*, in THE FUTURE OF THE LAW OF THE SEA 87, 95 (Gemma Andreone ed., 2017), https://link.springer.com/book/10.1007/978-3-319-51274-7. Turkey similarly only claims a 6 nm Territorial Sea in the Aegean. DoD MCRM—Turkey 2016 (full cite above).

[179] U.S. NAVY, MARINE CORPS & COAST GUARD, THE COMMANDER'S HANDBOOK ON THE LAW OF NAVAL OPERATIONS, NWP 1-14M/MCTP 11-10B/COMDTPUB P5800.7A, ¶¶ 1.5, 1.6, 2.6.1 to 2.6.2 (pp. 1-7, 1-8, 2-9) (2017), www.jag.navy.mil/distrib/instructions/CDRs_HB_on_Law_of_Naval_Operations_AUG17.pdf; THE FLETCHER SCHOOL OF LAW AND DIPLOMACY—TUFTS UNIVERSITY, LAW OF

[180] COMMANDER'S HANDBOOK, ¶¶ 1.1, 1.9, 2.7.2 (pp. 1-1, 1-10, 2-13) (full cite above); Raul (Pete) Pedrozo, *Military Activities in the Exclusive Economic Zone: East Asia Focus*, 90 INT'L. L. STUD. 514, 519-521 (2014), https://digital-commons.usnwc.edu/ils/vol90/iss1/15/.

[181] Int'l. Court of Justice (ICJ), *The Corfu Channel Case* (Merits) (United Kingdom of Great Britain and Northern Ireland and the People's Republic of Albania), Judgment of April 9th, 1949, 1949 I.C.J. Reports 4, 12, https://www.icj-cij.org/en/case/1.

[182] U.S. Dept. of State Foreign Affairs Manual (FAM) and Handbook (FAH), 7 FAM 034, *"Demarches"* (2005), https://fam.state.gov/FAM/07FAM/07FAM0030.html. *See generally* U.S. Dept. of State FAM/FAH Search, https://fam.state.gov/search.

[183] Chapter 9 discusses the Customary International Law (CIL) "duty to rescue" mariners from perils of the sea. This "duty to rescue" exists even if the States involved are not on friendly terms.

[184] The United Kingdom broke off diplomatic relations with Albania for 45 years (from 1946 -1991), which is comparable to the lack of diplomatic relations between the U.S. and Cuba (1961 - 2015).

[185] Chapter 2 discusses the primary sources of international law, including Customary International Law (CIL).

[186] Modern-day warnings to ships are often via a Notice to Mariners (aka NOTMAR). *See generally* National Geospatial-Intelligence Agency, Notice to Mariners, https://msi.nga.mil/NTM. Similar warnings to aircraft are via a Notice to Airmen (aka NOTAM).

[187] Albania finally agreed to pay $2M in reparations to the United Kingdom in 1992 (i.e., 43 years later)!

[188] Chapter 2 discusses the Third United Nations Conference on the Law of the Sea, which culminated in the 1982 UNCLOS.

[189] United Nations Convention on the Law of the Sea (UNCLOS) arts. 5 (normal baseline), 7 (straight baselines), 8 (internal waters), 10 (bays), 11 (ports and harbors, & 13 (low-tide elevations), Dec. 10, 1982, 1833 U.N.T.S. 397, https://www.un.org/Depts/los/convention_agreements/convention_overview_convention.htm.

[190] UNCLOS, art. 2 (full cite above). *See also* Dept. of Defense Law of War Manual § 13.2.2.2, pp. 881-882 (June 2015, updated Dec. 2016), https://www.hsdl.org/?view&did=797480.

[191] UNCLOS, art. 3 (full cite above); COMMANDER'S HANDBOOK, ¶¶ 1.3.2, 1.5.2, 2.5.2 & Figure 1-6 (pp. 1-3, 1-7, 1-8, 2-5) (full cite above). *See also* Richard Nixon, Statement About United States Oceans Policy (May 23, 1970), https://www.presidency.ucsb.edu/documents/statement-about-united-states-oceans-policy (calling for a multilateral treaty on the law of the sea, including a 12 nm Territorial Sea). Although the U.S. is not party to UNCLOS, President Reagan declared that the U.S. Territorial Sea extends out to 12 nm, and that in accordance with international law (as reflected in UNCLOS), the ships of all States enjoy the right of Innocent Passage through the U.S. Territorial Sea. Reagan Proclamation No. 5928, 3 C.F.R. 547 (1988), 54 Fed. Reg. 777 (Dec. 27. 1988), National Archives, Federal Register, Codification, Proclamations, Proclamation 5928—Territorial sea of the United States of America, https://www.archives.gov/federal-register/codification/proclamations/05928.html.

[192] United Nations Convention on the Law of the Sea (UNCLOS) art. 30, Dec. 10, 1982, 1833 U.N.T.S. 397, https://www.un.org/Depts/los/convention_agreements/convention_overview_convention.htm (recognizing that a Coastal State may require a non-complying warship to depart the Coastal State's Territorial Sea, which implies that warships possess the right of Innocent Passage); U.S. NAVY, MARINE CORPS & COAST GUARD, THE COMMANDER'S HANDBOOK ON THE LAW OF NAVAL OPERATIONS, NWP 1-14M/MCTP 11-10B/COMDTPUB P5800.7A, ¶ 2.7.1 (p. 2-13) (2017), www.jag.navy.mil/distrib/instructions/CDRs_HB_on_Law_of_Naval_Operations_AUG17.pdf. *See generally* William J. Aceves, *The Freedom of Navigation Program: A Study of the Relationship between Law and Politics*, 19 HASTINGS INT'L & COMP. L. REV. 259, 298-300 (1996), https://repository.uchastings.edu/hastings_international_comparative_law_review/vol19/iss2/2/ (providing a detailed example of how U.S. FONOPs in the Black Sea led to the "the signing of two bilateral agreements [between Russia and the U.S.] in 1989: the Agreement on the Prevention of Dangerous Military Activities and the Uniform Interpretation of Rules of International Law Governing Innocent Passage.").

[193] UNCLOS, art. 17 (full cite above); COMMANDER'S HANDBOOK, ¶¶ 2.5.2.1, 2.5.2.4, 3.11.2.2.3 (pp. 2-5 to 2-6, 3-12) (full cite above). The right of ships to conduct Innocent Passage does not depend on normal diplomatic relations between the States. For example, the U.S. does not have diplomatic relations with North Korea and Iran, yet North Korean and Iranian ships have the right to conduct Innocent Passage through U.S. Territorial Seas and *vice versa*.

[194] UNCLOS, art. 18(2) (full cite above). Continuous passage implies a ship not stopping unless necessary (e.g., to fix its position by taking navigational bearings off known landmarks, or if the vessel is in distress). COMMANDER'S HANDBOOK, ¶ 3.2.2 (p. 3-2) (full cite above). Expeditious passage means proceeding at a reasonable speed. The only exception to continuous and expeditious passage would be to render assistance to mariners in peril from dangers of the sea under Article 98. However, this exception would only apply if the location of the mariners in peril were reasonably known, and would not support searching for the lost mariners in a Coastal State's Territorial Sea without permission from the Coastal State.

[195] UNCLOS, art 19 (full cite above).

[196] *See also* Dept. of Defense Law of War Manual § 13.2.2.4, p. 883 (June 2015, updated Dec. 2016), https://www.hsdl.org/?view&did=797480; COMMANDER'S HANDBOOK, ¶ 2.5.2.1 (pp. 2-5 to 2-6) (full cite above).

[197] UNCLOS, art. 20 (full cite above). The primary reason why submarines must navigate on the surface while conducting Innocent Passage is because they are inherently threatening, especially when submerged. Chapter 9 discusses the importance of the "Flag State."

[198] Chapter 7 discusses Marine Scientific Research in more detail.

[199] UNCLOS, art. 21 (full cite above). Although the Coastal State has the right to adopt laws and regulations related to Innocent Passage, there is no support for the Coastal State requiring prior notification before foreign ships can conduct Innocent Passage, let alone prior permission/consent from the Coastal State. This is clear from the negotiating history of UNCLOS. A vote was taken to add the prior notification requirements for Innocent Passage, and the proposal was rejected. Nevertheless, quite a few States purport to require prior notification before conducting Innocent Passage, and even more States claim to require prior

permission to do so. Requiring either prior notification or prior permission for Innocent Passage would hamper Innocent Passage in violation of Article 24. Chapter 11 (Excessive Maritime Claims and Freedom of Navigation (FON) Programs) discusses such excessive requirements.

[200] UNCLOS, art. 22 (full cite above). *See generally* Aceves, *The FON Program*, p. 290 (full cite above) (providing a detailed example of a U.S. FON diplomatic protest to Finland regarding its sea lanes).

[201] UNCLOS, art. 25(1) (full cite above).

[202] UNCLOS, art. 25(2) (full cite above); COMMANDER'S HANDBOOK, ¶ 4.4.4.1.6 (p. 4-8) (full cite above). Under Articles 25(2) and 211(3), a Coastal State may set "conditions on port entry," which do not have to be reasonable. The U.S. requires the use of the Automatic Identification System (AIS), Notice of Arrival 96 hours prior to entering port, and a list of the five previous foreign ports. The U.S. Coast Guard (USCG) boards any high-interest vessels before they are permitted to enter U.S. Territorial Seas. Australia bans foreign whaling vessels, unless they pay for a special permit. As part of its "Nuclear Free Zone," New Zealand bans nuclear-powered vessels (including U.S. aircraft carriers) from entering its ports. New Zealand Nuclear Free Zone, Disarmament, and Arms Control Act 1987 § 11, http://www.legislation.govt.nz/act/public/1987/0086/latest/DLM115116.html#DLM 115147. *See also* 33 U.S. Code § 1228, https://www.law.cornell.edu/uscode/text; COMMANDER'S HANDBOOK, ¶ 2.6.6 (p. 2-12) (full cite above) (noting that "[t]he 1968 Nuclear Weapons Non-Proliferation Treaty, to which the United States is a party, acknowledges the right of groups of States to conclude regional treaties establishing nuclear-free zones. Such treaties are binding only on parties to them .... To the extent that the rights and freedoms of other States, including the high seas freedoms of navigation and overflight, are not infringed upon, such treaties are not inconsistent with international law."). Japan, Australia and the U.S. ban North Korean ships. The U.S. has also banned ships from Cuba, Iran, Libya, Sudan and Syria. *But see* COMMANDER'S HANDBOOK, ¶ 3.11.2.2.3 (p. 3-12) (full cite above) (indicating that "a coastal State may enforce reasonable, nondiscriminatory conditions on a vessel's entry into its ports."); DONALD R. ROTHWELL & TIM STEPHENS, THE INT'L. LAW OF THE SEA 57 (2nd ed. 2016) (noting that there are often reciprocal rights of port entry between States, and ports are generally open to commercial ships).

[203] UNCLOS, art. 25(3) (full cite above); COMMANDER'S HANDBOOK, ¶ 2.5.2.3 (p. 2-6) (full cite above).

[204] UNCLOS, art. 26 (full cite above); THE FLETCHER SCHOOL OF LAW AND DIPLOMACY—TUFTS UNIVERSITY, LAW OF THE SEA, A POLICY PRIMER 21 (2017), https://sites.tufts.edu/lawofthesea/introduction/.

[205] UNCLOS, art. 108 (full cite above); COMMANDER'S HANDBOOK, ¶¶ 3.4, 3.8, 3.11.4 to 3.11.4.3 (pp. 3-5, 3-7, 3-16 to 3-17) (full cite above). Chapter 9 discusses Flag States in more depth.

[206] UNCLOS, art. 28 (full cite above).

[207] UNCLOS, art. 24 (full cite above). The duty to warn of "any danger to navigation" is a direct result of, and implicit reference to the Corfu Channel case discussed earlier in this Chapter.

[208] UNCLOS, art. 30 (full cite above).

[209] *But see* TUFTS, LAW OF THE SEA, p. 22 (full cite above) (positing that "[d]ue to the sovereign immunity of warships ... the degree to which a coastal State can force a warship to exit its territorial waters in this situation is not clear.").

[210] United Nations Convention on the Law of the Sea (UNCLOS) art. 21(4), Dec. 10, 1982, 1833 U.N.T.S. 397, https://www.un.org/Depts/los/convention_agreements/convention_overview_convention.htm; Int'l. Maritime Organization (IMO), English, About IMO, Conventions, List of Conventions, Convention on the Int'l. Regulations for Preventing Collisions at Sea, 1972 (COLREGs), http://www.imo.org/en/About/Conventions/ListOfConventions/Pages/COLREG.aspx. The COLREGs are incorporated into UNCLOS by Article 94.

[211] Although the U.S. is not yet party to UNCLOS, it routinely participates as an observer at meetings of UNCLOS State Parties. *See, e.g.,* CarrieLyn D. Guymon (editor), DIGEST OF UNITED STATES PRACTICE IN INTERNATIONAL LAW 419 (2019), https://www.state.gov/digest-of-united-states-practice-in-international-law-2019.

[212] Reagan Proclamation No. 5928, 3 C.F.R. 547 (1988), 54 Fed. Reg. 777 (Dec. 27. 1988), National Archives, Federal Register, Codification, Proclamations, Proclamation 5928—Territorial sea of the United States of America, https://www.archives.gov/federal-register/codification/proclamations/05928.html. *See also* Richard Nixon, Statement About United States Oceans Policy (May 23, 1970), https://www.presidency.ucsb.edu/documents/statement-about-united-states-oceans-policy (calling for a multilateral treaty on the law of the sea, including a 12 nm Territorial Sea and "free transit through international straits").

[213] Donald R. Rothwell, *The Canadian-U.S. Northwest Passage Dispute: A Reassessment,* 26 CORNELL INT'L. L. J. 331, 348 (1993), https://scholarship.law.cornell.edu/cilj/vol26/iss2/2/.

[214] Letter Of Transmittal Forwarding The 1982 UN Law Of The Sea Convention To The United States Senate, DOS Commentary pp. 18-19 (William J. Clinton, Oct. 7, 1994) (S. Treaty Doc. 103–39), https://www.foreign.senate.gov/imo/media/doc/treaty_103-39.pdf.

[215] UNCLOS, art. 37 (full cite above). *See also* U.S. NAVY, MARINE CORPS & COAST GUARD, THE COMMANDER'S HANDBOOK ON THE LAW OF NAVAL OPERATIONS, NWP 1-14M/MCTP 11-10B/COMDTPUB P5800.7A, ¶ 2.5.3.1 (p. 2-7) (2017), www.jag.navy.mil/distrib/instructions/CDRs_HB_on_Law_of_Naval_Operations_AUG17.pdf (listing the 5 different types of straits).

[216] UNCLOS, art. 35(c) (full cite above); COMMANDER'S HANDBOOK, ¶ 2.5.3.1 (p. 2-7) (full cite above). *See also* Nilüfer Oral, Ukraine v. The Russian Federation: *Navigating Conflict over Sovereignty under UNCLOS,* 97 INT'L. L. STUD. 478, 479, 482 (2021), https://digital-commons.usnwc.edu/ils/vol97/iss1/25/ (noting that "the 1936 Montreux Convention ... creates a unique regime that imposes restrictions on the size and type of warships allowed in and out of the Black Sea and imposes limits on the duration of the stay of warships of non-Black Sea States. The Black Sea regime created under the Montreux Convention has roots in the ancient rule of the Ottoman sultans and the Soviet legal doctrine of 'closed sea.' The Montreux Convention reflects the view, especially that of the USSR, that the Black Sea is legally a closed sea, at least to foreign warships. ... [T]he Soviet position regarding the Black Sea was reflected in the closed sea doctrine, namely that in semi-enclosed or enclosed seas, coastal States should enjoy superior legal rights over non-coastal States. This meant that passage rights of foreign ships were to be established exclusively by the littoral States' concurrence. Non-contiguous States would have no legal rights of access unless expressly granted by the coastal States."); UNCLOS,

arts. 122-123 (full cite above) (encouraging States bordering an enclosed or semi-enclosed sea to cooperate).

[217] UNCLOS, art. 36 (full cite above); COMMANDER'S HANDBOOK, ¶¶ 2.5.3.1, 2.5.3.3 (pp. 2-7, 2-8) (full cite above).

[218] UNCLOS, art. 38(1) (full cite above); COMMANDER'S HANDBOOK, ¶ 2.5.3.1 (p. 2-7) (full cite above). Foreign ships still have the right of Innocent Passage through an island strait (e.g., Strait of Messina). UNCLOS, art. 45(1)(a) (full cite above). Italy purports to prohibit passage through the Strait of Messina by large vessels (10,000 tons or more) carrying oil and other pollutants. Dept. of Defense Maritime Claims Reference Manual (MCRM)—Italy 2014, http://www.jag.navy.mil/organization/code_10_mcrm.htm. Chapter 11 discusses excessive maritime claims, and Freedom of Navigation programs.

[219] UNCLOS, art. 38(2) (full cite above).

[220] UNCLOS, art. 36 (full cite above).

[221] UNCLOS, art. 37 (full cite above).

[222] UNCLOS, arts. 35(c) & 38(1) (full cite above).

[223] COMMANDER'S HANDBOOK, ¶ 2.5.3.2 (pp. 2-7 to 2-8) (full cite above).

[224] COMMANDER'S HANDBOOK, ¶ 2.7.1.1 (p. 2-13) (full cite above).

[225] UNCLOS, art. 39(1)(c) (full cite above); COMMANDER'S HANDBOOK, ¶ 2.5.3.2 (pp. 2-7 to 2-8) (full cite above).

[226] DOS Commentary, p. 19 (full cite above). *See also* UNCLOS, art. 39(1)(c) (full cite above); COMMANDER'S HANDBOOK, ¶ 2.5.3.2 (pp. 2-7 to 2-8) (full cite above); THE FLETCHER SCHOOL OF LAW AND DIPLOMACY—TUFTS UNIVERSITY, LAW OF THE SEA, A POLICY PRIMER 23 (2017), https://sites.tufts.edu/lawofthesea/introduction/.

[227] DOS Commentary, p. 17 (full cite above).

[228] COMMANDER'S HANDBOOK, ¶ 2.5.3.2 (pp. 2-7 to 2-8) (full cite above).

[229] UNCLOS, art. 36 (full cite above); COMMANDER'S HANDBOOK, ¶¶ 2.5.3.1, 2.5.3.3 (pp. 2-7, 2-8) (full cite above); DoD MCRM—Japan 2017 (full cite above). Specifically, Japan only claims a 3 nm Territorial Sea in the "Soya Strait, Tsugaru Strait, the eastern and western channels of the Tsushima Strait, and the Osumi Strait."

[230] Article 36 of UNCLOS provides that Transit Passage does not apply if a High Seas corridor exists through the strait. In addition, having a High Seas corridor would mean the strait doesn't satisfy the four-part test for International Straits because it would not have touching/overlapping Territorial Seas.

[231] COMMANDER'S HANDBOOK, ¶ 2.5.3.1, 2.5.3.2 (pp. 2-7 to 2-8) (full cite above).

[232] UNCLOS, art. 42(1)(a) (full cite above).

[233] UNCLOS, art. 42(1)(a) (full cite above). Although Coastal States bordering International Straits have the right to adopt laws and regulations related to Transit Passage, there is no support for a Coastal State to require prior notification before foreign ships can conduct Transit Passage, let alone prior permission/consent from the Coastal State, which will be discussed in Chapter 11.

[234] UNCLOS, art. 43(a) (full cite above).

[235] UNCLOS, art. 42(1)(b) (full cite above).

[236] UNCLOS, art. 43(b) (full cite above).

[237] UNCLOS, art. 40 (full cite above). Chapter 7 discusses Marine Scientific Research in more detail.

[238] UNCLOS, art. 42(1)(c) (full cite above).

[239] UNCLOS, art. 42(1)(d) (full cite above).

[240] United Nations Convention on the Law of the Sea (UNCLOS) art. 41, Dec. 10, 1982, 1833 U.N.T.S. 397, https://www.un.org/Depts/los/convention_agreements/convention_overview_convention.htm. *But see* U.S. NAVY, MARINE CORPS & COAST GUARD, THE COMMANDER'S HANDBOOK ON THE LAW OF NAVAL OPERATIONS, NWP 1-14M/MCTP 11-10B/COMDTPUB P5800.7A, ¶ 2.5.3.2 (pp. 2-7 to 2-8) (2017), www.jag.navy.mil/distrib/instructions/CDRs_HB_on_Law_of_Naval_Operations_AUG17.pdf (arguing that "sovereign-immune vessels … are not legally required to comply with such sea lanes and traffic separation schemes while in transit passage. Sovereign immune vessels, however, must exercise due regard for the safety of navigation. Warships and auxiliaries may, and often do, voluntarily comply with IMO-approved routing measures in international straits where practicable and compatible with the military mission."); THE FLETCHER SCHOOL OF LAW AND DIPLOMACY—TUFTS UNIVERSITY, LAW OF THE SEA, A POLICY PRIMER 24 (2017), https://sites.tufts.edu/lawofthesea/introduction/ (same).

[241] UNCLOS, art. 42(2) (full cite above); COMMANDER'S HANDBOOK, ¶ 2.5.3.2 (pp. 2-7 to 2-8) (full cite above).

[242] UNCLOS, art. 44 (full cite above). The duty to warn of "any danger to navigation" is a direct result of, and implicit reference to the Corfu Channel case discussed earlier in this Chapter.

[243] Letter Of Transmittal Forwarding The 1982 UN Law Of The Sea Convention To The United States Senate, DOS Commentary p. 19 (William J. Clinton, Oct. 7, 1994) (S. Treaty Doc. 103–39), https://www.foreign.senate.gov/imo/media/doc/treaty_103-39.pdf.

[244] DOS Commentary, p. 20 (full cite above).

[245] There are actually "five possible routes, with some variations that can be used to navigate the [Northwest] Passage…. Not all of these routes though are suitable for all vessels due to limitations caused by water depth and shoals. Of course, the polar conditions and presence of ice also impose severe limitations upon shipping. Thus, even during the summer months a vessel may require some ice breaking capacity to successfully complete the passage." Donald R. Rothwell, *The Canadian-U.S. Northwest Passage Dispute: A Reassessment*, 26 CORNELL INT'L. L. J. 331, 352-353 (1993), https://scholarship.law.cornell.edu/cilj/vol26/iss2/2/.

[246] Chart from ArcticEcon, Mining, Energy, Territorial Disputes, Climate, and more., *The Northwest Passage Dispute – Canada (Map with Exclusive Economic Zones)* (Jan. 13, 2012), https://arcticecon.wordpress.com/2012/01/13/the-northwest-passage-dispute-canada-map-with-exclusive-economic-zones/.

[247] Dept. of Defense Maritime Claims Reference Manual (MCRM)—Canada 2017, http://www.jag.navy.mil/organization/code_10_mcrm.htm.

[248] ArcGIS StoryMaps, *Canada's Sovereignty over the Northwest Passage: Who really owns it?* (Joel Fu & David Jiang, Jan. 5, 2020), https://storymaps.arcgis.com/stories/f2e7934cab2148da8400af23021f0fa9. *See also* Brown Political Review, *The U.S. – Canada Northwest Passage Dispute* (Daniel Steinfeld, Apr. 8, 2020), https://brownpoliticalreview.org/2020/04/the-u-s-canada-northwest-passage-dispute/; Quartz, *The US is picking a fight with Canada over a thawing Arctic shipping route* (Zoë Schlanger, June 28, 2019), https://qz.com/1653831/the-us-is-picking-a-fight-with-canada-over-an-arctic-shipping-route/.

[249] *See also* N. Nandan & D. H. Anderson, *Straits used for International Navigation: A Commentary on Part III of the United Nations Convention on the Law of the Sea 1982*, 60

BRIT. Y. B. INT'L L. 159, 169 (1990), https://www.semanticscholar.org/paper/Straits-Used-for-International-Navigation%3A-A-on-III-Nandan-Anderson/9b91234d4cc3960fde42e36f5d9bfafc46e73cdd (positing that the potential use of what would otherwise be an international strait is insufficient—there must be actual international use of the strait, although it does not have to be "regular or ... reach any predetermined level"); Tommy B. Koh, *The Territorial Sea, Contiguous Zone, Straits and Archipelagoes under the 1982 Convention on the Law of the Sea*, 29 MALAYA L. REV. 163, 178 (1987), https://www.jstor.org/stable/24865511 (same). *But see* Donat Pharand, *The Northwest Passage in International Law*, 17 CAN. Y.B. INT'L L. 99, 107-114 (1979), https://www.cambridge.org/core/journals/canadian-yearbook-of-international-law-annuaire-canadien-de-droit-international/article/abs/northwest-passage-in-international-law/733B392349A8B7A7AE20A07054F53B10 (arguing that "[t]he sufficiency of the use [of a potential international strait] is determined mainly, but not exclusively, by reference to two factors: the number of ships using the strait and the number of flag states represented. Both of these figures should normally reach the order of magnitude shown to exist in the Corfu Channel case. There, the ships using the North Corfu Channel averaged 137 a month, during a twenty-one-month period, and represented seven flag states.... [However, a special Polar standard could be applied to straits normally made impassable due to ice even during summer months, if there were a] brief history of transporting oil and gas by a few flag states"); Rothwell, *Northwest Passage Dispute*, p. 357 (full cite above) (concluding that "without further judicial guidance on the question of international straits, the determination of whether the [Northwest] Passage is or is not an international strait is extremely difficult. Those commentators who argue that the Northwest Passage is not an international strait rely upon an interpretation of the Corfu Channel case which is not universally accepted. They fail to adequately take into account that, because of polar conditions, a lesser volume of navigation through the Passage may still be sufficient to classify the strait as international.").

[250] DoD MCRM—Canada 2017 (full cite above).

[251] Photo: Image via Flickr (Coast Guard News), https://www.flickr.com/photos/coastguardnews/36478970050/in/photolist-XzwfTu-6Rr6DA-8gSRy3-bhwBcH-bhwBmP-bhwBug-37BpVq-5c4m2p-S5vDk4-7kihX9-bhwBSc-idAHvx-bhwC9p-bhwBia-e4KrUe-e4R3Y5-e4R3Rf-bWgfpL-r9Ziw1-AWvhcM-e4R4cu-e4R4ed-e4Ks7a-e4R49h-nvZuNE-yJNS4y-nRN5ov-MQcXgn-r9Ynij-e4R45A-e4KsgZ-oyDYcq-oR7to7-rrxKdg-dwwfnD-dwwfyp-rgnjxM-iUzS-7VZVsn-ARmKMQ-nRuY9g-2hp8gt8-qg1tu5-yXAu93-7TwvYX-78mXqV-5pnjpq-asRGXT-pFNVmn-iudENr.

[252] UNCLOS, art. 42(4) (full cite above).

[253] UNCLOS, art. 39(2)(a) (full cite above); Int'l. Maritime Organization (IMO), English, About IMO, Conventions, List of Conventions, Convention on the Int'l. Regulations for Preventing Collisions at Sea, 1972 (COLREGs), http://www.imo.org/en/About/Conventions/ListOfConventions/Pages/COLREG.aspx.

[254] UNCLOS, art. 39(3)(a) (full cite above).

[255] UNCLOS, art. 19(2)-(2)(a) (full cite above).

[256] UNCLOS, art. 39(1)(b) (full cite above).

[257] *But see* TUFTS, LAW OF THE SEA, p. 22 (full cite above) (positing that "[d]ue to the sovereign immunity of warships ... the degree to which a coastal State can force a warship to exit its territorial waters in this situation is not clear.").

[258] United Nations Convention on the Law of the Sea (UNCLOS) art. 42(5), Dec. 10, 1982, 1833 U.N.T.S. 397, https://www.un.org/Depts/los/convention_agreements/convention_overview_convention.htm.Chapter 9 discusses Flag States in more depth.

[259] UNCLOS, art. 39(1)(c) (full cite above); U.S. Navy, Marine Corps & Coast Guard, The Commander's Handbook on the Law of Naval Operations, NWP 1-14M/MCTP 11-10B/COMDTPUB P5800.7A, ¶ 2.5.3.2 (pp. 2-7 to 2-8) (2017), www.jag.navy.mil/distrib/instructions/CDRs_HB_on_Law_of_Naval_Operations_AUG17.pdf.

[260] Commander's Handbook, ¶ 2.5.3.2 (pp. 2-7 to 2-8) (full cite above).

[261] See, e.g., CNN, Middle East, 'Alter your course,' Iranians warned before seizing UK-flagged ship (Eliza Mackintosh, July 21, 2019), https://www.cnn.com/2019/07/21/middleeast/audio-recording-british-tanker-seized-iran-intl/index.html (noting that approximately 24% of global oil production passes through the Strait of Hormuz, which is the only way to ship oil out of the Persian (aka Arabian) Gulf).

[262] See, e.g., UNCLOS, art. 36 (full cite above); Commander's Handbook, Appendix C (pp. C-1 to C-2) (full cite above) (citing the 2015 Maritime Advisory warning that Iran has been harassing U.S.-flagged ships in the Strait of Hormuz); The Fletcher School of Law and Diplomacy—Tufts University, Law of the Sea, A Policy Primer 26-27 (2017), https://sites.tufts.edu/lawofthesea/introduction/ (detailing aggressive actions taken by Iran against U.S. warships in the Arabian Gulf and Strait of Hormuz).

[263] Vienna Convention on the Law of Treaties art. 2(1)(d), May 23, 1969, 1155 U.N.T.S. 331; Restatement (Third) of Foreign Relations § 313 cmt. a (1987); Restatement (Fourth) of Foreign Relations § 305 cmt. e (2018).

[264] Restatement (Third) of Foreign Relations § 313 cmt. b (1987).

[265] United Nations Treaty Collection, Depositary, Status of Treaties, Chapter XXI Law of the Sea, 6. United Nations Convention on the Law of the Sea, https://treaties.un.org/Pages/ViewDetailsIII.aspx?src=TREATY&mtdsg_no=XXI-6&chapter=21&Temp=mtdsg3&clang=_en. See also Dept. of Defense Maritime Claims Reference Manual (MCRM)—Iran 2014, http://www.jag.navy.mil/organization/code_10_mcrm.htm.

[266] Although the U.S. is not yet party to UNCLOS, it routinely participates as an observer at meetings of UNCLOS State Parties. See, e.g., CarrieLyn D. Guymon (editor), Digest of United States Practice in International Law 419 (2019), https://www.state.gov/digest-of-united-states-practice-in-international-law-2019.

[267] See, e.g., UNCLOS, art. 36 (full cite above); Commander's Handbook, Appendix C (pp. C-1 to C-2) (full cite above) (citing the 2015 Maritime Advisory warning that Iran has been harassing U.S.-flagged ships in the Strait of Hormuz); Tufts, Law of the Sea, pp. 26-27 (full cite above) (detailing aggressive actions taken by Iran against U.S. warships in the Arabian Gulf and Strait of Hormuz).

[268] Hugo Caminos & Vincent P. Cogliati-Bantz, Transit passage and customary law, in The Legal Regime of Straits: Contemporary Challenges and Solutions 452–472 (2014); The Law of the Sea: Costs of U.S. Accession to UNCLOS (June 14, 2012), https://www.heritage.org/testimony/the-law-the-sea-costs-us-accession-unclos; American Society of Int'l. Law (ASIL), 16 Insights 16, Transit Passage Rights in the Strait of Hormuz and Iran's Threats to Block the Passage of Oil Tankers (Nilufer Oral,

May 3, 2012), https://www.asil.org/insights/volume/16/issue/16/transit-passage-rights-strait-hormuz-and-iran%E2%80%99s-threats-block-passage.

[269] UNCLOS, art. 44 (full cite above); COMMANDER'S HANDBOOK, ¶ 2.5.3.2 (pp. 2-7 to 2-8) (full cite above).

[270] *See, e.g.,* UNCLOS, art. 36 (full cite above); COMMANDER'S HANDBOOK, Appendix C (pp. C-1 to C-2) (full cite above) (citing the 2015 Maritime Advisory warning that Iran has been harassing U.S.-flagged ships in the Strait of Hormuz); TUFTS, LAW OF THE SEA, pp. 26-27 (full cite above) (detailing aggressive actions taken by Iran against U.S. warships in the Arabian Gulf and Strait of Hormuz).

[271] CNN, Middle East, *Iran's Revolutionary Guards, explained* (Tamara Qiblawi, Apr. 8, 2019), https://www.cnn.com/2019/04/08/middleeast/iran-revolutionary-guards-explainer-intl/index.html.

[272] CNN, *'Alter your course'* (full cite above).

[273] CNN, *'Alter your course'* (full cite above).

[274] The Telegraph, World News, *Iranian commander warns British ship could be seized if oil tanker detained in Gibraltar is not released* (Roland Oliphant, July 5, 2019), https://www.telegraph.co.uk/news/2019/07/05/iranian-commander-warns-british-ship-could-seized-oil-tanker/.

[275] UNCLOS, art. 42 (full cite above).

[276] United Nations, Oceans & Law of the Sea, Division for Ocean Affairs and the Law of the Sea, Chronological lists of ratifications of, accessions and successions to the Convention and the related Agreements, https://www.un.org/Depts/los/reference_files/chronological_list, https://www.un.org/Depts/los/convention_agreements/convention_overview_convention.htm States in the World. *See, e.g.,* Independent States in the World Fact Sheet, U.S. Dept. of State Bureau of Intelligence and Research (March 27, 2019), https://www.state.gov/independent-states-in-the-world/; Frequently Asked Questions, Worldometers, https://www.worldometers.info/geography/how-many-countries-are-there-in-the-world/. Thus 168/195 or 86% of States are party to UNCLOS.

[277] Vienna Convention on the Law of Treaties (VCLT) art. 18, May 23, 1969, 1155 U.N.T.S. 331. Although the United States is not a party to the VCLT, it considers the VCLT to represent customary international law. Sean D. Murphy, The George Wash. Univ. Law Sch.: "Should the U.S. Join the International Criminal Court?" A Moderated Panel Discussion, Feb. 13, 2006. *See also* Letter Of Transmittal Forwarding The 1982 UN Law Of The Sea Convention To The United States Senate, DOS Commentary p. 17 (William J. Clinton, Oct. 7, 1994) (S. Treaty Doc. 103–39), https://www.foreign.senate.gov/imo/media/doc/treaty_103-39.pdf (noting that "[u]nder customary international law, as reflected in … the Vienna Convention on the Law of Treaties (92nd Congress; 1st Session, Senate Executive 'L')").

[278] Chapter 9 discusses the significance of Flag States.

[279] CNN, World, *How the Oman tanker attack played out* (Helen Regan, June 14, 2019), https://www.cnn.com/2019/06/14/middleeast/tanker-iran-us-timeline-intl-hnk/index.html.

[280] Statement from the President on the Designation of the Islamic Revolutionary Guard Corps as a Foreign Terrorist Organization (Apr. 8, 2019), https://www.whitehouse.gov/briefings-statements/statement-president-designation-islamic-revolutionary-guard-corps-foreign-terrorist-organization/.

[281] CNN, Politics, *Trump designates elite Iranian military force as a terrorist organization* (Nicole Gaouette, Apr. 8, 2019), https://www.cnn.com/2019/04/08/politics/iran–us–irgc–designation/index.html.

[282] *See, e.g.*, United Nations Convention on the Law of the Sea (UNCLOS) art. 36, Dec. 10, 1982, 1833 U.N.T.S. 397, https://www.un.org/Depts/los/convention_agreements/convention_overview_convention.htm; U.S. NAVY, MARINE CORPS & COAST GUARD, THE COMMANDER'S HANDBOOK ON THE LAW OF NAVAL OPERATIONS, NWP 1-14M/MCTP 11-10B/COMDTPUB P5800.7A, Appendix C (pp. C-1 to C-2) (2017), www.jag.navy.mil/distrib/instructions/CDRs_HB_on_Law_of_Naval_Operations_AUG17.pdf (citing the 2015 Maritime Advisory warning that Iran has been harassing U.S.-flagged ships in the Strait of Hormuz); THE FLETCHER SCHOOL OF LAW AND DIPLOMACY—TUFTS UNIVERSITY, LAW OF THE SEA, A POLICY PRIMER 26-27 (2017), https://sites.tufts.edu/lawofthesea/introduction/ (detailing aggressive actions taken by Iran against U.S. warships in the Arabian Gulf and Strait of Hormuz).

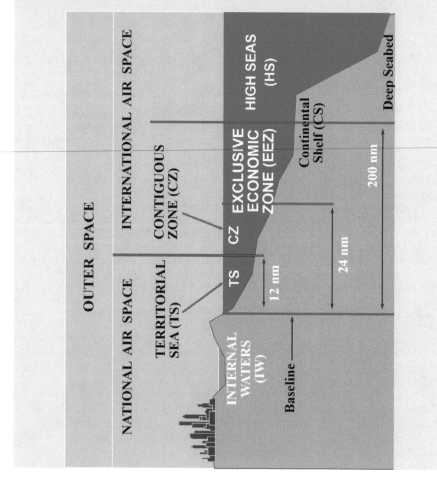

CHAPTER 4:
CONTIGUOUS ZONE, EXCLUSIVE ECONOMIC ZONE & ARCHIPELAGIC WATERS

"Our nation's exclusive zone [claimed under UNCLOS] would be larger than that of any country in the world—covering an area greater than the landmass of the lower 48 states."
— Henry Kissinger, George Schultz, James Baker III, Colin Powell, and Condoleeza Rice (former U.S. Secretaries of State)

U NCLOS CREATED THREE NEW MARITIME ZONES: the Contiguous Zone and Exclusive Economic Zone (which may be claimed by all States), and Archipelagic Waters (which may be claimed by States comprised of a number of islands, aka Archipelagic States). This Chapter discusses each of these maritime zones in turn. [NOTE: There is a diagram of the various maritime zones at the beginning of this Chapter.]

"Unlike the territorial sea, the contiguous zone is not subject to coastal State sovereignty; vessels and aircraft enjoy the same high seas freedom of navigation and overflight in the contiguous zone as in the EEZ."[283] Instead, the Contiguous Zone is a law enforcement buffer zone, usually related to the **inbound** movement of ships to **prevent infringement** of laws in the Coastal State's land territory or Territorial Sea, and the **outbound** movement of ships to **punish infringement** of laws that occurred in the Coastal State's land territory or Territorial Sea.[284] Article 33 is the only provision in UNCLOS pertaining to the Contiguous Zone:

Article 33 / Contiguous zone

1. In a zone contiguous to its territorial sea, described as the contiguous zone, the coastal State may exercise the control necessary to:

(a) prevent infringement of its customs, fiscal, immigration or sanitary laws and regulations within its territory or territorial sea;

(b) punish infringement of the above laws and regulations committed within its territory or territorial sea.

2. The contiguous zone may not extend beyond 24 nautical miles from the baselines from which the breadth of the territorial sea is measured. [emphasis added][285]

Thus, the Coastal State may enforce its laws out to 24 nm in four areas: Fiscal, Immigration, Sanitation and Customs (FISC), but only if the effects of the legal violations are felt either within the Coastal State's land territory or Territorial Seas (aka National Waters).[286] The Contiguous Zone grew out of Great Britain's "Hovering Acts" aimed at prosecuting foreign smuggler ships standing off the British coast, but with a "constructive presence" in Britain's National Waters when they sent small boats from the mother ship into Britain's Territorial Seas. This was also the foundation for the concept of "hot pursuit," which allows the pursuit and capture in International Waters for violations of law in the Territorial Seas.[287]

Not only is there only one article in UNCLOS dealing with the Contiguous Zone, which reflects a general lack of interest by States in creating a law enforcement "buffer" zone, but the Contiguous Zone is also the least popular zone as judged by the number of States which claim it. Out of 195 States in the world,[288] and 168 State Parties to UNCLOS,[289] only 90 of 150 Coastal States (i.e., States with a coastline) claim a Contiguous Zone.[290]

Although the Contiguous Zone was a new treaty right created by UNCLOS, President Clinton issued a proclamation in 1999 (i.e., five years after UNCLOS went into effect in 1994), claiming a 24 nm Contiguous Zone for the U.S. consistent with Article 33 of UNCLOS:

International law recognizes that coastal nations may establish zones contiguous to their territorial seas, known as contiguous zones.

The contiguous zone of the United States is a zone contiguous to the territorial sea of the United States, in which the United States may exercise the control necessary to prevent infringement of its customs, fiscal, immigration, or sanitary laws nd regulations within its territory or territorial sea, and to punish infringement of the above laws and regulations committed within its territory or territorial sea.

* * *

The contiguous zone of the United States extends to 24 nautical miles from the baselines of the United States determined in accordance with international law, but in no case within the territorial sea of another nation.[291]

Since the U.S. is not party to UNCLOS,[292] President Clinton implicitly based his claim to a U.S. Contiguous Zone on Customary International Law (CIL).

EXCLUSIVE ECONOMIC ZONE

Unlike the Contiguous Zone, which is a law enforcement zone, the Exclusive Economic Zone (EEZ) is a resource/economic zone. The **Coastal State (aka "littoral State") has exclusive ownership of ALL resources** (including any resources found on the surface of the ocean or in the "water column") of its EEZ, extending out to 200 nm from the baseline.[293] "Coastal States do not, however, exercise sovereignty over the EEZ."[294] The resources in the EEZ include *inter alia* (i.e., among other things):

> - all "natural resources" (including fishing);
> - "the production of energy from the water, currents and winds";[295]
> - "the establishment [i.e., construction and/or installation] and use of artificial islands, installations and structures"[296];
> - Marine Scientific Research (MSR);[297] and
> - environmental protection and preservation.[298]

A chart of the EEZs for each Coastal State (highlighted in light green above) reveals how extensive this Coastal State control over maritime resources actually is.[299]

The creation of the EEZ, recognizing the right of coastal States to jurisdiction over the resources of some 85 million square kilometers of ocean space, covering approximately 36 percent of the surface of the seas and accounting for almost 90 percent of fisheries, has been called one of the most revolutionary features of UNCLOS.[300]

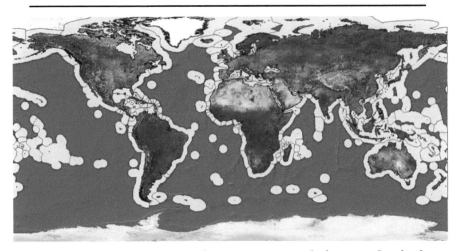

Notice that both the Contiguous Zone and the EEZ begin just outside the Territorial Seas, and can extend out to 24 nm and 200 nm respectively, regardless of the width of the Territorial Sea— they're measured from the baselines.[301] As mentioned earlier, the EEZ is a new maritime zone created by UNCLOS. "In negotiating UNCLOS, the [United States] argued that the EEZ was an extension inwards of the high seas while many coastal states viewed the EEZ as an extension outwards of their territorial sea. The compromise saw the EEZ established as a zone *sui generis* [i.e., unique]—neither high seas nor territorial sea subject to its own legal regime...."[302] President Reagan claimed a 200 nm EEZ for the U.S. in 1983,[303] implicitly basing the claim on Customary International Law (CIL). However, this was less than a year after the UNCLOS conference had concluded in 1982, and 11 years before UNCLOS went into effect in 1994. Since "[t]he establishment of the EEZ in the Convention represent[ed] a substantial change in the law of the sea,"[304] and the concept of an EEZ didn't even go into effect as a matter of treaty law (for the State Parties to UNCLOS) until 1994, it was a bit premature to claim that EEZ represented CIL at the time. Since then, based upon the number of States that claim a 200 nm EEZ (especially States, like the U.S., that are not yet parties to UNCLOS), the EEZ probably represents CIL today.

The EEZ of the United States is among the largest in the world, extending through considerable areas of the Atlantic, Pacific and Arctic Oceans, including those around U.S. insular territories. From the perspective of managing and conserving resources off its coasts, the United States gains more from the provisions on the EEZ in the Convention than perhaps any other State. [emphasis added][305]

In conjunction with the Coastal State's right to control the establishment and use of artificial islands, installations and structures, the Coastal State is also under an obligation to warn mariners (via a Notice to Mariners, or NOTMAR)[306] of such artificial structures and other hazards located in the EEZ,[307] which harkens back to the Corfu Channel case discussed in Chapter 3.

As discussed in Chapter 2, **outside the 12 nm Territorial Seas** (i.e., National Waters and National Airspace) **are International Waters**[308] **and International Airspace,**[309] over which the Coastal State exercises less and less sovereignty and control the further one travels from land. Thus, although the Coastal State owns all resources in its EEZ,[310] **other States enjoy all High Seas freedoms that are not resource-related in the Coastal State's EEZ**, including the freedom of navigation by ships, the freedom of overflight by aircraft, and the right to lay and repair submarine cables and pipelines.[311] Thus, of all the UNCLOS "provisions, perhaps the most important one [from a military perspective], is the fundamental principal of Freedom of Navigation. This has been the Navy's peacetime *raison d'être* [i.e., purpose for existing] for some time."[312]

In both of the maritime zones we've discussed previously (in Chapter 3), UNCLOS balances the Coastal State's rights with protecting other States' rights in those zones,[313] which was part of the UNCLOS "package deal."[314] Thus, in the Territorial Sea, where the Coastal State has almost complete sovereignty (subject primarily to the right of Innocent Passage by the ships of other States), the Coastal State has a duty not to hamper Innocent Passage.[315] Similarly, Coastal States bordering an International Strait have a duty not to hamper or suspend Transit Passage through that International Strait.[316]

Similarly, in the EEZ, where the Coastal State owns all resources, "the coastal State shall have due regard to the rights and duties of other States."[317] This means that the Coastal State has a duty not to interfere with non-resource-related High Seas freedoms, such as the freedoms of navigation, overflight, and laying/repairing submarine cables and pipelines.[318] Also, in exercising their rights in the EEZ, other "States shall have due regard to the rights and duties of the coastal State."[319] Thus, in the EEZ regime there exists a double-edged "due regard" standard, with Coastal States having due regard for the rights of other States (specifically non-resource-related High Seas freedoms), and other States having due regard to the rights of the Coastal State in managing its resources in the EEZ. If you think about it, not engaging in resource-related freedoms in another State's EEZ is an application of the due regard standard: respect the right of the Coastal State to manage economic resources in its EEZ.

Although this seems like a fairly clear division of rights and responsibilities in the EEZ (i.e., all resources belong to the Coastal State, but other States can still exercise all other High Seas freedoms), a number of States have passed domestic legislation that interferes with the navigational rights and freedoms in their EEZs.[320] Yet deliberations at the Third United Nations Conference on the Law of the Sea (which culminated in UNCLOS) expressly rejected Coastal States seeking to assert any jurisdiction (i.e., sovereignty) in their EEZs other than ownership of all resources.[321] Moreover, Article 58(2) specifically incorporates certain aspects of the High Seas regime,[322] including Article 89, which prohibits States from seeking to assert their sovereignty over the High Seas, and therefore (by extension) over their EEZs (other than ownership of all resources).[323]

Thus, can a Coastal State lawfully stop and search foreign fishing vessels in its EEZ, and/or require them to stow their fishing gear? Yes, absolutely! Because the Coastal State has the right to control all resources in its EEZ, including fishing.[324] Can a Coastal State lawfully limit hazardous cargo or propulsion (e.g., the transport of nuclear waste, or nuclear-propelled ships, such as U.S. naval aircraft carriers) in its EEZ? No! Because these ships have the High Seas freedom of navigation through another State's EEZ.[325] Can a Coastal State seek to lawfully limit foreign States conducting military exercises in its EEZ? Once again, no (!) for two reasons: (1) military exercises are not resource-related, and thus are not within the Coastal State's purview (within its EEZ), and (2) during the UNCLOS negotiations, "[m]ost nations agreed with the position advocated by the major maritime powers, that '[m]ilitary operations, exercises and activities have always been regarded as internationally lawful uses of the sea. The right to conduct such activities will continue to be enjoyed by all States in the exclusive economic zone.'"[326]

"Dissatisfied with the outcome of the [UNCLOS] negotiations, however, a few nations have sought to unilaterally expand their control in the EEZ, particularly by imposing restrictions on military operations and other lawful activities. These efforts impinge on traditional uses of the oceans by other States and are inconsistent with international law and State practice."[327] Chapter 11 discusses these excessive maritime claims in more depth.

Before moving to this Chapter's final sub-topic, let's analyze a maritime claim against what we've discussed thus far, in order to help cement our understanding. "The Principality of Sealand" is an

old sea fort ("HM Fort Roughs" or "Roughs Tower") built during World War II on a sandbar ("Rough Sands") 6 nm off the coast of England. The British Royal Navy stopped using the sea fort in 1956.

In the 1966-1967 timeframe, retired British Army Major Paddy Roy Bates relocated his pirate radio station to the sea fort in order to broadcast from international waters, converting "Roughs Tower into — at least in his view — a sovereign nation, The Principality of Sealand, with Bates bestowing upon himself the title Pri[n]ce Roy of Sealand."[328] Sealand has its own website (https://www.sealandgov.org/), where

it sells Sealand memorabilia, including certified copies of its constitution, and titles of nobility such as this one presented to the author by his former students.

When Major Bates fired "warning shots"[329] in 1968 at a buoy repair boat repairing a navigational buoy in Sealand's "territorial waters", he was prosecuted (as a British subject) by a British court for the unlawful possession and discharge of a firearm.[330] Apparently the British court determined that it lacked jurisdiction "because [the incident] occurred outside of Britain's ordinary territorial limits."[331] [NOTE: Britain's Territorial Seas were the same width as most States before UNCLOS: 3 nm.][332]

Let us assume that Great Britain "abandoned" the old sea fort,[333] and that Major Bates had a quasi-legitimate basis to salvage it under Admiralty Law.[334] Is there any validity to Major Bates' claim that "The Principality of Sealand" is a sovereign nation,[335] or can Great Britain assert some authority over Roughs Tower? As with most questions under UNCLOS, the first issue to resolve is in which maritime zone are we located? At the time Major Bates first occupied the sea fort in 1967, it lay beyond Great Britain's 3 nm Territorial Seas, and thus lay in International Waters. However, when Great Britain extended the width of its Territorial Seas from 3 nm to 12 nm in 1987, "Sealand" now lays within Great Britain's Territorial Seas.

The next issue to resolve is what type of formation is the sandbar "Rough Sands"? As discussed in Chapter 2, UNCLOS distinguishes between Islands, Rocks, and Low Tide Elevations (LTEs). Since naturally formed Islands are above water at high tide and can sustain human habitation (i.e., life), they are entitled to the same maritime zones as continental land masses (i.e., the mainland). Although Rocks are also above water at high tide, since they cannot sustain human habitation (i.e., life), they are only entitled to Territorial Seas and a Contiguous Zone.[336] Low Tide Elevations (LTEs) are also called "drying rocks" because they only "dry out" at low tide (i.e., they are above water only at low tide, and are submerged at high tide). A Low Tide Elevation is not entitled to any maritime zones, but it can be used to "bump out" the maritime zones (i.e., as a point on a straight baseline) if it is found within the Territorial Seas, and the Coastal State has constructed a lighthouse upon it.[337]

Chapter 12 discusses the requirements for claiming the status of an island in more depth in the context of the decision of an arbitral tribunal (sitting at the Permanent Court of Arbitration) in the South China Sea arbitration. BLUF: unless the sandbar "Rough Sands" has a natural source of potable water, and has had "sustained human habitation," it would not qualify as a natural island. As discussed in Chapter 2 and UNCLOS Article 121, artificial/man-made islands do not possess any maritime zones (i.e., you cannot "build" an island in order to claim maritime zones under UNCLOS).

If the sandbar "Rough Sands" remained above water at high tide, it would constitute a Rock, and thus would be considered a piece of land that could be owned. However, from the photo above, it does not appear that the sandbar "Rough Sands" remains above water at high tide. Thus, it would appear that "Sealand" is an "artificial island[], installation[or] structure[]," which is a type of resource owned by Great Britain,[338] whether it lies within Britain's Territorial Seas (where Britain has almost complete sovereignty, subject primarily to the right of Innocent Passage) or Britain's EEZ (where Britain owns all resources).[339]

Less than a year after the development of Sealand, Italian engineer Giorgio Rosa built a similar sea platform in 1967 at the edge of the Italian Territorial Seas, and claimed it as the Esperanta Respubliko de la Insulo de la Rozoj (The Esperanto Republic of Rose Island) in 1968. However, the Italian government was less

accommodating, and seized the sea platform 55 days after Rosa had declared independence; other Italian engineers and a storm conspired to sink the structure in 1969.[340]

ARCHIPELAGIC WATERS

This Chapter's third and final sub-topic is the special regime applicable to States comprised of a group of islands, known as archipelagoes, or Archipelagic States if they satisfy UNCLOS' objective, two-part test (discussed below). As discussed in Chapter 2, during the Third Conference on the Law of the Sea, UNCLOS was seen as a "package deal,"[341] and addressed the disparate requirements of a variety of States by providing tradeoffs or "something for everyone." One of the groups of States seeking to protect their unique interests were the archipelagoes (led by Indonesia and the Philippines),[342] who wanted some level of sovereignty over the waters between their islands. Indonesia is shown on the following chart (outlined in red, with its islands highlighted in white), and the Philippines (outlined in blue) are classic examples of Archipelagic States.

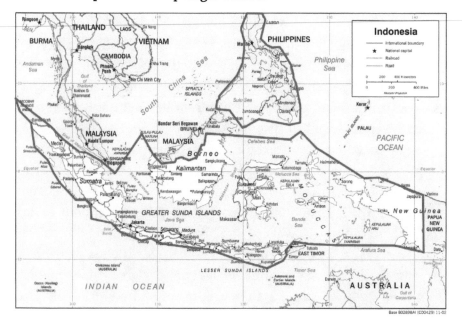

UNCLOS created a regime for Archipelagic States, which permits drawing "straight archipelagic baselines joining the outermost points of the outermost islands,"[343] thereby potentially encompassing huge swaths of ocean that were previously regarded as High Seas. However, in order to carefully limit the number of States eligible for this special status, **UNCLOS established an objective, two-part test for an Archipelagic State: (1) the ratio of water to land within the Archipelagic Baselines must be at least one to one, but no more than nine to one** (i.e., at least 50% water, up to 90% water),[344] **and (2) ninety-seven percent of the baselines shall not be longer than 100 nm, but the remaining three percent of the baselines can be up to 125 nm long** (i.e., the islands must be sufficiently close together).[345]

This UNCLOS formula is highly technical and specific because it was drafted so that only those States which had sought the status of an Archipelagic State during the Third Conference on the Law of the Sea would qualify. For example, Continental States with islands (e.g., the U.S. with Hawaii, or China with any of its "islands") would not satisfy the first criteria of the ratio of water to land.[346] On the other hand, Indonesia has a ratio of water to land of 1.2 to 1 (i.e., 55% water), and the Philippines has a ratio of water to land of 1.8 to 1 (i.e., 64% water).[347] States with islands too far away from each other similarly would not satisfy the second criteria of the length of the straight baselines connecting the outermost points of the outermost islands (e.g., the distance from Hawaii to the west coast of the U.S. is over 2,000 nm).[348] The second criteria is also designed to encourage very specific and detailed baseline claims (e.g., containing at least 101 points in order to form at least 100 baselines such that 3 baselines can be as long as 125 nm).

Indonesia was the first State to properly designate straight Archipelagic Baselines in accordance with UNCLOS in March, 2009,[349] although the Philippines quickly followed suit one month later.[350] The U.S. view is that only 20 States potentially qualify as Archipelagic States under the rigorous definition in UNCLOS:

Potential Archipelagic States under UNCLOS, Article 47	
1. Antigua & Barbuda	2. The Bahamas
3. Cape Verde	4. Comoros
5. Fiji	6. Grenada
7. Indonesia	8. Jamaica
9. Kiribati (in part)	10. Maldives
11. Marshall Islands (in part)	12. Papua New Guinea
13. Philippines	14. Saint Vincent and the Grenadines
15. Sao Tome & Principe	16. Seychelles
17. Solomon Islands (five archipelagos)	18. Tonga
19. Trinidad & Tobago	20. Vanuatu

[351]

The reasoning behind such a rigorous test for an Archipelagic State is that, unlike the other maritime zones which have distinct limits on their width (i.e., 12 nm for Territorial Seas, 24 nm for Contiguous Zones, and 200 nm for EEZs), "there is no designated [nautical] mile limit on the area of archipelagic waters."[352] Moreover, **each of the regular maritime zones are measured outwards from the Archipelagic Baselines**, rather than from a "normal" baseline drawn around each island.[353]

As discussed in Chapter 2, any waters inside the baseline are known as Internal Waters,[354] over which the Coastal State exercises "complete sovereignty" (i.e., the vessels of other States need permission/consent from the Coastal State to enter)[355] However, if Archipelagic Waters (i.e., waters inside Archipelagic Baselines) were treated as Internal Waters, this would severely hamper the rights of other States, such as the Freedom of Navigation through the Archipelagic Waters. Therefore, as part of the UNCLOS "package deal,"[356] in order to obtain sovereignty[357] over Archipelagic Waters inside Archipelagic Baselines, Archipelagic States were willing to compromise with other States desiring navigational freedoms through the Archipelagic Waters.

Thus, perhaps the best way to think of Archipelagic Waters is as an innovative compromise between island States wanting to control the waters between their islands, and other States not wanting to lose their navigational freedoms between them. So Archipelagic Waters are treated as if they were Territorial Seas, with the ships of other States able to conduct Innocent Passage through them.[358] In addition, "[a]n archipelagic State may designate sea lanes,"[359] although "[s]uch sea lanes ... shall include all normal passage routes used as routes for international navigation".[360] All ships and aircraft enjoy the right of Archipelagic Sea Lanes Passage (ASLP) through the sea lanes, which is akin to Transit Passage through International Straits.[361] The following diagram of a notional Archipelagic State may help visualize the new compromise regime of Archipelagic Waters.

The solid black lines are straight Archipelagic Baselines, connecting the outermost points of the outermost islands.[362] The Archipelagic State still has the regular maritime zones outside its straight archipelagic baselines (i.e., a 12 nm Territorial Sea, a 24 nm Contiguous Zone, and a 200 nm EEZ).[363] The waters inside the Archipelagic Baselines are Archipelagic Waters, through which the ships of all States enjoy the right of Innocent Passage.[364] An Archipelagic State may still have internal waters (e.g., inside a bay).[365] The Coastal State shall designate all normal passage routes as Archipelagic Sea Lanes,[366] by designating the center "axis line" of the Archipelagic Sea Lane (solid red line on the diagram). Ships and aircraft engaged in ASLP through the Archipelagic Sea Lanes

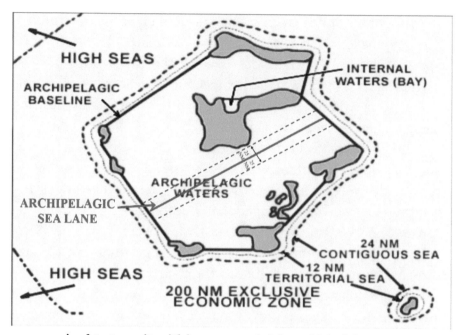

HIGH SEAS

ARCHIPELAGIC
BASELINE

INTERNAL
WATERS (BAY)

ARCHIPELAGIC
WATERS

ARCHIPELAGIC
SEA LANE

24 NM
CONTIGUOUS SEA

12 NM
TERRITORIAL SEA

HIGH SEAS

200 NM EXCLUSIVE
ECONOMIC ZONE

are required to transit within 25 nm of either side of the center axis (dashed red lines on the diagram above).[367] The right of ASLP is akin to Transit Passage through International Straits.[368] The duties of Archipelagic States and ships and aircraft engaged in ASLP are the same as in Transit Passage (e.g., the Archipelagic State must not hamper ASLP but it may designate traffic separation schemes, and ships and aircraft engaged in ASLP shall do so in their normal mode of continuous and expeditious transit while refraining from any threat or use of force against the Archipelagic State).[369]

The following table summarizes the different freedoms available in the various maritime zones. Green is good from a foreign ship's perspective (generally permitted), Yellow is cautionary (restricted), and Red is bad from a foreign ship's perspective (generally prohibited or very restricted).

	Freedom of Nav.	Over-flight	Sub-merged	Weps. & Intel	Exploit Resources	Obey Local Laws	Contin. & Exped.	Suspend-able
Legend: ● FAVORABLE ◣ MARGINAL ■ UNFAVORABLE								
HIGH SEAS FREEDOMS (ROUTINE OPS IN INT'L.)	●	●	●	●	●	N/A	N/A	NO
- EXCLUSIVE ECON. ZONE (200 nm)	●	●	●	●	■	N/A	N/A	NO
- CONTIGUOUS ZONE (24 nm)	●	●	●	●	■	◣	N/A	NO
INTERNATIONAL STRAITS (TRANSIT PASSAGE)	●	●	●	■	■	◣	YES	NO
TERRITORIAL SEAS (12 nm – INNOCENT PASS.)	◣	■	■	■	■	YES	YES	YES
ARCHIPELAGO – SEA LANE (ASLP)	●	●	●	■	■	◣	YES	NO
- INSIDE ARCHIPELAGO (INNOCENT PASSAGE)	◣	■	■	■	■	YES	YES	YES

[283] Letter Of Transmittal Forwarding The 1982 UN Law Of The Sea Convention To The United States Senate, DOS Commentary pp. 5, 23 (William J. Clinton, Oct. 7, 1994) (S. Treaty Doc. 103–39), https://www.foreign.senate.gov/imo/media/doc/treaty_103-39.pdf.

[284] DONALD R. ROTHWELL & TIM STEPHENS, THE INT'L. LAW OF THE SEA 83 (2nd ed. 2016); U.S. NAVY, MARINE CORPS & COAST GUARD, THE COMMANDER'S HANDBOOK ON THE LAW OF NAVAL OPERATIONS, NWP 1-14M/MCTP 11-10B/COMDTPUB P5800.7A, ¶¶ 1.3.3, 1.6.1, 2.6.1 (pp. 1-3, 1-9, 2-9) (2017), www.jag.navy.mil/distrib/instructions/CDRs_HB_on_Law_of_Naval_Operations_AUG17.pdf.

[285] United Nations Convention on the Law of the Sea (UNCLOS) art. 33, Dec. 10, 1982, 1833 U.N.T.S. 397, https://www.un.org/Depts/los/convention_agreements/convention_overview_convention.htm.

[286] Dept. of Defense Law of War Manual § 13.2.3.2, pp. 884-885 (June 2015, updated Dec. 2016), https://www.hsdl.org/?view&did=797480; COMMANDER'S HANDBOOK, ¶ 3.11.2.2.2 (p. 3-11) (full cite above).

[287] UNCLOS, art. 111 (full cite above); COMMANDER'S HANDBOOK, ¶¶ 3.10.1.2, 3.11.2.2.4 (pp. 3-8, 3-12) (full cite above). Chapter 8 discusses the right of hot pursuit related to maritime regulation and enforcement.

[288] There are generally considered to be 195 States in the World, although the inclusion of 2 States is disputed. *See, e.g.,* Independent States in the World Fact Sheet, U.S. Dept. of State Bureau of Intelligence and Research (March 27, 2019), https://www.state.gov/independent-states-in-the-world/ (including Kosovo but not Palestine, which has observer status at the UN similar to the Holy See); Frequently Asked Questions, Worldometers, https://www.worldometers.info/geography/how-many-countries-are-there-in-the-world/ (including Palestine, but not Kosovo since China and Russia are blocking its membership in the UN).

[289] Most recently, Azerbaijan ratified UNCLOS on June 16, 2016. United Nations, Oceans & Law of the Sea, Division for Ocean Affairs and the Law of the Sea, Chronological lists of ratifications of, accessions and successions to the Convention and the related Agreements, http://www.un.org/Depts/los/reference_files/chronological_lists_of_ratifications .htm#The%20United%20Nations%20Convention%20on%20the%20Law%20of%2 0the%20Sea.

[290] DONALD R. ROTHWELL & TIM STEPHENS, THE INT'L. LAW OF THE SEA 82, 88 (2nd ed. 2016).

[291] Clinton Proclamation No. 7219, 3 C.F.R. 7219 (Sep. 2, 1999), GovInfo, 3 CFR 7219 - Proclamation 7219 of September 2, 1999, https://www.govinfo.gov/content/pkg/CFR-2000-title3-vol1/pdf/CFR-2000-title3-vol1-proc7219.pdf. Before President Clinton's Proclamation 7219, "the U.S. contiguous zone and territorial sea claims [were] coterminous" (i.e., both out to 12 nm). Letter Of Transmittal Forwarding The 1982 UN Law Of The Sea Convention To The United States Senate, DOS Commentary p. 5 (William J. Clinton, Oct. 7, 1994) (S. Treaty Doc. 103–39), https://www.foreign.senate.gov/imo/media/doc/treaty_103-39.pdf.

[292] Although the U.S. is not yet party to UNCLOS, it routinely participates as an observer at meetings of UNCLOS State Parties. See, e.g., CarrieLyn D. Guymon (editor), DIGEST OF UNITED STATES PRACTICE IN INTERNATIONAL LAW 419 (2019), https://www.state.gov/digest-of-united-states-practice-in-international-law-2019.

[293] United Nations Convention on the Law of the Sea (UNCLOS) art. 57, Dec. 10, 1982, 1833 U.N.T.S. 397, https://www.un.org/Depts/los/convention_agreements/convention_overview_co nvention.htm; U.S. NAVY, MARINE CORPS & COAST GUARD, THE COMMANDER'S HANDBOOK ON THE LAW OF NAVAL OPERATIONS, NWP 1-14M/MCTP 11-10B/COMDTPUB P5800.7A, ¶¶ 1.3.4, 1.6.2, 2.6.2 (pp. 1-3, 1-9, 2-9) (2017), www.jag.navy.mil/distrib/instructions/CDRs_HB_on_Law_of_Naval_Operations _AUG17.pdf. See also Dept. of Defense Law of War Manual § 13.2.3.3, p. 885 (June 2015, updated Dec. 2016), https://www.hsdl.org/?view&did=797480.

[294] Raul (Pete) Pedrozo, Military Activities in the Exclusive Economic Zone: East Asia Focus, 90 INT'L. L. STUD. 514, 516 (2014), https://digital-commons.usnwc.edu/ils/vol90/iss1/15/. See also DOS Commentary, p. 6 (full cite above) (same).

[295] UNCLOS, art. 56(1)(a) (full cite above).

[296] UNCLOS, arts. 56(1)(b)(i) & 60(1)-(2) (full cite above).

[297] UNCLOS, art. 56(1)(b)(ii) (full cite above). Chapter 7 discusses marine scientific research in more depth.

[298] UNCLOS, art. 56(1)(b)(iii) (full cite above).

[299] THE FLETCHER SCHOOL OF LAW AND DIPLOMACY—TUFTS UNIVERSITY, LAW OF THE SEA, A POLICY PRIMER 13 (2017), https://sites.tufts.edu/lawofthesea/introduction/; Pedrozo, Military Activities in the EEZ, p. 515 (full cite above).

[300] Helmut Türk, Questions Relating to the Continental Shelf Beyond 200 Nautical Miles: Delimitation, Delineation, and Revenue Sharing, 97 INT'L. L. STUD. 231, 234 (2021), https://digital-commons.usnwc.edu/ils/vol97/iss1/18/.

[301] UNCLOS, arts. 33(2) & 57(3) (full cite above).

[302] Australian Strategic Policy Institute (ASPI)—The Strategist, Turning back the clock on UNCLOS (Sam Bateman, Aug. 20, 2015),

https://www.aspistrategist.org.au/turning-back-the-clock-on-unclos/; R. R. CHURCHILL & A. V. LOWE, THE LAW OF THE SEA 165-166 (1999).

[303] Reagan Proclamation No. 5030, 3 C.F.R. 22 (1983), 48 Fed. Reg. 10605 (Mar. 10, 1983), National Archives, Federal Register, Codification, Proclamations, Proclamation 5030—Exclusive Economic Zone of the United States of America, https://www.archives.gov/federal-register/codification/proclamations/05030.html. "Congress incorporated the [U.S. EEZ] claim in amending the Magnuson Fishery Conservation and Management Act, 16 U.S. Code § 1801 *et seq.*, Pub. L. 99-659." DOS Commentary, pp. 6, 42 (full cite above).

[304] DOS Commentary, p. 5 (full cite above).

[305] DOS Commentary, pp. 6, 23 (full cite above).

[306] *See generally* National Geospatial-Intelligence Agency, Notice to Mariners, https://msi.nga.mil/NTM.

[307] UNCLOS, art. 60(3) (full cite above).

[308] COMMANDER'S HANDBOOK, ¶¶ 1.5, 1.6, 2.6.1 to 2.6.2 (pp. 1-7, 1-8, 2-9) (full cite above); TUFTS, LAW OF THE SEA, pp. 30-31 (full cite above). *But see* The Strategist, *Turning back the clock on UNCLOS* (full cite above) (arguing that the U.S. should "stop talking about EEZs as 'international waters'", i.e., as an "extension inwards of the high seas" because that ignores the Coastal State's rights and duties in the EEZ).

[309] COMMANDER'S HANDBOOK, ¶¶ 1.1, 1.9, 2.7.2 (pp. 1-1, 1-10, 2-13) (full cite above); Pedrozo, *Military Activities in the EEZ*, pp. 519-521 (full cite above).

[310] UNCLOS, arts. 56(1)(a) & 68 (full cite above). Although Article 68 specifically excludes sedentary species from the EEZ regime, they are included in the resources owned by the Coastal State on the Continental Shelf, which generally lies beneath the EEZ. Chapter 6 discusses the Continental Shelf in more depth.

[311] UNCLOS, arts. 58(1) & 87 (full cite above). Chapter 5 discusses High Seas freedoms in more depth.

[312] Defense News, The Drift, *A Quick-Reference Guide on UNCLOS for Gen. Hyten: The Drift, Vol. XLIII,* (David B. Larter, Aug. 4, 2019), https://www.defensenews.com/naval/the-drift/2019/08/04/a-quick-reference-guide-on-unclos-for-gen-hyten-the-drift-vol-xliii/.

[313] TUFTS, LAW OF THE SEA, p. 2 (full cite above). *See also* U.S. Dept. of Defense, Under Secretary of Defense for Policy, OUSDP Offices, FON, DoD Annual Freedom of Navigation (FON) Reports, *Freedom of Navigation: FY 2020 Operational Assertions*, p. 2, https://policy.defense.gov/OUSDP-Offices/FON/ ("International law as reflected in the 1982 Law of the Sea Convention recognizes the rights and freedoms of all nations to engage in traditional uses of the sea. These rights and freedoms are deliberately balanced against coastal States' control over maritime activities. As a nation with both a vast coastline and a significant maritime presence, the United States is committed to preserving this legal balance as an essential part of the stable, rules-based international order.").

[314] UNCLOS, Introduction at p. 2 (full cite above) (noting that the "package deal" concept became a *leitmotif* (accompanying melody) that permeates throughout UNCLOS); TUFTS, LAW OF THE SEA, p. 9 (full cite above); ROTHWELL & STEPHENS, LAW OF THE SEA, pp. 13, 79 (full cite above). *See also* G.A. Res. 2750 (XXV), ¶ C, U.N. Doc A/AC.138/58 (Dec. 17, 1970), https://research.un.org/en/docs/ga/quick/regular/25 (noting "that the problems of ocean space are closely interrelated and need to be considered as a whole" when the United Nations General Assembly convened the Third United Nations Conference on the Law of the Sea); Permanent Court of

Arbitration, Cases, Past Cases, [2013-19] The South China Sea Arbitration (*The Republic of Philippines v. The People's Republic of China*), Documents, Award on Jurisdiction and Admissibility (Oct. 29, 2015) ¶¶ 107, 225 (pp. 37, 87-88), https://pcacases.com/web/sendAttach/2579.

[315] United Nations Convention on the Law of the Sea (UNCLOS) art. 24, Dec. 10, 1982, 1833 U.N.T.S. 397, https://www.un.org/Depts/los/convention_agreements/convention_overview_convention.htm. Chapter 3 discusses Innocent Passage through Territorial Seas in more depth.

[316] UNCLOS, art. 44 (full cite above); U.S. NAVY, MARINE CORPS & COAST GUARD, THE COMMANDER'S HANDBOOK ON THE LAW OF NAVAL OPERATIONS, NWP 1-14M/MCTP 11-10B/COMDTPUB P5800.7A, ¶ 2.5.3.2 (pp. 2-7 to 2-8) (2017), www.jag.navy.mil/distrib/instructions/CDRs_HB_on_Law_of_Naval_Operations_AUG17.pdf. Chapter 3 discusses Transit Passage through International Straits in more depth.

[317] UNCLOS, art. 56(2) (full cite above). *See also* HUGO GROTIUS, MARE LIBERUM [THE FREE SEA] (1609); DONALD R. ROTHWELL & TIM STEPHENS, THE INT'L. LAW OF THE SEA 95 (2nd ed. 2016).

[318] UNCLOS, arts. 58(1) & 87 (full cite above). Chapter 5 discusses High Seas Freedoms in more depth.

[319] UNCLOS, art. 58(3) (full cite above). *See also* Letter Of Transmittal Forwarding The 1982 UN Law Of The Sea Convention To The United States Senate, DOS Commentary p. 24 (William J. Clinton, Oct. 7, 1994) (S. Treaty Doc. 103-39), https://www.foreign.senate.gov/imo/media/doc/treaty_103-39.pdf (noting that "[i]t is the duty of the flag State, not the right of the coastal State, to enforce this 'due regard' obligation.").

[320] GROTIUS, MARE LIBERUM (full cite above). *See also* ROTHWELL & STEPHENS, LAW OF THE SEA, p. 98 (full cite above). Chapter 11 discusses excessive maritime claims and Freedom of Navigation programs.

[321] Raul (Pete) Pedrozo, *Military Activities in the Exclusive Economic Zone: East Asia Focus*, 90 INT'L. L. STUD. 514, 515 (2014), https://digital-commons.usnwc.edu/ils/vol90/iss1/15/, *citing* UNITED NATIONS CONVENTION ON THE LAW OF THE SEA 1982: A COMMENTARY, vol. II, 491, 529-30 (Satya N. Nandan & Shabtai Rosenne, eds., 1993). *See also* DOS Commentary, p. 24 (full cite above) (same).

[322] Chapter 5 discusses the "freedoms" of the High Seas.

[323] Pedrozo, *Military Activities in the EEZ*, p. 517 (full cite above).

[324] UNCLOS, art. 56(1) (full cite above); GROTIUS, MARE LIBERUM (full cite above). *See also* ROTHWELL & STEPHENS, LAW OF THE SEA, p. 93 (full cite above).

[325] UNCLOS, arts. 58(1) & 87 (full cite above); GROTIUS, MARE LIBERUM (full cite above). *See also* ROTHWELL & STEPHENS, LAW OF THE SEA, p. 99 (full cite above). Chapter 5 discusses High Seas freedoms in more depth.

[326] Pedrozo, *Military Activities in the EEZ*, pp. 515-16 (full cite above), *quoting* 17 Third UN Conference on the Law of the Sea, Plenary Meetings, Official Records, U.N. Doc. A/CONF.62/WS/37 and ADD.1-2, 244 (1973-1982). *See also* THE FLETCHER SCHOOL OF LAW AND DIPLOMACY—TUFTS UNIVERSITY, LAW OF THE SEA, A POLICY PRIMER 31 (2017), https://sites.tufts.edu/lawofthesea/introduction/; Brookings Institution, Center for East Asia Policy Studies, East Asia Policy Paper 9, *The U.S. FON Program in the South China Sea—A lawful and necessary response to China's strategic ambiguity*, pp. 7-8 (Lynn Kuok, June 2016), https://www.brookings.edu/research/the-u-s-fon-program-in-the-south-china-sea/.

[327] Pedrozo, *Military Activities in the EEZ*, p. 516 (full cite above).

[328] Now I Know, That's Half the Battle!, *The Principality of Sealand* (July 23, 2010), http://nowiknow.com/the-principality-of-sealand/. *See also* Sealand, Principality of Sealand, Our History, https://www.sealandgov.org/about/.

[329] Although not commonly used on land (due to their ineffectiveness), properly conducted warning shots are both commonly used and effective at sea for communicating a signal to stop, or else risk the next step up in the escalation or continuum of force (e.g., disabling fire). COMMANDER'S HANDBOOK, ¶ 3.11.5.1 (pp. 3-17 to 3-18) (full cite above). "When conducting maritime law enforcement operations, USCG personnel may use warning shots only as a signal to a vessel to stop, and only after all other available means of signaling have failed. USCG personnel may also discharge firearms to disable moving vessels or other maritime conveyances. However, before firing at or into a vessel, USCG personnel will first fire a gun as a warning signal unless they determine that firing a warning signal will unreasonably endanger persons or property in the vicinity of the vessel to be stopped. Warning shots and disabling fire are not intended to cause bodily injury. Accordingly, since warning shots and disabling fire are inherently dangerous, they should be used with all due care and with safety as the primary consideration. Additionally, if warning shots or disabling fire is warranted, each shot must have a defined target. ... Indiscriminate use of force would violate international law. In the 1929 *I'm Alone* case, an arbitration commission found that a USCG cutter crew's decision to intentionally sink a vessel was not justified under international law. In that case, the USCG pursued the vessel for two days for suspected smuggling of liquor. The USCG personnel then sank the vessel after the captain refused multiple orders and signals, including the use of warning shots and disabling fire, to heave to for boarding." Raul (Pete) Pedrozo, *Maritime Police Law of the People's Republic of China*, 97 INT'L. L. STUD. 465, 473-475 (2021), https://digital-commons.usnwc.edu/ils/vol97/iss1/24/. *See also* Military.com, Military News, *US Navy Fires Warning Shots at Iranian Fast Attack Craft* (Patricia Kime, Apr. 27, 2021), https://www.military.com/daily-news/2021/04/27/us-navy-fires-warning-shots-iranian-fast-attack-craft.html (describing how 2 U.S. patrol boats were harassed by armed IRGCN speed boats, and ultimately needed to fire warning shots to stop the harassment); Military.com, Military News, *Coast Guard Cutter Fires Warning Shots at Charging Iranian Speedboats* (Stephen Losey, May 10, 2021), https://www.military.com/daily-news/2021/05/10/coast-guard-cutter-fires-warning-shots-charging-iranian-speedboats.html (reporting that a group of 13 IRGCN speed boats armed with machine guns moved on opposite sides of a U.S. ship formation, and then 2 of the IRGCN speed boats uncovered and manned their machine guns before approaching the U.S. ships from behind at over 32 knots; the U.S. ships "made multiple bridge-to-bridge verbal warnings, five 'acoustic device' warnings, and five short horn blasts.... the internationally recognized signal for danger when trying to prevent collisions at sea. When those efforts were unsuccessful, ... the [U.S. Coast Guard patrol boat] Maui fired two volleys of warning shots from its .50-cal, totaling about 30 shots in all. The first volley was fired when the ships were within 300 yards, ... and the second when they were within 150 yards. After the second volley of warning shots, the 13 Iranian ships broke off contact." "This represents the second time in two weeks that American ships have fired warning shots at Iranian speedboats."). *But see* Jasenko Marin, Mišo Mudrić & Robert Mikac, *Private Maritime Security Contractors and Use of Lethal Force in Maritime Domain*, *in* THE FUTURE OF THE LAW OF THE SEA 191, 195, 197 (Gemma Andreone ed.,

2017), https://link.springer.com/book/10.1007/978-3-319-51274-7 (discussing the *Enrica Lexie* case, where the "warning shots" of 2 Italian marines killed 2 Indian fishermen in India's Contiguous Zone off the Indian port of Kochi/Cochin). The Indian courts charged the 2 Italian Marines with murder. The *Enrica Lexie* case remains an international controversy between Italy and India to the date of this writing. Permanent Court of Arbitration, Cases, Inter-State arbitrations, [2015-28] The 'Enrica Lexie' Incident (Italy v. India), https://pca-cpa.org/en/cases/117/.

[330] ThoughtCo., Humanities, Geography, *The Principality of Sealand* (Matt Rosenberg, Mar. 23, 2019), https://www.thoughtco.com/principality-of-sealand-1435434.

[331] Now I Know, That's Half the Battle!, *The Principality of Sealand* (July 23, 2010), http://nowiknow.com/the-principality-of-sealand/. *See also* Sealand, Principality of Sealand, https://www.sealandgov.org/about/.

[332] Great Britain extended the width of its Territorial Seas in 1987. Dept. of Defense Maritime Claims Reference Manual (MCRM)—United Kingdom 2014, http://www.jag.navy.mil/organization/code_10_mcrm.htm.

[333] Sealand, Principality of Sealand, Our History, https://www.sealandgov.org/about/.

[334] Int'l. Maritime Organization (IMO) Int'l. Convention on Salvage, Apr. 28, 1989, 1953 U.N.T.S. 165, https://www.jus.uio.no/lm/imo.salvage.convention.1989/doc.html#48.

[335] The requirements for claiming Statehood are not found in UNCLOS, but rather in Article 1 of the Montevideo Convention of 1933: "The State as a person of international law should possess the following qualifications: (a) a permanent population; (b) a defined territory; (c) government; and (d) capacity to enter into relations with the other States." Convention on Rights and Duties of States adopted by the Seventh Int'l. Conference of American States (Montevideo Convention), Dec. 26, 1933, 165 U.N.T.S. 19, https://treaties.un.org/pages/showDetails.aspx?objid=0800000280166aef. It is highly doubtful that the "Principality of Sealand" would satisfy these criteria for claiming Statehood. *See also* ThoughtCo., *Sealand* (full cite above) (reaching the same conclusion albeit by using eight criteria); Sealand, Principality of Sealand, https://sealandgov.org/ (official website of Sealand, with a commercial ".org" web address). *But see* Sealand, Principality of Sealand (full cite above) (citing documents that purportedly support Sealand's independence).

[336] Rocks are still considered pieces of land that can be owned, and thus are entitled to corresponding Territorial Seas and the limited enforcement provided for in the Contiguous Zone. Rocks are defined by UNCLOS as being above water at high tide, but incapable of sustaining human habitation. Thus, a sandbar that remains above water at high tide but cannot sustain human life would qualify as a Rock. THE FLETCHER SCHOOL OF LAW AND DIPLOMACY—TUFTS UNIVERSITY, LAW OF THE SEA, A POLICY PRIMER 16 (2017), https://sites.tufts.edu/lawofthesea/introduction/.

[337] United Nations Convention on the Law of the Sea (UNCLOS) arts. 7(4) & 13, Dec. 10, 1982, 1833 U.N.T.S. 397, https://www.un.org/Depts/los/convention_agreements/convention_overview_convention.htm; U.S. NAVY, MARINE CORPS & COAST GUARD, THE COMMANDER'S HANDBOOK ON THE LAW OF NAVAL OPERATIONS, NWP 1-14M/MCTP 11-10B/COMDTPUB P5800.7A, ¶ 1.5.3 & Figure 1-6 (pp. 1-7 to 1-8) (2017), www.jag.navy.mil/distrib/instructions/CDRs_HB_on_Law_of_Naval_Operations_AUG17.pdf. This is known as the "Norway exception," which was accepted by the

International Court of Justice (ICJ) in the 1951 Fisheries Case. Int'l. Court of Justice (ICJ), Fisheries (United Kingdom v. Norway), Judgement of Dec. 18, 1951 at p. 31, https://www.icj-cij.org/en/case/5.

[338] ThoughtCo., *Sealand* (full cite above).

[339] UNCLOS, arts. 56(1)(b)(i) & 60(1)-(2) (full cite above).

[340] Visit Rimini, free tourist information and news, When Italy went to war with the esperanto micro-nation Insulo de la Rozoj, https://www.visit-rimini.com/when-italy-went-to-war-with-the-esperanto-micro-nation-insulo-de-la-rozoj/. *See also* Damn Interesting, *The (Very Brief) Republic of Rose Island* (Marisa Brook, June 24, 2016), https://www.damninteresting.com/nugget/the-very-brief-republic-of-rose-island/.

[341] UNCLOS, Introduction at p. 2 (full cite above) (noting that the "package deal" concept became a *leitmotif* (accompanying melody) that permeates throughout UNCLOS); TUFTS, LAW OF THE SEA, p. 9 (full cite above); DONALD R. ROTHWELL & TIM STEPHENS, THE INT'L. LAW OF THE SEA 13, 79 (2nd ed. 2016). *See also* G.A. Res. 2750 (XXV), ¶ C, U.N. Doc A/AC.138/58 (Dec. 17, 1970), https://research.un.org/en/docs/ga/quick/regular/25 (noting "that the problems of ocean space are closely interrelated and need to be considered as a whole" when the United Nations General Assembly convened the Third United Nations Conference on the Law of the Sea); Permanent Court of Arbitration, Cases, Past Cases, [2013-19] The South China Sea Arbitration (*The Republic of Philippines v. The People's Republic of China*), Documents, Award on Jurisdiction and Admissibility (Oct. 29, 2015) ¶¶ 107, 225 (pp. 37, 87-88), https://pcacases.com/web/sendAttach/2579.

[342] Letter Of Transmittal Forwarding The 1982 UN Law Of The Sea Convention To The United States Senate, DOS Commentary p. 21 (William J. Clinton, Oct. 7, 1994) (S. Treaty Doc. 103−39), https://www.foreign.senate.gov/imo/media/doc/treaty_103-39.pdf.

[343] UNCLOS, art. 47(1) (full cite above).

[344] UNCLOS, art. 47(1) (full cite above); COMMANDER'S HANDBOOK, ¶ 1.5.4 & Figure 2-1 (pp. 1-8 to 1-9 & 2-10) (full cite above).

[345] UNCLOS, art. 47(2) (full cite above).

[346] DOS Commentary, p. 22 (full cite above).

[347] R. R. CHURCHILL & A. V. LOWE, THE LAW OF THE SEA 123 (1999).

[348] Nancy Barron, *Archipelagos and Archipelagic States under UNCLOS III: No Special Treatment for Hawaii*, 4 HASTINGS INT'L & COMP. L. REV. 509, 522-25 (1981), https://repository.uchastings.edu/hastings_international_comparative_law_review/vol4/iss3/3.

[349] Indonesia, Submission in Compliance with the Deposit Obligations Pursuant to the United Nations Convention on the Law of the Sea (UNCLOS), https://www.un.org/Depts/los/LEGISLATIONANDTREATIES/STATEFILES/IDN.htm.

[350] DoD MCRM—Philippines 2016 (full cite above); ROTHWELL & STEPHENS, LAW OF THE SEA, p. 276 (full cite above). *See also* Dept. of Defense Law of War Manual § 13.2.2.3, pp. 882-883 (June 2015, updated Dec. 2016), https://www.hsdl.org/?view&did=797480.

[351] DOS Commentary, p. 22 (full cite above).

[352] Barron, *Archipelagos and Archipelagic States*, p. 518 (full cite above).

[353] UNCLOS, art. 48 (full cite above); COMMANDER'S HANDBOOK, ¶ 1.5.4 & Figure 2-1 (pp. 1-8 to 1-9 & 2-10) (full cite above). Chapter 2 discussed the "normal" baseline for measuring maritime zones under Article 5 of UNCLOS.

[354] UNCLOS, art. 8(1) (full cite above).

[355] The concept that each State has exclusive sovereignty over its (land) territory originates from the 1648 Treaties of Westphalia (aka the Peace of Westphalia). Encyclopædia Britannica, European History, *Peace of Westphalia*, https://www.britannica.com/event/Peace-of-Westphalia; RESTATEMENT (THIRD) OF FOREIGN RELATIONS, pt. 1, introductory note (p. 17) (1987).

[356] United Nations Convention on the Law of the Sea (UNCLOS) Introduction at p. 2, Dec. 10, 1982, 1833 U.N.T.S. 397, https://www.un.org/Depts/los/convention_agreements/convention_overview_co nvention.htm; (noting that the "package deal" concept became a *leitmotif* (accompanying melody) that permeates throughout UNCLOS); THE FLETCHER SCHOOL OF LAW AND DIPLOMACY—TUFTS UNIVERSITY, LAW OF THE SEA, A POLICY PRIMER 9 (2017), https://sites.tufts.edu/lawofthesea/introduction/; DONALD R. ROTHWELL & TIM STEPHENS, THE INT'L. LAW OF THE SEA 13, 79 (2nd ed. 2016). *See also* G.A. Res. 2750 (XXV), ¶ C, U.N. Doc A/AC.138/58 (Dec. 17, 1970), https://research.un.org/en/docs/ga/quick/regular/25 (noting "that the problems of ocean space are closely interrelated and need to be considered as a whole" when the United Nations General Assembly convened the Third United Nations Conference on the Law of the Sea); Permanent Court of Arbitration, Cases, Past Cases, [2013-19] The South China Sea Arbitration (*The Republic of Philippines v. The People's Republic of China*), Documents, Award on Jurisdiction and Admissibility (Oct. 29, 2015) ¶¶ 107, 225 (pp. 37, 87-88), https://pcacases.com/web/sendAttach/2579.

[357] UNCLOS, art. 49 (full cite above).

[358] UNCLOS, art. 52 (full cite above); U.S. NAVY, MARINE CORPS & COAST GUARD, THE COMMANDER'S HANDBOOK ON THE LAW OF NAVAL OPERATIONS, NWP 1-14M/MCTP 11-10B/COMDTPUB P5800.7A, ¶ 2.5.4.2 & Figure 2-1 (pp. 2-9 to 2-10) (2017), www.jag.navy.mil/distrib/instructions/CDRs_HB_on_Law_of_Naval_Operations_AUG17.pdf; ROTHWELL & STEPHENS, LAW OF THE SEA, p. 269 (full cite above).

[359] UNCLOS, art. 53(1) (full cite above).

[360] UNCLOS, art. 53(4) (full cite above); COMMANDER'S HANDBOOK, ¶¶ 1.5.4, 2.5.4.1 & Figure 2-1 (pp. 1-8 to 1-9, 2-8 to 2-10) (full cite above).

[361] UNCLOS, arts. 53(2)-(3) (full cite above); COMMANDER'S HANDBOOK, ¶¶ 1.5.4, 2.5.4.1, 2.7.1.2 & Figure 2-1 (pp. 1-8 to 1-9, 2-8 to 2-10, 2-13) (full cite above).

[362] UNCLOS, art. 47(1) (full cite above); COMMANDER'S HANDBOOK, ¶¶ 1.5.4, 2.5.4.1 & Figure 2-1 (pp. 1-8 to 1-9, 2-8 to 2-10) (full cite above).

[363] UNCLOS, art. 48 (full cite above).

[364] UNCLOS, art. 52 (full cite above); COMMANDER'S HANDBOOK, ¶ 2.5.4.2 & Figure 2-1 (pp. 2-9 to 2-10) (full cite above).

[365] UNCLOS, art. 50 (full cite above).

[366] UNCLOS, art. 53(1) & (4) (full cite above); COMMANDER'S HANDBOOK, ¶¶ 1.5.4, 2.5.4.1 & Figure 2-1 (pp. 1-8 to 1-9, 2-8 to 2-10) (full cite above).

[367] UNCLOS, art. 53(5) (full cite above); COMMANDER'S HANDBOOK, ¶¶ 1.5.4, 2.5.4.1 & Figure 2-1 (pp. 1-8 to 1-9, 2-8 to 2-10) (full cite above). If an island juts into the Archipelagic Sea Lane, ships and aircraft engaged in ASLP are required to leave a 10% buffer (e.g., if an island extends 4 nm into the Archipelagic Sea Lane, then there is only 21 nm available on that side of the axis line, and ships and aircraft must remain at least 2.1 nm away from the coast).

[368] UNCLOS, art. 53(3) (full cite above); COMMANDER'S HANDBOOK, ¶¶ 1.5.4, 2.5.4.1 & Figure 2-1 (pp. 1-8 to 1-9, 2-8 to 2-10) (full cite above).

[369] UNCLOS, arts. 39, 44, & 53-54 (full cite above); COMMANDER'S HANDBOOK, ¶¶ 1.5.4, 2.5.4.1 & Figure 2-1 (pp. 1-8 to 1-9, 2-8 to 2-10) (full cite above); ROTHWELL &

STEPHENS, LAW OF THE SEA, pp. 273-274 (full cite above). Rather than repeating the duties of ships and aircraft, and the duties of Coastal States in the Archipelagic Sea Lanes Passage (ASLP) regime, Article 54 says the rules of Transit Passage "apply *mutatis mutandis* [i.e., modify as necessary without changing the underlying meaning] to archipelagic sea lanes passage." USLegal, Legal Definitions, Mutatis Mutandis, https://definitions.uslegal.com/m/mutatis-mutandis/.

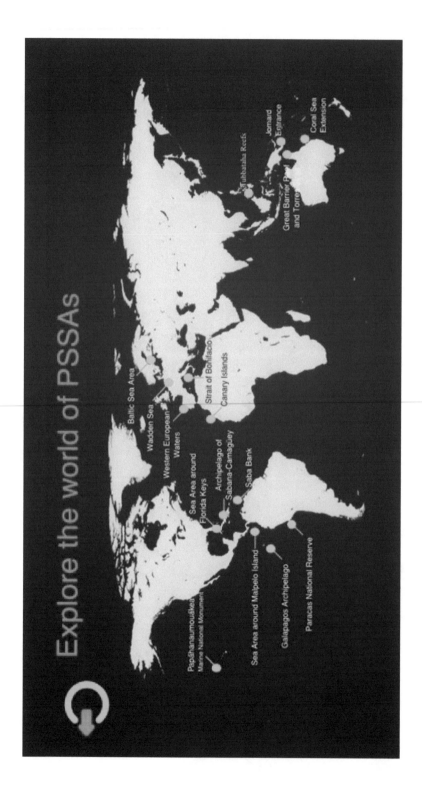

Explore the world of PSSAs

CHAPTER 5: HIGH SEAS & ENVIRONMENT

"The sea, the great unifier, is man's only hope.
Now, as never before, the old phrase has a literal
meaning: we are all in the same boat."
— Jacques Yves Cousteau, Oceanographer

HIGH SEAS FREEDOMS lie at the core of both the historical law of the sea and the UN Convention on the Law of the Sea (UNCLOS). As discussed in Chapter 2, Grotius argued for the **inclusive** use of the seas, especially freedom of the High Seas for international trade under the rubric *"Mare Liberum"* (the Free Sea). "As a principle, *mare liberum* reflects States' common economic interest in unhindered use of the high seas both as a route for trade and as a fishing ground; as well as maritime powers' interest in a regime 'permit[ting] unhindered passage of the[ir] naval fleets ... to areas of political and military influence.'"[370]

Under the "freedom of the seas" doctrine, oceans were broadly divided into two main areas: a Coastal State's Territorial Waters, and the High Seas beyond. This remained the guiding principle of the Law of the Sea until shortly after World War II, when States sought to vastly expand their sovereignty claims over the ocean itself, encroaching on the freedom of the seas that had existed for over 300 years. This led to the United Nations General Assembly convening the Third United Nations Conference on the Law of the Sea, which culminated in UNCLOS.[371]

Beyond Coastal States' extensive 200 nm Exclusive Economic Zones (EEZs) lie the High Seas, where all States may enjoy all High Seas freedoms,[372] including those freedoms enumerated in Article 87:

Article 87 / Freedom of the high seas
1. The high seas are open to all States, whether coastal or land-locked. Freedom of the high seas is exercised under the conditions laid down by this Convention and by other rules of international law. It comprises, *inter alia,* both for coastal and land-locked States:
    (a) freedom of navigation;
    (b) freedom of overflight;
    (c) freedom to lay submarine cables and pipelines, subject to Part VI [on the Continental Shelf];
    (d) freedom to construct artificial islands and other installations permitted under international law, subject to Part VI [on the Continental Shelf];
    (e) freedom of fishing, subject to the conditions laid down in section 2;
    (f) freedom of [marine] scientific research, subject to Parts VI and XIII.
    2. These freedoms shall be exercised by all States with due regard for the interests of other States in their exercise of the freedom of the high seas, and also with due regard for the rights under this Convention with respect to activities in the Area. [*emphasis added*][373]

Inter alia means "among other things," and thus Article 87(1)'s list of High Seas freedoms is not meant to be exhaustive. "Article 87 sets out the principal freedoms which all States enjoy in the high seas."[374] Thus, there are other High Seas freedoms that are not specifically enumerated, such as the freedom to conduct military operations, discussed in Chapter 10.

The easiest way to remember which High Seas freedoms apply in which maritime zone is that **ALL High Seas freedoms apply on**

the High Seas, and only those non-resource-related freedoms apply in the EEZ (i.e., beyond the 12 nm Territorial Seas).

International Waters ⟶	Exclusive Economic Zone (EEZ—Art. 58(1))	High Seas (Art. 87)
Freedom of Navigation (FON)	X	X
Freedom of Overflight	X	X
Freedom to lay submarine cables and pipelines	X	X
Other non-resource-related High Seas Freedoms (e.g., to conduct military operations)	X	X
Freedom to construct artificial islands and other installations		X
Freedom of fishing		X
Freedom of Marine Scientific Research (MSR)		X

As discussed in Chapter 4, there exists a double-edged "due regard" standard in the EEZ regime: "the coastal State shall have due regard to the rights and duties of other States"[375] (including the duty not to interfere with non-resource-related High Seas freedoms), and in exercising their rights in the EEZ, other "States shall have due regard to the rights and duties of the coastal State."[376] On the High Seas, there is a triple-edge "due regard" standard: each State shall have due regard for the High Seas freedoms of other States, and States shall have due regard for activities in "the Area" (aka on the Deep Seabed, discussed in Chapter 6).[377]

> All of these activities must be conducted with due regard for the rights of other States and the safe conduct and operation of other ships and aircraft. The exercise of any of these freedoms is subject to the conditions that they be taken with "reasonable" regard, according to the High Seas Convention, or "due" regard, according to the LOS Convention, for the interests of other nations in light of all relevant circumstances. There is no substantive difference between the two terms. The "reasonable regard/due regard" standard requires any using State to be cognizant of the interests of others in using a high seas area, to balance those interests with its own, and to refrain from activities that unreasonably interfere with the exercise of other States' high seas freedoms in light of that balancing of interests. [emphasis added][378]

Thus, States shall not interfere with other States exercising their High Seas freedoms (e.g., don't conduct military operations in the vicinity of fishing boats and vice versa), and States shall not interfere with Deep Seabed mining operations or Marine Scientific Research (e.g., bottom trawlers shouldn't fish in the vicinity of Deep Seabed mining operations, since bottom trawlers drag their large, weighted fishing nets across the seafloor, which would interfere with any mining operations or research being conducted on the seafloor).

As discussed above, Article 87 lists the principal High Seas freedoms,[379] and other High Seas freedoms include the right to conduct military operations, which we'll discuss in Chapter 10. A few examples might help cement our common understanding. The Freedom of Navigation means that any ship may navigate in whatever manner it desires, which need not be "continuous and expeditious" as is required for Innocent Passage through Territorial Seas and Transit Passage through International Straits (discussed in Chapter 3). So long as it does not interfere with the High Seas freedoms of other ships or with Deep Seabed mining or

Marine Scientific Research (MSR), a ship may navigate in circles (aka "drilling donut holes") on the High Seas; so long as it does not interfere with the Coastal State's right to manage its resources, a ship may "drill donut holes" in another State's EEZ as well. The same is true for aircraft exercising the Freedom of Overflight on the High Seas and in another State's EEZ. We shall discuss the High Seas freedom to lay submarine cables and pipelines in Chapter 6, and the High Seas freedoms of fishing (including whaling) and MSR in Chapter 7.

As discussed in Chapter 4, the Coastal State has exclusive ownership of all resources in its EEZ, including "the production of energy from the water, currents and winds";[380] and "the establishment [i.e., construction and/or installation] and use of artificial islands, installations and structures."[381] Article 87(1)(d) includes the latter freedom (constructing artificial islands and installations) as one of the enumerated principal High Seas freedoms. Thus, so long as it does not interfere with the High Seas freedoms of other States, or with Deep Seabed mining or MSR, or with any other international law, a State (or corporation or private citizens of any State) may construct an artificial island or structure on the High Seas.[382] Presumably a State (or corporation or private citizens of any State) could also harness energy from the water, currents and winds, so long as doing so didn't interfere with the High Seas freedoms of other States, or with Deep Seabed mining or MSR.

As discussed previously, the concept of High Seas freedoms includes "maritime powers' interest in a regime 'permit[ting] unhindered passage of the[ir] naval fleets ... to areas of political and military influence.'"[383]

> *Freedom to navigate and operate on, over, and under the high seas is a central requirement of the United States.*
>
> ** * **
>
> *Pursuant to article 87, all ships and aircraft, including warships and military aircraft, enjoy freedom of movement and operation on and over the high seas. For warships and military aircraft, this includes task force maneuvering, flight operations, military exercises, surveillance, intelligence gathering activities, and ordnance testing and firing. [emphasis added]*[384]

Thus, major maritime powers (including the U.S., Great Britain, France, China and Russia)[385] sought not only to protect the Freedom of Navigation of their naval fleets, but also their ability to conduct military exercises (aka "war games") and other military operations (such as those enumerated above) on the High Seas and in the EEZs of other Coastal States (again, subject to the due regard standards applicable in each regime). This is certainly the U.S. view, although as we will see in Chapter 11, the freedom to conduct military operations in another State's EEZ is not universally supported, despite the relatively clear negotiating history and text of UNCLOS.[386]

ENVIRONMENT

This Chapter's second sub-topic is the protection and preservation of the marine environment, both its living and non-living resources. For hundreds (if not thousands) of years, the seas were the epitome for the "Tragedy of the Commons," which Chapter 7 discusses in more depth in the context of fisheries. The seas were seen as vast, inexhaustible, and a good place in which to dispose of waste. "The solution to pollution is dilution" was the mantra for States seeking to dispose of waste, especially at sea. For example, a barge full of trash is a significant concern when it is in a Coastal State's river or bay (i.e., in its Internal Waters), or even in its Territorial Seas. But use ocean-going tugboats to push the barge full of trash out past the Coastal State's 12 nm Territorial Seas into International Waters, or even further past the 200 nm EEZ onto the High Seas, and a barge full of trash need only to quietly dispose of its malodorous cargo to solve the Coastal State's immediate problem, as the pollution would be "diluted" by the vast ocean's waters.[387] If the barge was full of food waste or even sewage, it would quickly dissipate and (arguably) provide nutrients to sea life. If the barge was full of other types of garbage, it could take far longer to break down.

Garbage Disposed at Sea	Time Require to Decompose
Paper	2-4 weeks
Cotton cloth	1-5 months
Rope	3-14 months
Wool cloth	1 year
Painted wood	13 years
Tin can	100 years
Aluminum can	200 years
Plastic bottle	450 years

A common misconception is that most maritime or marine pollution originates from ships and offshore oil rigs (i.e., pollution at sea). But pollution generated on land (both from land sources such as sewage pipes, and offshore dumping of land-generated wastes) accounts for more than half of marine pollution:[388]

Marine Pollution

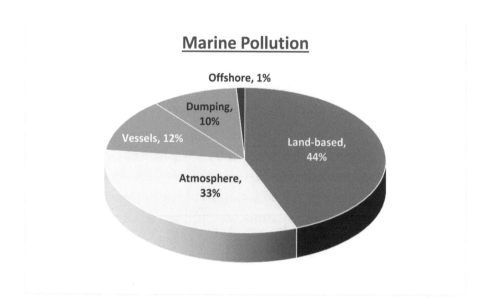

"Dumping was a type of ocean based pollution that was popular in the 1950s and 1960s to dispose of waste produced by activities on land."[389] Thirteen States even dumped 55 gallon drums

full of radioactive waste at sea for almost fifty years (1946-1993), totaling 1/3 of the radioactivity in the nuclear bomb dropped on Hiroshima. Which, by modern standards, is unfathomable (pun intended)!

After the nearly unanimous vote of the Third UN Conference on the Law of the Sea on April 30, 1982, UNCLOS was viewed as the "strongest comprehensive environmental treaty" of its time,[390] and certainly the first comprehensive environmental treaty governing the oceans.[391] "At the [3rd UNCLOS] Conference, the negotiators were ... hesitant to suggest too much detail in order not to upset a complicated negotiating process."[392] Thus, UNCLOS only includes six general definitions in Article 1, two of which deal with "pollution" and "dumping." Article 1(1)(4) defines "pollution of the marine environment" as:

[T]he introduction by man, directly or indirectly, of substances or energy into the marine environment, including estuaries, which results or is likely to result in such *deleterious effects* as harm to living resources and marine life, hazards to human health, hindrance to marine activities, including fishing and other legitimate uses of the sea, impairment of quality for use of sea water and reduction of amenities." [*emphasis added*][393]

Thus, UNCLOS does not seek to regulate **all** pollution, but only that pollution which either has, or is likely to have **deleterious effects** to the environment. Therefore, besides radioactive waste, other forms of marine pollution that UNCLOS regulates may include:

> ➢ pesticides and trace metals, which often originate from sewage, and runoff from farms;
> ➢ fat-soluble toxins, which may "bio-concentrate" or "bio-accumulate," particularly in birds and mammals, and pose human health risks (e.g., mercury in swordfish, shark, mackerel and tuna, with pregnant women advised to limit their consumption of these larger predator fish);
> ➢ bio-stimulants such as organic wastes and fertilizers that originate in sewage and runoff from farms and urban areas—higher nitrogen and warmer surface water fuels algae growth; when the algae dies, it depletes the

dissolved oxygen, which harms living resources such as fish;

➢ oil from land activities, shipping operations (e.g., pumping bilges), accidental spills,[394] offshore oil production, and even natural seepage from oil deposits beneath the seabed;

➢ radioactive isotopes originating from atmospheric fallout, industrial and military activities (e.g., penetration rounds made from heavy metals, used in this Close In Weapons System (CIWS), which has multiple  rotating barrels capable of firing up to 4,500 rounds/minute (75 rounds/ second), which forms a "wall of lead" that incoming missiles hopefully fly through and are destroyed);[395]

➢ sediments from farming, mining, and construction;

➢ plastics from dumping, ships, fishing nets, and containers, which entangle marine life or are ingested, and degrade beaches, wetlands and near-shore habitats;

➢ pathogens from sewage, livestock, and even wildlife, which pose health risks to swimmers and consumers of seafood (e.g., Giardia, a microscopic parasite that causes diarrhea when ingested);

- thermal waste from industry (e.g., power plants and manufacturing plants);
- noise from ships and sonar, which may disturb marine mammals;[396] and
- alien species from ballast water.

Article 1(1)(5) has a multi-part definition of "dumping":

Article 1 / Use of terms and scope
* * *
    (5) (a) "dumping" means:
        (i) any deliberate disposal of wastes or other matter from vessels, aircraft, platforms or other man-made structures at sea;
        (ii) any deliberate disposal of vessels, aircraft, platforms or other man-made structures at sea;
    (b) "dumping" does not include:
        (i) the disposal of wastes or other matter incidental to, or derived from the normal operations of vessels, aircraft, platforms or other man-made structures at sea and their equipment, other than wastes or other matter transported by or to vessels, aircraft, platforms or other man-made structures at sea, operating for the purpose of disposal of such matter or derived from the treatment of such wastes or other matter on such vessels, aircraft, platforms or structures;
        (ii) placement of matter for a purpose other than the mere disposal thereof, provided that such placement is not contrary to the aims of this Convention. [emphasis added][397]

Thus, "dumping" includes the disposal of wastes *from* ships when transported from land (but not any wastes generated onboard ships, which are covered by the Marine Pollution (MARPOL) Convention), and the disposal *of* ships, aircraft, platforms, or other artificial structures at sea (e.g., abandoning an offshore oil rig in place). However, "dumping" does not include the "placement ... for a purpose other than the mere disposal thereof," so long as it is consistent with UNCLOS. For example, the author served onboard *USS BELLEAU WOOD* (LHA 3) from 2003-2004. The amphibious "big deck helicopter carrier" was decommissioned and sunk in the 2006 Rim of the Pacific (RIMPAC) Live Fire Exercise (aka SINKEX). After two days of being used for target practice by more than forty ships and submarines from twenty-two States, she refused to sink—she was finally sunk by pre-rigged bombs laid by Explosive Ordnance Disposal (EOD) experts.[398] This did not constitute "dumping" because it was the "placement ... for a purpose other than the mere disposal thereof," specifically testing naval weapons and bombs.

Plastics dumped at sea are of particular concern, due to their lengthy decomposition period (and even then, they break down into "microplastics" smaller than 5 mm in size), as well as the fact that instead of sinking to the seafloor like other waste, plastics usually float throughout the water column (from the seafloor[399] to the ocean's surface). Rotating ocean currents known as "gyres" (i.e., whirlpools) concentrate plastics and other marine debris into "garbage patches" (aka "trash vortexes"). There are five ocean gyres (one in the Indian Ocean, and two each in the Atlantic and Pacific Oceans), each gyre with multiple garbage patches of varying sizes. The most infamous trash vortex is the "Great Pacific Garbage Patch" located between California and Hawaii in the Pacific Ocean.

 Besides the risk of wildlife ingesting or becoming entangled in plastic waste (like this turtle), discarded or lost fishing nets continue "ghost fishing" indefinitely. Humans may accidentally ingest microplastics as well, (e.g., from eating seafood). Discarded plastics can also become entangled in ships' propellers and/or clog water intakes. Unfortunately, the garbage patches are expected to grow in size as more debris is discarded at sea, unless or until the world's scientific community can develop cost effective technological methods for "taking the trash" out of the world's oceans.

For example, the U.S. National Oceanic and Atmospheric Administration (NOAA) "Marine Debris Program ... focus[es] on marine debris prevention and removal from shorelines and coastal areas where debris is easier to pick up. Prevention is key to solving the marine debris problem over time."[400] Taking a different approach is "The Ocean Cleanup," a Dutch non-profit organization, which is developing a variety of technological solutions to the "garbage patch" problem—from preventing plastic debris from entering the world's oceans in the first place (e.g., from rivers), to developing "a self-contained system in the

Great Pacific Garbage Patch that is using the natural forces of the ocean to passively catch and concentrate plastic."[401] The Ocean Cleanup launched its second proof of concept plastic garbage collection system from Vancouver in June 2019, and announced a short four months later that its "System 001/B" was successfully capturing and collecting plastic debris (including microplastics as small as 1 mm) from the Great Pacific Garbage Patch.[402] At least one estimate is that by 2048, "the amount of plastic in the oceans will outweigh the amount of fish."[403] Think about that.

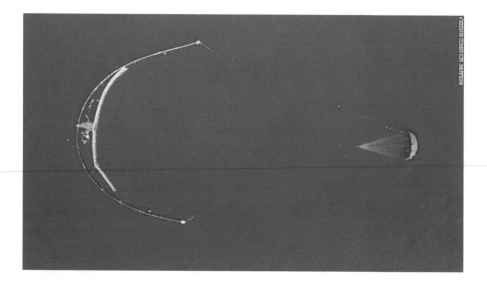

Another area of concern are Particularly Sensitive Sea Areas (PSSAs, such as the Australian Great Barrier Reef), where special environmental protection rules apply. Part XII of UNCLOS is entitled "Protection and Preservation of the Marine Environment." Article 194(5) provides that "[t]he measures taken in accordance with this Part shall include those necessary to protect and preserve rare or fragile ecosystems as well as the habitat of depleted, threatened or endangered species and other forms of marine life."

Article 211(6) amplifies these special protections where "coastal States have reasonable grounds for believing that a particular, clearly defined area of their respective exclusive economic zones is an area where the adoption of special mandatory measures for the prevention of pollution from vessels is required ...." A Coastal State seeking to have an area designated as a PSSA submits detailed "scientific and technical evidence in support" to the International Maritime Organization (IMO) for approval.[404] The IMO is the UN's specialized agency responsible for improving maritime safety and preventing pollution from ships.[405] The IMO has issued guidelines for proper designation of a PSSA, including: "ecological criteria, such as unique or rare ecosystem, diversity of the ecosystem or vulnerability to degradation by natural events or human activities; social, cultural and economic criteria, such as significance of the area for recreation or tourism; and scientific and educational criteria, such as biological research or historical value." The IMO website does a good job of defining PSSAs, and lists the 17 approved PSSAs (highlighted in the graphic at the beginning of this Chapter).[406]

In order to reach consensus at the Third Conference on the Law of the Sea,[407] even the relatively non-contentious area of PSSAs was intentionally left vague in UNCLOS, with the IMO being relied upon to establish and enforce the more detailed guidelines for proper designation of a PSSA. States participating in the Law of the Sea negotiations realized that if they tried to resolve every maritime issue, they would never achieve consensus on UNCLOS, and international standards would be more challenging to update if UNCLOS needed to be changed as new information became available (e.g., the need for stronger environmental protections in a particular region or against a particular pollutant). Thus, UNCLOS was viewed as a "framework" treaty especially with regard to maritime pollution[408] and international fisheries (discussed in

Chapter 7). Other multilateral treaties (between many States) would then establish more detailed (and more easily changed) international pollution and fishing standards. Article 197 alludes to this:

Article 197 / Cooperation on a global or regional basis
States shall cooperate on a global basis and, as appropriate, on a regional basis, directly or through competent international organizations, in formulating and elaborating international rules, standards and recommended practices and procedures consistent with this Convention, for the protection and preservation of the marine environment, taking into account characteristic regional features.[409]

UNCLOS then enumerates how to enforce domestic pollution laws and regulations, as well as international standards in Section 6 of Part XII, specifically with regard to enforcement against pollution from land-based sources,[410] seabed activities on the Continental Shelf[411] and Deep Seabed,[412] and dumping.[413] Section 6 of Part XII of UNCLOS also calls upon Flag States,[414] Port States,[415] and Coastal States[416] to enforce pollution standards against ships within their authority. Chapter 8 discusses enforcement of these pollution standards.

The only area where UNCLOS provides specific (and special) authority to Coastal States to regulate pollution is "in ice-covered areas within the limits of the exclusive economic zone" in Article 234. This special authority is based upon the sensitive ecology of these polar zones, and "was negotiated directly among the key states concerned (Canada, the United States and the Soviet Union)".[417] Thus, under Article 234, Canada may more closely regulate pollution by ships transiting through the Northwest Passage (discussed in Chapter 3) because of its sensitive ecology.[418] "In the Arctic Ocean, [UNCLOS] provides a clear framework for

Melting Arctic Sea Ice

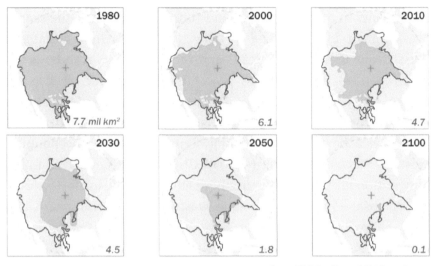

Source: U.S. National Geospatial-Intelligence Agency

determining boundaries and legal rights and responsibilities."[419] Canada and Russia have issued regulations pursuant to Article 234, seeking not only to regulate pollution, but also to exclude ships from their Territorial Seas, International Straits, and EEZs that do not comply with their domestic regulations. The U.S. disputes whether local regulations enacted pursuant to Article 234 can limit Innocent Passage, Transit Passage or High Seas freedoms.[420]

In addition to UNCLOS, the four major international maritime pollution treaties include the:

> - 1972 **London Dumping Convention** and its 1996 Protocol;
> - 1973/1978 **Marine Pollution Convention (MARPOL 73/78,** as amended in 1997);
> - 2001 **Anti-Fouling Convention**; and
> - 2004 **Ballast Water Convention**.

We will briefly discuss each of these maritime pollution treaties in turn.

Article 210 of UNCLOS establishes the framework for "Pollution by dumping," and admonishes "States [to] adopt laws and regulations to prevent, reduce and control pollution of the marine environment by dumping." Article 210 further directs States to "endeavour to establish global and regional rules, standards and recommended practices and procedures to prevent, reduce and control such pollution." This language implicitly referenced the London Dumping Convention passed 10 years earlier (in 1972), which was the first of the major, important maritime pollution treaties.[421] Prior to Article 1(5)(a) of UNCLOS, the London Dumping Convention also defined "dumping" as material transported to sea for disposal—it did not include wastes generated onboard ship (e.g., shipboard garbage and sewage, which was covered a year later by MARPOL 73/78, discussed next.) Under the London Dumping Convention, the enforcement against dumping is allocated between the Flag State of the dumping vessel, and the Coastal State of the waters where the material is dumped. The 1972 London Dumping Convention prohibited the dumping of materials which were judged to be most hazardous to the environment (aka the "black-list" in Annex I, including mercury, plastics, crude oil, and radioactive waste—so no more ocean disposal of radioactive waste, mentioned earlier in this Chapter). Annex I specifically exempted the disposal of "vessels and platforms or other man-made structures at sea"—thus, it permitted disposing offshore structures *in situ* (aka "in place"). The 1972 London Dumping Convention also permitted the dumping of materials which were judged to be less hazardous to the environment (aka the "grey-list" in Annex II, which require a special permit, including chemicals, pesticides, and "[c]ontainers, scrap metal and other bulky wastes liable to sink to the sea bottom)."

The 1996 Protocol to the London Dumping Convention turned the dumping regime on its head—"all dumping is prohibited, except for possibly acceptable wastes on the so-called 'reverse list'. This list includes the following:

1 [—] dredged material;

2 [—] sewage sludge;

3 [—] fish wastes;

4 [—] vessels and platforms;

5 [—] inert, inorganic geological material (e.g., mining wastes);

6 [—] organic material of natural origin;

7 [—] bulky items primarily comprising iron, steel and concrete; and

8 [—] carbon dioxide streams from carbon dioxide capture processes for sequestration."[422]

The 1996 Protocol to the London Dumping Convention no longer permits State Parties to export their wastes to other States—they are required to dump their wastes in their own waters. Now the trend is clearly toward **less** dumping at sea, rather than **more**. The vast majority (80-90%) of material dumped at sea is now dredged materials (e.g., sand, rock, and mud). Under UNCLOS, the Flag State may further restrict dumping at sea (e.g., the 1972 Ocean Dumping Act in the U.S.).[423] The U.S. is party to the 1972 London Dumping Convention, but not to the 1996 Protocol.[424]

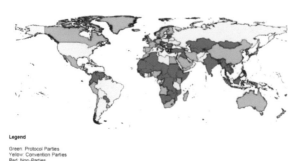

Map of Parties to the London Convention/Protocol

Legend
Green: Protocol Parties
Yellow: Convention Parties
Red: Non-Parties

Article 211 of UNCLOS establishes the framework for "Pollution from vessels," and admonishes States to "establish international rules and standards to prevent, reduce and control pollution of the marine environment from vessels." This was an implicit reference to the 1973/1978 Marine Pollution Convention (MARPOL 73/78, as amended in 1997).[425] MARPOL was meant to dovetail with the 1972 London Dumping Convention by specifically addressing wastes generated onboard ship (e.g., shipboard garbage and sewage). [NOTE: As discussed above, shipboard wastes were excluded from the definition of "dumping" in the London Convention and Protocol.] The MARPOL treaty is one of the more effective environmental treaties, and because it is intended to deal with all forms of intentional pollution of the sea **from** ships (other than dumping), it is very detailed. Ninety-nine percent of world merchant shipping Flag States (by tonnage) have ratified MARPOL, and thus it applies almost universally.[426] Detailed technical standards are contained in the six Annexes:

> **Mandatory Annex I – Oil:** no discharge of oil from vessels in certain areas (e.g., not in the Mediterranean, Baltic, and Black Seas).[427] [NOTE: after the major oil spills resulting from the Exxon Valdez running aground in Prince William Sound in the Gulf of Alaska in 1989, the IMO adopted Regulations 13G and 13H in 1992 which

phased out the use of single-hull oil tankers by 2010, in order to prevent oil spills when oil tankers run aground.]

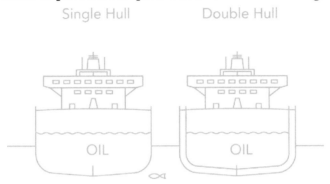

Single Hull   Double Hull

- ➤ **Mandatory Annex II – Noxious Liquid Substances Carried in Bulk:** dispose of in port facilities only (e.g., tank cleaning).
- ➤ **Annex III – Harmful Substances Carried in Packaged Form, or in Containers.**
- ➤ **Annex IV – Sewage from Ships:** not in the Baltic Sea, and not within 12 mm of land unless the vessel has an approved sewage treatment plant.

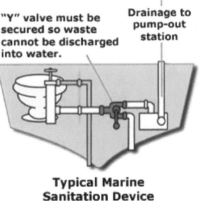

"Y" valve must be secured so waste cannot be discharged into water.

Drainage to pump-out station

Typical Marine Sanitation Device

- ➤ **Annex V – Garbage from Ships:** also based on the distance from land, no disposal of plastics, and not in certain areas (e.g., not in the Mediterranean, Baltic, Black, Red and North Seas).[428]
- ➤ **Annex VI – Air Pollution from Ships:** restricts emissions of sulfur and nitrogen oxide from marine engines, restricts use of ozone depleting substances, and prohibits certain shipboard incineration (e.g., PCBs).

As mentioned above, the MARPOL treaty is one of the more effective environmental treaties, and has led to the reduction of oil pollution from ships by seventy-five percent. However, enforcement remains a problem. For example, a General Accounting Office (GAO) report issued in 2000 found that in a six-year period, "cargo ships, tankers, cruise ships, and other commercial vessels registered, or 'flagged,' in foreign countries have been involved in almost 2,400 confirmed cases of illegally discharging oil, garbage, and other harmful substances into U.S. coastal waters."[429] Moreover, even when referrals are made to Flag States of polluting vessels, few enforcement actions are taken. "In 1992, for example, the State Department analyzed responses from flag states for alleged MARPOL V violations (dumping of garbage and/or plastics at sea). The study showed that of the 111 cases referred by the agency to Flag States from January 1989 through June 1992, the Flag States did not respond to or took no action on 99 cases (89 percent) and assessed small fines for only 2 of the remaining 12 cases."[430]

The U.S. is party to MARPOL except for Annex IV (Sewage).[431] The U.S. has also enacted the 1980 Act to Prevent Pollution from Ships (APPS) to incorporate MARPOL's provisions into U.S. domestic law.[432] In addition, "the Clean Water Act generally prohibits the discharge of any pollutant within 3 nautical miles of the United States and of oil and hazardous substances within 12 nautical miles of the United States."[433]

A ship's hull may become "fouled" (i.e., coated) with algae and barnacle growth (as in the photo below), which can reduce the ship's speed by up to ten percent, resulting in less fuel efficiency, and hence far greater fuel consumption.[434] Special "anti-fouling" paints "slowly 'leach' into the sea water, killing barnacles and other marine life that have attached to the ship or preventing their growth outright. But studies have shown that these compounds

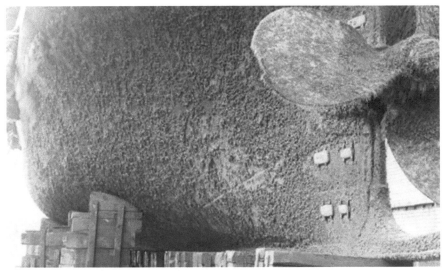

persist in the water, killing sea-life, harming the environment and possibly entering the food chain. One of the most effective anti-fouling paints, developed in the 1960s, contains the organotin tributyltin (TBT), which has been proven to cause deformations in oysters and sex changes in whelks."[435]

The international maritime shipping industry is usually fairly receptive to new international regulations so long as they are reasonably achievable. However, the Anti-Fouling System (AFS)

Convention was fairly remarkable and forward-thinking—when it was developed in 2001, there was no effective substitute for TBT anti-fouling paint. The AFS convention drove the research and development of more environmentally-friendly paints (i.e., the treaty drove technology)! The U.S. is party to the AFS Convention.[436] State Parties to the AFS Convention are required to prohibit and/or restrict the use of harmful anti-fouling systems on ships flying their flag, as well as ships which enter their ports or shipyards.[437] The U.S. Navy uses copper-based hull paint, which may eventually become an issue. In the author's experience, U.S. Navy ships may delay repainting their hulls until they are in a foreign port, due to the stricter U.S. environmental laws.

Another problem that ships routinely face is "ballasting and de-ballasting." In order to maintain proper stability, a ship may need to take on water ballast (aka "ballasting") to ride lower in the water, or discharge water ballast (aka "de-ballasting") to ride higher. Every time a cargo ship pulls into port and either onloads or offloads cargo, it needs to adjust how much ballast water it either takes on or discharges, in order to achieve an optimal level for stability, fuel efficiency, safety, etc. This is akin to putting air in a car's tires to maintain the optimal pressure.

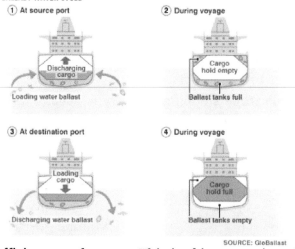

BALLAST WATER CYCLE

① At source port
Discharging cargo
Loading water ballast

② During voyage
Cargo hold empty
Ballast tanks full

③ At destination port
Loading cargo
Discharging water ballast

④ During voyage
Cargo hold full
Ballast tanks empty

SOURCE: GloBallast

The problem is that if ship discharges ballast water in a foreign port, it may also discharge small animals that were inadvertently swept up with the ballast water. Some of these species may be new or "alien" to that port, which runs contrary to UNCLOS.[438] This is a serious problem—for example, it is estimated that one new alien species is introduced every nine days into the Mediterranean Sea. "There is no doubt that shipping activities are the most important pathway of [Invasive Alien Species] in the Mediterranean. Ballast tanks of ships and the fouling on the outside of ships' hulls are significant vectors for marine bioinvasions in the Mediterranean."[439]

The 2004 Ballast Water Management (BWM) Convention, which entered into force in 2017, "aims to prevent the spread of harmful aquatic organisms from one region to another, by establishing standards and procedures for the management and control of ships' ballast water and sediments."[440] The BWM Convention applies to all ships involved in international shipping of the eighty-one Flag State Parties to the treaty. The U.S. is not yet party to the BWM Convention.[441]

Under the BWM Convention, ships are required to have "a ship-specific ballast water management plan," maintain "a ballast water record book," and carry "an international ballast water management certificate. The ballast water management standards will be phased in over a period of time. As an intermediate solution, ships should exchange ballast water mid-ocean. However, eventually most ships will need to install an on-board ballast water treatment system."[442] Exchanging ballast water mid-ocean is an application of the old mantra for waste disposal at sea: "the solution to pollution is dilution," but at least it should help prevent inadvertently introducing alien species into ports and enclosed seas. However, the eventual requirement of the BWM Convention to install onboard ballast water treatment plants is costly—ranging from $300K - $5M per ship![443]

Although the U.S. is not party to the BWM Convention, the U.S. had previously enacted the National Invasive Species Act of 1996, which the U.S. Coast Guard implemented by issuing the very detailed USCG Ballast Water Management Regulation. The USCG regulation requires ships to exchange their untreated ballast water outside of the 200 nm U.S. EEZ, or to have an approved Ballast Water Management System (BWMS).[444]

Although much work remains to protect and preserve the marine environment, States appear to be taking real action to address specific issues. UNCLOS is "[a] keystone of global environmental governance, ... protects the equilibrium of the world's oceans, and preserves access to the primary sources of food for over one billion people."[445] Although perhaps the ocean will always be seen as the archetypal "Tragedy of the Commons" (especially for marine pollution), we need to remember Jacques Cousteau's admonition that "we are all in the same boat."

[370] UNITED NATIONS CONVENTION ON THE LAW OF THE SEA, A COMMENTARY 679 (Alexander Proelss, ed., 2017), *quoting* NATALIE KLEIN, MARITIME SECURITY AND THE LAW OF THE SEA 14 (2011).

[371] G.A. Res. 2750 (XXV), ¶ C.2, U.N. Doc A/AC.138/58 (Dec. 17, 1970), https://research.un.org/en/docs/ga/quick/regular/25. The UN General Assembly debates and passes an annual omnibus resolution on oceans and the law of the sea. United Nations, Departments, Law of the Sea, Oceans and the Law of the Sea in the General Assembly of the United Nations, General Assembly resolutions and decisions, https://www.un.org/Depts/los/general_assembly/general_assembly_resolutions.htm.

[372] Dept. of Defense Law of War Manual § 13.2.3.4, pp. 885-886 (June 2015, updated Dec. 2016), https://www.hsdl.org/?view&did=797480; U.S. NAVY, MARINE CORPS & COAST GUARD, THE COMMANDER'S HANDBOOK ON THE LAW OF NAVAL OPERATIONS, NWP 1-14M/MCTP 11-10B/COMDTPUB P5800.7A, ¶¶ 1.3.5, 1.6.3, 2.6.3 (pp. 1-3, 1-7, 1-9, 2-11) (2017), www.jag.navy.mil/distrib/instructions/CDRs_HB_on_Law_of_Naval_Operations_AUG17.pdf.

[373] United Nations Convention on the Law of the Sea (UNCLOS) art. 87, Dec. 10, 1982, 1833 U.N.T.S. 397, https://www.un.org/Depts/los/convention_agreements/convention_overview_convention.htm.

[374] UNITED NATIONS CONVENTION ON THE LAW OF THE SEA 1982: A COMMENTARY, vol. III, 73 (Myron H. Nordquist, Satya N. Nandan & Shabtai Rosenne, eds., 1995).

[375] UNCLOS, art. 56(2) (full cite above). *See also* DONALD R. ROTHWELL & TIM STEPHENS, THE INT'L. LAW OF THE SEA 95 (2nd ed. 2016).

[376] UNCLOS, art. 58(3) (full cite above).

[377] UNCLOS, art. 87(2) (full cite above).

[378] Letter Of Transmittal Forwarding The 1982 UN Law Of The Sea Convention To The United States Senate, DOS Commentary p. 26 (William J. Clinton, Oct. 7, 1994) (S. Treaty Doc. 103–39), https://www.foreign.senate.gov/imo/media/doc/treaty_103-39.pdf.

[379] UNCLOS COMMENTARY, vol. III, p. 73 (full cite above).

[380] UNCLOS, art. 56(1)(a) (full cite above).

[381] UNCLOS, arts. 56(1)(b)(i) & 60(1)-(2) (full cite above).

[382] *See generally* The Seasteading Institute, Reimagining Civilization with Floating Cities, https://www.seasteading.org/.

[383] UNCLOS COMMENTARY, p. 679 (full cite above), *quoting* NATALIE KLEIN, MARITIME SECURITY AND THE LAW OF THE SEA 14 (2011).

[384] DOS Commentary, p. 26 (full cite above).

[385] It is interesting to note that these are also the five permanent members of the United Nations Security Council, which Chapter 9 discusses in the context of piracy.

[386] During the UNCLOS negotiations, "[m]ost nations agreed with the position advocated by the major maritime powers, that '[m]ilitary operations, exercises and activities have always been regarded as internationally lawful uses of the sea. The right to conduct such activities will continue to be enjoyed by all States in the exclusive economic zone.' ... Dissatisfied with the outcome of the [UNCLOS] negotiations, however, a few nations have sought to unilaterally expand their

control in the EEZ, particularly by imposing restrictions on military operations and other lawful activities. These efforts impinge on traditional uses of the oceans by other States and are inconsistent with international law and State practice." Raul (Pete) Pedrozo, *Military Activities in the Exclusive Economic Zone: East Asia Focus*, 90 INT'L. L. STUD. 514, 515-516 (2014), https://digital-commons.usnwc.edu/ils/vol90/iss1/15/, *quoting* 17 Third UN Conference on the Law of the Sea, Plenary Meetings, Official Records, U.N. Doc. A/CONF.62/WS/37 and ADD.1-2, 244 (1973–1982). *See also* THE FLETCHER SCHOOL OF LAW AND DIPLOMACY— TUFTS UNIVERSITY, LAW OF THE SEA, A POLICY PRIMER 30-34 (2017), https://sites.tufts.edu/lawofthesea/introduction/; Brookings Institution, Center for East Asia Policy Studies, East Asia Policy Paper 9, *The U.S. FON Program in the South China Sea—A lawful and necessary response to China's strategic ambiguity*, pp. 7-8 (Lynn Kuok, June 2016), https://www.brookings.edu/research/the-u-s-fon-program-in-the-south-china-sea/.

[387] U.S. Environmental Protection Agency (EPA), Environmental Topics, Learn about Ocean Dumping, https://www.epa.gov/ocean-dumping/learn-about-ocean-dumping.

[388] National Oceanic and Atmospheric Administration (NOAA), U.S. Dept. of Commerce, Ocean Facts, What is the biggest source of pollution in the ocean?, https://oceanservice.noaa.gov/facts/pollution.html (estimating that 80% of maritime pollution originates on land); Letter Of Transmittal Forwarding The 1982 UN Law Of The Sea Convention To The United States Senate, DOS Commentary p. 33 (William J. Clinton, Oct. 7, 1994) (S. Treaty Doc. 103–39), https://www.foreign.senate.gov/imo/media/doc/treaty_103-39.pdf (same).

[389] TUFTS, LAW OF THE SEA, p. 51 (full cite above).

[390] Letter Of Transmittal Forwarding The 1982 UN Law Of The Sea Convention To The United States Senate VI-VII (William J. Clinton, Oct. 7, 1994) (S. Treaty Doc. 103–39), https://www.foreign.senate.gov/imo/media/doc/treaty_103-39.pdf.

[391] TUFTS, LAW OF THE SEA, p. 49 (full cite above); American Society of Int'l. Law (ASIL), Resources, eResources - Insights and other E-Publications, Electronic Resource Guide (ERG), *Law of the Sea*, p. 4 (Barbara Bean, Apr. 27, 2015), https://www.asil.org/resources/electronic-resource-guide-erg.

[392] Helmut Türk, *Questions Relating to the Continental Shelf Beyond 200 Nautical Miles: Delimitation, Delineation, and Revenue Sharing*, 97 INT'L. L. STUD. 231, 253 (2021), https://digital-commons.usnwc.edu/ils/vol97/iss1/18/.

[393] United Nations Convention on the Law of the Sea (UNCLOS) art. 1(1)(4), Dec. 10, 1982, 1833 U.N.T.S. 397, https://www.un.org/Depts/los/convention_agreements/convention_overview_convention.htm.

[394] In 1989, the Exxon Valdez spilled nearly 11 million gallons of oil, which eventually covered 1,300 square miles of ocean. Although this was not the worst oil spill on record, it occurred in an isolated and enclosed area (Prince William Sound in the Gulf of Alaska), and thus the effects were concentrated, resulting in significant damage to the natural environment. The U.S. responded by enacting the 1990 Oil Pollution Act, which holds responsible parties strictly liable for removal costs and damages resulting from oil spills. 33 U.S. Code § 2701 *et seq.* (1990), https://www.law.cornell.edu/uscode/text; U.S. Environmental Protection Agency (EPA), Laws & Regulations, Summary of the Oil Pollution Act, https://www.epa.gov/laws-regulations/summary-oil-pollution-act.

395 *See generally* General Dynamics, Ordnance and Tactical Systems, Naval Platform Systems, Phalanx CIWS, https://www.gd-ots.com/armaments/naval-platforms-system/phalanx/; Raytheon, What We Do, Products and Services Listing, Phalanx Close-In Weapon System, https://www.raytheon.com/capabilities/products/phalanx.

396 TUFTS, LAW OF THE SEA, p. 57 (full cite above) (discussing the tension between environmental protection and national security, as typified by the U.S. Marine Mammal Protection Act (MMPA), and its impact on the U.S. Navy's use of low frequency sonar). The U.S. Navy goes to great lengths to be effective environmental stewards. For example, the U.S. Navy employs a Marine Mammal Monitoring (M3R) system using underwater acoustic sensors "to detect, identify, and track marine mammals that might be approaching Navy testing ranges. This enables the Navy to both protect marine mammals and improve its understanding of the animals' behavior ... ." Safety 4 Sea, US Navy deploys marine mammal monitoring system (Feb. 26, 2020), https://safety4sea.com/us-navy-deploys-marine-mammal-monitoring-system/. The Navy also participates in Marine Mammal studies. America's Navy, Press Office, News Stories, *USS Cole Supports Marine Mammal Study* (Asheka Lawrence-Reid, July 24, 2020), https://www.navy.mil/Press-Office/News-Stories/display-news/Article/2302555/uss-cole-supports-marine-mammal-study/ (describing the controlled use of active sonar to monitor the reactions of marine mammals).

397 UNCLOS, art. 1(1)(5) (full cite above).

398 YouTube, Sinking Exercise during Rim of the Pacific · Twenty-two Nations, More Than 40 Ships & Submarines, https://www.youtube.com/watch?v=imwLc2T3oks; Naval History and Heritage Command, Belleau Wood (LHA 3), https://www.history.navy.mil/content/history/nhhc/research/histories/ship-histories/danfs/b/belleau-wood-lha-3-ii.html; HullNumber.com, Find Your Shipmates, U.S.S. BELLEAU WOOD, https://www.hullnumber.com/LHA-3; USCarriers.net, USS BELLEAU WOOD (LHA 3), http://www.uscarriers.net/lha3history.htm; NavSource Online: Amphibious Photo Archive, USS Belleau Wood (LHA-3), http://www.navsource.org/archives/10/07/0703.htm.

399 The Atlantic, *History's Largest Mining Operation Is About to Begin* (Wil S. Hylton, January/February 2020), https://www.theatlantic.com/magazine/archive/2020/01/20000-feet-under-the-sea/603040/; The Atlantic, A Troubling Discovery in the Deepest Ocean Trenches (Ed Yong, Feb. 27, 2019), https://www.theatlantic.com/science/archive/2019/02/deepest-ocean-trenches-animals-eat-plastic/583657/.

400 National Oceanic and Atmospheric Administration (NOAA), U.S. Dept. of Commerce, Marine Debris Program, Office of Response and Restoration, Garbage Patches, https://marinedebris.noaa.gov/info/patch.html. The U.S. Save Our Seas (SOS) Act of 2018 granted a $10M annual budget to NOAA's Marine Debris Program for an additional 5 years to identify, prevent, reduce, remove and address adverse impacts of Marine Debris. It also authorizes NOAA to release federal funds to U.S. states for cleanup of Severe Marine Debris Events.

401 The Ocean Cleanup, About Us, https://theoceancleanup.com/about/.

402 The Ocean Cleanup, Updates, The Ocean Cleanup Successfully Catches Plastic in the Great Pacific Garbage Patch, https://theoceancleanup.com/updates/the-

ocean-cleanup-successfully-catches-plastic-in-the-great-pacific-garbage-patch/; CNN Business, Mission: Ahead, *A floating device created to clean up plastic from the ocean is finally doing its job, organizers say* (David Williams, Oct. 3, 2019), https://www.cnn.com/2019/10/02/tech/ocean-cleanup-catching-plastic-scn-trnd/index.html.

[403] Zed, Books, *An interview with Captain Peter Hammarstedt of Catching Thunder* (Apr. 13, 2018), https://www.zedbooks.net/media/show/interview-captain-peter-hammarstedt-catching-thunder/.

[404] "The International Maritime Organization is a specialized agency of the United Nations which is responsible for measures to improve the safety and security of international shipping and to prevent pollution from ships. It is also involved in legal matters, including liability and compensation issues and the facilitation of international maritime traffic." Int'l. Maritime Organization (IMO), English, About IMO, FAQs, http://www.imo.org/en/About/Pages/FAQs.aspx.

[405] Int'l. Maritime Organization (IMO), English, About IMO, Introduction to IMO, http://www.imo.org/en/About/Pages/Default.aspx; American Society of Int'l. Law (ASIL), Resources, eResources - Insights and other E-Publications, Electronic Resource Guide (ERG), *Law of the Sea*, pp. 9-10 (Barbara Bean, Apr. 27, 2015), https://www.asil.org/resources/electronic-resource-guide-erg.

[406] Int'l. Maritime Organization (IMO), English, Our Work, Marine Environment, Particularly Sensitive Sea Areas, http://www.imo.org/en/OurWork/Environment/PSSAs/Pages/Default.aspx.

[407] United Nations Convention on the Law of the Sea (UNCLOS) Introduction at p. 3, Dec. 10, 1982, 1833 U.N.T.S. 397, https://www.un.org/Depts/los/convention_agreements/convention_overview_convention.htm (noting that reaching consensus was "adopted as the principal means by which decisions [at the Third Conference on the Law of the Sea] were to be taken," including "exhaust[ing] all efforts to reach consensus before any voting on questions of substance could take place," and even delaying votes by the use of "cooling off" periods because "[b]y delaying the voting as long as possible, it was hoped that the divergent positions might be reconciled in the interim, thus obviating the need to vote at all.").

[408] *See* UNCLOS, art. 237 (full cite above) (mentioning "agreements which may be concluded in furtherance of the general principles set forth in this Convention.").

[409] UNCLOS, art. 197 (full cite above).

[410] UNCLOS, art. 213 (full cite above).

[411] UNCLOS, art. 214 (full cite above).

[412] UNCLOS, art. 215 (full cite above).

[413] UNCLOS, art. 216 (full cite above).

[414] UNCLOS, arts. 216(1)(b) & 217 (full cite above). Chapter 9 discusses Flag States in more depth.

[415] UNCLOS, arts. 216(1)(c) & 218-219 (full cite above).

[416] UNCLOS, arts. 216(1)(a) & 220 (full cite above).

[417] Letter Of Transmittal Forwarding The 1982 UN Law Of The Sea Convention To The United States Senate, DOS Commentary p. 40 (William J. Clinton, Oct. 7, 1994) (S. Treaty Doc. 103–39), https://www.foreign.senate.gov/imo/media/doc/treaty_103-39.pdf.

[418] *See also* U.S. Navy, Marine Corps & Coast Guard, The Commander's Handbook on the Law of Naval Operations, NWP 1-14M/MCTP 11-10B/COMDTPUB P5800.7A, ¶¶ 2.6.5.1 to 2.6.5.2 (p. 2-12) (2017),

www.jag.navy.mil/distrib/instructions/CDRs_HB_on_Law_of_Naval_Operations _AUG17.pdf (noting that the Arctic and Antarctic are special areas not subject to claims of sovereignty).

[419] THE FLETCHER SCHOOL OF LAW AND DIPLOMACY—TUFTS UNIVERSITY, LAW OF THE SEA, A POLICY PRIMER 59-60 (2017), https://sites.tufts.edu/lawofthesea/introduction/. The 5 Coastal States bordering the Arctic Ocean ("Arctic 5": Canada, Denmark, Norway, Russia and the United States) "met at the political level on 28 May 2008 in Ilulissat, Greenland ... [and] adopted the following declaration: ... We remain committed to [the UNCLOS] legal framework ... [and] therefore see no need to develop a new comprehensive international legal regime to govern the Arctic Ocean." Arctic Portal, Stories, Ilulissat Declaration, https://arcticportal.org/images/stories/pdf/Ilulissat-declaration.pdf. See also Michael W. Lodge (Secretary-General of the International Seabed Authority), Enclosure of the Oceans versus the Common Heritage of Mankind: The Inherent Tension between the Continental Shelf Beyond 200 Nautical Miles and the Area, 97 INT'L. L. STUD. 803, 823 (2021), https://digital-commons.usnwc.edu/cgi/viewcontent.cgi?article=2971&context=ils (noting that "[e]ven the United States, although not a party to UNCLOS, has agreed with this position. This implies that any areas of the seabed beyond national jurisdiction in the Arctic Ocean would be considered part of the Area and subject to the legal regime set out in Part XI of UNCLOS and the 1994 Agreement, as well as the rules, regulations, and procedures of the ISA concerning mineral exploration and exploitation. How much of the seabed of the Arctic Ocean lies beyond national juris-diction remains to be seen. All five Arctic coastal States (Canada, Denmark, Norway, the Russian Federation, and the United States) assert entitlements to continental shelves in the Arctic Ocean extending beyond 200 nautical miles. Submissions to the CLCS by Canada, Denmark, Norway, and the Russian Federation are in various stages of consideration, and no State has yet established final and binding outer limits. The United States has gathered technical data to substantiate its entitlement to a continental shelf but, as a non-party, has not made a submission to the CLCS.... All parties have committed to the orderly settlement of these claims on the basis of the Ilulissat Declaration, which recognizes that UNCLOS provides the legal framework delineating the outer limits of the continental shelf in the Arctic. The prevailing view, based on all published sources, is that there will be two small areas of seabed remaining beyond national jurisdiction that will form part of the Area.").

[420] TUFTS, LAW OF THE SEA, pp. 61-63 (full cite above). The U.S. has also conducted a Freedom of Navigation Operation (FONOP, discussed in Chapter 11) through the Barents Sea in the Arctic. Military.com, News, Headlines, Navy Ships Transit Through Barents Sea Near Russia for 1st Time Since Cold War (Gina Harkins, May 5, 2020), https://www.military.com/daily-news/2020/05/05/navy-ships-transit-through-barents-sea-near-russia-1st-time-cold-war.html?ESRC=eb_200506.nl.

[421] Int'l. Maritime Organization (IMO), English, Our Work, Marine Environment, London Convention and Protocol, http://www.imo.org/en/ourwork/Environment/LCLP/Pages/default.aspx

[422] Int'l. Maritime Organization (IMO), London Convention and Protocol Information Leaflet, http://www.imo.org/en/OurWork/Environment/LCLP/Documents/22780LDC%20L eaflet%20without%2040%20Anniv%20logo2012Web1.pdf.

[423] Also called the Marine Protection, Research and Sanctuaries Act, the U.S. Ocean Dumping Act (ODA) supplements the London Convention and further

restricts dumping at sea. The ODA requires a permit to dump materials in the ocean, and imposes civil penalties up to $125,000 (e.g., for dumping medical waste), and criminal penalties for knowing violations. *See generally* United States Environmental Protection Agency, EPA History: Marine Protection, Research and Sanctuaries Act (Ocean Dumping Act), https://www.epa.gov/history/epa-history-marine-protection-research-and-sanctuaries-act-ocean-dumping-act.

[424] Int'l. Maritime Organization (IMO), Map of Current London Convention and London Protocol Parties (February 2019), http://www.imo.org/en/OurWork/Environment/LCLP/Documents/Parties%20to%20the%20LCLP%20February%202019.pdf.

[425] Int'l. Maritime Organization (IMO), English, About IMO, Conventions, List of Conventions, Int'l. Convention for the Prevention of Pollution from Ships (MARPOL), http://www.imo.org/en/About/Conventions/ListOfConventions/Pages/International-Convention-for-the-Prevention-of-Pollution-from-Ships-(MARPOL).aspx.

[426] Int'l. Maritime Organization (IMO), English, About IMO, Conventions, Status of Conventions, Ratifications by treaty, http://www.imo.org/en/About/Conventions/StatusOfConventions/Documents/StatusOfTreaties.pdf; THE FLETCHER SCHOOL OF LAW AND DIPLOMACY—TUFTS UNIVERSITY, LAW OF THE SEA, A POLICY PRIMER 52 (2017), https://sites.tufts.edu/lawofthesea/introduction/. Chapter 9 discusses Flag States in more depth.

[427] Int'l. Maritime Organization (IMO), English, Our Work, Marine Environment, Special Areas Under MARPOL, http://www.imo.org/en/OurWork/Environment/SpecialAreasUnderMARPOL/Pages/Default.aspx.

[428] IMO, Special Areas Under MARPOL (full cite above).

[429] U.S. General Accounting Office (GAO), Marine Pollution: Progress Made to Reduce Marine Pollution by Cruise Ships, but Important Issues Remain (Feb. 2000), p. 3, https://www.gao.gov/products/RCED-00-48.

[430] GAO, Progress Made to Reduce Marine Pollution by Cruise Ships (full cite above). Chapter 9 discusses Flag States in more depth.

[431] Int'l. Maritime Organization (IMO), English, About IMO, Conventions, Status of Conventions, http://www.imo.org/en/About/Conventions/StatusOfConventions/Pages/Default.aspx. There are 143 State Parties to Annex IV (Sewage) of MARPOL, representing over 96% of world merchant shipping by tonnage. IMO, Ratifications by treaty (full cite above).

[432] 33 U.S. Code §§ 1905-1915 (1980), https://www.law.cornell.edu/uscode/text. The 1980 Act to Prevent Pollution from Ships (APPS) prohibits discharge of oil within 3 nm of the U.S. coast, and the discharge of garbage (Annex V) within the 200 nm U.S. EEZ. APPS requires the use of port reception facilities to discharge oil, and imposes civil and criminal penalties for violations. It also applies Annex V (garbage and plastic limitations) to sovereign immune vessels (such as U.S. or foreign warships)!

[433] GAO, Progress Made to Reduce Marine Pollution by Cruise Ships, p. 7 (full cite above).

[434] Safety4Sea, *Understanding marine biofouling: How anti-fouling systems prevent growth* (Dec. 13, 2018), https://safety4sea.com/cm-understanding-marine-biofouling-how-anti-fouling-systems-prevent-growth/.

435 Int'l. Maritime Organization (IMO), English, About IMO, Conventions, Int'l. Convention on the Control of Harmful Anti-fouling Systems on Ships, http://www.imo.org/en/About/Conventions/ListOfConventions/Pages/Internationa l-Convention-on-the-Control-of-Harmful-Anti-fouling-Systems-on-Ships-(AFS).aspx.

436 IMO, Status of Conventions (full cite above). There are 89 State Parties to the AFS Convention, representing over 96% of world merchant shipping by tonnage. IMO, Ratifications by treaty (full cite above).

437 IMO, Anti-fouling Convention (full cite above).

438 United Nations Convention on the Law of the Sea (UNCLOS) art. 196, Dec. 10, 1982, 1833 U.N.T.S. 397, https://www.un.org/Depts/los/convention_agreements/convention_overview_co nvention.htm.

439 Mediterranean Information Office for Environment, Culture and Sustainable Development (MIO-ECSDE), Aliens in the Mediterranean, pp. 6, 16 (Thomais Vlachogianni, Milan Vogrin & Michael Scoullos 2013) http://mio-ecsde.org/project/vlachogianni-t-vogrin-m-scoullos-m-aliens-in-the-mediterranean-mio-ecsde-athens-2013/.

440 Int'l. Maritime Organization (IMO), English, About IMO, Conventions, Int'l. Convention for the Control and Management of Ships' Ballast Water and Sediments (BWM), http://www.imo.org/en/About/conventions/listofconventions/pages/international-convention-for-the-control-and-management-of-ships'-ballast-water-and-sediments-(bwm).aspx. *See generally* United Nations, Oceans & Law of the Sea, Division for Ocean Affairs and the Law of the Sea, The Nippon Foundation of Japan Fellowship Programme ~ Human Resources Development and Advancement of the Legal Order of the World's Oceans ~, The Fellows and their Thesis [sic], Reports, *The Role of the Brazilian Ports in the Improvement of the National Ballast Water Management Program According the Provisions of the International Ballast Water Convention* (Uirá Cavalcante Oliveira, 2008), https://www.un.org/depts/los/nippon/unnff_programme_home/fellows_pages/r eports_index.htm.

441 Int'l. Maritime Organization (IMO), English, About IMO, Conventions, Status of Conventions, http://www.imo.org/en/About/Conventions/StatusOfConventions/Pages/Default.as px. There are 81 State Parties to the BWM Convention, representing almost 81% of world merchant shipping by tonnage. IMO, Status of Conventions (full cite above).

442 IMO, Ballast Water Convention (full cite above).

443 gCaptain, *Ballast Water Treatment Costs Could Promote Accelerated Ship Scrapping* (McQuilling, Nov. 21, 2013), https://gcaptain.com/ballast-water-treatment-costs/; Riviera Maritime Media, Opinion, *Counting the cost of ballast treatment* (Mar. 7, 2016), https://www.rivieramm.com/opinion/opinion/counting-the-cost-of-ballast-treatment-33924.

444 33 CFR Part 151; 46 CFR Part 162 (2012). *See also* gCaptain, *Ballast Water Treatment Costs* (full cite above); Bio-Sea, IMO/USCG BWM Regulation, USCG Ballast Water Management Regulation, https://www.ballast-water-treatment.com/en/ballast-water-management-regulation/uscg-bwm-standards.

445 TUFTS, LAW OF THE SEA, p. 58 (full cite above).

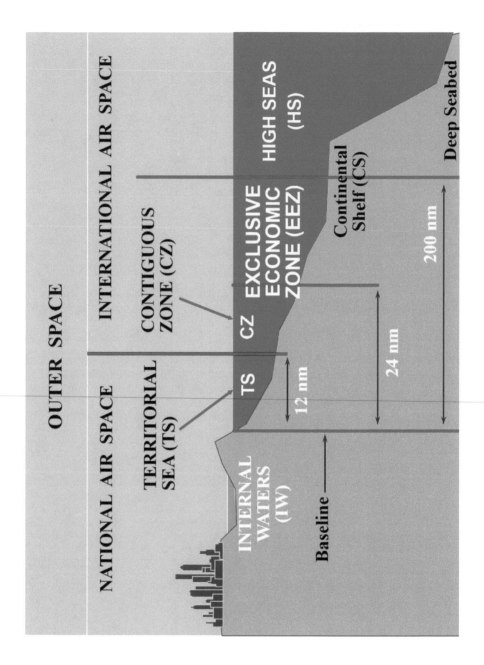

CHAPTER 6: CONTINENTAL SHELF & DEEP SEABED

"The convention is the only means for international recognition and acceptance of our extended continental shelf claims in the Arctic, and we are the only Arctic nation that is not a party to the [Law of the Sea] convention."
—*Leon Panetta (former U.S. Secretary of Defense)*

THE RESOURCES OF THE SEAFLOOR are at least as vast as those in the water column, such as fisheries. There are extensive mineral and petroleum resources on the seafloor, both in areas controlled by States (on the Continental Shelf that generally lies beneath the Exclusive Economic Zone), and beneath the High Seas on the Deep Seabed. Ninety percent of the hydrocarbons (i.e., oil) that lie beneath the sea lie on the Continental Shelf, where we will learn that the Coastal State (aka "littoral State") owns all resources. [NOTE: There is a diagram of the various maritime zones at the beginning of the Chapter.]

As discussed in Chapter 2, Grotius' "freedom of the seas" doctrine remained the guiding principle of the Law of the Sea until President Truman issued Proclamation 2667 on September 28, 1945,[446] unilaterally extending U.S. jurisdiction over the natural resources found on the "the continental shelf [which] may be regarded as an extension of the land-mass of the coastal nation".[447] President Truman's proclamation became "instant" Customary International Law as other States quickly followed suit.[448] The flurry of Continental Shelf claims were viewed as encroaching on the resources of the Deep Seabed, such as polymetallic manganese nodules (discussed subsequently).

This potential encroachment on the resources of the Deep Seabed concerned other States, particularly the smaller and newly independent States, who saw these resources as being the "common heritage of mankind,"[449] and therefore not subject to any one State's possession or control.[450] These concerns led to the United Nations General Assembly adopting Resolution 2750 in 1970 to convene the Third United Nations Conference on the Law of the Sea,[451] which culminated in the 1982 United Nations Convention on the Law of the Sea (UNCLOS).

Whereas Chapters 3, 4 and 5 focused on maritime zones dealing with the "water column" (i.e., Territorial Seas, Contiguous Zone, Exclusive Economic Zone (EEZ), and High Seas), this Chapter focuses on the seafloor. This area of UNCLOS has some of the most technical rules—unless the reader is particularly interested in the technical details, you should simply focus on understanding the overarching concepts.

The first area of the seafloor we'll discuss is the Continental Shelf, which by default extends beneath the EEZ (i.e., out to 200 nm from the baseline).[452] Although UNCLOS uses the more common term "Continental Shelf" to describe the seafloor beneath the EEZ, Article 76 recognizes that this technically constitutes the scientific "continental margin," which is comprised of the scientific continental shelf, continental slope, and continental rise, as seen in the following graphic. "Worldwide, there is wide variation in the breadths of these areas."[453] The "Abyssal Plain" is also known as the Deep Seabed.

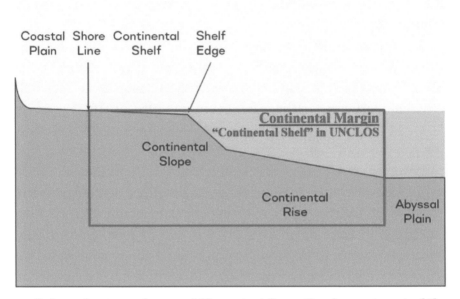

Coastal Plain / Shore Line / Continental Shelf / Shelf Edge / Continental Margin "Continental Shelf" in UNCLOS / Continental Slope / Continental Rise / Abyssal Plain

It is easier to understand if we start from the deepest part of the ocean floor. Imagine Superman standing on the Abyssal Plain, and starting to walk towards dry land. Superman would first start walking up the gradual continental rise, where rocks, sand and sediment have accumulated over millennia, but at a relatively gentle rise. Eventually he would reach the bottom of the steeper continental slope, which is like an underwater ski slope. After Superman climbed the steep continental slope, he would reach the scientific continental shelf, which is a submerged plateau or shoulder of land just off the coast, averaging about 500 feet deep (i.e., accessible by an experienced scuba diver). The scientific continental shelf, continental slope, and continental rise are collectively called the continental margin. It would have been simpler (and more scientifically accurate) if UNCLOS had used the term continental margin to describe the seafloor lying beneath the EEZ.[454] However, the States negotiating the text of UNCLOS took nine years to reach an acceptable compromise,[455] and chose to use the term "Continental Shelf," since it had been used historically (since 1877)[456] and had become the accepted term.[457]

By default, UNCLOS recognizes the Continental Shelf as extending out to 200 nm from the baseline (i.e., beneath the EEZ).[458] This is internally consistent: the Coastal State owns all economic resources in the water column out to 200 nm (i.e., in its EEZ), and owns all economic resources on the seabed beneath it (i.e., on the Continental Shelf) out to 200 nm.

However, recognizing that a State's actual "Continental Shelf" might extend beyond 200 nm from the baseline, **UNCLOS permits States to claim an Outer (or Extended) Continental Shelf if they can prove it!** Once again, Article 76 is one of most scientifically technical Articles in UNCLOS, and thus can be very confusing. We are only going to focus on the highlights. Article 76(4) requires the Coastal State to define the outer limits of its continental margin if it seeks an Outer Continental Shelf beyond 200 nm.[459] The Coastal State has the choice of two formulas[460] for defining the outer edge of its Outer Continental Shelf—either: (1) 60 nm from the foot of the continental slope (the Hedberg formula), or (2) out to a point where the thickness of the sediment on the seafloor is 1% of the distance to the foot of the continental slope (the Irish or Gardiner formula).[461] For example, if the Coastal State has unusually thick sediment on the seabed off its coast (e.g., 4,253 feet thick, which equates to .7 nm) out to a series of points 70 nm from the foot of the continental slope, it could claim those points as the outer edge of its Outer Continental Shelf.

However, regardless of how many Guinness® beers one must drink in order to understand these two formulas, the maximum width of the Outer Continental Shelf generally cannot exceed 350 nm.[462] Moreover, Coastal States are required to provide extensive scientific data supporting their Outer Continental Shelf claims,

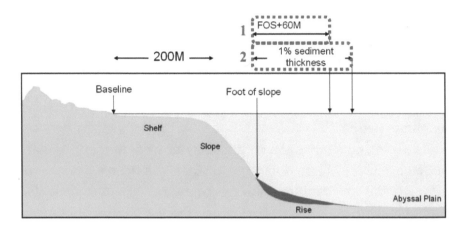

which are reviewed by the twenty-one scientific/technical experts on the Commission on the Limits of the Continental Shelf (CLCS).[463]

Although it is the coastal State that is entitled to establish the outer limits of its continental shelf beyond 200 nautical miles, ... these limits ... only become "final and binding" if adopted "on the basis of" recommendations by the CLCS. ... The term "on the basis of," suggested by the United States, allows the coastal State some, but perhaps not too much flexibility concerning the implementation of the recommendations of the CLCS.[464]

To date, there have been 88 Outer Continental Shelf claims submitted to the CLCS, with many Coastal States making multiple claims.[465] The CLCS has only been able to make recommendations in 35 of those submissions, and only 9 States have deposited charts with geographical coordinates with the ISA Secretary General showing the limits of their OCS.[466] "Given its current workload, it may take decades for the CLCS to make all the recommendations regarding the submissions by coastal States with respect to the outer limits of the continental shelf."[467] Moreover, the CLCS only makes recommendations based upon their independent scientific analysis of the data provided—it is up to States to resolve their Continental Shelf disputes through delimitation[468] (discussed in Chapter 8). "[W]here there are delimitation disputes between States—and there are quite a few—the final determination of the outer limits [of their Continental Shelves] may be delayed for an indefinite period."[469]

As the introductory quote to this Chapter from former Secretary of Defense Leon Panetta indicates, UNCLOS "is the only means for international recognition and acceptance of our extended continental shelf claims in the Arctic, and we are the only Arctic nation that is not a party to the [Law of the Sea] convention."[470] Although the U.S. is not party to UNCLOS yet,[471] it has already made Outer Continental Shelf claims (following graphic), although the U.S. has not submitted them to the CLCS for approval.[472]

While it seems clear that the entitlement to a continental shelf in paragraph 1 of Article 76 is part of customary international law, it is less clear that the detailed provisions and related obligations set out in paragraphs 2–7 [for claiming an extended or outer continental shelf] also have the status of customary international law ....

... In respect of the United States, some authors have suggested that a claim to a continental shelf beyond 200 nautical miles could be made based on customary international law as reflected in the Truman Declaration and the 1958 Geneva Convention on the Continental Shelf. According to this view, while nothing in UNCLOS prohibits the United States from making a submission to the CLCS, notwithstanding its status as a non-party to UNCLOS, it is not obliged to do so in order to benefit from customary international law. It is also unclear whether non-parties would be bound by the provisions of Article 84(2), although one presumes that it could only be in their interests to deposit information on the outer limits of their continental shelves with both the United Nations and ISA.[473]

Thus, whether or not the U.S. can effectively claim an Outer or Extended Continental Shelf under international law remains an open question.[474]

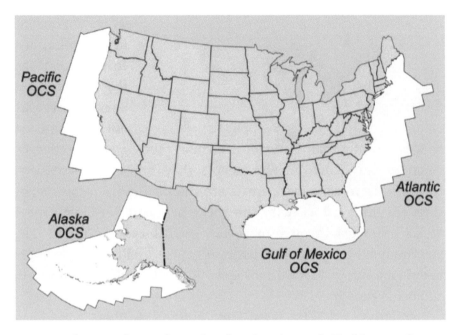

Now that we know how far the Continental Shelf extends, we need to discuss which resources it includes. Article 77 grants exclusive ownership rights to the Coastal State over the following resources (whether or not it expressly claims or exploits them):

> ➤ Mineral resources (e.g., hydrocarbons, precious metals),
> ➤ Other non-living resources (e.g., hydrothermal vents), and
> ➤ Sedentary species (e.g., sponges, coral).

Although "minerals" are not defined by UNCLOS, they generally include hydrocarbons (i.e., oil and gas), and metals (e.g., iron, manganese, cobalt). For example, cobalt-rich ferromanganese crusts[475] are found near volcanic seamounts (i.e., underwater volcanoes), and are thought to be formed by the precipitation of

minerals from seawater. Ferromanganese crusts are up to 25 cm (10 inches) in thickness, and cover up to 2% of the seafloor. Since they are often found in shallower water than manganese nodules (400-4,000 meters deep versus 4,000-6,000 meters deep), they are more accessible. However, ferromanganese crusts are still difficult to recover since they are often attached to the rocky seafloor. Ferromanganese crusts are a good source of cobalt, manganese and nickel. The environmental impacts of crust mining are similar to manganese nodule mining (discussed subsequently), but would be confined to smaller areas.[476]

Similarly, UNCLOS does not define "[o]ther non-living resources," but this would normally include non-minerals found on the Continental Shelf such as hydrothermal (i.e., warm water) vents, which were first discovered in 1977 (i.e., in the middle of UNCLOS negotiations).[477] Hydrothermal vents often form "chimneys" that support unique and complex ecosystems,[478] and thus are useful for Marine Scientific Research (MSR, discussed in Chapter 7). Hydrothermal vents are essentially small underwater geysers, and thus potentially could be tapped as an energy source as well (since the pressurized seawater can reach temperatures of over 750° F (400° C) without boiling.[479] Hydrothermal vents are thought to come in two varieties: "'Black smokers' are chimneys formed from deposits of iron sulfide, which is black. 'White smokers' are chimneys formed from deposits of barium, calcium, and silicon, which are white."[480]

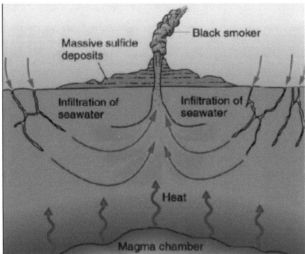

Hydrothermal vents are surrounded by valuable minerals, such as the accumulation of millions of tons of polymetallic sulfides[481] containing lead, zinc, copper, gold and silver,[482] which also could be harvested by the Coastal State on the Continental Shelf. Many of the known hydrothermal vents lie within 200 nm of Coastal States (i.e., on their Continental Shelves).[483]

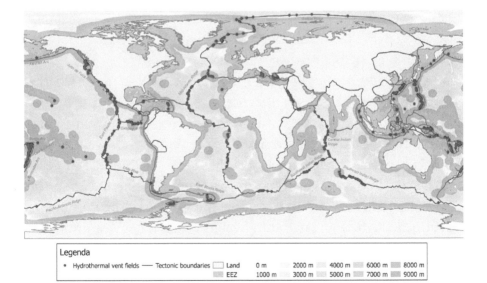

The final type of resource over which UNCLOS grants exclusive ownership rights to the Coastal State is "sedentary species," for which Article 77(4) provides a fairly specific definition: "[S]edentary species, that is to say, organisms which, at the harvestable stage, either are immobile on or under the seabed or are unable to move except in constant physical contact with the seabed or the subsoil." This would certainly seem to include sea cucumbers, sponges, and most types of mollusks (e.g., snails, clams, scallops, oysters and mussels). Whether or not "sedentary species" includes crustaceans (e.g., crabs and lobsters) would depend on whether they "are unable to move except in constant physical contact with the seabed or the subsoil." Some types of crabs can swim (e.g., blue crabs), and although lobsters usually crawl across the seafloor, they can flee danger by swimming backward quickly by flexing their muscular tail. On the U.S. Continental Shelf, the Magnuson Fishery Conservation and Management Act (MFCMA) includes a long list of Cnidaria (aka Corals), Crustacea (including Tanner Crabs, King Crabs, Dungeness Crabs, Stone Crabs and Lobsters), Mollusks (including Abalones, Queen Conch, Surf Clam and Ocean Quahog), and various Sponges as "Continental Shelf fishery resources."[484]

Within 200 nm, it would not appear to matter much whether crabs and lobsters are sedentary species governed by the Continental Shelf regime, or a living resource in the water column (i.e., a type of fisheries) governed by the EEZ regime—either way, UNCLOS grants exclusive ownership rights to the Coastal State. However, if a Coastal State claims an Outer Continental Shelf that is approved by the Commission on the Limits of the Continental Shelf (CLCS), the Coastal State would retain exclusive ownership rights of sedentary species on the Outer Continental Shelf as well. Thus, if crabs and lobsters are sedentary species, the Coastal State retains ownership of them on its Outer Continental Shelf. However, if crabs and lobsters are not considered sedentary species, then every State would have the right to capture them on the High Seas (i.e., in the water column beyond the Coastal State's 200 nm EEZ).[485] However, the Coastal State is responsible for making international royalty payments on "the exploitation of the non-living resources of the continental shelf beyond 200 nautical miles" (i.e., on the Outer Continental Shelf (OCS)) to "the Authority," which we shall see controls mineral resources in "the Area" (i.e., on the Deep Seabed) for the benefit of mankind.[486]

Besides the requirement to make international royalty payments for the exploitation of non-living resources on the OCS, another Continental Shelf issue is the laying and repair of submarine cables and pipelines.

Submarine cables include telegraph, telephone, and high-voltage power cables, which are essential to modern communications. In light of the extraordinary costs and increasing importance to the world economy of undersea telecommunications cables, particularly the new fiber-optic cables, it is significant that the Convention strengthens the protections for tlie owners and operators of these cables in the event of breakage.

Pipelines include those which deliver water, oil and natural gas, and other commodities. The Convention recognizes that pipelines may pose an environmental threat to the coastal State and, therefore, increases the authority of the coastal State on its continental shelf over the location of pipelines and with respect to pollution therefrom.[487]

The submarine cable industry has consistently supported U.S. accession to UNCLOS,[488] which has eight different UNCLOS articles protecting submarine cables and pipelines. This reflects their importance to States negotiating the text of UNCLOS:

➢ Article 21: The right of a Coastal State to enact laws protecting cables and pipelines in its Territorial Sea;

➢ Article 58(1): The right of all States to lay submarine cables and pipelines in the EEZ of another State;

➢ Article 79(1): The right of all States to lay submarine cables and pipelines on the Continental Shelf of another State, subject only to the ***Coastal State's consent regarding the course of pipelines***, and due regard to existing submarine cables and pipelines already in place;[489]

➢ Articles 87 and 112: The freedom of all States to lay submarine cables and pipelines beneath the High Seas (i.e., on the Deep Seabed), subject to due regard to other States' High Seas freedoms;

➢ Articles 79(5) and 87(1)(c): States shall not impair other States' ability to repair existing submarine cables and pipelines already in place on the Continental Shelf or on the Deep Seabed;

➢ Article 113: Requirement for Flag States to enact laws imposing liability on ships negligently or intentionally breaking or damaging submarine cables and pipelines;

➢ Article 114: Requirement for States to enact laws imposing liability on owners of submarine cables and pipelines to bear the cost of repairing any other submarine cables and pipelines they may damage; and

➢ Article 115: Requirement for Flag States to enact laws indemnifying ship owners who sacrifice gear (e.g., an anchor, net, or fishing gear) to avoid damaging submarine cables and pipelines by the owners of those submarine cables and pipelines.

A couple examples might help cement our common understanding of the right to lay and repair submarine cables and pipelines. The first example is if Russia wanted to export oil to Canada, could Russia lay a submarine oil pipeline across the U.S. Continental Shelf off the Alaskan coast in order to do so? The 1945 Truman Proclamation (claiming a Continental Shelf in order to secure "new sources of petroleum and other minerals")[490] did not address submarine cables and pipelines.[491] However, the U.S. is party to the 1958 Convention on the Continental Shelf,[492] which provides in Article 4 that: "Subject to its right to take reasonable measures for the exploration of the continental shelf and the exploitation of its natural resources, the coastal State may not impede the laying or maintenance of submarine cables or pipelines on the continental shelf." Thus, under the 1958 Convention on the Continental Shelf, Russia could lay a submarine oil pipeline across the U.S. Continental Shelf off the Alaskan coast in order to export oil to Canada, although perhaps the U.S. could delineate the course of the pipeline as a "reasonable measure[] for the exploration of the continental shelf and the exploitation of its natural resources." Although UNCLOS does not apply to the U.S. as a matter of treaty law (since the U.S. has not yet ratified the treaty), as discussed in Chapter 2 President Reagan issued a statement that UNCLOS includes provisions *"which generally confirm existing maritime law and practice and fairly balance the interests of all states"*[493] which is generally viewed as a declaration that the U.S. views most UNCLOS provisions (especially its "navigational bill of rights")[494] as reflecting existing Customary International Law (CIL), with which the United States will comply.[495] Under UNCLOS, Russia could lay a submarine oil pipeline across the U.S. Continental Shelf off the Alaskan coast in order to export oil to Canada, and all the U.S. could do would be to delineate the course of the submarine oil pipeline (e.g., to avoid sensitive maritime areas or areas that the U.S. wanted to explore and/or exploit).

The second example is if Russia wanted to export communist television to Cuba, could Russia lay a submarine cable to Cuba over the U.S. Continental Shelf? Absolutely! Under the 1958 Convention on the Continental Shelf, perhaps the U.S. could direct that the submarine cable avoid certain areas as a "reasonable measure[] for the exploration of the continental shelf and the exploitation of its natural resources." Under UNCLOS, the U.S. would have no say in the matter whatsoever. In both examples, Russia must have due regard to existing submarine cables and pipelines already in place (e.g., not laying the submarine oil pipeline directly on top of submarine cables, thereby effectively burying them, possibly damaging them, and preventing their repair).

We should all be supportive of the right to lay and repair submarine cables, since 99% of international data, including telecommunications (i.e., international telephone calls) is transmitted via submarine cables.[496] Modern submarine cables are about the diameter of a garden hose, and are surprisingly vulnerable to a number of threats, including driftnet fishing,

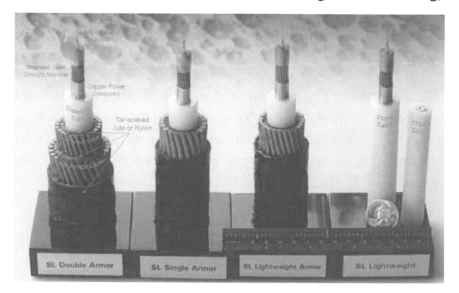

anchoring, being cut (either accidentally or intentionally), and even possibly tapped into for eavesdropping purposes![497]

The final Continental Shelf issue is who has the right to drill or construct artificial islands on the Continental Shelf? The answer to this question is merely a repetition of the Coastal State's exclusive ownership rights over resources in the EEZ and on the Continental Shelf, including the construction of artificial islands,[498] and drilling on the Continental Shelf.[499]

DEEP SEABED

This Chapter's second sub-topic is the Deep Seabed, which lies beneath the High Seas[500] and is also known as "the Area" in Part XI of UNCLOS. As discussed in Chapter 5, the States negotiating UNCLOS could only agree on including six general definitions. Article 1(1)(1) defines "[the] Area" as: "the seabed and ocean floor and subsoil thereof, beyond the limits of national jurisdiction," which is thus the Deep Seabed beyond all States' Continental Shelves, including all confirmed claims to Outer Continental Shelves (OCS). "[T]he Area itself is a residual space, comprising only what is left over after coastal States have taken their share."[501] Because most of the OCS claims have yet to be resolved, "the boundary between national jurisdiction and the international seabed Area still remains largely undefined."[502] This is the source of "a deep-seated underlying tension that continues to exist at the heart of UNCLOS. This tension lies between the delineation of the continental shelf beyond 200 nautical miles under Article 76 of UNCLOS and the delineation of the extent of the Area as defined in Article 1(1)."[503] At a minimum, the Deep Seabed (highlighted in orange in the following graphic) covers more than 50% of the Earth's surface,[504] and ranges from 20,000 to almost 36,000 feet deep (in the Marianas Trench off the coast of Guam). The Deep Seabed is truly the bottom of the ocean.[505] [NOTE: the apparent "holes" in the Deep Seabed represent the Continental Shelves of islands, such as the island of Bermuda off the east coast of the U.S.]

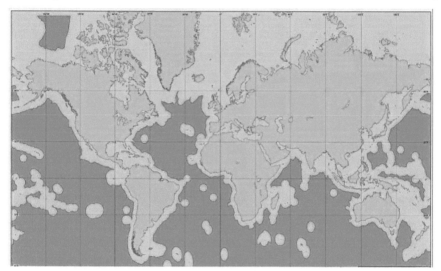

As discussed earlier in this Chapter, Coastal States are required to make international royalty payments to "the Authority" on any non-living resources they mine or exploit on the Outer Continental Shelf.

As a quid pro quo *for the reduction by some thirty million square kilometers of the geographical extent of the Area caused by the recognition of national jurisdiction over the continental margin beyond 200 nautical miles, the broad-shelf States had to agree to a system of revenue sharing between coastal States and the international community in respect of the exploitation of non-living resources of the extended continental shelf. This compromise is enshrined in Article 82 of UNCLOS..*
***

A formula for sharing revenue specifically derived from the shelf beyond 200 nautical miles was originally proposed at the second session of UNCLOS III in 1974. The United States suggested it as "a way to

Article 156 established "The Authority" as the "International Seabed Authority" (ISA), which has its headquarters in Kingston, the capital of Jamaica.[507] The ISA is charged with "organiz[ing] and control[ling] activities in the Area, particularly with a view to administering the resources of the Area."[508] Unlike Coastal State-owned resources on the Continental Shelf (which include mineral and non-living resources, and sedentary species), "resources" in "the Area" (i.e., the Deep Seabed) controlled by the ISA only include minerals. Thus, non-living resources and sedentary species found on the Deep Seabed are beyond the purview of the ISA, and are generally available to all States to explore and exploit as a High Seas freedom.[509] It is estimated that the Deep Seabed "contain[s] more valuable minerals than all the continents combined."[510]

Although "minerals" are not defined by UNCLOS, "[t]hose resources are all solid, liquid or gaseous mineral resources on or under the seabed."[511] Thus, they would include hydrocarbons (i.e.,

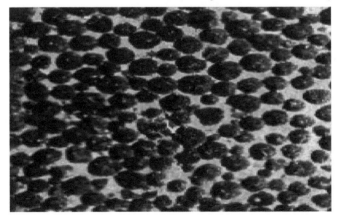

oil and gas), and metals (e.g., iron, manganese, cobalt). Article 133 specifically includes "polymetallic nodules" in its definition of resources controlled by the ISA in the Area. Manganese nodules are poly-metallic rocks (i.e., they contain many metals), with up to 30% manganese, 20% iron, and a variety of other metals including nickel, copper, cobalt, and aluminum. Manganese nodules vary from ¼ inch to 10 inches (.5 to 25 centimeters) in diameter, and were first found by the HMS Challenger scientific expedition in 1873.[512] If we cut Manganese nodules in half and look at their cross-sections, they often show concentric layers or growth rings around a core, just like the rings of a tree. Manganese nodules are thought

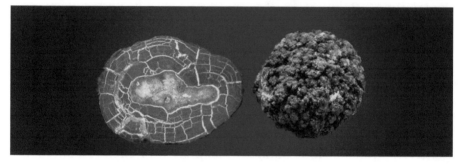

to precipitate from seawater as a result of chemical reactions, with the possible involvement of bacteria. The growth rate of manganese nodules is very slow—nodules in the Pacific Ocean are estimated to be 2-3 million years old.

Manganese nodules form in the deep ocean (4,000-6,000 meters), particularly in the Pacific where they cover 30-50% of the seafloor. Nevertheless, it is estimated that there are only 3-10 sites with a sizeable quantity of "good nodules" with sufficiently high concentrations of nickel, copper, manganese and cobalt to be worth collecting or "mining." Manganese is used to strengthen steel, and in batteries. In fact, scientists theorize that the ability to effectively mine manganese nodules would assist in the transition from fossil fuels to battery power (e.g., used in electric and hybrid vehicles).[513]

The ISA controls mining for manganese nodules, and all other minerals in "the Area" (i.e., the Deep Seabed) for the benefit of all

mankind. UNCLOS repeats that the mineral resources on the Deep Seabed (and related rights, such as Marine Scientific Research (MSR), discussed in Chapter 7) are the common heritage of mankind 14 times(!),[514] including in Article 136:

Article 136 / Common heritage of mankind
The Area and its resources are the common heritage of mankind.[515]

Sharing in the resources of the Deep Seabed was obviously very important to the Group of 77 Developing States who participated in negotiating the text of UNCLOS at the Third Conference on the Law of the Sea! The Group of 77 also convinced other State Parties to include a provision for the transfer of Deep Seabed mining technology to developing States.[516] However, as this technology transfer provision was one of the primary U.S. concerns

Group of 77 members and participants as of 2013. Note that China "participates" with the G-77 but is not a member.

about ratifying UNCLOS, the 1994 Implementing Agreement (aka Part XI Agreement) softened this provision by indicating that "developing States wishing to obtain deep seabed mining technology, shall seek to obtain such technology on fair and reasonable commercial terms and conditions on the open market, or through joint-venture arrangements" in order to protect intellectual property rights.[517] The 1994 Implementing Agreement also negated the mandatory technology transfer provisions contained in Article 5 of Annex III to UNCLOS, Basic Conditions of Prospecting, Exploration and Exploitation.[518] As discussed in Chapter 2, President Reagan's former Secretary of State George

Shultz confirmed that the 1994 Implementing Agreement adequately addressed all of the American concerns about ratifying UNCLOS.[519] "Significant improvements to the decision-making structure of the Authority ... made it possible for the United States and other industrialized States to have confidence that such rules and regulations will protect their interests."[520] "[T]hese revisions satisfactorily address the objections raised by the United States and other industrialized countries to Part XI."[521]

Just as a Coastal State can protect and preserve the marine environment in its Exclusive Economic Zone (EEZ),[522] the ISA may adopt rules to protect and preserve the marine environment in "the Area" (i.e., on the Deep Seabed).[523] The ISA is attempting to write a comprehensive "Mining Code" for mining operations in "the Area."[524] UNCLOS also includes a special provision for the protection of archaeological objects found on the Deep Seabed (e.g., shipwrecks):

Article 149 / Archaeological and historical objects
All objects of an archaeological and historical nature found in the Area shall be preserved or disposed of for the benefit of mankind as a whole, particular regard being paid to the preferential rights of the State or country of origin, or the State of cultural origin, or the State of historical and archaeological origin.[525]

Thus, while shipwrecks "shall be preserved or disposed of for the benefit of mankind as a whole," **the country of origin** of the ship, or of the cultural objects found onboard **shall have preferential treatment** (e.g., Spain would have preferential rights on the preservation or disposal of a Spanish galleon found on the Deep Seabed, especially if it was full of Spanish gold bullion).[526]

As we have seen, Part XI of UNCLOS details the ISA's rights and responsibilities in controlling activities in "the Area" (i.e., on the Deep Seabed), particularly controlling the exploitation of its mineral resources.[527] Section 3 of Part XI of UNCLOS provides detailed provisions on the development and exploitation of mineral resources on the Deep Seabed (e.g., production policies, production ceilings, quantities of production, etc.),[528] many of which were "scaled down" by the 1994 Implementing Agreement to make them more palatable to the U.S.[529] The ISA has entered into 15-year contracts for mineral exploration with 30 contractors,[530] sixteen of which are for the exploration of manganese nodules in the Clarion-Clipperton Fracture Zone extending from Mexico to Hawaii. Reviewing the list of contractors on the ISA website reveals that there are somewhat surprisingly NO American companies involved![531] This is because each contractor requires a Sponsoring State which is a State Party to UNCLOS,[532] and the U.S. has yet to ratify UNCLOS. American companies may also be unwilling to invest billions of dollars in the research and development of Deep Seabed mining technology, since the legal status of their claims would be on shaky ground, at least until the U.S. accedes to UNCLOS.[533] A 1986 study argued that the metal prices of nickel, copper, cobalt and ferromanganese would have to double before the rate of return on Deep Seabed mining of polymetallic nodules would attract the necessary investment capital for this high-risk venture.[534] However, there is some indication that the companies exploring mining manganese nodules in the Clarion-Clipperton Fracture Zone will transition to "industrial-scale extraction" once the ISA implements its comprehensive "Mining Code."[535]

The environmental impacts of mining minerals in "the Area" (i.e., on the Deep Seabed) are similar to those for mining minerals on a Coastal State's Continental Shelf. The major environmental impact would come from releasing the unwanted sediment that is collected along with the minerals—the sediment plume would then drift on the ocean currents and blanket hundreds of miles of the Deep Seabed, especially if the sediment is discharged near the surface instead of being pumped back down to the Deep Seabed.[536]

Finally, any disputes regarding deep seabed mining are not subject to the mandatory dispute settlement provisions (discussed in Chapter 12), but are referred to the Seabed Disputes Chamber of the International Tribunal for the Law of the Sea (ITLOS).[537]

In summary, **the Coastal State owns extensive mineral and non-living resources, and sedentary species on the Continental Shelf**. Similarly, **the ISA controls** the exploration, and production of **mineral resources on the Deep Seabed**, but **for the benefit of all mankind**.

---

[446] Elliot L. Richardson, Power, Mobility and the Law of the Sea, J. FOREIGN AFF., 902, 903 (1980). *See also* Michael W. Lodge (Secretary-General of the International Seabed Authority), Enclosure of the Oceans versus the Common Heritage of Mankind: The Inherent Tension between the Continental Shelf Beyond 200 Nautical Miles and the Area, 97 INT'L. L. STUD. 803, 831 (2021), https://digital-commons.usnwc.edu/cgi/viewcontent.cgi?article=2971&context=ils (noting that "[i]n many ways, the history of the law of the sea, starting with the unintended and ill-thought-out consequences of the Truman Declaration, has been one of an erosion of the doctrine of the freedom and commonality of the sea towards enclosure. This is perhaps ironic given that the original impetus for UNCLOS came from those nations interested in preserving freedom of navigation against the creeping jurisdiction of other States.").

[447] Truman Proclamation No. 2667, 10 Fed. Reg. 12,305, codified as Executive Order 9633 (Sep. 28, 1945), Harry S. Truman Library, Executive Order 9633, https://www.trumanlibrary.gov/library/executive-orders/9633/executive-order-9633.

[448] DONALD R. ROTHWELL & TIM STEPHENS, THE INT'L. LAW OF THE SEA 105 & 114 (2nd ed. 2016). In 1945 when President Truman issued Proclamation 2667 claiming a U.S. Continental Shelf, only the scientific continental shelf existed, since it preceded both the 1958 Convention on the Continental Shelf (which failed to define its outer limits), and the 1982 UNCLOS. ROTHWELL & STEPHENS, LAW OF THE SEA, p. 8 (full cite above). The White House Press Release that accompanied President Truman's Proclamation provided that: "Generally, submerged land which is contiguous to the continent and which is covered by no more than 100 fathoms (600 feet) of water is considered as the continental shelf." *See also* Helmut Türk, *Questions Relating to the Continental Shelf Beyond 200 Nautical Miles: Delimitation, Delineation, and Revenue Sharing*, 97 INT'L. L. STUD. 231, 237 (2021), https://digital-

commons.usnwc.edu/ils/vol97/iss1/18/ (noting that before UNCLOS was negotiated, the term Continental Shelf referred to the scientific continental shelf).

[449] United Nations Convention on the Law of the Sea (UNCLOS) Preamble unnumbered ¶ 7 & arts. 125(1), 136, 137(2), 140(1), 143(1), 149, 150(i), 153(1), 155(1)(a), 155(2), 246(3), 311(6) & 1994 Implementing Agreement Preamble ¶ 2, Dec. 10, 1982, 1833 U.N.T.S. 397, https://www.un.org/Depts/los/convention_agreements/convention_overview_convention.htm; THE FLETCHER SCHOOL OF LAW AND DIPLOMACY—TUFTS UNIVERSITY, LAW OF THE SEA, A POLICY PRIMER 8 (2017), https://sites.tufts.edu/lawofthesea/introduction/.

[450] Tullio Treves, Introductory Note to the United Nations Convention on the Law of the Sea, AUDIOVISUAL LIBRARY OF INT'L. LAW, http://legal.un.org/avl/ha/uncls/uncls.html.

[451] G.A. Res. 2750 (XXV), ¶ C.2, U.N. Doc A/AC.138/58 (Dec. 17, 1970), https://research.un.org/en/docs/ga/quick/regular/25. The UN General Assembly debates and passes an annual omnibus resolution on oceans and the law of the sea. United Nations, Departments, Law of the Sea, Oceans and the Law of the Sea in the General Assembly of the United Nations, General Assembly resolutions and decisions, https://www.un.org/Depts/los/general_assembly/general_assembly_resolutions.htm.

[452] UNCLOS, art. 76(1) (full cite above).

[453] Letter Of Transmittal Forwarding The 1982 UN Law Of The Sea Convention To The United States Senate, DOS Commentary p. 52 (William J. Clinton, Oct. 7, 1994) (S. Treaty Doc. 103–39), https://www.foreign.senate.gov/imo/media/doc/treaty_103-39.pdf.

[454] See Türk, Questions Relating to the Continental Shelf Beyond 200 Nautical Miles, pp. 233, 236 (full cite above) (noting that the ICJ's decision in the 1969 North Sea Continental Shelf Case used the term "natural prolongation" in referring to the Continental Shelf (as did the 1945 Truman Proclamation), which States "equated ... with the notion of the continental margin, that is, the geophysical shelf, the slope, and the rise, a view that would later find its way into UNCLOS.").

[455] Türk, Questions Relating to the Continental Shelf Beyond 200 Nautical Miles, p. 236 (full cite above).

[456] United Nations, Oceans & Law of the Sea, Division for Ocean Affairs and the Law of the Sea, The Nippon Foundation of Japan Fellowship Programme ~ Human Resources Development and Advancement of the Legal Order of the World's Oceans ~, The Fellows and their Thesis [sic], Reports, Overlapping Claims for an Extended Continental Shelf in the Northeastern Part of South America Facing the Atlantic Ocean 2, footnote 2 (Raul Curiel, 2010), https://www.un.org/depts/los/nippon/unnff_programme_home/fellows_pages/reports_index.htm.

[457] ROTHWELL & STEPHENS, LAW OF THE SEA, pp. 102 & 112 (full cite above).

[458] UNCLOS, art. 76(1) (full cite above); U.S. NAVY, MARINE CORPS & COAST GUARD, THE COMMANDER'S HANDBOOK ON THE LAW OF NAVAL OPERATIONS, NWP 1-14M/MCTP 11-10B/COMDTPUB P5800.7A, ¶ 1.7 (p. 1-10) (2017), www.jag.navy.mil/distrib/instructions/CDRs_HB_on_Law_of_Naval_Operations_AUG17.pdf.

[459] One esteemed author (a former ITLOS judge, President of the Assembly of the International Seabed Authority, and Austrian delegate to the 3rd UNCLOS conference)

clarifies that "there is in law only a single continental shelf rather than an inner shelf and a separate or outer continental shelf." Helmut Türk, *Questions Relating to the Continental Shelf Beyond 200 Nautical Miles: Delimitation, Delineation, and Revenue Sharing*, 97 INT'L. L. STUD. 231, 233 (2021), https://digital-commons.usnwc.edu/ils/vol97/iss1/18/ (citing arbitral tribunal and ITLOS decisions, as well as Articles 76 and 83 of UNCLOS). *But see* Türk, *Questions Relating to the Continental Shelf Beyond 200 Nautical Miles*, p. 233 (full cite above), (noting that although legally there is only a single Continental Shelf, the Coastal State's legal *obligations* differ on the regular Continental Shelf versus the Outer Continental Shelf). To most readers, this may seem like a distinction without a difference.

[460] DONALD R. ROTHWELL & TIM STEPHENS, THE INT'L. LAW OF THE SEA 113 (2nd ed. 2016).

[461] Türk, *Questions Relating to the Continental Shelf Beyond 200 Nautical Miles*, p. 237 (full cite above); THE FLETCHER SCHOOL OF LAW AND DIPLOMACY—TUFTS UNIVERSITY, LAW OF THE SEA, A POLICY PRIMER 13 (2017), https://sites.tufts.edu/lawofthesea/introduction/. *See generally* United Nations, Oceans & Law of the Sea, Division for Ocean Affairs and the Law of the Sea, The Nippon Foundation of Japan Fellowship Programme ~ Human Resources Development and Advancement of the Legal Order of the World's Oceans ~, The Fellows and their Thesis [sic], Reports, *A Practical Overview of Article 76 of the United Nations Convention on the Law of the Sea* (Sharveen Persand, 2005), https://www.un.org/depts/los/nippon/unnff_programme_home/fellows_pages/reports_index.htm. The two different formulas obviously can result in different claims. The Diplomat, Flashpoints, Security, Southeast Asia, *Malaysia's New Game in the South China Sea* (Nguyen Hong Thao, Dec. 21, 2019), https://thediplomat.com/2019/12/malaysias-new-game-in-the-south-china-sea/ (noting the divergence between Vietnam's and Malaysia's Outer Continental Shelf claims, owing to their choice of formulas). *See also* Türk, *Questions Relating to the Continental Shelf Beyond 200 Nautical Miles*, p. 238 (full cite above) (noting that "[e]xperience has shown that the application of the two specific formulae contained in Article 76 for determining the outer edge of the continental margin is an often quite complicated, cost-intensive process requiring a high level of expert knowledge, a process that in some cases may take many years. ... there are inherent difficulties in determining the thickness of sedimentary rocks and the foot of the continental slope. ... Article 76 reflect[ed] the state of scientific knowledge at the time of its elaboration and that subsequently gaps in that Article have been identified that introduce 'a measure of subjectivity' into the process of the determination of the outer limit of the continental shelf. The outer edge of the continental margin may thus not always be as readily determined as had been contended at the Conference by some of the proponents of these two formulae. The author of the Irish formula, Tony Gardiner, repeatedly tried to convince delegates ... that the practical application of his proposal would not cause particular difficulties.").

[462] United Nations Convention on the Law of the Sea (UNCLOS) arts. 76(5)-(6), Dec. 10, 1982, 1833 U.N.T.S. 397, https://www.un.org/Depts/los/convention_agreements/convention_overview_convention.htm; U.S. NAVY, MARINE CORPS & COAST GUARD, THE COMMANDER'S HANDBOOK ON THE LAW OF NAVAL OPERATIONS, NWP 1-14M/MCTP 11-10B/COMDTPUB P5800.7A, ¶ 1.7 (p. 1-10) (2017), www.jag.navy.mil/distrib/instructions/CDRs_HB_on_Law_of_Naval_Operations

_AUG17.pdf; ROTHWELL & STEPHENS, LAW OF THE SEA, p. 115 (full cite above). *But see* Letter Of Transmittal Forwarding The 1982 UN Law Of The Sea Convention To The United States Senate, DOS Commentary p. 56 (William J. Clinton, Oct. 7, 1994) (S. Treaty Doc. 103–39), https://www.foreign.senate.gov/imo/media/doc/treaty_103-39.pdf (noting that "the outer limit of the continental shelf shall not exceed 350 miles from the coast on submarine ridges, provided that this limitation on the use of either alternative limit set forth in paragraph 5 does not apply 'to submarine elevations that are natural components of the continental margin, such as its plateaux, rises, caps, banks and spurs' (paragraph 6). The United States understands that features such as the Chukchi plateau and its component elevations, situated to the north of Alaska, are covered by this exemption, and thus not subject to the 350 mile limitation set forth in paragraph 6. Because of the potential for significant oil and gas reserves in the Chukchi plateau, it is important to recall the U.S. statement made to this effect on April 3, 1980 during a Plenary session of the Third United Nations Conference on the Law of the Sea....").

[463] United Nations, Division for Ocean Affairs and the Law of the Sea, Commission on the Limits of the Continental Shelf (CLCS), https://www.un.org/Depts/los/clcs_new/clcs_home.htm.

[464] Türk, *Questions Relating to the Continental Shelf Beyond 200 Nautical Miles*, pp. 245-246 (full cite above). *See also* DOS Commentary, pp. 56-57 (full cite above) (noting that "Coastal States with continental shelves extending beyond 200 miles are to provide information on those limits to the Commission on the Limits of the Continental Shelf, an expert body established· by Annex II to the Convention. The Commission is to make recommendations to coastal States on these limits. The coastal State is not bound to accept these recommendations, but if it does, the limits of the continental shelf established by a coastal State on the basis of these recommendations are final and binding on all States Parties to the Convention and on the International Seabed Authority.... thus providing stability to these claims which may not be contested.").

[465] United Nations, Division for Ocean Affairs and the Law of the Sea, Commission on the Limits of the Continental Shelf (CLCS), Submissions, through the Secretary-General of the United Nations, to the Commission on the Limits of the Continental Shelf, pursuant to article 76, paragraph 8, of the United Nations Convention on the Law of the Sea of 10 December 1982, https://www.un.org/Depts/los/clcs_new/commission_submissions.htm; ROTHWELL & STEPHENS, LAW OF THE SEA, p. 103 (full cite above). "At the [3rd UNCLOS] Conference, the negotiators were led to believe that no more than thirty to thirty-five States would be able to claim an entitlement to a continental shelf beyond 200 nautical miles. ... It has been estimated that the total number of submissions by coastal States will approach 120." Türk, *Questions Relating to the Continental Shelf Beyond 200 Nautical Miles*, pp. 248-249 (full cite above). *See also* DOS Commentary, p. 52 (full cite above) (noting that "Only a limited number of coastal States, including the United States, have significant areas of adjacent continental margin that extend beyond 200 miles from the coast. Many States preferred a universal limit at 200 miles for all."); DOS Commentary (full cite above), p. 56 (noting that "For the United States, the continental shelf extends beyond 200 miles in a variety of areas, including notably the Atlantic coast, the Gulf of Mexico, the Bering Sea and the Arctic Ocean. Other States with broad margins include Argentina, Australia, Brazil, Canada, Iceland, India, Ireland, Madagascar, Mexico, New Zealand, Norway, the Russian Federation and the United Kingdom.").

466 United Nations, Division for Ocean Affairs and the Law of the Sea, Commission on the Limits of the Continental Shelf (CLCS), Submissions, through the Secretary-General of the United Nations, to the Commission on the Limits of the Continental Shelf, pursuant to article 76, paragraph 8, of the United Nations Convention on the Law of the Sea of 10 December 1982, https://www.un.org/Depts/los/clcs_new/commission_submissions.htm; Michael W. Lodge (Secretary-General of the International Seabed Authority), *Enclosure of the Oceans versus the Common Heritage of Mankind: The Inherent Tension between the Continental Shelf Beyond 200 Nautical Miles and the Area,* 97 INT'L. L. STUD. 803, 810-811 (2021), https://digital-commons.usnwc.edu/cgi/viewcontent.cgi?article=2971&context=ils (noting that "[t]hese nine States are Australia, Croatia, France (concerning Martinique, Guadeloupe, Guyana, La Reunion, New Caledonia, St Paul and Amsterdam, and the Kerguelen islands), Ireland, Mauritius, Mexico, Niue, Pakistan, and the Philippines.").

467 Helmut Türk, *Questions Relating to the Continental Shelf Beyond 200 Nautical Miles: Delimitation, Delineation, and Revenue Sharing,* 97 INT'L. L. STUD. 231, 250 (2021), https://digital-commons.usnwc.edu/ils/vol97/iss1/18/. *See also* Lodge, *Enclosure of the Oceans,* pp. 809-810 (full cite above) (noting that "the slow progress in the work of the CLCS ... is caused by two main factors. First, during UNCLOS III, it was estimated that no more than thirty-five States would be able to claim an entitlement to a[n extended] continental shelf .... This was a significant underestimate. As of March 31, 2020, the CLCS had received a total of ninety-two submissions, including seven revised submissions, from seventy-one States parties.... With at least forty-six submissions left to be considered, the work of the CLCS could well continue to the middle of the century. Second, and related to the first, is the fact that the UNCLOS negotiators, since they did not foresee the large number of submissions, did not make adequate provision for the work of the CLCS. Unlike ITLOS and ISA, which were established as permanent institutions with autonomous budgets and appropriate governance structures, the CLCS was established as a body of experts to be elected by the States parties every five years .... Membership in the CLCS is not a full-time job, and members are expected to combine frequent and lengthy meetings of the CLCS in New York with their regular professional commitments. The CLCS has no budget and the States parties that nominated the members have the responsibility to defray the expenses of those members while in performance of CLCS duties.... A further exacerbating factor, as reported by the current chair of the CLCS is that 'improvements in science and technology, coupled with deeper knowledge of continental shelf areas, has increased the complexity of submissions, requiring more time and analysis by the Commission.'").

468 THE FLETCHER SCHOOL OF LAW AND DIPLOMACY—TUFTS UNIVERSITY, LAW OF THE SEA, A POLICY PRIMER 61-62 (2017), https://sites.tufts.edu/lawofthesea/introduction/.

469 Türk, *Questions Relating to the Continental Shelf Beyond 200 Nautical Miles,* p. 251 (full cite above).

470 Joint Chiefs of Staff, Media, Speeches, https://www.jcs.mil/Media/Speeches/Article/571928/sec-panetta-and-gen-dempseys-remarks-at-the-forum-on-the-law-of-the-sea-convent/. *See also* U.S. Dept. of State, Office of Ocean and Polar Affairs, U.S. Extended Continental Shelf Project, https://www.state.gov/u-s-extended-continental-shelf-project/; Lodge, *Enclosure of the Oceans,* p. 823 (full cite above) (noting that "[e]ven the United States,

182

although not a party to UNCLOS, has agreed with this position. This implies that any areas of the seabed beyond national jurisdiction in the Arctic Ocean would be considered part of the Area and subject to the legal regime set out in Part XI of UNCLOS and the 1994 Agreement, as well as the rules, regulations, and procedures of the ISA concerning mineral exploration and exploitation. How much of the seabed of the Arctic Ocean lies beyond national juris-diction remains to be seen. All five Arctic coastal States (Canada, Denmark, Norway, the Russian Federation, and the United States) assert entitlements to continental shelves in the Arctic Ocean extending beyond 200 nautical miles. Submissions to the CLCS by Canada, Denmark, Norway, and the Russian Federation are in various stages of consideration, and no State has yet established final and binding outer limits. The United States has gathered technical data to substantiate its entitlement to a continental shelf but, as a non-party, has not made a submission to the CLCS.... All parties have committed to the orderly settlement of these claims on the basis of the Ilulissat Declaration, which recognizes that UNCLOS provides the legal framework delineating the outer limits of the continental shelf in the Arctic. The prevailing view, based on all published sources, is that there will be two small areas of seabed remaining beyond national jurisdiction that will form part of the Area."). Part of the concern that the U.S. is the only Arctic nation that is not a party to UNCLOS, and that UNCLOS "is the only means for international recognition and acceptance of our extended continental shelf claims in the Arctic," is that an estimated "16-26% of the Earth's undiscovered [oil and natural gas] reserves" are believed to lie beneath the Arctic. BBC Future, *Why Russia is sending robotic submarines to the Arctic* (David Hambling, Nov. 21, 2017), https://www.bbc.com/future/article/20171121-why-russia-is-sending-robotic-submarines-to-the-arctic.

[471] Although the U.S. is not yet party to UNCLOS, it routinely participates as an observer at meetings of UNCLOS State Parties. *See, e.g.,* CarrieLyn D. Guymon (editor), DIGEST OF UNITED STATES PRACTICE IN INTERNATIONAL LAW 419 (2019), https://www.state.gov/digest-of-united-states-practice-in-international-law-2019.

[472] "There is the further question of those States that are not or not yet parties to UNCLOS and might also have claims to continental shelf entitlements beyond 200 nautical miles. It would seem that nothing prohibits these States from making a submission to the CLCS. It would then be up to it, as an autonomous body, to decide whether to consider the submission. ... [S]hould a non-party file a submission with the CLCS, it might be wise for the Commission to consider it and appropriately apprise the Meeting of States Parties of the submission. In any case, if a non-party wishes to engage in such a course of action, it would not make sense from the point of view of the interests of the international community to prevent that State from doing so. It would also seem reasonable that in such a case the non-party would be asked to defray the costs of processing its application, the amount to be determined by the Meeting of States Parties." Türk, *Questions Relating to the Continental Shelf Beyond 200 Nautical Miles,* p. 249 (full cite above).

[473] Lodge, *Enclosure of the Oceans,* pp. 811–812 (full cite above).

[474] *See e.g.,* Türk, *Questions Relating to the Continental Shelf Beyond 200 Nautical Miles,* pp. 238–239 (full cite above) (noting that the ICJ held in the 2012 *Nicaragua v. Colombia* judgment that it considers Article 76(1) as Customary International Law (CIL), and that "[t]here are good arguments to support paragraphs 2–7 of the Article, which provide the detailed rules that implement the continental margin criterion of paragraph 1, also being part of customary law" .... It can thus be

concluded that the applicable law for determining the spatial extent of the continental shelf is the same for all coastal States, whether they are a party to UNCLOS or not."). *See also* Bjarni Már Magnússon, *Can the United States Establish the Outer Limits of Its Extended Continental Shelf Under International Law?*, 78 J. OF OCEAN DEV. & INT'L. LAW 1 (2017), https://www.tandfonline.com/doi/abs/10.1080/00908320.2017.1265361; THE FLETCHER SCHOOL OF LAW AND DIPLOMACY—TUFTS UNIVERSITY, LAW OF THE SEA, A POLICY PRIMER 84 (2017), https://sites.tufts.edu/lawofthesea/introduction/; The Heritage Foundation, Report Europe, Ariel Cohen, *From Russian Competition to Natural Resources Access: Recasting U.S. Arctic Policy* (2010), https://www.heritage.org/europe/report/russian-competition-natural-resources-access-recasting-us-arctic-policy; The Heritage Foundation, Backgrounder, Steven Groves, *U.S. Accession to U.N. Convention on the Law of the Sea Unnecessary to Develop Oil and Gas Resources* (2012), https://www.heritage.org/report/us-accession-un-convention-the-law-the-sea-unnecessary-develop-oil-and-gas-resources. Part of the problem is a definitional one, since the U.S. enacted "The Outer Continental Shelf Lands Act (OCSLA)[, which] defines the outer continental shelf as any and all submerged lands lying beyond state coastal waters, greater than three miles offshore, which are under United States jurisdiction." This Act codified President Truman's Proclamation 2667 claiming a U.S. Continental Shelf, and clarified when federal or a particular U.S. state's workers' compensation law applies. Schechter, McElwee, Shaffer & Harris, L.L.P., OCSLA Lawyers (Outer Continental Shelf Lands Act), https://maintenanceandcure.com/ocsla-lawyers/; The Ammons Law Firm, OCSLA, https://www.ammonslaw.com/maritime-offshore-injury/outer-continental-shelf-lands-act-ocsla/; 43 U.S. Code §§ 1301(a), 1331(a) (1953), https://www.law.cornell.edu/uscode/text; U.S. Dept. of the Interior, Bureau of Ocean Energy Management, https://www.boem.gov/. Thus, U.S. domestic law conflates the UNCLOS concepts of the Continental Shelf versus the Outer Continental Shelf. Moreover, the U.S. Department of State makes a superficial argument that the U.S. Extended/Outer Continental Shelf claim is based upon Customary International Law. U.S. Dept. of State, Office of Ocean and Polar Affairs, U.S. Extended Continental Shelf Project, Frequently Asked Questions – U.S. Extended Continental Shelf Project, https://www.state.gov/frequently-asked-questions-u-s-extended-continental-shelf-project/. *See also* Int'l. Court of Justice (ICJ), *Territorial and Maritime Dispute (Nicaragua v. Colombia)*, Judgment of November 19th, 2012, 2012 I.C.J. Reports 624, 666 (¶¶ 114-118), https://www.icj-cij.org/files/case-related/124/124-20121119-JUD-01-00-EN.pdf (concluding that Art. 76(1) of UNCLOS (setting the default Continental Shelf at 200 nm) represents Customary International Law without any analysis whatsoever!).

[475] Michael W. Lodge (Secretary-General of the International Seabed Authority), *Enclosure of the Oceans versus the Common Heritage of Mankind: The Inherent Tension between the Continental Shelf Beyond 200 Nautical Miles and the Area*, 97 INT'L. L. STUD. 803, 805-806 (2021), https://digital-commons.usnwc.edu/cgi/viewcontent.cgi?article=2971&context=ils (noting that "[t]he International Seabed Authority (ISA) has introduced regulations governing access to mineral resources that had not even been discovered when UNCLOS was negotiated," including cobalt-rich ferromanganese crusts).

[476] DONALD R. ROTHWELL & TIM STEPHENS, THE INT'L. LAW OF THE SEA 131 (2nd ed. 2016).

[477] National Oceanic and Atmospheric Administration (NOAA), U.S. Dept. of Commerce, Ocean Facts, *What is a hydrothermal vent?*, https://oceanservice.noaa.gov/facts/vents.html; National Geographic, Resource Library, Video, *Deep Sea Hydrothermal Vents*, https://www.nationalgeographic.org/media/deep-sea-hydrothermal-vents/; The Atlantic, *History's Largest Mining Operation Is About to Begin* (Wil S. Hylton, January/February 2020), https://www.theatlantic.com/magazine/archive/2020/01/20000-feet-under-the-sea/603040/; Woods Hole Oceanographic Institution, oceanus magazine, *The Discovery of Hydrothermal Vents* (Evan Lubofsky, June 11, 2018), https://www.whoi.edu/oceanus/feature/the-discovery-of-hydrothermal-vents/; Woods Hole Oceanographic Institution, Know Your Ocean, Ocean Topics, Ocean Life, *Life at Vents & Seeps*, https://www.whoi.edu/know-your-ocean/ocean-topics/ocean-life/life-at-vents-seeps/.

[478] Smithsonian, Ocean Find Your Blue, *The Microbes That Keep Hydrothermal Vents Pumping* (Lyndsy Gazda, Mar. 2016), https://ocean.si.edu/ecosystems/deep-sea/microbes-keep-hydrothermal-vents-pumping. Some scientists theorize that life on earth may have originated near hydrothermal vents. Oceana, Protecting the World's Oceans, Marine Science and Ecosystems, *Deep Hydrothermal Vent*, https://oceana.org/marine-life/marine-science-and-ecosystems/deep-hydrothermal-vent; Woods Hole, *The Discovery of Hydrothermal Vents* (full cite above).

[479] Woods Hole Oceanographic Institution, *Hydrothermal Vents*, https://www.whoi.edu/know-your-ocean/ocean-topics/seafloor-below/hydrothermal-vents/.

[480] NOAA, *What is a hydrothermal vent?* (full cite above).

[481] Lodge, *Enclosure of the Oceans*, pp. 805-806 (full cite above) (noting that "[t]he International Seabed Authority (ISA) has introduced regulations governing access to mineral resources that had not even been discovered when UNCLOS was negotiated," including polymetallic sulfides).

[482] ROTHWELL & STEPHENS, LAW OF THE SEA, pp. 130-131 (full cite above). In fact, the giant copper mines found on Cyprus, which have been mined since the 4th millennium B.C. (i.e., beginning of the Bronze Age), were formed by hydrothermal vents millions of years ago. Woods Hole, *Hydrothermal Vents* (full cite above); Chesterfield Resources, *Cyprus Mining History*, https://www.chesterfieldresourcesplc.com/operations/cyprus-mining-history/. Black Smokers appear to be more economically viable because some vents are closer to shore in shallow water and contain very high grades of minerals. Black Smokers can grow up to 30 cm (12 inches) per day and chimneys can reach 40-60 meters high, before they topple over and the process starts all over again. Hydrothermal vents support a variety of organisms, which are 10-100,000 times more plentiful than the surrounding barren seafloor. Bacteria synthesize the chemicals into organic material, which attracts larger and larger animals, including deep sea mega fauna. There is even an "iron-sulfur world" theory by Günter Wächtershäuser (a German chemist turned patent lawyer) that life originated in thermal vents on the Deep Seabed. Space.com, News, Search for Lives, *Earth Life May Have Originated at Deep-Sea Vents* (Garret Fitzpatrick, Jan. 25, 2013), https://www.space.com/19439-origin-life-earth-hydrothermal-vents.html; Astrobiology Magazine, Exploring Origins of Life on Earth & Beyond, Extreme Life, Jailhouse Rock, *Metal cells may have*

held the chemicals of life's origin captive (Leslie Mullen, Jan. 16, 2003), https://www.astrobio.net/extreme-life/jailhouse-rock/.

[483] Wikimedia Commons, *Distribution of hydrothermal vent fields* (DeDuijn, Mar. 12, 2016), https://commons.wikimedia.org/w/index.php?curid=47480973; InterRidge Vents Database Ver. 3.34, Vent Fields, http://vents-data.interridge.org/.

[484] 16 U.S. Code § 1802(7), https://www.law.cornell.edu/uscode/text. *See also* Letter Of Transmittal Forwarding The 1982 UN Law Of The Sea Convention To The United States Senate, DOS Commentary p. 46 (William J. Clinton, Oct. 7, 1994) (S. Treaty Doc. 103–39), https://www.foreign.senate.gov/imo/media/doc/treaty_103-39.pdf.

[485] "The rights of the coastal State over the continental shelf do not affect the legal status of the superjacent waters or of the air space above those waters." United Nations Convention on the Law of the Sea (UNCLOS) art. 78(1), Dec. 10, 1982, 1833 U.N.T.S. 397, https://www.un.org/Depts/los/convention_agreements/convention_overview_convention.htm. Thus, the waters above a Coastal State's Outer Continental Shelf (which would be, by definition, beyond the Coastal State's 200 nm EEZ) would still be considered High Seas, and the air above would still be International Airspace.

[486] UNCLOS, art. 82 (full cite above). Article 82 provides that the first five years of production at a particular site on the Outer Continental Shelf are royalty-free. International royalty payments are first due at the end of the 6th year of production starting at 1% of either the value of production or volume of annual production, if paying in kind (i.e., in resources instead of with money), and then increase by an additional 1% each year up until the 12th year, when the international royalty payments plateau at 7% of either the value or volume of annual production. "With the benefit of hindsight, the five-year grace period thought to be a reasonable time during which the operator would be able to recover development costs is probably somewhat too short given the enormous financial outlay required for deep-sea mining in great depths." Helmut Türk, *Questions Relating to the Continental Shelf Beyond 200 Nautical Miles: Delimitation, Delineation, and Revenue Sharing*, 97 INT'L. L. STUD. 231, 253 (2021), https://digital-commons.usnwc.edu/ils/vol97/iss1/18/. However, as the author heard one mining company representative testify at a Senate hearing on UNCLOS, "99% of a lot is better than 100% of nothing," which may be all a U.S. company would get without UNCLOS. For example, with an estimated "16-26% of the Earth's undiscovered [oil and natural gas] reserves" believed to lie beneath the Arctic, U.S. petroleum companies would prefer to get 99% of that revenue (from drilling on the U.S. Outer/Extended Continental Shelf, rather than "100% of nothing." BBC Future, *Why Russia is sending robotic submarines to the Arctic* (David Hambling, Nov. 21, 2017), https://www.bbc.com/future/article/20171121-why-russia-is-sending-robotic-submarines-to-the-arctic. DONALD R. ROTHWELL & TIM STEPHENS, THE INT'L. LAW OF THE SEA 124 (2nd ed. 2016). This Chapter subsequently discusses the Deep Seabed in more depth. *See also* Michael W. Lodge (Secretary-General of the International Seabed Authority), *Enclosure of the Oceans versus the Common Heritage of Mankind: The Inherent Tension between the Continental Shelf Beyond 200 Nautical Miles and the Area*, 97 INT'L. L. STUD. 803, 807, 826–830 (2021), https://digital-commons.usnwc.edu/cgi/viewcontent.cgi?article=2971&context=ils (noting that Article 82's revenue-sharing provisions have yet to be implemented by the ISA); DOS Commentary, p. 52 (full cite above) (noting that "The Convention balances the extension of coastal State control over the natural resources of the continental margin seaward of 200 miles with a modest obligation to share revenues

from successful minerals development seaward of 200 miles. The potential economic benefits of these resources to the coastal State greatly exceed any limited revenue sharing that may occur in the future."); DOS Commentary, p. 58 (full cite above) ("The requisite payments are a small percentage of the value of the resources extracted at the site. That value is itself a small percentage of the total economic benefits derived by the coastal State from offshore resources development.").

[487] DOS Commentary, pp. 30-31 (full cite above).

[488] For example, Hibernia Atlantic – a trans-Atlantic submarine cable network company – voiced its support for accession to UNCLOS in a letter to the Senate in October 2007.

[489] UNCLOS, arts. 79(3) & (5) (full cite above). ROTHWELL & STEPHENS, LAW OF THE SEA, p. 125 (full cite above).

[490] Türk, *Questions Relating to the Continental Shelf Beyond 200 Nautical Miles*, p. 235 (full cite above).

[491] Truman Proclamation No. 2667, 10 Fed. Reg. 12,305, codified as Executive Order 9633 (Sep. 28, 1945), Harry S. Truman Library, Executive Order 9633, https://www.trumanlibrary.gov/library/executive-orders/9633/executive-order-9633.

[492] United Nations Treaty Collection, Depositary, Status of Treaties, Chapter XXI Law of the Sea, 4. Convention on the Continental Shelf, https://treaties.un.org/Pages/ViewDetails.aspx?src=TREATY&mtdsg_no=XXI-4&chapter=21&clang=_en. The 1958 Convention on the Continental Shelf entered into force on June 10, 1964. United Nations Convention on the Continental Shelf, Apr. 29, 1958, 499 U.N.T.S. 311, http://legal.un.org/diplomaticconferences/1958_los/. States which are party to both the 1958 law of the sea conventions and the 1982 United Nations Convention on the Law of the Sea (UNCLOS) are bound by the latter. UNCLOS, art. 311 (full cite above). However, since the U.S. is not yet party to UNCLOS, the provisions of the 1958 law of the sea conventions (to which the U.S. is a party) still apply to the U.S.

[493] Ronald Reagan Presidential Library & Museum, Statement on United States Ocean Policy (Mar. 10, 1983), https://www.reaganlibrary.gov/research/speeches/31083c; U.S. NAVY, MARINE CORPS & COAST GUARD, THE COMMANDER'S HANDBOOK ON THE LAW OF NAVAL OPERATIONS, NWP 1-14M/MCTP 11-10B/COMDTPUB P5800.7A, ¶ 2.8 (p. 2-15) (2017), www.jag.navy.mil/distrib/instructions/CDRs_HB_on_Law_of_Naval_Operations_AUG17.pdf. *See also* U.S. Dept. of Defense, Under Secretary of Defense for Policy, OUSDP Offices, FON, DoD Annual Freedom of Navigation (FON) Reports, *Freedom of Navigation: FY 2020 Operational Assertions*, p. 2, https://policy.defense.gov/OUSDP-Offices/FON/ ("International law as reflected in the 1982 Law of the Sea Convention recognizes the rights and freedoms of all nations to engage in traditional uses of the sea. These rights and freedoms are deliberately balanced against coastal States' control over maritime activities. As a nation with both a vast coastline and a significant maritime presence, the United States is committed to preserving this legal balance as an essential part of the stable, rules-based international order.").

[494] United States Senate Committee on Foreign Relations (SFRC), Chairman's Press, *"24 Star" Military Witnesses Voice Strong Support for Law of the Sea Treaty* (June 14, 2012), https://www.foreign.senate.gov/press/chair/release/24-star-military-witnesses-voice-strong-support-for-law-of-the-sea-treaty (quoting then SFRC-Chairman John Kerry as stating "There's a reason every living Chief of Naval Operations supports U.S. accession to the Law of the Sea.... They know the United

States needs the Treaty's 'navigational bill of rights' for worldwide access to get our troops to the fight, to sustain them during the fight, and to get back home without the permission of other countries.").

[495] U.S. Navy, Marine Corps & Coast Guard, The Commander's Handbook on the Law of Naval Operations, NWP 1-14M/MCTP 11-10B/COMDTPUB P5800.7A, ¶ 1.2 (p. 1-1)   (2017), www.jag.navy.mil/distrib/instructions/CDRs_HB_on_Law_of_Naval_Operations_AUG17.pdf; The Fletcher School of Law and Diplomacy—Tufts University, Law of the Sea, A Policy Primer 2 (2017), https://sites.tufts.edu/lawofthesea/introduction/. See also U.S. Dept. of Defense, Under Secretary of Defense for Policy, OUSDP Offices, FON, DoD Annual Freedom of Navigation (FON) Reports, Freedom of Navigation: FY 2020 Operational Assertions, p. 1, https://policy.defense.gov/OUSDP-Offices/FON/ (using the mantras "International law as reflected in the 1982 Law of the Sea Convention" and "customary international law as reflected in the Law of the Sea Convention"); CarrieLyn D. Guymon (editor), Digest of United States Practice in International Law 419 (2019), https://www.state.gov/digest-of-united-states-practice-in-international-law-2019 (statement by counselor for legal affairs for the U.S. Mission to the United Nations that "[t]he United States underscores the central importance of international law as reflected in the Law of the Sea Convention").

[496] Newsweek, Tech & Science, Undersea Cables Transport 99 Percent of International Data (Douglas Main, Apr. 2, 2015), https://www.newsweek.com/undersea-cables-transport-99-percent-international-communications-319072.   See   also Builtvisible, Messages in the Deep: The Remarkable Story of the Underwater Internet (Liam   Fisher,   Dani   Mansfield   &   Darren   Kingman,   undated), https://builtvisible.com/messages-in-the-deep/ (providing a detailed summary of submarine cables).

[497] See, e.g., Military.com, Off Duty, History, Operation Ivy Bells (Matthew Carle, 2020), https://www.military.com/history/operation-ivy-bells.html (summarizing the classified operation "Ivy Bells" in the early 1970s that apparently located and attached a listening device to a Soviet submarine cable "carry[ing] secret Soviet communications between military bases."); The National Interest, The Buzz, How a Super-Secret U.S. Navy Submarine Tapped Russia's Underwater Communications Cables (Kyle Mizokami, June 29, 2017), https://nationalinterest.org/blog/the-buzz/how-super-secret-us-navy-submarine-tapped-russias-underwater-21370   (same); Popular Mechanics, Technology, Security, How Secret Underwater Wiretapping Helped End   the   Cold   War   (Matt   Blitz,   Mar.   30,   2017), https://www.popularmechanics.com/technology/security/a25857/operation-ivy-bells-underwater-wiretapping/ (same). See also Center for Strategic & Int'l. Studies (CSIS), Int'l. Security Program, Global Threats and Regional Stability, Contested Seas: Maritime Domain Awareness in Northern Europe, pp. V, 7, 20 (Andrew Metrick & Kathleen H. Hicks, Mar. 28, 2018), https://www.csis.org/programs/international-security-program/global-threats-and-regional-stability/contested-seas (concluding that submarine cables "are an integral part of MDA [Maritime Domain Awareness]," and are threatened by Russia's ability to potentially tap them).

[498] United Nations Convention on the Law of the Sea (UNCLOS) arts. 60 & 80, Dec.   10,   1982,   1833   U.N.T.S.   397, https://www.un.org/Depts/los/convention_agreements/convention_overview_convention.htm.

[499] UNCLOS, art. 81 (full cite above).

[500] Article 135 confirms that the water above the Deep Seabed is still High Seas with all High Seas freedoms, and the air above is still International Airspace.

[501] Michael W. Lodge (Secretary-General of the International Seabed Authority), *Enclosure of the Oceans versus the Common Heritage of Mankind: The Inherent Tension between the Continental Shelf Beyond 200 Nautical Miles and the Area*, 97 INT'L. L. STUD. 803, 813 (2021), https://digital-commons.usnwc.edu/cgi/viewcontent.cgi?article=2971&context=ils.

[502] Helmut Türk, *Questions Relating to the Continental Shelf Beyond 200 Nautical Miles: Delimitation, Delineation, and Revenue Sharing*, 97 INT'L. L. STUD. 231, 251 (2021), https://digital-commons.usnwc.edu/ils/vol97/iss1/18/.

[503] Lodge, *Enclosure of the Oceans*, p. 806 (full cite above).

[504] Türk, *Questions Relating to the Continental Shelf Beyond 200 Nautical Miles*, p. 251 (full cite above). *See also* Letter Of Transmittal Forwarding The 1982 UN Law Of The Sea Convention To The United States Senate, DOS Commentary p. 60 (William J. Clinton, Oct. 7, 1994) (S. Treaty Doc. 103–39), https://www.foreign.senate.gov/imo/media/doc/treaty_103-39.pdf (noting that "[t]he Area ... comprises approximately 60 percent of the seabed.").

[505] For a fascinating visual depiction of marine life, follow the link below and scroll down to 10,924 meters deep to see the "Challenger Deep," which is the deepest part of the Marianas Trench, and the deepest known part of the ocean. Neal.fun, *The Deep Sea* (Neal Agarwal), https://neal.fun/deep-sea/?fbclid=IwAR1PGbjLD-MJjouPfnH3MBuejnqsUExh8NyrQK4l7qKa3XcnNr4f1hKHOiE. *See also* DONALD R. ROTHWELL & TIM STEPHENS, THE INT'L. LAW OF THE SEA 130 (2ⁿᵈ ed. 2016).

[506] Lodge, *Enclosure of the Oceans*, pp. 826-830 (full cite above) (also noting that "UNCLOS provides little guidance as to how Article 82 might be implemented in practice.... The basic idea behind the provision is quite straight-forward. But even a cursory examination of the text shows that it suffers from a lack of precision and raises numerous questions of interpretation. Definitions for key terms, such as 'value,' 'volume,' 'site,' 'payments,' and 'contributions in kind' are lacking. Some of these terms may be understood differently in States with a continental shelf beyond 200 nautical miles. Article 82 has also been characterized as having 'textual ambiguities and process gaps that can be expected to constrain implementation.' It has been suggested that the negotiators at UNCLOS III were hesitant to suggest too much detail in order not to upset a complicated negotiating process. They were also aware they were legislating for an unknown point in time in the future and further believed that some issues were better left for future implementation.... [T]hese difficult issues should not be postponed indefinitely. The fact is that with increased scientific knowledge, we can expect more and more discoveries of non-living resources on the continental shelf, and we can also expect that advances in technology will make exploitation of these resources commercially viable. The interpretation and application of Article 82 raise difficult questions that need to be further considered and resolved.... Nevertheless, States parties have shown reluctance to confront the issues associated with Article 82 head-on.").

[507] Int'l. Seabed Authority (ISA), The Authority-Details, https://www.isa.org.jm/authority-details. The ISA also has Permanent Observer status at the United Nations in New York. Int'l. Seabed Authority, The Authority, https://www.isa.org.jm/authority. *See generally* Letter Of Transmittal Forwarding The 1982 UN Law Of The Sea Convention To The United States Senate, DOS Commentary pp. 61-63 (William J. Clinton, Oct. 7, 1994) (S. Treaty Doc. 103–39),

https://www.foreign.senate.gov/imo/media/doc/treaty_103-39.pdf (discussing the various "organs" of the ISA).

[508] United Nations Convention on the Law of the Sea (UNCLOS) art. 157(1), Dec. 10, 1982, 1833 U.N.T.S. 397, https://www.un.org/Depts/los/convention_agreements/convention_overview_convention.htm.

[509] "[A]rticle 141 declares the Area to be open to use by all States. Only mining activities are subject to regulation by the International Seabed Authority .... Other activities on the deep seabed, including military activities, telecommunications and marine scientific research, may be conducted freely in accordance with principles of the Convention pertaining to the high seas, including the duty to have reasonable regard to other uses." DOS Commentary, p. 61 (full cite above). Even if an activity unrelated to collecting mineral resources has an effect on the Deep Seabed (e.g., deep sea trawling), it is not governed by the ISA, which only has jurisdiction over "activities in the Area." DONALD R. ROTHWELL & TIM STEPHENS, THE INT'L. LAW OF THE SEA 143 (2nd ed. 2016).

[510] The Atlantic, *History's Largest Mining Operation Is About to Begin* (Wil S. Hylton, January/February 2020), https://www.theatlantic.com/magazine/archive/2020/01/20000-feet-under-the-sea/603040/.

[511] DOS Commentary, p. 60 (full cite above).

[512] ROTHWELL & STEPHENS, LAW OF THE SEA, p. 130 (full cite above); ISA, Minerals, Polymetallic Nodules, https://www.isa.org.jm/mineral-resources/55. The Challenger expedition was the primogenitor of modern oceanography. Woods Hole Oceanographic Institution, Dive and Discover Expeditions to the Seafloor, *History of Oceanography*, https://divediscover.whoi.edu/history-of-oceanography/; Emmanuella Doussis, *Marine Scientific Research: Taking Stock and Looking Ahead*, in THE FUTURE OF THE LAW OF THE SEA 87, 87 (Gemma Andreone ed., 2017), https://link.springer.com/book/10.1007/978-3-319-51274-7.

[513] The Atlantic, *History's Largest Mining Operation* (full cite above). *See also* Mining.com, *Mining's Tesla moment: DeepGreen harvests clean metals from the seafloor* (June 5, 2017), https://www.mining.com/web/minings-tesla-moment-deepgreen-harvests-clean-metals-seafloor/ (the battery for each electric car "require[s] 187 pounds of copper, 123 pounds of nickel, and 15 pounds each of manganese and cobalt. On a planet with 1 billion cars, the conversion to electric vehicles would require several times more metal than all existing land-based supplies").

[514] UNCLOS, Preamble unnumbered ¶ 7 & arts. 125(1), 136, 137(2), 140(1), 143(1), 149, 150(i), 153(1), 155(1)(a), 155(2), 246(3), 311(6) & 1994 Implementing Agreement Preamble ¶ 2 (full cite above); THE FLETCHER SCHOOL OF LAW AND DIPLOMACY—TUFTS UNIVERSITY, LAW OF THE SEA, A POLICY PRIMER 8 (2017), https://sites.tufts.edu/lawofthesea/introduction/.

[515] UNCLOS, art. 136 (full cite above). However, the concept that the Deep Seabed is open to use by all States is also an American concept: "Article 136 provides that the Area and its resources are the common heritage of mankind. This principle, reflects the fact that the Area and its resources are beyond the territorial jurisdiction of any nation and are open to use by all in accordance with commonly accepted rules. This principle has its roots in political and legal opinion dating back to the earliest days of the Republic. President John Adams stated that 'the oceans and its treasures are the common property of all men'. With respect to the seabed in particular, President Lyndon Johnson declared that 'we must ensure that the deep

seas and the ocean bottoms are, and remain, the legacy of all human beings.' The United States joined in the adoption, by consensus, of the United Nations General Assembly Resolution 2749 (XXV)(1970), which set forth this principle. The Deep Seabed Hard Mineral Resources Act of 1980 (30 U.S.C. § 1401 et seq.) (DSHMRA) incorporated this principle into U.S. law." DOS Commentary, pp. 60-61 (full cite above). *See also* 30 U.S. Code § 1401(a)(7), https://www.law.cornell.edu/uscode/text (Congress finding that "on December 17, 1970, the United States supported (by affirmative vote) the United Nations General Assembly Resolution 2749 (XXV) declaring inter alia the principle that the mineral resources of the deep seabed are the common heritage of mankind, with the expectation that this principle would be legally defined under the terms of a comprehensive international Law of the Sea Treaty yet to be agreed upon").

[516] UNCLOS, art. 144 (full cite above).

[517] UNCLOS, 1994 Implementing Agreement, Annex Section 5 Transfer of Technology, ¶¶ 1(a)-(b) (full cite above). "Part XI, as modified by the [1994] Agreement, gives specific meaning to the common heritage principle as it applies to the mineral resources of the seabed beyond coastal State jurisdiction. It is worth noting that the Agreement, by restructuring the seabed mining regime along free market lines, endorses the consistent view of the United States that the common heritage principle fully comports with private economic activity in accordance with market principles." DOS Commentary, p. 61 (full cite above).

[518] UNCLOS, Annex III Art. 5 & 1994 Implementing Agreement, Annex Section 5 Transfer of Technology, ¶ 2 (full cite above). The 1994 Implementing Agreement negated other provisions contained in Annex III to UNCLOS (Basic Conditions of Prospecting, Exploration and Exploitation), such as Arts. 6(5), & 7. Thus, the 2 documents should be read together, especially with regard to the Deep Seabed mining provisions. *See also* DOS Commentary, p. 73 (full cite above) (detailing how the 1994 Agreement eliminated the original technology transfer provisions).

[519] *The Law of the Sea Convention (Treaty Doc. 103-39): Hearing Before the Comm. on Foreign Relations, U.S. Senate, 112th Cong.* 12 (May 23, 2012) (prepared statement of Sec. of State Hon. Hillary Rodham Clinton), https://www.govinfo.gov/content/pkg/CHRG-112shrg77375/html/CHRG-112shrg77375.htm (noting that "[t]he United States signed the Agreement on the deep seabed mining provisions in 1994. As George P. Shultz, Secretary of State to President Reagan, said in a letter to Senator Lugar in 2007: 'The treaty has been changed in such a way with respect to the deep sea-beds that it is now acceptable, in my judgment. Under these circumstances, and given the many desirable aspects of the treaty on other grounds, I believe it is time to proceed with ratification.' Indeed, every former Secretary of State since Secretary Shultz, Democrat and Republican alike, has called for the United States to secure and advance our national interests by joining the Convention."). President Reagan's specific concerns about the Deep Seabed mining regime included:

"— Provisions that would actually deter future development of deep seabed mineral resources, when such development should serve the interest of all countries.

— A decision[-]making process that would not give the United States or others a role that fairly reflects and protects their interests.

— Provisions that would allow amendments to enter into force for the United States without its approval. This is clearly incompatible with the United States approach to such treaties.

— Stipulations relating to mandatory transfer of private technology and the possibility of national liberation movements sharing in benefits.

— The absence of assured access for future qualified deep seabed miners to promote the development of these resources." Ronald Reagan Presidential Library & Museum, Statement on United States Actions Concerning the Conference on the Law of the Sea (July 9, 1982), https://www.reaganlibrary.gov/research/speeches/70982b.

[520] Letter Of Transmittal Forwarding The 1982 UN Law Of The Sea Convention To The United States Senate, DOS Commentary p. 63 (William J. Clinton, Oct. 7, 1994) (S. Treaty Doc. 103–39), https://www.foreign.senate.gov/imo/media/doc/treaty_103-39.pdf.

[521] DOS Commentary, p. 75 (full cite above). *See also* DOS Commentary, p. 79 (full cite above) (noting that "the Agreement clearly revises Part XI in a manner that satisfies these criteria. Of particular importance in this context are the elimination of production controls, mandatory technology transfer by operators, the annual U.S. $1,000,000 fee during exploration and the onerous economic rent provisions of Part XI; the provision to U.S. entities of non-discriminatory access to deep seabed mineral resources on terms no less favorable than those provided for registered pioneer investors; the limitations on contract modifications; the restraints imposed on the operation of the Enterprise; and the revisions to the decision-making provisions of Part XI that will allow the United States to protect its interests and those of U.S. citizens.").

[522] United Nations Convention on the Law of the Sea (UNCLOS) art. 56(1)(b)(iii), Dec. 10, 1982, 1833 U.N.T.S. 397, https://www.un.org/Depts/los/convention_agreements/convention_overview_convention.htm. Chapter 7 discusses the Coastal State's duty to conserve natural resources, especially living resources in the EEZ regime. However, there is no similar requirement in the Continental Shelf regime. *Compare* UNCLOS, art. 61(2) (full cite above) ("The coastal State ... shall ensure through proper conservation and management measures that the maintenance of the living resources in the exclusive economic zone is not endangered by over-exploitation.") *with* UNCLOS art. 77(1) ("The coastal State exercises over the continental shelf sovereign rights for the purpose of exploring it and exploiting its natural resources." (i.e., no mention of over-exploitation)). "This is consistent with the theory of the Continental Shelf as a natural prolongation of land territory, [where] there is no general duty to conserve resources." DONALD R. ROTHWELL & TIM STEPHENS, THE INT'L. LAW OF THE SEA 125 (2nd ed. 2016). Thus, arguably, a Coastal State may harvest sedentary species on the Continental Shelf to extinction consistent with UNCLOS!

[523] UNCLOS, art. 145 (full cite above).

[524] Int'l. Seabed Authority (ISA), Legal Authorities, The Mining Code, https://www.isa.org.jm/mining-code. *See also* The Atlantic, *History's Largest Mining Operation Is About to Begin* (Wil S. Hylton, January/February 2020), https://www.theatlantic.com/magazine/archive/2020/01/20000-feet-under-the-sea/603040/. The Coronavirus 2019 (COVID-19) Pandemic delayed negotiations on the ISA's Mining Code. China Dialogue, Ocean, Extractive Industries, *Covid-19 throws seabed mining negotiations off track* (Todd Woody, May 7, 2020), https://chinadialogueocean.net/13685-covid-19-could-throw-seabed-mining-negotiations-off-track/.

525 UNCLOS, art. 149 (full cite above). *See also* UNCLOS, art. 303 (imposing a general duty on State Parties to cooperate in protecting shipwrecks); DOS Commentary, p. 94 (full cite above) (same).

526 Hexapolis, *Treasure hunters come across a very rare Spanish gold coin in a million-dollar worth hoard* (Dattatreya Mandal, July 29, 2015), https://www.hexapolis.com/2015/07/29/treasure-hunters-come-across-a-very-rare-spanish-gold-coin-in-a-million-dollar-worth-hoard/. *See also* UNCLOS, art. 303 (full cite above). *See also* CarrieLyn D. Guymon (editor), DIGEST OF UNITED STATES PRACTICE IN INTERNATIONAL LAW 424 (2019), https://www.state.gov/digest-of-united-states-practice-in-international-law-2019 (noting that the U.S. accepted the Agreement Concerning the Shipwrecked Vessel Royal Mail Ship ("RMS") Titanic, which went into effect on November 18, 2019 and "protect[s] the integrity of the wreck site from unregulated salvage and other activities" and "preserve[s] the wreck site as an international maritime memorial to the men, women, and children who perished aboard the ship"); U.S. Dept. of State, Multilateral Treaties, 2019 Treaties and Agreements, Multilateral (19-1118) – Agreement Concerning the Shipwrecked Vessel RMS Titanic, https://www.state.gov/multilateral-19-1118.

527 UNCLOS, art. 157(1) (full cite above).

528 UNCLOS, arts. 150-155 (full cite above).

529 UNCLOS, 1994 Implementing Agreement, Annex Section 6 Production Policy (full cite above). *See also* DOS Commentary, pp. 59-60 (full cite above) (noting that "The decline in commercial interest in deep seabed mining, due to relatively low metals prices over the last decade, created an opening for reform of Part XI. This waning interest and resulting decline in exploration activity led most States to recognize that the large bureaucratic structure and detailed provisions on commercial exploitation contained in Part XI were unnecessary. This made possible the negotiation of a scaled-down regime to meet the limited needs of the present, but one capable of evolving to meet those of the future, coupled with general principles on economic and commercial policy that will serve as the basis for more detailed rules when interest in commercial exploitation re-emerges.... The Agreement fully meets the objections of the United States and other industrialized States to Part XI."). *See also* DOS Commentary, p. 68 (full cite above) (noting that "decision-making was one of the key areas of concern for the United States and other industrialized States in the reform of Part XI. In particular, the United States objected to the absence of a guaranteed seat in the 36-member Council, to the possibility that the Assembly could dominate decisions within the Authority ... and to the fact that industrialized countries did not have influence on the Council commensurate with their interests. ... The United States is now guaranteed a seat on the Council in perpetuity. Section 3(15) of the Annex to the Agreement provides that the consumer chamber in the Council shall include the State that, upon the entry into force of the Convention, has the largest economy in terms of gross domestic product. ... Because the requirements for representation of developing countries and for equitable geographic distribution set forth in article 161 of the Convention would likely produce a majority of developing States on the Council, the United States and other industrialized States sought to change the voting rules to ensure that the United States, and others with special interests that would be affected by decisions of the Authority, would have special voting rights in the Council. ... Section 3(5) of the Annex to the Agreement provides that, when consensus cannot be reached in the Council. This chambered voting arrangement will ensure that the United States and two other consumers, or three investors or

producers acting in concert, can block substantive decisions in the Council. ... The requirement that [the 4 exceptions to this rule] be made by consensus in effect gives the United States a veto with respect to them.").

[530] *See, e.g.,* Michael W. Lodge (Secretary-General of the International Seabed Authority), *Enclosure of the Oceans versus the Common Heritage of Mankind: The Inherent Tension between the Continental Shelf Beyond 200 Nautical Miles and the Area,* 97 INT'L. L. STUD. 803, 815-818 (2021), https://digital-commons.usnwc.edu/cgi/viewcontent.cgi?article=2971&context=ils (providing a brief description of the ISA entering into a 15-year exploration contract (through 2030) with a Brazilian State corporation to explore cobalt-rich ferromanganese crusts in the Rio Grande Rise off the coast of Brazil; unfortunately, Brazil subsequently submitted a revised OCS submission to the CLCS that overlapped with the Rio Grande Rise—the status of the 15-year exploration contract is thus in limbo until the CLCS opines on the matter). *See also* Letter Of Transmittal Forwarding The 1982 UN Law Of The Sea Convention To The United States Senate, DOS Commentary pp. 65-67 (William J. Clinton, Oct. 7, 1994) (S. Treaty Doc. 103-39), https://www.foreign.senate.gov/imo/media/doc/treaty_103-39.pdf (detailing the application process, and explaining how the 15-year exploration contracts can be extended "in additional five-year increments at the request of the contractor.").

[531] ISA, Contractors, Polymetallic Nodules, https://www.isa.org.jm/deep-seabed-minerals-contractors?qt-contractors_tabs_alt=0#qt-contractors_tabs_alt. *See also* Mining.com, *Mining's Tesla moment: DeepGreen harvests clean metals from the seafloor* (June 5, 2017), https://www.mining.com/web/minings-tesla-moment-deepgreen-harvests-clean-metals-seafloor/.

[532] United Nations Convention on the Law of the Sea (UNCLOS) art. 153(2)(b), Dec. 10, 1982, 1833 U.N.T.S. 397, https://www.un.org/Depts/los/convention_agreements/convention_overview_convention.htm. *See also* DOS Commentary, p. 64 (full cite above).

[533] *See, e.g.,* Lodge, *Enclosure of the Oceans,* p. 805 (full cite above) (noting that "there have been no unilateral [deep seabed mining] claims outside the regime established by UNCLOS.").

[534] P.D. Ingham, *The Economic Viability of Deep-Seabed Mining of Polymetallic Nodules,* working paper submitted for the Preparatory Commission for the Int'l. Sea-Bed Authority (ISA) and for the Int'l. Tribunal for the Law of the Sea (ITLOS) (1986), https://trove.nla.gov.au/work/18590699?selectedversion=NBD4434993; https://catalogue.nla.gov.au/Record/511387.

[535] Int'l. Seabed Authority (ISA), Legal Authorities, The Mining Code, https://www.isa.org.jm/mining-code. *See also* The Atlantic, *History's Largest Mining Operation Is About to Begin* (Wil S. Hylton, January/February 2020), https://www.theatlantic.com/magazine/archive/2020/01/20000-feet-under-the-sea/603040/.

[536] The Atlantic, *History's Largest Mining Operation* (full cite above).

[537] DOS Commentary, p. 87 (full cite above).

CHAPTER 7: FISHERIES & MARINE SCIENTIFIC RESEARCH

"Neither nature nor art has partitioned the sea into empires. The ocean and its treasures are the common property of all men. Upon this deep and strong foundation do I build, and with this cogent and irresistible argument do I fortify our rights and liberties."
—President John Adams

UNFORTUNATELY, THE "TRAGEDY OF THE COMMONS" is the most apt description of international fisheries.[538] The "Tragedy of the Commons" is an old economic concept that a shared resource open to use by all—such as the public land (aka "commons" or "village green") in the middle of an English town, on which all farmers were allowed to let their livestock graze—is over-depleted as each user maximizes their own self-interest, thereby depleting the shared resource (e.g., killing all of the grass through over-grazing).[539] Fishing in international waters is a classic "Tragedy of the Commons" situation due to a historic lack of shared responsibility through regulation and enforcement, and the ease of avoiding both by savvy commercial fishermen seeking to maximize their short-term profits. One way that commercial fishermen maximize profits is by using indiscriminate nets that literally catch anything in their wake.[540]

This is a photo of a large purse seine net, which closes up like a purse and captures anything caught inside that is too large to swim through the net (which depends on the size of the "mesh" or openings in the net).

Another type of net is called a drift net, because it hangs vertically in the water and drifts along (i.e., it has floats on the top of the net and weights at the bottom, but it is not anchored in one place)—marine life is captured when it gets tangled in the nets. The problem with drift nets (aka "curtains of death") is that they are also indiscriminate, and result in a large "by-catch" problem, such as this large sea turtle which was unintentionally caught along with the intended school of Skipjack Tuna.[541] The United

Nations General Assembly has adopted a number of resolutions, seeking to ban the use of drift nets due to their indiscriminate nature.[542]

The United States was also instrumental in promoting the adoption, by consensus, of United Nations General Assembly Resolutions 441225, 45/297 and 46/215, which have effectively created a moratorium on the use of large-scale driftnets on the high seas. In pressing for the adoption of these resolutions, the United States relied heavily on the fact that large-scale driftnets in the North Pacific Ocean intercepted salmon of U.S. origin in violation of article 66 of [UNCLOS] and indiscriminately killed large numbers of other species, including marine mammals and birds, in violation of the basic conservation and related obligations contained in the Convention. In creating the moratorium, the international community implemented obligations flowing from these provisions of the Convention.[543]

The by-catch problem is particularly bad for shrimp fishing (due to the small mesh size used in bottom trawling nets), with up to 6-20 pounds of by-catch for every 1 pound of shrimp caught, as typified in this photo.

The Food and Agriculture Organization (FAO) is a specialized agency of the United Nations charged with eliminating hunger worldwide. Within the FAO's broad mandate are a number of lines of effort, including the "Climate and Natural Resources," which includes the "Fisheries and Aquaculture Department."[544] The "flagship" publication of the Fisheries and Aquaculture Department is the biennial "The State of World Fisheries & Aquaculture," (aka SOFIA) report. The most recent (224 page!) SOFIA report was issued in 2020, with data through 2018.[545]

The 2020 SOFIA report suggests that many of the United Nations' "Sustainable Development Goals" are directly related to

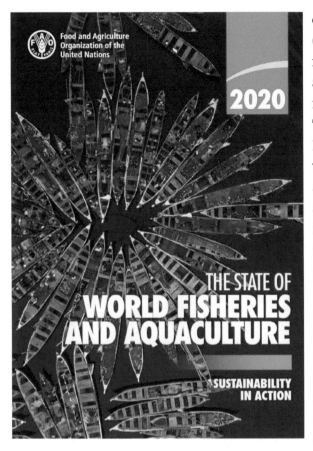

capture fisheries (i.e., wild-caught fish) and aquaculture (i.e., farm-raised fish). The 2020 SOFIA Report is replete with fisheries and aquaculture data and statistics, including the fact that not only did global fish production (including both wild capture and aquaculture) reach an all-time high in 2018, but the *per capita* consumption of fish also reached an all-time high of 20.5 kg (45 pounds) of fish consumed per person in 2018![546] So not only is the increasing world population demanding a greater supply of fish as a readily available and healthy source of protein, but people around the world are also consuming more fish on an individual basis.

As the following chart reveals, in 1950, limited fishing technology and low prices for fish (fish was regarded as the "poor man's protein") meant relatively low worldwide catches—around 20 million metric tons / year. As the world's population grew, and people started eating more fish, prices rose, and technology gradually improved.[547] By 1970 the worldwide catch was 60 million

FIGURE 1 WORLD CAPTURE FISHERIES AND AQUACULTURE PRODUCTION

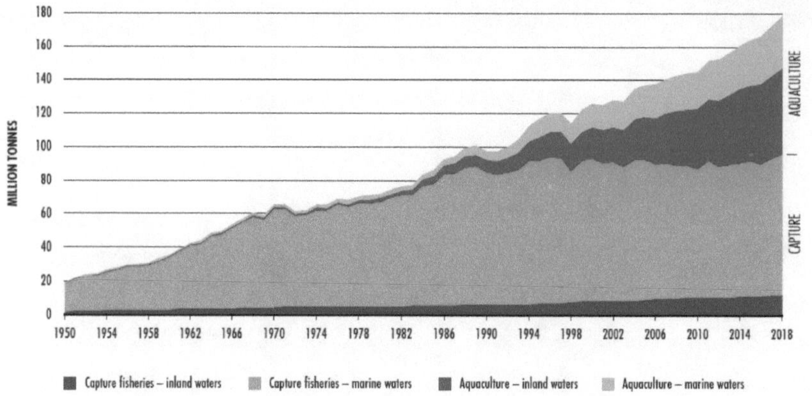

Legend: Capture fisheries – inland waters | Capture fisheries – marine waters | Aquaculture – inland waters | Aquaculture – marine waters

NOTE: Excludes aquatic mammals, crocodiles, alligators and caimans, seaweeds and other aquatic plants.
SOURCE: FAO.

metric tons/year. By the late 1980s the world catch stabilized at around 86-93 million metric tons/year, where it has remained for the past 30 years.[548] Despite more modern fishing technology (e.g., satellite navigation and electronic "recorders" at the mouth of nets that inform the fishing boat's skipper how much and what type of fish they are catching), fishing fleets are capturing about the same tonnage of wild fish today. There's also been more attention paid to overfishing since 1990. The overall demand for fish continued to increase along with the increase in the world's population, and since wild capture wasn't keeping up with demand, fish farming or "aquaculture" stepped up to fill the void, especially in China (the world's largest aquaculture producer).[549] In fact, **aquaculture provides more fish for human consumption than fish captured in the wild, and has done so since 2014.**[550] This trend is expected to continue indefinitely.

Nevertheless, marine capture production (i.e., fish caught in the oceans) "remains an essential source of animal proteins, micronutrients and omega-3 fatty acids, which are vital in low-income food-deficit countries (LIFDCs) and Small Island Developing States (SIDS), where diets are heavily reliant on fish."[551] China is by far the world's top producer, catching 15% of the total wild caught fish, which is as much as the next two largest producers (Indonesia and Peru) combined. The top 8 producers account for 53% of total captures.[552] International commercial fishermen catch over 1,700 species of fish, cephalopods (e.g., squid and octopus), mollusks (e.g., oysters, mussels, and scallops), and crustaceans (e.g., lobsters, crabs and shrimps).[553] Marine capture production is quite varied between species, with the top three species of fish captured (Peruvian Anchoveta, Alaskan Pollock, and Skipjack Tuna) only representing 14% of the total wild capture, and the top 14 major species only accounting for approximately 39% of the total.[554]

Unfortunately, 34% of fish stocks are being fished beyond biological sustainability (i.e., overfishing, shown in orange in the following chart), reflecting the "Tragedy of the Commons" (i.e., a shared resource with little shared responsibility). Sixty percent of fish stocks are being fully fished/utilized (i.e., to their "Maximum Sustainable Yield (MSY)." The MSY is the largest catch that can be sustained over time without depleting the stock—it is like winning the lottery jackpot, and only living on the interest without touching the principal. MSY is addressed in UNCLOS Article 61(3)). There's not much room to increase marine capture production, as only 6% of fish stocks are underfished. The traditional fishing areas which have been overfished the worst are the Mediterranean and Black Sea (each at 63% overfished), Southeast Pacific (55% overfished), and Southwest Atlantic (53% overfished)—sadly, the majority of fish stocks in each of these areas have been overfished beyond the point of biological sustainability.[555]

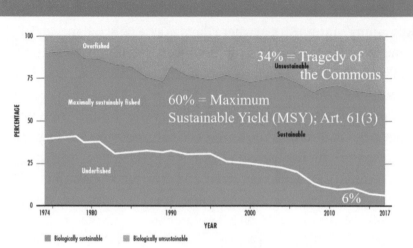

SOURCE: FAO.

The reader can see from the preceding chart that in the last 40 years, the percentage of fully fished fish stocks has remained relatively constant at 50-60%, while the percentage of overfished fish stocks has risen dramatically, and the percentage of underfished fish stocks has decreased dramatically. The bottom line is "that the successes achieved in some countries and regions have not been sufficient to reverse the global trend of overfished stocks".[556] Consumers can help reverse this trend by only eating sustainable seafood—such as those species recommended by the Monterey Bay Aquarium's "Seafood Watch" website and mobile application.[557]

Despite the importance of fishing to individual States,[558] to the world economy, and to global development, there are only 8 articles in UNCLOS specifically related to fishing, all in the Exclusive Economic Zone (EEZ). This is because UNCLOS was viewed as a "framework" treaty, especially with regard to maritime pollution (discussed in Chapter 5) and international fisheries. Other multilateral treaties (i.e., between many States) would then establish more detailed (and more easily changed) international pollution and fishing standards. Article 61(2) alludes to this when it provides that the Coastal State shall ensure that living resources in the EEZ are not over-exploited, and that "the coastal State and competent international organizations, whether subregional, regional or global, shall cooperate to this end."

There are a few reasons why the 8 UNCLOS articles specifically related to fishing all deal with fishing in the EEZ. First, the vast majority of fish stocks are found within the EEZ.[559] Second, fishing in other maritime zones is somewhat beyond the scope of UNCLOS. As discussed in Chapter 2, Coastal States have "complete sovereignty" over Internal Waters (which are akin to land territory).[560] Thus, managing resources within Internal Waters (including fishing) is one of the "matters which are essentially within the domestic jurisdiction of any state," and thus beyond even the authority of the United Nations to intervene.[561] Similarly, as discussed in Chapter 3, a Coastal State exercises almost complete sovereignty over its Territorial Seas (which are considered national waters), subject primarily to the right of all ships to conduct Innocent Passage. Article 19 defines Innocent Passage in the negative by providing specific examples of what violates Innocent Passage, including "any fishing activities."[562] Thus, fishing within the Territorial Sea is also solely within the Coastal State's purview to regulate. As discussed in Chapter 4, Archipelagic Waters are treated as if they were Territorial Seas, with the ships of other States able to conduct Innocent Passage through them, and would similarly be violated by fishing.[563] Thus, Archipelagic States control fishing within their Archipelagic Waters, except that UNCLOS requires them to "recognize traditional fishing rights" of neighboring States.[564] In contrast, fishing on the High Seas is one of the enumerated High Seas Freedoms (discussed in Chapter 5).[565] Only Flag States would have jurisdiction to enforce fishing regulations on the High Seas, especially those fishing regulations implementing the Flag State's treaty obligations.[566] "The freedom of high seas fishing has never been an unfettered right, however. The High Seas Convention, for example, required this freedom to be exercised by all States with 'reasonable regard to the interests of other States in their exercise of the freedom of the high seas.'"[567] Chapter 5 discussed UNCLOS' triple-edge "due regard" standard on the High Seas.

Therefore, the 8 UNCLOS articles specifically related to fishing all deal with fishing in the EEZ. Article 61 is entitled "Conservation of the living resources [in the EEZ]," and provides the Coastal State with exclusive authority to "determine the allowable catch of the living resources in its exclusive economic zone."[568] The "Total Allowable Catch (TAC) is the tool used to establish maximum fishing limits during a certain timeframe and for each one of the species controlled by management plans."[569] However, establishing a TAC is somewhat of a blunt instrument for a Coastal State to use to control fishing, even when it is species specific, because setting a "TAC without further regulations, invariably leads to a rush for the fish, resulting in even fiercer competition than under the open-access fisheries. These are aptly described as 'Derby' or 'Olympic'-fisheries and are bound to inflict great pressure on the captain, crew and the vessel until the TAC is exhausted." Methods used to mitigate this "race to the TAC" include limiting the number of days that fishing vessels can remain at sea, and/or setting individual quotas for each vessel or fishing company.[570] Another criticism of using TACs is that Coastal States may ignore scientific recommendations in setting them.[571]

Article 62(2) directs a Coastal State to also determine whether its domestic fishing industry has the capacity to fully utilize the fish stocks contained in its EEZ.[572] If so, the Coastal State is under no obligation to permit foreign vessels to fish in the Coastal State's

EEZ! "In fact, because the harvesting capacity of the U.S. domestic fishing industry has in recent years been estimated to equal the total allowable catch of all relevant species subject to U.S. management authority, the United States has had no surplus to allocate to potentially interested States."[573] If the Coastal State lacks the capacity to fully utilize any particular fish stocks contained in its EEZ, the Coastal State has "wide discretion in choosing which other States will be allocated a share of any surplus."[574] The U.S. requires a foreign state to have a "governing international fishery agreement" (GIFA) with the U.S. before the foreign State could potentially be allocated a portion of any future surplus in fish stocks within the U.S. EEZ.[575]

Besides setting the TAC and determining whether to allocate any of the surplus, Coastal States may take other conservation or "control" measures pursuant to Article 62(4), including:

(a) licensing of fishermen, fishing vessels and equipment, including *payment of fees* and other forms of remuneration, which, in the case of developing coastal States, may consist of adequate compensation in the field of financing, equipment and technology relating to the fishing industry;

(b) determining the species which may be caught, and *fixing quotas of catch,* whether in relation to particular stocks or groups of stocks or catch per vessel over a period of time or to the catch by nationals of any State during a specified period;

(c) regulating seasons and areas of fishing, the types, sizes and amount of gear, and the types, sizes and number of fishing vessels that may be used;

(d) fixing the age and size of fish and other species that may be caught;

(e) specifying information required of fishing vessels, including catch and effort statistics and vessel position reports;

(f) requiring, under the authorization and control of the coastal State, the conduct of specified fisheries research programmes and regulating the conduct of such research, including the *sampling of*

catches, *disposition of samples and reporting of associated scientific data;*

 (g) the placing of observers or trainees on board such vessels by the coastal State; [576]

 (h) the landing of all or any part of the catch by such vessels in the ports of the coastal State;

 (i) terms and conditions relating to joint ventures or other cooperative arrangements;

 (j) requirements for the training of personnel and the transfer of fisheries technology, including enhancement of the coastal State's capability of undertaking fisheries research;

 (k) enforcement procedures. [emphasis added][577]

As we can see from this excerpt from Article 62(4), this is a fairly comprehensive list of Coastal State conservation/control measures for fishing in its EEZ! If foreign vessels are permitted to fish in the Coastal State's EEZ, they are obligated to comply with these Coastal State conservations measures.[578] Moreover, setting these conservation/control measures for fishing in its EEZ are an aspect of the Coastal State's exclusive sovereignty over resources in the EEZ, and thus are entirely within its discretion, with no ability to appeal the Coastal State's conservation/control measures or their application (i.e., mandatory dispute settlement is not available to resolve any disputes regarding their reasonableness or lack thereof).[579]

For example, the U.S. National Oceanic and Atmospheric Administration (NOAA) Fisheries, also known as the National Marine Fisheries Service,[580] is the U.S. federal agency responsible for the management, conservation, and protection of living marine resources within the U.S. The "NOAA Fisheries Service prevents overfishing by limiting the total harvest in every fishery through the establishment of annual catch limits,"[581] and by enforcing over 40 U.S. marine conservation laws in the U.S. EEZ.[582] NOAA Fisheries enforces specific rules and regulations (including conservation/control measures) for each of the U.S. coastal fisheries.[583] For example, rules and regulations for "Atlantic Highly Migratory Species" include a prohibition against taking any Bluefin, Bigeye, or Yellowfin Tuna with a "curved fork length" less than 27 inches, which equates to a weight of approximately 14 pounds.[584] NOAA Fisheries also restricts the use of "fish aggregation devices … to attract ocean going pelagic[585] fish such as marlin, tuna and mahi-mahi."[586] A foreign fishing company may only challenge these conservation/control measures in U.S. federal court, and not by submitting the dispute to mandatory dispute settlement under UNCLOS.[587]

The remaining UNCLOS articles specifically related to fishing establish the framework for the conservation of a variety of fisheries:[588]

> ➤ Shared Fish Stocks between the EEZs of neighboring States;[589]
> ➤ Straddling Fish Stocks between a Coastal State's EEZ and the High Seas;[590]
> ➤ Highly Migratory Species that regularly migrate throughout one or more fishing regions (such as tuna);[591]
> ➤ Marine Mammals (including cetaceans, i.e., whales, dolphins, and porpoises);[592]
> ➤ Anadromous Fish Stocks, which are saltwater fish that spawn in fresh water (such as Salmon);[593] and
> ➤ Catadromous Fish Stocks, which are fresh water fish that spawn in saltwater (such as eels).[594]

As discussed earlier in this Chapter, a Coastal State shall seek to conserve the living resources in its EEZ, and "shall ensure through proper conservation and management measures that the maintenance of the living resources in the exclusive economic zone is not endangered by over-exploitation."[595] However, as discussed in Chapter 6, there is no similar requirement for a Coastal State to conserve natural resources found on the Continental Shelf: "The coastal State exercises over the continental shelf sovereign rights for the purpose of exploring it and exploiting its natural resources" (with no mention of protecting against over-exploitation).[596] "This is consistent both with the earlier Continental Shelf Convention,[597] and with the theory of the Continental Shelf as a natural prolongation of land territory, [where] there is no general duty to conserve resources."[598] Since sedentary species are specifically included in the resources of the Continental Shelf, and not in the EEZ,[599] consistent with UNCLOS a Coastal State may harvest sedentary species (such as sea cucumbers, sponges, mollusks, and possibly crustaceans such as crabs and lobsters) on the Continental Shelf to extinction!

A prime example of an international fishing treaty that was drafted in accordance with the UNCLOS framework is the 1995 Straddling Fish Stocks and Highly Migratory Fish Stocks Agreement (aka 1995 Straddling/Migratory Fish Stocks Agreement).[600] UNCLOS established the framework for Coastal States and States fishing on the High Seas—for Straddling Fish Stocks (between a Coastal State's EEZ and the High Seas) and for Highly Migratory Species—to cooperate and agree on conservation measures "with a view to ensuring conservation and promoting the objective of optimum utilization of such species" both within and beyond the EEZ.[601] Some of these species are listed in Annex I to UNCLOS, and include a variety of species of tuna,[602] marlin, swordfish, and dolphin fish (aka *Mahi-mahi* in Hawaiian, and *Dorado* in Spanish—not to be confused with dolphins, which are marine mammals). Article 18 of the 1995 Straddling/Migratory Fish Stocks Agreement imposes a duty on Flag States to regulate the fishing activities of their vessels to ensure compliance.[603]

What is remarkable about the 1995 Straddling/Migratory Fish Stocks Agreement is that State Parties were able to reach an agreement (under the auspices of the UN General Assembly) on how to implement UNCLOS provisions "Relating to the Conservation and Management of Straddling Fish Stocks and Highly Migratory Fish Stocks" less than 10 months after UNCLOS entered into force.[604] The 1995 Agreement "sets out principles for the conservation and management of those fish stocks and establishes that such management must be based on the precautionary approach and the best available scientific information."

The Precautionary Approach is commonly used in Environmental Law treaties to ensure progress on environmental protection is not delayed while waiting for perfect scientific proof of potential environmental damage.[605] The Precautionary Approach is generally defined as:

> *When an activity raises threats of harm to human health or the environment, precautionary measures should be taken even if some cause and effect relationships are not fully established scientifically.*
>
> *In this context the proponent of an activity, rather than the public, should bear the burden of proof.*[606]

Thus, the lack of full scientific certainty is not a sufficient reason to postpone cost-effective measures to prevent harm to the environment (i.e., there is no reason to wait for perfect information before doing something now to protect the environment). Article 6(2) of the 1995 Straddling/Migratory Fish Stocks Agreement provides that "[t]he absence of adequate scientific information shall not be used as a reason for postponing or failing to take conservation and management measures."[607]

Article 7(2) of the 1995 Straddling/Migratory Fish Stocks Agreement imposes a duty on Coastal States and States fishing on the High Seas to cooperate in "achieving compatible measures" both in the Coastal States' EEZs and on the High Seas. The 1995 Agreement does this "by establishing ... detailed minimum international standards for the conservation and management of straddling fish stocks and highly migratory fish stocks" which are "compatible and coherent" between Coastal States' EEZs and on the High Seas, including "effective mechanisms for compliance and enforcement of those measures."[608]

In terms of enforcing its provisions, Article 18 of the 1995 Straddling/Migratory Fish Stocks Agreement imposes duties on Flag States to ensure that fishing vessels flying their flag comply with all conservation and management measures related to the 1995 Agreement, and provides detailed measures to control fishing on the High Seas by vessels flying their flag to enforce compliance (e.g., licensing, reporting, catch verification, etc.). There are now

91 State Parties to the 1995 Straddling/Migratory Fish Stocks Agreement, including 8 of the top 10 commercial fishing States (including Indonesia, U.S. and Russia), but not yet including the world's top producer—China.[609]

There are a large number of international fishing treaties that deal with the conservation of specific species, including by-catch species (e.g., sea turtles,[610] and dolphins[611]). For example, the Patagonian Toothfish is a large deep sea[612] predator that can reach over 2 meters (7 feet) long and weigh 100 kg (220 pounds).[613]

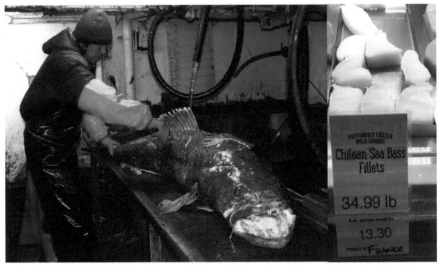

Patagonian Toothfish has a firm texture, fairly mild flavor, is high in fat, and was considered a by-catch until the 1970's when more popular types of fish became more difficult to catch. The Patagonian Toothfish was *rebranded* as "Chilean Sea Bass" in 1977, and its popularity soared.[614] By the late 1990's, Patagonian Toothfish had been overfished, and American Chefs were asked to "Take a Pass on Chilean Sea Bass."[615] Nevertheless, unscrupulous fishermen engaging in Illegal, Unreported and Unregulated (IUU) fishing, continued to overfish Patagonian Toothfish (which they called "White Gold" due to its profitability). One particularly notorious IUU fisherman of Patagonian Toothfish was Antonio Garcia Perez. Perez used longlines more than 15 miles long, with up to 15,000 baited hooks to catch up to 40 tons of Patagonian Toothfish per day. Caught *in flagrante delicto* (in the act), Australian patrol boats engaged in hot pursuit for over 4,000 nm before catching Perez.[616] Due to the lucrativeness of fishing for Patagonian Toothfish, and the remoteness of their Antarctic habitat, chasing their IUU fishermen have set all recent hot pursuit records (discussed in more depth in Chapter 8).

Commercial fishing of Patagonian Toothfish is now managed by a Regional Fishery Management Organization (RFMO),[617] the Commission for the Conservation of Antarctic Marine Living Resources (CCAMLR), and by Coastal States (e.g., Argentina, Chile, and Uruguay) taking CCAMLR management practices into account in setting and enforcing their own national standards. IUU fishing of the species has been nearly eliminated since 2015.[618] Longline fishing of Patagonian Toothfish now follows strict compliance measures, such as: fishing within Total Allowable Catch (TAC) limits; licensing; inspecting and monitoring vessels, ports and transshipments; a Catch Document Scheme[619] to reduce the scope for trade in IUU fish; and by-catch avoidance measures, such as seabird exclusion devices.[620] Thanks to these coordinated efforts, the stocks of the slow-maturing and slow-reproducing Patagonian Toothfish are once again rising, and over 60% of the global catch is now from sustainable fisheries.[621] Even Seafood Watch notes the success in allowing some Patagonian Toothfish stocks to recover, and lists a number of responsible sources for acquiring the highly sought-after fish.[622] The main takeaway is that international fishing treaties and conservation measures can make a difference!

Up until 2019, the conservation of marine mammals, especially cetaceans (i.e., whales, dolphins, and porpoises), had similar cause for guarded optimism. Whales have been hunted for thousands of years, possibly starting as early as 2200 BC.[623] Over-exploitation and recognition "that whales were 'the wards of the entire world', a 'common resource' that must be conserved," led to the development of three whaling conventions, the most recent and comprehensive one in 1946.[624]

Article 65 of UNCLOS discusses the conservation and management of marine mammals in the EEZ, and Article 120 applies Article 65 to the conservation and management of marine mammals on the High Seas. Articles 65 and 120 implicitly refer to the 1946 International Convention for the Regulation of Whaling (1946 Whaling Convention), which is a long-standing multilateral treaty designed to prevent the overhunting of whales in order to "provide for the proper conservation of whale stocks and thus make possible the orderly development of the whaling industry."[625] The 1946 Whaling Convention created the International Whaling Commission (IWC), whose 88 members[626] (representing every State Party to the 1946 Whaling Convention) meet every 2 years,[627] with the next meeting scheduled to be held in Slovenia in 2021.[628]

The 1946 Whaling Convention includes a binding Schedule which "sets out catch limits for commercial and aboriginal subsistence whaling" (similar to Total Allowable Catch for fisheries), as well as other detailed control measures (e.g., protected species; hunting seasons and waters; size limits; time, methods and intensity of whaling; gear types and specifications; and record-keeping).[629] The IWC may amend the binding Schedule at one of its biennial meetings with a ¾ supermajority vote.[630] "The Commission receives advice on sustainability from its Scientific Committee and this assists it in deciding catch limits.... In 1982 the IWC decided that there should be a pause in commercial whaling on all whale species and populations (known as 'whale stocks') from the 1985/1986 season onwards. This pause is often referred to as the commercial whaling moratorium, and it remains in place today."[631] In essence, the IWC set a zero-catch limit on whales, and converted the treaty into an "Anti-Whaling" Convention, at least temporarily.[632] However, three State Parties to the 1946 Whaling Convention exercised their right to "opt-out"[633] of the moratorium on whaling, and two of them (Norway and Iceland) continue to take whales commercially within their EEZs.[634]

"The whaling regime under the [1946 Whaling] Convention provides for three types of whaling: commercial (at present zero 'quotas'); aboriginal (indigenous whaling); and scientific [research] whaling."[635] Thus, besides Norway and Iceland continuing to take whales under their right to "opt-out" of the moratorium on commercial whaling, other States continue to take whales either for "research" purposes, or for aboriginal subsistence purposes. A State Party to the 1946 Whaling Convention "may grant to any of its nationals a special permit authorizing that national to kill, take and treat whales for purposes of scientific research."[636] Japan was the only State Party to grant special "research" permits to take whales since 2007.[637] Of course, any whales taken for "research" are still "processed" for human or animal consumption.[638]

The third exception to the moratorium on whaling is for aboriginal subsistence purposes. "From the outset, the IWC recognised that indigenous or aboriginal subsistence whaling is not the same as commercial whaling. Aboriginal whaling does not seek to maximise catches or profit. ... The IWC recognises that its regulations have the potential to impact significantly on traditional cultures, and great care must be taken in discharging this responsibility. In summary, the IWC objectives for management of aboriginal subsistence whaling are to ensure that hunted whale populations are maintained at (or brought back to) healthy levels, and to enable native people to hunt whales at levels that are

appropriate to cultural and nutritional requirements in the long term."[639] Thus, the binding Schedule to the 1946 Whaling Convention sets "catch limits for aboriginal subsistence whaling" in specific whale fisheries (i.e., by species and location). Besides setting specific "strike limits," the binding Schedule requires that "the meat and products of such whales are to be used exclusively for local consumption by the aborigines."[640] "Currently, the [International Whaling] Commission permits aboriginals from Denmark (Greenland), the Russian Federation, St. Vincent and the Grenadines, and the United States to engage in this type of whaling on certain whale stocks. The United States is subject to domestic legal requirements and works with the indigenous communities in Alaska and Washington to ensure that the catch limits established through the Commission meet their cultural and subsistence needs."[641]

Thus, after the 1985 commercial whaling moratorium, with exceptions for Norway and Iceland to "opt-out," Japan to conduct limited whale "research," and the indigenous people of 4 States to engage in limited aboriginal subsistence whaling, there was guarded optimism for the conservation of whales. However, 9 States have withdrawn from the 1946 Whaling Convention as a result of the moratorium.[642] When Japan was unable to convince the other State Parties at the 2018 International Whaling Commission (IWC) meeting to lift the ban on commercial whaling,

Japan withdrew from the 1946 Convention, and resumed commercial whaling in its EEZ![643] Unfortunately, "[t]he IWC is riddled with irreconcilable problems and has become a divisive body."[644]

MARINE SCIENTIFIC RESEARCH

This Chapter's second sub-topic is Marine Scientific Research (MSR), which was another contentious issue during UNCLOS negotiations. In some respects, MSR has come quite far since the HMS Challenger scientific expedition in the 1870s (discussed in Chapter 6); MSR now encompasses a range of scientific disciplines. However, in other respects, MSR is still quite literally operating in the dark:

While scientific understanding of the role of the oceans has considerably progressed since the nineteenth century, we still know very little of this huge, abyssal, and often inaccessible, natural asset. Although oceans represent a very essential part of our planet, paradoxically they are the least known and thus the least understood geographical and geomorphological areas. As one commentator has, quite eloquently, noticed: "until quite recently we did not know what was at the bottom of the oceans. Nor did we know what the bottom of the ocean was made of. In most areas, we did not even know where the bottom of the ocean actually was."[645]

MSR is addressed in Part XIII of UNCLOS. Even though Part XIII includes 28 articles, it leaves MSR itself undefined,[646] "despite the number of proposals that were made for a definition during the negotiations for the Convention."[647] However, MSR is generally viewed as including:

> Oceanography, which is the overarching branch of science dealing with the oceans, their biological, chemical, and physical characteristics, and exploitation of their resources;

> Marine biology, which is the study of organisms living in the oceans;[648]

> Fisheries research, which assesses fish stocks;

> Scientific ocean drilling and coring in order to understand seafloor and plate tectonics; and

> Geological/geophysical scientific surveying, which studies the topography, composition, and electromagnetic fields of the seafloor, including mineral and energy exploration.[649]

Because MSR typically is related to one or more economic resources (e.g., marine organisms, fish stocks, minerals and energy), MSR is subject to various levels of Coastal State control/consent in each of its maritime zones, and by the International Seabed Authority (ISA) in "the Area" (i.e., on the Deep Seabed, discussed in Chapter 6).[650] Before UNCLOS, scientific researchers recognized that they needed to request permission to conduct MSR in a Coastal State's (aka "littoral State's") waters or on its Continental Shelf, but MSR requests were routinely either denied or simply ignored. The U.S. had one of the few deep-water research fleets at the time, so the U.S. tried to keep the UNCLOS language somewhat ambiguous in order to be able to interpret it in a particular way (i.e., differentiating between MSR and military surveys, discussed below). UNCLOS "confirms the rights of coastal

States to require consent for marine scientific research undertaken in marine areas under their jurisdiction. These rights are balanced by specific criteria to ensure that the consent authority is exercised in predictable and reasonable fashion so as to promote maximum access for research activities."[651]

As discussed in Chapter 3, a Coastal State exercises almost complete sovereignty in its Territorial Sea, subject primarily to the right of all ships to conduct Innocent Passage. Thus, MSR in the Territorial Sea requires the express consent of the Coastal State,[652] especially since MSR would otherwise violate Innocent Passage.[653] Coastal State consent is similarly required to conduct MSR in the Coastal State's EEZ or on its Continental Shelf.[654] However, such consent shall normally be given,[655] even in the absence of normal diplomatic relations between the Coastal and Researching States.[656] The Coastal State may condition its consent to conduct MSR in its

EEZ or on its Continental Shelf upon the Coastal State's right to participate in the MSR (including posting observers onboard the maritime research vessels, such as NOAA's Ship Pisces pictured here),[657] receipt of preliminary and final reports of scientific findings, and access to all data and samples.[658] Failure to abide by these Coastal State conditions is a valid basis for the Coastal State to suspend or terminate its consent to conduct MSR in its EEZ or on its Continental Shelf.[659] All States are free to conduct MSR on the High Seas (especially since MSR is one of the enumerated High Seas Freedoms), and on the Deep Seabed.[660]

Now that UNCLOS has been in effect for over 25 years,[661] there is a fairly clear process for submitting MSR requests.[662] Scientific researchers still need to request permission to conduct MSR via "appropriate official channels"[663] (i.e., via their State to the Coastal State), but MSR requests can no longer simply be ignored by the Coastal State, which should normally grant reasonable requests to conduct MSR in the Coastal State's EEZ or on its Continental Shelf.[664] Article 248 enumerates the information that the Requesting/Researching State shall provide at least 6 months in advance of the MSR's commencement, including a full description of the project. The Coastal State has 4 months to respond, otherwise its consent to conduct the MSR may be implied.[665] [NOTE: thus if a Coastal State simply ignores the MSR request, it has implicitly granted it after 4 months of silence, which still provides the researchers another 2 months to finalize preparations before they had planned to commence their research.] Moreover, Coastal States are required to adopt reasonable rules, regulations and procedures to facilitate MSR beyond their Territorial Sea.[666]

Requests to conduct MSR in U.S. waters or on the U.S. Continental Shelf are managed by the Department of State's Office of Ocean and Polar Affairs (OPA). "The Office of Ocean and Polar Affairs (OPA) ... formulates and implements U.S. policy related to the conduct of marine scientific research in the territorial sea (up to 12 nautical miles from shore), in the exclusive economic zone (from 12 to 200 nautical miles from shore), and on the continental shelf (from 12 to, in some cases, beyond 200 nautical miles from shore)."[667] OPA serves as the "appropriate official channel" for about 400 American research requests annually to conduct MSR in foreign Coastal State waters (i.e., outbound requests), and for only about 70 foreign research requests annually to conduct MSR in U.S. waters (i.e., inbound requests).[668] The primary reason why there are so few foreign research requests is the OPA policy that U.S. consent is only required to conduct 5 types of MSR in the U.S. EEZ:

> "Any portion of the MSR within the U.S. EEZ is conducted within a **national marine sanctuary, a marine national monument, or other marine protected areas**;
> Any portion of the MSR within the U.S. EEZ involves the study of **marine mammals or endangered species**;
> Any portion of the MSR within the U.S. EEZ requires **taking commercial quantities of marine resources**;
> Any portion of the MSR within the U.S. EEZ involves **contact with the U.S. continental shelf**; or
> Any portion of the MSR within the U.S. EEZ involves **ocean dumping research**. (emphasis added)"[669]

"American policy has long been to make the waters of the U.S. exclusive economic zone open and available to the activities of foreign scientists. In many cases, it does not even require a permit or advance notice to undertake MSR. ... [T]his policy is admirable for its robust endorsement of maritime freedom. ..."[670] This is fairly remarkable considering that the U.S. has the largest EEZ in the world![671]

If the planned MSR falls within one of these 5 types, or within the U.S. Territorial Sea, the foreign researcher is required to submit their application "to OPA via the Research Application Tracking System (RATS), an online data management system designed to improve the transparency and efficiency of OPA's implementation of the marine scientific research consent regime."[672] Besides applying for MSR permits (either inbound or outbound) on RATS, researching scientists can also track their applications, receive the authorizing permits, and submit the required preliminary and final reports on RATS.[673] OPA provides a link to detailed coordinates of U.S. maritime zones.[674] OPA also provides guidance on supporting documentation to provide for outbound MSR requests, with specific guidance for specific Coastal States (e.g., for MSR requests submitted to China, it is better for a Chinese research partner to solely submit the MSR application directly to the Chinese "State Oceanic Administration, not via the U.S. Embassy").[675] The U.S. National Oceanic and Atmospheric Administration (NOAA) assists in reviewing inbound MSR requests to conduct MSR in U.S. waters. Understandably, for inbound MSR requests "[t]he United States reserves the right to participate in research activities conducted in the U.S. territorial sea and/or EEZ, and on the U.S. continental shelf."[676]

As mentioned earlier in this Chapter, the U.S. tried to keep the UNCLOS language on MSR ambiguous in order to be able to differentiate between **Marine Scientific *Research*** and

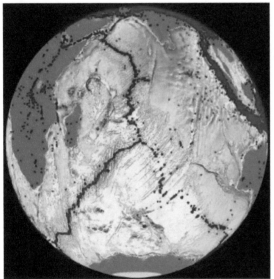

hydrographic and military *surveys*. "The United States has identified some marine data collection activities that are not marine scientific research. These include ... hydrographic surveys (for enhancing the safety of navigation); [and] military activities including military surveys."[677] Hydrographic surveys include mapping the ocean floor[678] and potential hazards to navigation; and measuring the direction and force of currents, heights and times of tides. Military surveys include measuring thermoclines (i.e., the boundary between the more turbulent surface water and calmer deep water), as well as underwater acoustics for more effective submarine operations.

The U.S. and United Kingdom (U.K.) posit that although hydrographic and military surveys may use the same equipment and measure the same type of data as oceanographic research, since the MSR provisions in UNCLOS only mention "research" and not "survey," and since the purpose behind conducting hydrographic and military surveys is to produce nautical charts and support safety of navigation and not the exploitation of marine resources, hydrographic and military surveys do not constitute MSR subject to Coastal State consent. Thus, the U.S. and U.K. view is that hydrographic and military surveys may be conducted in another State's Exclusive Economic Zone (EEZ) without informing the Coastal State, let alone seeking its consent!

In support of this position, **UNCLOS appears to differentiate between "*research*" and "*surveys.*"**[679] For example, in listing the acts that are prejudicial to conducting Innocent Passage through Territorial Seas, Article 19(2)(j) includes "the carrying out of research or survey activities." Similarly Article 21(1)(g) permits the Coastal State to adopt laws and regulations related to Innocent Passage through its Territorial Seas specifically regarding "marine scientific research and hydrographic surveys." Similarly Article 40 provides that: "During transit passage, foreign ships, including marine scientific research and hydrographic survey ships, may not carry out any research or survey activities without the prior authorization of the States bordering straits," and Article 54 makes this applicable to ships and aircraft engaged in Archipelagic Sea Lanes Passage (ASLP). By including both "research" and "survey," these UNCLOS articles arguably differentiate between the two activities.

Yet the MSR provisions in UNCLOS only provide Coastal State control over *research*. For example, Article 56(1)(b)(ii) provides that the Coastal State has jurisdiction over "marine scientific research" in its EEZ, with no mention of hydrographic or military surveys. Similarly, Article 143 discusses MSR in "the Area" (i.e., on the Deep Seabed),[680] with no mention of hydrographic or military surveys. Part XIII of UNCLOS (Article 238-265) consistently discusses Marine Scientific *Research* without once mentioning hydrographic or military surveys.[681] Even the revised United Nations guide on MSR notes that "survey activities" are dealt with elsewhere in UNCLOS, rather than in Part XIII dealing with MSR; and that the freedom to conduct MSR on the **High** Seas and on the Deep Seabed "also extends to such activities as hydrographic surveys" (i.e., continuing to differentiate between *"research"* and *"surveys"*).[682]

Another potential differentiation is between different levels of scientific research. Some MSR is conducted as "pure research" (aka basic or fundamental research), where the objective is simply to understand the marine environment and the natural forces at work therein, and to openly publish any scientific findings. However, much MSR is conducted as "applied research" (aka "profit-driven science" or "resource-related"),[683] which seeks to develop practical applications for the newly discovered phenomena. Examples of MSR abound: from sequencing the DNA of bacteria and viruses found in seawater in order to create synthetic microbes beneficial to humans, such as antibiotics;[684] to discovering uses of "Green Fluorescent Protein" isolated from jellyfish as a potential biological marker;[685] to "bioprospecting to discover pharmaceutical products," such as analyzing enzymes found in "extremophile" organisms that thrive in the extremely high pressures and high temperatures around hydrothermal vents,[686] or bacteria found in shipworms consuming 60,000 year-old Bald Cypress trees preserved off the coast of Alabama;[687] to studying a rare mineral found in the teeth of a large chiton (a type of mollusk) known as a "wandering meatloaf."[688]

One MSR success story that has received a bit of attention is research involving the blue blood of the Atlantic/American Horseshoe Crab (*Limulus polyphemus*). The term "Horseshoe Crab" is a bit of a misnomer, since they are more closely related to scorpions and spiders than to crabs. Horseshoe Crabs have been in existence for 450 million years, which is at least 100 million years older than the dinosaurs! Horseshoe Crabs migrate from the Continental Shelf to the shoreline in the late spring/early summer to spawn.[689] Horseshoe Crabs "lay millions upon millions of tiny, pearly, green or pink eggs" at high tide, which "play an important ecological role in the food web for migrating shorebirds"[690] and other marine animals.[691] For hundreds of years, Horseshoe Crabs were largely ignored, except when they were collected either to use as fertilizer, livestock feed or as bait for commercial fishing.[692]

Then in 1956, Dr. Frederik Bang,[693] a medical researcher at Johns Hopkins and "pioneer in applying marine biology to medical research",[694] discovered that Horseshoe Crabs are fairly resistant to infection, because the Horseshoe Crabs' blue blood clots to wall off bacteria.[695] [NOTE: Horseshoe Crab blood is fairly unique in that it is based on copper instead of iron, and thus it is colored cerulean blue instead of crimson red.] Dr. Bang noticed that Horseshoe Crab blood was particularly sensitive to "Gram-negative" bacteria (like E Coli), which is resistant to sterilization techniques (such as high heat and chemicals), and thus can be particularly dangerous. Further research developed the ultra-sensitive and fast-acting "Limulus amebocyte lysate (LAL) test, which could test for bacterial endotoxins using horseshoe crab blood." The LAL test is now the gold standard used worldwide to ensure the safety of "all intravenous fluids, [injectable] drugs, and implantable medical devices before they are used in patients. Overall, revenue from the

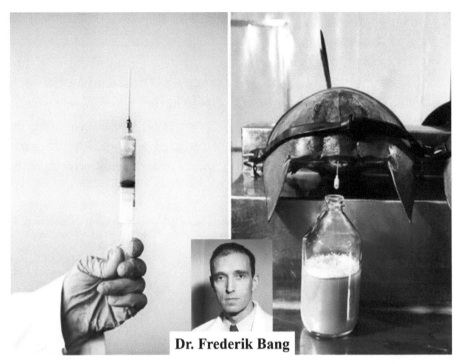
Dr. Frederik Bang

Horseshoe Crab portion of the biomedical industry is estimated to be approximately $250 million annually."[696]

Horseshoe Crab blood is collected by capturing approximately 575,000 Horseshoe Crabs each year, and taking about 1/3 of their blood before releasing them back into the wild to hopefully survive (with an estimated 70-90% survival rate) and reproduce. [NOTE: Horseshoe Crabs are thought to live 20-40 years, although it is uncertain how taking 1/3 of their blood affects them.] LAL costs approximately $15,000 per quart (or liter). Although a synthetic substitute (recombinant factor C (rFC)) for LAL has been available since 2003, it is not as effective, and only one drug has been approved by the U.S. Food and Drug Administration (FDA) after using the synthetic substitute (rFC) instead of LAL to test its safety. Because the Horseshoe Crabs are not being collected for human consumption, there are no quotas or Total Allowable Catch (TAC) limits on collecting them for biomedical purposes.[697] For this reason, the American Horseshoe Crab is "vulnerable" (i.e., one notch below endangered).[698]

In summary, although the "Tragedy of the Commons" is the most apt description of international fisheries, there is some basis for guarded optimism,[699] although perhaps less so for the conservation of whales. The future for Marine Scientific Research (MSR), however, is bright, with unlimited potential to develop practical applications for the newly discovered phenomena.

---

[538] Fisheries are "[a] geographic area that is associated with a population of aquatic organisms (fish, mollusks, crustaceans, etc.) which are harvested for their commercial or recreational value." National Oceanic and Atmospheric Administration (NOAA), U.S. Dept. of Commerce, Sea Earth Atmosphere (SEA) Educational Resources, *What are fisheries*, https://coast.noaa.gov/psc/sea/content/what-are-fisheries.html.

[539] *See, e.g.*, Investopedia, Economics, Microeconomics, Tragedy Of The Commons, *What is Tragedy Of The Commons?* (Jim Chappelow, May 10, 2019) https://www.investopedia.com/terms/t/tragedy-of-the-commons.asp. The "Tragedy of the Commons" economic theory is not without its detractors. *See, e.g.*, Scientific American, *The Tragedy of the Tragedy of the Commons* (Matto Mildenberger, Apr. 23, 2019), https://blogs.scientificamerican.com/voices/the-tragedy-of-the-tragedy-of-the-commons/; Climate and Capitalism, *The Myth of the Tragedy of the Commons* (Ian Angus, Aug. 25, 2008), https://climateandcapitalism.com/2008/08/25/debunking-the-tragedy-of-the-commons/.

[540] *See, e.g.*, Foreign Policy, *The Hunt for the Last Chilean Sea Bass Poachers* (Christopher Pala, June 17, 2015), https://foreignpolicy.com/2015/06/17/chilean-sea-bass-toothfish-thunder-sea-shepherd/ (noting that the Sea Shepherd ships that harassed the illegal *Fishing Vessel (F/V) Thunder* for 110 days recovered 45 miles of deep sea gill nets, which had captured "50 tons of marine life, of which only a quarter was [the sought-after Patagonian] toothfish."). Chapter 8 discusses the "hot pursuit" of illegal fishing vessels.

[541] Food and Agriculture Organization (FAO), http://www.fao.org/3/t0502e/t0502e01.htm; Oceana, Protecting the World's Oceans, Our Work, *Illegal Fishing: Driftnets*, https://eu.oceana.org/en/our-work/driftnets/overview.

[542] United Nations, Division for Ocean Affairs and the Law of the Sea, Oceans and the Law of the Sea in the General Assembly of the United Nations, General Assembly resolutions and decisions, https://www.un.org/Depts/los/general_assembly/general_assembly_resolutions.htm.

[543] Letter Of Transmittal Forwarding The 1982 UN Law Of The Sea Convention To The United States Senate, DOS Commentary p. 47 (William J. Clinton, Oct. 7,

1994) (S. Treaty Doc. 103–39), https://www.foreign.senate.gov/imo/media/doc/treaty_103-39.pdf.

[544] FAO, About FAO, Departments, http://www.fao.org/about/who-we-are/departments/en/.

[545] FAO, Fisheries and Aquaculture Dept., The State of World Fisheries and Aquaculture 2020 (SOFIA 2020), http://www.fao.org/fishery/sofia/en.

[546] FAO, SOFIA 2020, p. 9 & Table 1 (full cite above).

[547] THE FLETCHER SCHOOL OF LAW AND DIPLOMACY—TUFTS UNIVERSITY, LAW OF THE SEA, A POLICY PRIMER 7 (2017), https://sites.tufts.edu/lawofthesea/introduction/; HARRY SCHEIBER, ECONOMIC USES OF THE OCEANS AND THE IMPACTS ON MARINE ENVIRONMENTS: PAST TRENDS AND CHALLENGES AHEAD 3 (2011).

[548] FAO, SOFIA 2020, pp. 8-9 & Figures 1 & 4, (full cite above).

[549] FAO, SOFIA 2020, p. 10 (full cite above). Fish farms raise a relatively diverse range of different species of finfish, crustaceans, molluscs, and other aquatic animals. However, different species of Carp and Tilapia account for over 44% of the finfish raised, different species of Shrimp and Prawns account for 66% of the crustaceans raised, different species of Oysters and Mussels account for 42% of the molluscs raised, and Chinese Softshell Turtles and Japanese Sea Cucumbers account for 54% of all other aquatic animals raised (all by weight). However, as a percentage of total aquaculture production (by weight), different species of Carp and Tilapia account for over 29% of the total aquaculture production, different species of Oysters and Mussels account for 9% of the total aquaculture production, and different species of Shrimp and Prawns account for 7.5% of the total aquaculture production. The other species of finfish, crustaceans, molluscs, and other aquatic animals account for the other 54% of the total aquaculture production. FAO, SOFIA 2020, pp. 30-31 & Table 8 (full cite above).

[550] FAO, SOFIA 2020 – In Brief, p. 7 (full cite above).

[551] FAO, SOFIA 2020, p. 2 (full cite above).

[552] China, Norway, Vietnam, India, Chile and Thailand are the major exporters of fish and fish products. The European Union (EU), U.S. and Japan are the largest markets for fish and fish products, accounting for 57% of the total value of world imports. FAO, SOFIA 2020, pp. 6, 8, 10-13, 18, Table 2 & Figure 5 (full cite above).

[553] FAO, SOFIA 2020, p. 10 (full cite above).

[554] FAO, SOFIA 2020, pp. 10, 14 & Table 3 (full cite above).

[555] FAO, SOFIA 2020, Foreword, pp. 47, 49 & Figure 20, (full cite above).

[556] FAO, SOFIA 2020, pp. vi, 47-48 & Figure 19 (full cite above).

[557] Monterey Bay Aquarium Seafood Watch, *Helping people make better seafood choices for a healthy ocean*, https://www.seafoodwatch.org/.

[558] Fishing is so important to some States that they have appointed a Minister of Fisheries. *See, e.g.,* **Australian** Government, Agriculture, Assistant Minister for Forestry and Fisheries, https://minister.agriculture.gov.au/Duniam; Government of the People's Republic of **Bangladesh**, Ministry of Fisheries And Livestock, https://mofl.gov.bd/; **Canada**, Fisheries and Oceans, Media Room, Minister, http://www.dfo-mpo.gc.ca/about-notre-sujet/minister-ministre-eng.htm; Ministry of Fisheries **Fiji**, About Us, Minister for Fisheries Profile, http://www.fisheries.gov.fj/index.php/about-mof/minister-for-fisheries-profile; Government of **Iceland**, Ministries, Minister of Fisheries and Agriculture, https://www.government.is/ministries/ministry-of-industries-and-innovation/minister-of-fisheries-and-agriculture/; Government of **India**, Ministry of Fisheries, Animal Husbandry & Dairying,

https://pib.gov.in/newsite/PrintRelease.aspx?relid=194814; Republic of **Indonesia**, Ministry of Marine Affairs and Fisheries, https://kkp.go.id/; Republic of **Korea**, Ministry of Oceans and Fisheries, Message from the Minister, http://www.mof.go.kr/eng/content/view.do?menuKey=474&contentKey=278; **Maldives**, Ministries, Ministry of Fisheries, Marine Resources and Agriculture, https://www.fishagri.gov.mv/; Republic of **Namibia**, Fisheries and Marine Resources, About Us, Management Profile, Minister, https://www.mfmr.gov.na/minister; **New Zealand** Ministry for Primary Industries, About us, Our structure, Ministers, Minister of Fisheries, https://www.mpi.govt.nz/about-us/our-structure/ministers/; **Norway**, Ministries, Ministry of Trade, Industry and Fisheries, Organisation, https://www.regjeringen.no/en/dep/nfd/organisation/minister-of-fisheries-and-seafood-harald-t.-nesvik/id2608225/.

[559] Letter Of Transmittal Forwarding The 1982 UN Law Of The Sea Convention To The United States Senate, DOS Commentary p. 41 (William J. Clinton, Oct. 7, 1994) (S. Treaty Doc. 103–39), https://www.foreign.senate.gov/imo/media/doc/treaty_103-39.pdf (estimating that "90 percent of living marine resources are harvested within 200 miles of the coast. By authorizing the establishment of EEZs, and by providing for the sovereign rights and management authority of coastal States over living resources within their EEZs, the Convention has brought most living marine resources under the jurisdiction of coastal States."; Zed, Books, *An interview with Captain Peter Hammarstedt of Catching Thunder* (Apr. 13, 2018), https://www.zedbooks.net/media/show/interview-captain-peter-hammarstedt-catching-thunder/ (same).

[560] United Nations Convention on the Law of the Sea (UNCLOS) art. 8(1), Dec. 10, 1982, 1833 U.N.T.S. 397, https://www.un.org/Depts/los/convention_agreements/convention_overview_convention.htm. The concept that each State has exclusive sovereignty over its (land) territory originates from the 1648 Treaties of Westphalia (aka the Peace of Westphalia). Encyclopædia Britannica, European History, *Peace of Westphalia*, https://www.britannica.com/event/Peace-of-Westphalia; RESTATEMENT (THIRD) OF FOREIGN RELATIONS, pt. 1, introductory note (p. 17) (1987).

[561] United Nations, Charter of the United Nations, art. 2(7), https://www.un.org/en/charter-united-nations/. Chapter 9 discusses the United Nations Charter and its framework.

[562] UNCLOS, art. 19(2)(i) (full cite above).

[563] UNCLOS, art. 52 (full cite above). DONALD R. ROTHWELL & TIM STEPHENS, THE INT'L. LAW OF THE SEA 269 (2nd ed. 2016).

[564] UNCLOS, art. 51(1) (full cite above).

[565] UNCLOS, arts. 87(1)(e) & 116 (full cite above).

[566] UNCLOS, art. 116(a) (full cite above). Chapter 9 discusses Flag States in more depth.

[567] DOS Commentary, p. 46 (full cite above).

[568] UNCLOS, art. 61(1) (full cite above).

[569] Oceana, Protecting the World's Oceans, Our Work, *Total Allowable Catches (TACs)*, https://eu.oceana.org/en/total-allowable-catches-tacs.

[570] Food and Agriculture Organization of the United Nations (FAO), *Fisheries management and safety*, http://www.fao.org/3/X9656E/X9656E03.htm.

[571] Oceana, *Total Allowable Catches* (full cite above).

228

572 UNCLOS, art. 62(2) (full cite above).

573 DOS Commentary, p. 43 (full cite above).

574 DOS Commentary p. 42 (full cite above).

575 DOS Commentary p. 43 (full cite above).

576 Serving as an observer on a commercial fishing vessel is a particularly challenging occupation. See, e.g., National Oceanic and Atmospheric Administration (NOAA), U.S. Dept. of Commerce, NOAA Fisheries, Keeping Fishery Observers Safe from Harassment (Dec. 11, 2019), https://www.fisheries.noaa.gov/feature-story/keeping-fishery-observers-safe-harassment.

577 UNCLOS, art. 62(4) (full cite above).

578 UNCLOS, arts. 58(3) & 62(4) (full cite above). Chapter 9 discusses Flag States in more depth.

579 UNCLOS, art. 297(3)(a) (full cite above). Chapter 12 discusses mandatory dispute settlement in more depth.

580 NOAA, U.S. Dept. of Commerce, NOAA Fisheries, About Us, Overall, https://www.fisheries.noaa.gov/about-us.

581 NOAA, U.S. Dept. of Commerce, Sea Earth Atmosphere (SEA) Educational Resources, What are fisheries, https://coast.noaa.gov/psc/sea/content/what-are-fisheries.html.

582 NOAA, U.S. Dept. of Commerce, NOAA Fisheries, Enforcement, Overview, https://www.fisheries.noaa.gov/topic/enforcement. As discussed in Chapter 4, President Reagan claimed a 200 nm EEZ for the U.S. in 1983. Reagan Proclamation No. 5030, 3 C.F.R. 22 (1983), 48 Fed. Reg. 10605 (Mar. 10, 1983), National Archives, Federal Register, Codification, Proclamations, Proclamation 5030—Exclusive Economic Zone of the United States of America, https://www.archives.gov/federal-register/codification/proclamations/05030.html.

583 NOAA, U.S. Dept. of Commerce, NOAA Fisheries, Rules & Regulations, Fisheries, https://www.fisheries.noaa.gov/rules-and-regulations.

584 50 CFR Part 635, § 635.20(c), https://www.ecfr.gov/cgi-bin/text-idx?SID=7c298bed7921bcbb07e00ff3d1e949c1&mc=true&node=se50.12.635_120&rgn=div8. See also Montauk Marine Basin, How To Determine The Weight of a Tuna, http://www.marinebasin.com/other_pages.html&key=TUNAFISH.

585 Pelagic fish live in the pelagic zone (aka the open sea/ocean), which isn't near either the shoreline or the seabed. National Oceanic and Atmospheric Administration (NOAA), U.S. Dept. of Commerce, Ocean Facts, What are pelagic fish?, https://oceanservice.noaa.gov/facts/pelagic.html.

586 NOAA, What are fisheries (full cite above).

587 UNCLOS, art. 297(3)(a) (full cite above). Chapter 12 discusses mandatory dispute settlement in more depth.

588 Article 73 deals with the enforcement of the Coastal State's fishing laws and regulations, which Chapter 8 discusses in more depth.

589 UNCLOS, art. 63(1) (full cite above).

590 UNCLOS, art. 63(2) (full cite above). UNCLOS distinguishes between Straddling Fish Stocks and Highly Migratory Species (HMS): "One justification for this distinction rests on the biological differences between the two categories of stocks. Broadly speaking, 'straddling' stocks, such as cod in the Northwest Atlantic and pollock in the Bering Sea, occur primarily in the EEZs of a very few coastal States. Outside the EEZs, these stocks are fished in relatively discrete areas of the adjacent high seas. Accordingly, it seems reasonable for the coastal State 'unilaterally' to determine conservation and management measures applicable in

its EEZ, while the high seas fishing States and the coastal State(s) jointly develop such measures applicable in the adjacent areas. Most HMS, by contrast, migrate through thousands of miles of open ocean. They are fished in the EEZs of large numbers of coastal States and in many areas of the high seas. No single coastal State could adopt effective conservation and management measures for such a stock as a whole. As a result, international cooperation is necessary in the development of such measures for these stocks throughout their range, both within and beyond the EEZ." Letter Of Transmittal Forwarding The 1982 UN Law Of The Sea Convention To The United States Senate, DOS Commentary p. 50 (William J. Clinton, Oct. 7, 1994) (S. Treaty Doc. 103–39), https://www.foreign.senate.gov/imo/media/doc/treaty_103-39.pdf. This distinction may have been made somewhat less significant by the implementation of the 1995 Straddling/Migratory Fish Stocks Agreement.

[591] United Nations Convention on the Law of the Sea (UNCLOS) art. 64 & Annex I, Dec. 10, 1982, 1833 U.N.T.S. 397, https://www.un.org/Depts/los/convention_agreements/convention_overview_convention.htm. Somewhat remarkably, the U.S. initially took a contrarian view of the management of Highly Migratory Species (HMS), arguing that Article 64's admonition for "international management of HMS throughout their migratory range" meant that foreign vessels could essentially chase HMS (like tuna) into a foreign EEZ and continue fishing them, notwithstanding UNCLOS' comprehensive framework for allocating exclusive authority to the Coastal State over the living resources in its EEZ. "The predominant view was that HMS are treated exactly the same as all other. living resources in the sense that they fall within exclusive coastal State authority in the territorial sea and EEZ". Fortunately, "the United States amended the [Magnuson Fishery Conservation and Management Act] to include HMS among all other species over which it asserts sovereign rights and exclusive fishery management authority while such species occur within the U.S. EEZ (16 U.S.C. § 1812). That amendment also recognized, at least implicitly, the right of other coastal States to assert the same sovereign rights and authority over HMS within their EEZs. With this amendment, a long-standing juridical dispute came to an end." DOS Commentary, p. 49 (full cite above).

[592] UNCLOS, arts. 65 & 120 (full cite above). See also DOS Commentary, p. 44 (full cite above) (noting that "U.S. law, including the Marine Mammal Protection Act of 1972 ... and the Whaling Convention Act of 1949 ... strictly limits the exploitation of marine mammals within the U.S. territorial sea and EEZ and by U.S. vessels and persons subject to U.S. jurisdiction elsewhere.").

[593] UNCLOS, art. 66 (full cite above). See also DOS Commentary, pp. 44–45 (full cite above) (noting that Article 66 "reflects a major U.S. policy accomplishment," because it determines that the "States in whose rivers anadromous stocks originate shall have the primary interest in and responsibility for such stocks" and "to set total allowable catches for anadromous stocks originating in its rivers. ... [T]he combined effect of the LOS Convention and these two treaties [governing the North Pacific and the North Atlantic] precludes any fishery for U.S.-origin salmon, or any other salmon, on the high seas, a major benefit to the United States.").

[594] UNCLOS, art. 67 (full cite above). See also DOS Commentary, p. 45 (full cite above) (noting that "[t]he United States exercises exclusive fishery management authority over catadromous stocks within the U.S. EEZ under the general provisions of the [Magnuson Fishery Conservation and Management Act]").

[595] UNCLOS, art. 61(2) (full cite above).

[596] UNCLOS, art. 77(1) (full cite above).

[597] United Nations Convention on the Continental Shelf art. 2(4), Apr. 29, 1958, 499 U.N.T.S. 311, https://treaties.un.org/doc/Treaties/1964/06/19640610%2002-10%20AM/Ch_XXI_01_2_3_4_5p.pdf. *See also* DOS Commentary, p. 46 (full cite above).

[598] DONALD R. ROTHWELL & TIM STEPHENS, THE INT'L. LAW OF THE SEA 125 (2nd ed. 2016).

[599] UNCLOS, arts. 68 & 77 (full cite above).

[600] United Nations Treaty Collection, Depositary, Status of Treaties, Chapter XXI Law of the Sea, 7. Agreement for the Implementation of the Provisions of the United Nations Convention on the Law of the Sea of 10 December 1982 relating to the Conservation and Management of Straddling Fish Stocks and Highly Migratory Fish Stocks, https://treaties.un.org/Pages/ViewDetails.aspx?src=TREATY&mtdsg_no=XXI-7&chapter=21&clang=_en. *See also* Michael W. Lodge (Secretary-General of the International Seabed Authority), *Enclosure of the Oceans versus the Common Heritage of Mankind: The Inherent Tension between the Continental Shelf Beyond 200 Nautical Miles and the Area*, 97 INT'L. L. STUD. 803, 805 (2021), https://digital-commons.usnwc.edu/cgi/viewcontent.cgi?article=2971&context=ils (noting that the 1995 high seas fisheries agreement is 1 of 2 UNCLOS implementing agreements, the other one being the 1994 Implementing Agreement that modified the deep seabed mining provisions in order to seek U.S. ratification of UNCLOS).

[601] UNCLOS, art. 64(1) & Annex I (full cite above); Straddling Fish Stocks Convention, art. 18 (full cite above).

[602] "Tunas are of great importance because of their high catches, high economic value and extensive international trade. Moreover, their sustainable management is subject to additional challenges owing to their highly migratory and often straddling distributions. ... In 2017, among the seven principal tuna species, 33.3 percent of the stocks were estimated to be fished at biologically unsustainable levels, while 66.6 percent were fished within biologically sustainable levels. ... Market demand for tuna remains high, and tuna fishing fleets continue to have significant overcapacity. Effective management, including the implementation of harvest control rules, is needed to restore overfished stocks and to maintain others at sustainable levels." FAO, Fisheries and Aquaculture Dept., The State of World Fisheries and Aquaculture 2020 (SOFIA 2020) p. 49, http://www.fao.org/fishery/sofia/en.

[603] United Nations, Division for Ocean Affairs and the Law of the Sea, The United Nations Agreement for the Implementation of the Provisions of the United Nations Convention on the Law of the Sea of 10 December 1982 relating to the Conservation and Management of Straddling Fish Stocks and Highly Migratory Fish Stocks (in force as from 11 December 2001) art. 18, https://www.un.org/Depts/los/convention_agreements/convention_overview_fish_stocks.htm.

[604] Straddling Fish Stocks Convention, Overview (full cite above). "Agenda 21, adopted by the 1992 United Nations Conference on Environment and Development, called upon the United Nations to convene a conference specifically devoted to [Straddling Fish Stocks and Highly Migratory Species, with] ... the resulting United Nations Conference on Straddling Fish Stocks and Highly Migratory Fish Stocks ... all participating States have agreed that any such outcome must be consistent with the LOS Convention." Letter Of Transmittal Forwarding The 1982 UN Law Of The Sea Convention To The United States Senate, DOS Commentary p. 51 (William J.

Clinton, Oct. 7, 1994) (S. Treaty Doc. 103–39), https://www.foreign.senate.gov/imo/media/doc/treaty_103-39.pdf.

[605] The Precautionary Approach is akin to the Expected Value of Perfect Information (EVPI) in economics and decision theory. EVPI recognizes that a certain level of uncertainty always exists, and questions whether the value of perfect information (which eliminates all uncertainty) is worth the cost. *See, e.g.,* wisdomjobs.com, Home, Quantitative Techniques For Management Tutorial, Expected Value With Perfect Information (EVPI) - Quantitative Techniques for Management, *Evpi Formula,* https://www.wisdomjobs.com/e-university/quantitative-techniques-for-management-tutorial-297/expected-value-with-perfect-information-evpi-10071.html; Chegg Study Textbook Solutions, home, study, math, statistics and probability, statistics and probability definitions, *expected value of perfect information,* https://www.chegg.com/homework-help/definitions/expected-value-of-perfect-information-31.

[606] Science and Environmental Health Network, Wingspread Conference on the Precautionary Principle (Jan. 26, 1998), https://www.sehn.org/sehn/wingspread-conference-on-the-precautionary-principle.

[607] *See also* Michael W. Lodge (Secretary-General of the International Seabed Authority), *Enclosure of the Oceans versus the Common Heritage of Mankind: The Inherent Tension between the Continental Shelf Beyond 200 Nautical Miles and the Area,* 97 INT'L. L. STUD. 803, 805-806 (2021), https://digital-commons.usnwc.edu/cgi/viewcontent.cgi?article=2971&context=ils (noting that "[t]he International Tribunal for the Law of the Sea (ITLOS) has also demonstrated its willingness to clarify and interpret the law in line with progressive environmental concepts such as the precautionary approach.").

[608] United Nations, Division for Ocean Affairs and the Law of the Sea, The United Nations Agreement for the Implementation of the Provisions of the United Nations Convention on the Law of the Sea of 10 December 1982 relating to the Conservation and Management of Straddling Fish Stocks and Highly Migratory Fish Stocks (in force as from 11 December 2001) art. 18, https://www.un.org/Depts/los/convention_agreements/convention_overview_fis h_stocks.htm.

[609] Straddling Fish Stocks Convention (full cite above).

[610] National Oceanic and Atmospheric Administration (NOAA), U.S. Dept. of Commerce, NOAA Fisheries, Endangered Species Conservation, Inter-American Convention for the Protection and Conservation of Sea Turtles, https://www.fisheries.noaa.gov/national/endangered-species-conservation/inter-american-convention-protection-and-conservation-sea.

[611] Inter-American Tropical Tuna Commission (IATTC), Int'l. Dolphin Conservation Program (IDCP), Agreement on the Int'l. Dolphin Conservation Program (AIDCP), https://www.iattc.org/IDCPENG.htm.

[612] For a fascinating visual depiction of marine life, follow the link below and scroll down to 3,912 meters deep to see the Patagonian Toothfish. Neal.fun, *The Deep Sea* (Neal Agarwal), https://neal.fun/deep-sea/?fbclid=IwAR1PGbjLD-MJjouPfnH3MBuejnqsUExh8NyrQK4l7qKa3XcnNr4f1hKHOiE.

[613] Oceana, Protecting the World's Oceans, Marine Life, Ocean Fishes, *Patagonian Toothfish,* https://oceana.org/marine-life/ocean-fishes/patagonian-toothfish.

[614] Other species of formerly by-catch fish that were "rebranded" include Slimehead as "Orange Roughy," and Goosefish as "Monkfish," both of which are

now also vulnerable to over-exploitation. Priceonomics, *The Invention of the Chilean Sea Bass* (Alex Mayyasi), https://priceonomics.com/the-invention-of-the-chilean-sea-bass/. *See also* The Atlantic, *History's Largest Mining Operation Is About to Begin* (Wil S. Hylton, January/February 2020), https://www.theatlantic.com/magazine/archive/2020/01/20000-feet-under-the-sea/603040/.

[615] Marine Stewardship Council, Patagonian Toothfish Story, *Back on the menu* (Jan. 2018), http://patagonian-toothfish-story.msc.org/; Foreign Policy, *The Hunt for the Last Chilean Sea Bass Poachers* (Christopher Pala, June 17, 2015), https://foreignpolicy.com/2015/06/17/chilean-sea-bass-toothfish-thunder-sea-shepherd/.

[616] Priceonomics, *The Invention of the Chilean Sea Bass* (full cite above). Chapter 8 discusses the Coastal State's right of "hot pursuit" in more depth.

[617] *See generally* United Nations, Oceans & Law of the Sea, Division for Ocean Affairs and the Law of the Sea, The Nippon Foundation of Japan Fellowship Programme ~ Human Resources Development and Advancement of the Legal Order of the World's Oceans ~, The Fellows and their Thesis [sic], Reports, *Establishment and Implementation of a Conservation and Management Regime for High Seas Fisheries, With Focus on the Southeast Pacific and Chile* (M. Cecilia Engler, 2007), https://www.un.org/depts/los/nippon/unnff_programme_home/fellows_pages/reports_index.htm. There are currently 17 RFMOs. An RFMO "is an international body made up of countries that share a practical and/or financial interest in managing and conserving fish stocks in a particular region. These include coastal States, whose waters are home to at least part of an identified fish stock, and 'distant water fishing nations' (DWFN), whose fleets travel to areas where a fish stock is found." The PEW Charitable Trusts, Fact Sheet, *FAQ: What is a Regional Fishery Management Organization?* (Feb. 23, 2012), https://www.pewtrusts.org/en/research-and-analysis/fact-sheets/2012/02/23/faq-what-is-a-regional-fishery-management-organization. RFMOs complement Flag State enforcement of IUU fishing. Food and Agriculture Organization of the United Nations (FAO), Legal Papers Online #61, *The "Genuine Link" Concept in Responsible Fisheries: Legal Aspects and Recent Developments* 12 (Ariella D'andrea, Nov. 2006), http://www.fao.org/documents/card/en/c/5299785c-bbe2-4af1-b614-5837fe3b2be0. *See also* U.S. Dept. of State, Key Topics, Office of Marine Conservation, International Fisheries Management, https://www.state.gov/key-topics-office-of-marine-conservation/international-fisheries-management/.

[618] The Sea Shepherd takes credit for its 110-day record-setting "hot pursuit" of the *Fishing Vessel (F/V) Thunder* (which was one of the "Bandit Six" IUU fishing vessels taking Patagonian Toothfish) as "galvanizing government action against the other five bandits .... Within two years of the F/V Thunder chase, all of the 'Bandit Six' had been brought to justice." Zed, Books, *An interview with Captain Peter Hammarstedt of Catching Thunder* (Apr. 13, 2018), https://www.zedbooks.net/media/show/interview-captain-peter-hammarstedt-catching-thunder/.

[619] A Catch Document Scheme (CDS) tracks Patagonian Toothfish from the point of landing throughout the trade cycle to the point of sale. The CDS requires verification and authorization by national authorities at regular intervals in the trade cycle.

[620] Seabirds (such as albatrosses) try to take bait off the longline hooks, and often get hooked themselves to become the bait as the longlines descend into the depths of the ocean.

[621] Commission for the Conservation of Antarctic Marine Living Resources (CCAMLR), Home, Fisheries, *Toothfish fisheries*, https://www.ccamlr.org/en/fisheries/toothfish-fisheries; Marine Stewardship Council, Home, Media Centre, Press Releases, *Australian Heard Island and McDonald Islands Toothfish continues to meet global sustainability standard* (July 19, 2017), https://www.msc.org/media-centre/press-releases/australian-heard-island-and-mcdonald-islands-toothfish-continues-to-meet-global-sustainability-standard; MSC, Patagonian Toothfish Story, *Back on the menu* (Jan. 2018), http://patagonian-toothfish-story.msc.org/; FishChoice, Seafood Guides, *Patagonian Toothfish*, https://fishchoice.com/buying-guide/patagonian-toothfish.

[622] Monterey Bay Aquarium Seafood Watch, Helping people make better seafood choices for a healthy ocean, Seafood Recommendations, *Toothfish Recommendations*, https://www.seafoodwatch.org/seafood-recommendations/groups/toothfish?q=Toothfish,%20Patagonian&type=patagonian. *See also* Environmental Defense Fund, EDF Seafood Selector, *Chilean Sea Bass*, http://seafood.edf.org/chilean-sea-bass.

[623] United Nations, Legal, Audiovisual Library of Int'l. Law, Environmental Law, Int'l. Convention for the Regulation of Whaling, Introductory Note 1 (Malgosia Fitzmaurice 2017), https://legal.un.org/avl/ha/icrw/icrw.html.

[624] Int'l. Convention for the Regulation of Whaling 1-2, Feb. 12, 1946, 161 U.N.T.S. 72, https://iwc.int/convention.

[625] UN, Whaling Convention, unnumbered preambular ¶ 8 (full cite above).

[626] Int'l. Whaling Commission (IWC), home, https://iwc.int/home; IWC, Commission, General Information, Membership & Contracting Governments, https://iwc.int/members.

[627] Whaling Convention, arts. III.1 & III.8 (full cite above).

[628] International Whaling Commission, Commission, Meetings, https://iwc.int/meetingsmain; IWC, Documents & Publications, List of Events & Workshops, 2020, https://iwc.int/events-and-workshops?year=2020; IWC, 68th Meeting of the International Whaling Commission (IWC68), https://sdg.iisd.org/events/68th-meeting-of-the-international-whaling-commission-iwc68/.

[629] Whaling Convention, art. V.1 (full cite above).

[630] Whaling Convention, arts. III.2 & V.1 (full cite above).

[631] IWC, Conservation & Management, Whaling, Commercial Whaling, https://iwc.int/commercial.

[632] Whaling Convention, Introductory Note, pp. 3-4 (full cite above).

[633] Whaling Convention, art. V.3 (full cite above); IWC, Commercial Whaling (full cite above). Including the ability to "opt-out" of changes to the binding Schedule (such as the 1985 zero-catch limit) was necessary to get the U.S., Netherlands, France and the Soviet Union to sign the 1946 Whaling Convention. Whaling Convention, Introductory Note, p. 1 (full cite above).

[634] IWC, Conservation & Management, Whaling, Aboriginal subsistence whaling, Catch Limits, Catches taken: Under Objection, https://iwc.int/table_objection; Whaling Convention, Introductory Note, p. 4 (full cite above).

[635] Whaling Convention, Introductory Note, p. 3 (full cite above). *See also* National Oceanic and Atmospheric Administration (NOAA), U.S. Dept. of Commerce, NOAA

Fisheries, Int'l. Affairs, IWC, https://www.fisheries.noaa.gov/international-affairs/international-whaling-commission.

[636] Whaling Convention, art. VIII.1 & p. 4 (full cite above).

[637] IWC, Conservation & Management, Whaling, Aboriginal subsistence whaling, Catch Limits, Scientific Permit Whaling, https://iwc.int/table_permit. The Int'l. Court of Justice (ICJ) put a temporary halt to Japan's scientific "research" whaling in 2014 when it ruled that Japan had failed to prove the scientific research justification for its whaling. The Guardian, *Japan told to halt Antarctic whaling by international court* (Mar. 31, 2014), https://www.theguardian.com/environment/2014/mar/31/japanese-whaling-halt-antarctic-international-court. *See also* BBC News, *Japan to resume whaling in Antarctic despite court ruling* (28 November 2015), https://www.bbc.com/news/world-asia-34952538; Int'l. Court of Justice (ICJ), Whaling in the Antarctic (Australia v. Japan: New Zealand intervening), https://www.icj-cij.org/en/case/148; Whaling Convention, Introductory Note, pp. 5-6 (full cite above).

[638] Whaling Convention, art. VIII.2 (full cite above).

[639] IWC, Conservation & Management, Whaling, Aboriginal subsistence whaling, https://iwc.int/aboriginal; IWC, Commission General Information, Commission Sub-groups, Aboriginal Subsistence Whaling Sub-Committee, https://iwc.int/aboriginal-subsistence-whaling-sub-committee.

[640] Whaling Convention, Schedule ¶ 13(b)(1)-(4) (full cite above).

[641] NOAA, IWC (full cite above). *See also* IWC, Conservation & Management, Whaling, Aboriginal subsistence whaling, Catch Limits, Catches taken: ASW, https://iwc.int/table_aboriginal; IWC, Conservation & Management, Whaling, Aboriginal subsistence whaling, Information on hunts, https://iwc.int/information-on-hunts.

[642] Canada withdrew in 1982 (soon after the moratorium on whaling), Jamaica withdrew in 1984, Mauritius and Philippines withdrew in 1988, Egypt withdrew in 1989, Seychelles withdrew in 1995, Venezuela withdrew in 1999, Greece withdrew in 2013, and Japan withdrew in 2019. IWC, Membership (full cite above).

[643] The Guardian, World, Japan, *Japan launches bid to end ban on commercial whaling* (Justin McCurry & Graham Readfearn, Sep. 11, 2018), https://www.theguardian.com/world/2018/sep/11/japan-launches-bid-to-end-ban-on-commercial-whaling; BBC News, News, World, Asia, *Japan resumes commercial whaling after 30 years* (July 1, 2019), https://www.bbc.com/news/world-asia-48821797; NBC News, World, *Japan resumes commercial whaling after three decades* (Yuliya Talmazan, July 1, 2019), https://www.nbcnews.com/news/world/japan-resume-commercial-whaling-n1025046.

[644] Whaling Convention, Introductory Note, p. 4 (full cite above).

[645] Emmanuella Doussis, *Marine Scientific Research: Taking Stock and Looking Ahead*, *in* THE FUTURE OF THE LAW OF THE SEA 87, 87-88 (Gemma Andreone ed., 2017), https://link.springer.com/book/10.1007/978-3-319-51274-7, citing David Kenneth Leary, INT'L. LAW AND THE GENETIC RESOURCES OF THE DEEP SEA 8 (2006), https://brill.com/view/title/13344.

[646] U.S. Dept. of State, Bureau of Oceans and Int'l. Environmental and Scientific Affairs, Policy Issues, The Ocean and Polar Affairs, Key Topics, Marine Science, Marine Scientific Research Consent Overview, https://www.state.gov/marine-scientific-research-consent-overview/. *See also* Emmanuella Doussis, *Marine Scientific Research: Taking Stock and Looking Ahead*, *in* THE FUTURE OF THE LAW OF THE

SEA 99 (Gemma Andreone ed., 2017), https://link.springer.com/book/10.1007/978-3-319-51274-7 (noting that the lack of an MSR definition means that "there is no clear answer" whether it includes military surveys and bioprospecting).

[647] UNITED NATIONS OFFICE FOR OCEAN AFFAIRS AND THE LAW OF THE SEA, THE LAW OF THE SEA, MARINE SCIENTIFIC RESEARCH: A REVISED GUIDE TO THE IMPLEMENTATION OF THE RELEVANT PROVISIONS OF THE UNITED NATIONS CONVENTION ON THE LAW OF THE SEA 4-6 (2010), https://www.un.org/Depts/los/doalos_publications/publicationstexts/msr_guide%202010_final.pdf.

[648] MarineBio, Marine Life, A History of the Study of Marine Biology (Feb. 16, 2019), https://marinebio.org/creatures/marine-biology/history-of-marine-biology/.

[649] National Oceanic and Atmospheric Administration (NOAA), U.S. Dept. of Commerce, Office of General Counsel, Marine Scientific Research, https://www.gc.noaa.gov/gcil_marine_research.html.

[650] Michael W. Lodge (Secretary-General of the International Seabed Authority), *Enclosure of the Oceans versus the Common Heritage of Mankind: The Inherent Tension between the Continental Shelf Beyond 200 Nautical Miles and the Area*, 97 INT'L. L. STUD. 803, 825 (2021), https://digital-commons.usnwc.edu/cgi/viewcontent.cgi?article=2971&context=ils.

[651] Letter Of Transmittal Forwarding The 1982 UN Law Of The Sea Convention To The United States Senate, DOS Commentary pp. 79-80 (William J. Clinton, Oct. 7, 1994) (S. Treaty Doc. 103–39), https://www.foreign.senate.gov/imo/media/doc/treaty_103-39.pdf.

[652] United Nations Convention on the Law of the Sea (UNCLOS) arts. 21(1)(g), 40, 54 & 245, Dec. 10, 1982, 1833 U.N.T.S. 397, https://www.un.org/Depts/los/convention_agreements/convention_overview_convention.htm; Emmanuella Doussis, *Marine Scientific Research: Taking Stock and Looking Ahead*, *in* THE FUTURE OF THE LAW OF THE SEA 87, 91-92 (Gemma Andreone ed., 2017), https://link.springer.com/book/10.1007/978-3-319-51274-7; DOS Commentary, p. 81 (full cite above).

[653] UNCLOS, art. 19(2)(j) (full cite above).

[654] UNCLOS, arts. 56(1)(b)(ii), 62(4)(f), & 246(1)-(2) (full cite above); Doussis, *Marine Scientific Research*, p. 92 (full cite above).

[655] UNCLOS, art. 246(3) (full cite above).

[656] UNCLOS, art. 246(4) (full cite above); DOS Commentary, p. 81 (full cite above). For example, the U.S. could potentially grant a permit to Iranian scientists to conduct MSR in the U.S. EEZ off the coast of Guam, even though the U.S. and Iran do not have diplomatic relations. U.S. Dept. of State, Countries & Areas, Iran, Bilateral Relations Fact Sheet, https://www.state.gov/u-s-relations-with-iran/; WorldAtlas, Politics, Countries With Whom The U.S. Has No Diplomatic Relations, https://www.worldatlas.com/articles/countries-with-whom-the-us-has-no-diplomatic-relations.html.

[657] NOAA Ocean Exploration and Research, Science & Technology, Vessels, NOAA Ship Pisces, https://oceanexplorer.noaa.gov/technology/vessels/pisces/pisces.html. There is also an American Academic Research Fleet, coordinated by the University-National Oceanographic Laboratory System. University-National Oceanographic Laboratory System (UNOLS), Vision, Mission, and Top Issues, https://www.unols.org/what-unols/vision-mission-and-top-issues. The U.S. National Science Foundation (NSF) and U.S. Navy Office of Naval Research fund a

number of academic MSR projects, and even "own research vessels that are operated by civilian institutes and incorporated into UNOLS." China also has a fleet of 50 maritime research vessels. The National Interest, *Chinese Scientists Want to Conduct Research in U.S. Waters—Should Washington Let Them?* (Ryan Martinson & Peter Dutton, Nov. 4, 2018), https://nationalinterest.org/feature/chinese-scientists-want-conduct-research-us-waters%E2%80%94should-washington-let-them-34997.

[658] UNCLOS, art. 249 (full cite above).

[659] UNCLOS, art. 253 (full cite above).

[660] UNCLOS, arts. 87(1)(f), 143, & 256-257 (full cite above); Doussis, *Marine Scientific Research*, p. 93 (full cite above). *But see* Doussis, *Marine Scientific Research*, p. 101 (full cite above) (noting that UNCLOS strikes the balance between Coastal States and researching States in favor of the former: "in the case of MSR, the balance seems to weigh more on the side of the coastal States. As it was eloquently noted: 'freedom of MSR has ceased to exist in the law of the sea.' Admittedly, MSR is not yet free but largely controlled by the coastal States even in some parts of the high seas. This might explain why our knowledge on many issues concerning the role of the oceans is still limited.").

[661] As discussed in Chapter 2, UNCLOS entered into force in 1994.

[662] United Nations Educational, Scientific, and Cultural Organization (UNESCO), Intergovernmental Oceanographic Commission, Resources, Meetings, Documents, People, Marine Scientific Research, Practices of Member States, http://ioc-unesco.org/index.php?option=com_content&view=article&id=310&Itemid=100025; UN, MSR: A REVISED GUIDE, (full cite above).

[663] UNCLOS, art. 250 (full cite above).

[664] UNCLOS, art. 246(3) (full cite above).

[665] UNCLOS, art. 252 (full cite above). *But see* Doussis, *Marine Scientific Research*, pp. 87, 92 (full cite above) (noting that "the possibility of a presumed and an implied consent [for MSR] ... have been ignored by State practice.").

[666] UNCLOS, art. 255 (full cite above). *But see* Doussis, *Marine Scientific Research*, p. 94 (full cite above) (noting that "only few coastal States have enacted special national legislation to prescribe procedures necessary for conducting MSR, but overall it seems that their practice is more or less consistent with the UNCLOS requirements.").

[667] U.S. Dept. of State, Bureau of Oceans and Int'l. Environmental and Scientific Affairs, Policy Issues, The Ocean and Polar Affairs, Key Topics, Marine Science, Marine Scientific Research Consent Overview, https://www.state.gov/marine-scientific-research-consent-overview/.

[668] U.S. Dept. of State, MSR Consent Overview (full cite above); U.S. Dept. of State, Bureau of Oceans and Int'l. Environmental and Scientific Affairs, Policy Issues, The Ocean and Polar Affairs, Key Topics, Marine Science, Marine Scientific Research, https://www.state.gov/marine-scientific-research/.

[669] U.S. Dept. of State, MSR Consent Overview (full cite above). *But see* The National Interest, *Chinese Scientists* (full cite above). (arguing that the U.S. "needs to update its MSR policy to better cope with the China challenge. It should focus on two key aims. First, it should strive to better understand which Chinese operations are for scientific advancement and which are military surveys. ... By requiring permission for states to conduct MSR in American waters, U.S. authorities would be better able to identify those Chinese vessels that are operating in U.S. waters to achieve a purely military objective. Second, the United States should insist on

reciprocity. Simply put, U.S. ships conducting military surveys in Chinese waters should be accorded the same respectful treatment that Chinese vessels have always received in U.S. waters. Thus, this shift in policy would advance two important objectives—it would impose more clarity about the nature of Chinese operations in American waters and it would establish a stronger basis for reciprocal respect for American military surveys in Chinese waters.").

[670] The National Interest, *Chinese Scientists Want to Conduct Research in U.S. Waters—Should Washington Let Them?* (Ryan Martinson & Peter Dutton, Nov. 4, 2018), https://nationalinterest.org/feature/chinese-scientists-want-conduct-research-us-waters%E2%80%94should-washington-let-them-34997. *See also* Letter Of Transmittal Forwarding The 1982 UN Law Of The Sea Convention To The United States Senate, DOS Commentary p. 80 (William J. Clinton, Oct. 7, 1994) (S. Treaty Doc. 103–39), https://www.foreign.senate.gov/imo/media/doc/treaty_103-39.pdf.

[671] THE FLETCHER SCHOOL OF LAW AND DIPLOMACY—TUFTS UNIVERSITY, LAW OF THE SEA, A POLICY PRIMER 13 (2017), https://sites.tufts.edu/lawofthesea/introduction/ (estimating the U.S. EEZ at 3.4M square nm); DOS Commentary, p. 6 (full cite above).

[672] U.S. Dept. of State, Bureau of Oceans and Int'l. Environmental and Scientific Affairs, Policy Issues, The Ocean and Polar Affairs, Key Topics, Marine Science, Marine Scientific Research Consent Overview, https://www.state.gov/marine-scientific-research-consent-overview/. *See also* U.S. Dept. of State, Bureau of Oceans and Int'l. Environmental and Scientific Affairs, Policy Issues, The Ocean and Polar Affairs, Key Topics, Marine Science, Marine Scientific Research, About the Research Application Tracking System, https://www.state.gov/research-application-tracking-system/; U.S. Dept. of State, Marine Science Research Application Tracking System, https://rats.state.gov/PublicFunctionality/Login.aspx?ReturnUrl=%2f.

[673] U.S. Dept. of State, About the Research Application Tracking System (full cite above).

[674] National Oceanic and Atmospheric Administration (NOAA), U.S. Dept. of Commerce, Office of Coast Survey, Data, U.S. Maritime Limits & Boundaries, https://www.nauticalcharts.noaa.gov/data/us-maritime-limits-and-boundaries.html.

[675] U.S. Dept. of State, Bureau of Oceans and Int'l. Environmental and Scientific Affairs, Policy Issues, The Ocean and Polar Affairs, Key Topics, Marine Science, Marine Scientific Research, Guidance on Supporting Documentation, https://www.state.gov/guidance-on-supporting-documentation/.

[676] U.S. Dept. of State, MSR Consent Overview (full cite above). "NOAA seeks to leverage and benefit from the marine scientific research conducted by foreign scientists in waters subject to U.S. jurisdiction by routinely requesting the data and reports that such research generates." NOAA, Office of General Counsel, Marine Scientific Research, https://www.gc.noaa.gov/gcil_marine_research.html.

[677] TUFTS, LAW OF THE SEA, p. 32 (full cite above). *See also* DOS Commentary, p. 80 (full cite above).

[678] America's Navy, Forged by the Sea, News, *Diagramming the Deep: Navy-Sponsored Scientist Awarded for Sea-Floor Mapping* (Warren Duffie, Jr., Feb. 6, 2019), https://www.navy.mil/submit/display.asp?story_id=108543.

[679] Raul (Pete) Pedrozo, *Military Activities in the Exclusive Economic Zone: East Asia Focus*, 90 INT'L. L. STUD. 514, 525-526 (2014), https://digital-commons.usnwc.edu/ils/vol90/iss1/15/ (noting that: "The distinction between MSR

and other forms of marine data collection articulated in UNCLOS reflect centuries of State practice. ... U.S. naval units have plied the world's oceans for more than 180 years conducting military marine data collection since the Dept. of Charts and Instruments was first established in 1830.").

[680] Michael W. Lodge (Secretary-General of the International Seabed Authority), *Enclosure of the Oceans versus the Common Heritage of Mankind: The Inherent Tension between the Continental Shelf Beyond 200 Nautical Miles and the Area*, 97 INT'L. L. STUD. 803, 825 (2021), https://digital-commons.usnwc.edu/cgi/viewcontent.cgi?article=2971&context=ils.

[681] DONALD R. ROTHWELL & TIM STEPHENS, THE INT'L. LAW OF THE SEA 330-331 (2nd ed. 2016); U.S. NAVY, MARINE CORPS & COAST GUARD, THE COMMANDER'S HANDBOOK ON THE LAW OF NAVAL OPERATIONS, NWP 1-14M/MCTP 11-10B/COMDTPUB P5800.7A, ¶ 2.6.2.2 (p. 2-11) (2017), www.jag.navy.mil/distrib/instructions/CDRs_HB_on_Law_of_Naval_Operations _AUG17.pdf. *But see* ROTHWELL & STEPHENS, LAW OF THE SEA, p. 92 (full cite above) (noting that China includes intelligence gathering and surveys in its EEZ as MSR requiring Coastal State consent); Dept. of Defense Maritime Claims Reference Manual (MCRM)—China 2017 p.3, http://www.jag.navy.mil/organization/code_10_mcrm.htm. In order to remain somewhat internally consistent, China apparently attempts to disguise its own military surveys in the U.S. EEZ as MSR. The National Interest, *Chinese Scientists* (full cite above).

[682] UNITED NATIONS OFFICE FOR OCEAN AFFAIRS AND THE LAW OF THE SEA, THE LAW OF THE SEA, MARINE SCIENTIFIC RESEARCH: A REVISED GUIDE TO THE IMPLEMENTATION OF THE RELEVANT PROVISIONS OF THE UNITED NATIONS CONVENTION ON THE LAW OF THE SEA 6 ¶ 14 & 16 ¶ 56 (2010), https://www.un.org/Depts/los/doalos_publications/publicationstexts/msr_guide %202010_final.pdf.

[683] The Atlantic, *History's Largest Mining Operation Is About to Begin* (Wil S. Hylton, January/February 2020), https://www.theatlantic.com/magazine/archive/2020/01/20000-feet-under-the-sea/603040/; Emmanuella Doussis, *Marine Scientific Research: Taking Stock and Looking Ahead, in* THE FUTURE OF THE LAW OF THE SEA 87, 89, 98 (Gemma Andreone ed., 2017), https://link.springer.com/book/10.1007/978-3-319-51274-7.

[684] The Atlantic, *History's Largest Mining Operation* (full cite above).

[685] JSTOR Daily, where news meets its scholarly match, Science & Technology, *The Wildest Inventions in Scientific Research* (James MacDonald, Apr. 24, 2018), https://daily.jstor.org/the-wildest-inventions-in-scientific-research/.

[686] ROTHWELL & STEPHENS, LAW OF THE SEA, p. 1 (full cite above); Woods Hole Oceanographic Institution, oceanus magazine, *The Discovery of Hydrothermal Vents* (Evan Lubofsky, June 11, 2018), https://www.whoi.edu/oceanus/feature/the-discovery-of-hydrothermal-vents/; Woods Hole, Know Your Ocean, Ocean Topics, Ocean Life, *Life at Vents & Seeps*, https://www.whoi.edu/know-your-ocean/ocean-topics/ocean-life/life-at-vents-seeps/.

[687] NOAA, Ocean Exploration and Research, Expeditions, *Bioprospecting for Industrial Enzymes and Drug Compounds in an Ancient Submarine Forest* (Aug.-Dec. 2020), https://oceanexplorer.noaa.gov/explorations/20ancient-forest/welcome.html; CNN, Live, *Scientists uncover a 60,000-year-old forest underwater and think its preserved trees may help pioneer new medicines* (Alicia Lee, Apr. 8, 2020), https://www.cnn.com/2020/04/07/us/ancient-underwater-forest-

alabama-scn-trnd/index.html. *See also* U.S. Dept. of State, Bureau of Oceans and Int'l. Environmental and Scientific Affairs, Policy Issues, The Ocean and Polar Affairs, Key Topics, Marine Science, Marine Scientific Research Consent Overview, https://www.state.gov/marine-scientific-research-consent-overview/. *See also* Emmanuella Doussis, *Marine Scientific Research: Taking Stock and Looking Ahead, in* THE FUTURE OF THE LAW OF THE SEA 87, 99 (Gemma Andreone ed., 2017), https://link.springer.com/book/10.1007/978-3-319-51274-7 (noting that the lack of an MSR definition means that "there is no clear answer" whether it includes military surveys and bioprospecting).

[688] CNN, World, *This 'wandering meatloaf' chiton has a rare mineral in its teeth* (Ashley Strickland, May 31, 2021), https://www.cnn.com/2021/05/31/world/rare-mineral-chiton-mollusk-teeth-scn/index.html?utm_term=1622543628560f14b54496986&utm_source=cnn_Five+Things+for+Tuesday%2C+June+1%2C+2021&utm_medium=email&bt_ee=FBS%2B3TaLqR7ARcP%2FJYCBR1N9Dq4IhwRjyK8FjTiGgoItlIE15rZ1%2BtV6sBpGL%2BKE&bt_ts=1622543628562.

[689] The National Wildlife Foundation, Educational Resources, Wildlife Guide, Invertebrates, *Horseshoe Crab*, https://www.nwf.org/Educational-Resources/Wildlife-Guide/Invertebrates/Horseshoe-Crab.

[690] National Oceanic and Atmospheric Administration (NOAA), U.S. Dept. of Commerce, NOAA Fisheries, News, *Horseshoe Crabs: Managing a Resource for Birds, Bait, and Blood* (July 31, 2018), https://www.fisheries.noaa.gov/feature-story/horseshoe-crabs-managing-resource-birds-bait-and-blood.

[691] Cool Green Science, Smarter by Nature, Fish & Fisheries, *The Underwater Secrets of Horseshoe Crabs* (Joe Smith, July 26, 2017), https://blog.nature.org/science/2017/07/26/underwater-secrets-horseshoe-crabs-spawning/.

[692] The Atlantic, Technology, *The Blood Harvest* (Alexis C. Madrigal, February 26, 2014), https://www.theatlantic.com/technology/archive/2014/02/the-blood-harvest/284078/; Atlantic States Marine Fisheries Commission, Management, *Horseshoe Crab*, http://www.asmfc.org/species/horseshoe-crab.

[693] Getty Images (left); Andrew Tingle (right).

[694] The Golden Goose Award, Celebrating Scientific Success Stories, Awardees, 2019: The Blood of the Horseshoe Crab, *The Blood of the Horseshoe Crab: Its Improbable Contribution to International Public Health*, https://www.goldengooseaward.org/awardees/horseshoe-crab-blood.

[695] Johns Hopkins, Bloomberg School of Public Health, About, History, Heroes of Public Health, Frederik Bang, MD, https://www.jhsph.edu/about/history/heroes-of-public-health/frederik-bang.html. Dr. Bang and his collaborator, Dr. Jack Levin, were awarded the "Golden Goose" award in 2019, which recognizes federally funded researchers "for breakthroughs in the development of life-saving medicines and treatments; game-changing social and behavioral insights; and major technological advances related to national security, energy, the environment, communications, and public health." The Golden Goose Award, Celebrating Scientific Success Stories, About, History, https://www.goldengooseaward.org/history; The Golden Goose Award, Celebrating Scientific Success Stories, Awardees, 2019: The Blood of the Horseshoe Crab, *The Blood of the Horseshoe Crab: Its Improbable Contribution to International Public Health*, https://www.goldengooseaward.org/awardees/horseshoe-crab-blood.

[696] The Golden Goose Award, Celebrating Scientific Success Stories, Awardees, 2019: The Blood of the Horseshoe Crab, *The Blood of the Horseshoe Crab: Its Improbable Contribution to International Public Health*, https://www.goldengooseaward.org/awardees/horseshoe-crab-blood.

[697] Atlantic States Marine Fisheries Commission, *Horseshoe Crab* (full cite above).

[698] The Atlantic, *The Blood Harvest* (full cite above); Popular Mechanics, Science, Health, *This Crab's Blood Is the Reason You're Alive* (Caren Chesler, Aug. 23, 2019), https://www.popularmechanics.com/science/health/a26038/the-blood-of-the-crab/?utm_source=pocket-newtab.

[699] *But see* Zed, Books, *An interview with Captain Peter Hammarstedt of Catching Thunder* (Apr. 13, 2018), https://www.zedbooks.net/media/show/interview-captain-peter-hammarstedt-catching-thunder/ (arguing that "[i]f current trends continue, then by 2048 all of the world's major fisheries will collapse.").

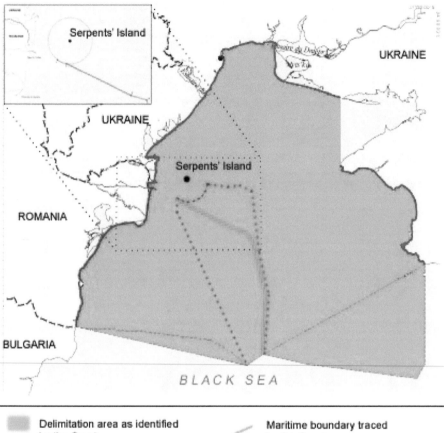

▦	Delimitation area as identified by the Court	╱ Maritime boundary traced by the Court
—	Romania's relevant coasts	⋯ Romania's claim
—	Ukraine's relevant coasts	⋯ Ukraine's claim

700

CHAPTER 8:
DELIMITATION, REGULATION & ENFORCEMENT

"We made it Son—International Waters, the land that law forgot.—Homer Simpson
"Wow! You can do anything out here."—Bart Simpson (television character)

BEFORE UNCLOS, the only effective maritime zone was the Customary International Law (CIL) norm of Coastal States (aka "littoral States") claiming sovereignty over a 3 nautical mile (nm) Territorial Sea.[701] Therefore, the only States which needed to define (or "delimit") their maritime borders were generally neighboring States (i.e., those States whose coastlines are adjoining or side-by-side, such as the east coasts of Romania and Ukraine on the preceding chart). Delimitation of maritime borders was therefore less significant and less controversial before UNCLOS went into effect in 1994.

As discussed in Chapters 3, 4 and 6, besides extending Territorial Seas to 12 nm, UNCLOS created the new 200 nm Exclusive Economic Zone (EEZ), and pushed out the default Continental Shelf to 200 nm (with the possibility of a Coastal State extending its Continental Shelf even further if it can prove it). Moreover, now under UNCLOS, Coastal States own all resources within 200 nm (either under the EEZ or Continental Shelf regimes), and all mineral resources, non-living resources, and sedentary species on any Outer Continental Shelf claims. Therefore, UNCLOS not only created more overlapping maritime claims (with 200 nm EEZs and Continental Shelves much more likely to overlap than 3 nm Territorial Seas), but also put much more at stake (i.e., extensive resources in the EEZ and on the Continental Shelf), making the delimitation of maritime borders much more significant and potentially much more controversial! Thus, there is a far greater need under UNCLOS to reduce uncertainty[702] between bordering States, and to resolve any conflicts peacefully in delimiting their maritime borders.

Of the 195 States in the world,[703] 45 of them are "landlocked" (i.e., they have no coastlines bordering the ocean), which leaves 150 Coastal States. These 150 Coastal States have approximately 400 maritime borders with other States, of which approximately 200 (50%) have not yet been delimited between neighboring States![704] For example, the U.S. has maritime borders with 11 States, and has treaties and other international agreements delimiting maritime boundaries with each of them (although the 2 asterisked below have not yet gone into effect):

1) **Canada**;   2) **Cook Islands**;
3) **Cuba** (*including the Continental Shelf in the Eastern Gulf of Mexico beyond 200 Nautical Miles);
4) **Kiribati**;   5) Federated States of **Micronesia**;
6) **Mexico** (*including the Maritime Boundary in the Eastern Gulf of Mexico);
7) **New Zealand**; 8) **Niue**; 9) **Russia**n Federation;
10) **United Kingdom**; and 11) **Venezuela**.[705]

Before UNCLOS, with only 3 nm Territorial Sea borders to define, the main theory of delimitation was "equity." The most common equitable resolution was a line equidistant from each State (i.e., a median line, drawn half-way between each State).[706] However, equidistance was not always the most equitable solution if special circumstances existed,[707] such as in the very narrow Straits of Johor between Malaysia and Singapore. In 1928, the British Prime Minister and the Sultan of Johor agreed to use the middle of the main deep water navigable channel (*Thalweg*, pronounced "*tall-vegg*"), which was equitable, but not equidistant (i.e., sometimes it is closer to the Malaysian coastline, and sometimes to the Singapore coastline).[708]

Another pre-UNCLOS maritime border delimitation was the landmark 1969 North Sea Continental Shelf Case before the World Court—the International Court of Justice (ICJ). The 7 States bordering the North Sea could not agree on what was an "equitable" division of the scientific Continental Shelf in the North Sea, which contained huge submarine oil deposits. Article 6 of the 1958 Convention on the Continental Shelf provided that the "median line" or "equidistance" was the default delimitation of Continental Shelf claims, unless "special circumstances" exist. Germany argued for a just and equitable share of the Continental Shelf based upon special circumstances, but Denmark and the Netherlands didn't agree, wanting Germany to be limited to a small Continental Shelf "box" based upon equidistance and German's concave coastline in the North Sea (which is shaped like a backwards "L").

The 7 Coastal States involved agreed to submit their dispute to the ICJ, asking the World Court not to necessarily delimit the States' borders, but to provide the applicable principles and rules of International Law. In the 1969 North Sea Continental Shelf Case, the World Court held:

1) Article 6 of the 1958 Convention on the Continental Shelf did not apply, because Germany was not yet a party (Germany had signed but not yet ratified the treaty).[709]

2) Nor did Article 6 of the 1958 Convention on the Continental Shelf represent Customary International Law (CIL).

3) Delimitation of maritime borders must be by agreement between States, who had an:
   a. obligation to negotiate in good faith,
   b. taking into account all relevant circumstances,
   c. in order to arrive at an equitable solution.

4) All relevant circumstances included:

a. The general configuration of the coastlines of the Parties;

b. The presence of any special or unusual features;

c. The physical and geological structure and natural resources of the Continental Shelf areas involved; and

d. A reasonable degree of proportionality (e.g., the size of Germany as a State).[710]

After the 1969 ICJ decision in the North Sea Continental Shelf Case, the 7 States involved arrived at this "equitable" solution.

Projectie: Europe Lambert Conformal Conic - ED 1950

Another pre-UNCLOS maritime border delimitation was the Gulf of Maine, which is shared between the U.S. and Canada. [NOTE: white represents land and grey represents water in the first chart on the left—the colors are inverted on the chart on the right.] The

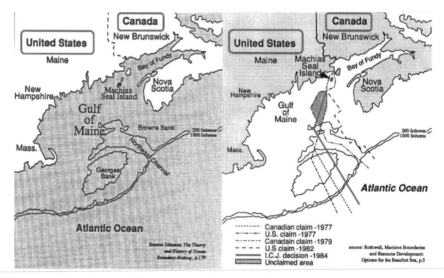

U.S. and Canada could not agree how to delimit the border, but they agreed to let the ICJ decide. The chart on the right depicts where the ICJ delimited the border in 1984, in a 300-page decision (including detailed charts and lists of resources, claims, currents, etc.).[711]

The UNCLOS articles on delimitation vary by maritime zone. In the Territorial Seas, Article 15 specifies that:

Article 15 / Delimitation of the territorial sea between States with opposite or adjacent coasts

Where the coasts of two States are opposite or adjacent to each other, neither of the two States is entitled, failing agreement between them to the contrary, to extend its territorial sea beyond the median line every point of which is equidistant from the nearest points on the baselines from which the breadth of the territorial seas of each of the two

States is measured. The above provision does not apply, however, where it is necessary by reason of historic title or other special circumstances to delimit the territorial seas of the two States in a way which is at variance therewith. [emphasis added][712]

Thus, (1) the default delimitation of Territorial Sea claims between neighboring Coastal States is the median line/equidistance, unless (2) the States reach another equitable agreement,[713] or (3) historic title, or (4) special circumstances exist.

As discussed in Chapter 4, Article 33 is the only provision in UNCLOS pertaining to the Contiguous Zone. However, Article 33 does not mention delimiting the Contiguous Zones between neighboring States because the Contiguous Zone overlaps with the Exclusive Economic Zone (EEZ), and any EEZ delimitations would encompass overlapping Contiguous Zones as well.

Delimiting EEZs is addressed in Article 74, which provides no default delimitation of EEZ claims between neighboring Coastal States.[714] Instead, Article 74(1) provides that "[t]he delimitation of the exclusive economic zone between States with opposite or adjacent coasts shall be effected by agreement on the basis of international law, as referred to in Article 38 of the Statute of the International Court of Justice, in order to achieve an equitable solution." This expressly incorporates the 4 sources of International Law discussed in Chapter 2 and considered by the World Court, especially treaties and Customary International Law (CIL).[715] Article 74(2) provides that "[i]f no agreement can be reached within a reasonable period of time, the States concerned shall resort to the procedures provided for in Part XV" (Settlement of Disputes, discussed in Chapter 12). Thus, (1) there is no default delimitation under UNCLOS of EEZ claims between neighboring Coastal States, (2) who are admonished to reach an agreement, (3) in order to achieve an equitable solution, and if no agreement, (4) to resort to mandatory dispute settlement.

The problem (as we shall see in Chapter 12), is that States have the ability to "opt out" of mandatory dispute settlement for the delimitation of their maritime borders.[716] Thus, if neighboring Coastal States cannot reach an agreement to delimit their EEZ claims, and one or both of them have opted out of mandatory dispute settlement for the delimitation of their maritime borders, the neighboring Coastal States are back to the diplomatic negotiating table to reach an equitable agreement, and there is no way to force a resolution "within a reasonable period of time."

For delimiting Continental Shelf claims, Article 83 repeats the language from Article 74 verbatim, and simply substitutes "Continental Shelf" for "EEZ." Thus, the same process applies,[717] with the same issue if one or both of them have opted out of mandatory dispute settlement for the delimitation of their maritime borders.[718] The delimitation of EEZ and Continental Shelf claims harken back to the 1969 decision in the North Sea Continental Shelf case, where the ICJ held that delimitation of maritime borders must be by agreement between States, who have an obligation to negotiate in good faith, taking into account all relevant circumstances, in order to arrive at an equitable solution.

The delimitation decisions made by international tribunals and the delimitation rules in UNCLOS are very general in nature, which means it is not always straight-forward to apply them to precisely resolve a specific problem (i.e., their application is necessarily fact- and situation-specific). In other words, the concepts of equidistance and equitable factors[719] as applied to delimitation of maritime claims seems logical enough in theory, but actually applying them to real world geography is much more complicated.

One modern example of maritime borders that still need to be delimited post-UNCLOS are the maritime borders between North and South Korea in the Western (aka Yellow) Sea. The 1953 Korean Armistice Agreement established a military demarcation line on land at the 38th parallel of Latitude, but did not delimit a maritime border in the Western Sea between North and South Korea. The U.S.-led United Nations (UN) military forces unilaterally set the "Northern Limit Line" north of the South Korean islands, labeled as blue line A in the chart below. In 1999 (46 years later), North Korea unilaterally asserted a maritime Military Demilitarization Line, labeled as red line B below, which provides South Korea with very narrow (3 nm wide) maritime "corridors" to reach its islands. In 2006, South Korea "opted out" of mandatory dispute settlement for delimitations of maritime borders (discussed in Chapter 12).

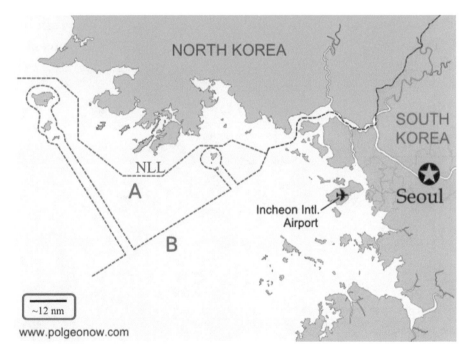

www.polgeonow.com

Like the U.S., North Korea is not party to UNCLOS. Unlike the U.S., however, there is no indication that North Korea considers UNCLOS in general to represent Customary International Law

(CIL), let alone the specific provisions for delimiting maritime border claims between neighboring Coastal States. Thus, the only means of delimiting their maritime borders in the Western Sea would be for North and South Korea to negotiate an agreement in good faith in order to achieve an equitable solution. As discussed in Chapter 1, until international relations between North and South Korea "normalize" and they are able to negotiate an equitable settlement, the maritime border between North and South Korea is likely to remain in limbo.

Another modern example of a maritime border that still needs to be delimited post-UNCLOS is the Territorial Sea boundary between Iraq and Iran. Below is a chart of the Northern Arabian (aka Persian) Gulf (NAG), including the two Iraqi offshore gas and oil platforms (GOPLATs): the *Khawr al Amiyah* Oil Terminal (KAAOT) and the *Al Basrah* Oil Terminal (ABOT). Eighty percent of

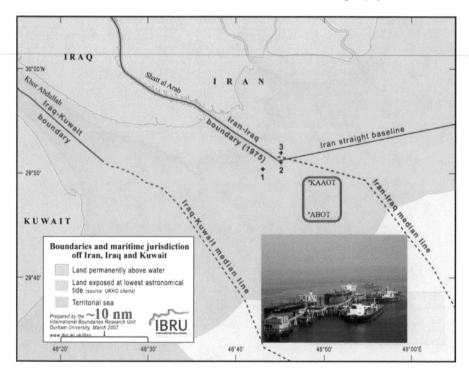

Iraq's Gross Domestic Product flows through these two GOPLATs, which are essentially "gas stations at sea" that fill up oil tankers to export Iraq's oil. Although Iran and Iraq established a land border along the *Thalweg* in the *Shatt al Arab* (SAA) river in 1975,[720] they did not delimit their Territorial Sea boundary. Although Iran signed UNCLOS, it has not yet ratified UNCLOS. Iran is also not party to the 1958 Convention on the Territorial Sea and the Contiguous Zone (unlike the U.S.).[721] Also unlike the U.S., there is no indication that Iran considers UNCLOS in general to represent Customary International Law (CIL), let alone the specific provisions for delimiting maritime border claims between neighboring Coastal States. Thus, despite the "Iran-Iraq median line" marked as a red-dashed line on the preceding chart, there is no indication that Iran and Iraq have accepted this median line as the default delimitation of their Territorial Seas boundary. [NOTE: when the author deployed to the NAG in 2004, he advised the Expeditionary Strike Group Three Commander, Brigadier General Joe Medina, who established the "Medina Line" extending the

Thalweg (just north of Iraq's KAAOT GOPLAT) as the *de facto* Territorial Sea maritime boundary between Iran and Iraq.][722] In fact, Iran's straight baseline claim (marked as a solid black line on the preceding chart), would appear to argue against Iran accepting the median line as the delimitation of Iran and Iraq's Territorial Sea boundary. Thus, the only means of delimiting their maritime borders in the NAG would be for Iran and Iraq to negotiate an agreement in good faith in order to achieve an equitable solution. Given the current closer diplomatic relations between Iran and Iraq, this may be possible.

REGULATION & ENFORCEMENT

This Chapter's second sub-topic is a Coastal State's ability both to regulate and to enforce its regulations in each of its maritime zones. The bottom line up front (BLUF) is that a Coastal State can enact and enforce laws and regulations to the extent it exercises control over each of its maritime zones (thus it varies by maritime zone), but jurisdiction is limited, and if only civil (i.e., monetary) penalties are available, then the Coastal State must "promptly release" any arrested vessels and their crews if the ship's Master or Flag State posts a reasonable "bond."

The first issue is the level of Flag State control over vessels flying that State's flag. This issue will be discussed more fully in Chapter 9, but the BLUF is that a Flag State has primary jurisdiction over vessels flying that State's flag everywhere, including on the High Seas.[723] Therefore, the U.S. can enforce its laws and regulations on American-flagged vessels anywhere in the world.[724] So Homer and Bart Simpson's dialogue in this Chapter's introductory quotation—that "anything goes" in international waters—is incorrect. An American-flagged vessel can be stopped, boarded, and inspected by a U.S. Coast Guard (USCG) vessel anywhere it finds the American-flagged vessel.[725]

The larger issue is the level of **Coastal State** control over foreign flagged vessels. Against foreign flagged vessels, a Coastal State can basically enforce what sovereignty/control it has over each maritime zone. In convoluted UNCLOS language, a Coastal State can enforce "the rights for the protection of which the zone was established."[726]

As discussed in Chapter 3, a Coastal State exercises almost complete sovereignty in its Territorial Sea, subject primarily to the right of all ships to conduct Innocent Passage. Therefore, the Coastal State may enforce all of its laws (including criminal laws) and regulations in the Territorial Sea. However, UNCLOS imposes a duty on the Coastal State not to hamper Innocent Passage,[727] which harkens back to the Corfu Channel case also discussed in Chapter 3. Therefore, a Coastal State needs to judge the severity of the infraction and its impact on the Coastal State before seeking to enforce its laws and regulations onboard a foreign flagged vessel.

For example, Article 27 provides that a Coastal State should not enforce its criminal laws onboard a foreign flagged vessel engaged in innocent passage (i.e., "only passing through the territorial sea") unless:

> ➢ the consequences of the crime impact the Coastal State (e.g., are felt in the Coastal State's land territory or Territorial Seas, such as if the victim of the crime is a national of the Coastal State);
> ➢ the crime is so severe that it "disturbs the peace of the country or the good order of the territorial sea" (e.g., murder onboard the vessel or in the Territorial Seas);
> ➢ the ship's master or Flag State has requested assistance;
> ➢ to "suppress[] illicit traffic in narcotic drugs or psychotropic substances"[728]; or

> the foreign vessel just departed internal waters (e.g., a port) with a suspected criminal onboard.

Similarly, Article 28 provides that a Coastal State should not generally enforce its civil laws onboard a foreign flagged vessel engaged in innocent passage (i.e., "only passing through the territorial sea") unless the foreign vessel just departed internal waters (e.g., a port) with a suspected civil violator onboard.

As discussed in Chapter 4, the Contiguous Zone is a law enforcement buffer zone, usually related to the **inbound** movement of ships to **prevent infringement** of laws in the Coastal State's territory or Territorial Sea, and the **outbound** movement of ships to **punish infringement** of laws that occurred in the Coastal State's territory or Territorial Sea.[729] Article 33 permits the Coastal State to enforce its laws out to 24 nm onboard foreign flagged vessels, but only in four areas: Fiscal, Immigration, Sanitation and Customs (FISC), and only if the effects of the legal violations are felt either within the Coastal State's land territory or Territorial Seas. The Contiguous Zone grew out of Great Britain's "Hovering Acts" aimed at prosecuting foreign smuggler ships standing off the British coast, but with a "constructive presence" in Britain's Territorial Seas when they sent small boats from the mother ship into Britain's Territorial Seas. This was also the foundation for the concept of "hot pursuit," discussed subsequently.[730]

Also as discussed in Chapter 4, the Coastal State has exclusive ownership of ALL resources (including any resources found on the surface of the ocean or in the "water column") of its Exclusive Economic Zone (EEZ), extending out to 200 nm from the baseline.[731] Similarly, Chapter 6 discussed a State's "ownership of all resources" on the Continental Shelf (i.e., the seabed beneath the EEZ, and possibly extending further). Therefore, the Coastal State may enact and enforce all of its **resource-related** laws and regulations in its EEZ (e.g., illegal fishing, such as fishing without a permit) and on its Continental Shelf (e.g., conducting MSR that touches the Continental Shelf without seeking the Coastal State's consent) onboard foreign flagged vessels.[732] However, Article 73 imposes certain caveats on the enforcement of resource-related laws and regulations:

Article 73 / Enforcement of laws and regulations of the coastal State

1. The coastal State may, in the exercise of its sovereign rights to explore, exploit, conserve and manage the living resources in the exclusive economic zone, take such measures, including boarding, inspection, arrest and judicial proceedings, as may be necessary to ensure compliance with the laws and regulations adopted by it in conformity with this Convention.

2. Arrested vessels and their crews shall be promptly released upon the posting of reasonable bond or other security.

3. Coastal State penalties for violations of fisheries laws and regulations in the exclusive economic zone may not include imprisonment, in the absence of agreements to the contrary by the States concerned, or any other form of corporal punishment.

4. In cases of arrest or detention of foreign vessels the coastal State shall promptly notify the flag State, through appropriate channels, of the action taken and of any penalties subsequently imposed.[733]

Therefore, Article 73 permits boarding, inspecting, arresting, and instituting judicial proceedings against foreign flagged vessels. However, the Coastal State must "promptly release" any arrested vessels and their crews if the ship's Master or Flag State posts a reasonable "bond" (i.e., either insurance, or an amount of money that would potentially cover the anticipated fine, similar to being released on bail after being arrested if one posts a bond as surety of payment).

Thus, all State Parties to UNCLOS may enforce what sovereignty they have over each maritime zone (e.g., over FISC matters in the

Contiguous Zone, and over resources in the EEZ and on the Continental Shelf) against foreign flagged vessels.[734] However, some States seek to expand their sovereignty over their maritime zones even beyond what UNCLOS provides. For example, not only does China have excessive maritime claims (discussed in Chapter 11), but it appears that China may be trying to assert more sovereignty in its EEZ than UNCLOS provides. For example, China was considering national legislation that would purport to require foreign submarines to: obtain prior approval before entering the Chinese EEZ; report to Chinese authorities when in the Chinese EEZ (which UNCLOS does not even require for submarines conducting Innocent Passage through Territorial Seas, as this would hamper Innocent Passage); and operate on the surface while in China's EEZ.[735] Imposing such requirements would exceed the Coastal State's authority under UNCLOS.

UNCLOS provides more specific guidance for enforcing pollution standards, discussed in Chapter 5 and Section 6 of Part XII of UNCLOS: "Protection and Preservation of the Marine Environment." "In this respect, the Convention goes beyond and strengthens existing international agreements, many of which do not have express enforcement clauses."[736] UNCLOS enumerates how to enforce domestic pollution laws and regulations, as well as international standards, specifically with regard to pollution from land-based sources,[737] seabed activities on the Continental Shelf[738] and Deep Seabed,[739] and dumping.[740] Section 6 of Part XII of UNCLOS also calls upon Flag States,[741] Port States,[742] and Coastal States[743] to enforce pollution standards against ships within their authority.

For example, Article 220 provides very detailed guidance for Coastal States to enforce pollution standards against foreign vessels suspected of polluting in the Coastal State's waters. BLUF: **the Coastal State has less sovereignty and control the further away**

from shore, and pollution must be that much more serious in order for the Coastal State to "escalate" enforcement measures— from asking for information from the ship's master (via bridge-to-bridge radio), to inspecting the vessel, to instituting civil proceedings for money damages against the foreign ship, and ultimately to detaining the vessel and crew. Once again, however, the Coastal State must release the vessel and her crew if they post a bond as surety/security of payment for the money damages, civil penalty and/or fine. Thus, "Article 220 balances the interests of coastal States in taking enforcement action with rights and freedoms of navigation of flag States."[744]

The following table seeks to explain this complicated article (Article 220), and the potential escalation of pollution enforcement actions by the Coastal State. So, for example, if there are "clear grounds" to believe that a Chinese ship has polluted in the U.S. EEZ (e.g., by leaking bunker fuel), and the Chinese ship is still in the U.S. EEZ or Territorial Seas, Article 220(3) would only permit the U.S. Coast Guard[745] to query the ship's master for additional information (such as the name of the ship, its Flag State (aka Chinese registry), where it is coming from ("last port of call"), and where it is going to ("next port of call"—highlighted in light blue in the following table). The U.S. may use this information to contact

China (as the Flag State) to investigate the incident further, and if Chinese authorities find sufficient evidence of a violation, for them to institute civil proceedings on behalf of the U.S., and to impose penalties of sufficient severity to discourage further violations.[746]

UNCLOS Art. 220: Coastal State Enforcement of Pollution Laws & Regulations

Location of Pollution	Location of Polluting Ship (aka Polluter)	Query for Information (Identity, Registry, Last & Next Ports of Call)	Physical Inspection of the Vessel	Institute Civil Proceedings (including Detention)	Release Vessel if Bond Posted
Exclusive Economic Zone (EEZ)	Exclusive Economic Zone (EEZ) or Territorial Seas (TS)	**220(3):** if clear grounds to believe a violation of international standards or conforming domestic pollution laws or regulations	**220(3) & (5):** if clear grounds to believe a violation of international standards or conforming domestic pollution laws or regulations, resulting in a substantial discharge causing or threatening significant pollution, and either refusal to provide information or inconsistent information	**220(3) & (6):** if clear objective evidence to believe a violation of international standards or conforming domestic pollution laws or regulations, resulting in a discharge causing or threatening major damage	**220(7):** the Coastal State shall release the vessel and allow the vessel to proceed if a bond or other financial security has been posted / assured
Territorial Seas (TS)	Territorial Seas (TS)		**220(2):** if clear believe a violation pollution laws	grounds to of domestic or regulations	
TS or EEZ	Port			**220(1):** for any violation of domestic pollution laws and regulations	

260

In order for the U.S. Coast Guard to escalate the enforcement action by stopping the Chinese vessel to inspect it (highlighted in green in the preceding table), the discharge would need to be "substantial" and either cause or threaten "significant" pollution, but only if the master of the Chinese ship either refused to provide pertinent information, or provided information that is inconsistent with the observable facts.[747]

In order for the U.S. to escalate the enforcement action one step further by instituting civil proceedings in a U.S. federal district court, there would need to be "clear objective evidence" (presumably of sufficient strength to use as evidence in court— such as a video of the Chinese ship leaving an oily trail taken by a U.S. Navy maritime patrol aircraft,[748] and chemical analysis of the oil spill), and the discharge would need to be of even greater severity (to cause or threaten "major damage" to the U.S. coastline, resources, or related interests; highlighted in yellow in the preceding table). The U.S. could also detain the vessel and its crew, but if China posts a bond that would cover the potential fine and monetary damages, the U.S. would be required to promptly release the vessel and its crew.[749] Moreover, if China institutes proceedings against the Chinese barge within 6 months for polluting in the U.S. EEZ, the U.S. would be obliged to *suspend* its proceedings;[750] once China's proceedings have concluded (e.g., by imposing a nominal fine on the Chinese barge), the U.S. would be obliged to *terminate* (i.e., dismiss) its proceedings.[751]

Another example of a State seeking to expand its sovereignty over its maritime zones beyond what UNCLOS provides is Iran. As discussed previously, Iran has signed but not yet ratified UNCLOS. However, Article 18 of the Vienna Convention on the Law of Treaties (VCLT) imposes a requirement on treaty signatories (even before ratification) to "refrain from acts which would defeat the object and purpose of a treaty."[752] Yet, as discussed in Chapter 3,

Iran repeatedly uses military force in the Strait of Hormuz in a manner inconsistent with UNCLOS.[753] In January 2021, the Islamic Revolutionary Guard Corps Navy (IRGCN) seized a South Korean oil/chemical tanker in the Strait of Hormuz allegedly for "creating environmental and chemical pollution in the Persian Gulf." However, an Iranian spokesman made it clear that Iran seized the vessel to use as diplomatic leverage to get South Korea to release $7 billion of Iranian funds that were frozen in South Korean banks.[754] Regardless of the underlying reason for seizing the tanker, Iran appears to have skipped a few steps in the UNCLOS Article 220 process outlined above.

Regardless of the byzantine Article 220 process, Article 221 preserves the Coastal State's right to take action to protect its coastline and economic interests threatened by a maritime casualty which may result in "major harmful consequences." This would apply in the case of an oil spill, or a vessel collision at sea that released significant amounts of pollutants. After the 1989 Exxon Valdez oil spill (of nearly 11 million gallons of oil in the Prince William Sound of the Gulf of Alaska), the U.S. enacted the 1990 Oil Pollution Act, which holds responsible parties (e.g., the ship owner, operator, and/or charterer) **strictly liable** for removal costs and damages resulting from oil spills. Oil tankers operating in U.S. waters are also required to have double hulls.[755]

The International Maritime Organization (IMO) adopted the double hull requirement for oil tankers operating worldwide in 1992, with a phase-out schedule (for old single hull oil tankers) that has been repeatedly accelerated.[756] Thanks to the requirement for oil tankers to have double hulls, the maritime shipping industry now claims that less oil is spilled at sea than is "poured down the drain by mechanics changing their engine oil."[757]

In order to effectively enforce their laws and regulations, Article 111 of UNCLOS recognizes the right of Coastal States to engage in the "hot pursuit" of suspected violators.[758] If "the competent authorities of the coastal State have good reason to believe that the [foreign flagged] ship has violated the laws and regulations of that State," and the foreign vessel is located in an area where the Coastal State can enforce its laws and regulations (e.g., enforcing resource-related laws and regulations in the EEZ), then:

> the Coastal State must provide "a visual or auditory signal to stop" to the foreign ship;[759]
> if the foreign ship ignores the signal to stop, it may be pursued "by warships or military aircraft, or other ships or aircraft clearly marked and identifiable as being on government service and authorized to that effect";[760]
> the pursuit must be continuous and uninterrupted (including by electronic means such as radar)[761]; and
> "[t]he right of hot pursuit ceases as soon as the ship pursued enters the territorial sea of its own State or of a third State."[762]

The significance of hot pursuit is that if it is properly conducted and leads to successful interdiction of the vessel being pursued, it preserves the coastal State's law enforcement jurisdiction over that vessel, even if the vessel is no longer present in the maritime zone in which it violated that State's law or regulations.[763]

A classic example of hot pursuit at sea was the pursuit of the *Fishing Vessel (F/V) South Tomi* by an Australian patrol boat. With a coastline longer than the U.S. (and the 8th longest in the world),[764] Australia divides its traditional coast guard duties across a variety of federal, state and local agencies. To augment its coast guard efforts, Australia occasionally charters private vessels to perform these functions, such as in 2001 when the Australian Fisheries

Management Authority (AFMA) chartered the civilian *Patrol Vessel (P/V) Southern Supporter* to conduct customs and fisheries patrols in the Southern Ocean bordering Antarctica.

The *F/V South Tomi* was a fishing boat registered in Togo, which is a flag of convenience,[765] especially for fishing vessels engaged in Illegal, Unreported and Unregulated (IUU) fishing. The *F/V South Tomi* departed the port of Fremantle, Australia (just south of Perth). Two and a half weeks later, the *P/V Southern Supporter* caught the *F/V South Tomi* fishing for Patagonian Toothfish[766] illegally in the Australian EEZ off the coast of Heard Island (900 miles north of Antarctica). The Australian patrol boat directed the fishing vessel to return to Fremantle for civil proceedings. The *F/V South Tomi* initially obeyed the order and turned towards Fremantle, Australia (as if to return to port as directed), but once she reached the High Seas, she changed course toward Africa (presumably trying to

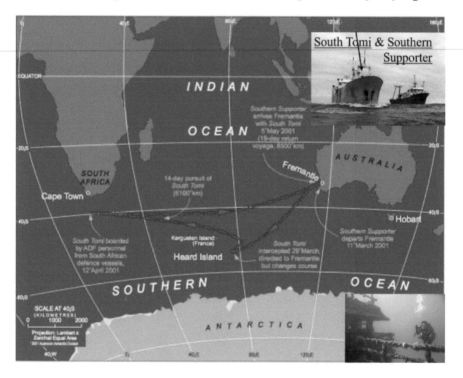

outrun the *P/V Southern Supporter* and reach sanctuary in South African Territorial Seas). The Australian patrol boat continued its hot pursuit, and also enlisted the aid of France (off the Kerguelen or Desolation Islands) to keep track of the fishing vessel. Australian Defence Force (ADF) personnel flew to Cape Town, South Africa to board South African defence vessels in order to intercept the *F/V South Tomi* 3,300 nm and 2 weeks later at a location 320 nm south of Cape Town (i.e., still on the High Seas). The *P/V Southern Supporter* took another 3 weeks to escort the *F/V South Tomi* back to Fremantle, where her Spanish skipper Leonardo Manuel Aviles plead guilty to illegal fishing, and received the largest fine at that time for illegal fishing ($136,000). Australia recovered the costs of the chase by seizing the fishing vessel and her catch (worth $1.5M), eventually selling her at auction and sinking her as an artificial reef off the coast of Geraldton, Australia.[767]

Due to the lucrativeness of fishing for Patagonian Toothfish, and the remoteness of their Antarctic habitat, chasing their IUU fishermen have set hot pursuit records. Two years after the *P/V Southern Supporter* captured the *F/V South Tomi*, the civilian patrol vessel caught another IUU fishing boat (the *F/V Viarsa 1*) with 96 tons of illegally fished Patagonian Toothfish onboard (worth $1M) after a 3,900 nm/3-week hot pursuit into an Antarctic storm.[768] A notorious non-governmental organization (NGO) known as the Sea Shepherd Conservation Society[769] (discussed subsequently in Chapter 9), harassed and pursued another boat illegally fishing for Patagonian Toothfish (*F/V Thunder*) for 10,000 nm/110 days in 2015, from 80 nm north of Antarctica up past the Equator.[770] The illegal fishing vessel's crew finally scuttled (i.e., sank) their own fishing boat in the Gulf of Guinea off the west coast of Africa in an attempt to destroy the evidence of their crimes![771] Her 40-member crew relied on the Customary International Law (CIL) norm (also expressed in Article 98 of UNCLOS) of Sea Shepherd's *Motor Yacht*

(M/Y) Bob Barker having a "duty to rescue" them from perils of the sea (discussed in Chapter 9).[772]

In summary, the delimitation of maritime boundaries are normally based on equity, with equidistance (i.e., a median line) often being the most equitable, and also the default for delimiting Territorial Seas. A Coastal State may enforce the level of sovereignty it possesses in each maritime zone over foreign flagged vessels. However, the Coastal State only has limited criminal jurisdiction onboard foreign flagged vessels (generally only if the effects are felt ashore), and in civil cases, the ship can post a bond which requires the Coastal State to let the ship and crew depart port.

---

[700] The Hague Justice Portal, *Maritime Delimitation in the Black Sea (Romania v. Ukraine): A Commentary* (Alex Oude Elferink, Mar. 27, 2009), http://www.haguejusticeportal.net/index.php?id=10407. *See also* Nilüfer Oral, *Ukraine v. The Russian Federation: Navigating Conflict over Sovereignty under UNCLOS*, 97 INT'L. L. STUD. 478, 481-486 (2021), https://digital-commons.usnwc.edu/ils/vol97/iss1/25/ (providing a brief history of the Black Sea from the Ottoman Empire to the Soviet Union).

[701] As early as 1793, U.S. Secretary of State (later President) Thomas Jefferson claimed exclusive control over maritime resources out to 3 nm from shore. PHILIP C. JESSUP, THE LAW OF TERRITORIAL WATERS AND MARITIME JURISDICTION 5-6 (1927). DONALD R. ROTHWELL & TIM STEPHENS, THE INT'L. LAW OF THE SEA 7 (2nd ed. 2016). Some authors called this the "cannon shot rule," as 3 nm was generally considered to be the maximum range that a shore battery could control with its guns. *See, e.g.,* THE FLETCHER SCHOOL OF LAW AND DIPLOMACY—TUFTS UNIVERSITY, LAW OF THE SEA, A POLICY PRIMER 6 (2017), https://sites.tufts.edu/lawofthesea/introduction/; R. R. CHURCHILL & A. V. LOWE, THE LAW OF THE SEA 77-78 (1999).

[702] The UNCLOS framers tried to establish a legal framework for the seas specifically to avoid legal uncertainty. Helmut Türk, *Questions Relating to the Continental Shelf Beyond 200 Nautical Miles: Delimitation, Delineation, and Revenue Sharing*, 97 INT'L. L. STUD. 231, 251 (2021), https://digital-commons.usnwc.edu/ils/vol97/iss1/18/.

[703] There are generally considered to be 195 States in the World, although the inclusion of 2 States is disputed. *See, e.g.,* Independent States in the World Fact Sheet, U.S. Dept. of State Bureau of Intelligence and Research (March 27, 2019), https://www.state.gov/independent-states-in-the-world/ (including Kosovo but not Palestine, which has observer status at the UN similar to the Holy See); Frequently Asked Questions, Worldometers, https://www.worldometers.info/geography/how-many-countries-are-there-in-the-world/ (including Palestine, but not Kosovo since China and Russia are blocking its membership in the UN).

704 *See generally* Emmanuella Doussis, *Marine Scientific Research: Taking Stock and Looking Ahead, in* THE FUTURE OF THE LAW OF THE SEA 87, 94–97 (Gemma Andreone ed., 2017), https://link.springer.com/book/10.1007/978-3-319-51274-7 (positing that States may prefer to ***not*** delimit their maritime borders, especially between their EEZs, in order to leave the situation ambiguous in order to exploit the resources up to the Territorial Seas of their neighboring States, or perhaps because they hesitate to open a "Pandora's Box" of political, diplomatic and economic issues between them).

705 U.S. Dept. of State, Key Topics, Office of Ocean and Polar Affairs, U.S. Maritime Boundaries: Agreements and Treaties, https://www.state.gov/u-s-maritime-boundaries-agreements-and-treaties/. *See also* Letter Of Transmittal Forwarding The 1982 UN Law Of The Sea Convention To The United States Senate, DOS Commentary p. 89 (William J. Clinton, Oct. 7, 1994) (S. Treaty Doc. 103–39), https://www.foreign.senate.gov/imo/media/doc/treaty_103-39.pdf (opining that "U.S. maritime boundary positions are fully consistent with the rules reflected in the Convention. These positions were determined through an interagency process in the late 1970s, prior to the U.S. extension of its maritime jurisdiction to 200 miles. As a result of that process, the United States determined that equidistance was the appropriate boundary in most cases, but that three situations required a boundary other than the equidistant line: with Canada in the Gulf of Maine/Georges Bank area; with the USSR {now the Russian Federation) in the Bering and Chukchi Seas and North Pacific Ocean; and with the Bahamas north of the Straits of Florida.").

706 *See generally The Three Equidistance Lines in Maritime Delimitation: What and Why?* (Danychannraksmeychhoukroth, Sep. 5, 2015), https://danychannraksmeychhoukroth.wordpress.com/2015/09/05/the-three-equidistance-lines-in-maritime-delimitation-what-and-why/. "[T]he United States determined that equidistance was the appropriate boundary in most cases, but that three situations required a boundary other than the equidistant line: with Canada in the Gulf of Maine/Georges Bank area; with the USSR {now the Russian Federation) in the Bering and Chukchi Seas and North Pacific Ocean; and with the Bahamas north of the Straits of Florida." DOS Commentary, p. 89 (full cite above).

707 *See, e.g.,* United Nations Convention on the Continental Shelf art. 6, Apr. 29, 1958, 499 U.N.T.S. 311, https://treaties.un.org/doc/Treaties/1964/06/19640610%2002-10%20AM/Ch_XXI_01_2_3_4_5p.pdf (providing that the "median line" or "equidistance" is the default delimitation of continental shelf claims, unless "special circumstances" exist).

708 *See generally*, Dept. of Defense Maritime Claims Reference Manual (MCRM)— Singapore 2014, http://www.jag.navy.mil/organization/code_10_mcrm.htm.

709 In fact, Germany is still not a party to the 1958 Convention on the Continental Shelf, and thus its provisions are still not binding on Germany. Continental Shelf Convention (full cite above).

710 Int'l. Court of Justice (ICJ), North Sea Continental Shelf (Federal Republic of Germany/Denmark & Federal Republic of Germany/Netherlands), https://www.icj-cij.org/en/case/51 & https://www.icj-cij.org/en/case/52.

711 Int'l. Court of Justice (ICJ), Delimitation of the Maritime Boundary in the Gulf of Maine Area (Canada/United States of America), https://www.icj-cij.org/en/case/67.

712 United Nations Convention on the Law of the Sea (UNCLOS) art. 15, Dec. 10, 1982, 1833 U.N.T.S. 397,

https://www.un.org/Depts/los/convention_agreements/convention_overview_co nvention.htm.

713 This is an example of *lex specialis*, where a more specific rule prevails over a more general rule. Int'l. Committee of the Red Cross (ICRC), Casebook, *How Does Law Protect in War?*, Lex specialis, https://casebook.icrc.org/glossary/lex-specialis. Thus, a more specific agreement between Coastal States delimiting their Territorial Sea borders would prevail over the general rule provided in Article 15 of UNCLOS.

714 States may seek to establish their own default delimitation of EEZ claims between neighboring Coastal States. For example, Bahamas claims that in the "absence of agreements with bordering States, territorial sea and EEZ boundaries will not extend beyond the median line." Dept. of Defense Maritime Claims Reference Manual (MCRM)—Bahamas 2015, http://www.jag.navy.mil/organization/code_10_mcrm.htm.

715 Statute of the Int'l. Court of Justice (ICJ) art. 38(1), https://www.icj-cij.org/en/statute. *See also* RESTATEMENT (THIRD) OF FOREIGN RELATIONS § 102(1) (1987) (listing the 4 sources of international law).

716 United Nations Convention on the Law of the Sea (UNCLOS) art. 298(1)(a)(i), Dec. 10, 1982, 1833 U.N.T.S. 397, https://www.un.org/Depts/los/convention_agreements/convention_overview_co nvention.htm.

717 *See* Helmut Türk, *Questions Relating to the Continental Shelf Beyond 200 Nautical Miles: Delimitation, Delineation, and Revenue Sharing*, 97 INT'L. L. STUD. 231, 240-244 (2021), https://digital-commons.usnwc.edu/ils/vol97/iss1/18/ (discussing the "historical" decision by ITLOS in the *Bangladesh v. Myanmar* case).

718 The lack of a default delimitation of Continental Shelf claims under UNCLOS differs from Article 6 of the 1958 Convention on the Continental Shelf, which provided that the "median line" or "equidistance" is the default delimitation of continental shelf claims, unless "special circumstances" exist. Continental Shelf Convention, art. 6 (full cite above). However, States may seek to establish their own default delimitation of Continental Shelf claims. For example, Belgium claims that the Continental Shelf "[b]oundary with neighboring States [is] to be established by the principle of equidistance." DoD MCRM—Belgium 2019 (full cite above).

719 "[T]he equidistance/relevant circumstances method, which in recent years has become the preferred method used by international courts and tribunals to achieve an equitable solution as required by Article 83, paragraph 1, UNCLOS [to delimit the Continental Shelf]. ... There can be no doubt that, whenever possible, a single boundary line delimiting both the seabed and the water column is preferable, which has also become general practice. ... The potential problems that may arise from areas of overlap between a State's continental shelf and EEZ rights of another State, resulting in so-called 'grey areas,' are a matter to which the negotiators at the Conference obviously did not devote sufficient attention." Türk, *Questions Relating to the Continental Shelf Beyond 200 Nautical Miles*, pp. 243-244, 257 (full cite above) (discussing the ITLOS decision in the *Bangladesh v. Myanmar* case).

720 Algiers Accord, United Nations Treaty Series, Vol. 1017, No. 14903, p. 54, https://treaties.un.org/doc/Publication/UNTS/Volume%201017/v1017.pdf.

721 United Nations Convention on the Territorial Sea and the Contiguous Zone, Apr. 29, 1958, 516 U.N.T.S. 205, http://legal.un.org/docs/?path=../ilc/texts/instruments/english/conventions/8_1_1958_territorial_sea.pdf&lang=EF.

[722] *See generally* AmericanGrit, Stories, Military, *The "General's Armada"- One of the most brilliant Naval campaigns and the Marine who led it* (Faisal Sipra, Aug, 2, 2019), https://www.americangrit.com/2019/08/02/the-generals-armada-one-of-the-most-brilliant-naval-campaigns-and-the-marine-who-led-it/; America's Navy, Forged by the Sea, News, *Brig. Gen. Jensen Relieves Brig. Gen. Medina as ESG 3 Commander* (Zack Baddorf, June 2, 2005), https://www.navy.mil/submit/display.asp?story_id=18589.

[723] UNCLOS, arts. 94, 97, 109, 110, 216(1)(b), 217, & 228 (full cite above); YOSHIFUMI TANAKA, THE INT'L. LAW OF THE SEA 190 (3rd ed. 2019).

[724] U.S. NAVY, MARINE CORPS & COAST GUARD, THE COMMANDER'S HANDBOOK ON THE LAW OF NAVAL OPERATIONS, NWP 1-14M/MCTP 11-10B/COMDTPUB P5800.7A, ¶ 3.11.2.1 (p. 3-11) (2017), www.jag.navy.mil/distrib/instructions/CDRs_HB_on_Law_of_Naval_Operations_AUG17.pdf; THE FLETCHER SCHOOL OF LAW AND DIPLOMACY—TUFTS UNIVERSITY, LAW OF THE SEA, A POLICY PRIMER 54 (2017), https://sites.tufts.edu/lawofthesea/introduction/.

[725] "The U.S. Coast Guard (USCG) ... is tasked with making inquiries, examinations, inspections, searches, seizures, and arrests upon the high seas and in waters over which the United States has jurisdiction for the prevention, detection, and suppression of violations of U.S. laws. In the execution of these duties, USCG personnel may board any vessel subject to U.S. jurisdiction; address inquiries to those on board; examine the ship's documents and papers; examine, inspect, and search the vessel; and use all necessary force to compel compliance. USCG personnel may also arrest persons on board and seize the vessel if they determine that U.S. laws have been violated. However, USCG personnel may only use the force that is objectively reasonable considering the facts and circumstances confronting them at the time force is applied. In this regard, reasonableness is judged from the perspective of a reasonable officer on the scene, not with the 20/20 vision of hindsight. Accordingly, there is a range of responses that may be reasonable and appropriate under a particular set of circumstances. Once physical force is used, it will be discontinued when resistance ceases or when the incident is under control." Raul (Pete) Pedrozo, *Maritime Police Law of the People's Republic of China*, 97 INT'L. L. STUD. 465, 471-472 (2021), https://digital-commons.usnwc.edu/ils/vol97/iss1/24/.

[726] UNCLOS, art. 111(1) (full cite above); COMMANDER'S HANDBOOK, ¶¶ 3.10.1.2, 3.11.2.2.4 (pp. 3-8, 3-12) (full cite above).

[727] UNCLOS, art. 24 (full cite above).

[728] UNCLOS, art. 108 (full cite above); COMMANDER'S HANDBOOK, ¶¶ 3.4, 3.8, 3.11.4 to 3.11.4.3 (pp. 3-5, 3-7, 3-16 to 3-17) (full cite above).

[729] DONALD R. ROTHWELL & TIM STEPHENS, THE INT'L. LAW OF THE SEA 83 (2nd ed. 2016).

[730] UNCLOS, art. 111 (full cite above); COMMANDER'S HANDBOOK, ¶¶ 3.10.1.2, 3.11.2.2.4 (pp. 3-8, 3-12) (full cite above).

[731] UNCLOS, art. 57 (full cite above).

[732] Although there are no express enforcement provisions for the Continental Shelf, they may be implied. ROTHWELL & STEPHENS, LAW OF THE SEA, p. 431 (full cite above).

[733] UNCLOS, art. 73 (full cite above). *See also* Letter Of Transmittal Forwarding The 1982 UN Law Of The Sea Convention To The United States Senate, DOS Commentary p. 46 (William J. Clinton, Oct. 7, 1994) (S. Treaty Doc. 103–39), https://www.foreign.senate.gov/imo/media/doc/treaty_103-39.pdf (noting that

"[t]he provisions of the Convention prohibiting imprisonment or corporal punishment for fishing violations responded to the severe treatment meted out to foreign fishermen in some places. Although the Convention limits the ability of the United States to impose prison sentences on foreign fishermen who violate U.S. fishery laws, the Convention promotes a major U.S. objective in protecting U.S. fishermen seized by other States from the imposition of prison sentences. On balance, these provisions of the Convention serve U.S. interests overall, given that many U.S. fishermen are actively engaged in fishing within foreign EEZs, while no foreign fishing is authorized within the U.S. EEZ at present.").

734 United Nations Convention on the Law of the Sea (UNCLOS) art. 111(1), Dec. 10, 1982, 1833 U.N.T.S. 397, https://www.un.org/Depts/los/convention_agreements/convention_overview_convention.htm; U.S. NAVY, MARINE CORPS & COAST GUARD, THE COMMANDER'S HANDBOOK ON THE LAW OF NAVAL OPERATIONS, NWP 1-14M/MCTP 11-10B/COMDTPUB P5800.7A, ¶¶ 3.10.1.2, 3.11.2.2.4 (pp. 3-8, 3-12) (2017), www.jag.navy.mil/distrib/instructions/CDRs_HB_on_Law_of_Naval_Operations _AUG17.pdf.

735 Quartz, Topside Watch, *China wants foreign submarines to stop traveling below the surface in the vast waters it claims* (Steve Mollman, Feb. 20, 2017), https://qz.com/915110/china-wants-foreign-submarines-to-stop-traveling-below-the-surface-in-the-south-china-sea-and-other-waters-it-claims/. *But see* Dept. of Defense Maritime Claims Reference Manual (MCRM)—China 2017, http://www.jag.navy.mil/organization/code_10_mcrm.htm (making no mention of this requirement as having been imposed yet).

736 Letter Of Transmittal Forwarding The 1982 UN Law Of The Sea Convention To The United States Senate, DOS Commentary p. 36 (William J. Clinton, Oct. 7, 1994) (S. Treaty Doc. 103–39), https://www.foreign.senate.gov/imo/media/doc/treaty_103-39.pdf.

737 UNCLOS, art. 213 (full cite above).

738 UNCLOS, art. 214 (full cite above).

739 UNCLOS, art. 215 (full cite above).

740 UNCLOS, art. 216 (full cite above).

741 UNCLOS, arts. 216(1)(b) & 217 (full cite above). Chapter 9 discusses Flag States.

742 UNCLOS, arts. 216(1)(c) & 218-219 (full cite above).

743 UNCLOS, arts. 216(1)(a) & 220 (full cite above).

744 DOS Commentary, p. 37 (full cite above).

745 UNCLOS recognizes that enforcing laws and regulations against foreign flagged vessels can only be done by "officials or by warships, military aircraft, or other ships or aircraft clearly marked and identifiable as being on government service and authorized to that effect." UNCLOS, art. 224 (full cite above).

746 UNCLOS, arts. 216(1)(b), 217(4)-(8) & 231 (full cite above). Chapter 9 discusses Flag State responsibilities in more depth.

747 UNCLOS, arts. 220(3) & (5) (full cite above).

748 The U.S. Navy is transitioning to Boeing's P-8A as its primary Maritime Patrol (MARPAT) aircraft. *See, e.g.,* Naval Air Systems Command (NAVAIR), P-8A Poseidon, https://www.navair.navy.mil/product/P-8A-Poseidon; Commander, Naval Air Forces, Patrol Squadron (PATRON) FOUR SEVEN, P-8 Information, https://www.public.navy.mil/airfor/vp47/Pages/P-8-Information.aspx; Boeing, Defense, Maritime Surveillance, P-8A Poseidon,

https://www.boeing.com/defense/maritime-surveillance/p-8-poseidon/index.page.

[749] UNCLOS, arts. 220(3), (6) & (7) & 231 (full cite above). If a Coastal State fails to "prompt[ly] release ... the vessel or its crew upon the posting of a reasonable bond," the Flag State may submit the matter to a court or tribunal under Article 292 of UNCLOS for expedited dispute settlement. DOS Commentary, p. 85 (full cite above). Chapter 12 discusses Mandatory Dispute Settlement.

[750] DOS Commentary, p. 39 (full cite above).

[751] UNCLOS, art. 228(1) (full cite above); THE FLETCHER SCHOOL OF LAW AND DIPLOMACY—TUFTS UNIVERSITY, LAW OF THE SEA, A POLICY PRIMER 55 (2017), https://sites.tufts.edu/lawofthesea/introduction/.

[752] Vienna Convention on the Law of Treaties (VCLT) art. 18, May 23, 1969, 1155 U.N.T.S. 331. Although the United States is not a party to the VCLT, it considers the VCLT to represent customary international law. Sean D. Murphy, The George Wash. Univ. Law Sch.: "Should the U.S. Join the International Criminal Court?" A Moderated Panel Discussion, Feb. 13, 2006. See also DOS Commentary, p. 17 (full cite above) (noting that "[u]nder customary international law, as reflected in ... the Vienna Convention on the Law of Treaties (92nd Congress; 1st Session, Senate Executive 'L')").

[753] See, e.g., UNCLOS, art. 36 (full cite above); COMMANDER'S HANDBOOK, Appendix C (pp. C-1 to C-2) (full cite above) (citing the 2015 Maritime Advisory warning that Iran has been harassing U.S.-flagged ships in the Strait of Hormuz); TUFTS, LAW OF THE SEA, pp. 26-27 (full cite above) (detailing aggressive actions taken by Iran against U.S. warships in the Arabian Gulf and Strait of Hormuz).

[754] CNN, Five Things, *Armed Iranian troops boarded South Korean tanker, ship's owner says* (Jake Kwon, Gawon Bae & Zamira Rahim, Jan. 5, 2021), https://www.cnn.com/2021/01/05/asia/south-korea-anti-piracy-unit-iran-ship-seized-intl-hnk-mil/index.html?utm_term=160984627848574a284d4d1c3&utm_source=cnn_Five+Things+for+Tuesday%2C+January+5%2C+2021&utm_medium=email&utm_campaign=1609846278486&bt_ee=wO5oNaF1nsAFesn2ReknFkskxMo5nk9X%2B7gE6duitbiDJinEow0PVlWdUhRmF0vZ&bt_ts=1609846278486; Military.com, Daily News, *South Korean Tanker Was Boarded by Armed Iran Guard Forces* (Hyung-Jin Kim & Jon Gambrell, Jan. 5, 2021), https://www.military.com/daily-news/2021/01/05/south-korean-tanker-was-boarded-armed-iran-guard-forces.html?ESRC=eb_210105.nl.

[755] 33 U.S. Code § 2701 et seq. (1990), https://www.law.cornell.edu/uscode/text; U.S. Environmental Protection Agency (EPA), Laws & Regulations, Summary of the Oil Pollution Act, https://www.epa.gov/laws-regulations/summary-oil-pollution-act.

[756] Int'l. Maritime Organization (IMO), English, Our Work, Marine Environment, Pollution Prevention, Oil Pollution, Construction Requirements for Oil Tankers, http://www.imo.org/en/OurWork/Environment/PollutionPrevention/OilPollution/Pages/constructionrequirements.aspx.

[757] Rose George, NINETY PERCENT OF EVERYTHING 8 (2013).

[758] COMMANDER'S HANDBOOK, ¶¶ 3.10.1.2, 3.11.2.2.4 (pp. 3-8, 3-12) (full cite above).

[759] UNCLOS, art. 111(4) (full cite above); COMMANDER'S HANDBOOK, ¶¶ 3.10.1.2, 3.11.2.2.4 to 3.11.2.2.4.1 (full cite above).

[760] UNCLOS, art. 111(5) (full cite above); COMMANDER'S HANDBOOK, ¶¶ 3.10.1.2, 3.11.2.2.4 (full cite above).

[761] U.S. NAVY, MARINE CORPS & COAST GUARD, THE COMMANDER'S HANDBOOK ON THE LAW OF NAVAL OPERATIONS, NWP 1-14M/MCTP 11-10B/COMDTPUB P5800.7A, ¶ 3.11.2.2.4.2 (p. 3-12) (2017), www.jag.navy.mil/distrib/instructions/CDRs_HB_on_Law_of_Naval_Operations _AUG17.pdf.
[762] United Nations Convention on the Law of the Sea (UNCLOS) art. 111(3), Dec. 10, 1982, 1833 U.N.T.S. 397, https://www.un.org/Depts/los/convention_agreements/convention_overview_co nvention.htm; COMMANDER'S HANDBOOK, ¶ 3.11.2.2.4.3 (p. 3-12) (full cite above). But see COMMANDER'S HANDBOOK, ¶ 3.5.3.2 (p. 3-6) (full cite above) (positing that while pursuing a fleeing pirate vessel that proceeds into another State's Territorial Seas or Archipelagic Waters, "every effort should be made to obtain the consent of the State having sovereignty over these zones to continue pursuit .... The inviolability of the territorial integrity of sovereign States makes the decision of a warship or military aircraft to continue pursuit into these areas without such consent a serious matter. However, the international nature of the crime of piracy may allow continuation of pursuit if contact cannot be established in a timely manner with the coastal State to obtain its consent. In such a case, pursuit must be broken off immediately upon request of the coastal State, and, in that event, the right to seize the pirate vessel or aircraft and to prosecute the pirates devolves on the State having sovereignty over the territorial seas, archipelagic waters, or airspace."). Although the Commander's Handbook cites to no authority for this bold proposition, perhaps it is a reflection of the informal mantra of the U.S. Navy: "it is better to seek forgiveness than to seek permission." See generally A.V. Lowe, The Commander's Handbook on the Law of Naval Operations and the Contemporary Law of the Sea, in 64 U.S. NAVAL WAR COLLEGE INT'L. L. STUD.: THE LAW OF NAVAL OPERATIONS, 126 (Horace B. Robertson, Jr., ed., 1991), https://archive.org/details/lawofnavaloperat64robe/page/126/mode/2up (noting a similar discrepancy between the Commander's Handbook and the generally-recognized contemporary law of the sea).
[763] COMMANDER'S HANDBOOK, ¶ 3.11.2.2.4 (p. 3-12) (full cite above).
[764] WorldAtlas, World Facts, Countries With The Longest Coastline, https://www.worldatlas.com/articles/countries-with-the-most-coastline.html. "[N]ote: the Canadian Arctic Archipelago - consisting of 36,563 islands, several of them some of the world's largest - contributes to Canada easily having the longest coastline in the world". U.S. Central Intelligence Agency (CIA.gov), World Factbook, https://www.cia.gov/the-world-factbook/field/coastline/.
[765] Chapter 9 discusses Flags of convenience or "open registries" in more depth.
[766] As discussed in Chapter 7, Patagonian Toothfish was rebranded as "Chilean Sea Bass" in 1977, and its popularity soared. Priceonomics, The Invention of the Chilean Sea Bass (Alex Mayyasi), https://priceonomics.com/the-invention-of-the-chilean-sea-bass/.
[767] Australian Government, Dept. of the Environment and Energy, Australian Antarctic Division: Leading Australia's Antarctic Program, Australian Antarctic Magazine, Int'l., Another one that didn't get away! (Ian Hay, Spring 2001), http://www.antarctica.gov.au/magazine/2001-2005/issue-2-spring-2001/international/another-one-that-didnt-get-away!.
[768] Priceonomics, The Invention of the Chilean Sea Bass (full cite above); Australian Government, Dept. of the Environment and Energy, Australian Antarctic Division: Leading Australia's Antarctic Program, Australian Antarctic Magazine, Feature,

Poachers pursued over 7,000 kilometers (Autumn 2004), http://www.antarctica.gov.au/magazine/2001-2005/issue-6-autumn-2004/feature/poachers-pursued-over-7-000-kilometers; stop illegal fishing, Press/Links, *End of the line for Spain's most notorious illegal fishing family* (Joe Duggan, July 14, 2016), https://stopillegalfishing.com/press-links/end-line-spains-notorious-illegal-fishing-family/.

[769] Sea Shepherd, Who We Are, https://seashepherd.org/. *See also* Maclean's, *Thunder gone under: The story of the world's longest maritime chase* (Jonathon Gatehouse & Amanda Shendruk, Apr. 16, 2015), https://www.macleans.ca/news/canada/thunder-gone-under-the-story-of-the-worlds-longest-maritime-chase/ (describing the Sea Shepherd Conservation Society as an "environmental guerrilla group").

[770] The Sea Shepherd's *Motor Yacht (M/Y) Bob Barker* is not a "warship[] ... or other ship[] ... clearly marked and identifiable as being on government service and authorized to that effect." Therefore, her harassment and pursuit of the *F/V Thunder* did not qualify as "hot pursuit" under Article 111(5) of UNCLOS. Nevertheless, the Sea Shepherd's pursuit was effective, as it prompted the illegal fishing vessel's crew to scuttle (i.e., sink) their own fishing boat. Nevertheless, the Sea Shepherd's crew were able to secure incriminating evidence from the slowly sinking fishing boat. The Sea Shepherd's efforts ultimately resulted in 3-year criminal sentences and $17M in fines for the boat's captain and two senior crew members, and a $10M fine for the illegal fishing boat's Spanish owner. TakePart, *One of the World's Most Notorious Illegal Fishing Crews Is Fined $17 Million* (Taylor Hill, Oct. 13, 2015), http://www.takepart.com/article/2015/10/13/illegal-fishing-vessel-sentenced-sea-shepherd/; Maritime Executive, *Owner of F/V Thunder Hit with Fine in Spain* (Apr. 18, 2018), https://www.maritime-executive.com/article/owner-of-f-v-thunder-hit-with-fine-in-spain. *See also* Foreign Policy, *The Hunt for the Last Chilean Sea Bass Poachers* (Christopher Pala, June 17, 2015), https://foreignpolicy.com/2015/06/17/chilean-sea-bass-toothfish-thunder-sea-shepherd/ (noting that the Sea Shepherd "ships had no internationally recognized authority to board or detain the poachers, but they were prepared to physically prevent the pirates from fishing, to chase them out of the fishing grounds, and to collect evidence of illegal fishing and present it to authorities.").

[771] The Guardian, *Captain deliberately sank illegal fishing vessel, claim Sea Shepherd rescuers* (Oliver Milman, Apr. 7, 2015), https://www.theguardian.com/environment/2015/apr/07/captain-deliberately-sank-illegal-fishing-vessel-claim-sea-shepherd-rescuers; Maclean's, *Thunder gone under*, (full cite above); Sea Shepherd, *Another Impossible Mission Made Possible by Sea Shepherd* (Paul Watson Apr. 7, 2015), https://seashepherd.org/2015/04/07/another-impossible-mission-made-possible-by-sea-shepherd/; Foreign Policy, *Last Chilean Sea Bass Poachers* (full cite above); TakePart, *One of the World's Most Notorious Illegal Fishing Crews*, (full cite above); Maritime Executive, *Owner of F/V Thunder Hit with Fine* (full cite above).

[772] Military.com, News, Headlines, *Navy Touts US Merchant Ship's Rescue of Iranians After Others Left Them Adrift* (Gina Harkins, Dec. 28, 2019), https://www.military.com/daily-news/2019/12/28/navy-touts-us-merchant-ships-rescue-iranians-after-others-left-them-adrift.html?ESRC=eb_191230.nl.

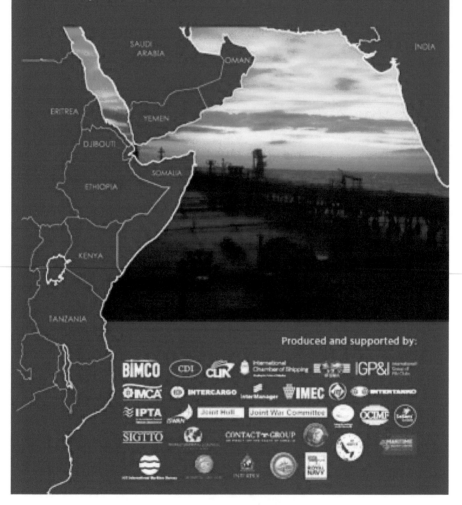

CHAPTER 9: PIRACY & OTHER ILLEGAL MARITIME ACTIVITIES

"Oceans are the biggest crime scene in the world."
—*Admiral (retired) James Stavridis*

B LUF: PRIMARY JURISDICTION/ENFORCEMENT RESTS WITH THE FLAG STATE, including over piracy and other illegal maritime activities. Historically, a ship that does not fly the flag of any particular State is considered a "ship without nationality" (aka "stateless"), "enjoys no protection in international law,"[773] and is subject to be boarded on the High Seas by a warship from any State.[774] Therefore, ship and yacht owners generally recognize the need to register their vessel with a Flag State, and to fly its flag on their vessel.[775] Article 91 of UNCLOS provides that "[s]hips have the nationality of the State whose flag they are entitled to fly. There must exist a genuine link between the State and the ship." "The genuine link was originally intended as an economic and social connection between the owner of the vessel and the state of registration."[776] For example, a "genuine link" between a ship and a particular State (such that flying its flag is defensible) would include the location of the ship's homeport, the nationality of the operating company and/or the ship's owner, etc. However, "genuine link" is not defined by UNCLOS, and a subsequent 1986 [Ship] Registration Convention (which would provide more specific guidance) has not yet entered into force.[777] Moreover, the International Tribunal for the Law of the Sea (ITLOS) held in the 1999 *Motor Vessel (M/V) Saiga* case that the lack of an apparent "genuine link" between a particular vessel and a particular State may not be challenged by another State.[778]

The lack of enforcement of the "genuine link" requirement between vessels and Flag States has led to "flags of convenience" (aka "open registries" or "open registers").[779] "Open-registry states are those nations where the requirements set for ship registration are flexible and generally not based on nationality. Often being developing countries, these states do not have the ability and the resources to ensure control of all the ships flying their flag, which increases the number of potential [Illegal, Unreported and Unregulated] fishing vessels."[780] Flags of convenience are also viewed by some as "national flags flown by mercenary ships that have been registered in countries other than those of their owners in order to escape high domestic wages and taxation and stringent regulations on safety, manning, employment and related requirements."[781] Utilizing a flag of convenience is akin to incorporating a U.S. company in Delaware,

#1 Panama

#2 Liberia

#3 Marshall Islands

with corporate-friendly tax laws (i.e., no corporate income tax), a corporate-friendly Court of Chancery (with only judges, and no juries) to resolve issues related to the law of corporations, limited personal liability, and protections of privacy/anonymity.[782] The top 3 flags of convenience are Panama, Liberia,[783] and the Marshall Islands (although the 2nd and 3rd Flag States often swap back and forth).[784]

According to the International Maritime Organization (IMO) and the International Chamber of Shipping (ICS), the 8 largest flags of convenience represent 64% of the world merchant fleet! However, the largest flags of convenience are considered "low risk" because of their regular ship inspections and compliance with IMO requirements. In fact, the IMO is less worried about flags of convenience these days, so long as the "open registries" accept traditional Flag State responsibility for their vessels.[785] "We have moved beyond 'flags of convenience' ... they have become international registries with international responsibilities."[786]

Article 94 of UNCLOS sets out the detailed duties of Flag States, including:

> ➤ Maintaining a **registry** of ships flying its flag;
> ➤ Assuming **domestic jurisdiction** "over each ship flying its flag and its master, officers and crew";
> ➤ Ensuring **safety at sea** by regulating:
>   - ○ "the **construction, equipment and seaworthiness** of ships";
>   - ○ "the **manning** of ships, labour conditions and the **training** of crews";[787]
>   - ○ "the use of **signals**, the maintenance of **communications** and the **prevention of collisions**";[788]
>   - ○ **regular inspection**/survey "by a qualified surveyor of ships";
>   - ○ the inventory "on board [of] such **charts**, nautical publications and **navigational equipment** and instruments as are appropriate for the **safe navigation** of the ship";

- o "that each ship is in the charge of a **master and officers who possess appropriate qualifications**, in particular in seamanship, navigation, communications and marine engineering:
- o "that the **crew is appropriate in qualification and numbers** for the type, size, machinery and equipment of the ship"; and
- o "that the master, officers and ... the crew are fully conversant with and required to **observe the applicable international regulations** concerning the safety of life at sea, the prevention of collisions, the prevention, reduction and control of marine pollution, and the maintenance of communications by radio."[789]

➢ **Investigating alleged violations** by Flag State vessels (alleged by other States);

➢ **Investigating "every marine casualty** or incident of navigation on the high seas involving a ship flying its flag and **causing loss of life or serious injury** to nationals of another State **or serious damage** to ships or installations of another State or to the marine environment"; and

➢ **Cooperating "in the conduct of any inquiry** held by ... [an]other State into any such marine casualty or incident of navigation."[790]

Article 217 reiterates that Flag States are to ensure that their vessels comply with international rules and standards preventing pollution from ships.[791] However, UNCLOS "does not specifically oblige flag states to ensure responsible fisheries."[792]

In addition, Article 98 of UNCLOS imposes an additional duty to Flag States: to ensure that ships flying its flag:

(a) "… render assistance to any person found at sea in danger of being lost;

(b) … proceed with all possible speed to the rescue of persons in distress, if informed of their need of assistance, in so far as such action may reasonably be expected of him;

(c) after a collision, … render assistance to the other ship, its crew and its passengers and, where possible, to inform the other ship of the name of his own ship, its port of registry and the nearest port at which it will call."

This is simply the codification of the longstanding Customary International Law (CIL) "**duty to rescue**" mariners from perils of the sea.[793] This "duty to rescue" exists even if the States, or even the individual ships involved, are not on friendly terms.[794] As discussed in Chapter 8, the Sea Shepherd Conservation Society's[795] *Motor Yacht (M/Y) Bob Barker* harassed and pursued the *Fishing Vessel (F/V) Thunder* (which was illegally fishing for Patagonian Toothfish) for 10,000 nm/110 days in 2015, from 80 nm north of Antarctica up past the Equator.[796] The illegal fishing vessel's crew finally scuttled (i.e., sank) their own fishing boat in the Gulf of Guinea off the west coast of Africa in an attempt to destroy the evidence of their crimes.[797] The *M/Y Bob Barker* nevertheless abided by their "duty to rescue" the 40-member fishing crew.

However, despite the CIL norm and UNCLOS treaty obligation imposing a "duty to rescue," apparently not all ship masters abide by it. For example, despite the strained relations between the U.S. and Iran, a U.S.-flagged merchant vessel rescued 3 distressed Iranian mariners, who had been floating in a large plastic water tank 80 nm off the coast of Oman for almost 3 weeks in late 2019. A spokesman for the American shipping company said: "Sadly, the Iranians said that in the course of being adrift over 19 days, several other ships had stopped, provided them with food and water, but refused to take them aboard. Whether this was to avoid the cost of delays associated with rescue efforts or for other reasons we can never know."[798] (Photo Courtesy of the U.S. Navy)

Under Article 92(1) of UNCLOS, Flag States (including flags of convenience) have exclusive jurisdiction over their vessels on the High Seas (including criminal jurisdiction over collisions),[799] with only a very few exceptions:

1) A **"stateless" ship** (that does not fly the flag of any particular State), or "quasi-stateless" ship ("which sails under the flags of two or more States, using them according to convenience") are subject to be boarded on the High Seas by any State's warship.[800]

2) Although a Flag State shall "prevent and punish the transport of **slaves** in ships authorized to fly its flag," a warship may board a foreign ship it encounters on the High Seas if the foreign ship is reasonably suspected of engaging in human trafficking or human smuggling.[801] However, once

the warship sets free any victims found onboard, the Flag State retains jurisdiction over the foreign ship.[802]

3) Universal jurisdiction over **piracy**—discussed subsequently.

4) Although the Flag State retains jurisdiction over its vessels reasonably suspected of engaging in "illicit **traffic in narcotic drugs** or psychotropic substances," it "may request the cooperation of other States to suppress such traffic."[803]

5) "**Unauthorized broadcasting**" of "radio or television broadcasts from a ship or installation on the high seas intended for reception by the general public contrary to international regulations." However, only States with a connection to the unauthorized broadcasting (e.g., based upon the nationality of the ship, installation, persons transmitting or receiving the broadcasts, or "any State where authorized radio communication is suffering interference") have jurisdiction to arrest suspected persons or vessels on the High Seas, and to prosecute them.[804]

Exclusive jurisdiction by a Flag State over its vessels on the High Seas means that no other State has jurisdiction to board that vessel on the High Seas except for the Flag State, unless one of the 5 enumerated exceptions applies. So if an American national owns a fishing boat that is registered in Panama, and the Panamanian-flagged fishing boat is fishing on the High Seas with a Russian crew, only a Panamanian military vessel may board the fishing boat—neither a Russian warship nor a U.S. Coast Guard vessel can do so, unless the fishing boat is reasonably suspected of engaging in piracy, or one of the other exceptions to exclusive Flag State jurisdiction. Thus, **Flag States serve as the primary means of enforcement under UNCLOS.**[805] Since Panama only has 20 boats in its maritime forces, including 9 riverine patrol boats and only 11 seagoing swift boats (U.S. leftovers from the Vietnam War),[806] it is unlikely that any State has both the lawful authority and the operational capability to board your Panamanian-flagged fishing boat lawfully fishing on the High Seas.

Therefore, there are **generally only two instances when a warship need not worry about violating Flag State jurisdiction on the High Seas—a warship may board: 1) any "stateless" or "quasi-stateless" ship** (since there is no legitimate Flag State involved, this is not technically an exception to exclusive Flag State jurisdiction);[807] **and 2) any ship reasonably suspected of engaging in piracy.**[808] Stateless vessels are far too common, and smaller boats often don't fly a flag. For example, the *USS Forrest Sherman* (DDG 98), an American guided-missile destroyer, "was conducting routine maritime operations" (discussed in Chapter 10) in late 2019 in the Arabian Sea "when sailors noticed a small boat exhibiting behavior similar to other vessels involved in smuggling" (i.e., suspicious behavior). Since the small boat "was not flying a flag, ... Navy and Coast Guard personnel boarded it for inspection and flag verification — a process allowed under international law." The boarding team discovered and "seized a 'significant cache' of suspected Iranian guided missile parts headed to [Houthi] rebels in Yemen," in "violation of a U.N. Security Council resolution." The boarding team transferred the Yemeni crew to the custody of the Yemeni Coast Guard.[809] Two months later in early 2020, the *USS Normandy* (CG 60), an American guided-missile cruiser, boarded a stateless "*dhow*"[810] in the Arabian Sea, and seized over 150 Iranian missiles and missile parts once again headed to Houthi rebels in Yemen in violation of an UNSCR "barring weapons transfers to the Houthis."[811]

The second primary exception to Flag State jurisdiction on the High Seas is piracy, which holds a unique place in maritime law.

Pirates have been considered *hostis humani generis* (pronounced "*hoss-tees hew-man-ee jen-er-iss*," i.e., the enemy of mankind) **for time immemorial.**[813] Piracy is the classic example of a crime that is "international in scope," (i.e., "the crime [] threatens the international system as a whole if it were to go unpunished, or the prohibited acts [are] of an international character and of serious concern to the international community as a whole. ... The assertion of universal jurisdiction for ... these international crimes is based upon multilateral treaties that provide for 'domestic jurisdiction over extraterritorial offenses regardless of the actors' nationalities,' and thus implicitly allow for universal jurisdiction, despite the fact that they lack 'any reference to the universality principle.'"[814]

UNCLOS is one such multilateral treaty that provides for domestic jurisdiction over an international crime (i.e., piracy) outside a State's territory regardless of the suspected criminals' nationalities, "and thus implicitly allow for universal jurisdiction." Thus, Article 105 provides:

> Article 105 / Seizure of a pirate ship or aircraft
> On the high seas, or in any other place outside the jurisdiction of any State, every State may seize a pirate ship or aircraft, or a ship or aircraft taken by piracy and under the control of pirates, and arrest the persons and seize the property on board. The courts of the State which carried out the seizure may decide upon the penalties to be imposed, and may also

determine the action to be taken with regard to the ships, aircraft or property, subject to the rights of third parties acting in good faith.[815]

Thus, a warship encountering a suspected pirate vessel in international waters does not need to have any relationship to the Flag State of the pirate vessel, or the State of nationality of a pirated vessel or its crew being held hostage, or even the State of nationality of the suspected pirates. Article 105's admonition that "every State may seize a pirate ship" is a clear statement that **universal jurisdiction exists over piracy**—i.e., every State may board a suspected pirate vessel, seize the vessel, arrest her crew, seize the property onboard, prosecute the suspected pirates, and dispose of the pirate vessel.[816]

Piracy is defined in Article 101 as:

1) "any **illegal acts of violence or detention**, or any act of depredation" (i.e., attacking or plundering),
2) "committed for **private ends**"
3) "by the crew ... of a **private ship**"
4) against a ship "on the high seas or ... in a place outside the jurisdiction of any State" (i.e., **in International Waters**).[817]

As discussed in Chapter 2, outside the 12 nm Territorial Seas (i.e., National Waters and National Airspace) are International Waters[818] and International Airspace,[819] over which the Coastal State (aka "littoral State") exercises less and less sovereignty and control the further one travels from land.[820] In order to constitute piracy, the illegal acts committed by a private ship for private ends must be carried out in International Waters. The same illegal acts committed by a private ship for private ends in Territorial Seas is generally described as "**armed robbery at sea**," and is a matter entirely within the Coastal State's jurisdiction.[821]

Although movie producers tend to romanticize pirates as historical characters, the truth about piracy is that it is a violent crime where innocent people are attacked and killed every year.[822] The International Chamber of Commerce established the International Maritime Bureau (IMB) "in 1981 to act as a focal point in the fight against all types of maritime crime," including piracy.[823] The IMB "established the 24 hour IMB Piracy Reporting Centre (PRC) in Kuala Lumpur, Malaysia" in order "to provide a free service to the seafarer."[824] The IMB PRC analyzes the hundreds of piracy incidents that are reported worldwide every year, and generates a detailed annual "Piracy and Armed Robbery Against Ships" report.[825] The IMB also maintains a website with a live piracy map (although there is a seasonal component to piracy incidents, related to at-sea weather conditions), including narratives of recent attacks.[826]

It is important to note that violent actions taken against another ship in International Waters need not have a pecuniary (i.e., monetary or financial) motive in order to constitute piracy. One controversial example is the Sea Shepherd Conservation Society, which touts itself as "an international non-profit, marine wildlife conservation organization."[827] However, the Sea Shepherd's aggressive tactics have been routinely criticized, even by other conservation groups. "For decades, Mr. Watson and his Sea Shepherd Conservation Society have rammed, sabotaged, shot water can[n]ons at and thrown stink bombs on whalers and commercial fishing vessels. ... [Even] Greenpeace criticized Watson and his tactics as 'morally wrong' and counter-productive because 'If there's one way to harden Japanese public opinion and ensure whaling continues, it's to use violent tactics against their fleet.'" Sea Shepherd's alleged actions include sinking 10 whaling vessels in port, and seeking to disable the world's largest whale factory ship in treacherous Antarctic waters.[828]

The Japanese "Institute of Cetacean Research" (ICR, under which Japan captured hundreds of whales each year in the name of

The Japanese whaling vessel Yushin Maru No. 2 shoots its water cannons at a Sea Shepherd craft during an altercation on Feb. 12, 2012. The photo was released by the Sea Shepherd Conservation Society.

"research") sued the Sea Shepherd Conservation Society in the U.S. federal District Court in Seattle, Washington. After their case was dismissed, the ICR appealed to the U.S. 9th Circuit Court of Appeals, which "concluded that the district court had misinterpreted the phrase 'private ends' and the word 'violence' under the United Nations Convention on the Law of the Sea's (UNCLOS) definition of piracy."[829]

It probably didn't help that the Sea Shepherd painted its ships "with giant shark-like teeth that make it look rather like, well, a pirate ship."[831] After the U.S. Supreme Court refused to hear their appeal, the Sea Shepherd Conservation Society finally agreed to pay $2.55M to the ICR for attacking their whaling ships.[832]

However, the Sea Shepherd Conservation Society takes credit for serving as the impetus behind Australia bringing the Japanese whaling case to the ICJ:

For 10 years, Sea Shepherd had been pursuing the Japanese whaling fleet in the Antarctic, high-profile campaigns that ultimately resulted in the government of Australia taking the government of Japan to the International Court of Justice (ICJ) in The Hague. The ICJ ruled that the Japanese whaling program was illegal and thus the Japanese whaling industry took a one-year hiatus from whaling as they re-worked their whaling program in [a] bid to subvert the ICJ ruling. That one-year hiatus gave Sea Shepherd the opportunity to focus on a different Antarctic poaching issue altogether — namely the poaching of Patagonian and Antarctic Toothfish.[833]

Nevertheless, the Sea Shepherd has apparently abandoned its anti-whaling campaign, because the Japanese whaling fleet started to use satellites to track the location of Sea Shepherd's vessels, and merely avoided all contact.[834]

Before discussing the international response to piracy, it is necessary to understand the United Nations (UN) Charter framework, the role of the UN Security Council (UNSC), and how to read UNSC Resolutions (UNSCRs).

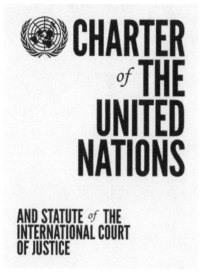

CHARTER *of* **THE UNITED NATIONS**

AND STATUTE *of* THE INTERNATIONAL COURT OF JUSTICE

The UN Charter was drafted and signed during World War II, and entered into force 52 days after the end of World War II on October 24, 1945. A subsequent treaty normally prevails over an earlier treaty, such as the 1982 UNCLOS treaty prevailing over the 1958 Law of the Sea Conventions for those States which are party to both.[835] However, the UN Charter is considered a "super treaty" because it trumps any conflicting treaty provisions, even if the other treaty entered into force later in time: "In the event of a conflict between the obligations of the Members of the United Nations under the present Charter and their obligations under any other international agreement, their obligations under the present Charter shall prevail."[836]

The UN Charter outlaws the "offensive" use of warfare: "All Members shall refrain in their international relations from the threat or use of force against the territorial integrity or political independence of any state, or in any other manner inconsistent with the Purposes of the United Nations."[837] One of the founding principles of the UN is that member States shall settle their disputes peacefully.[838] Another founding principle is that member States "confer on the Security Council primary responsibility for the maintenance of international peace and security, and agree that in carrying out its duties under this responsibility the Security Council acts on their behalf."[839] If States are unable to settle their disputes peacefully, the UN Security Council (UNSC) may take action pursuant to Chapter VI of the UN Charter, in order to ensure the peaceful settlement of a dispute between States.

However, once a dispute between States has escalated to the level of a "threat to the peace, breach of the peace, or act of aggression," the UNSC may take action pursuant to Chapter VII of the UN Charter in order to maintain or enforce international peace and security.[840] In order to act under Chapter VII, the UNSC must first determine if Chapter VII has been "triggered" (UN Charter, Article 39) by a threat to the peace, breach of the peace or act of aggression.[841] The UNSC may do so by *expressly* referencing Article 39, or by making a determination that there is a threat to the peace, breach of the peace or act of aggression. The UNSC may also do so *impliedly* simply by taking action pursuant to Chapter VII. If a UNSC Resolution (UNSCR) does not mention "acting under Chapter VII," then the UNSC is acting under Chapter VI (i.e., peaceful settlement of disputes).

Once the UNSC has determined that it needs to take an "enforcement" action under Chapter VII of the UN Charter, the UNSC must next consider whether non-military measures may be effective in restoring peace (e.g., imposing economic sanctions, restricting communications and severing diplomatic relations), under Article 41 of the UN Charter.[842]

If the UNSC determines that non-military measures "would be inadequate or have proved to be inadequate," the UNSC finally considers whether military measures may be necessary to restore international peace and security (i.e., authorizing Member States to use military force), under Article 42 of the UN Charter.[843]

The UNSC is comprised of 15 members, including 5 permanent members (the major Allied victors of World War II):[844] China, France, the Russian Federation, the United Kingdom, and the United States. The remaining 10 non-permanent members are elected for two-year terms by the General Assembly (with the end of each State's term noted):

1) Estonia (2021);
2) India (2022);
3) Ireland (2022);
4) Kenya (2022);
5) Mexico (2022);
6) Niger (2021);
7) Norway (2022);
8) Saint Vincent and the Grenadines (2021);
9) Tunisia (2021); and
10) Vietnam (2021)."[845]

UNSC decisions on **procedural** matters require a 3/5 supermajority vote (i.e., 9 of the 15 members). UNSC decision "on all other matters [i.e., on **substantive** matters] shall be made by an affirmative vote of nine members including the concurring votes of the permanent members."[846] Requiring the "affirmative vote" of the 5 permanent UNSC members essentially conveys on each of them the authority to "veto" any draft UNSC decision with which they disagree. However, an "affirmative vote" has been interpreted as the absence of a negative vote. In other words, if one of the 5 permanent members "abstains" from a substantive vote, that does not prevent the UNSCR from passing if 9 of the 15 members, including the other 4 permanent members, approve it.

Now that we've discussed the UN Charter framework, and the role of the UN Security Council (UNSC), we need to review how to read UNSC Resolutions (UNSCRs). A couple examples should help.

Five days after North Korea conducted its first nuclear weapons test in October 2006, the UNSC determined North Korea's actions constituted a clear

North Korea's first nuclear weapons test— October 2006

Unanimous vote by UN Security Council in favor of UNSCR 1718

threat to international peace and security, and unanimously voted in UNSCR 1718 to take action pursuant to Chapter VII of the UN Charter.[847]

At the beginning of any UNSCR are a number of preambular or prefatory paragraphs in the *"chapeau"* (i.e., hat). These paragraphs

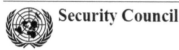

United Nations   S/RES/1718 (2006)

Security Council

Distr.: General
14 October 2006

Resolution 1718 (2006)

Adopted by the Security Council at its 5551st meeting, on 14 October 2006

The Security Council,

Recalling its previous relevant resolutions, including resolution 825 (1993), resolution 1540 (2004) and, in particular, resolution 1695 (2006), as well as the statement of its President of 6 October 2006 (S/PRST/2006/41),

Reaffirming that proliferation of nuclear, chemical and biological weapons, as well as their means of delivery, constitutes a threat to international peace and security,

Expressing the gravest concern at the claim by the Democratic People's Republic of Korea (DPRK) that it has conducted a test of a nuclear weapon on 9 October 2006, and at the challenge such a test constitutes to the Treaty on the Non-Proliferation of Nuclear Weapons and to international efforts aimed at strengthening the global regime of non-proliferation of nuclear weapons, and the danger it poses to peace and stability in the region and beyond,

---

are not numbered, and typically begin with italicized verbs such as "recalling," "reaffirming," and "expressing." The preambular or prefatory paragraphs in the *"chapeau"* set the stage for the rest of the UNSCR, referring to previous UNSCRs, proclaiming the importance of adhering to international law, and expressing the concerns of the UNSC members especially as to how the State actions addressed may threaten international peace and security.

Only the last 2 preambular paragraphs are of particular importance, because they identify whether Article 39 has been triggered due to a "threat to international peace and security," and whether the UNSC is acting under Chapter VI (peaceful settlement of disputes) or Chapter VII of the UN Charter (enforcement actions).

> *Expressing* profound concern that the test claimed by the DPRK has generated increased tension in the region and beyond, and *determining* therefore that there is a clear threat to international peace and security.
>
> *Acting* under Chapter VII of the Charter of the United Nations, and taking measures under its Article 41.

In UNSCR 1718, the UNSC is clearly acting not only under Chapter VII of the UN Charter, but specifically under Article 41: non-military measures.

In order to determine what specific actions the UNSC has approved in UNSCR 1718, it is necessary to read the operative (i.e., binding or important) paragraphs, which are always numbered.

> 8.   *Decides* that:
>
> (a)   All Member States shall prevent the direct or indirect supply, sale or transfer to the DPRK, through their territories or by their nationals, or using their flag vessels or aircraft, and whether or not originating in their territories, of:
>
> (i)   Any battle tanks, armoured combat vehicles, large calibre artillery systems, combat aircraft, attack helicopters, warships, missiles or missile systems as defined for the purpose of the United Nations Register on Conventional Arms, or related materiel including spare parts, or items as determined by the Security Council or the Committee established by paragraph 12 below (the Committee);
>
> (ii)   All items, materials, equipment, goods and technology as set out in the lists in documents S/2006/814 and S/2006/815, unless within 14 days of adoption of this resolution the Committee has amended or completed their provisions also taking into account the list in document S/2006/816, as well as other items, materials, equipment, goods and technology, determined by the Security Council or the Committee, which could contribute to DPRK's nuclear-related, ballistic missile-related or other weapons of mass destruction-related programmes;
>
> (iii)   Luxury goods;

Thus, paragraph 8 of UNSCR 1718 banned exporting any "luxury goods" to North Korea (*inter alia*), which is a form of economic sanction or "non-military measure" under Article 41. "Luxury goods" is generally interpreted as including any form of alcohol.[848] This is why Dutch officials in the port of Rotterdam seized 90,000 pint bottles of Russian vodka that were destined for North Korea in 2019—the bottles of vodka were "luxury goods" which were banned from export to North Korea by UNSCR 1718.[849] The Netherlands was merely abiding by its treaty obligation (i.e., the UN Charter) to enforce UNSCR 1718. Thus, UNSCR 1718 is an example of the UNSC imposing **non-military measures** under Article 41.

Dutch officials seize 90K bottles of vodka headed for North Korea

By Yaron Steinbuch   February 26, 2019 | 2:19pm | Updated

An example of the UNSC imposing **military measures** under Article 42 of the UN Charter was done in response to the situation in Kosovo. In the 1990's, Yugoslavian President Slobodan Milosevic had a policy of "ethnic cleansing" of Albanians in Kosovo. The UN Security Council determined Yugoslavia's actions constituted a threat to international peace and security, and voted in UNSCR 1244 to take action pursuant to Chapter VII.[850] Again, only the last 2 preambular paragraphs are of particular importance, because they identify whether Art. 39 has been triggered due to a "threat to international peace & security," and whether the UNSC is acting under Chapter VI (peaceful settlement of disputes) or Chapter VII of the UN Charter (enforcement actions).

UNITED
NATIONS   S

Security Council
                                                          Distr.
                                                          GENERAL

                                                          S/RES/1244 (1999)
                                                          10 June 1999

RESOLUTION 1244 (1999)

Adopted by the Security Council at its 4011th meeting,
on 10 June 1999

The Security Council,

    Bearing in mind the purposes and principles of the Charter of the United Nations, and the primary responsibility of the Security Council for the maintenance of international peace and security,

* * *

Determining that the situation in the region continues to constitute a threat to international peace and security,

Determined to ensure the safety and security of international personnel and the implementation by all concerned of their responsibilities under the present resolution, and *acting* for these purposes under Chapter VII of the Charter of the United Nations,

In UNSCR 1244, the UNSC is clearly acting under Chapter VII of the UN Charter (enforcement actions).

In order to determine what specific actions the UNSC has approved in UNSCR 1244, it is necessary to read the operative numbered paragraphs. One military measure that the UNSC can authorize under Article 42 is sending in UN Peacekeepers (aka "blue helmets"), as it did to restore/maintain peace in Kosovo:

5. *Decides* on the deployment in Kosovo, under United Nations auspices, of international civil and security presences, with appropriate equipment and personnel as required, and welcomes the agreement of the Federal Republic of Yugoslavia to such presences;

* * *

7. *Authorizes* Member States and relevant international organizations to establish the international security presence in Kosovo as set out in point 4 of annex 2 with all necessary means to fulfil its responsibilities under paragraph 9 below;

* * *

9. *Decides* that the responsibilities of the international security presence to be deployed and acting in Kosovo will include:

(a) Deterring renewed hostilities, maintaining and where necessary enforcing a ceasefire, and ensuring the withdrawal and preventing the return into Kosovo of Federal and Republic military, police and paramilitary forces, except as provided in point 6 of annex 2;

(b) Demilitarizing the Kosovo Liberation Army (KLA) and other armed Kosovo Albanian groups as required in paragraph 15 below;

(c) Establishing a secure environment in which refugees and displaced persons can return home in safety, the international civil presence can operate, a transitional administration can be established, and humanitarian aid can be delivered;

(d) Ensuring public safety and order until the international civil presence can take responsibility for this task;

* * *

The UN Security Council's authorization to use "all necessary means" in paragraph 7 of UNSCR 1244 implies the use of military force. Thus, UNSCR 1244 is an example of the UNSC authorizing the use of military force under Article 42.

Now that we've discussed the UN Charter framework, the role of the UNSC, and how to read UNSCRs, we have laid the foundation to discuss the international response to piracy, especially off the coast of Somalia. Historically, piracy had always been a problem in certain areas, e.g., in the Strait of Malacca between Singapore, Malaysia, and Indonesia;[851] in the Caribbean; and to a lesser extent, off the African coasts, especially off the coast of Somalia[852] (which is considered one of the world's failed States).[853]

"Modern pirates tend to attack and hijack cargo ships and fishing vessels, which have commodities readily sellable on the black market, and therefore rarely direct their attention towards cruise ships. 'Smaller pirate gangs, who do not have the resources to seize the cargo being transported, instead often board a ship to steal substantial amounts of the cash ships carry for payroll and port fees, and the recent trend is more frequent kidnappings of crewmembers to be exchanged for ransom money'."[854] The piracy problem off the coast of Somalia started spreading after 2005,

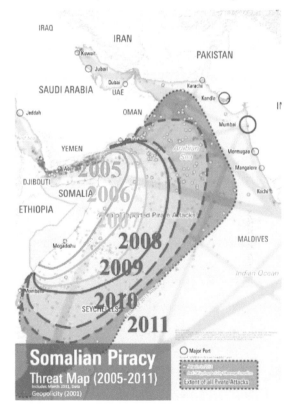

Somalian Piracy
Threat Map (2005-2011)
Includes March 2011, Data
Geopolicity (2001)

both in terms of greater frequency of attacks and in terms of a wider area of attacks, as shown in this chart.[855] Somali pirates even brazenly attacked a U.S. warship in 2010 mistaking it for a cargo ship.[856] "Somalia has been without an effective government since 1991, when warlords overthrew a dictatorship and then turned on one another. The lawlessness has allowed piracy to flourish off the coast, with bandits in speed boats launching attacks on foreign shipping, bringing in millions of dollars in ransom."[857] Lack of a central government, lawlessness, and poor harvests led to country-wide famine in Somalia, which required 40,000 metric tons of World Food Program (WFP) food every month simply for Somalia's population to survive.[858] Ninety percent of WFP food aid to Somalia was shipped by sea, and unfortunately, pirates targeted WFP ships as well. "Before the escorts started in 2007, six ships with WFP food were hijacked over three years."[859]

Part of the piracy problem was the fact that maritime shipping companies simply considered piracy to be a cost of doing business, especially when compared to the value of each vessel and its cargo.[860] The probability of any particular ship getting hijacked was fairly small, the insurance rates were relatively low,[861] and even if one of their ships was hijacked, the crew wouldn't be treated too badly;[862] after paying a few million dollars in ransom, the ship would be released in a few months.

Another part of the piracy problem was that maritime shipping companies weren't always willing to take measures necessary to make their vessels more difficult to pirate. For example, they didn't avoid areas with high-pirate activity, and they didn't instruct their vessels to take evasive maneuvers or speed up to try to outrun pirate attempts.[863] Maritime shipping companies were initially loathe to arm their crewmembers because it represented a paradigm shift in how they had always conducted business,[864] they were worried about potential liability,[865] and "because it [was] feared this would increase the likelihood of crew members getting killed or injured" by pirates.[866] Maritime shipping companies didn't even raise the height of the deck (aka "freeboard") in order to make it more difficult for pirates to climb onboard.[867] For example, the *Motor Vessel (M/V) Maersk Alabama*) was hijacked while it was bringing donated food for the WFP in 2009.[868] Because the ship was U.S.-flagged with an American crew, U.S. Navy SEALs were involved in rescuing the American crew (which formed the basis for the "Captain Phillips" movie released in 2013). As seen in the following photo, the *M/V Maersk Alabama* only had a 20 feet freeboard[869]—not very challenging for a properly motivated pirate with a ladder!

An unprecedented international response to piracy off the coast of Somalia began in 2008, when the UNSC got involved and started passing resolutions to combat "[t]he situation in Somalia." In UNSCR 1814, the UNSC took action under Chapter VII of the UN Charter by authorizing non-military measures under Article 41 of the UN Charter that focused on assisting in rebuilding Somalia's government, and holding free and democratic elections, as well as calling upon States and regional organizations to protect WFP ships delivering humanitarian aid to Somalia.[870] Less than 3 weeks later, the UNSC took action under Chapter VII in UNSCR 1816 and authorized military measures to combat piracy off the coast of Somalia in operative paragraph 7. The resulting "[i]nternational cooperation in response to Somali piracy has been remarkable."[871]

United Nations   S/RES/1816 (2008)*

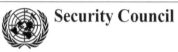 **Security Council**   Distr.: General
                                                                 2 June 2008

Resolution 1816 (2008)

Adopted by the Security Council at its 5902nd meeting on 2 June 2008

The Security Council,

Recalling its previous resolutions and the statements of its President concerning the situation in Somalia,

* * *

Determining that the incidents of piracy and armed robbery against vessels in the territorial waters of Somalia and the high seas off the coast of Somalia exacerbate the situation in Somalia which continues to constitute a threat to international peace and security in the region.

Acting under Chapter VII of the Charter of the United Nations.

* * *

As discussed earlier in this Chapter, in order to constitute piracy, illegal acts committed by a private ship for private ends must be carried out in International Waters. The same illegal acts committed by a private ship for private ends in National Waters (i.e., in Territorial Seas, Internal Waters, or Archipelagic Waters) is generally described as "armed robbery at sea,"[872] and is a matter entirely within the Coastal State's jurisdiction. However, since Somalia is incapable of effectively patrolling its Territorial Seas and combating "armed robbery at sea," Paragraph 7 of UNSCR 1816 basically permits foreign States to treat Somalia's Territorial Seas as if they were International Waters for combating piracy and armed robbery at sea.[873]

Also as discussed earlier in this Chapter, "all necessary means to repress acts of piracy and armed robbery" authorizes the use of military force in doing so.[874] Notice also that paragraph 8 of UNSCR 1816 reminds States to ensure their actions do not hamper the right of Innocent Passage through Somalia's Territorial Seas, consistent with UNCLOS.[875] Paragraph 9 of UNSCR 1816 reminds States that the other strictures of international law still apply, namely that:

1) Combating piracy and armed robbery at sea off the coast of Somalia is a unique situation;

2) The authorization to enter Somalia's Territorial Seas is at the specific behest/request of the Transitional Federal Government (TFG) of Somalia (since otherwise taking military action in another State's Territorial Seas would not only violate Innocent Passage, but would also constitute an act of war, discussed in Chapter 10); and

3) Such actions neither add a "gloss"[876] on the interpretation of UNCLOS, nor contribute to the formation of Customary International Law (CIL—i.e., they are of no precedential value).

Moreover, "[n]ations entering Somali waters to fight piracy and robbery along the country's 1,880-mile coastline ... must first obtain approval from the Somali government and give advance notice to UN secretary general Ban Ki-moon."[877]

Four months later, the UNSC provided an update on actions taken to combat armed robbery at sea off the coast of Somalia in UNSCR 1838, and called upon States to combat piracy on the High Seas as well.[878] Less than two months later, the UNSC recognized the efforts taken by the North Atlantic Treaty Organization (NATO) and the European Union (EU) to combat piracy and armed robbery at sea off the coast of Somalia in UNSCR 1846 (December 2, 2008). Paragraph 10 of UNSCR 1846 renewed the authority to enter Somalia's Territorial Seas to combat piracy and armed robbery at sea for another 12 months, and repeated operative paragraph 7 of UNSCR 1816 practically verbatim in operative paragraph 10 of UNSCR 1846.[879]

However, 2 weeks later the UNSC passed UNSCR 1851, again acting under Chapter VII of the UN Charter, with an even stronger operative paragraph 6:

> 6.   In response to the letter from the TFG of 9 December 2008, *encourages* Member States to continue to cooperate with the TFG in the fight against piracy and armed robbery at sea, *notes* the primary role of the TFG in rooting out piracy and armed robbery at sea, and *decides* that for a period of twelve months from the date of adoption of resolution 1846, States and regional organizations cooperating in the fight against piracy and armed robbery at sea off the coast of Somalia for which advance notification has been provided by the TFG to the Secretary-General may undertake all necessary measures that are appropriate in Somalia, for the purpose of suppressing acts of piracy and armed robbery at sea, pursuant to the request of the TFG, provided, however, that any measures undertaken pursuant to the authority of this paragraph shall be undertaken consistent with applicable international humanitarian and human rights law;

For the first time, the UNSC had authorized not merely "entry" into Somalia's Territorial Seas and the "use of all necessary means" therein to combat piracy and armed robbery at sea, but to "**undertake all necessary measures that are appropriate** *in* *Somalia*" (emphasis added).[880] This prompted a chorus of responses (by the author at NATO Headquarters and by other surprised international law practitioners and commentators): holy cr@n—the UN Security Council just authorized 'boots ashore' (i.e., military force on land) to combat piracy![881]

The U.S. had proposed even stronger draft language.[882] In her remarks after the UNSC meeting on the "situation in Somalia," U.S. Secretary of State (SECSTATE) Condoleeza Rice commented that "I was sent here to get authorization to go ashore so that we did not create a dividing line that was a maritime-to-land sanctuary for the pirates. And that is a position that is supported by the United States Government as a whole." SECSTATE Rice admitted that although it was in the waning days of President George W. Bush's presidency (which ended barely a month later), the U.S.

government "would raise in consultations" with other States a UNSCR authorizing another UN peacekeeping mission in Somalia,[883] which never happened. Instead, newly-elected President Obama simply decided to declare a national emergency 16 months later, in order to freeze any al-Shabaab (the terrorist group allegedly financing many of the Somali pirates) assets in the U.S.[884]

The UN Security Council (UNSC) has renewed the authorizations to treat Somalia's Territorial Seas as if they were International Waters for combating piracy and armed robbery at sea, and to use military force on land "*in Somalia*" to combat piracy (i.e., the authorizations contained in UNSCRs 1846 and 1851) every year since 2008, and will likely do so again this year.[885]

One would think that having ships from the European Union (EU), North Atlantic Treaty Organization (through 2016), Russia, China, and other States (at an annual cost of one billion dollars)[886] combating piracy since 2009 would imply that piracy off the coast of Somalia remains a rampant problem. But that is not the case— if anything, maritime patrols off the coast of Somalia and around the Horn of Africa (HOA) have been quite successful at drastically reducing Somali piracy.[887] As we can see from the red shaded "hat" in this chart, Somali piracy was a significant problem from 2007 through 2012, but has been eliminated since then.[888] In contrast, Southeast Asia[889] (highlighted in orange) always has been, and remains a hot bed of piracy activity. The rest of Africa (mostly in the Gulf of Guinea, highlighted in yellow)) has also been a consistent problem for the past 25 years.[890] Nevertheless, efforts to combat piracy in these areas do not benefit from any special UNSC treatment, involvement, or authorizations.

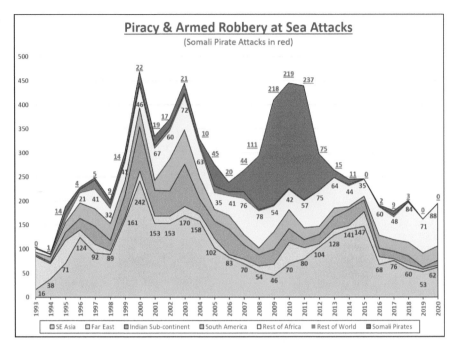

Piracy & Armed Robbery at Sea Attacks
(Somali Pirate Attacks in red)

Take Nigeria[891] for example, which shares many characteristics with Somalia: "chronic lawlessness,"[892] high unemployment,[893] famine, perhaps a failed State[894] that is unable to effectively patrol its Territorial Seas,[895] with a significant piracy problem in the Gulf of Guinea (averaging 51 pirate attacks each year for the past 20 years,[896] and "accounts for almost 82% of crew kidnappings globally")[897] that is affecting international maritime commerce and poses a major threat to maritime security. In addition, Nigeria appears unwilling to prosecute captured pirates.[898] Yet Nigeria in particular, and piracy in the Gulf of Guinea in general, has received very little UNSC attention.[899] In 2011, the UNSC "[e]xpress[ed] its deep concern about the threat that piracy and armed robbery at sea in the Gulf of Guinea pose to international navigation, security and the economic development of states in the region." Yet the UNSC took no enforcement actions pursuant to Chapter VII of the UN Charter, and instead merely encouraged States in the area to cooperate in countering piracy.[900] Four months later, the UNSC welcomed regional initiatives "to enhance maritime safety and security in the Gulf of Guinea." Yet once again, the UNSC took no enforcement actions pursuant to Chapter VII of the UN Charter, and instead merely encouraged States in the area to cooperate in countering piracy (once again), and international partners to provide support.[901] Thus, twice encouraged, States in the region convened a Heads of State Conference on Maritime Safety and Security in the Gulf of Guinea, and adopted a Code of Conduct in Yaounde, Cameroon in 2013.[902] The UNSC touted the 2013 Yaounde (pronounced "*yow-un-dee*") Code of Conduct as "pav[ing] the way" for States in the Region to develop a comprehensive strategy to combat piracy and armed robbery at sea.[903] Yet the language in the 2013 Yaounde Code of Conduct (taken from a similar Djibouti Code of Conduct for combating piracy in the Gulf of Aden) seems fairly watered down (pun intended):

Article 2 / Purpose and Scope
1. Consistent with their available resources and related priorities, their respective national laws and regulations, and applicable rules of international law, the Signatories intend to co-operate to the fullest extent in the repression of transnational organized crime in the maritime domain, maritime terrorism, IUU fishing and other illegal activities at sea....[904]

The State signatories do not even grant permission to either combat piracy in each other's Territorial Seas, or even to continue in hot pursuit of suspected pirates into each other's Territorial Seas.[905]

Other States have engaged in joint naval exercises to bolster and train the Gulf of Guinea Coastal States' navies and coast guards.[906]

However, other States have been unwilling to support counter-piracy missions[907] in the Gulf of Guinea on the *west coast of Africa*, even though this would appear no more logistically challenging than supporting counter-piracy missions in the Gulf of Aden/Horn of Africa on the *east coast of Africa*, especially since both have similar geographical locations (i.e., from the equator up to approximately 10° North Latitude). However, although the piracy problem in the Gulf of Guinea is significant, it is unclear whether any of its 16 Coastal States (i.e., Guinea-Bissau, Guinea, Sierra Leone, Liberia, Côte d'Ivoire, Ghana, Togo, Benin, Nigeria,[908] Cameroon, Sao Tome and Principe, Equatorial Guinea, Gabon, Republic of the Congo, Democratic Republic of the Congo, and Angola) have requested assistance as Somalia did,[909] even though each of these Coastal States have had pirate attacks reported in their territorial waters, especially Nigeria (averaging 27 pirate attacks each year for the past 20 years).[910]

Perhaps it is because the African pirates operating in the Gulf of Guinea only demand fairly "reasonable" ransom payments in the thousands of dollars[911] (rather than the millions of dollars demanded by Somali pirates), which the maritime shipping companies are more than willing to pay as simply a cost of doing business:

[T]he combined cost of insuring the ship, the cargo and the crew (for kidnapping and ransom) for a voyage to Nigeria is typically no more than the cost of half a day's fuel. It can be cheaper not to bother with armed guards. Premiums are so low in part because Nigerian pirates, unlike those in Somalia, have priced their ransoms just right: for many companies they can be written off as a cost of doing business.[912]

Perhaps it is because the 16 Coastal States bordering the Gulf of Guinea have regular 12 nm Territorial Sea claims, consistent with UNCLOS. [NOTE: unlike Somalia, which claims a 200 nm Territorial Sea,[913] and thus any counter-piracy operations within 200 nm would violate Somalia's excessive Territorial Sea claim, except as permitted by a UNSCR.] Or perhaps it is because "[t]he Gulf of Guinea, unlike the Malacca Strait or the Gulf of Aden, is not a choke point for international trade,"[914] and thus is of little international consequence. Finally, perhaps it is because African pirates operating in the Gulf of Guinea have not had the audacity to attack a World Food Program (WFP) ship delivering food aid on behalf of the UN.

In summary, jurisdiction over illegal maritime activities primarily rests with the Flag State, including flags of convenience. In fact, Flag States have exclusive jurisdiction over their vessels on the High Seas with two primary exceptions—a warship may board: 1) any "stateless" or "quasi-stateless" ship (although, since there is no legitimate Flag State involved, this is not really an exception to exclusive Flag State jurisdiction); and 2) any ship reasonably suspected of engaging in piracy, since all States have universal jurisdiction over a suspected pirate (aka the enemy of mankind). Due to a surge in piracy off the coast of Somalia, the UNSC has issued robust authorizations (from 2008 to the present) to treat Somalia's Territorial Seas as if they were International Waters for combating piracy and armed robbery at sea, and to use military force on land "*in Somalia*" to combat piracy. As a result, maritime patrols off the coast of Somalia have eliminated piracy in that region. However, piracy remains a significant threat to maritime security in Southeast Asia, and in the Gulf of Guinea on the west coast of Africa.

[773] Ukrainian Maritime Bar Association, Newsroom, *The Concept of «Genuine Link»* in the *International Maritime Law* (Olena Ptashenchuk, 2014), http://www.umba.org.ua/en/newsroom/articles/article3.htm.
[774] United Nations Convention on the Law of the Sea (UNCLOS) arts. 92(2) & 110(1)(d), Dec. 10, 1982, 1833 U.N.T.S. 397, https://www.un.org/Depts/los/convention_agreements/convention_overview_convention.htm; U.S. NAVY, MARINE CORPS & COAST GUARD, THE COMMANDER'S HANDBOOK ON THE LAW OF NAVAL OPERATIONS, NWP 1-14M/MCTP 11-10B/COMDTPUB P5800.7A, ¶ 3.11.2.3 (p. 3-13) (2017), www.jag.navy.mil/distrib/instructions/CDRs_HB_on_Law_of_Naval_Operations_AUG17.pdf.
[775] *See, e.g.,* Boat, Luxury Yacht Advice, *How to choose your yacht's flag state* (Kenny Wooton, Jan. 21, 2015), https://www.boatinternational.com/yachts/luxury-yacht-advice/how-to-choose-your-yachts-flag-state--615. Although somewhat controversial, luxury yachts were also favored by some billionaires as a place of isolation during the Coronavirus 2019 (COVID-19) Pandemic. CNN Travel, Article, *Are billionaires really self-isolating on superyachts?* (Tamara Hardingham-Gill, Apr. 15, 2020), https://www.cnn.com/travel/article/billionaires-self-isolating-superyachts/index.html?utm_term=15870340425436ef9078eab37&utm_source=Coronavirus+Update+-+April+16%2C+2020&utm_medium=email&utm_campaign=198851_15870340425 46&bt_ee=DYtCPphEqvZW59jFcilXjd6j4NDamS4mP1d0Wgu%2BuZBWa4eyeec5U9 1pdUZG26O2&bt_ts=1587034042546.
[776] Food and Agriculture Organization of the United Nations (FAO), Legal Papers Online #61, *The "Genuine Link" Concept in Responsible Fisheries: Legal Aspects and Recent Developments* 1 (Ariella D'andrea, Nov. 2006), http://www.fao.org/documents/card/en/c/5299785c-bbe2-4af1-b614-5837fe3b2be0.
[777] FAO, *The "Genuine Link" Concept,* (full cite above); United Nations Treaty Collection, Depositary, Status of Treaties, Chapter XXI Law of the Sea, 7. United Nations Convention on Conditions for Registration of Ships, https://treaties.un.org/Pages/ViewDetails.aspx?src=TREATY&mtdsg_no=XII-7&chapter=12&clang=_en.
[778] FAO, *The "Genuine Link" Concept,* (full cite above); Int'l. Tribunal for the Law of the Sea (ITLOS), The *M/V "SAIGA"* (No. 2) Case (*Saint Vincent and the Grenadines v. Guinea*), Judgment of 1 July 1999, ¶¶ 82-83, https://www.itlos.org/cases/list-of-cases/case-no-2/. In addition, repeated "requests to further discuss and clarify the genuine link concept" have gone unheeded. FAO, *The "Genuine Link" Concept,* (full cite above). "[I]n the *M/V Saiga* judgment, the International Tribunal for the Law of the Sea found that the use of force by a Guinean patrol boat to stop and board the *Saiga* for an alleged violation of Guinean customs laws, both before and after the boarding, was excessive and unreasonable, and endangered human life. The Tribunal determined that international law requires that the use of force must be avoided if possible and, if the use of force is unavoidable, it must not go beyond what is reasonable and necessary in the circumstances. When boarded on the high seas, the *Saiga*, a coastal tanker, was fully laden with gas oil and had recently provided fuel to fishing vessels in Guinea's contiguous zone. The Guinean patrol boat opened fire on the tanker with live ammunition using solid shot from large-caliber automatic weapons without issuing any signal or warning, as required by

international law and practice. The Tribunal also found that the boarding party's use of weapons was excessive given that the tanker's crew did not resist and did not threaten the boarding party." Raul (Pete) Pedrozo, *Maritime Police Law of the People's Republic of China*, 97 INT'L. L. STUD. 465, 475 (2021), https://digital-commons.usnwc.edu/ils/vol97/iss1/24/.

[779] Rose George, NINETY PERCENT OF EVERYTHING 8 (2013).

[780] Food and Agriculture Organization of the United Nations (FAO), Legal Papers Online #61, *The "Genuine Link" Concept in Responsible Fisheries: Legal Aspects and Recent Developments* 1 (Ariella D'andrea, Nov. 2006), http://www.fao.org/documents/card/en/c/5299785c-bbe2-4af1-b614-5837fe3b2be0.

[781] Ukrainian Maritime Bar Association, Newsroom, *The Concept of «Genuine Link»* in the International Maritime Law (Olena Ptashenchuk, 2014), http://www.umba.org.ua/en/newsroom/articles/article3.htm.

[782] Medium.com, *How Delaware Became the State Where Companies Incorporate* (Elaine Zelby, Jan. 30, 2019), https://medium.com/useless-knowledge-daily/why-most-companies-incorporate-in-delaware-b8eae1e528a3.

[783] THE FLETCHER SCHOOL OF LAW AND DIPLOMACY—TUFTS UNIVERSITY, LAW OF THE SEA, A POLICY PRIMER 54 (2017), https://sites.tufts.edu/lawofthesea/introduction/.

[784] Lloyd's List, Maritime intelligence, Top 10 flag states 2020, (Dec. 3, 2020), https://lloydslist.maritimeintelligence.informa.com/LL1134965/Top-10-flag-states-2020.

[785] Int'l. Chamber of Shipping (ICS), Home, Press Releases, *New Edition of ICS Flag State Performance Table Shows Impressive Performance for All Major Flag Registers* (Feb. 9, 2016), https://www.ics-shipping.org/news/press-releases/view-article/2016/02/09/new-edition-of-ics-flag-state-performance-table-shows-impressive-performance-for-all-major-flag-registers; FAO, *The "Genuine Link" Concept*, (full cite above) (noting that "the genuine link concept ... seems to have lost significance in terms of its perceived effectiveness in the fight against reflagging and IUU fishing.").

[786] Int'l. Chamber of Shipping (ICS), ICS Conference 2015, *What Does ICS Expect of a Responsible Flag?* slide 11 of 12 (Arthur Bowring, 2015, citing IMO Secretary General, Marine Environment Protection Committee (MEPC), http://www.ics-shipping.org/docs/default-source/ICS-Conference-2015/bowring.pdf.

[787] Although UNCLOS assigns the responsibility for ensuring safety at sea to the Flag State, China has sought to impose its own safety conditions on vessels sailing through its waters. Raul (Pete) Pedrozo, *China's Revised Maritime Traffic Safety Law*, 97 INT'L. L. STUD. 956, 961 (2021), https://digital-commons.usnwc.edu/ils/vol97/iss1/39/.

[788] Int'l. Maritime Organization (IMO), English, About IMO, Conventions, List of Conventions, Convention on the Int'l. Regulations for Preventing Collisions at Sea, 1972 (COLREGs), http://www.imo.org/en/About/Conventions/ListOfConventions/Pages/COLREG.aspx. The COLREGs are incorporated into UNCLOS by Article 94.

[789] Safety onboard a vessel cannot be overemphasized, as even well-run vessels can run into trouble. For example, a large and apparently well-run commercial dive boat was anchored off Santa Cruz Island (about 90 miles northwest of Los Angeles) for the night in September 2019 when a fire broke out at 3:00 AM. Thirty-three scuba divers and one crew member were awake in the berthing compartments on the lowest deck, but couldn't escape via the single narrow ladder—only the 5

crewmembers sleeping on the deck escaped. Military.com, Military News, Coast Guard, *At Least 25 Confirmed Dead in Boat Fire in California: Coast Guard* (Stefanie Dazio, Sep. 3, 2019), https://www.military.com/daily-news/2019/09/03/least-25-confirmed-dead-boat-fire-california-coast-guard.html. As a result, the Captain of the vessel "was charged ... with 34 counts of seaman's manslaughter," and the U.S. Coast Guard implemented 7 new requirements for U.S.-flagged small passenger vessels, "including mandatory checks on roving watches [i.e., a watchstander whose job is to walk around the vessel whenever passengers are below deck to check on things], better [interconnected] smoke detector systems, mandatory safety management systems and improved emergency exits." Military.com, Military News, *Coast Guard to Enact Sweeping Safety Reforms in Wake of Deadly Conception Boat Fire* (Richard Winton, Feb. 11, 2021), https://www.military.com/daily-news/2021/02/11/coast-guard-enact-sweeping-safety-reforms-wake-of-deadly-conception-boat-fire.html?ESRC=eb_210212.nl. Unfortunately, these types of incidents are all too common. *See, e.g.*, Taucher.net, Magazin, News, *Egypt: Red Sea Aggressor 1 burning* (Michael Houben, Nov. 6., 2019), https://taucher.net/diveinside-egypt__red_sea_aggressor_1_burning-kaz8119. The woman who died (Trish Sulzbach), was a friend of the author. Ever Loved, In memory of Patricia Marie Kessler (Sulzbach), https://everloved.com/life-of/patricia-kessler-sulzbach/obituary/.

[790] United Nations Convention on the Law of the Sea (UNCLOS) art. 94, Dec. 10, 1982, 1833 U.N.T.S. 397, https://www.un.org/Depts/los/convention_agreements/convention_overview_convention.htm.

[791] UNCLOS, art. 217 (full cite above).

[792] FAO, *The "Genuine Link" Concept*, (full cite above).

[793] Letter Of Transmittal Forwarding The 1982 UN Law Of The Sea Convention To The United States Senate, DOS Commentary p. 28 (William J. Clinton, Oct. 7, 1994) (S. Treaty Doc. 103–39), https://www.foreign.senate.gov/imo/media/doc/treaty_103-39.pdf. There is even a duty to rescue a person in distress inside another State's Territorial Seas: "ships [and aircraft, such as helicopters] have the duty to enter into a foreign State's territorial sea without the permission of the coastal State when there is reasonable certainty (based on the best available information) that a person is in distress, their location in reasonably well known [i.e., not conducting a wide-spread search operation], and the rescuing unit is in position to render timely and effective assistance. ... Though the ship or aircraft conducting the rescue shall not request approval from the coastal State to enter the State's territorial sea to conduct a rescue operation, it shall provide timely notification to the coastal State's search and rescue authorities." U.S. NAVY, MARINE CORPS & COAST GUARD, THE COMMANDER'S HANDBOOK ON THE LAW OF NAVAL OPERATIONS, NWP 1-14M/MCTP 11-10B/COMDTPUB P5800.7A, ¶¶ 2.5.2.6, 3.2 to 3.2.1.2 (pp. 2–6 to 2-7, 3-2) (2017), www.jag.navy.mil/distrib/instructions/CDRs_HB_on_Law_of_Naval_Operations_AUG17.pdf.

[794] COMMANDER'S HANDBOOK, ¶ 3.2.1.1 (p. 3-2) (full cite above).

[795] Sea Shepherd, Who We Are, https://seashepherd.org/. *See also* Maclean's, *Thunder gone under: The story of the world's longest maritime chase* (Jonathon Gatehouse & Amanda Shendruk, Apr. 16, 2015), https://www.macleans.ca/news/canada/thunder-gone-under-the-story-of-the-

worlds-longest-maritime-chase/ (describing the Sea Shepherd Conservation Society as an "environmental guerrilla group").

[796] The Sea Shepherd's *Motor Yacht (M/Y) Bob Barker* is not a "warship[] ... or other ship[] ... clearly marked and identifiable as being on government service and authorized to that effect." Therefore, her harassment and pursuit of the *F/V Thunder* did not qualify as "hot pursuit" under Article 111(5) of UNCLOS. Nevertheless, the Sea Shepherd's pursuit was effective, as it prompted the illegal fishing vessel's crew to scuttle (i.e., sink) their own fishing boat, and the Sea Shepherd's crew were able to secure incriminating evidence from the slowly sinking fishing boat. The Sea Shepherd's efforts ultimately resulted in 3-year criminal sentences and $17M in fines for the boat's captain and two senior crew members, and a $10M fine for the illegal fishing boat's Spanish owner. TakePart, *One of the World's Most Notorious Illegal Fishing Crews Is Fined $17 Million* (Taylor Hill, Oct. 13, 2015), http://www.takepart.com/article/2015/10/13/illegal-fishing-vessel-sentenced-sea-shepherd/; Maritime Executive, *Owner of F/V Thunder Hit with Fine in Spain* (Apr. 18, 2018), https://www.maritime-executive.com/article/owner-of-f-v-thunder-hit-with-fine-in-spain. *See also* Foreign Policy, *The Hunt for the Last Chilean Sea Bass Poachers* (Christopher Pala, June 17, 2015), https://foreignpolicy.com/2015/06/17/chilean-sea-bass-toothfish-thunder-sea-shepherd/ (noting that the Sea Shepherd "ships had no internationally recognized authority to board or detain the poachers, but they were prepared to physically prevent the pirates from fishing, to chase them out of the fishing grounds, and to collect evidence of illegal fishing and present it to authorities.").

[797] The Guardian, *Captain deliberately sank illegal fishing vessel, claim Sea Shepherd rescuers* (Oliver Milman, Apr. 7, 2015), https://www.theguardian.com/environment/2015/apr/07/captain-deliberately-sank-illegal-fishing-vessel-claim-sea-shepherd-rescuers; Maclean's, *Thunder gone under: The story of the world's longest maritime chase* (Jonathon Gatehouse & Amanda Shendruk, Apr. 16, 2015), https://www.macleans.ca/news/canada/thunder-gone-under-the-story-of-the-worlds-longest-maritime-chase/; Sea Shepherd, *Another Impossible Mission Made Possible by Sea Shepherd* (Paul Watson Apr. 7, 2015), https://seashepherd.org/2015/04/07/another-impossible-mission-made-possible-by-sea-shepherd/; Foreign Policy, *The Hunt for the Last Chilean Sea Bass Poachers* (full cite above); TakePart, *One of the World's Most Notorious Illegal Fishing Crews* (full cite above); Maritime Executive, *Owner of F/V Thunder Hit with Fine* (full cite above).

[798] Military.com, News, Headlines, *Navy Touts US Merchant Ship's Rescue of Iranians After Others Left Them Adrift* (Gina Harkins, Dec. 28, 2019), https://www.military.com/daily-news/2019/12/28/navy-touts-us-merchant-ships-rescue-iranians-after-others-left-them-adrift.html?ESRC=eb_191230.nl.

[799] United Nations Convention on the Law of the Sea (UNCLOS) art. 97, Dec. 10, 1982, 1833 U.N.T.S. 397, https://www.un.org/Depts/los/convention_agreements/convention_overview_convention.htm; U.S. NAVY, MARINE CORPS & COAST GUARD, THE COMMANDER'S HANDBOOK ON THE LAW OF NAVAL OPERATIONS, NWP 1-14M/MCTP 11-10B/COMDTPUB P5800.7A, ¶ 3.11.2.2.1 (p. 3-11) (2017), www.jag.navy.mil/distrib/instructions/CDRs_HB_on_Law_of_Naval_Operations_AUG17.pdf.

[800] UNCLOS, arts. 92(2) & 110(1)(d) (full cite above); COMMANDER'S HANDBOOK, ¶¶ 3.11.2.3 to 3.11.2.4, 4.4.4.1.4 to 4.4.4.1.5 (full cite above).
[801] COMMANDER'S HANDBOOK, ¶¶ 3.4, 3.6, 4.4.4.1.4 (pp. 3-5, 3-7, 4-7) (full cite above); THE FLETCHER SCHOOL OF LAW AND DIPLOMACY—TUFTS UNIVERSITY, LAW OF THE SEA, A POLICY PRIMER 45-46 (2017), https://sites.tufts.edu/lawofthesea/introduction/.
[802] UNCLOS, arts. 99 & 110(1)(b) (full cite above). Letter Of Transmittal Forwarding The 1982 UN Law Of The Sea Convention To The United States Senate, DOS Commentary pp. 28-29 (William J. Clinton, Oct. 7, 1994) (S. Treaty Doc. 103–39), https://www.foreign.senate.gov/imo/media/doc/treaty_103-39.pdf. Unfortunately, slavery is still a problem, not only in terms of human trafficking (up to 4M people each year), but also as "sea slaves" used (and abused) as free labor on fishing boats. TUFTS, LAW OF THE SEA, p. 46 (full cite above). For example, Thai fishing boats are notorious for using sea slaves, who "are beaten for the smallest transgressions, like stitching a torn net too slowly or mistakenly placing a mackerel into a bucket for herring, according to a United Nations survey of about 50 Cambodian men and boys sold to Thai fishing boats. Of those interviewed in the 2009 survey, 29 said they had witnessed their captain or other officers kill a worker." The New York Times, World, The Outlaw Ocean, 'Sea Slaves': The Human Misery That Feeds Pets and Livestock (Ian Urbina, July 27, 2015), https://www.nytimes.com/2015/07/27/world/outlaw-ocean-thailand-fishing-sea-slaves-pets.html; Human Rights Watch, Hidden Chains, Rights Abuses and Forced Labor in Thailand's Fishing Industry (Jan. 23, 2018), https://www.hrw.org/report/2018/01/23/hidden-chains-rights-abuses-and-forced-labor-thailands-fishing-industry.
[803] UNCLOS, art. 108 (full cite above); COMMANDER'S HANDBOOK, ¶¶ 3.4, 3.8, 3.11.4 to 3.11.4.3, 4.4.4.1.4 (pp. 3-5, 3-7, 3-16 to 3-17, 4-7) (full cite above); TUFTS, LAW OF THE SEA, pp. 43-44 (full cite above). See also United Nations Office on Drugs and Crime (UNODC), United Nations Convention against Illicit Traffic in Narcotic Drugs and Psychotropic Substances, 1988, https://www.unodc.org/unodc/en/treaties/illicit-trafficking.html; United Nations Treaty Collection, Depositary, Status of Treaties, Chapter VI Narcotic Drugs and Psychotropic Substances, 19. United Nations Convention against Illicit Traffic in Narcotic Drugs and Psychotropic Substances, https://treaties.un.org/Pages/ViewDetails.aspx?src=TREATY&mtdsg_no=VI-19&chapter=6&clang=_en. The U.S. has negotiated a number of bilateral ship boarding agreements with other States in order to board their vessels reasonably suspected of engaging in international drug trafficking. "While the general rule of exclusive flag State jurisdiction over vessels on the high seas has long standing in international law, the United States and other members of the international community have developed procedures for resolving problems that have arisen in certain contexts, including drug smuggling, illegal immigration and fishing, when States are unable or unwilling to exercise responsibility over vessels flying their flag. These procedures, several of which are contained in international agreements, typically seek to ensure that the flag State gives expeditious permission to other States for the purpose of boarding, inspection and, where appropriate, taking law enforcement action with respect to its vessels." DOS Commentary, pp. 27, 29-30 (full cite above).
[804] UNCLOS, arts. 109 & 110(1)(c) (full cite above); COMMANDER'S HANDBOOK, ¶¶ 3.4, 3.7, 4.4.4.1.4 (pp. 3-5, 3-7, 4-7) (full cite above).

[805] United Nations Convention on the Law of the Sea (UNCLOS) arts. 94, 97, 109, 110, 216(1)(b), 217, & 228, Dec. 10, 1982, 1833 U.N.T.S. 397, https://www.un.org/Depts/los/convention_agreements/convention_overview_co nvention.htm; YOSHIFUMI TANAKA, THE INT'L. LAW OF THE SEA 190 (3rd ed. 2019).

[806] Global Firepower, Total Naval Strength by Country, https://www.globalfirepower.com/navy-ships.asp; Global Firepower, Panama Military Strength, https://www.globalfirepower.com/country-military-strength-detail.asp?country_id=panama; Global Security, Military, World, Central America, Panama, National Aero-Naval Service, https://www.globalsecurity.org/military/world/centam/pa-navy.htm; Military Factory, Naval Warfare, Patrol Craft Fast (PCF) (Swift Boat) (July 27, 2017), https://www.militaryfactory.com/ships/detail.asp?ship_id=Swift-Boat-PCF.

[807] UNCLOS, arts. 92(2) & 110(1)(d) (full cite above); U.S. NAVY, MARINE CORPS & COAST GUARD, THE COMMANDER'S HANDBOOK ON THE LAW OF NAVAL OPERATIONS, NWP 1-14M/MCTP 11-10B/COMDTPUB P5800.7A, ¶¶ 3.11.2.3 to 3.11.2.4 (pp. 3-13 to 3-14) (2017), www.jag.navy.mil/distrib/instructions/CDRs_HB_on_Law_of_Naval_Operations_AUG17.pdf.

[808] COMMANDER'S HANDBOOK, ¶¶ 3.4 to 3.5.3.3, 4.4.4.1.4 (pp. 3-5 to 3-7, 4-7) (full cite above).

[809] NBC News, News, Military, *Officials: U.S. Navy seizes suspected Iranian missile parts set for Yemen* (Mosheh Gains & Adiel Kaplan, Dec. 4, 2019), https://www.nbcnews.com/news/military/officials-u-s-navy-seizes-suspected-iranian-missile-parts-set-n1096096.

[810] A "dhow" is a traditional, sturdy wooden sailing vessel, often built by hand, that has been used in the Middle East for thousands of years. CNN World, Global Gateway, Middle East, *'World's biggest dhow' to set sail from Dubai* (Gisella Deputato & Sophie Morlin-Yron, Mar. 2, 2017), https://www.cnn.com/2017/03/01/middleeast/dubai-biggest-wooden-dhow/index.html.

[811] Military.com, News, Headlines, *Navy Cruiser Seizes Huge Iranian Arms Cache in Arabian Sea* (Richard Sisk, Feb. 13, 2020), https://www.military.com/daily-news/2020/02/13/navy-cruiser-seizes-huge-iranian-arms-cache-arabian-sea.html.

[812] Letter Of Transmittal Forwarding The 1982 UN Law Of The Sea Convention To The United States Senate, DOS Commentary p. 29 (William J. Clinton, Oct. 7, 1994) (S. Treaty Doc. 103–39), https://www.foreign.senate.gov/imo/media/doc/treaty_103-39.pdf.

[813] A Pyrate's Life—facts, legends and myths, *The Golden Age of Piracy*, http://pirates.hegewisch.net/GoldenAge.html.

[814] James Benoit, *The Evolution of Universal Jurisdiction Over War Crimes*, 53 NAVAL L. REV. 259, 262-63 (2006), https://heinonline.org/HOL/LandingPage?handle=hein.journals/naval53&div=9&id=&page=.

[815] UNCLOS, art. 105 (full cite above).

[816] COMMANDER'S HANDBOOK, ¶¶ 3.4 to 3.5.3.3, 4.4.4.1.4 (pp. 3-5 to 3-7, 4-7) (full cite above).

[817] UNCLOS, art. 101 (full cite above). *See also* THE FLETCHER SCHOOL OF LAW AND DIPLOMACY—TUFTS UNIVERSITY, LAW OF THE SEA, A POLICY PRIMER 44-45 (2017), https://sites.tufts.edu/lawofthesea/introduction/; American Society of Int'l. Law

(ASIL), Resources, eResources - Insights and other E-Publications, Electronic Resource Guide (ERG), *International Piracy*, p. 7 (Douglas Guilfoyle, July 31, 2014), https://www.asil.org/resources/electronic-resource-guide-erg (asserting that UNCLOS "is now generally accepted as stating the applicable customary international law as regards both the definition of piracy and the extent of permissible action by States to repress it").

⁸¹⁸ COMMANDER'S HANDBOOK, ¶¶ 1.5, 1.6, 2.6.1 to 2.6.2 (pp. 1-7, 1-8, 2-9) (full cite above); TUFTS, LAW OF THE SEA, pp. 30-31 (full cite above).

⁸¹⁹ COMMANDER'S HANDBOOK, ¶¶ 1.1, 1.9, 2.7.2 (pp. 1-1, 1-10, 2-13) (full cite above); Raul (Pete) Pedrozo, *Military Activities in the Exclusive Economic Zone: East Asia Focus*, 90 INT'L. L. STUD. 514, 519-521 (2014), https://digital-commons.usnwc.edu/ils/vol90/iss1/15/.

⁸²⁰ Dept. of Defense Law of War Manual § 13.2.3, p. 883 (June 2015, updated Dec. 2016), https://www.hsdl.org/?view&did=797480.

⁸²¹ COMMANDER'S HANDBOOK, ¶ 3.5.2.1 (p. 3-6) (full cite above).

⁸²² Int'l. Scientific Journal "Security & Future", *Maritime Piracy and Armed Robbery Evolution in 2008-2017*, p. 20 (Adelina Tumbarska, July 2018), https://www.researchgate.net/publication/326972932_MARITIME_PIRACY_AND_ARMED_ROBBERY_EVOLUTION_IN_2008-2017. *See also* Market Watch, Economy & Politics, *Forget Somalia — this is the new sea piracy hot spot* (Sara Sjolin, Oct. 7, 2015), https://www.marketwatch.com/story/forget-somalia-this-the-new-sea-piracy-hot-spot-2015-10-07 (describing violent pirate attacks in the Strait of Malacca). *See generally* National Geospatial-Intelligence Agency, Maritime Safety Information, Worldwide Threats to Shipping Reports, https://msi.nga.mil/Piracy.

⁸²³ Int'l. Chamber of Commerce (ICC), Commercial Crime Services, Int'l. Maritime Bureau (IMB), https://icc-ccs.org/icc/imb.

⁸²⁴ Int'l. Chamber of Commerce (ICC), Commercial Crime Services, Maritime Piracy, https://www.icc-ccs.org/.

⁸²⁵ The reader can request a copy of IMB's most current detailed annual "Piracy and Armed Robbery Against Ships" report, which includes data for the past 5 years. Int'l. Chamber of Commerce (ICC), Commercial Crime Services, Int'l. Maritime Bureau (IMB), Request Piracy & Armed Robbery Report, https://icc-ccs.org/piracy-reporting-centre/request-piracy-report.

⁸²⁶ ICC, Maritime Piracy (full cite above).

⁸²⁷ Sea Shepherd, Who We Are, https://seashepherd.org/. *See also* Maclean's, *Thunder gone under: The story of the world's longest maritime chase* (Jonathon Gatehouse & Amanda Shendruk, Apr. 16, 2015), https://www.macleans.ca/news/canada/thunder-gone-under-the-story-of-the-worlds-longest-maritime-chase/ (describing the Sea Shepherd Conservation Society as an "environmental guerrilla group").

⁸²⁸ The Christian Science Monitor, World, Global News, *Whale Wars: The aggressive tactics of Sea Shepherd Paul Watson* (Dan Murphy, 6 Jan. 2010), https://www.csmonitor.com/World/Global-News/2010/0106/Whale-Wars-The-aggressive-tactics-of-Sea-Shepherd-Paul-Watson. *See also* treehugger, Living, Culture, *5 Ways Sea Shepherd's Controversial Methods are Changing the World For Whales* (Blythe Copeland, Feb. 23, 2011), https://www.treehugger.com/culture/5-ways-sea-shepherds-controversial-methods-are-changing-the-world-for-whales.html (noting that while "we aren't entirely on board with the methods used by the Sea Shepherd Conservation Society in their fight against the Japanese whaling fleet," they have been effective).

829 Environmental Law Review, Lewis & Clark Law School, Institute of Cetacean Research v. Sea Shepherd Conservation Society, 725 F.3d 940 (9th Cir. 2013), https://elawreview.org/case-summaries/2013/institute-of-cetacean-research-v-sea-shepherd-conservation-society-725-f-3d-940-9th-cir-2013/.

830 ICR v Sea Shepherd, 725 F.3d 940 (9th Cir. 2013) (Chief Judge Kozinski), https://caselaw.findlaw.com/us-9th-circuit/1632126.html; American Society of Int'l. Law (ASIL), Resources, eResources - Insights and other E-Publications, Electronic Resource Guide (ERG), *International Piracy*, p. 5 (Douglas Guilfoyle, July 31, 2014), https://www.asil.org/resources/electronic-resource-guide-erg.

831 Foreign Policy, *The Hunt for the Last Chilean Sea Bass Poachers* (Christopher Pala, June 17, 2015), https://foreignpolicy.com/2015/06/17/chilean-sea-bass-toothfish-thunder-sea-shepherd/.

832 Takepart, Articles, *Sea Shepherd to Pay Millions to Whale Killers* (David Kirby, June 9, 2015), http://www.takepart.com/article/2015/06/09/sea-shepherd-has-pay-millions-japanese-whalers.

833 The Sea Shepherd takes credit for its 110-day record-setting "hot pursuit" of the *Fishing Vessel (F/V) Thunder* (which was one of the "Bandit Six" IUU fishing vessels taking Patagonian Toothfish) as "galvanizing government action against the other five bandits .... Within two years of the F/V Thunder chase, all of the 'Bandit Six' had been brought to justice." Zed, Books, *An interview with Captain Peter Hammarstedt of Catching Thunder* (Apr. 13, 2018), https://www.zedbooks.net/media/show/interview-captain-peter-hammarstedt-catching-thunder/. Chapter 8 discussed the poaching of Patagonian and Antarctic Toothfish.

834 Real Faces of Animal Rights, Spotlight on the Activists of Animal Rights, *Top wildlife conservation group Sea Shepherd admits defeat in whaling battle* (Sep. 11, 2017), https://realfacesofanimalrights.com/animal-rights-activism/sea-shepherd-admits-defeat-in-whaling-battle/.

835 States which are party to both the 1958 law of the sea conventions and the 1982 UNCLOS are bound by the latter. United Nations Convention on the Law of the Sea (UNCLOS) art. 311, Dec. 10, 1982, 1833 U.N.T.S. 397, https://www.un.org/Depts/los/convention_agreements/convention_overview_convention.htm.

836 United Nations, Charter of the United Nations, art. 103, https://www.un.org/en/charter-united-nations/.

837 UN Charter, art. 2(4) (full cite above); U.S. Navy, Marine Corps & Coast Guard, The Commander's Handbook on the Law of Naval Operations, NWP 1-14M/MCTP 11-10B/COMDTPUB P5800.7A, ¶ 4.2 (p. 4-1) (2017), www.jag.navy.mil/distrib/instructions/CDRs_HB_on_Law_of_Naval_Operations_AUG17.pdf. *See also*, United Nations, Codification Division Publications, Repertory of Practice of United Nations Organs, Charter of the United Nations, Chapter VII, Article 2, https://legal.un.org/repertory/art2.shtml. *See also* Dept. of Defense Law of War Manual § 1.11.3, pp. 43-44 (June 2015, updated Dec. 2016), https://www.hsdl.org/?view&did=797480.

838 UN Charter, art. 2(3) (full cite above); Commander's Handbook, ¶ 4.2 (p. 4-1) (full cite above)

839 UN Charter, art. 24(1) (full cite above); Commander's Handbook, ¶ 4.2 (p. 4-1) (full cite above).

[840] UN Charter, arts. 39-51 (full cite above); COMMANDER'S HANDBOOK, ¶ 4.2 (p. 4-1) (full cite above). *See also* DoD Law of War Manual, § 1.11.2, pp. 42-43 (full cite above).

[841] UN Charter, art. 39 (full cite above); COMMANDER'S HANDBOOK, ¶ 4.2 (p. 4-1) (full cite above). *See also*, UN, Repertory of Practice, Article 39, https://legal.un.org/repertory/art39.shtml.

[842] UN Charter, art. 41 (full cite above); COMMANDER'S HANDBOOK, ¶¶ 4.2 to 4.3.3 (p. 4-2 to 4-3) (full cite above). *See also*, UN, Repertory of Practice, Article 41, https://legal.un.org/repertory/art41.shtml.

[843] UN Charter, art. 42 (full cite above); COMMANDER'S HANDBOOK, ¶¶ 4.2, 4.4 (p. 4-2, 4-3) (full cite above). *See also*, UN, Repertory of Practice, Article 42, https://legal.un.org/repertory/art42.shtml. A State may also use military force in self-defense against an "armed attack" under Article 51 of the UN Charter.

[844] Encyclopædia Britannica, Allied Powers, Int'l. Alliance, https://www.britannica.com/topic/Allied-Powers-international-alliance#ref754272.

[845] United Nations Security Council, Members, Current Members, https://www.un.org/securitycouncil/content/current-members; UN Charter, art. 23 (full cite above).

[846] UN Charter, art. 27 (full cite above). *See also*, UN, Repertory of Practice, Article 27, https://legal.un.org/repertory/art27.shtml.

[847] United Nations Security Council Resolution (UNSCR) 1718, Non-proliferation/Democratic People's Republic of Korea (Oct. 14, 2006), http://unscr.com/en/resolutions/1718.

[848] NKHumanitarian, UN Sanctions, *Definitions of "Luxury Goods"* (Apr. 28, 2019), https://nkhumanitarian.wordpress.com/un-sanctions-definition-of-luxury-goods/.

[849] New York Post, News, *Dutch officials seize 90K bottles of vodka headed for North Korea* (Yaron Steinbuch, Feb. 26, 2019), https://nypost.com/2019/02/26/dutch-officials-seize-90k-bottles-of-vodka-headed-for-north-korea/; The Telegraph, News, *Rotterdam seizes 90,000 bottles of Russian vodka believed to be intended for Kim Jong-un* (Alec Luhn & Simon Taylor, Feb. 26, 2019), https://www.telegraph.co.uk/news/2019/02/26/rotterdam-seizes-90000-bottles-russian-vodka-believed-intended/.

[850] United Nations Security Council Resolution (UNSCR) 1244, The situation relating Kosovo (June 10, 1999), http://unscr.com/en/resolutions/1244.

[851] ASIL, *International Piracy*, p. 3 (full cite above).

[852] One novel suggestion is to commission privateers to combat Somali pirates. *See generally* Todd Emerson Hutchins, *Structuring a Sustainable Letters of Marque Regime: How Commissioning Privateers can Defeat the Somali Pirates*, 99 CALIFORNIA L. REV. 819 (2011), https://scholarship.law.berkeley.edu/californialawreview/vol99/iss3/2/ (exploring the historical development of letters of marque and reprisal, and arguing that the U.S. could incentivize privateers to help dismantle pirate networks).

[853] The Christian Science Monitor, World, Africa, *Should ground troops hunt pirates in Somalia?* (Shashank Bengali, Dec. 17, 2008), https://www.csmonitor.com/World/Africa/2008/1217/p25s04-woaf.html.

[854] Int'l. Scientific Journal "Security & Future", *Maritime Piracy and Armed Robbery Evolution in 2008-2017*, p. 20 (Adelina Tumbarska, July 2018), https://www.researchgate.net/publication/326972932_MARITIME_PIRACY_AND

_ARMED_ROBBERY_EVOLUTION_IN_2008-2017, (quoting WorldAtlas, Modern Day Pirate Attacks by Country (Jan. 2018), https://www.worldatlas.com/articles/modern-day-pirates-countries-with-the-most-maritime-piracy-today.html).

[855] American Society of Int'l. Law (ASIL), Resources, eResources - Insights and other E-Publications, Electronic Resource Guide (ERG), *International Piracy*, p. 4 (Douglas Guilfoyle, July 31, 2014), https://www.asil.org/resources/electronic-resource-guide-erg.

[856] The pirates received prison sentences ranging from 33 years to life imprisonment. The Virginian-Pilot, U.S. Military News, *2 Somali pirates receive life sentences for attacking USS Ashland; third gets 33 years* (Brock Vergakis, Nov. 7, 2016), https://www.pilotonline.com/military/article_0482a38e-d4e1-55b9-8390-ac08ff53a364.html; The Maritime Executive, Intellectual Capital for Leaders, Article, *Pirates Get Life for Attacking USS Ashland* (Nov. 8, 2016), https://www.maritime-executive.com/article/pirates-get-life-for-attacking-uss-ashland.

[857] United Nations on NBCNews.com, *U.N.: Piracy threatens food aid to Somalia* (Apr. 15, 2009), http://www.nbcnews.com/id/30231035/ns/world_news-united_nations/t/un-piracy-threatens-food-aid-somalia/. *See also* The Christian Science Monitor, World, Africa, 2008, *Getting food ships past Somalian pirates* (Rob Crilly, Sep. 26, 2008), https://www.csmonitor.com/World/Africa/2008/0926/p01s01-woaf.html (noting that "[a]lmost two decades after the 1991 collapse of Somalia's last functioning government, the lawlessness and fighting among Somali warlords has now spread to the waters off the coast. Criminal gangs, armed with AK-47s and rocket-propelled grenades, now patrol the sea. By some estimates, there are nearly 1,000 pirates plundering ships in the area.").

[858] UN News, *NATO navy escorts protect UN-shipped food aid to Somalia against pirates* (Nov. 11, 2008), https://news.un.org/en/story/2008/11/281242-nato-navy-escorts-protect-un-shipped-food-aid-somalia-against-pirates.

[859] NBCNews.com, *U.N.: Piracy threatens food aid to Somalia* (full cite above).

[860] The Guardian, Business, Economics, Int'l. Trade, *In the Gulf of Aden, a pirate ransom becomes the cost of doing business* (Simon Goodley, Nov. 19, 2010), https://www.theguardian.com/business/2010/nov/19/pirate-ransom-cost-of-doing-business.

[861] Christian Science Monitor, *Getting food ships past Somalian pirates* (full cite above) (noting that insurance rates have gone up ten-fold). The International Maritime Bureau estimates that half of pirate attacks go unreported, either because of concerns of rising insurance rates, or that individual vessels will be delayed in port pending investigations. The Economist, Int'l., *The Gulf of Guinea is now the world's worst piracy hotspot* (June 29, 2019), https://www.economist.com/international/2019/06/29/the-gulf-of-guinea-is-now-the-worlds-worst-piracy-hotspot; THE FLETCHER SCHOOL OF LAW AND DIPLOMACY—TUFTS UNIVERSITY, LAW OF THE SEA, A POLICY PRIMER 45 (2017), https://sites.tufts.edu/lawofthesea/introduction/; WAYNE K. TALLEY, MARITIME SAFETY, SECURITY AND PIRACY 97 (2008); World Economic Forum, Agenda, 2019, *West Africa is becoming the world's piracy capital. Here's how to tackle the problem* (June 28, 2019), https://www.weforum.org/agenda/2019/06/west-africa-is-becoming-the-world-s-piracy-capital-here-s-how-to-tackle-the-problem/.

862 National Public Radio (NPR), American University Radio, Planet Money, *Behind The Business Plan Of Pirates Inc.* (Chana Joffe-Wolt, Apr. 30, 2009), https://www.npr.org/templates/story/story.php?storyId=103657301.

863 The IMO published "BMP5: Best Management Practices to Deter Piracy and Enhance Maritime Security in the Red Sea, Gulf of Aden, Indian Ocean and Arabian Sea" (cover graphic at the beginning of the Chapter), which lists a number of "Ship Protection Measures" (SPM), including:

- Implementing a 3-layered defense, including:
  o remaining vigilant at keeping a good look out to detect pirates, including binoculars, thermal imagery optics, night vision aids, and radar;
  o installing physical barriers (e.g., double roll of razor wire) and fixed search lights around the outside of the ship, and "dummy" crewmembers ("to give the impression of greater numbers of crew on watch") to deter boarding;
  o maneuvering the vessel, increasing the ship's speed, and raising the freeboard to make it more difficult to board;
  o considering hiring a Private Maritime Security Company (PMSC) or Privately Contracted Armed Security Personnel (PCASP);
  o hardening the doors to the ship's bridge and internal compartments, adding a gate or grate in front of the doors as another barrier, and installing either a motion sensor and/or Closed Circuit Television (CCTV) as a secondary layer of defense;
  o creating a "citadel" (which "is designed and constructed to resist forced entry") within the ship as the last layer of defense, with additional hardened doors, reliable communications, and control of propulsion and steering.
- Using avoidance maneuvers to create "hydrostatic pressure" between the vessel and the pirate's boat.
- Using "[t]he ship's alarms [to] inform the ship's crew that an attack is underway and warn the attacker that the ship is aware and is reacting. In addition, continuous sounding of the ship's whistle may distract the attackers."
- Using remotely operated, fixed "water spray and/or foam monitors ... [to] deter[] or delay[] any attempt to illegally board a ship. The use of water can make it difficult for an unauthorised boat to remain alongside and makes it significantly more difficult to climb aboard."
- Installing sandbags on the "bridge wings" to protect external watchstanders.
- "[C]ontrol[ling] access routes to the accommodation and machinery spaces to deter or delay entry."
- Being able to secure doors and hatches from the inside.
- Securing tools and equipment on the upper deck, to prevent their use by pirates.

Int'l. Maritime Organization (IMO), English, Our Work, Maritime Security and Piracy, Piracy, Piracy and armed robbery against ships, Best Management Practices (BMP5), pp. 11-20, http://www.imo.org/en/OurWork/Security/PiracyArmedRobbery/Documents/BMP5%20small.pdf. *See also* Int'l. Maritime Organization (IMO), English, Our Work,

Maritime Security and Piracy, Piracy, Private Armed Security, http://www.imo.org/en/OurWork/Security/PiracyArmedRobbery/Pages/Private-Armed-Security.aspx (admitting that the IMO's position on Private Armed Security has "evolved"); BIMCO, Contracts and clauses, Contracts, GUARDCON, https://www.bimco.org/contracts-and-clauses/bimco-contracts ("GUARDCON is an agreement for the hire of the services of private maritime security guards on ships – either armed or unarmed."); Human Rights at Sea, Rules for the Use of Force (RUF), The 100 Series Rules for the Use of Force, https://www.humanrightsatsea.org/rules-for-the-use-of-force-ruf/; American Society of Int'l. Law (ASIL), Resources, eResources - Insights and other E-Publications, Electronic Resource Guide (ERG), *International Piracy*, p. 5 (Douglas Guilfoyle, July 31, 2014), https://www.asil.org/resources/electronic-resource-guide-erg; Jasenko Marin, Mišo Mudrić & Robert Mikac, *Private Maritime Security Contractors and Use of Lethal Force in Maritime Domain*, in THE FUTURE OF THE LAW OF THE SEA 191, 191-212 (Gemma Andreone ed., 2017), https://link.springer.com/book/10.1007/978-3-319-51274-7 (discussing the issues associated with hiring private maritime security contractors, such as regulating their use of force, excessive self-defense, setting standards and guidelines, and ensuring the reasonability and proportionality of force).

[864] Marin, Mudrić & Mikac, *Private Maritime Security Contractors* (full cite above) (noting that "up to that point, it was in principle prohibited for private actors to carry arms—the notable exception (recognized by the relevant international maritime law and law of the sea conventions and relevant domestic law maritime codes and acts) allows the Masters of Vessels and First Officers to make use of personal firearms that have to be kept under lock and key at all times.").

[865] Maritime Accident Casebook, *Maersk: We Don't Need Security* (Apr. 11, 2009), http://maritimeaccident.org/tags/maersk-alabama-freeboard/.

[866] The Guardian, World, Africa, *Somali pirates pick on the wrong ship* (Matthew Weaver, Apr. 9, 2009), https://www.theguardian.com/world/2009/apr/09/somali-pirates-maersk-alabama-shane-murphy.

[867] World Economic Forum, Agenda, 2019, *West Africa is becoming the world's piracy capital. Here's how to tackle the problem* (June 28, 2019), https://www.weforum.org/agenda/2019/06/west-africa-is-becoming-the-world-s-piracy-capital-here-s-how-to-tackle-the-problem/.

[868] United Nations on NBCNews.com, *U.N.: Piracy threatens food aid to Somalia* (Apr. 15, 2009), http://www.nbcnews.com/id/30231035/ns/world_news-united_nations/t/un-piracy-threatens-food-aid-somalia/.

[869] National Public Radio (NPR), American University Radio, Author Interviews, *Surviving A Somali Pirate Attack On The High Seas* (Dave Davies interviewing Captain Richard Phillips, Apr. 6, 2010), https://www.npr.org/transcripts/125507354.

[870] United Nations Security Council Resolution (UNSCR) 1814, The situation in Somalia (May 15, 2008), http://unscr.com/en/resolutions/1814.

[871] American Society of Int'l. Law (ASIL), Resources, eResources - Insights and other E-Publications, Electronic Resource Guide (ERG), *International Piracy*, p. 4 (Douglas Guilfoyle, July 31, 2014), https://www.asil.org/resources/electronic-resource-guide-erg.

[872] Int'l. Maritime Organization (IMO), English, Our Work, Maritime Security and Piracy, Piracy, Piracy and armed robbery against ships, http://www.imo.org/en/OurWork/Security/PiracyArmedRobbery/Pages/Default.aspx.

873 As Chapter 11 discusses, Somalia claims a 200 nm Territorial Sea, and purports to require "Foreign warships [to] obtain permission prior to transiting" through its Territorial Sea. Dept. of Defense Maritime Claims Reference Manual (MCRM)—Somalia 2020, http://www.jag.navy.mil/organization/code_10_mcrm.htm. Thus, the UNSCRs permitting foreign States to combat piracy in international waters and armed robbery at sea in Somalia's Territorial Seas were particularly necessary, due to Somalia's excessive Territorial Sea claims.

874 UNSCR 1816 ¶ 7, The situation in Somalia (June 2, 2008), http://unscr.com/en/resolutions/1816.

875 UNSCR 1816, ¶ 8 (full cite above); United Nations Convention on the Law of the Sea (UNCLOS) arts. 24-26, Dec. 10, 1982, 1833 U.N.T.S. 397, https://www.un.org/Depts/los/convention_agreements/convention_overview_convention.htm.

876 "Adding a gloss" to a text (such as the U.S. Constitution, or an international treaty) means adding an interpretation of the text, in order to avoid conflicts with related language, to put the text in context, and/or to add one's own perspective to the text.

877 Express, News, World, US leads push to hunt down pirates (Dec. 11, 2008), https://www.express.co.uk/news/world/75208/US-leads-push-to-hunt-down-pirates.

878 UNSCR 1838 ¶¶ 2-3, The situation in Somalia (Oct. 7, 2008), http://unscr.com/en/resolutions/1838.

879 UNSCR 1846 ¶ 10, The situation in Somalia (Dec. 2, 2008), http://unscr.com/en/resolutions/1846 (merely adding "and regional organizations" after States in the first paragraph, and "into" territorial waters in sub-paragraph (a)).

880 UNSCR 1851 ¶ 6, The situation in Somalia (Dec. 16, 2008), http://unscr.com/en/resolutions/1851.

881 ASIL, International Piracy, p. 4 (full cite above); Marin, Mudrić & Mikac, Private Maritime Security Contractors (full cite above) (stating that "overt in-land combat activities as conducted by the Joint Special Operations Command ... have by far most contributed to the elimination of the pirate outposts in the region"); The New York Times, World, Africa, Toughening Its Stand, European Union Sends Forces to Strike Somali Pirate Base (Jeffrey Gettleman, May 15, 2012), https://www.nytimes.com/2012/05/16/world/africa/european-forces-strike-pirate-base-in-somalia.html?auth=login-email&login=email (reporting that "[t]he European Union, which had vowed to take a tougher stand against the scourge of Somali piracy, took the fight to the pirates' home base for the first time on Tuesday, destroying several of their signature fiberglass skiffs as they lay on the beach in a notorious pirate den. The Europeans struck via combat helicopter, with forces never actually landing in Somalia"); Naval History and Heritage Command, Piracy Off the Horn of Africa: Congressional Research Service Report for Congress 35 (Lauren Ploch, Christopher M. Blanchard, Ronald O'Rourke, R. Chuck Mason & Rawle O. King, Sep. 28, 2009), https://www.history.navy.mil/content/history/nhhc/research/library/online-reading-room/title-list-alphabetically/p/piracy-off-horn-africa-crs.html ("Ultimately, piracy is a problem that starts ashore and requires an international solution ashore. We made this clear at the offset of our efforts. We cannot guarantee safety in this vast region." Vice Admiral William Gortney, Commander, U.S. Naval

Forces Central Command, Testimony before the House Armed Services Committee, Mar. 5, 2009).

[882] "In one of the Bush administration's last major foreign policy initiatives, the US circulated a draft United Nations resolution seeking international authorisation to hunt down Somali pirates on land. … The US-drafted UN Security Council resolution is to be presented at a session on Somalia … with secretary of state Condoleezza Rice. It proposes that for a year nations 'may take all necessary measures ashore in Somalia, including in its airspace, to interdict those who are using Somali territory to plan, facilitate or undertake acts of piracy and armed robbery at sea and to otherwise prevent those activities.'" Express, News, World, *US leads push to hunt down pirates* (Dec. 11, 2008), https://www.express.co.uk/news/world/75208/US-leads-push-to-hunt-down-pirates.

[883] U.S. Dept. of State, Archive, Situation in Somalia, Secretary Condoleezza Rice, Remarks Following the UN Security Council Meeting on the Situation in Somalia (Dec. 16, 2008), https://2001-2009.state.gov/secretary/rm/2008/12/113272.htm; U.S. Dept. of State, Archive, Combating the Scourge of Piracy, Secretary Condoleezza Rice (Dec. 16, 2008), https://2001-2009.state.gov/secretary/rm/2008/12/113269.htm; United Nations, Meetings Coverage and Press Releases, Press Release, Security Council, Security Council Authorizes States to Use Land-Based Operations in Somalia, as Part of Fight Against Piracy Off Coast, Unanimously Adopting 1851 (2008) (SC/9541, Dec. 16, 2008), https://www.un.org/press/en/2008/sc9541.doc.htm.

[884] Executive Order 13536: Blocking Property of Certain Persons Contributing to the Conflict in Somalia (Pres. Barack Obama, Apr. 12, 2010), 75 Fed. Reg. 19,869, https://www.archives.gov/federal-register/executive-orders/2010.html.

[885] United Nations Security Council Resolution (UNSCR) 1897 ¶ 7, The situation in Somalia (Nov. 30, 2009), http://unscr.com/en/resolutions/1897; UNSCR 1950 ¶ 7, The situation in Somalia (Nov. 23, 2010), http://unscr.com/en/resolutions/1950; UNSCR 2020 ¶ 9, The situation in Somalia (Nov. 22, 2011), http://unscr.com/en/resolutions/2020; UNSCR 2077 ¶ 12, The Situation in Somalia (Nov. 21, 2012), http://unscr.com/en/resolutions/2077; UNSCR 2125 ¶ 12, Somalia (Nov. 18, 2013), http://unscr.com/en/resolutions/2125; UNSCR 2184 ¶ 13, Somalia (Nov. 12, 2014), http://unscr.com/en/resolutions/2184; UNSCR 2246 ¶ 14, Somalia (Nov. 10, 2015), http://unscr.com/en/resolutions/2246; UNSCR 2316 ¶ 14, The situation in Somalia (Nov. 9, 2016), http://unscr.com/en/resolutions/2316; UNSCR 2383 ¶ 14, The situation in Somalia (Nov. 7, 2017), http://unscr.com/en/resolutions/2383; UNSCR 2442 ¶ 14, The situation in Somalia (Nov. 6, 2018), http://unscr.com/en/resolutions/2442; UNSCR 2500 ¶ 14, The situation in Somalia (Dec. 4, 2019), http://unscr.com/en/resolutions/2500; UNSCR 2554 ¶ 14, The situation in Somalia (Dec. 4, 2020), https://undocs.org/S/RES/2554(2020). *See also* United Nations, Division for Ocean Affairs and the Law of the Sea, United Nations Documents on Piracy, *Report of the Special Adviser to the Secretary-General on Legal Issues Related to Piracy off the Coast of Somalia*, S/2011/30 (Jack Lang, Jan. 20., 2011), https://www.un.org/depts/los/piracy/piracy_documents.htm.

[886] The Economist, Int'l., *The Gulf of Guinea is now the world's worst piracy hotspot* (June 29, 2019), https://www.economist.com/international/2019/06/29/the-gulf-of-guinea-is-now-the-worlds-worst-piracy-hotspot.

887 American Society of Int'l. Law (ASIL), Resources, eResources - Insights and other E-Publications, Electronic Resource Guide (ERG), *International Piracy*, p. 4 (Douglas Guilfoyle, July 31, 2014), https://www.asil.org/resources/electronic-resource-guide-erg. *But see* The Economist, *The Gulf of Guinea* (full cite above) (noting that "In Somalia pirates still scour the oceans, looking for unprotected ships, so the frigates and private guards will be needed as long as chaos reigns on land.").

888 The last hostages held by Somali pirates weren't released until August 2020, "mark[ing] the end of an era of Somali piracy." Private Iranian donors funded the $180,000 ransom paid to release the "three Iranian crewmen from the Siraj fishing boat ... [who] had been in captivity since March 2015 when their vessel was hijacked off the Somali coast. ... At the peak of the piracy outbreak in January 2011, Somali pirates held 736 hostages and 32 boats. Between 2010 and 2019, more than 2,300 crew [members] were taken." National News, World, Europe, *Last hostages held by Somali pirates released after five and a half years* (Nicky Harley, Aug. 31, 2020), https://www.thenationalnews.com/world/europe/last-hostages-held-by-somali-pirates-released-after-five-and-a-half-years-1.1070903.

889 However, "the littoral countries [i.e., Coastal States of Southeast Asia] are all richer and far better-run. Historically, piracy had thrived because of their reluctance to work together. Joint patrols first started in 2004; after the surge in 2014 Malaysia and Indonesia sent a joint rapid-response team to the Malacca Strait. The two countries also agreed to joint patrols with the Philippines in the Sulu Sea, where Philippine separatist groups had made a foray into piracy. In 2015 Indonesia caught a ringleader with Malaysian help. Two years later it detained 15 other pirates following a tip-off from Singapore. Calm returned [to Southeast Asia]." The Economist, *The Gulf of Guinea* (full cite above).

890 Int'l. Chamber of Commerce (ICC), Commercial Crime Services, Int'l. Maritime Bureau (IMB), Piracy and Armed Robbery Against Ships, 2004, 2008, 2012, 2015, 2019 & 2020 Reports. The reader can request a copy of IMB's most current detailed annual "Piracy and Armed Robbery Against Ships" report, which includes data for the past 5 years. Int'l. Chamber of Commerce (ICC), Commercial Crime Services, Int'l. Maritime Bureau (IMB), Request Piracy & Armed Robbery Report, https://icc-ccs.org/piracy-reporting-centre/request-piracy-report.

891 "The pirates have struck across the region, but are primarily a Nigerian problem. They mostly operate out of the labyrinthine waterways in the Niger delta, near which most of west Africa's attacks occur." The Economist, *The Gulf of Guinea* (full cite above).

892 The Economist, *The Gulf of Guinea* (full cite above). *See also* World Economic Forum, Agenda, 2019, *West Africa is becoming the world's piracy capital. Here's how to tackle the problem* (June 28, 2019), https://www.weforum.org/agenda/2019/06/west-africa-is-becoming-the-world-s-piracy-capital-here-s-how-to-tackle-the-problem/ (noting that "[q]uite paradoxically, the discovery of large amounts of offshore hydrocarbons has generated poverty rather than wealth. It has exacerbated social tensions and increased environmental pollution. Only the central government, oil companies, and local elites have benefitted from oil production. Those excluded from the benefits have turned to organised crime in the form of 'petro piracy.' This form of piracy is aimed at stealing crude-oil from tankers and pipelines so as to process the gains in illegally set up refineries. ... In Nigeria in particular, weak law enforcement capacity, corruptible officials, and a largely unregulated oil market makes it easy for criminal

organisations to move stolen and refined products back onto legitimate markets. Corruption and fraud are rampant in [the] Nigerian oil sector and the lines between legal and illegal supplies can sometimes be blurry.").

[893] World Economic Forum, Agenda, 2019, *West Africa is becoming the world's piracy capital. Here's how to tackle the problem* (June 28, 2019), https://www.weforum.org/agenda/2019/06/west-africa-is-becoming-the-world-s-piracy-capital-here-s-how-to-tackle-the-problem/ (noting that "[m]ost often, ships are hijacked for amassing monetary gains. Due to lack of jobs, when people see there is nothing on the ground for them to benefit from, they go to any length and use any means to disturb the economic activities that bring money into the nation.").

[894] The Guardian, Features, *Is it fair to call Nigeria a failed state?* (Yemisi Adegoke, Apr. 11, 2018), https://guardian.ng/features/is-it-fair-to-call-nigeria-a-failed-state/; Vanguard, *Why 'NIGERIA' is now qualified as a failed state* (Ben Nwabueze, Feb. 3, 2018), https://www.vanguardngr.com/2018/02/nigeria-now-qualified-failed-state/; U.S. Dept. of State, Bureau of Consular Affairs, Int'l. Travel, Country Information, Nigeria Int'l. Travel Information, Travel Advisory, Nigeria – Level 3: Reconsider Travel (Oct. 29, 2019), https://travel.state.gov/content/travel/en/international-travel/International-Travel-Country-Information-Pages/Nigeria.html. *But see* The Economist, Int'l., *The Gulf of Guinea is now the world's worst piracy hotspot* (June 29, 2019), https://www.economist.com/international/2019/06/29/the-gulf-of-guinea-is-now-the-worlds-worst-piracy-hotspot (noting that "Nigeria, a democracy whose government—for all its flaws—is far less impotent than Somalia's"). "Nigeria boasts Africa's largest economy and is the most populous country on the continent. It also has strong ties to the US: The two countries have been allies in fighting terrorism and cyber crime in Nigeria, and the US has been Nigeria's main trading partner for 60 years." Good Morning From CNN (Feb. 3, 2020), https://www.cnn.com/2020/02/03/us/five-things-february-3-trnd/index.html.

[895] The Economist, *The Gulf of Guinea* (full cite above).

[896] IMB, Piracy and Armed Robbery Against Ships, 2004, 2008, 2012, 2015, 2019 & 2020 Reports (full cite above). *See also* The Economist, *The Gulf of Guinea* (full cite above); THE FLETCHER SCHOOL OF LAW AND DIPLOMACY—TUFTS UNIVERSITY, LAW OF THE SEA, A POLICY PRIMER 45 (2017), https://sites.tufts.edu/lawofthesea/introduction/.

[897] gCaptain, *VLCC Attack Underscores Piracy Problem Off Nigeria* (Olivia Konotey-Ahulu, Dec. 5, 2019), https://gcaptain.com/vlcc-attack-off-nigeria-underscores-piracy-issue-in-region/; Lloyd's List, Maritime intelligence | Informa, Nigeria, Piracy and Security, *Piracy problem is a threat to Nigeria's maritime economy* (Linton Nightingale, Sep. 11, 2019), https://lloydslist.maritimeintelligence.informa.com/LL1129132/Piracy-problem-is-a-threat-to-Nigerias-maritime-economy.

[898] "Nigeria has yet to make piracy a specific criminal offence. Pirates captured by the navy are often quietly released. Around 300 people have been prosecuted in Somalia for piracy. By contrast, the UN Office on Drugs and Crime (UNODC) says it does not know of a single prosecution in Nigeria." The Economist, *The Gulf of Guinea* (full cite above).

[899] American Society of Int'l. Law (ASIL), Resources, eResources - Insights and other E-Publications, Electronic Resource Guide (ERG), *International Piracy*, p. 5 (Douglas Guilfoyle, July 31, 2014), https://www.asil.org/resources/electronic-resource-guide-erg.

900 United Nations Security Council Resolution (UNSCR) 2018, Peace and security in Africa (Oct. 31, 2011), http://unscr.com/en/resolutions/2018. One difference between Nigeria and Somalia is that the former State has "rolled back" its excessive Territorial Sea claim from 30 nm to 12 nm, consistent with UNCLOS, whereas the latter State claims a 200 nm Territorial Sea, which is excessive. Dept. of Defense Maritime Claims Reference Manual (MCRM)—Nigeria 2016 & Somalia 2020, http://www.jag.navy.mil/organization/code_10_mcrm.htm. Thus, perhaps an UNSCR is less necessary to combat piracy and armed robbery at sea in Nigerian waters than it is in Somali waters.

901 UNSCR 2039, Peace consolidation in West Africa (Feb. 29, 2012), http://unscr.com/en/resolutions/2039.

902 All Africa, Stories, *Cameroon: Gulf of Guinea! - Security Code of Conduct Evaluated* (Elizabeth Mosima, Aug. 17, 2017), https://allafrica.com/stories/201708180197.html.

903 United Nations, Meetings Coverage and Press Releases, Meetings Coverage, Security Council, Security Council, in Statement, Welcomes Adoption of Code of Conduct by Regional Leaders to Prevent Piracy in Gulf of Guinea (Aug. 13, 2013), https://www.un.org/press/en/2013/sc11091.doc.htm.

904 Yaounde Code of Conduct Concerning the Repression of Piracy, Armed Robbery Against Ships, and Illicit Maritime Activity in West and Central Africa art. 2 (June 25, 2013), www.imo.org/en/OurWork/Security/WestAfrica/Documents/code_of_conduct%20signed%20from%20ECOWAS%20site.pdf.

905 Yaounde Code of Conduct, arts. 6-7 (full cite above). *See also* Int'l. Maritime Organization (IMO), English, Our Work, Maritime Security and Piracy, West and Central Africa, Regional Agreements and Information Sharing, http://www.imo.org/en/OurWork/Security/WestAfrica/Pages/Code-of-Conduct-against-illicit-maritime-activity.aspx; Djibouti Code of Conduct Concerning the Repression of Piracy and Armed Robbery Against Ships in the Western Indian Ocean and the Gulf of Aden Arts. 4-5 (Jan. 29, 2009), www.imo.org/en/OurWork/Security/PIU/Documents/DCoC%20English.pdf.

906 Insurance Journal, News, *The Mounting Cost of Piracy off Coast of West Africa: Opinion* (Tobin Harshaw, July 3, 2019), https://www.insurancejournal.com/news/international/2019/07/03/531288.htm; World Economic Forum, *West Africa is becoming the world's piracy capital* (full cite above).

907 The Economist, *The Gulf of Guinea* (full cite above). However, when a U.S.-led naval exercise encountered a pirated oil tanker, "Navies from the United States, Ghana, Togo and Nigeria tracked the hijacked tanker through waters off five countries before Nigerian naval forces stormed aboard Saturday Feb. 20, 2016 amid a shootout that killed one of the pirates." Insurance Journal, *The Mounting Cost of Piracy* (full cite above).

908 The Economist, *The Gulf of Guinea* (full cite above) (noting that "Nigeria, a democracy whose government—for all its flaws—is far less impotent than Somalia's, is bound to resent foreign navies or mercenaries off its coast.").

909 Although Nigeria may be "open to the idea." Lloyd's List, *Nigeria, Piracy and Security* (full cite above) (quoting the "director-general of the Nigeria Maritime Administration and Safety Agency" as saying "that Nigeria was open to the idea of a naval coalition in the Gulf of Guinea. 'We are welcome to all options to tackling piracy in the Gulf of Guinea, as it is a matter that deserves priority and attention, and so any sort of partnership will not be ignored.'").

[910] Int'l. Chamber of Commerce (ICC), Commercial Crime Services, Int'l. Maritime Bureau (IMB), Piracy and Armed Robbery Against Ships, 2004, 2008, 2012, 2015, 2019 & 2020 Reports. The reader can request a copy of IMB's most current detailed annual "Piracy and Armed Robbery Against Ships" report, which includes data for the past 5 years. Int'l. Chamber of Commerce (ICC), Commercial Crime Services, Int'l. Maritime Bureau (IMB), Request Piracy & Armed Robbery Report, https://icc-ccs.org/piracy-reporting-centre/request-piracy-report.

[911] Insurance Journal, News, *The Mounting Cost of Piracy off Coast of West Africa: Opinion* (Tobin Harshaw, July 3, 2019), https://www.insurancejournal.com/news/international/2019/07/03/531288.htm (noting that "the economic cost of seaborne crime off West Africa – including such things as lost goods, contracted security, insurance and 'captivity pay' to crew members held hostage – totaled $818 million in 2017).

[912] The Economist, Int'l., *The Gulf of Guinea is now the world's worst piracy hotspot* (June 29, 2019), https://www.economist.com/international/2019/06/29/the-gulf-of-guinea-is-now-the-worlds-worst-piracy-hotspot.

[913] Dept. of Defense Maritime Claims Reference Manual (MCRM)—Somalia 2020, http://www.jag.navy.mil/organization/code_10_mcrm.htm.

[914] The Economist, *The Gulf of Guinea* (full cite above).

CHAPTER 10: MILITARY USES OF THE SEA & NAVAL WARFARE

"When word of crisis breaks out in Washington, it's no accident the first question that comes to everyone's lips is: where is the nearest [aircraft] carrier?"
—*President Bill Clinton*

D UE TO THE VASTNESS OF THE SEAS AND THEIR STRATEGIC IMPORTANCE, from at least as far back as the Peloponnesian War between Athens and Sparta in 431-404 BC, Coastal States have recognized the need to have a powerful Navy in order to ensure their maritime security.[915] This book will use the term "maritime security" to refer to a State's use of military power to defend the State's interests, including its national territory and possessions, economic interests (including commercial shipping, energy and natural resources), freedom of navigation of its vessels, its nationals (i.e., a State's residents and citizens, including those living abroad), and potentially to defend similar interests of the State's allies.[916] A related concept is

"Maritime Domain Awareness" (MDA), which is "defined by the United States as the effective understanding of anything associated with the maritime domain that could impact the security, safety, economy, or environment of a nation or region, [and thus] is an exceptionally broad concept" that "means many things to many people."[917]

Due to the preeminent role of the Navy in maintaining maritime security and MDA, it is not surprising that the drafters of the United Nations Convention on the Law of the Sea (UNCLOS) ensured that UNCLOS addressed the rights and duties of warships. As discussed in Chapter 5, UNCLOS includes very few definitions. However, the drafters of UNCLOS felt it of sufficient importance to define warships in Article 29:

Article 29 / Definition of warships
For the purposes of this Convention, "warship" means a ship belonging to the armed forces of a State bearing the external marks distinguishing such ships of its nationality, under the command of an officer duly commissioned by the government of the State and whose name appears in the appropriate service list or its equivalent, and manned by a crew which is under regular armed forces discipline. [emphasis added][918]

Thus the UNCLOS test for a warship is:

1) A ship belonging to an armed force (i.e., a **military ship**);
2) **with distinctive external marks** (such as painting the hull grey and flying an American flag);
3) **under the command of a commissioned officer** (such as a Navy Commander or Captain);
4) **whose name is on the appropriate list of vessels in the military service** (such as the Naval Vessel Register);[919] and

5) **with a military crew** (e.g., Navy officers and enlisted sailors).[920]

U.S. Navy ships (with the ship prefix of *United States Ship* or *USS*) clearly meet this 5-part definition, such as the "grey hulls" in the background in this photo. What about the *U.S. Coast Guard Cutter (USCGC) LEGARE (WMEC 912)* in the foreground—is she a warship?

By U.S. law, "[t]he Coast Guard, established January 28, 1915, shall be a military service and a branch of the armed forces of the United States at all times."[921] The *USCGC LEGARE* certainly has distinctive external marks (white hull with a thick orange and thin blue racing stripes painted on her bow), and she is under the command of a commissioned officer (a USCG Commander) with a military crew.[922] The U.S. Coast Guard also maintains a list of Cutters in each Area (i.e., Atlantic or Pacific).[923] Article 29 was specifically expanded by the drafters from "naval" forces to "armed forces" to accommodate different States' integration of their various branches (e.g., "the operation of seagoing craft by some armies and air forces, and the existence of a coast guard as a separate unit of the armed forces of some nations, such as the United States."[924] Thus, a USCG Cutter would also qualify as a warship under UNCLOS.[925]

What about the *United States Naval Ship (USNS) SUPPLY (T-AOE-6)* pictured in this next photograph? The *USNS SUPPLY* is operated by the U.S. Navy's Military Sealift Command (MSC) as part of MSC's Naval Fleet *Auxiliary* Force.[926] Supply ships often deploy with Carrier Strike Groups (CSGs), replenishing the CSG ships with fuel, ammunition, and food.[927] Auxiliary ships are typically under the

command of a civilian master, with a combined civilian/military crew. Auxiliary ships therefore do not qualify as "warships" under UNCLOS' 5-part test.[928]

Articles 32 and 95 provide for the sovereign immunity[929] of warships in the Territorial Seas and on the High Seas (respectively), and articles 32 and 96 provide for the sovereign immunity of "government ships operated for non-commercial purposes," which would include naval auxiliary ships (like those operated by MSC),[930] as well as government Marine Scientific Research (MSR) vessels (discussed in Chapter 7).

In general terms, only the Flag State has jurisdiction over military warships and other government vessels. As discussed in Chapter 3, the right of Innocent Passage through Territorial Seas extends to military warships and other government vessels.[931] However, the Coastal State (aka "littoral State") may adopt laws and regulations in the Territorial Sea related to:

> the safety of navigation, preserving the environment, and preventing and controlling pollution;[932]

> establishing sea lanes and traffic separation schemes to ensure the safety of navigation of foreign ships exercising Innocent Passage;[933]

> preventing non-innocent passage (i.e., preventing violations of Innocent Passage);[934]

> setting conditions on port entry;[935]

> temporarily suspending Innocent Passage in specific areas of the Territorial Sea, when essential to protect its security, and after due publicity (e.g., when conducting weapons exercises);[936] and

> levying charges against foreign ships for actual services rendered (e.g., pilotage, providing fuel).[937]

These Coastal State authorities are contained in Subsection A "Rules Applicable to All Ships" of Section 3 "Innocent Passage in the Territorial Sea" of Part II of UNCLOS ("Territorial Sea and Contiguous Zone"), and thus apply to "all ships," including military warships, other government vessels, and commercial vessels engaged in Innocent Passage through Territorial Seas.

In contrast, Article 30 is in Subsection C "Rules Applicable to Warships and Other Government Ships…" and provides:

Thus, if a foreign military warship violates Coastal State laws and regulations in the Territorial Sea related to the topics mentioned above, the Coastal State can only request the foreign military warship to comply (e.g., via bridge-to-bridge radio), and if the foreign military warship disregards the Coastal State's request for compliance, the Coastal State may "require" the foreign military warship to depart the Territorial Sea. Besides "ordering" the foreign warship to depart, this implies that the Coastal State may use reasonable military force to enforce such an order (e.g., having a Coastal State warship "shoulder" the foreign military warship to convince it to depart the Territorial Sea).[939] Article 31 provides that the Flag State bears responsibility for any damage to the Coastal State caused by the non-compliance of a military warship or other government vessel (e.g., damage from pollution).

The U.S. Navy also asserts that U.S. warships, government vessels, and military aircraft possess sovereign immunity in foreign ports and airports (e.g., by not submitting to searches or inspections by foreign authorities,[940] and not paying any foreign "taxes," etc.) based upon Article 32 of UNCLOS.[941] If the foreign port authorities insist upon such measures, the U.S. warship or government vessel simply announces its intention to depart port.[942] Usually the local authorities see the wisdom of foregoing such measures in favor of the revenue generated by hundreds or thousands of thirsty, hungry sailors spending a few days in port!

As discussed in Chapter 3, "**all ships and aircraft** enjoy the right of transit passage" through International Straits,[943] which includes military warships and military aircraft in their "normal modes of continuous and expeditious transit."[944] Thus, submarines can transit submerged, warship strike groups can navigate in formation, and warships can launch and recover aircraft (e.g., helicopters, or fighter jets off aircraft carriers).[945] Although military warships and military aircraft are not required to comply with sea lanes and traffic separation schemes while engaged in Transit Passage through International Straits, they must still ensure the safety of navigation, and often voluntarily comply with IMO-approved routing measures.[946]

As discussed in Chapter 4, a Coastal State owns all resources in its Exclusive Economic Zone (EEZ), but other States may still exercise all other High Seas freedoms. Article 58(1) provides that "[i]n the EEZ, all States ... enjoy ... the freedoms referred to in article 87 of navigation and overflight ... and other internationally lawful uses of the sea related to these freedoms, such as those associated with the operation of ships, [and] aircraft ...." Thus, all ships and all aircraft (including military warships and airplanes, and other government vessels and aircraft) enjoy the High Seas freedoms of navigation and overflight in International Waters (i.e., including in foreign EEZs), as well as other related freedoms:

These "other internationally lawful uses of the seas" may be undertaken without coastal State notice or consent and include a broad range of military activities such as: intelligence, surveillance and reconnaissance (ISR) operations; military marine data collection and naval oceanographic surveys; war games and military exercises; bunkering and underway replenishment; testing and use of weapons; aircraft carrier flight operations and submarine operations; acoustic and sonar operations; naval control and protection of shipping; establishment and maintenance of military-related artificial installations; ballistic missile defense operations and ballistic missile test support; maritime interdiction operations (e.g., visit, board, search and seizure); conventional and ballistic missile testing; belligerent rights in naval warfare (e.g., right of visit and search); strategic arms control verification; maritime security operations (e.g., counter-terrorism and counter-proliferation); and sea control.

States may also conduct a number of non-resource-related maritime law enforcement activities in foreign EEZs without coastal State consent pursuant to Article 58(2), which provides that "Articles 88 to 115 and other pertinent rules of international law apply to the EEZ in so far as they are not incompatible..." with Part V. These constabulary operations include actions taken to counter the slave trade (Article 99) and repress piracy (Articles 100–107), suppression of unauthorized broadcasting (Article 109), suppression of narcotics trafficking (Articles 108), the exercise of the peacetime right of approach and visit (Article 110), the duty to render assistance (Article 98), and the right of hot pursuit (Article 111). Article 86 of the Convention confirms this broad interpretation.[947]

Nevertheless, some States purport to limit the freedoms of navigation and overflight by foreign military warships and aircraft in their EEZs. However, during the UNCLOS negotiations, "[m]ost nations agreed with the position advocated by the major maritime powers, that '[m]ilitary operations, exercises and activities have always been regarded as internationally lawful uses of the sea. The right to conduct such activities will continue to be enjoyed by all States in the exclusive economic zone.'"[948] "Dissatisfied with the outcome of the [UNCLOS] negotiations, however, a few nations have sought to unilaterally expand their control in the EEZ, particularly by imposing restrictions on military operations and other lawful activities. These efforts impinge on traditional uses of the oceans by other States and are inconsistent with international law and State practice."[949] Chapter 11 discusses these excessive maritime claims in more depth.

Nor does UNCLOS' "[r]eservation of the high seas for peaceful purposes" in Article 88, and its admonition to only use the seas for "[p]eaceful uses" in Article 301 prohibit military operations, so long as the military operations are conducted in accordance "with the principles of international law embodied in the Charter of the United Nations."[950]

As discussed in Chapter 9 (and mentioned in the quote above), military warships and military aircraft and "other ships or aircraft clearly marked and identifiable as being on government service and authorized to that effect" possess:

> the right to *seize* a foreign vessel "on account of piracy" pursuant to Article 107 of UNCLOS;

> the right to *approach and visit* a foreign vessel when there are reasonable grounds for suspecting a ship is "engaged in piracy," "is without nationality" (i.e., is stateless or quasi-stateless), or is engaged in other international crimes pursuant to Article 110;[951]

> the right to engage in "*hot pursuit*" of a foreign vessel in International Waters when there is "good reason to believe that the [foreign] ship has violated the laws and regulations of that [Coastal] State" pursuant to Article 111; and

> the powers of *enforcement to protect the maritime environment* pursuant to Article 224 (as discussed in Chapter 8).

Although all military vessels are authorized to board foreign vessels in these circumstances, the U.S. Coast Guard boarding "teams are the 'subject matter experts' when it comes to boarding ships," particularly target vessels that are either uncooperative or who oppose the boarding outright. In a permissive boarding situation, the master of the target vessel has consented (i.e., given permission or acquiesced to being boarded);[952] the ship maintains a steady course and constant speed, and has a clear deck—all of which facilitates boarding. A non-compliant (or non-permissive) boarding typically involves the Master of the target vessel not facilitating boarding either by repeatedly changing course, speeding up and then slowing down, and/or "fouling" their deck with anything that might make boarding the target vessel more dangerous. An opposed boarding involves the target vessel using some type of force in an attempt to try to prevent the boarding.

The U.S. Coast Guard trains specialized Maritime Security Response Teams (MSRTs) and Advanced Interdiction Teams to board ships with "non-compliant crews," either "by fast-roping from helicopters [aka 'top-down'] or the old-fashioned way, using grappling hooks and climbing hand-over-hand up the side [aka 'bottom-up']." "Typically, Coast Guard Advanced Interdiction Teams serve to augment Navy Visit, Board, Search and Seizure [VBSS] teams, providing training and backup. When a Level III VBSS is required, meaning the target ship may offer resistance [i.e., an opposed boarding], the Advanced Interdiction Teams are assigned the task."[953] Navy SEALs can also participate in opposed boardings.

Although military warships are authorized to board foreign vessels in these circumstances, one has to wonder if that is the best use of a military asset. States do not invest significant resources in military warships primarily to enforce their rights and duties under UNCLOS. Instead, States invest in expensive military warships[954] in order to have the capability to conduct naval warfare. The Law of Naval Warfare is a branch of the Law of Armed Conflict (LOAC), which was historically known as the Law of War (LOW), and more modernly as International Humanitarian Law (IHL).[955] Following is a chart of International Law, which can be viewed as a series of dichotomies, including Private International Law (between Companies) versus Public International Law (between governments); and within Public International Law between LOAC and "other" Public International Law, such as the Public International Law governing civil aviation (under the International Civil Aviation Organization or ICAO), or that governing international trade (under the World Trade Organization or WTO).

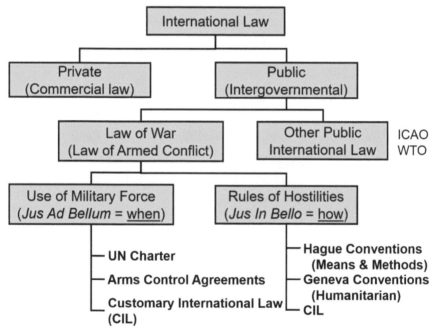

The Law of War (LOW) (aka Law of Armed Conflict (LOAC)) is defined as "that part of international law that regulates the resort to armed force."[956] Within LOAC, there is a distinction or dichotomy between the law related to *when* **a State can use military force** (*jus*

ad bellum, pronounced "*yoose add bell-um*") and the rules applicable to *how* **that conflict/hostilities are conducted** (*jus in bello*, pronounced "*yoose in bell-oh*").[957] An easy way to remember this final distinction is that *jus IN bello* applies when parties are already *IN* a conflict.

Jus ad bellum, or the legal justification to use military force (i.e., **when is a State permitted to go to war**)[958] is beyond the scope of this book. **Jus in bello** deals with the rules applicable to **how to conduct military hostilities** (i.e., how to use military force),[959] which include 4 basic LOAC principles applicable to all branches of warfare (i.e., land, naval, aerial, and space):

1) **Military Necessity:** it is only permissible to seize or destroy enemy property if doing so is necessary for a military purpose (e.g., an oil refinery, if the oil is being used to support the enemy's war effort; or an enemy radio station, if it is broadcasting enemy troop movements).[960]

2) **Distinction:** distinguish between military objectives and military personnel (aka combatants) on the one hand (both of which can be attacked), and protected property and civilian personnel (aka noncombatants) on the other hand (which cannot be attacked). The principle of distinction therefore prohibits indiscriminate attacks (i.e., attacks which are incapable of distinguishing between combatants and

noncombatants, or between military objectives and civilian objects). The principle of distinction also requires combatants to distinguish themselves from noncombatants, for example by wearing a distinctive uniform or insignia.[961]

3) **Proportionality**: the loss of life and damage to civilian property that is reasonably anticipated to occur must not be excessive vis-à-vis the concrete and direct military advantage that is expected to be gained from a military attack. The principle of proportionality seeks to minimize incidental or collateral damage to civilians and civilian objects from legitimate military attacks.[962]

4) **Unnecessary Suffering**: it is forbidden to use weapons that are calculated to cause unnecessary suffering. For example, projectiles made from (or filled with) clear plastic or glass are generally prohibited, as clear plastic or glass fragments would be undetectable by field X-ray equipment, and thus would prevent the proper treatment of wounds.[963]

These 4 basic LOAC principles are found in 3 primary sources:

1) **The Hague Conventions/Regulations** regulate the "means and methods" of warfare.[964]

2) **The 4 Geneva Conventions of 1949** protect the "victims" of war: Wounded and Sick, Shipwrecked at Sea, Prisoners of War, and Civilians. After the Vietnam War, 2 Additional Protocols were adopted by States in order to "fill in the gaps" in the Geneva Conventions: **Additional Protocol I** (AP I) applicable to International Armed Conflict (IAC) between States, and **Additional Protocol II** (AP II) applicable to Non-International Armed Conflict (NIAC).[965]

3) **Other LOAC Treaties** such as the 1954 Cultural Property Convention; 1972 Biological Weapons Convention; 1980 Certain Conventional Weapons Treaty; and the 1993 Chemical Weapons Convention (CWC).[966]

The 4 basic LOAC principles (military necessity, distinction, proportionality, and unnecessary suffering) and the 3 primary sources (Hague, Geneva, and other LOAC treaties) are condensed into (and implemented by) operational rules that can be readily understood and applied by deployed military forces. These condensed operational rules are known as Rules of Engagement (ROE). American military forces are subject to the Standing ROE (SROE) in all military operations.[967] The SROE are augmented by supplemental, mission-specific ROE, which are often classified.[968]

As mentioned previously, "[a]ll armed conflicts are covered by the basic rules and principles of international humanitarian law, wherever the theatre of operations might be, land, sea or air. Nevertheless, some treaty and customary law specifically refers to certain aspects of naval and aerial warfare."[969] Thus, the Law of Naval Warfare has a few peculiarities that make it *lex specialis* (i.e., specialized law), or even *sui generis* (i.e., unique law), such as Deceptive Lighting and Naval Blockade.[970]

Although "[d]eception is as old as warfare itself,"[971] States distinguish between permissible "ruses of war," and impermissible "perfidy" (e.g., pretending to have a different "status," such as wearing civilian garb, or fighting while wearing the enemy's uniform—either of which would presumably forestall attack):[972]

12.1.1 Permitted Deceptions
Ruses of war are methods, resources, and techniques that can be used either to convey false information or deny information to opposing forces. They can include ... means, such as electronic warfare measures; flares, smoke, and chaff; camouflage; deceptive lighting; dummy ships and other armament; decoys; simulated forces; feigned attacks and withdrawals; ambushes; false intelligence information; and utilization of enemy codes, passwords, and countersigns. [emphasis added]

The use of unlawful deceptions is called 'perfidy.' Acts of perfidy are acts that invite the confidence of the enemy to lead him to believe that he is entitled to, or is obliged to accord, protected status under the law of armed conflict, with the intent to betray that confidence. Perfidy is prohibited because it may undermine the protections afforded by the law of war to certain classes of persons and objects .... Feigning surrender and then attacking; feigning an intent to negotiate under a flag of truce and then attacking; and feigning death or incapacitation by wounds or sickness and then attacking are examples of acts of perfidy.[973]

Thus, wearing camouflage uniforms in order to blend in to the natural environment is permissible. Similarly, using Deceptive Lighting in Naval Warfare is also permissible.[974] Although the 1972 Convention on the International Regulations for Preventing Collisions at Sea (COLREGs, which are incorporated into UNCLOS by article 94)[975] requires navigation or "running" lights to be used at night (between sunset and sunrise) by all vessels in order to prevent collisions,[976] "warships are generally exempt from compliance with COLREGs."[977] Therefore, States have long used Deceptive Lighting as a legitimate ruse of war.

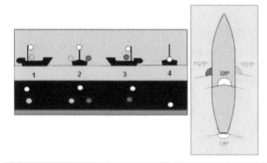

1) Basic lighting configuration—starboard
2) Vessel facing directly towards observer
3) Basic lighting configuration—port
4) Vessel facing away from observer

The idea behind using Deceptive Lighting is to make a military warship appear to be a different type of vessel at night (when all one can see visually is whatever lights the ship is using). Deceptive Lighting may be as simple as lowering the "masthead light" from the top of the mast in order to appear to be a much smaller fishing vessel, for example in order to break a Naval Blockade (discussed next). Whether or not the use of such Deceptive Lighting constitutes perfidy must be evaluated on a case-by-case basis.[978] Even aircraft carriers may effectively use deceptive lighting in order to appear to be another type of vessel (e.g., a large cargo vessel).[979] With advancements in technology, it may eventually be possible to use "[d]igital displays ... in daylight hours to complete the deception ... [using] active camouflage.... A ship's freeboard and superstructure could be covered in conformal LED paneling to display an image of a merchant or some other vessel, provided it is not protected by international treaties like a hospital ship."[980]

Before moving to the 2nd primary peculiarity of Naval Warfare (Naval Blockade), let us consider another maritime example that would appear to cross the line into perfidy: Russia hiding advanced weapons systems in shipping containers:

In the maritime domain, there are numerous ways of hiding in plain sight. One of the most troubling is the containerization of advanced missile systems. Russia has recently showcased several containerized missile systems that outwardly appear indistinguishable from a normal shipping container. A number of these containers could be seeded throughout the ... region at both port facilities and on Russian-operated vessels. Locating and tracking these specific containers would be incredibly difficult. This deceptive capability would enable Russian leadership to mass considerable combat power in the region without raising alarm.[981]

Russia also has a number of State-owned, "non-military" vessels that could be used "for a range of military missions ... [such as] potentially insert[ing] small teams of special operations forces."[982]

Both of these Russian subterfuges (hiding military weapons systems in what otherwise appear to be civilian shipping containers, and using State-owned "non-military" vessels for military missions) appear to be perfidious as they "invite the confidence of the enemy to lead him to believe that he is entitled to, or is obliged to accord, protected status under the law of armed conflict, with the intent to betray that confidence."[983] Another country engaged in armed conflict with Russia generally could not attack what appear to be civilian objects (shipping containers and civilian ships) under the Law of War (LOW) principle of distinction: i.e., the requirement to distinguish between military objectives on the one hand (which can be attacked), and protected civilian property on the other hand (which cannot be attacked).

The 2nd primary peculiarity of Naval Warfare is the use of a Naval Blockade. A Naval Blockade is a belligerent operation (i.e., use of military force or "method of warfare")[984] to deny vessels and/or aircraft of all States – both enemy and neutral – from entering or exiting specific ports, airfields or coastal areas belonging to (or under the control of) an enemy State. While land blockades are not unheard of (e.g., the Soviet Union's land blockade of West Germany after World War II), most blockades are at sea. Blockades should be distinguished from the belligerent right of visit and search[985] during an armed conflict. Visit and search is targeted at certain contraband items/goods (e.g., oil and ammunition being supplied to the enemy), whereas blockades target ALL vessels and aircraft, regardless of cargo.

The Law of Naval Warfare has specialized rules that apply to Naval Blockades, reflecting a balance between the right of a belligerent that commands the sea lanes to *close enemy ports* and coastlines with the right of neutral States to carry out *neutral commerce* with the least possible interference from belligerent forces. Therefore, a Naval Blockade must satisfy certain established criteria in order to be valid:[986]

Thus, a Naval Blockade is a good example of a belligerent act that makes the Law of Naval Warfare *sui generis* (i.e., unique law). It can be a bit disconcerting, therefore, when politicians suggest that the U.S. impose Naval Blockades against States with which we are not at war—imposing the Naval Blockade itself would be an Act  (and therefore Declaration) of War! For example, Democrat Senator Carl Levin (representing Michigan from 1979-2015) proposed having the U.S. Navy impose a Naval Blockade off the coast of Iran in 2012 in order to pressure Iran to forego its nuclear program by blocking Iranian oil exports. Senator Levin characterized his proposed Naval Blockade as a non-combat measure,[987] which is ludicrous! To make matters worse, Senator Levin was the Chairman of the U.S. Senate Armed Services Committee (SASC) at the time, which not only lends his statement more gravitas, but also implies that he should have been better-informed about the Law of Armed Conflict.[988] Unfortunately, diplomats and politicians are notoriously quite cavalier about using military force—they are very quick to suggest the use of military force as a potential solution, despite the fact that many of them have never served in the military. In contrast, most military leaders view the use of military force as the **last resort**, because they bear the brunt of the conflict, as is typified by this quote from General Patton.

> ON THE CONTRARY, THE SOLDIER, ABOVE ALL OTHER PEOPLE, PRAYS FOR PEACE, FOR HE MUST SUFFER AND BEAR THE DEEPEST WOUNDS AND SCARS OF WAR.
>
> GENERAL DOUGLAS MACARTHUR

Within the U.S., it is ultimately the decision of the President and Congress whether to use military force. However, before the President and Congress can legitimately decide to use military force, they need to have the authority to do so on 2 different planes (i.e., levels): internationally and domestically (within the U.S.). As discussed in Chapter 9, there are only 3 situations that justify a State's use of military force under modern international law (specifically *jus ad bellum*):

1) when authorized by the UN Security Council pursuant to Article 42 of the UN Charter (i.e., the use of military measures to enforce international peace and security, under Chapter VII of the UN Charter);

2) when exercising the State's inherent right of self-defense under Article 51 of the UN Charter;[989] or

3) when requested by the State where the military force is to be used (which is a form of collective self-defense).[990]

For example, using military force to combat piracy and armed robbery at sea off the coast of Somalia (discussed in Chapter 9) is both authorized by the UN Security Council pursuant to Article 42 of the UN Charter (i.e., the use of military measures to enforce international peace and security), and by the specific request of the Transitional Federal Government (TFG) of Somalia. Thus, combating piracy and armed robbery at sea off the coast of Somalia rests upon 2 solid justifications under *jus ad bellum*.

In fact, on the international plane, a UN Security Council Resolution (UNSCR) authorizing the use of military force under Chapter VII is the "gold standard" (i.e., the strongest authority). Self-defense under Article 51 of the UN Charter is not quite as solid of a foundation for the use of military force, as self-defense is easy to claim, and therefore rife with abuse. For example, Russia invaded both the South Ossetia region of Georgia in 2008, and the Crimean peninsula in Ukraine in 2014 claiming that it was exercising its right to defend Russian citizens in both foreign States.[991] However, both Russian self-defense claims are considered pretextual and nebulous by the international community, particularly since Russia issued Russian passports to hundreds of thousands of Georgian and Ukrainian nationals shortly before the 2 invasions in order to claim that they were Russian citizens (i.e., to bolster its self-defense argument). Some States (like the U.S. and Israel) don't wait for an armed attack before exercising their right of self-defense under Article 51 of the UN Charter, and instead either anticipate an imminent attack (i.e., anticipatory self-defense), or even seek to prevent a future attack (i.e., preemptive self-defense)—both of which are also met with criticism by the international community.

However, even if the potential use of military force is authorized on the international plane, there still needs to be domestic authority for using military force. For example, the U.S.

Constitution deliberately divides war powers between Congress (which has the powers to declare war, raise and support an Army, provide for and maintain a Navy, and to authorize military spending by making the necessary "appropriations") and the President (who "shall be Commander in Chief of the Army and Navy of the United States," and thus is entitled to defend the U.S.).[992] Therefore, on the domestic plane, a Congressional declaration of war (which hasn't happened since World War II) or Authorization to Use Military Force (AUMF, e.g., in 2001 against Terrorists and in 2002 against Iraq) is the "gold standard" (i.e., the strongest authority). Yet in 1950 President Truman exercised his Commander in Chief (CINC) powers to order U.S. forces to become involved in the Korean War without a congressional declaration of war. And a succession of 5 U.S. Presidents "ratcheted up ... U.S. involvement in the decades-long [Vietnam] conflict,"[993] once again without a congressional declaration of war.

Towards the end of the Vietnam conflict, Congress became increasingly concerned that President Nixon was exceeding his authority (e.g., by secretly bombing Cambodia without notifying Congress). In 1973, Congress pass the War Powers Resolution (WPR) over President Nixon's veto by a 2/3 majority in both Houses of Congress. The WPR reiterates Congress' authority to declare war and to authorize the use of military force, but permits the President to introduce American troops for 60-90 days without congressional authorization. However, the President must notify Congress within 48 hours after "United States Armed Forces are introduced ... into hostilities" or "into the territory, airspace or waters of a foreign nation, while equipped for combat").[994]

Every President since the WPR was enacted in 1973 has only grudgingly complied with it, and only to a certain extent. Each subsequent President has also questioned whether the WPR constitutes an unconstitutional infringement on the President's

CINC powers. For example, President Obama ignored the WPR in conducting U.S. military operations in Libya in 2011, and both President Obama and President Trump ignored the WPR in introducing U.S. ground forces into Syria (2012-2017). Because the President requires domestic authority to go to war, Congress can seek to block the President from doing so.[995]

If the U.S. President decides to use military force (with or without congressional authorization), what are the President's options? There are now 6 U.S. military forces (listed in order of their creation):[996]

1) Army (June 14, 1775)
2) Navy (October 13, 1775)
3) Marine Corps (November 10, 1775)
4) Coast Guard (August 4, 1790)
5) Air Force (September 18, 1947)
6) Space Force (December 20, 2019)

The Space Force is still being formed,[997] and the Coast Guard primarily has law enforcement and safety missions (e.g., drug and migrant interdiction, search and rescue, etc.).[998] That leaves the U.S. President 4 options to project military force abroad: Army, Navy, Marine Corps and Air Force (in addition to Special Forces, which are intended for special "surgical" missions).

The U.S. Army is designed to fight land wars, and measures "its warfighting capacity in terms of brigade combat teams"[999] or BCTs.

A BCT averages 4,500 soldiers depending on its variant: Stryker, Armored, or Infantry. A Stryker BCT is a mechanized infantry force organized around the Stryker combat vehicle [i.e., an 8-wheeled armored vehicle with a 2-man crew that can carry a squad of 9 infantry soldiers]. Armored BCTs are the Army's primary armored units and employ the M1 Abrams Main Battle Tank and the M2 Bradley Fighting Vehicle [i.e., armored personnel carrier]. An Infantry BCT is a highly maneuverable dismounted unit. Variants of the Infantry BCT are the Airmobile BCT, optimized for helicopter assault, and the Airborne BCT, optimized for parachute forcible entry operations.[1000]

The Army is intended to be able to fight 2 wars simultaneously. However, some of the Army's equipment is outdated, especially vis-à-vis comparable weaponry of "top-tier potential adversaries like China and Russia" (e.g., artillery), and "[m]ost experts agree that the Army is too small."[1001] For example, the Heritage Foundation (a conservative think tank based in Washington, D.C. that strenuously opposes U.S. accession to UNCLOS)[1002] argues that the Army needs 50 BCTs, yet currently only has 35 BCTs, of which only 28 are ready to "deploy" (i.e., to be sent overseas on a military mission) at any one time.[1003]

The U.S. Army has 2 challenges: logistics and foreign sovereignty. Even deploying a single BCT (with about 4,500 soldiers), involves establishing a large "footprint" on foreign soil (i.e., establishing a Forward Operating Base (FOB) from which to operate), and significant logistics support to maintain (e.g., fuel, food, ammunition, water, etc.). All of this can easily take 30-45 days to accomplish (i.e., to deploy a U.S.-based BCT overseas).[1004] The Army's rapid deployment forces (e.g., the 82nd Airborne Division and the 75th Ranger Regiment) are supposed to be deployable within 18 hours. However, they too need to establish a FOB on foreign soil from which to operate, which either requires that State's consent, or would constitute the use of military force by itself.

The U.S. Air Force is designed to establish "air superiority" (i.e., control of air warfare) with fighter jets in order for its bombers to drop ordnance (i.e., bombs) anywhere in the world (aka "global strike"); it measures its warfighting capacity in terms of number of aircraft. Like the Army, the Air Force has a smaller capacity than what it needs to fight a major conflict, let alone 2 major conflicts. In fact, the Heritage Foundation estimates that the Air Force requires approximately 250 more "combat-coded" (i.e., combat-ready) fighter aircraft over the 951 in inventory at the end of Fiscal Year (FY) 2019, which would represent a 26% increase.[1005]

The force required to fight, fuel, and resupply a war with China across the vast expanse of the Pacific would need to be much larger than the force that was employed in Desert Storm. The tanker bridge would need to be much longer and more robust, and the airlift capacity required to move and sustain those assets would be greater even without the plethora of air bases that were available to the allied force in 1991. It is hard to fathom how the current number of total force tanker and strategic airlift aircraft assets would be sufficient to fulfill the associated requirements.[1006]

The U.S. Air Force faces the same 2 challenges: logistics and foreign sovereignty. Its planes need to either land at a friendly airfield every few hours to refuel, or get aerial refueling from "tankers." The further the "target area" is from a friendly airfield (such as Andersen Air Force Base in Guam), the longer would be the necessary "tanker bridge" to refuel the bombers and fighter escorts in both directions (outbound and inbound). The challenges of establishing an airfield on foreign soil are akin to those faced by the Army in establishing FOBs on foreign soil—requiring either the foreign State's consent, or using military force to secure the airfield.

Unless the Army can establish a large "footprint" on foreign soil and/or the Air Force can sustain a lengthy "tanker bridge" to sustain flight operations abroad, that leaves the U.S. President with only 2 remaining options to project military force overseas: the Navy and Marine Corps, both of which are part of the Department of the Navy. A quote seen in a Navy exhibit in the halls of the Pentagon sums up the efficacy of using the "Blue-Green Team" to project military force abroad:

> **COMING FROM THE SEA,**
> **WE GET THERE SOONER,**
> **STAY THERE LONGER,**
> **BRING EVERYTHING WE NEED WITH US,**
> **AND DON'T HAVE TO ASK ANYONE'S PERMISSION.**

The Blue-Green Team "is capable of supporting a wide range of Navy/Marine Corps missions across the spectrum of conflict, from peacetime operations like humanitarian assistance/disaster relief, defense support of civil authorities and theater security cooperation; to non-combatant evacuation operations; to full combat operations in support of Marine landing forces."[1007]

The U.S. Council on Foreign Relations (CFR)[1008] publishes an annual survey of foreign policy experts on conflicts that potentially threaten American interests.[1009] "The ... annual Preventive Priorities Survey (PPS) evaluates ongoing and potential conflicts based on their likelihood of occurring in the coming year and their impact on U.S. interests ... to help the U.S. policymaking community prioritize competing conflict prevention and crisis mitigation demands."[1010] In the following chart, the CFR has identified the States highlighted in red as "Tier I (High Priority)," orange as "Tier II (Moderate)," and yellow as "Tier III (Low Priority)."

If the U.S. President decides to use military force abroad (with or without congressional authorization), besides the limitations mentioned previously (e.g., the Army needing to establish a large "footprint" on foreign soil), "a sense of collective fatigue … [has set in for] land interventions in the Middle East that began with the 1991 liberation of Kuwait …. At a cost of 7,000 lives and several trillion dollars for remarkably little demonstrable result, those interventions have not been a happy experience."[1011] However, it is highly unlikely that the U.S. would become isolationist once again as it did after the First World War.[1012]

Instead, we will project power across large swaths of the earth the way maritime empires have done so throughout history: using our Navy. The Navy is our "away team," as Obama-era Secretary of the Navy Ray Mabus liked to say. You can move an aircraft carrier strike group – with almost a half-dozen big warships, thousands of sailors and enough weaponry to destroy an entire city – from one conflict zone to another with the media barely noticing. We do it all the time. But to move a commensurate number of soldiers and their equipment is impossible without a debate in Congress, or a front-page headline. Given the moral taboo against the use of nuclear weapons, the Navy is the United States' primary strategic instrument, projecting power 24/7 around the globe.
    * * *

A naval century is upon us, in keeping with an era of globalization that depends on safe and secure sea lines of communication for container shipping. But nobody should assume it will be peaceful.[1013]

The preeminence of using naval forces to project power (aka "forward presence"), and the Navy and Marine Corps' ability to deploy quickly (i.e., to be sent overseas on a military mission) is typified by the introductory quote to this Chapter from former President Bill Clinton: "When word of a crisis breaks out in Washington, it's no accident that the first question that comes to everyone's lips is: 'Where's the nearest [aircraft] carrier?'"[1014] Thus, perhaps it is no surprise that the U.S. Department of Defense (DoD) aspires to restore the size of the U.S. Navy to 500 ships.[1015]

The versatility of naval forces should not be underestimated. In fact, politicians, military leaders, and even Sailors and Marines themselves can be quite creative in their suggestions for how best to effectively utilize naval forces. For example, as discussed in Chapter 3, tensions have been rising between the U.S. and Iran,[1016] particularly after Iran attacked a handful of oil tankers in the summer of 2019 with naval mines, and the Islamic Revolutionary Guard Corps Navy (IRGCN) seized the British-flagged oil tanker *M/V Stena Impero* in July 2019.[1017]

The U.S. Navy issued a Notice to Mariners (NOTMAR)[1018] on May 18, 2020 warning other vessels to maintain at least a 100 meter "standoff" from U.S. Naval vessels:

181603Z MAY 2020
1478/20(62,63).
ARABIAN SEA.
GULF OF OMAN.
PERSIAN GULF.
DNC 03, DNC 10.

U.S. NAVAL FORCES ARE CONDUCTING ROUTINE OPERATIONS IN THE REGION WITH A COMMITMENT TO FREEDOM OF NAVIGATION AND THE FREE FLOW OF MARITIME COMMERCE. DUE TO RECENT EVENTS, IN ORDER TO ENHANCE SAFETY, MINIMIZE AMBIGUITY, AND REDUCE OPPORTUNITIES FOR MISCALCULATION, ALL VESSELS ARE ADVISED TO MAINTAIN A SAFE DISTANCE OF AT LEAST 100 METERS FROM U.S. NAVAL VESSELS IN INTERNATIONAL WATERS/STRAITS. ARMED VESSELS APPROACHING WITHIN 100 METERS OF A U.S. NAVAL VESSEL MAY BE INTERPRETED AS A THREAT AND SUBJECT TO LAWFUL DEFENSIVE MEASURES. MARINERS ARE REMINDED TO OPERATE IN ACCORDANCE WITH INTERNATIONAL LAW AND WITH DUE REGARD FOR THE SAFE NAVIGATION OF OTHER VESSELS. ALL VESSELS OPERATING IN THE VICINITY OF U.S. NAVAL VESSELS ARE ADVISED TO CLEARLY COMMUNICATE INTENTIONS, RESPOND TO QUERIES CONCERNING COURSE AND SPEED, EXERCISE PRINCIPLES OF PRUDENT SEAMANSHIP AS REQUIRED UNDER INTERNATIONAL LAW, AND REMAIN AT THE MAXIMUM AVAILABLE DISTANCE FROM U.S. NAVAL FORCES. [emphasis added][1019]

Thus, due to sustained and rising tensions in the Arabian Gulf, ships and aircraft of all States need to conduct detailed planning before conducting Transit Passage through the Strait of Hormuz. American ships in particular need to be prepared to respond to the full continuum of potential Iranian challenges and threats during their transit.[1020] "Sadly, harassment by the IGRC Navy is not a new

phenomenon .... It is something that all our commanding officers and crews of our vessels are trained for, when serving in the Central Command area of responsibility, particularly in and around the [Persian] Gulf."[1021] Therefore, it should not be surprising that when the U.S. Navy's Military Sealift Command (MSC) time-chartered a vessel (i.e., paid for the exclusive use of the vessel for a specific period of time versus paying to ship specific cargo), MSC embarked U.S. Marines onboard the civilian vessel in order to provide security during its Transit Passage through the Strait of Hormuz.[1022] Using military forces to protect private and merchant vessels is not unprecedented:

[I]nternational law also contemplates the use of force in peacetime in certain circumstances to protect private and merchant vessels, private property, and persons at sea from acts of unlawful violence. The legal doctrines of individual and collective self-defense and protection of nationals provide the authority for U.S. Armed Forces to protect U.S. and, in some circumstances, foreign flag vessels, aircraft, property, and persons from violent and unlawful acts of others.[1023]

Similarly, when the *USS BOXER* (LHD 4) (an amphibious "big deck helicopter carrier") transited through the Strait of Hormuz, instead of the embarked Marines just sitting around, they tied down Light Armored Vehicles (LAVs) on both of the aircraft elevators in order to improve the ship's ability to detect small boats and to respond to a small boat attack with chain guns and machine guns.[1024] The U.S. Navy regional commander indicated that "[w]e are focused on maintaining strong defenses and exposing nefarious actors. We are not seeking conflict, but we will be prepared to defend ourselves and respond to attacks on U.S. forces and our interests."[1025]

Contrast these creative (but still legitimate) uses of military force to defend American ships conducting Transit Passage through the Strait of Hormuz, with the suggestion from a former member of President George W. Bush's senior staff (and adjunct professor of public policy and international affairs at Georgetown University) to use commercial ships with military crews and embarked special forces as decoys in the Strait of Hormuz to respond "with overwhelming force against those seeking to hijack, kidnap or otherwise harm the crew or the ship."[1026] Despite his pedigree, this idea to use "decoy ships" would blur the distinction between combatants and civilians, in violation of the Law of Armed Conflict (LOAC) principle of distinction, similar to the Russian subterfuges discussed earlier.[1027] Although the U.S. and Iran are not engaged in armed conflict (i.e., at war) at the time of this writing, if Iran attempted to seize a commercial ship "decoy," and the decoy ship's military crew "respond[ed] with overwhelming force," *the*

U.S. and Iran would be 1 step closer to (if not already at) war, and the actions of both States (arguably) would have violated LOAC.

Against this LOAC backdrop, let us analyze a real world example: when Iran shot down a U.S. drone in the Strait of Hormuz in June 2019.[1028] The U.S. Air Force regional commander indicated that:

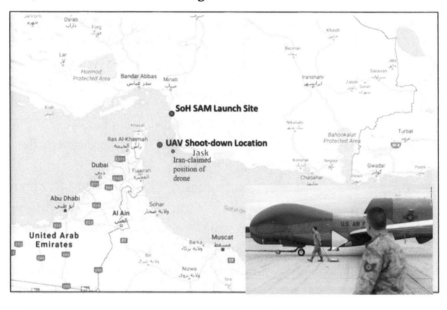

A U.S. Navy RQ-4 was flying over the Gulf of Oman and the Strait of Hormuz on a surveillance mission in international airspace in the vicinity of recent IRGC maritime attacks when it was shot down by an IRGC surface to air missile fired from a location in the vicinity of Goruk, Iran. This was an unprovoked attack on a U.S. surveillance asset that had not violated Iranian airspace at any time during its mission.

This attack is an attempt to disrupt our ability to monitor the area following recent threats to international shipping and free flow of commerce.

Iranian reports that this aircraft was shot down over Iran are categorically false. The aircraft was over the Strait of Hormuz and fell into international waters. At the time of the intercept, the RQ-4 was operating at high-altitude approximately 34 kilometers from the nearest point of land on the Iranian coast.

> *This dangerous and escalatory attack was irresponsible and occurred in the vicinity of established air corridors between Dubai, UAE, and Muscat Oman, possibly endangering innocent civilians.*[1029]

"[U]nmanned aerial vehicles (UAV) and remotely piloted vehicles are generally considered to be military aircraft. As such, they enjoy the same navigational rights and protections of applicable domestic and international law as manned aircraft."[1030] Therefore the U.S. drone was a military aircraft entitled to conduct Transit Passage through the International Strait of Hormuz.[1031]

Based upon the official press statements, it appears that a U.S. Navy RQ-4 drone was collecting Imagery Intelligence (IMINT) while engaged in Transit Passage through the Strait of Hormuz. As discussed in Chapter 3, ships and aircraft enjoy the right of Transit Passage "solely for the purpose of continuous and expeditious transit of the [international] strait."[1032] which does not include collecting IMINT. Moreover, the right of Transit Passage through International Straits does not otherwise "affect the legal status of the waters forming such straits"—i.e., they remain Territorial Seas.[1033] Article 19 of UNCLOS explains that "[p]assage of a foreign ship shall be considered to be prejudicial to the peace, good order or security of the coastal State if in the territorial sea it engages in ... any act aimed at collecting information to the prejudice of the defence or security of the coastal State." By analogy, this prohibition on collecting intelligence would also seem to apply to foreign military aircraft conducting Transit Passage through an International Strait, especially since collecting intelligence is not part of a military aircraft's "normal mode[] of continuous and expeditious transit."

Thus, it would appear that the U.S. Navy RQ-4 violated the rights of the Coastal States when the drone was engaged in collecting IMINT (i.e., a spy plane taking photographs) while engaged in

Transit Passage through the Strait of Hormuz. However, it appears that the drone only flew through the waters of Oman and the United Arab Emirates (UAE), and *not Iran!* As discussed in Chapter 3, although a Coastal State may use the minimum military force necessary to compel a noncompliant foreign warship to depart the Territorial Sea,[1034] there is no corresponding right to forcibly eject a noncompliant foreign warship or aircraft from an International Strait. Instead, if a foreign warship or aircraft violates Transit Passage (e.g., by collecting intelligence), "[t]he flag State … shall bear international responsibility for any loss or damage which results to States bordering straits."[1035] Therefore, Iran was not justified in shooting down the American drone in the Strait of Hormuz. If Iran bore "any loss or damage" from the American drone's violation of Transit Passage, Iran could seek to hold the U.S. "international[ly] responsible."

One area where American leaders have chosen to project power is in the South China Sea against China's expanding naval power:

In July 2013, the Chinese Communist Party held a Politburo meeting devoted to the topic of transforming China into a "maritime great power" (海洋强国). Rather than centering his remarks on the cooperative spirit of UNCLOS, General Secretary Xi Jinping conjured themes of national struggle against competing states: "Historical experience tells us that countries that embrace the sea prosper, while countries that forsake the sea decline."
* * *
Since Xi Jinping came to power in 2012, China has invested vast resources to build itself into a world-class naval power. Once largely confined to the waters of the First Island Chain, the Chinese navy is now preparing to compete with American sea power in the western and central Pacific and in the Indian Ocean beyond the umbrella of its shore-based aircraft and missile batteries.[1036]

The U.S. Navy operates about half of the world's "aircraft carriers" (broadly defined as including ships that can launch fixed-wing aircraft from full-length flight decks, and "smaller carriers that operate helicopters").[1037] China's top military leader has "stated that war with the United States is inevitable".[1038] There is some concern that China could negate the U.S. Navy's advantage with long-range, precision-guided anti-ship missiles.[1039] However, there are a number of hurdles that China would need to overcome before it could successfully attack U.S. aircraft carriers:

U.S. carrier strike groups maintain a dense defensive perimeter in the air around their locations that includes interceptor aircraft, networked surface-to-air missiles, surveillance planes and airborne jammers. No Chinese aircraft is likely to get close enough to a carrier to establish a sustained target track. The same applies to Chinese surface vessels and submarines, which are even more vulnerable to preemption by the strike group than airborne assets.

So the vital early steps of simply finding and fixing the carriers would not be easy. .... Any weapons dispatched against the intended target would need to negotiate multiple layers of active and passive defenses, including electronic countermeasures and, in the future, beam weapons.

Some observers have stressed the danger posed by China's recent deployment of anti-ship ballistic missiles with maneuvering warheads. The Navy takes the threat seriously, and in response has moved most of its missile-defense warships to the Pacific. As a practical matter, though,

these weapons make little difference to the balance of power if China cannot first find, fix, track and target a carrier.
* * *

The bottom line is that China is nowhere near overcoming the hurdles required for successful attacks against U.S. aircraft carriers. Whether those carriers are engaged in projecting air power ashore or maintaining control of sea lanes, Beijing will be hard-pressed to impede their operation in wartime. And it's a safe bet that whatever assets China may have for executing such a mission on the first day of war will be quickly reduced by the combined efforts of the U.S. joint force, whether they be deployed on land, at sea, or in orbit.[1040]

Besides deploying aircraft carriers to the Persian (aka Arabian) Gulf and the South China Sea, the U.S. also deploys them to other areas of strategic concern, including, for the first time in nearly 30 years, to the Arctic Circle/Norwegian Sea. In 2018, the *USS HARRY S. TRUMAN* (CVN 75) sailed through "the 'GIUK Gap,' waters around Greenland, Iceland and the United Kingdom [that are] considered vital if [an] American warship must rush to Europe to aid allies. It is also a key route for Russian submarines slipping into the North Atlantic."[1041] Besides using "Naval presence"[1042] as a "show of force" to Russia, the U.S. deployed the Truman Strike Group to "reacquaint[] a new generation of officers and sailors with what

Source: Finnish Institute of International Affairs

could become a maritime battlefield. ... It's not just about training for this kind of warfare but specifically training the location that we may have to fight. ... So you are going to see more large-scale training in the Mediterranean, training in the Arctic and training in the western Pacific."[1043]

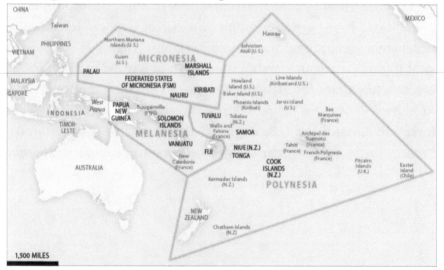

The value and versatility of Naval presence cannot be overstated:

One measure the United States may use to protect its maritime interests in peacetime is naval presence. Naval forces constitute a key and unique element of the U.S. national military capability. The mobility of forces operating at sea, combined with the versatility of naval force composition—from units operating individually to multicarrier strike group formations—provide the President and Secretary of Defense with the flexibility to tailor U.S. military presence as circumstances may require.

Naval presence, ranging from showing the flag during port visits to forces deployed in response to contingencies or crises, can be tailored to exert the precise influence best suited to U.S. interests. Depending upon the magnitude and immediacy of the problem, naval forces may be positioned near areas of potential discord as a show of force, or as a symbolic expression of support and concern. Unlike land-based forces, naval forces may be so employed without political entanglement, and without the necessity of seeking consent from littoral States. So long as they remain in international waters and international airspace, U.S. warships and military aircraft enjoy the full spectrum of the high seas freedoms of navigation and overflight, including the right to conduct naval maneuvers. Deployment of a naval strike group into areas of tension and augmentation of U.S. naval forces to deter interference with U.S. commercial shipping in an area of armed conflict provide graphic illustrations of the use of U.S. naval forces in peacetime to deter violations of international law and to protect U.S. flag vessels. Peacetime naval missions such as these are becoming more important to fulfill critical 21st century strategic goals.[1044]

In summary, whether the U.S. is preparing for potential conflict with Russia, Iran, North Korea, or China, the efficacy of using the "Blue-Green Team" to project military force abroad cannot be overstated. "To back up friends, to warn potential enemies, to neutralize similar deployments by other naval powers, to exert influence in ambiguous situations, to demonstrate resolve through a deployment of palpable force-all these are tasks that naval power is uniquely able to perform. For these purposes the advantages of naval power over land or air power are clear."[1045]

---

[915] *See, e.g.*, MARC G. DE SANTIS, A NAVAL HISTORY OF THE PELOPONNESIAN WAR (2018). The term "maritime security" can be used in a variety of contexts. However, at a minimum, "maritime security" encompasses a number of related disciplines,

covering the gamut from international and regional threats to the maritime domain (which is perhaps the widest aperture/definition of the term), to national security, to military power projection using naval forces, to force protection of vessels and offshore platforms (which is perhaps the narrowest aperture/definition of the term). THE FLETCHER SCHOOL OF LAW AND DIPLOMACY—TUFTS UNIVERSITY, LAW OF THE SEA, A POLICY PRIMER 41 (2017), https://sites.tufts.edu/lawofthesea/introduction/.

⁹¹⁶ *See generally* United States Dept. of Transportation, Maritime Administration (MARAD), Office of Maritime Security, https://www.maritime.dot.gov/ports/office-security/office-maritime-security.

⁹¹⁷ Center for Strategic & Int'l. Studies (CSIS), Int'l. Security Program, Global Threats and Regional Stability, *Contested Seas: Maritime Domain Awareness in Northern Europe*, pp. V, 1-2, 12-21 (Andrew Metrick & Kathleen H. Hicks, Mar. 28, 2018), https://www.csis.org/programs/international-security-program/global-threats-and-regional-stability/contested-seas (noting that "[t]he modern history of MDA begins in the United States, with Homeland Security Presidential Directive – 13 (HSPD-13) / National Security Presidential Directive – 41 (NSPD-41) issued in 2004 by President George W. Bush. The document lays out core interests for the United States to enhance security in the maritime domain and creates a cooperative framework to support MDA operations across different spheres."). Maritime Situational Awareness (MSA) is the North Atlantic Treaty Organization (NATO) variant of MDA. CSIS, *Contested Seas* (full cite above).

⁹¹⁸ United Nations Convention on the Law of the Sea (UNCLOS) art. 29, Dec. 10, 1982, 1833 U.N.T.S. 397, https://www.un.org/Depts/los/convention_agreements/convention_overview_convention.htm.

⁹¹⁹ Naval Vessel Register, The Official Inventory of US Naval Ships and Service Craft, https://www.nvr.navy.mil/.

⁹²⁰ U.S. NAVY, MARINE CORPS & COAST GUARD, THE COMMANDER'S HANDBOOK ON THE LAW OF NAVAL OPERATIONS, NWP 1-14M/MCTP 11-10B/COMDTPUB P5800.7A, ¶ 2.2.1 (pp. 2-1 to 2-2) (2017), www.jag.navy.mil/distrib/instructions/CDRs_HB_on_Law_of_Naval_Operations_AUG17.pdf. The UNCLOS definition of a warship is similar to the 4-part test for who is entitled to prisoner of war (POW) status (other than members of the regular armed forces, who are automatically entitled to POW status) under Article 4 of the Third Geneva Convention: "Members of other militias ... provided that such militias ... fulfil the following conditions:

  (a) that of being commanded by a person responsible for his subordinates;

  (b) that of having a fixed distinctive sign [e.g., insignia or uniform] recognizable at a distance;

  (c) that of carrying arms [i.e., weapons] openly;

  (d) that of conducting their operations in accordance with the laws and customs of war. Int'l. Committee of the Red Cross (ICRC), Treaties, States Parties and Commentaries, Treaties and Documents, Geneva Conventions of 1949 and Additional Protocols, and their Commentaries, Convention (III) relative to the Treatment of Prisoners of War Art 4. (Geneva, Aug. 12 1949), https://ihl-databases.icrc.org/ihl/WebART/375-590007?OpenDocument.

⁹²¹ 14 U.S. Code § 1, https://www.law.cornell.edu/uscode/text. Following a declaration of war, either the President or Congress may direct that the U.S. Coast Guard "operate as a service in the Navy." 14 U.S. Code § 103(b), https://www.law.cornell.edu/uscode/text.

922 U.S. Dept. of Homeland Security, United States Coast Guard Atlantic Area, Our Organization, Area Cutters, CGLEGARE, https://www.atlanticarea.uscg.mil/Area-Cutters/CGCLEGARE/.
923 U.S. Dept. of Homeland Security, United States Coast Guard, https://www.uscg.mil/.
924 Letter Of Transmittal Forwarding The 1982 UN Law Of The Sea Convention To The United States Senate, DOS Commentary p. 17 (William J. Clinton, Oct. 7, 1994) (S. Treaty Doc. 103–39), https://www.foreign.senate.gov/imo/media/doc/treaty_103-39.pdf.
925 COMMANDER'S HANDBOOK, ¶ 2.2.1 (pp. 2-1 to 2-2) (full cite above).
926 TUFTS, LAW OF THE SEA, pp. 38-39 (full cite above); Rob McLaughlin, An Incident in the South China Sea, 96 INT'L. L. STUD. 505, 518 (2020), https://digital-commons.usnwc.edu/ils/vol96/iss1/16/.
927 America's Navy, Forged by the Sea, United States Navy Fact File, Fast Combat Support Ships T-AOE, https://www.navy.mil/navydata/fact_display.asp?cid=4400&tid=300&ct=4%20.
928 COMMANDER'S HANDBOOK, ¶ 2.2.1 (pp. 2-1 to 2-2) (full cite above). UNCLOS only explicitly mentions "naval auxiliary" ships once: Article 236 explains that warships, naval auxiliaries and "government ships used only on government non-commercial service" have sovereign immunity (i.e., are exempt) from the requirements to protect and preserve the marine environment in Part XII of UNCLOS (discussed in Chapter 5). UNCLOS, art. 236 (full cite above). Article 96 also mentions that "ships used only on government non-commercial service" (e.g., U.S. Naval Supply ships, and NOAA vessels) have sovereign immunity on the High Seas. See also TUFTS, LAW OF THE SEA, pp. 36-37 (full cite above); COMMANDER'S HANDBOOK, ¶¶ 2.2.1, 2.3.1 (pp. 2-1 to 2-3) (full cite above). Bangladesh and Ecuador claim that "sovereign immunity does not relieve a State from the obligation ... in accepting responsibility and liability for compensation and relief in respect of damage caused by pollution of the marine environment ...." This claim is not recognized by the U.S. Dept. of Defense Maritime Claims Reference Manual (MCRM)—Bangladesh 2019 & Ecuador 2017, http://www.jag.navy.mil/organization/code_10_mcrm.htm); U.S. Dept. of State, Limits in the Seas No. 147 (full cite above). Canada has also imposed "[r]egulations [that] require mandatory ship reporting and regulation of foreign-flagged vessels entering and transiting certain areas within Canada's claimed EEZ and territorial sea, without exemption for all sovereign immune vessels." DoD MCRM—Canada 2017 (full cite above). Chapter 11 discusses excessive maritime claims, and Freedom of Navigation programs.
929 "Sovereign immunity in international law makes one State's property immune from interference by another State in two ways: jurisdictional immunity, which limits the adjudicatory power of national courts against a foreign State, and enforcement immunity, which limits the taking of or interference with State property by executive authorities of foreign States." TUFTS, LAW OF THE SEA, p. 37 (full cite above).
930 COMMANDER'S HANDBOOK, ¶¶ 2.2.1, 2.3.1 (pp. 2-1 to 2-3) (full cite above). TUFTS, LAW OF THE SEA, pp. 36-37 (full cite above); COMMANDER'S HANDBOOK, ¶¶ 2.1-2.1.1 (p. 2-1) (full cite above); McLaughlin, An Incident in the South China Sea (full cite above).
931 UNCLOS, art. 17 (full cite above); COMMANDER'S HANDBOOK, ¶¶ 2.5.2.1, 2.5.2.4 (pp. 2-5 to 2-6) (full cite above).
932 UNCLOS, art. 21 (full cite above). Although the Coastal State has the right to adopt laws and regulations related to Innocent Passage, there is no support for the

Coastal State requiring prior notification before foreign ships can conduct Innocent Passage, let alone prior permission/consent from the Coastal State. This is clear from the negotiating history of UNCLOS. A vote was taken to add the prior notification requirements for Innocent Passage, and the proposal was rejected. Nevertheless, 10 States purport to require prior notification before conducting Innocent Passage, and 29 States claim to require prior permission to do so. Requiring either prior notification or prior permission for Innocent Passage would hamper Innocent Passage in violation of Article 24. Chapter 11, Excessive Maritime Claims and Freedom of Navigation (FON) Programs, discusses such excessive requirements.

[933] United Nations Convention on the Law of the Sea (UNCLOS) art. 22, Dec. 10, 1982, 1833 U.N.T.S. 397, https://www.un.org/Depts/los/convention_agreements/convention_overview_convention.htm. *See generally* William J. Aceves, *The Freedom of Navigation Program: A Study of the Relationship between Law and Politics*, 19 HASTINGS INT'L & COMP. L. REV. 259, 290 (1996), https://repository.uchastings.edu/hastings_international_comparative_law_review/vol19/iss2/2/ (providing a detailed example of a U.S. FON diplomatic protest to Finland regarding its sea lanes).

[934] UNCLOS, art. 25(1) (full cite above).

[935] UNCLOS, art. 25(2) (full cite above); U.S. NAVY, MARINE CORPS & COAST GUARD, THE COMMANDER'S HANDBOOK ON THE LAW OF NAVAL OPERATIONS, NWP 1-14M/MCTP 11-10B/COMDTPUB P5800.7A, ¶ 4.4.4.1.6 (p. 4-8) (2017), www.jag.navy.mil/distrib/instructions/CDRs_HB_on_Law_of_Naval_Operations_AUG17.pdf. Under Articles 25(2) and 211(3), a Coastal State may set "conditions on port entry," which do not have to be reasonable. The U.S. requires the use of the Automatic Identification System (AIS), Notice of Arrival 96 hours prior to entering port, and a list of the five previous foreign ports. The U.S. Coast Guard (USCG) boards any high-interest vessels before they are permitted to enter U.S. Territorial Seas. Australia bans foreign whaling vessels, unless they pay for special permit. As part of its "Nuclear Free Zone," New Zealand bans nuclear-powered vessels (including U.S. aircraft carriers) from entering its ports. New Zealand Nuclear Free Zone, Disarmament, and Arms Control Act 1987 § 11, http://www.legislation.govt.nz/act/public/1987/0086/latest/DLM115116.html#DLM115147. *See also* 33 U.S. Code § 1228, https://www.law.cornell.edu/uscode/text; COMMANDER'S HANDBOOK, ¶ 2.6.6 (p. 2-12) (full cite above) (noting that "[t]he 1968 Nuclear Weapons Non-Proliferation Treaty, to which the United States is a party, acknowledges the right of groups of States to conclude regional treaties establishing nuclear-free zones. Such treaties are binding only on parties to them .... To the extent that the rights and freedoms of other States, including the high seas freedoms of navigation and overflight, are not infringed upon, such treaties are not inconsistent with international law."). Japan, Australia and the U.S. ban North Korean ships. The U.S. has also banned ships from Cuba, Iran, Libya, Sudan and Syria. *But see* COMMANDER'S HANDBOOK, ¶ 3.11.2.2.3 (p. 3-12) (full cite above) (indicating that "a coastal State may enforce reasonable, nondiscriminatory conditions on a vessel's entry into its ports."); DONALD R. ROTHWELL & TIM STEPHENS, THE INT'L. LAW OF THE SEA 57 (2nd ed. 2016) (noting that there are often reciprocal rights of port entry between States, and ports are generally open to commercial ships).

[936] COMMANDER'S HANDBOOK, ¶ 2.5.2.3 (p. 2-6) (full cite above).

[937] UNCLOS, art. 26 (full cite above); THE FLETCHER SCHOOL OF LAW AND DIPLOMACY—TUFTS UNIVERSITY, LAW OF THE SEA, A POLICY PRIMER 21 (2017), https://sites.tufts.edu/lawofthesea/introduction/.

[938] UNCLOS, art. 30 (full cite above).

[939] Shouldering or "riding off is a tolerated maritime law enforcement and maritime security measure". Rob McLaughlin, An Incident in the South China Sea, 96 INT'L. L. STUD. 505, 525-526 (2020), https://digital-commons.usnwc.edu/ils/vol96/iss1/16/.

[940] COMMANDER'S HANDBOOK, ¶¶ 2.1-2.1.1 (p. 2-1) (full cite above); TUFTS, LAW OF THE SEA, p. 37 (full cite above).

[941] COMMANDER'S HANDBOOK, ¶¶ 2.2.2-2.2.3, 2.4.2 (pp. 2-2, 2-4) (full cite above); TUFTS, LAW OF THE SEA, p. 37 (full cite above).

[942] COMMANDER'S HANDBOOK, ¶¶ 2.1, 3.11.2.2.3 (pp. 2-1, 3-12) (full cite above).

[943] UNCLOS. art. 38 (full cite above).

[944] UNCLOS, art. 39(1)(c) (full cite above); COMMANDER'S HANDBOOK ¶¶ 2.5.3.2, 2.7.1.1 (pp. 2-7 to 2-8, 2-13) (full cite above).

[945] UNCLOS, art. 39(1)(c) (full cite above); COMMANDER'S HANDBOOK, ¶ 2.5.3.2 (pp. 2-7 to 2-8) (full cite above); TUFTS, LAW OF THE SEA, p. 23 (full cite above).

[946] COMMANDER'S HANDBOOK, ¶ 2.5.3.2 (pp. 2-7 to 2-8) (full cite above) (arguing that "sovereign-immune vessels ... are not legally required to comply with such sea lanes and traffic separation schemes while in transit passage. Sovereign immune vessels, however, must exercise due regard for the safety of navigation. Warships and auxiliaries may, and often do, voluntarily comply with IMO-approved routing measures in international straits where practicable and compatible with the military mission."); TUFTS, LAW OF THE SEA, p. 24 ((full cite above) (same).

[947] Raul (Pete) Pedrozo, Military Activities in the Exclusive Economic Zone: East Asia Focus, 90 INT'L. L. STUD. 514, 517-518 & 540-541 (2014), https://digital-commons.usnwc.edu/ils/vol90/iss1/15/. Military exercises can be quite extensive, such as the "Large Scale Exercise 2021" scheduled for late summer 2021, which is planned to involve "[a]ircraft carriers, submarines, planes, unmanned vessels, and about 25,000 personnel ... [and] will span 17 time zones with sailors and Marines in the U.S., Africa, Europe and the Pacific joining." Military.com, Military News, Biggest Navy Exercise in a Generation Will Include 25,000 Personnel Across 17 Time Zones (Gina Harkins, May 21, 2021), https://www.military.com/daily-news/2021/05/21/biggest-navy-exercise-generation-will-include-25000-personnel-across-17-time-zones.html?ESRC=navy-a_210526.nl.

[948] Pedrozo, Military Activities in the EEZ, pp. 515-16 (full cite above), quoting 17 Third UN Conference on the Law of the Sea, Plenary Meetings, Official Records, U.N. Doc. A/CONF.62/WS/37 and ADD.1-2, 244 (1973–1982). See also TUFTS, LAW OF THE SEA, p. 31 ((full cite above); Brookings Institution, Center for East Asia Policy Studies, East Asia Policy Paper 9, The U.S. FON Program in the South China Sea—A lawful and necessary response to China's strategic ambiguity, pp. 7-8 (Lynn Kuok, June 2016), https://www.brookings.edu/research/the-u-s-fon-program-in-the-south-china-sea/.

[949] Pedrozo, Military Activities in the EEZ, pp. 516-518 (full cite above) (examining the travaux préparatoires (i.e., negotiating record) of the Third UN Conference on the Law of the Sea, which culminated in UNCLOS).

[950] UNCLOS. art. 301 (full cite above); John Norton Moore, Navigational Freedom: The Most Critical Common Heritage, 93 INT'L. L. STUD. 251, 258 (2017), https://digital-commons.usnwc.edu/ils/vol93/iss1/8/; Pedrozo, Military Activities in the EEZ, pp. 532-

536 (full cite above); Letter Of Transmittal Forwarding The 1982 UN Law Of The Sea Convention To The United States Senate, DOS Commentary p. 94 (William J. Clinton, Oct. 7, 1994) (S. Treaty Doc. 103-39), https://www.foreign.senate.gov/imo/media/doc/treaty_103-39.pdf.

⁹⁵¹ "This is a right of great importance to the United States. Article 110 permits the right of visit to be exercised if there are reasonable grounds for suspecting that a foreign flag vessel is engaged in piracy, the slave trade, or unauthorized broadcasting; is without nationality; or is, in reality, of the same nationality as the warship. The maintenance and continued respect for these rights are essential to maritime counter-narcotics and alien smuggling interdiction operations." DOS Commentary, p. 30 (full cite above).

⁹⁵² U.S. NAVY, MARINE CORPS & COAST GUARD, THE COMMANDER'S HANDBOOK ON THE LAW OF NAVAL OPERATIONS, NWP 1-14M/MCTP 11-10B/COMDTPUB P5800.7A, ¶¶ 3.11.2.5 to 3.11.2.5.2, 4.4.4.1.3 (pp. 3-14, 4-7) (2017), www.jag.navy.mil/distrib/instructions/CDRs_HB_on_Law_of_Naval_Operations _AUG17.pdf.

⁹⁵³ Military.com, Daily News, 'The Night Is Ours:' Inside the Elite World of Coast Guard Ship-Boarding Teams (Richard Sisk, Apr. 4, 2019), https://www.military.com/daily-news/2019/04/04/night-ours-inside-elite-world-coast-guard-ship-boarding-teams.html.

⁹⁵⁴ The United States invests an average of $1-2 Billion per new Navy warship, with new aircraft carriers costing $11-13 Billion. Navy Times, Pentagon & Congress, A 308-ship Navy to cost $566 billion, CBO estimates (Shawn Snow, Feb. 24, 2017), https://www.navytimes.com/news/pentagon-congress/2017/02/24/a-308-ship-navy-to-cost-566-billion-cbo-estimates/; Congressional Budget Office, Nonpartisan Analysis for the U.S. Congress, An Analysis of the Navy's Fiscal Year 2019 Shipbuilding Plan (Oct. 18, 2018), https://www.cbo.gov/publication/54564.

⁹⁵⁵ Dept. of Defense Law of War Manual § 1.3.1.2, p. 8 (June 2015, updated Dec. 2016), https://www.hsdl.org/?view&did=797480; COMMANDER'S HANDBOOK, ¶ 5.6 (p. 5-8) (full cite above).

⁹⁵⁶ DoD Law of War Manual, § 1.3, p. 7 (full cite above).

⁹⁵⁷ DoD Law of War Manual, §§ 1.11 & 3.5, pp. 39-40 & 86-89 (full cite above); COMMANDER'S HANDBOOK, ¶¶ 5.1 to 5.1.2.2 (pp. 5-1 to 5-2) (full cite above).

⁹⁵⁸ DoD Law of War Manual, § 1.11, pp. 39-40 (full cite above).

⁹⁵⁹ DoD Law of War Manual, § 1.11, pp. 39-40 (full cite above).

⁹⁶⁰ DoD Law of War Manual, § 2.2, pp. 52-58 (full cite above); COMMANDER'S HANDBOOK, ¶ 5.3.1 (p. 5-3) (full cite above); INT'L. AND OPERATIONAL LAW DEPT., THE JUDGE ADVOCATE GENERAL'S LEGAL CENTER AND SCHOOL (TJAGLCS), U.S. DEP'T. OF ARMY, 2011 OPERATIONAL LAW HANDBOOK Ch. 2 ¶ V.A (pp. 10-11), https://www.loc.gov/rr/frd/Military_Law/pdf/operational-law-handbook_2011.pdf.

⁹⁶¹ DoD Law of War Manual, § 2.5, pp. 62-65 (full cite above); COMMANDER'S HANDBOOK, ¶ 5.3.4 (p. 5-4) (full cite above); TJAGLCS, 2011 OPLAW HANDBOOK Ch. 2 ¶ V.B (pp. 11-12) (full cite above); LOUISE DOSWALD-BECK, SAN REMO MANUAL ON INT'L. LAW APPLICABLE TO ARMED CONFLICTS AT SEA ¶¶ 39-41 (1994).

⁹⁶² DoD Law of War Manual, §§ 2.4 & 5.10-5.12, pp. 60-62 & 241-270 (full cite above); COMMANDER'S HANDBOOK, ¶ 5.3.3 (p. 5-4) (full cite above); TJAGLCS, 2011 OPLAW HANDBOOK Ch. 2 ¶ V.C (p. 12) (full cite above).

⁹⁶³ DoD Law of War Manual, §§ 6.6.1-6.6.2, pp. 358-360 (full cite above); COMMANDER'S HANDBOOK, ¶ 5.3.2 (p. 5-3) (full cite above); TJAGLCS, 2011 OPLAW

HANDBOOK Ch. 2 ¶ V.D (pp. 12-13) (full cite above). *See also* ICRC Study on Customary Int'l. Humanitarian Law, Rule 70, https://ihl-databases.icrc.org/customary-ihl/eng/docs/v2_rul_rule70; SAN REMO MANUAL, ¶ 42 (full cite above).

⁹⁶⁴ Hague Convention IV Respecting the Laws and Customs of War on Land, Oct. 18, 1907, 36 Stat. 2277; Hague Convention V Respecting the Rights and Duties of Neutral Powers and Persons in Case of War on Land, Oct. 18, 1907; Hague Convention IX, Concerning Bombardment by Naval Forces in Time of War, Oct. 18, 1907, 36 Stat. 2314. *See generally* TJAGLCS, 2011 OPLAW HANDBOOK Ch. 2 ¶ VII (pp. 10-11) (full cite above).

⁹⁶⁵ Geneva Convention for the Amelioration of the Condition of the Wounded and Sick in Armed Forces in the Field, Aug. 12, 1949, 6 U.S.T. 3114, T.I.A.S. 3362, 75 U.N.T.S. 31; Geneva Convention for the Amelioration of the Condition of Wounded, Sick, and Shipwrecked Members, Aug. 12, 1949, 6 U.S.T. 3217, T.I.A.S. 3363, 75 U.N.T.S. 85; Geneva Convention Relative to the Treatment of Prisoners of War, Aug. 12, 1949, 6 U.S.T. 3316, T.I.A.S. 3364, 75 U.N.T.S. 135; Geneva Convention, Relative to the Protection of Civilian Persons in Time of War, Aug. 12, 1949, 6 U.S.T. 3516, T.I.A.S. 3365, 75 U.N.T.S. 287; Protocol Additional to the Geneva Conventions of 12 August 1949, and Relating to the Protection of Victims of Int'l. Armed Conflicts (Protocol I), June 8, 1977 (not ratified by the United States); Protocol Additional to the Geneva Conventions of 12 August 1949, and Relating to the Protection of Victims of Non- Int'l. Armed Conflicts (Protocol II), June 8, 1977 (not ratified by the United States). *See generally* TJAGLCS, 2011 OPLAW HANDBOOK Ch. 2 ¶ VII (pp. 10-11) (full cite above). *See also* DoD Law of War Manual, §§ 7.1-11.23, pp. 433-838 (full cite above).

⁹⁶⁶ 1954 Hague Convention for the Protection of Cultural Property in the Event of Armed Conflict, May 14, 1954, 249 U.N.T.S. 216; Convention on the Prohibition of the Development, Production and Stockpiling of Bacteriological (Biological) and Toxin Weapons and on Their Destruction, Apr. 10, 1972, 26 U.S.T. 583; Convention on Prohibitions or Restrictions of the Use of Certain Conventional Weapons Which May be Deemed to be Excessively Injurious or to Have Indiscriminate Effects, Oct. 10, 1980, 19 I.L.M. 1523; Convention on the Prohibition of the Development, Production, Stockpiling and Use of Chemical Weapons and on Their Destruction, Jan. 13, 1993, 32 I.L.M. 800. *See generally* TJAGLCS, 2011 OPLAW HANDBOOK Ch. 2 ¶ VII (pp. 14-16) (full cite above).

⁹⁶⁷ DoD Law of War Manual, § 1.10, p. 36 (full cite above).

⁹⁶⁸ CHAIRMAN OF THE JOINT CHIEFS OF STAFF INSTR. 3121.01B, STANDING RULES OF ENGAGEMENT/STANDING RULES FOR THE USE OF FORCE FOR U.S. FORCES (13 June 2005). *See generally* TJAGLCS, 2011 OPLAW HANDBOOK Ch. 5 (pp. 73-102) (full cite above); SAN REMO MANUAL ¶ 42 (full cite above); DoD Law of War Manual § 1.6.5, pp. 26-27 (full cite above).

⁹⁶⁹ Int'l. Committee of the Red Cross (ICRC), Air and naval warfare (Oct. 29, 2010), https://www.icrc.org/en/doc/war-and-law/conduct-hostilities/air-naval-warfare/overview-air-and-naval-warfare.htm.

⁹⁷⁰ DoD Law of War Manual, § 13.13, pp. 915-916 (full cite above). *See generally* U.S. NAVAL WAR COLLEGE INT'L. L. STUD.: THE LAW OF NAVAL OPERATIONS, 126 (Horace B. Robertson, Jr., ed., 1991), https://archive.org/details/lawofnavaloperat64robe/mode/2up.

⁹⁷¹ Center for Strategic & Int'l. Studies (CSIS), Int'l. Security Program, Global Threats and Regional Stability, *Contested Seas: Maritime Domain Awareness in Northern Europe*, p. 5 (Andrew Metrick & Kathleen H. Hicks, Mar. 28, 2018),

https://www.csis.org/programs/international-security-program/global-threats-and-regional-stability/contested-seas.

[972] U.S. NAVY, MARINE CORPS & COAST GUARD, THE COMMANDER'S HANDBOOK ON THE LAW OF NAVAL OPERATIONS, NWP 1-14M/MCTP 11-10B/COMDTPUB P5800.7A, ¶ 5.3.5 & Chapter 12 (pp. 5-4 & 12-1 to 12-4) (2017), www.jag.navy.mil/distrib/instructions/CDRs_HB_on_Law_of_Naval_Operations_AUG17.pdf.

[973] COMMANDER'S HANDBOOK, ¶¶ 12.1.1, 12.1.2 (p. 12-1) (full cite above). See also LOUISE DOSWALD-BECK, SAN REMO MANUAL ON INT'L. LAW APPLICABLE TO ARMED CONFLICTS AT SEA ¶¶ 109-111 (1994); Dept. of Defense Law of War Manual § 5.22.1, p. 320 (June 2015, updated Dec. 2016), https://www.hsdl.org/?view&did=797480.

[974] DoD Law of War Manual, § 5.25.2, p. 327-328 (full cite above).

[975] Int'l. Maritime Organization (IMO), English, About IMO, Conventions, List of Conventions, Convention on the Int'l. Regulations for Preventing Collisions at Sea, 1972 (COLREGs), http://www.imo.org/en/About/Conventions/ListOfConventions/Pages/COLREG.aspx.

[976] Convention on the Int'l. Regulations for Preventing Collisions at Sea, 1972 (COLREGs), Rules 20-23, https://treaties.un.org/doc/Publication/UNTS/Volume%201050/volume-1050-I-15824-English.pdf.

[977] Lieutenant Mike Madden, *Naval Chameleons? Re-evaluating the Legality of Deceptive Lighting under International Humanitarian Law*, 6 CANADIAN NAVAL REV. 4, 5 (2011), https://www.yumpu.com/en/document/read/33349661/full-issue-in-pdf-format-canadian-naval-review. *But see* COMMANDER'S HANDBOOK, ¶ 2.9.1 (pp. 2-15 to 2-16) (full cite above) (asserting that the COLREGs are applicable to warships).

[978] "The deceptive lighting of warships should not be categorized generally as either legal or illegal under IHL [International Humanitarian Law, aka Law of Armed Conflict (LOAC)]; rather, individual scenarios contemplating the use of deceptive lighting must be evaluated on a case-by-case basis in order to determine their conformity with IHL's perfidy laws." Madden, *Naval Chameleons*, pp. 6-8 (full cite above) (arguing that a warship rigging lights to appear to be a fishing vessel "would satisfy the definition of perfidy," but "a warship that alters its lighting configuration to deceive the enemy regarding its identity, but not its status as a power-driven vessel (that may or may not be a combatant), does not engage in perfidy. Such ruses do not cause the enemy to believe that the deceiving vessel is protected under IHL – they merely make the enemy's task of identifying combatants from within the class of power-driven vessels more difficult.").

[979] America's Navy, Forged by the Sea, News, *Enterprise Completes Deceptive Lighting Drill* (Tracey L. Whitley, Apr. 13, 2010), https://www.navy.mil/submit/display.asp?story_id=52563.

[980] The Maritime Executive, Intellectual Capital for Leaders, Article, *Camouflage: You Ain't Screen Nothin' Yet* (James Drennan, Sep. 18, 2014), https://www.maritime-executive.com/article/Camouflage-You-Aint-Screen-Nothin-Yet-2014-09-18.

[981] Center for Strategic & Int'l. Studies (CSIS), Int'l. Security Program, Global Threats and Regional Stability, *Contested Seas: Maritime Domain Awareness in Northern Europe*, p. 5 (Andrew Metrick & Kathleen H. Hicks, Mar. 28, 2018), https://www.csis.org/programs/international-security-program/global-threats-and-regional-stability/contested-seas.

[982] CSIS, MDA in Northern Europe, pp. 5-6 (full cite above).

[983] COMMANDER'S HANDBOOK, ¶ 12.1.2 (p. 12-1) (full cite above). *See also* SAN REMO MANUAL, ¶¶ 109-111 (full cite above); DoD Law of War Manual, § 5.22.1, p. 320 (full cite above).

[984] SAN REMO MANUAL, ¶¶ 93-104 (full cite above).

[985] The belligerent right of visit and search during an armed conflict is not unlike a Coastal State's right to enforce all of its resource-related laws and regulations in its EEZ during peacetime, including by boarding, inspecting, arresting, and instituting judicial proceedings against foreign flagged vessels (discussed in Chapter 8). It is also similar to a warship boarding any "stateless" or "quasi-stateless" ships it encounters on the High Seas, or any ship reasonably suspected of engaging in piracy in International Waters (discussed in Chapter 9). As discussed earlier in this Chapter, boardings may be conducted by U.S. Coast Guard or U.S. Navy boarding teams, including Navy SEALs (especially for opposed boardings). *See generally* Craig H. Allen, *The Peacetime Right of Approach and Visit and Effective Security Council Sanctions Enforcement at Sea*, 95 INT'L. L. STUD. 400 (2019), https://digital-commons.usnwc.edu/ils/vol95/iss1/13/.

[986] A Naval Blockade must generally satisfy 6 criteria:

1) Establishment: A Naval Blockade is established by a belligerent power, which is usually accomplished through some form of declaration or démarche (i.e., a formal written diplomatic protest) specifying the date it is to begin, its geographic limits, and the grace period granted neutral vessels to leave the designated area.

2) Notification: A belligerent State must provide notification of its Naval Blockade, usually either by publishing its declaration in news media and/or via a neutral State.

3) Effectiveness: The blockade itself must be effective. This does not mean the blockading force must be present 100% of the time, or that every possible avenue of approach must be covered/denied. However, it does require maintenance by a combination of surface, subsurface and air assets employing lawful means of warfare sufficient to render ingress and egress hazardous.

4) Impartiality: The belligerent State imposing a Naval Blockade must not discriminate either for or against vessels from any neutral Flag State, but must impose the Naval Blockade impartially.

5) Military Purpose: The belligerent State imposing a Naval Blockade must not have as its sole purpose the denial of goods essential for the survival of the civilian population.

6) Neutral Ports: Finally, the Naval Blockade must not bar access to, or departure from, any neutral ports. Indeed, neutral States retain the right to engage in commerce between one another, so long as that trade is not destined for the blockaded area. *See generally* COMMANDER'S HANDBOOK, ¶¶ 7.7 to 7.7.5 (pp. 7-10 to 7-12) (full cite above); SAN REMO MANUAL, ¶¶ 93-104 (full cite above). *See also* DoD Law of War Manual, § 13.10, pp. 903-908 (full cite above); U.S. Dept. of State Foreign Affairs Manual (FAM) and Handbook (FAH), 7 FAM 034, "*Demarches*" (2005), https://fam.state.gov/FAM/07FAM/07FAM0030.html. *See generally* U.S. Dept. of State FAM/FAH Search, https://fam.state.gov/search. *Cf.* COMMANDER'S HANDBOOK, ¶ 4.4.8 (p. 4-10) (full cite above) (contrasting the U.S. 1-time use of a "maritime quarantine" during the Cuban-missile crisis in 1962 with the much-more widely-recognized Naval Blockade).

[987] Reuters, *US senator says naval blockade of Iran should be considered* (Jim Wolf, Mar. 9, 2012), https://www.reuters.com/article/iran-usa-blockade/us-senator-says-naval-blockade-of-iran-should-be-considered-idUSL2E8E9F0Y20120309.

988 To make matters even worse, Senator Levin was arguing for the imposition of a Naval Blockade in order to enforce UN Security Council Resolution 1984 (9JUN2011) against Iran. However, UNSCR 1984 specifically said that the UNSC was acting under Article 41, non-military measures (i.e., economic sanctions against Iran over its nuclear program), and thus did NOT authorize the use of military force such as a Naval Blockade!

989 Int'l. Committee of the Red Cross (ICRC), Casebook, Self-defence, https://casebook.icrc.org/glossary/self-defence; U.S. NAVY, MARINE CORPS & COAST GUARD, THE COMMANDER'S HANDBOOK ON THE LAW OF NAVAL OPERATIONS, NWP 1-14M/MCTP 11-10B/COMDTPUB P5800.7A, ¶¶ 4.2, 4.4.1 to 4.4.1.1 (p. 4-2, 4-3 to 4-4) (2017), www.jag.navy.mil/distrib/instructions/CDRs_HB_on_Law_of_Naval_Operations_AUG17.pdf.

990 Dept. of Defense Law of War Manual §§ 1.11.4 & 18.12.3, pp. 45-46 & 197 (June 2015, updated Dec. 2016), https://www.hsdl.org/?view&did=797480; COMMANDER'S HANDBOOK, ¶ 5.1.1 (p. 5-1) (full cite above). States have sought to expand the 3 accepted international bases for using military force by claiming other bases for doing so, including:

- "humanitarian intervention" (e.g., NATO bombing Kosovo in 1999);
- "violation of a UN ceasefire" (e.g., U.S. invading Iraq in 2003 based upon a 1990 UNSCR, which is why subsequent UNSCRs have included sunset provisions, such as those authorizing States to combat piracy off the coast of Somalia, discussed in Chapter 9); and
- "Responsibility to Protect" (R2P) "the world's most vulnerable populations from the most heinous international crimes: genocide, war crimes, ethnic cleansing and crimes against humanity" (i.e., "When a state is 'manifestly failing' to protect its own populations then the international community has a responsibility to protect and may take collective action in a timely manner even to the point of using force as a last resort.").

Australian Red Cross, *International Humanitarian Law and the Responsibility to Protect: A handbook* p. 11 (2011), https://www.redcross.org.au/getmedia/d0338aa5-27c9-4de9-92ce-45e4c8f4d825/IHL-R2P-responsibility-to-protect.pdf.aspx. *See also* United Nations General Assembly Resolution (UNGAR) 60/1. 2005 World Summit Outcome ¶¶ 138-139, Responsibility to protect populations from genocide, war crimes, ethnic cleansing and crimes against humanity (Oct. 24, 2005), http://daccess-ods.un.org/access.nsf/Get?OpenAgent&DS=A/RES/60/1&Lang=E; United Nations, Past Conferences, Meetings and Events, The 2005 World Summit, https://www.un.org/en/events/pastevents/worldsummit_2005.shtml; Int'l. Coalition for the Responsibility to Protect (ICRtoP), Home, http://responsibilitytoprotect.org/; Washington Post, News, Monkey-cage, *The Responsibility to Protect doctrine is faltering. Here's why* (Dec. 8, 2015), https://www.washingtonpost.com/news/monkey-cage/wp/2015/12/08/the-responsibility-to-protect-doctrine-is-failing-heres-why/.

991 The New Republic, *Here's What International Law Says About Russia's Intervention in Ukraine* (Ashley Deeks, Mar. 2. 2014), https://newrepublic.com/article/116819/international-law-russias-ukraine-intervention. *See also* Nilüfer Oral, Ukraine v. The Russian Federation: *Navigating Conflict over Sovereignty under UNCLOS*, 97 INT'L. L. STUD. 478, 479, 481, 507 (2021), https://digital-commons.usnwc.edu/ils/vol97/iss1/25/ (noting that Ukraine initiated 3 cases against Russia under UNCLOS; "The common thread in these three

cases is the conflict between Ukraine and Russia over sovereignty in Crimea. ... The real issue in these cases is whether Ukraine or Russia has sovereignty over Crimea, but the legal analysis is skillfully couched within the language of UNCLOS. ... There is no doubt that Ukraine is utilizing UNCLOS and its compulsory dispute settlement mechanism to gain recognition of its sovereignty, even if implicitly, over Crimea through the international adjudicative process.").

[992] The Constitution of the United States, The Bill of Rights & All Amendments, https://constitutionus.com/.

[993] History.com, News, U.S. Presidents, Vietnam War Escalation, *How the Vietnam War Ratcheted Up Under 5 U.S. Presidents* (Jesse Greenspan, Mar. 14, 2019), https://www.history.com/news/us-presidents-vietnam-war-escalation.

[994] Public Law 93-148 (Nov. 7, 1973), http://www.gpo.gov/fdsys/pkg/STATUTE-87/pdf/STATUTE-87-Pg555.pdf.

[995] For example, the Democrat-controlled House of Representatives was worried about then-President Trump going to war with Iran, so it included Section 1229 in the Fiscal Year (FY) 2020 National Defense Authorization Act (NDAA), which is the Department of Defense's (DoD's) annual budget. Section 1229 recognized that if Iran acquired a nuclear weapon, that would pose a grave threat to the U.S. and its allies, and that Iran is a leading state sponsor of terrorism, but reminded the President that only Congress can authorize going to war. In fact, Section 1229 mentioned the WPR 4 times and mentioned that it is NOT authorizing the use of military force against Iran 4 times (lest the Trump administration try to make that argument). President Trump asked his Secretary of Defense to write a letter to the House Armed Services Committee (HASC) and the Senate Armed Services Committee (SASC) saying that Section 1229 undermined the President's authority to defend the U.S., and that it may actually embolden Iran to be more provocative. Still concerned about President Trump's intentions with regard to using military force against Iran, even the Republican-controlled Senate passed a resolution that included a "generalized statement declaring that Congress has the sole power to declare war. The resolution also direct[ed] Trump to terminate [the] use of military force against Iran or any part of its government without approval from Congress." Military.com, News, Headlines, *Senate Moves to Limit Trump on Military Force Against Iran* (Matthew Daly, Feb. 13, 2020), https://www.military.com/daily-news/2020/02/13/senate-moves-limit-trump-military-force-against-iran.html.

[996] Military.com, Join the Military, Service Choices, *What Are the Branches of the U.S. Military?*, https://www.military.com/join-armed-forces/us-military-branches-overview.html.

[997] United States Space Force, https://www.spaceforce.mil/.

[998] Gocoastguard.com, Home, About the Coast Guard, USCG: A Multi-Mission Force, https://www.gocoastguard.com/about-the-coast-guard/discover-our-roles-missions; COMMANDER'S HANDBOOK, ¶ 3.11 (p. 3-9) (full cite above).

.

[999] The Heritage Foundation, *2021 Index of U.S. Military Strength*, (Nov. 17, 2020), p. 326, https://www.heritage.org/military-strength/download-the-index.

[1000] Heritage, *2021 Index of U.S. Military Strength*, p. 326 (full cite above).

[1001] Heritage, *2021 Index of U.S. Military Strength*, p. 327 (full cite above).

[1002] Mark E. Rosen, *U.S. International Oceans Law and Policy Interests in the South China Sea Arbitration: Implications for the U.S. Administration in the South China Sea and Elsewhere*, 22 J. OF CHINESE POLIT. SCI. 251, online unnumbered pp. 2-3 (2017), https://www.readcube.com/articles/10.1007/s11366-017-9468-9.

[1003] The Heritage Foundation, *2021 Index of U.S. Military Strength*, (Nov. 17, 2020), pp. 331-332, https://www.heritage.org/military-strength/download-the-index.

[1004] War on the Rocks, *Rapid Deployment: The Army and American Strategy* (Robert Killebrew, Dec. 9, 2013), https://warontherocks.com/2013/12/rapid-deployment-the-army-and-american-strategy/; Defense Science Board Task Force on Mobility 82 (Sep. 2005), https://apps.dtic.mil/dtic/tr/fulltext/u2/a441079.pdf.

[1005] Heritage, *2021 Index of U.S. Military Strength*, p. 413 (full cite above).

[1006] Heritage, *2021 Index of U.S. Military Strength*, p. 412 (full cite above).

[1007] America's Navy, News Archive, *USS America's 'Blue-Green Team' Demonstrates Capability During Rim of the Pacific 2016* (Capt. Michael W. Baze, Fall 2016), https://www.public.navy.mil/surfor/lha6/Pages/USS-Americas-Blue-Green-Team-Demonstrates-Capability-During-Rim-of-the-Pacific-2016.aspx; U.S. NAVY, MARINE CORPS & COAST GUARD, THE COMMANDER'S HANDBOOK ON THE LAW OF NAVAL OPERATIONS, NWP 1-14M/MCTP 11-10B/COMDTPUB P5800.7A, ¶ 3.10.3 (p. 3-9) (2017), www.jag.navy.mil/distrib/instructions/CDRs_HB_on_Law_of_Naval_Operations_AUG17.pdf.

[1008] The Council on Foreign Relations describes itself as "an independent, nonpartisan membership organization, think tank, and publisher dedicated to being a resource for its members, government officials, business executives, journalists, educators and students, civic and religious leaders, and other interested citizens in order to help them better understand the world and the foreign policy choices facing the United States and other countries. Founded in 1921, CFR takes no institutional positions on matters of policy. Our goal is to start a conversation in this country about the need for Americans to better understand the world." Council on Foreign Relations, About CFR, Mission Statement, https://www.cfr.org/about.

[1009] Council on Foreign Relations, Center for Preventive Action, *Conflicts to Watch in 2021* (Paul B. Stares, Jan. 14, 2021), https://www.cfr.org/report/conflicts-watch-2021.

[1010] CFR, *Conflicts to Watch in 2021*, p. 2 (full cite above). Of 9 Tier I contingencies on the PPS 2021 survey, only 1 is considered both highly likely to occur, and to have a high impact on U.S. interests: heightened military tensions on the Korean peninsula due to North Korea's further development of nuclear weapons. CFR, *Conflicts to Watch in 2021*, p. 6 (full cite above).

[1011] The Washington Post, Global Opinions, *The coming era of U.S. security policy will be dominated by the Navy* (Robert D. Kaplan, Mar. 13, 2019), https://www.washingtonpost.com/opinions/2019/03/13/coming-era-us-security-policy-will-be-dominated-by-navy/?noredirect=on.

[1012] U.S. Dept. of State, Office of the Historian, *American Isolationism in the 1930s*, https://history.state.gov/milestones/1937-1945/american-isolationism.

[1013] The Washington Post, *The coming era of U.S. security policy* (full cite above).

[1014] Task & Purpose, Military Tech, Navy Aircraft Carrier History, *How Navy aircraft carriers have projected US military might all over the world for nearly a century* (Benjamin Brimelow, Oct. 6, 2020)), https://taskandpurpose.com/military-tech/navy-aircraft-carrier-history/. Another commentator implies that Naval dominance by English-speaking countries has changed the course of history: "Since [the battle of] Trafalgar, Anglo-Saxon command of the seas has facilitated the free flow of trade and commerce, and the rule of law across the maritime commons, which not coincidentally, has paralleled the greatest period of economic growth and technological development in human history." The National Interest, Security,

374

Americas, *The Impact of Great Power Competition on the U.S. Navy* (John S. Van Oudenaren, Apr. 10, 2019), https://nationalinterest.org/feature/impact-great-power-competition-us-navy-51877.

[1015]Military.com, Military News, *7 Things to Know About the Pentagon's New Plan for a 500-Ship Navy Fleet* (Gina Harkins, Oct. 7, 2020), https://www.military.com/daily-news/2020/10/07/5-things-know-about-pentagons-new-plan-500-ship-navy-fleet.html. Military.com, Military News, *Navy Forges Ahead with 500-Ship Plan in Wake of Esper's Firing* (Gina Harkins, Nov. 15, 2020), https://www.military.com/daily-news/2020/11/15/navy-forges-ahead-500-ship-plan-wake-of-espers-firing.html. When the author joined in 1994, the U.S. Navy had 400 ships.

[1016] The U.S. unilaterally withdrew from the Iran nuclear deal in May 2018, and President Trump designated the Islamic Revolutionary Guard Corps (IRGC) as a Foreign Terrorist Organization in April 2019. Statement from the President on the Designation of the Islamic Revolutionary Guard Corps as a Foreign Terrorist Organization (Apr. 8, 2019), https://www.whitehouse.gov/briefings-statements/statement-president-designation-islamic-revolutionary-guard-corps-foreign-terrorist-organization/. President Trump re-imposed economic sanctions on Iran in May 2019, and Iran responded by declaring "the United States as a terrorist sponsored government and ... all its affiliated [military] forces as terrorist groups." CNN, Politics, *Trump designates elite Iranian military force as a terrorist organization* (Nicole Gaouette, Apr. 8, 2019), https://www.cnn.com/2019/04/08/politics/iran-us-irgc-designation/index.html. Iran also increased its production and stockpile of low-enriched uranium, exceeding the limits set in the defunct 2015 Iran nuclear deal.

[1017] Most international commentators considered the seizure to be retaliation for Britain's seizure of the Iranian oil tanker M/V Grace 1 two weeks earlier because the Grace 1 was transporting crude oil to Syria in violation of European Union (EU) sanctions against Syria. CNN, Middle East, *'Alter your course,' Iranians warned before seizing UK-flagged ship* (Eliza Mackintosh, July 21, 2019), https://www.cnn.com/2019/07/21/middleeast/audio-recording-british-tanker-seized-iran-intl/index.html.

[1018] *See generally* National Geospatial-Intelligence Agency, Notice to Mariners, https://msi.nga.mil/NTM.

[1019] National Geospatial-Intelligence Agency, Notice to Mariners, NTMS 22/2020 at p. 44, https://msi.nga.mil/NTM.

[1020] *See, e.g.,* United Nations Convention on the Law of the Sea (UNCLOS) art. 36, Dec. 10, 1982, 1833 U.N.T.S. 397, https://www.un.org/Depts/los/convention_agreements/convention_overview_convention.htm; COMMANDER'S HANDBOOK, Appendix C (pp. C-1 to C-2) (full cite above) (citing the 2015 Maritime Advisory warning that Iran has been harassing U.S.-flagged ships in the Strait of Hormuz); THE FLETCHER SCHOOL OF LAW AND DIPLOMACY— TUFTS UNIVERSITY, LAW OF THE SEA, A POLICY PRIMER 26-27 (2017), https://sites.tufts.edu/lawofthesea/introduction/ (detailing aggressive actions taken by Iran against U.S. warships in the Arabian Gulf and Strait of Hormuz).

[1021] Military.com, Military News, *Coast Guard Cutter Fires Warning Shots at Charging Iranian Speedboats* (Stephen Losey, May 10, 2021), https://www.military.com/daily-news/2021/05/10/coast-guard-cutter-fires-warning-shots-charging-iranian-speedboats.html.

[1022] America's Navy, Forged by the Sea, *Marines Embark Merchant Vessel to Provide Security in Strait of Hormuz Transit* (Oct. 31, 2019),

https://www.navy.mil/submit/display.asp?story_id=111328&utm_source=phplist4
029&utm_medium=email&utm_content=HTML&utm_campaign=U.S.+Navy+Top
+Stories.

[1023] U.S. NAVY, MARINE CORPS & COAST GUARD, THE COMMANDER'S HANDBOOK ON THE
LAW OF NAVAL OPERATIONS, NWP 1-14M/MCTP 11-10B/COMDTPUB P5800.7A, ¶¶ 3.10
to 3.10.2 (pp. 3-8 to 3-9) (2017),
www.jag.navy.mil/distrib/instructions/CDRs_HB_on_Law_of_Naval_Operations
_AUG17.pdf.

[1024] Military.com, News, Headlines, *Marines Use Armored Vehicle to Defend Navy
Ship from Small Boats off Iranian Coast* (Gina Harkins, Aug. 15, 2019),
https://www.military.com/daily-news/2019/08/15/marines-use-armored-vehicle-
defend-navy-ship-small-boats-iranian-coast.html?ESRC=eb_190816.nl.

[1025] America's Navy, Forged by the Sea, *Marines Embark Merchant Vessel to Provide
Security in Strait of Hormuz Transit* (Oct. 31, 2019),
https://www.navy.mil/submit/display.asp?story_id=111328&utm_source=phplist4
029&utm_medium=email&utm_content=HTML&utm_campaign=U.S.+Navy+Top
+Stories.

[1026] "America and our allies should announce that decoy ships will be deployed
in the Strait of Hormuz and elsewhere there are threats to commercial shipping.
These ships would appear to be commercial ships and will fly the flags of their
nations, but the crews will be military and special forces who will only respond to
threats. Once a threat is made then the crews would respond with overwhelming
force against those seeking to hijack, kidnap or otherwise harm the crew or the ship.

"By deploying decoys, the Iranians will never know which is a true commercial
vessel and which may be a ship chock full of military personnel and weapons to
repel any threat.

"If America and our allies embarked on this strategy, I bet the aggression of the
Iranians would cease immediately. Iran is a bully and a coward. While they seek to
provoke, the last thing they want is a confrontation. If the Iranians respect
international laws and conventions of free passage, then there will be no incidents.
If they choose the wrong victim, they will be sorely mistaken." Fox News, Opinion,
*Bradley Blakeman: Iran has been hostile to ships near the Strait of Hormuz – It's time for
THIS solution* (Bradley Blakeman, Aug. 6, 2019),
https://www.foxnews.com/opinion/bradley-blakeman-iran-hostile-ships-strait-
of-hormuz-solution.

[1027] COMMANDER'S HANDBOOK, ¶ 12.1.2 (p. 12-1) (full cite above). *See also* LOUISE
DOSWALD-BECK, SAN REMO MANUAL ON INT'L. LAW APPLICABLE TO ARMED CONFLICTS AT SEA
¶¶ 109-111 (1994). *See also* Dept. of Defense Law of War Manual § 5.22.1, p. 320 (June
2015, updated Dec. 2016), https://www.hsdl.org/?view&did=797480.

[1028] "Iran's Revolutionary Guard said it had shot down an 'intruding American
spy drone' after it entered into the country's territory ...." CNN, World, *Iran shoots
down US drone aircraft, raising tensions further in Strait of Hormuz* (Joshua Berlinger,
Mohammed Tawfeeq, Barbara Starr, Shirzad Bozorgmehr & Frederik Pleitgen, June
20, 2019), https://www.cnn.com/2019/06/20/middleeast/iran-drone-claim-hnk-
intl/index.html. A spokesman for the U.S. regional commander confirmed that: "A
U.S. Navy Broad Area Maritime Surveillance (or BAMS-D) ISR [Intelligence,
Surveillance and Reconnaissance] aircraft was shot down by an Iranian surface-to-
air missile system while operating in international airspace over the Strait of
Hormuz .... Iranian reports that the aircraft was over Iran are false. This was an
unprovoked attack on a U.S. surveillance asset in international airspace." USNI

News, Home, Aviation, VIDEO: *Iran Shoots Down Navy Surveillance Drone in 'Unprovoked Attack'* (Sam LaGrone, June 20, 2019), https://news.usni.org/2019/06/20/iran-shoots-down-120m-navy-surveillance-drone-in-unprovoked-attack-u-s-disputes-claims-it-was-over-iranian-airspace; Breaking Defense, Air Warfare, Threats, *US: Iran Shoots Down Global Hawk; Second Drone Down This Month* (Paul McLeary, June 20, 2019), https://breakingdefense.com/2019/06/us-iran-shoots-down-global-hawk-second-drone-down-this-month/. The BAMS-D is the Navy version of the RQ-4A Global Hawk High-Altitude, Long, Endurance (HALE) UAV costing $110M and designed to collect IMINT (Imagery Intelligence).

[1029] U.S. Central Command, Home, Media, Statements, Statements View, *U.S. Air Forces Central Command Statement on the Shoot Down of a U.S. RQ-4* (June 20, 2019), https://www.centcom.mil/MEDIA/STATEMENTS/Statements-View/Article/1882519/us-air-forces-central-command-statement-on-the-shoot-down-of-a-us-rq-4/.

[1030] COMMANDER'S HANDBOOK, ¶¶ 2.2.2-2.2.3, 2.4.2 (pp. 2-2, 2-4) (full cite above); THE FLETCHER SCHOOL OF LAW AND DIPLOMACY—TUFTS UNIVERSITY, LAW OF THE SEA, A POLICY PRIMER 37-38 (2017), https://sites.tufts.edu/lawofthesea/introduction/.

[1031] As discussed in Chapter 2, even though the U.S. is not party to UNCLOS (and therefore is not bound by UNCLOS as a matter of treaty law), the U.S. follows UNCLOS navigational regimes (i.e., the rules of the various maritime zones, including Transit Passage through International Straits) as a matter of Customary International Law (CIL). TUFTS, LAW OF THE SEA, p. 10 (full cite above). As discussed in Chapter 3, although Iran is also not party to UNCLOS (and therefore is not bound by UNCLOS as a matter of treaty law, having signed but not yet ratified UNCLOS), Article 18 of the Vienna Convention on the Law of Treaties (VCLT) imposes a requirement on treaty signatories (even before ratification) to "refrain from acts which would defeat the object and purpose of a treaty." Vienna Convention on the Law of Treaties (VCLT) art. 18, May 23, 1969, 1155 U.N.T.S. 331. Although the United States is not a party to the VCLT, it considers the VCLT to represent customary international law. Sean D. Murphy, The George Wash. Univ. Law Sch.: "Should the U.S. Join the International Criminal Court?" A Moderated Panel Discussion, Feb. 13, 2006. *See also* Letter Of Transmittal Forwarding The 1982 UN Law Of The Sea Convention To The United States Senate, DOS Commentary p. 17 (William J. Clinton, Oct. 7, 1994) (S. Treaty Doc. 103-39), https://www.foreign.senate.gov/imo/media/doc/treaty_103-39.pdf (noting that "[u]nder customary international law, as reflected in ... the Vienna Convention on the Law of Treaties (92nd Congress; 1st Session, Senate Executive 'L')").

[1032] United Nations Convention on the Law of the Sea (UNCLOS) arts. 38(2), 39(1)(c), Dec. 10, 1982, 1833 U.N.T.S. 397, https://www.un.org/Depts/los/convention_agreements/convention_overview_convention.htm; COMMANDER'S HANDBOOK, ¶ 2.5.3.2 (pp. 2-7 to 2-8) (full cite above).

[1033] UNCLOS, art. 34(1) (full cite above).

[1034] *But see* TUFTS, LAW OF THE SEA, p. 22 (full cite above) (positing that "[d]ue to the sovereign immunity of warships ... the degree to which a coastal State can force a warship to exit its territorial waters in this situation is not clear.").

[1035] UNCLOS, art. 42(5) (full cite above).

[1036] The National Interest, *Chinese Scientists Want to Conduct Research in U.S. Waters—Should Washington Let Them?* (Ryan Martinson & Peter Dutton, Nov. 4, 2018), https://nationalinterest.org/feature/chinese-scientists-want-conduct-research-us-waters%E2%80%94should-washington-let-them-34997.

[1037] Popular Mechanics, Military, Navy Ships, *Here Is Every Aircraft Carrier in the World* (Kyle Mizokami, Jan. 25, 2016), https://www.popularmechanics.com/military/navy-ships/g2412/a-global-roundup-of-aircraft-carriers/.

[1038] Military.com, Military News, *As China Declares War with US Inevitable, Army General Highlights Need for Fighting Vehicles* (Matthew Cox, Mar. 11, 2021), https://www.military.com/daily-news/2021/03/11/china-declares-war-us-inevitable-army-general-highlights-need-fighting-vehicles.html?ESRC=eb_210312.nl.

[1039] China also seeks to have a "world-class military" (by the end of the year 2049) that could compete with the U.S. military. China already has the largest Navy in the world, produces the most ships in the world (by tonnage), is increasing its shipbuilding capacity, and is already "nearly self-sufficient for all [its] shipbuilding needs." U.S. Dept. of Defense, Office of the Secretary of Defense, *Annual Report To Congress: Military and Security Developments Involving the People's Republic of China 2020*, pp. vi-vii, 143, https://media.defense.gov/2020/Sep/01/2002488689/-1/-1/1/2020-DOD-CHINA-MILITARY-POWER-REPORT-FINAL.PDF.

[1040] Forbes, Editors' Pick, *Why China Can't Target U.S. Aircraft Carriers* (Loren Thompson, Aug. 9, 2019), https://www.forbes.com/sites/lorenthompson/2019/08/09/why-china-cant-target-u-s-aircraft-carriers/?utm_source=Sailthru&utm_medium=email&utm_campaign=EBB%2008.12.19&utm_term=Editorial%20-%20Early%20Bird%20Brief#4ed2e325716a. *But see* The Sunday Times, *US 'would lose any war' fought in the Pacific with China* (Michael Evans, May 16, 2020), https://www.thetimes.co.uk/article/us-would-lose-any-war-fought-in-the-pacific-with-china-7j90bjs5b.

[1041] Navy Times, News, Your Navy, *The Navy sends a carrier back to Russia's Arctic haunts* (Geoff Ziezulewicz & David B. Larter, Oct. 19, 2018), https://www.navytimes.com/news/your-navy/2018/10/19/the-navy-sends-a-carrier-back-to-russias-arctic-haunts/. *See also* America's Navy, Forged by the Sea, News, *U.S., and British Ships Conduct Anti-submarine Exercise Above Arctic Circle* (May 1, 2020), https://www.navy.mil/submit/display.asp?story_id=112823&utm_source=phplist5567&utm_medium=email&utm_content=HTML&utm_campaign=Headlines.

[1042] U.S. NAVY, MARINE CORPS & COAST GUARD, THE COMMANDER'S HANDBOOK ON THE LAW OF NAVAL OPERATIONS, NWP 1-14M/MCTP 11-10B/COMDTPUB P5800.7A, ¶ 4.4.2 (p. 4-5) (2017), www.jag.navy.mil/distrib/instructions/CDRs_HB_on_Law_of_Naval_Operations_AUG17.pdf.

[1043] Navy Times, *The Navy sends a carrier back to Russia's Arctic haunts* (full cite above). *See also* America's Navy, Forged by the Sea, News, *USS Donald Cook Applies Lessons for Second Trip to Arctic* (Sarah Claudy & Teresa Meadows, May 14, 2020), https://www.navy.mil/submit/display.asp?story_id=112964&utm_source=phplist5723&utm_medium=email&utm_content=HTML&utm_campaign=Headlines.

[1044] COMMANDER'S HANDBOOK, ¶ 4.4.2 (p. 4-5) (full cite above).

[1045] Elliot L. Richardson, Power, Mobility and the Law of the Sea, J. FOREIGN AFF., 902, 905 (1980).

CHAPTER 11: EXCESSIVE MARITIME CLAIMS & FREEDOM OF NAVIGATION PROGRAMS

"Joining the [Law of the Sea] convention will protect us from ongoing and persistent efforts on the part of a number of nations ... to advance their national laws and set precedents that could restrict our maritime activities, particularly within the bounds of their exclusive economic zones."
—Admiral (retired) James A. Winnefeld Jr.

A LTHOUGH SOME UNCLOS PROVISIONS ARE INHERENTLY SUBJECTIVE (e.g., the situations where a Coastal State is justified in drawing straight baselines, discussed in Chapter 2), most UNCLOS provisions are fairly definitive, especially those dealing with maritime zones (e.g., the 12 nautical mile (nm)

Territorial Sea discussed in Chapter 3, and the 200 nm Exclusive Economic Zone discussed in Chapter 4). Yet numerous States make maritime claims that appear excessive vis-à-vis a plain reading of the relevant UNCLOS provisions, and therefore difficult to justify as a matter of good faith treaty interpretation.[1046]

As mentioned in Chapter 2, the easiest place to find each State's maritime claims is in the online U.S. Department of Defense (DoD) Maritime Claims Reference Manual, regularly maintained by the U.S. Navy Judge Advocate General's (JAG) Corps' National Security Law (NSL) division (aka Code 10).[1047] A more in-depth, though less regularly updated, reference is the U.S. Department of State Limits in the Seas series.[1048] These two sets of references summarize the maritime claims of each of the 150 Coastal States (i.e., States with a coastline or "littoral States"), and provide helpful links to the underlying domestic statutes, regulations, decrees, etc. A detailed review of these two references reveals that the U.S. believes that just over half of the Coastal States (78 out of 150) have excessive maritime claims. As this Chapter will discuss, there are numerous examples of excessive maritime claims for each maritime zone.

As discussed in Chapter 2, a Coastal State may use "straight baselines" in order to reduce the complexity (i.e., simplify) irregular coastlines. As discussed in Chapter 4, an Archipelagic State (comprised of a group of islands that satisfies UNCLOS' objective, two-part test) may draw "straight archipelagic baselines joining the outermost points of the outermost islands."[1049] Excessive straight baseline claims, therefore:

> ➤ Are drawn in situations where there are no fringing islands or a deeply indented coastline that would justify using a straight baseline under Article 7(1) of UNCLOS;

> ➤ Deviate from the general direction of the coastline, contrary to Article 7(3) of UNCLOS; or

> Include straight archipelagic baselines that are too long, contrary to Article 47(2) of UNCLOS.

Thus, excessive baseline claims are drawn from something other than the low-water line (i.e., the normal baseline in accordance with Article 5 of UNCLOS), without adequate justification. From a U.S. "strict constructionist" perspective, *most Coastal States' straight baseline claims lack a valid basis.*[1050] *A number of States also claim "historic waters" or "historic bays" as lying inside their baselines, again without adequate justification* (discussed in Chapter 2).[1051] Each year, the U.S. and other States contest many of these excessive baseline claims via numerous Freedom of Navigation (FON) operations,[1052] which this Chapter will discuss subsequently.

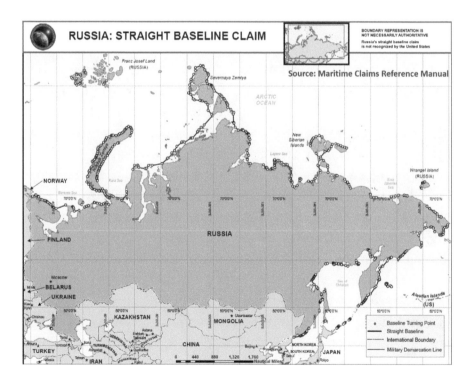

RUSSIA: STRAIGHT BASELINE CLAIM

Source: Maritime Claims Reference Manual

It would appear to be conceptually impossible to misread the plain language in Article 3 of UNCLOS regarding the breadth of the Territorial Sea (discussed in Chapter 3):

Every State has the right to establish the breadth of its territorial sea up to a limit not exceeding 12 nautical miles, measured from baselines determined in accordance with this Convention.[1053]

Fortunately, "for the most part aberrant and vague area claims and claims beyond permissible limits for the territorial sea and economic zone seem to be slowly receding as the Convention takes greater hold each and every year."[1054] Thus, "[s]ince 1983, State practice in asserting territorial sea claims has largely coalesced around the 12 mile maximum breadth set by the Convention."[1055] Seventeen Coastal States have "rolled back" their Territorial Seas to 12 nautical miles (nm): Albania (from 15 nm),[1056] Angola (from 20 nm),[1057] Argentina[1058] and Benin[1059] (each from 200 nm), Cabo Verde (from 100 nm),[1060] Cameroon (from 50 nm),[1061] Republic of the Congo,[1062] Ecuador,[1063] El Salvador[1064] and Liberia[1065] (each from 200 nm), Mauritania (from 70 nm),[1066] Nicaragua (from 200 nm),[1067] Nigeria (from 30 nm),[1068] Panama[1069] and Sierra Leone (each from 200 nm),[1070] Syria (from 35 nm),[1071] and Tanzania (from 50 nm).[1072] *Yet there are still a few States that continue to make Territorial Sea claims in excess of 12 nm.* Although the small African nation of Togo claims a 30 nm Territorial Sea,[1073] more egregious examples are Peru[1074] and Somalia,[1075] each of which claims a 200 nm Territorial Sea, and the Republic of the Philippines, whose Territorial Sea claims vary by location up to 285 nm![1076] Of these excessive Territorial Sea claims, only Peru's claim is potentially defensible, as Peru has neither signed nor ratified UNCLOS, and thus is not bound by it as a matter of treaty law. And only the Philippines purports to defend its excessive Territorial Sea claim based upon "historical" title pre-dating UNCLOS. As we can see from the following notional chart, such excessive Territorial Sea claims purport to claim sovereignty over a wide swath of ocean that otherwise would be considered international waters, over which the Coastal State normally would exercise less and less sovereignty and control the further one travels from land (as discussed in Chapter 2).

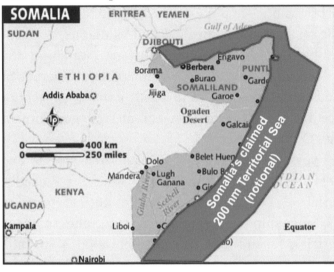

Another type of excessive maritime claim vis-à-vis Territorial Seas relates to Coastal States' purported limits on ships conducting Innocent Passage. Although a Coastal State has the right to adopt laws and regulations related to Innocent Passage pursuant to Article 21 of UNCLOS, there is no support for a Coastal State requiring prior notification before foreign ships can conduct Innocent Passage, let alone prior permission/consent from the Coastal State.[1077] This is clear from the negotiating history of UNCLOS. A vote was taken to add the prior notification requirement for Innocent Passage, and the proposal was rejected.[1078] Requiring either prior notification or prior permission for Innocent Passage would hamper Innocent Passage in violation of UNCLOS Article 24's admonition not to hamper Innocent Passage. Yet *quite a few*

383

States purport to require prior <u>notification</u> before foreign warships or other foreign vessels may engage in Innocent Passage through their Territorial Seas:

> ➢ **Warships:** Argentina,[1079] Croatia (24-hour prior notice and no more than 3 warships concurrently),[1080] Denmark,[1081] Egypt,[1082] Estonia,[1083] India,[1084] Libya,[1085] Montenegro (24-hour prior notice and limitation on the number of warships concurrently),[1086] Slovenia (24-hour prior notice and must use designated sea lanes or traffic separation schemes),[1087] and Vietnam.[1088]

> ➢ **Warships and other vessels:** Guyana (warships and ships carrying nuclear or other inherently dangerous or noxious substances),[1089] and South Korea (3-day prior notice for warships or non-commercial government vessels).[1090]

> ➢ **Other vessels:** Djibouti (nuclear-powered vessels and vessels carrying nuclear or other radioactive material),[1091] Pakistan (supertankers, nuclear-powered ships, and ships carrying nuclear or other noxious materials),[1092] and UAE (nuclear-powered ships and ships carrying nuclear, radioactive, "or other inherently dangerous or noxious substances").[1093]

Lest the reader believe that "nuclear-powered vessel" is completely synonymous with "warship," the list of over 160 nuclear-powered vessels in the world currently includes warships (primarily submarines and aircraft carriers), Russian icebreakers, and 1 Russian freighter (for delivering goods to Arctic regions).[1094]

Even more egregious than those States which purport to require prior <u>notification</u> before foreign warships or other foreign vessels may engage in Innocent Passage through their Territorial Seas, are those ***States that purport to require prior <u>permission/consent</u>***

before foreign warships or other foreign vessels may engage in Innocent Passage through their Territorial Seas:

> **Warships:** Albania,[1095] Algeria (15-day prior notice),[1096] Antigua and Barbuda,[1097] Bangladesh,[1098] Barbados,[1099] Burma/Myanmar,[1100] Chile (reciprocal for vessels of Flag States which require prior permission/consent for warships),[1101] China,[1102] Colombia,[1103] Latvia (30 days and special coordination for foreign warships with nuclear propulsion or nuclear weapons),[1104] Lithuania (only requires prior permission for Innocent Passage by foreign warships on a reciprocal basis—i.e., if the foreign Flag State imposes such a requirement),[1105] North Korea,[1106] Pakistan,[1107] Romania,[1108] Sierra Leone,[1109] Somalia,[1110] Sri Lanka,[1111] St. Vincent and Grenadines,[1112] Sudan,[1113] UAE,[1114] and Vanuatu.[1115]

> **Warships and other vessels:** Ecuador (warships, nuclear-powered ships, or ships transporting radioactive, toxic, hazardous or harmful substances),[1116] Iran (warships/ submarines, nuclear-powered ships and any ship carrying nuclear or other dangerous or noxious substances),[1117] Maldives (warships, nuclear-powered ships and ships carrying any nuclear or other inherently dangerous or noxious substances),[1118] Malta (warships, nuclear-powered vessels, and ships carrying nuclear or

other inherently dangerous or noxious substances),[1119] Oman (warships, submarines, nuclear-powered vessels, and vessels carrying dangerous substances),[1120] Seychelles (warships and nuclear-powered or nuclear-carrying cargo ships),[1121] Syria (warships and submarines, and ships of a "dangerous nature," defined as "nuclear-powered ships or ships carrying materials dangerous for the environment or prejudicial to national security"),[1122] and Yemen (warships and nuclear-powered ships).[1123]

➢ **Other vessels:** Egypt (nuclear-powered ships and ships carrying nuclear or other inherently dangerous and noxious substances),[1124] Estonia (nuclear-powered ships and ships carrying nuclear weapons or radioactive substances),[1125] Malaysia (nuclear-powered vessels or vessels carrying nuclear material),[1126] Samoa (vessels carrying nuclear/dangerous cargoes),[1127] and Saudi Arabia (nuclear-powered vessels and vessels carrying nuclear materials, dangerous, or noxious substances).[1128]

The height of hubris is reached by those *States which outright prohibit certain vessels from engaging in Innocent Passage through their Territorial Seas:*

➢ **Dominican Republic** (ships carrying radioactive or toxic cargo),[1129]

➢ **Estonia** (ships carrying certain hazardous substances),[1130]

➢ **Haiti** ("any vessel transporting wastes, refuse, residues or any other materials likely to endanger the health of the country's population and to pollute the marine, air and land environment"),[1131]

➢ **Italy** (prohibits vessels 10,000 tons or more carrying oil and other pollutants from exercising the right of

Innocent Passage through the island Strait of Messina (discussed in Chapter 3),[1132]

> **Mexico** (nuclear-powered and nuclear-armed ships),[1133]
> **Romania** (ships carrying nuclear, chemical or other weapons of mass destruction or "any other products prohibited by the laws of Romania"),[1134]
> **Saudi Arabia** (claims that Innocent Passage does not apply in Territorial Seas when a High Seas or EEZ route exists which is equally suitable regarding navigational and hydrographic features),[1135]

> **Somalia** (prohibits passage by vessels of States not recognized by Somalia),[1136] and
> **UAE** (vessels over 20 years old).[1137]

Perhaps because the right of Transit Passage through International Straits is a new treaty right established by UNCLOS, or perhaps because there are only about 200 International Straits in the world (as discussed in Chapter 3), there appear to be only 4 remaining[1138] excessive maritime claims related to International Straits:

> **Argentina** (requires prior notice by warships before conducting Transit Passage through the Straits of Magellan),[1139]
> **Iran** (declared that "only parties to the Convention shall be entitled to benefit from the contractual rights created therein," which would limit the right of Transit Passage in the Strait of Hormuz to the 168 State Parties to UNCLOS, which does not yet include the U.S.),[1140]
> **Oman** (claims to only permit Innocent Passage through the Strait of Hormuz instead of Transit Passage),[1141] and

➢ **Sweden** (restricts Transit Passage in Aaland Strait to surface traffic only).[1142]

Since the U.S. view is that only 19 States potentially qualify as Archipelagic States under the rigorous definition in UNCLOS (discussed in Chapter 4), it is not surprising that there are also only 4 excessive maritime claims related to Archipelagic Waters:

➢ **Antigua and Barbuda** (prior authorization before warships may enter Archipelagic Waters),[1143]

➢ **Dominican Republic** (does not recognize Archipelagic Sea Lanes Passage),[1144]

➢ **Indonesia** (only provided partial list of Archipelagic Sea Lanes, and limits other lanes to Innocent Passage),[1145] and

➢ **Maldives** (requires prior permission for overflight of Archipelagic Waters by foreign military aircraft).[1146]

The unpopular Contiguous Zone (claimed by only 90 of 150 Coastal States)[1147] generates a surprisingly large number of excessive maritime claims (almost as many as excessive EEZ claims, discussed next). As discussed in Chapter 4, a Coastal State may enforce its Fiscal, Immigration, Sanitation and Customs (FISC) laws out to 24 nm, but only if the effects of the legal violations are felt either within the Coastal State's land territory or Territorial Seas (aka National Waters). Yet Sierra Leone tries to prevent infringement of its environmental laws in addition to its FISC laws.[1148] Another example is North Korea, which established "military boundary zones" up to 50 nm in the East Sea/Sea of Japan and up to 200 nm in the West/Yellow Sea, where it prohibits foreign military vessels and planes, and requires prior permission for civilian ships and planes (not including fishing boats).[1149] A number of other States claim similar "security zones" or claim jurisdiction over "security matters":[1150] Bangladesh,[1151] Burma/Myanmar,[1152] Cambodia,[1153] China,[1154] Colombia,[1155] Egypt,[1156] Haiti,[1157] India,[1158]

Iran,[1159] Nicaragua (15-day prior notice for entry of warships and military aircraft, and 7-day prior notice for entry of civilian vessels into the security zone),[1160] Pakistan,[1161] Saudi Arabia,[1162] Sri Lanka,[1163] Sudan,[1164] Syria,[1165] UAE,[1166] Venezuela,[1167] and Yemen.[1168]

There is no basis in the Convention, or other sources of international law, for coastal States to establish security zones in peacetime that would restrict the exercise of non-resource-related high seas freedoms beyond the territorial sea. Accordingly, the United States does not recognize the peacetime validity of any claimed security or military zone seaward of the territorial sea which purports to restrict or regulate the high seas freedoms of navigation and overflight, as well as other lawful uses of the sea..[1169]

As discussed in Chapter 4, the Exclusive Economic Zone (EEZ) is a new maritime zone created by UNCLOS wherein Coastal States possess complete ownership of all resources[1170] in a huge swath (200 nm from the baselines, representing 38% of the world's oceans).[1171] Otherwise, as discussed in Chapter 2, outside the 12 nm Territorial Seas (i.e., National Waters and National Airspace) are International Waters[1172] and International Airspace,[1173] wherein other States enjoy all High Seas freedoms that are not resource-

related, including the freedom of navigation by ships, the freedom of overflight by aircraft, and the right to lay and repair submarine cables and pipelines.[1174]

Thus, UNCLOS balances the Coastal State's economic rights in the EEZ with protecting other States' freedoms in International Waters,[1175] which was part of the UNCLOS "package deal."[1176] As discussed in Chapter 4, there exists a double-edged "due regard" standard in the EEZ, with Coastal States having due regard for the rights of other States (specifically non-resource-related High Seas freedoms),[1177] and other States having due regard to the rights of the Coastal State in managing its resources in the EEZ.[1178]

Although this seems like a fairly clear division of rights and responsibilities in the EEZ (i.e., all resources belong to the Coastal State, but other States can still exercise all other High Seas freedoms), "[t]he EEZ is the most misunderstood of all the maritime zones by policymakers in States around the world."[1179] More specifically, a number of States have passed domestic legislation that interferes with High Seas Freedoms in their EEZs.[1180] Yet deliberations at the Third United Nations Conference on the Law of the Sea (which culminated in UNCLOS) expressly rejected Coastal States seeking to assert any jurisdiction in their EEZs other than ownership of all resources.[1181] This rejection of Coastal State control in the EEZ is most likely due to the fact that over 50% of all Coastal States are "zone-locked," in that they can only reach the High Seas by navigating through the EEZs of neighboring States. "Understandably, this large block of coastal nations does not want to be turned into the functional equivalent of land-locked states with access controlled by their neighbors."[1182]

Moreover, Article 58(2) specifically incorporates certain aspects of the High Seas regime,[1183] including Article 89, which prohibits States from seeking to assert their sovereignty over the High Seas, and therefore (by extension) over their EEZs (other than ownership of all resources).[1184]

One High Seas Freedom that is particularly contentious is conducting military operations (e.g., military exercises) in a foreign State's EEZ. Yet during the UNCLOS negotiations, "[m]ost nations agreed with the position advocated by the major maritime powers, that '[m]ilitary operations, exercises and activities have always been regarded as internationally lawful uses of the sea. The right to conduct such activities will continue to be enjoyed by all States in the exclusive economic zone.'"[1185] "Dissatisfied with the outcome of the [UNCLOS] negotiations, however, a few nations have sought to unilaterally expand their control in the EEZ, particularly by imposing restrictions on military operations and other lawful activities. These efforts impinge on traditional uses of the oceans by other States and are inconsistent with international law and State practice."[1186]

Thus, the most common infringement into High Seas freedoms in the EEZ are Coastal States which purport to require prior consent for foreign States to conduct military exercises: Bangladesh,[1187] Brazil,[1188] China,[1189] Dominican Republic,[1190] Ecuador,[1191] India,[1192] Iran,[1193] Malaysia,[1194] Pakistan,[1195] Thailand,[1196] Uruguay,[1197] and Venezuela.[1198] For example, the statement by the People's Republic of China's Ministry of Foreign Affairs spokesman (made in response to planned military exercises by the U.S. and South Korea in the Yellow Sea) is representative of restrictive views towards military activities in the EEZ: "We hold a consistent and clear-cut stance on the issue. We oppose any party to take any military actions in our exclusive economic zone without permission."[1199] Similarly, India objects to U.S. "Freedom of Navigation" operations (FONOPs, discussed subsequently in this Chapter) in its EEZ without prior consent.[1200]

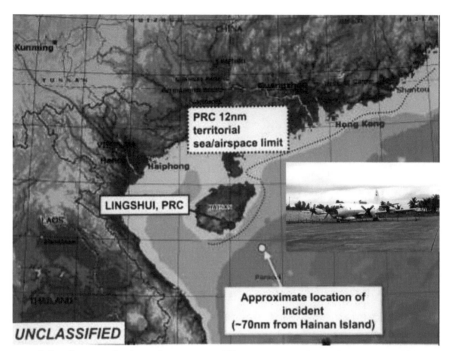

PRC 12nm territorial sea/airspace limit

LINGSHUI, PRC

Approximate location of incident (~70nm from Hainan Island)

China's restrictive views on military operations led to a collision between a Chinese fighter jet and an American reconnaissance airplane in China's EEZ. In 2001, a U.S. EP-3 reconnaissance airplane was collecting "Signals Intelligence" (SIGINT) 70 nm away from China's Hainan Island. Although China owns all resources in its EEZ, under UNCLOS other States (including the U.S.) enjoy all High Seas freedoms that are not resource-related, including the freedom of overflight by aircraft (including military aircraft), and military operations as a traditional use of the oceans. A People's Liberation Army (PLA) F-8 fighter jet came out to intercept the American spy plane, as is typical (in order to ensure that the foreign military aircraft is not beginning an armed attack, and to harass the spy plane). The Chinese F-8 got too close and bumped into the American EP-3. The Chinese F-8 crashed, killing its pilot. The American pilot was barely able to control his EP-3, and was forced to conduct an emergency landing on Hainan Island, as permitted by international law.[1201] China detained the 24-member crew for 11 days, stripped all high-tech SIGINT gear from the American spy plane, and only agreed to release the damaged American aircraft after the U.S. promised to dismantle it instead of flying it off the island—all counter to international law.[1202]

China's Minister of Foreign Affairs said that the collision occurred above China's EEZ, that the U.S. plane threatened China's national security interests,[1203] and called for the U.S. to apologize. The U.S. emphasized its right to operate in airspace above the EEZ, and continues to fly these intelligence collection missions over China's EEZ today.[1204] Although China continues to harass ships and aircraft conducting military operations in its EEZ, China has begun to conduct similar military operations in other States' EEZs![1205]

The remaining excessive EEZ claims run the gamut from the types of excessive maritime claims already discussed (e.g., prior notice, prior consent, etc.), to novel ones:

> **Australia** (EEZ claims infringe on Antarctic territory),[1206]
> **China** (claims security jurisdiction in the EEZ, and prior approval of all surveying and mapping activities in the EEZ),[1207]
> **Costa Rica** (requires a permit for a foreign fishing vessel to merely sail through the EEZ),[1208]
> **Ecuador** (prior authorization for warships, nuclear-powered, or ships transporting radioactive, toxic, hazardous or harmful substances to enter the EEZ),[1209]
> **Guyana** (claims authority to establish sea lanes, traffic separation schemes, etc., for foreign ships to pass through designated areas),[1210]
> **Haiti** (prohibits entry into EEZ of "any vessel transporting wastes, refuse, residues or any other materials likely to endanger the health of the country's

population and to pollute the marine, air and land environment."),[1211]

➤ **India** (requires 24-hour prior notice from vessels entering its EEZ with cargoes "including dangerous goods and chemicals, oil, noxious liquid and harmful substances and radioactive material"),[1212]

➤ **Maldives** (requires prior permission for all foreign vessels to enter its EEZ),[1213]

➤ **North Korea** (claims that "[n]o foreign person, vessel or aircraft may ... take photographs, investigate, ... [or] survey" in the EEZ without prior approval),[1214]

➤ **Pakistan** (foreign state aircraft flying through the EEZ must file flight plans with civil aviation authority),[1215] and

➤ **Seychelles** (any act of pollution qualifies as prejudicial to peace, good order and security).[1216]

The final area of excessive maritime claims is the Continental Shelf, which (as discussed in Chapter 6) is the seabed lying beneath the EEZ.[1217] Just as a Coastal State owns all economic resources in the water column out to 200 nm (i.e., in its EEZ), a Coastal State owns all economic resources on the seabed beneath it (i.e., on the Continental Shelf) out to 200 nm, including mineral resources (e.g., oil, gas, and metals), other non-living resources (e.g., hydrothermal vents), and sedentary species (e.g., sponges).[1218] States negotiating the text of UNCLOS devoted eight different UNCLOS articles to protecting the laying and repair of submarine cables and pipelines, including the right of all States to lay submarine cables and pipelines in the EEZ,[1219] and on the Continental Shelf of another State,[1220] subject only to the *Coastal State's consent regarding the course of pipelines*, and due regard to existing submarine cables and pipelines already in place on the Continental Shelf, including the ability to repair them.[1221]

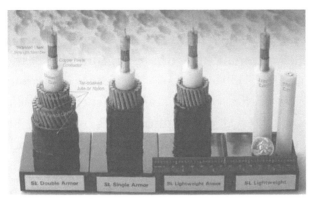

Nevertheless, 7 States claim the right not only to delineate the course of submarine pipelines, but also submarine cables, which are about the diameter of a garden hose: Angola,[1222] Cabo Verde,[1223] Cambodia,[1224] China,[1225] Syria,[1226] Uruguay,[1227] and Vietnam.[1228]

The remaining excessive Continental Shelf claims run the gamut from the types of excessive maritime claims already discussed (e.g., "security" jurisdiction, consent for military exercises, etc.), to novel ones:

➢ **Australia** (Continental Shelf claims infringe on Antarctic territory),[1229]

➢ **China** (claims security jurisdiction on the Continental Shelf),[1230]

➢ **Chile** (claimed Outer Continental Shelf for Easter and *Sala y Gomez* Islands out to 350 nm without submitting the claims to the Commission on the Limits of the Continental Shelf (CLCS)[1231] for review),[1232]

➢ **Ecuador** (claimed Outer Continental Shelf along the undersea Carnegie Ridge to include the Galapagos Archipelago),[1233]

➢ **India** (prior consent for foreign States to conduct military exercises),[1234]

➢ **Iran** (prior consent for foreign States to conduct military exercises),[1235] and

➢ **Nicaragua** (claims that its sovereignty "embraces and extends over the airspace as well as all islands, keys, shoals, reefs and other geographic irregularities existing within the defined limits..., be they exposed or submerged, adherent to or emergent from the continental shelf.").[1236]

Aside from being Law of the Sea "purists," why should the U.S. be concerned about such excessive maritime claims by almost 80 other States? The answer lies in the U.S. position in the world, both geographically and diplomatically:

Throughout its history, the United States has been aware of its dependence on unrestricted passage through the world's oceans. America's geographic position, the locations of its major allies, its reliance on international trade, and the importance of the oceans as sources of food, energy, and minerals provide a compelling rationale for this traditional reliance on the freedom of the seas. In addition, the United States status as a global power is dependent upon its sea power. Writing at the end of the 19th century, Admiral Alfred Thayer Mahan acknowledged the critical relationship between national power, foreign policy, and sea power. In his view, no state aspiring for great leadership status could ignore the importance of sea power. More recently, the U.S. Department of Defense noted in the white paper National Security and the Convention on the Law of the Sea *that "[t]he United States has always been a maritime nation and we must have substantial air and sealift capabilities to enable our forces to be where and when needed." To ensure these capabilities, a principal element of U.S. maritime policy is the "[a]ssurance that key sea and air lines of communication will remain open as a matter of international legal right and not contingent upon approval by coastal or island nations."[1237]*

As the introductory quote to this Chapter (from former Vice Chairman of the U.S. Joint Chiefs of Staff, Admiral James A. "Sandy" Winnefeld Jr.) indicates, excessive maritime claims by other States attempt to "restrict our maritime activities, particularly within the bounds of their exclusive economic zones."

For example, requiring prior notification and/or consent before U.S. warships may engage in Innocent Passage through the Territorial Seas of foreign States would limit their Freedom of Navigation, either by publicizing their intended course/track (and thereby making them more susceptible to attack), or by delaying or denying their planned movement. Arguably, "navigational freedom ... is quite literally the most important common heritage in the world's oceans .... UNCLOS is truly a gift to the World and its greatest legacy is protecting navigational freedom on the World's oceans. That is a legacy to protect!"[1238]

More importantly, if such excessive maritime claims remained unchallenged, they could add a "gloss"[1239] on the interpretation of UNCLOS (i.e., subsequent treaty practice as a means of interpreting the treaty language).[1240] Article 31 of the Vienna Convention on the Law of Treaties (VCLT) indicates that a treaty should be interpreted in context, including "[a]ny subsequent practice in the application of the treaty which establishes the agreement of the parties regarding its interpretation."[1241]

'Excessive maritime claims' are attempts by coastal States to restrict unlawfully the rights and freedoms of navigation and overflight and other lawful uses of the sea. These claims are made through laws, regulations, or other pronouncements that are inconsistent with international law as reflected in the Law of the Sea Convention. If left unchallenged, excessive maritime claims could permanently infringe upon the freedom of the seas enjoyed by all nations.[1242]

Moreover, "a new rule of customary international law may emerge to modify the provisions of a treaty. International law is not static."[1243] Thus, subsequent State practice may modify how States actually interpret a treaty—for example, if foreign warships abided by Coastal State requirements to provide notice before conducting Innocent Passage through their Territorial Seas, even though this is not required by UNCLOS, that practice could be used to define how States interpret Innocent Passage by warships![1244] "If the United States fails to consistently assert i[t]s maritime rights under international law, these [rights] might be lost over time."[1245]

FREEDOM OF NAVIGATION PROGRAMS

Former ITLOS Judge Helmut Türk: "Experience ... has ... shown that most members of the international community are quite reluctant to react to maritime boundaries established by other States when their immediate interests are not involved."[1246]

Former U.S. Secretary of Defense Mark Esper: "We will also maintain a routine military presence in the South China Sea, to demonstrate the seriousness of our commitment. We will not accept attempts to assert unlawful maritime claims at the expense of law-abiding nations. The United States military will continue to fly, sail, and operate wherever international law allows, and we will encourage other nations to affirm their rights in the same manner. Freedom of Navigation Operations remain central to our demonstration of leadership in upholding the rules-based order."[1247]

In order to prevent State practice that is consistent with such excessive maritime claims and thereby add a "gloss" on the interpretation of UNCLOS, the U.S. has been conducting "Freedom of Navigation" operations (FONOPs) since the 1970s[1248] (i.e., before UNCLOS was even finalized in 1982).[1249] President Jimmy Carter formally established the 2-step U.S. FON program in 1979,[1250] which has been referred to as a "feather and hammer" approach:[1251]

1) A diplomatic protest by the U.S. Department of State, via a diplomatic note, *démarche* (written or oral),[1252] *note verbale*, or *aide-mémoire* (informal diplomatic message as a reminder);

2) coupled with a subsequent operational assertion or challenge, usually by U.S. Navy warships or U.S. Air Force aircraft, and sometimes by U.S. Coast Guard vessels.[1253]

The "purpose [of FONOPs] is to reinforce international law peacefully and in a principled, unbiased manner."[1254] The U.S. Department of Defense (DoD) publicizes FONOPs in its annual FON Report to Congress, for all the world to see (i.e., to let foreign States know that the U.S. has challenged their excessive maritime claims in the past year).[1255] U.S. FONOPs are:

1) deliberately planned well in advance (with an appropriate level of legal review, as well as high level approval for "particularly sensitive challenges"[1256]);

2) professionally conducted and non-provocative[1257] (i.e., vessels observe all UNCLOS rules, such as not threatening the Coastal State while engaged in Innocent Passage through their Territorial Seas, and following strict guidelines if challenged during a FONOP);[1258]

3) politically neutral (i.e., the U.S. conducts FONOPs as often against our allies (e.g., Albania, Canada), and partners (e.g., Philippines) as we do against our competitors (e.g., China, Iran, and Russia[1259]); and

4) not tied to current events, but are usually planned in conjunction with operational deployments (e.g., the U.S. is unlikely to send ships or aircraft out of their way "in a fiscally-constrained environment"[1260] to challenge Peru's

excessive 200 nm Territorial Sea claim, but if there is a planned military deployment off the west coast of South America, operational planners might include a FONOP within 200 nm of Peru's coastline, such as a military exercise).[1261]

The 2020 FON report to Congress explains that the U.S. "challenged the excessive maritime claims of 19 claimants" in Fiscal Year (FY) 2020, some of them multiple times (marked with an asterisk). The 2020 FON report includes citations to "each claimants' specific laws, regulations, and other proclamations articulating the excessive maritime claims".[1262]

Freedom of Navigation Operational Challenges Fiscal Year 2020		
Claimant	**Excessive Maritime Claim** An asterisk indicates multiple operational challenges to the excessive claim.	**Geographic Area or Location**
Algeria	Requires foreign warships request permission at least 15 days prior to conducting innocent passage, except in cases of force majeure. [Decree No. 72-194 of October 5, 1972 for the Peacetime Regulation of the Passage of Foreign Warships through the Territorial Waters and of their Calls]	Mediterranean Sea
Argentina	* Prior notification required before warships enter the approaches to the Strait of Magellan. [Declaration upon Ratification of the 1982 Law of the Sea Convention, Dec. 1, 1995.]	Strait of Magellan

Brazil	Prior consent required for military exercises or maneuvers, in particular those involving the use of weapons or explosives, in the exclusive economic zone. [Law No. 8,617 of January 4, 1993, on the Territorial Sea, the Contiguous Zone, the Exclusive Economic Zone and the Continental Shelf.]	South Atlantic Ocean
China	* Straight baseline claims. [Declaration of the Government of the People's Republic of China on the Baselines of the Territorial Sea of the People's Republic of China, May 15, 1996.]	South China Sea
	* Restrictions on foreign aircraft flying through an Air Defense Identification Zone (ADIZ) without the intent to enter national airspace. [Ministry of National Defense Announcement, Nov. 23, 2013.]	East China Sea
	* Criminalization of surveying and mapping activities by foreign entities which do not obtain approval from or cooperate with the People's Republic of China (PRC). [Surveying and Mapping Law of the People's Republic of China, Apr. 27, 2017.]	South China Sea and East China Sea
	* Jurisdiction over all surveying and mapping activities "in the territorial air, land, and waters, as well as other sea areas under PRC jurisdiction," without distinction between marine scientific research and military surveys. [Surveying and Mapping Law of the People's Republic of China, Apr. 27, 2017.]	South China Sea and East China Sea

China (continued)	* Security jurisdiction over the contiguous zone. [Law on the Territorial Sea and Contiguous Zone, Feb. 25, 1992.]	South China Sea and East China Sea
	* Prior permission required for innocent passage of foreign military ships through the territorial sea. [Law on the Territorial Sea and Contiguous Zone, Feb. 25, 1992.]	South China Sea
	* Territorial sea and airspace around features not so entitled (*i.e.*, low-tide elevations). [Actions and statements implying such a claim.]	South China Sea
Ecuador	Express consent required for military exercises or maneuvers of any type in the exclusive economic zone. [Declaration upon Accession to the 1982 Law of the Sea Convention, Sep. 24, 2012.]	South Pacific Ocean
Haiti	Unpublished but inferred straight baseline claims. [Decree No. 38 of 8 April 1977.]	Gulf of Gonave
Iran	* Restrictions on the right of transit passage through the Strait of Hormuz to Parties of the United Nations Convention on the Law of the Sea. [Declaration upon Signature of the 1982 Law of the Sea Convention, Dec. 10, 1982.]	Strait of Hormuz
	* Prohibition on foreign military activities and practices in the exclusive economic zone. [Act on the Marine Areas of the Islamic Republic of Iran in the Persian Gulf and the Oman Sea, article 16, Apr. 20, 1993.]	Persian Gulf

Japan	Straight baseline claims. [Enforcement Order of the Law on the Territorial Sea and the Contiguous Zone (Cabinet Order No. 210 of 1977, as amended by Cabinet Order No. 383 of 1993, Cabinet Order No. 206 of 1996 and Cabinet Order No. 434 of 2001).]	Tsushima Strait
Malaysia	Prior authorization of passage required before nuclear-powered vessels enter the territorial sea. [Declaration upon Ratification of the 1982 Law of the Sea Convention, Oct. 14, 1996.]	Strait of Malacca
	* Prior consent required for military exercises or maneuvers in the exclusive economic zone. [Declaration upon Ratification of the 1982 Law of the Sea Convention, Oct. 14, 1996.]	South China Sea
Maldives	* Prior authorization required for all foreign vessels to enter the exclusive economic zone. [Maritime Zones of Maldives Act No. 6/96.]	Indian Ocean
Nicaragua	Straight baseline claims. [Presidential Decree 17-2018, Decree of Reform to Decree No. 33-2013, "Baselines of the Maritime Spaces of the Republic of Nicaragua in the Caribbean Sea," 10 October 2018.]	Caribbean Sea
Pakistan	* Prior consent required for military exercises or maneuvers in the exclusive economic zone. [Declaration upon Ratification of the 1982 Law of the Sea Convention, Feb. 26, 1997.]	North Arabian Sea
Republic of Korea	Straight baseline claims. [Territorial Sea and Contiguous Zone Act, Law No. 3037, promulgated on 31 December 1977, as amended by Law No. 14607, promulgated on 21 March 2017.]	Yellow Sea

Samoa	Prior authorization required for vessels carrying radioactive wastes or other inherently dangerous, noxious or hazardous wastes, or substances harmful to the environment, through the territorial sea. [Maritime Zones Act 1999, No. 18, Aug. 25, 1999.]	South Pacific Ocean
Taiwan	* Prior notification required for foreign military or government vessels to enter the territorial sea. [Law on the Territorial Sea and the Contiguous Zone, article 7, Jan. 21, 1998.]	South China Sea
Uruguay	Prior authorization required for foreign military exercises or any other military activities, particularly those involving the use of arms, explosives or other aggressive or polluting means, in the exclusive economic zone. [Act 17.033 of 20 November 1998.]	Atlantic Ocean
Vietnam	* Prior notification required for foreign warships to enter the territorial sea. [Law of the Sea of Vietnam, Law No. 18/2012/QH13, article 12, June 21, 2012.]	South China Sea
Venezuela	* Prior permission required for military operations in the exclusive economic zone and Flight Identification Region (FIR). [Actions and statements implying such claims.]	Caribbean Sea
	Attempted enforcement of a security zone beyond the lawful limit of the territorial sea. [Actions and statements implying such a claim, contrary to the repeal of article 3 of the Territorial Sea, Continental Shelf, Fisheries Protection and Airspace Act of 27 July 1956.]	Caribbean Sea

Yemen	* Prior permission required for foreign warships to transit the territorial sea. [Declaration upon Ratification of the 1982 Law of the Sea Convention, July 21, 1987.]	Bab al-Mandeb Strait

"FON operations help to ensure that the hard-earned compromises reached during the Third United Nations Conference on the Law of the Sea (1973-1982) are maintained both by word and deed."[1263] Yet for almost 40 years, the U.S. was the only State that conducted Freedom of Navigation Operations (FONOPs). Other States were unwilling to expend the time, effort, financial, domestic political capital, and international diplomatic costs involved with conducting FONOPs. However, in the last few years[1264] a few other States have begun to conduct FONOPs in the South China Sea (including Australia, the United Kingdom, and France)[1265] to challenge China's excessive maritime claims. "The involvement of countries other than the United States helps to take the edge off U.S.-China rivalry and sends the important message that these countries care about maintaining open seas and [that] rules matter. It also helps debunk Beijing's claim that the dispute

HMAS Success and HMAS Toowoomba recently conducted FoN Operations in the South China Sea

is one that only concerns claimants to territorial features and that other powers have no valid interests in the South China Sea."[1266]

> FONOPs, even joint FONOPs with other nations, will not by itself roll back China's expansion in the South China Sea. But more FONOPs conducted by more nations will globalize the dispute beyond U.S.-China relations and make China incur new costs for its policies. Hopefully, they will also cause China to think twice about further regional expansionism.[1267]

FONOPs in the South China Sea is a good example of their underlying purpose: to "ensur[e] that the US military can fly, sail, and operate wherever international law allows."[1268] The South China Sea dispute began in earnest in May 2009, when Malaysia and Vietnam submitted a joint declaration to the Commission on the Limits of the Continental Shelf (CLCS), supporting their Outer Continental Shelf claims "in the southern part of the South China Sea."[1269] The next day, China responded via a 2-page *note verbale*, including this paragraph and the chart following:

> China has indisputable sovereignty over the islands in the South China Sea and the adjacent waters, and enjoys sovereign rights and jurisdiction over the relevant waters as well as the seabed and subsoil thereof (see attached map). The above position is consistently held by the Chinese Government, and is widely known by the international community.

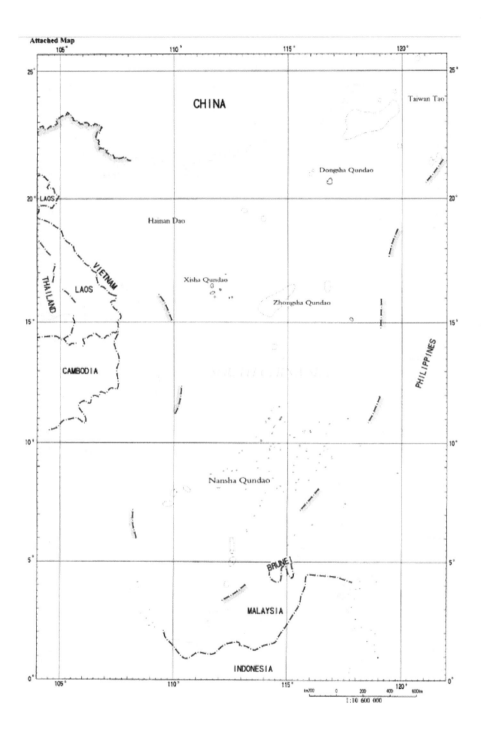

"This was the first time this map, which claims almost all of the South China Sea, including features and waters within it under Chinese sovereignty, has been presented within the framework of the United Nations."[1270] China has neither clarified the nature or scope of its claimed historic rights, nor the specific meaning of its "9-dash line,"[1271] although China has claimed sovereignty over the enclosed seabed,[1272] and has implemented domestic legislation that would permit it to enforce Chinese law over the entire area.[1273] For a State with 3,500 years of written history,[1274] China's claims to "historic" rights within its "cow tongue" claim (which has varied between 9- and 11-dashes)[1275] only appear to extend back to 1947-1948,[1276] when it sought to "re-assert[] control over the island groups of the South China Sea in the immediate post-war period and the pre-empting of potential interference by third States."[1277]

The South China Sea includes the Spratly and Paracel Islands and other disputed geographic features.[1278] China's "9-dash line" encompasses 85% of the South China Sea,[1279] or about 3.7 million

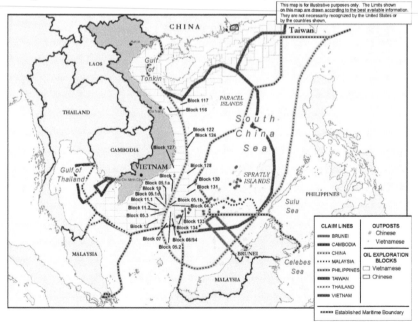

square kilometers (the size of Mexico or Saudi Arabia), and China estimates the resources inside are worth $1 trillion.[1280] As we can see on this detailed chart, Vietnam, Malaysia, Brunei, the Philippines and China have overlapping claims to the islands and waters in the South China Sea. Moreover, approximately 80% of the crude oil that is shipped to China, Japan, South Korea and Taiwan uses shipping lanes in the South China Sea.[1281]

Before an international arbitral tribunal ruled on the South China Sea dispute (discussed in Chapter 12), the U.S. took no position on competing claims by Asian States, but routinely conducts FONOPs there to demonstrate the freedoms of navigation and overflight, and to support the Rule of Law.[1282] In doing so, the U.S. followed its 2-step "feather and hammer" approach:[1283] a diplomatic protest by the U.S. Department of State, followed by a subsequent operational assertion or challenge, typically conducted by U.S. Navy warships.[1284] The U.S. protested China's prior permission requirement (before a warship may conduct Innocent Passage through China's Territorial Seas) by oral *démarche* delivered in August 1992 in Beijing.[1285] The U.S. "provided an aide-mémoire to Chinese officials concerning China's assertion that military activities in the EEZ required its prior consent."[1286] The U.S. protested China's straight baseline claims by "State Department telegram 96 State 181478, delivered August 21, 1996."[1287]

China routinely opposes U.S. FONOPs in the South China Sea, which resulted in a near collision between U.S. and People's Republic of China (PRC) warships in October 2018.[1288] The near collision put a further strain on U.S./China diplomatic relations. Yet a month later, China permitted the USS RONALD REAGAN (CVN 76) aircraft carrier to conduct a Hong Kong port visit. China did this as a goodwill gesture just a few days before the Group of 20 (G20) summit in Buenos Aires, Argentina, which included both the

American and Chinese leaders. This highlights the diplomatic component of military operations in general, especially naval presence, and FONOPs in particular.[1289] China similarly uses naval presence as a means of sending diplomatic messages.[1290]

Perhaps not too surprisingly, U.S. FONOPs in the South China Sea ("the most contentious region for FON operations")[1291] increased under Republican President Trump versus under his Democrat predecessor, President Obama,[1292] although President Obama also supported the idea of Freedom of Navigation.[1293] "The Obama administration authorized two FONOPs in 2015 and three in 2016. "Under President Trump, the U.S. military enhanced its presence in the South China Sea", and appeared to have "streamlin[ed] the approval process for FONOPs,"[1294] with the Navy conducting six FONOPs in 2017 and five in 2018." And "[t]he Navy conducted nine FONOPs in the South China Sea" in 2019, more "than in any year since the U.S. began more aggressively challenging China's claims in the South China Sea in 2015."[1295]

The Navy conducted its first FONOP of 2020 on Jan. 25, sending the littoral combat ship Montgomery past Chinese claims in the Spratly Islands. During that operation, China sent two fighter-bombers scrambling overhead to intimidate the Montgomery, according to the country's state media.

The U.S. Navy frames these FONOPs as challenging excessive claims by all powers in the region, and the Jan. 25 patrol was officially aimed at China, Taiwan and Vietnam. Specifically, the Navy challenged the notion that innocent passage through claimed territorial waters requires previous notification.[1296]

Besides harassing the U.S. warships,[1297] China typically responds to U.S. FONOPs in the South China Sea by releasing press statements that reiterate its sweeping claims to the area, such as the following:

> We urge (the United States) to stop these provocative actions to avoid any unforeseeable accidents. ... China has indisputable sovereignty over the South China Sea islands and its surrounding area.
>
> * * *
>
> The U.S. actions severely damage China's sovereignty and safety, destroy the peace and stability in the South China Sea, and we express our resolute opposition.[1298]

One could argue that U.S. FONOPs are becoming more aggressive in challenging China's excessive maritime claims in the South China Sea. Yet "[s]uch operations may ... be better framed as assertions of maritime rights (so that these rights are reinforced and not detracted from in the future), rather than as challenges to excessive maritime claims. This recasting is particularly appropriate in the Spratlys where China has been especially vague about its maritime claims."[1299] Dr. Lynn Kuok argues that instead of U.S. FONOPs in the South China Sea being "unnecessarily provocative," the U.S. FON program is a measured response to China's expansive claims. Dr. Kuok provides a number of helpful suggestions for *expanding* U.S. FONOPs in the South China Sea:

> ➤ Expand FONOPs beyond merely exercising a warship's right to engage in Innocent Passage through Territorial Seas (without either seeking authorization or providing prior notice) to "exercis[ing] high sea freedoms around features like Mischief Reef in the Spratlys ... [which] is not entitled to a territorial sea."

Figure 30: Aerial Photograph of Structure on Mischief Reef
Supplemental Written Submission, Vol. II, p. 126.

➤ "[E]xercis[ing] high sea freedoms through the Paracels and Spratlys outside of potential territorial seas" ... [in order to] reiterate that China's established [straight] baselines are without legitimacy."

➤ More "[c]learly put on record the maritime right the United States is asserting at the time of a FON operation" by providing "[d]etails such as where the operation took place, what the operation did, and what right(s) the United States was asserting should be expeditiously, clearly and consistently made public."[1300]

➤ "Publish a consolidated list of all diplomatic protests made in respect of excessive maritime claims," which will "more clearly set out the United States rationale for regarding certain claims as excessive." This Department of State list of diplomatic protests could be similar to the annual DoD FON report to Congress. In other words, the U.S. should be more obvious as to what it is asserting, both operationally and diplomatically.[1301]

Thus, so long as States make excessive maritime claims that are difficult to "square" with a plain reading of the relevant UNCLOS provisions, the U.S. and other similarly minded States will continue to conduct Freedom of Navigation Operations (FONOPs) in order to challenge these excessive maritime claims, assert States' freedoms of navigation and overflight, and prevent adding a "gloss" on the interpretation of UNCLOS (i.e., subsequent treaty practice as a means of interpreting the treaty language). "The South China Sea dispute is about much more than mere 'rocks'. It is about maritime rights and the preservation of the system of international law. More broadly, how the United States and China interact in the South China Sea has important implications for their relationship elsewhere and on other issues."[1302] The next, and final Chapter discusses the South China Sea dispute in more depth.

[1046] Vienna Convention on the Law of Treaties (VCLT) art. 26, May 23, 1969, 1155 U.N.T.S. 331 (providing the treaty maxim *pacta sunt servanda*: "Every treaty in force is binding upon the parties to it and must be performed by them in good faith."). Put simply: agreements must be kept. *See also* Dept. of Defense Law of War Manual § 1.10.1.1, p. 36 (June 2015, updated Dec. 2016), https://www.hsdl.org/?view&did=797480. Although the United States is not a party to the VCLT, it considers the VCLT to represent customary international law. Sean D. Murphy, The George Wash. Univ. Law Sch.: "Should the U.S. Join the International Criminal Court?" A Moderated Panel Discussion, Feb. 13, 2006. *See also* Letter Of Transmittal Forwarding The 1982 UN Law Of The Sea Convention To The United States Senate, DOS Commentary p. 17 (William J. Clinton, Oct. 7, 1994) (S. Treaty Doc. 103–39), https://www.foreign.senate.gov/imo/media/doc/treaty_103-39.pdf (noting that "[u]nder customary international law, as reflected in ... the Vienna Convention on the Law of Treaties (92nd Congress; 1st Session, Senate Executive 'L')").

[1047] Dept. of Defense Maritime Claims Reference Manual (MCRM), http://www.jag.navy.mil/organization/code_10_mcrm.htm. *See generally* U.S. Navy Judge Advocate General's Corps, About Us, Organization, National Security Law (Code 10), https://www.jag.navy.mil/organization/code_10.htm (explaining the mission, functions and references maintained by Code 10).

[1048] U.S. Dept. of State, Bureau of Oceans and Int'l. Environmental and Scientific Affairs, Policy Issues, The Ocean and Polar Affairs, Key Topics, Limits in the Seas (LIS), https://www.state.gov/limits-in-the-seas/.

[1049] United Nations Convention on the Law of the Sea (UNCLOS) art. 47(1), Dec. 10, 1982, 1833 U.N.T.S. 397, https://www.un.org/Depts/los/convention_agreements/convention_overview_co nvention.htm.

[1050] Dept. of Defense Maritime Claims Reference Manual (MCRM)—Albania 2018 & LIS No. 116, Argentina 2016 & LIS No. 44, Bangladesh 2019, Burma/Myanmar 2019, Cambodia 2016, Canada 2017, China 2017 & LIS No. 127, Colombia 2016 & LIS No. 103, Comoros 2020, Costa Rica 2017 & LIS No. 111, Cuba 2016 & LIS No. 76, Djibouti 2013 & LIS No. 113, Dominican Republic 2020 & LIS No. 130, Ecuador 2017 & LIS No. 42 & 147, Egypt 2019 & LIS No. 116, Faroe Islands (Denmark) 2014, Gabon 2014, Guinea-Bissau 2018, Haiti 2017, Honduras 2014 & LIS No. 124, Iran 2014 & LIS No. 114, Japan 2017, Kenya 2020, Malta 2018, Mauritania 2019 & LIS No. 8, Mexico 2014 & LIS No. 4, Nicaragua 2016, Oman 2016 & LIS No. 113, Pakistan 2014 & LIS No. 118, Philippines 2016 & LIS Nos. 33 & 142, Portugal 2019 & LIS No. 27, Russian Federation 2016 & LIS Nos. 107 & 109, Saudi Arabia 2014 & LIS No. 20, South Korea 2018 & LIS Nos. 82 & 121, Sudan 2020, Thailand 2014 & LIS No. 31, Tunisia 2020, Uruguay 2017 & LIS No. 123, Venezuela 2016 & LIS No. 21, Vietnam 2016, http://www.jag.navy.mil/organization/code_10_mcrm.htm. *See also* U.S. Dept. of State, Bureau of Oceans and Int'l. Environmental and Scientific Affairs, Policy Issues, The Ocean and Polar Affairs, Key Topics, Limits in the Seas (LIS), https://www.state.gov/limits-in-the-seas/; United States Institute of Peace, *What's in a Name: Burma or Myanmar* (Andrew Selth & Adam Gallagher, June 21, 2018), https://www.usip.org/blog/2018/06/whats-name-burma-or-myanmar. The U.S. protested China's straight baseline claims by "State Dept. telegram 96 State 181478, delivered August 21, 1996." Brookings Institution, Center for East Asia Policy Studies, East Asia Policy Paper 9, *The U.S. FON Program in the South China Sea—A lawful and necessary response to China's strategic ambiguity*, pp. 12-13 (Lynn Kuok, June 2016), https://www.brookings.edu/research/the-u-s-fon-program-in-the-south-china-sea/.

[1051] DoD MCRM—Australia 2019, Cambodia 2016 & LIS Nos. 99 & 112, Canada 2017, China 2017 & LIS No. 143, Dominican Republic 2020 & LIS No. 130, Egypt 2019 & LIS No. 22, India 2016, Italy 2014, Kenya 2020, Libya 2014 & LIS No. 112, Panama 2014, Russian Federation 2016, Sri Lanka 2014, Thailand 2014 & LIS No. 31, Venezuela 2016, Vietnam 2016 & LIS No. 99 (full cite above). *See also* U.S. Dept. of State, Limits in the Seas (full cite above).

[1052] *See, e.g.*, Military.com, Military News, *USS John S. McCain Challenges Russia's Claims to Peter the Great Bay in Sea of Japan* (Caitlin Doornbos, Nov. 24, 2020), https://www.military.com/daily-news/2020/11/24/uss-john-s-mccain-challenges-russias-claims-peter-great-bay-sea-of-japan.html.

[1053] UNCLOS, art. 3 (full cite above).

[1054] John Norton Moore, *Navigational Freedom: The Most Critical Common Heritage*, 93 INT'L. L. STUD. 251, 259 (2017), https://digital-commons.usnwc.edu/ils/vol93/iss1/8/.

[1055] Letter Of Transmittal Forwarding The 1982 UN Law Of The Sea Convention To The United States Senate, DOS Commentary p. 5 (William J. Clinton, Oct. 7, 1994) (S. Treaty Doc. 103–39), https://www.foreign.senate.gov/imo/media/doc/treaty_103-39.pdf.

[1056] DoD MCRM—Albania 2018 (full cite above).

[1057] DoD MCRM—Angola 2017 (full cite above).

[1058] DoD MCRM—Argentina 2016 (full cite above).

[1059] DoD MCRM—Benin 2020 (full cite above).
[1060] DoD MCRM—Cabo Verde 2017 (full cite above).
[1061] DoD MCRM—Cameroon 2013 (full cite above).
[1062] DoD MCRM—Congo (full cite above).
[1063] DoD MCRM—Ecuador 2017 (full cite above); U.S. Dept. of State, Limits in the Seas No. 147 (full cite above).
[1064] DoD MCRM—El Salvador 2014 (full cite above).
[1065] DoD MCRM—Liberia 2018 (full cite above).
[1066] DoD MCRM—Mauritania 2019 (full cite above).
[1067] DoD MCRM—Nicaragua 2016 (full cite above).
[1068] DoD MCRM—Nigeria 2016 (full cite above).
[1069] DoD MCRM—Panama 2014 (full cite above).
[1070] DoD MCRM—Sierra Leone 2014 (full cite above).
[1071] DoD MCRM—Syria 2017 (full cite above).
[1072] DoD MCRM—Tanzania 2016 (full cite above).
[1073] DoD MCRM—Togo 2020 (full cite above).
[1074] DoD MCRM—Peru 2014 (full cite above).
[1075] DoD MCRM—Somalia 2020 (full cite above).
[1076] DoD MCRM—Philippines 2016 (full cite above).
[1077] DOS Commentary, p. 15 (full cite above).
[1078] Brookings Institution, *U.S. FON Program in the South China Sea* (full cite above). *See also* Raul (Pete) Pedrozo, *China's Revised Maritime Traffic Safety Law*, 97 INT'L. L. STUD. 956, 965-966 (2021), https://digital-commons.usnwc.edu/ils/vol97/iss1/39/ (noting that "Prior notification was discussed during the UNCLOS negotiations. Efforts by a handful of States to include a prior notification or prior consent requirement in Article 21 failed to achieve a majority vote, so the proponents agreed not to pursue the matter as it was clear that there was insufficient support to adopt the proposal. Shortly before the conclusion of the negotiations in 1982, the conference president, Ambassador Tommy Koh, confirmed that all ships have a 'right of innocent passage through the territorial sea, and there is no need ... to acquire the prior consent or even notification of the coastal State.'").
[1079] DoD MCRM—Argentina 2016 (full cite above).
[1080] DoD MCRM—Croatia 2013 (full cite above).
[1081] DoD MCRM—Denmark 2015 (full cite above).
[1082] DoD MCRM—Egypt 2019 (full cite above).
[1083] DoD MCRM—Estonia 2020 (full cite above).
[1084] DoD MCRM—India 2016 (full cite above).
[1085] DoD MCRM—Libya 2014 (full cite above).
[1086] DoD MCRM—Montenegro 2018 (full cite above).
[1087] DoD MCRM—Slovenia 2020 (full cite above). *Cf.* UNCLOS, art. 22 (full cite above) (permitting a Coastal State to "require foreign ships exercising the right of innocent passage through its territorial sea to use such sea lanes and traffic separation schemes ... [i]n particular, tankers, nuclear-powered ships and ships carrying nuclear or other inherently dangerous or noxious substances or materials ...."). Thus, while Slovenia may have a basis under UNCLOS for requiring vessels with dangerous means of propulsion (e.g., nuclear-powered aircraft carriers) or dangerous cargoes (e.g., radioactive waste) to use designated sea lanes or traffic separation schemes, there is no clear basis for requiring all foreign warships to do so.

[1088] Dept. of Defense Maritime Claims Reference Manual (MCRM)—Vietnam 2016, http://www.jag.navy.mil/organization/code_10_mcrm.htm.

[1089] DoD MCRM—Guyana 2014 (full cite above).

[1090] DoD MCRM—South Korea 2018 (full cite above); U.S. Dept. of State, Bureau of Oceans and Int'l. Environmental and Scientific Affairs, Policy Issues, The Ocean and Polar Affairs, Key Topics, Limits in the Seas No. 121, https://www.state.gov/limits-in-the-seas/.

[1091] DoD MCRM—Djibouti 2013 (full cite above).

[1092] DoD MCRM—Pakistan 2014 (full cite above).

[1093] DoD MCRM—United Arab Emirates 2016 (full cite above).

[1094] World Nuclear Association, Home, Information Library, Non-power Nuclear Applications, Transport, Nuclear-Powered Ships (Dec. 2019), https://www.world-nuclear.org/information-library/non-power-nuclear-applications/transport/nuclear-powered-ships.aspx. *See also* Letter Of Transmittal Forwarding The 1982 UN Law Of The Sea Convention To The United States Senate, DOS Commentary p. 15 (William J. Clinton, Oct. 7, 1994) (S. Treaty Doc. 103–39), https://www.foreign.senate.gov/imo/media/doc/treaty_103-39.pdf (estimating that "some 40 per cent of U.S. Navy combatant ships use nuclear propulsion.").

[1095] DoD MCRM—Albania 2018 (full cite above).

[1096] DoD MCRM—Algeria 2018 (full cite above).

[1097] DoD MCRM—Antigua and Barbuda 2020 (full cite above).

[1098] DoD MCRM—Bangladesh 2019 (full cite above).

[1099] DoD MCRM—Barbados 2017 (full cite above).

[1100] DoD MCRM—Burma/Myanmar 2019 (full cite above). *See also* United States Institute of Peace, *What's in a Name: Burma or Myanmar* (Andrew Selth & Adam Gallagher, June 21, 2018), https://www.usip.org/blog/2018/06/whats-name-burma-or-myanmar.

[1101] DoD MCRM—Chile 2013 (full cite above).

[1102] DoD MCRM—China 2017 (full cite above); U.S. Dept. of State, Limits in the Seas No. 43 (full cite above). The United States protested this requirement by oral démarche delivered in August 1992 in Beijing. Brookings Institution, Center for East Asia Policy Studies, East Asia Policy Paper 9, *The U.S. FON Program in the South China Sea—A lawful and necessary response to China's strategic ambiguity*, p. 7 (Lynn Kuok, June 2016), https://www.brookings.edu/research/the-u-s-fon-program-in-the-south-china-sea/. *See also* Raul (Pete) Pedrozo, *Maritime Police Law of the People's Republic of China*, 97 INT'L. L. STUD. 465, 466-468 (2021), https://digital-commons.usnwc.edu/ils/vol97/iss1/24/ (noting that "the Maritime Police Law of the People's Republic of China (MPL), which took effect on February 1, 2021 … authorizes the [Chinese coastal police agencies (CCG)] to take enforcement measures in the territorial sea, 'such as detention, forced removal, and forced towing.' Without defining the meaning of illegal entry, the law could be used as a subterfuge to hamper the right of innocent passage, which is guaranteed to all ships of all States and cannot be impaired or denied by China except in accordance with UNCLOS."); Raul (Pete) Pedrozo, *China's Revised Maritime Traffic Safety Law*, 97 INT'L. L. STUD. 956, 964 (2021), https://digital-commons.usnwc.edu/ils/vol97/iss1/39/ (noting that China's Revised Maritime Traffic Safety Law purports to "impose[] a prior notification requirement of certain foreign ships entering or leaving China's territorial sea. These ships include (1) submersibles; (2) nuclear-powered ships; (3) ships carrying radioactive materials or other toxic and hazardous materials; and (4) other vessels that may endanger China's maritime traffic safety as prescribed by

Chinese laws or regulations, or the State Council. These classes of ships are further required to hold relevant certificates when passing through China's territorial sea, take special precautionary measures in compliance with the Chinese laws, regulations, and rules, and accept the instructions and supervision of the maritime ad-ministrative agency.").

[1103] DoD MCRM—Colombia 2016 (full cite above).
[1104] DoD MCRM—Latvia 2018 (full cite above).
[1105] DoD MCRM—Lithuania 2018 (full cite above).
[1106] DoD MCRM—North Korea 2016 (full cite above).
[1107] DoD MCRM—Pakistan 2014 (full cite above).
[1108] DoD MCRM—Romania 2014 (full cite above). *See generally* William J. Aceves, *The Freedom of Navigation Program: A Study of the Relationship between Law and Politics*, 19 HASTINGS INT'L & COMP. L. REV. 259, 288-289 (1996), https://repository.uchastings.edu/hastings_international_comparative_law_revi ew/vol19/iss2/2/ (providing a detailed example of a U.S. FON diplomatic protest to Romania).
[1109] DoD MCRM—Sierra Leone 2014 (full cite above).
[1110] DoD MCRM—Somalia 2020 (full cite above).
[1111] DoD MCRM—Sri Lanka 2014 (full cite above).
[1112] DoD MCRM—Saint Vincent and the Grenadines 2014 (full cite above); U.S. Dept. of State, Limits in the Seas No. 144 (full cite above).
[1113] DoD MCRM—Sudan 2020 (full cite above).
[1114] DoD MCRM—United Arab Emirates 2016 (full cite above).
[1115] DoD MCRM—Vanuatu 2014 (full cite above).
[1116] DoD MCRM—Ecuador 2017 (full cite above); U.S. Dept. of State, Limits in the Seas No. 147 (full cite above).
[1117] DoD MCRM—Iran 2014 (full cite above); U.S. Dept. of State, Limits in the Seas No. 114 (full cite above).
[1118] DoD MCRM—Maldives 2017 (full cite above).
[1119] DoD MCRM—Malta 2018 (full cite above).
[1120] DoD MCRM—Oman 2016 (full cite above).
[1121] DoD MCRM—Seychelles 2014 (full cite above).
[1122] DoD MCRM—Syria 2017 (full cite above).
[1123] DoD MCRM—Yemen 2016 (full cite above).
[1124] DoD MCRM—Egypt 2019 (full cite above).
[1125] DoD MCRM—Estonia 2020 (full cite above).
[1126] DoD MCRM—Malaysia 2016 (full cite above).
[1127] DoD MCRM—Samoa 2020 (full cite above).
[1128] DoD MCRM—Saudi Arabia 2014 (full cite above).
[1129] DoD MCRM—Dominican Republic 2020 (full cite above); U.S. Dept. of State, Limits in the Seas No. 130 (full cite above).
[1130] DoD MCRM—Estonia 2020 (full cite above).
[1131] DoD MCRM—Haiti 2017 (full cite above). *See generally* Aceves, *The FON Program*, pp. 291-293 (full cite above) (providing a detailed example of a U.S. FON diplomatic protest to Haiti).
[1132] DoD MCRM—Italy 2014 (full cite above).
[1133] DoD MCRM—Mexico 2014 (full cite above).
[1134] DoD MCRM—Romania 2014 (full cite above). *See generally* Aceves, *The FON Program*, pp. 288-289 (full cite above) (providing a detailed example of a U.S. FON diplomatic protest to Romania).

[1135] Dept. of Defense Maritime Claims Reference Manual (MCRM)—Saudi Arabia 2014, http://www.jag.navy.mil/organization/code_10_mcrm.htm.

[1136] DoD MCRM—Somalia 2020 (full cite above). So not only does Somalia still try to claim a 200 nm Territorial Sea, but it requires "[f]oreign warships [to] obtain permission prior to transiting" through its Territorial Sea, and attempts to prohibit the "passage by vessels of nations not recognized by Somalia" through its Territorial Sea. What makes these claims particularly preposterous is the fact that Somalia's Coast Guard is apparently very small, and thus would find it quite challenging to patrol Somalia's long coastline out to 12 nm, let alone out to 200 nm! European Union, External Action, EUCAP Somalia, About Us, Fact Sheet, *European Union Capacity Building Mission in Somalia* (Sep. 19, 2019), https://www.eucap-som.eu/fact-sheet/ (noting that the European Union has a capacity building mission in Somalia that "supports the development of coast guard and maritime police functions in and around the main Somali ports.").

[1137] DoD MCRM—United Arab Emirates 2016 (full cite above).

[1138] Australia had sought to impose a compulsory pilotage requirement in the Torres Strait near the Great Barrier Reef (i.e., any vessel seeking to engage in Transit Passage through the International Strait would be required to take onboard an Australian pilot familiar with the Torres Strait). However, the International Maritime Organization (IMO) concluded that there was no "international legal basis for compulsory pilotage," and thus Australia may only "recommend" taking onboard a local pilot before engaging in Transit Passage. DoD MCRM—Australia 2019, p. 5 (full cite above). *See also* Int'l. Maritime Organization (IMO), English, Our Work, Marine Safety, Navigation, Pilotage, http://www.imo.org/en/OurWork/Safety/Navigation/Pages/Pilotage.aspx; Raul (Pete) Pedrozo, *China's Revised Maritime Traffic Safety Law*, 97 Int'l. L. Stud. 956, 960 (2021), https://digital-commons.usnwc.edu/ils/vol97/iss1/39/ (noting that "[c]ompulsory pilotage is normally associated with ports and internal waters as a condition of port entry. It is inconsistent with international law, including Article 24 of UNCLOS, to require compulsory pilotage for foreign ships engaged in innocent passage that do not intend to enter the coastal State's ports or internal waters. Such a requirement would have the practical effect of denying or impairing the right of innocent passage.").

[1139] DoD MCRM—Argentina 2016 (full cite above).

[1140] DoD MCRM—Iran 2014 (full cite above).

[1141] DoD MCRM—Oman 2016 (full cite above).

[1142] DoD MCRM—Sweden 2014 (full cite above).

[1143] DoD MCRM—Antigua and Barbuda 2020 (full cite above).

[1144] DoD MCRM—Dominican Republic 2020 (full cite above); U.S. Dept. of State, Bureau of Oceans and Int'l. Environmental and Scientific Affairs, Policy Issues, The Ocean and Polar Affairs, Key Topics, Limits in the Seas No. 130, https://www.state.gov/limits-in-the-seas/.

[1145] DoD MCRM—Indonesia 2018 (full cite above).

[1146] DoD MCRM—Maldives 2017 (full cite above); U.S. Dept. of State, Limits in the Seas No. 126 (full cite above).

[1147] Donald R. Rothwell & Tim Stephens, The Int'l. Law of the Sea 82 & 88 (2nd ed. 2016).

[1148] DoD MCRM—Sierra Leone 2014 (full cite above).

[1149] DoD MCRM—North Korea 2016 (full cite above); Raul (Pete) Pedrozo, *Military Activities in the Exclusive Economic Zone: East Asia Focus*, 90 INT'L. L. STUD. 514, 539-540 (2014), https://digital-commons.usnwc.edu/ils/vol90/iss1/15/.

[1150] *See, e.g.*, U.S. NAVY, MARINE CORPS & COAST GUARD, THE COMMANDER'S HANDBOOK ON THE LAW OF NAVAL OPERATIONS, NWP 1-14M/MCTP 11-10B/COMDTPUB P5800.7A, ¶ 2.6.4 (pp. 2-11 to 2-12) (2017), www.jag.navy.mil/distrib/instructions/CDRs_HB_on_Law_of_Naval_Operations_AUG17.pdf (arguing that security zones "have no basis in international law in time of peace, and are not recognized by the United States.").

[1151] DoD MCRM—Bangladesh 2019 (full cite above).

[1152] DoD MCRM—Burma/Myanmar 2019 (full cite above). *See also* United States Institute of Peace, *What's in a Name: Burma or Myanmar* (Andrew Selth & Adam Gallagher, June 21, 2018), https://www.usip.org/blog/2018/06/whats-name-burma-or-myanmar.

[1153] DoD MCRM—Cambodia 2016 (full cite above).

[1154] DoD MCRM—China 2017 (full cite above).

[1155] DoD MCRM—Colombia 2016 (full cite above).

[1156] DoD MCRM—Egypt 2019 (full cite above); U.S. Dept. of State, Limits in the Seas No. 22 (full cite above).

[1157] DoD MCRM—Haiti 2017 (full cite above). *See generally* William J. Aceves, *The Freedom of Navigation Program: A Study of the Relationship between Law and Politics*, 19 HASTINGS INT'L & COMP. L. REV. 259, 291-293 (1996), https://repository.uchastings.edu/hastings_international_comparative_law_review/vol19/iss2/2/ (providing a detailed example of a U.S. FON diplomatic protest to Haiti).

[1158] DoD MCRM—India 2016 (full cite above).

[1159] DoD MCRM—Iran 2014 (full cite above); U.S. Dept. of State, Limits in the Seas No. 114 (full cite above).

[1160] DoD MCRM—Nicaragua 2016 (full cite above).

[1161] DoD MCRM—Pakistan 2014 (full cite above).

[1162] DoD MCRM—Saudi Arabia 2014 (full cite above).

[1163] DoD MCRM—Sri Lanka 2014 (full cite above).

[1164] DoD MCRM—Sudan 2020 (full cite above).

[1165] DoD MCRM—Syria 2017 (full cite above).

[1166] DoD MCRM—United Arab Emirates 2016 (full cite above).

[1167] DoD MCRM—Venezuela 2016 (full cite above).

[1168] DoD MCRM—Yemen 2016 (full cite above).

[1169] Letter Of Transmittal Forwarding The 1982 UN Law Of The Sea Convention To The United States Senate, DOS Commentary p. 26 (William J. Clinton, Oct. 7, 1994) (S. Treaty Doc. 103–39), https://www.foreign.senate.gov/imo/media/doc/treaty_103-39.pdf.

[1170] United Nations Convention on the Law of the Sea (UNCLOS) arts. 56(1)(a) & 68, Dec. 10, 1982, 1833 U.N.T.S. 397, https://www.un.org/Depts/los/convention_agreements/convention_overview_convention.htm. Although Article 68 specifically excludes sedentary species from the EEZ regime, they are included in the resources owned by the Coastal State on the Continental Shelf, which generally lies beneath the EEZ. Chapter 6 discusses the Continental Shelf in more depth.

[1171] THE FLETCHER SCHOOL OF LAW AND DIPLOMACY—TUFTS UNIVERSITY, LAW OF THE SEA, A POLICY PRIMER 13 (2017), https://sites.tufts.edu/lawofthesea/introduction/;

Raul (Pete) Pedrozo, *Military Activities in the Exclusive Economic Zone: East Asia Focus*, 90 Int'l. L. Stud. 514, 515 (2014), https://digital-commons.usnwc.edu/ils/vol90/iss1/15/; United Nations Convention on the Law of the Sea (UNCLOS) art. 57, Dec. 10, 1982, 1833 U.N.T.S. 397, https://www.un.org/Depts/los/convention_agreements/convention_overview_convention.htm.

[1172] U.S. Navy, Marine Corps & Coast Guard, The Commander's Handbook on the Law of Naval Operations, NWP 1-14M/MCTP 11-10B/COMDTPUB P5800.7A, ¶¶ 1.5, 1.6, 2.6.1 to 2.6.2 (pp. 1-7, 1-8, 2-9) (2017), www.jag.navy.mil/distrib/instructions/CDRs_HB_on_Law_of_Naval_Operations_AUG17.pdf; The Fletcher School of Law and Diplomacy—Tufts University, Law of the Sea, A Policy Primer 30-31 (2017), https://sites.tufts.edu/lawofthesea/introduction/. *But see* Australian Strategic Policy Institute (ASPI)—The Strategist, *Turning back the clock on UNCLOS* (Sam Bateman, Aug. 20, 2015), https://www.aspistrategist.org.au/turning-back-the-clock-on-unclos/ (arguing that the U.S. should "stop talking about EEZs as 'international waters'", i.e., as an "extension inwards of the high seas" because that ignores the Coastal State's rights and duties in the EEZ).

[1173] Commander's Handbook, ¶¶ 1.1, 1.9, 2.7.2 (pp. 1-1, 1-10, 2-13) (full cite above); Pedrozo, *Military Activities in the EEZ*, pp. 519-521 (full cite above).

[1174] UNCLOS, arts. 58(1) & 87 (full cite above). Chapter 5 discusses High Seas freedoms in more depth.

[1175] Tufts, Law of the Sea, p. 2 (full cite above). *See also* U.S. Dept. of Defense, Under Secretary of Defense for Policy, OUSDP Offices, FON, DoD Annual Freedom of Navigation (FON) Reports, *Freedom of Navigation: FY 2020 Operational Assertions*, p. 2, https://policy.defense.gov/OUSDP-Offices/FON/ ("International law as reflected in the 1982 Law of the Sea Convention recognizes the rights and freedoms of all nations to engage in traditional uses of the sea. These rights and freedoms are deliberately balanced against coastal States' control over maritime activities. As a nation with both a vast coastline and a significant maritime presence, the United States is committed to preserving this legal balance as an essential part of the stable, rules-based international order.").

[1176] UNCLOS, Introduction at p. 2 (full cite above) (noting that the "package deal" concept became a *leitmotif* (accompanying melody) that permeates throughout UNCLOS); Tufts, Law of the Sea, p. 9 (full cite above); Donald R. Rothwell & Tim Stephens, The Int'l. Law of the Sea 13, 79 (2nd ed. 2016). *See also* G.A. Res. 2750 (XXV), ¶ C, U.N. Doc A/AC.138/58 (Dec. 17, 1970), https://research.un.org/en/docs/ga/quick/regular/25 (noting "that the problems of ocean space are closely interrelated and need to be considered as a whole" when the United Nations General Assembly convened the Third United Nations Conference on the Law of the Sea); Permanent Court of Arbitration, Cases, Past Cases, [2013-19] The South China Sea Arbitration (*The Republic of Philippines v. The People's Republic of China*), Documents, Award on Jurisdiction and Admissibility (Oct. 29, 2015) ¶¶ 107, 225 (pp. 37, 87-88), https://pcacases.com/web/sendAttach/2579.

[1177] UNCLOS, art. 56(2) (full cite above). *See also* Rothwell & Stephens, Law of the Sea, p. 95 (full cite above).

[1178] UNCLOS, art. 58(3) (full cite above).

[1179] Tufts, Law of the Sea, p. 13 (full cite above).

[1180] Rothwell & Stephens, Law of the Sea, p. 98 (full cite above).

1181 Pedrozo, *Military Activities in the EEZ*, p. 515 (full cite above), *citing* United Nations Convention On The Law Of The Sea 1982: A Commentary, vol. II, 491, 529-30 (Satya N. Nandan & Shabtai Rosenne, eds., 1993).

1182 John Norton Moore, *Navigational Freedom: The Most Critical Common Heritage*, 93 Int'l. L. Stud. 251, 254-255 (2017), https://digital-commons.usnwc.edu/ils/vol93/iss1/8/.

1183 Chapter 5 discusses the "freedoms" of the High Seas.

1184 Pedrozo, *Military Activities in the EEZ*, p. 517 (full cite above).

1185 Pedrozo, *Military Activities in the EEZ*, pp. 515-16 (full cite above), *quoting* 17 Third UN Conference on the Law of the Sea, Plenary Meetings, Official Records, U.N. Doc. A/CONF.62/WS/37 and ADD.1-2, 244 (1973–1982). *See also* Tufts, Law Of The Sea, p. 31 (full cite above); Brookings Institution, Center for East Asia Policy Studies, East Asia Policy Paper 9, *The U.S. FON Program in the South China Sea—A lawful and necessary response to China's strategic ambiguity*, pp. 7-8 (Lynn Kuok, June 2016), https://www.brookings.edu/research/the-u-s-fon-program-in-the-south-china-sea/.

1186 Pedrozo, *Military Activities in the EEZ*, p. 516 (full cite above); Tufts, Law Of The Sea, pp. 30-34 (full cite above).

1187 Dept. of Defense Maritime Claims Reference Manual (MCRM)—Bangladesh 2019, http://www.jag.navy.mil/organization/code_10_mcrm.htm.

1188 DoD MCRM—Brazil 2013 (full cite above).

1189 DoD MCRM—China 2017 (full cite above). "In January 2007, the United States provided an aide-mémoire to Chinese officials concerning China's assertion that military activities in the EEZ required its prior consent." Brookings Institution, *U.S. FON Program in the South China Sea*, pp. 8-9 (full cite above).

1190 DoD MCRM—Dominican Republic 2020 (full cite above).

1191 DoD MCRM—Ecuador 2017 (full cite above); U.S. Dept. of State, Bureau of Oceans and Int'l. Environmental and Scientific Affairs, Policy Issues, The Ocean and Polar Affairs, Key Topics, Limits in the Seas No. 147, https://www.state.gov/limits-in-the-seas/.

1192 DoD MCRM—India 2016 (full cite above).

1193 DoD MCRM—Iran 2014 (full cite above).

1194 DoD MCRM—Malaysia 2016 (full cite above).

1195 DoD MCRM—Pakistan 2014 (full cite above).

1196 DoD MCRM—Thailand 2014 (full cite above).

1197 DoD MCRM—Uruguay 2017 (full cite above); U.S. Dept. of State, Limits in the Seas No. 123 (full cite above).

1198 DoD MCRM—Venezuela 2016 (full cite above).

1199 Global Research, Centre for Research on Globalization, *US-South Korea military drills. China opposes any military acts in exclusive economic zone without permission* (Nov. 26, 2010), https://www.globalresearch.ca/us-south-korea-military-drills-china-opposes-any-military-acts-in-exclusive-economic-zone-without-permission/22121.

1200 Military.com, Military News, *India Objects to US Navy Ship's Patrol Without Consent* (Apr. 9, 2021), https://www.military.com/daily-news/2021/04/09/india-objects-us-navy-ships-patrol-without-consent.html?ESRC=navy-a_210414.nl.

1201 Commander's Handbook, ¶ 2.7.1 (p. 2-13) (full cite above); Tufts, Law Of The Sea, p. 34 (full cite above).

1202 Commander's Handbook, ¶ 2.7.1 (p. 2-13) (full cite above).

1203 Pedrozo, *Military Activities in the EEZ*, p. 527 (full cite above).

¹²⁰⁴ *See generally* THE FLETCHER SCHOOL OF LAW AND DIPLOMACY—TUFTS UNIVERSITY, LAW OF THE SEA, A POLICY PRIMER 30-32, 34 (2017), https://sites.tufts.edu/lawofthesea/introduction/ (outlining the dispute regarding the U.S. conducting military activities in China's EEZ); Raul (Pete) Pedrozo, *Military Activities in the Exclusive Economic Zone: East Asia Focus*, 90 INT'L. L. STUD. 514, 528 (2014), https://digital-commons.usnwc.edu/ils/vol90/iss1/15/ (arguing that "in accordance with a generally accepted principle of international law—any act that is not prohibited in international law is permitted (the Lotus principle)—States may lawfully engage in intelligence collection, oceanographic surveys and other military activities in and over the EEZ without coastal State notice or consent.").

¹²⁰⁵ Pedrozo, *Military Activities in the EEZ*, pp. 541-542 (full cite above).

¹²⁰⁶ Dept. of Defense Maritime Claims Reference Manual (MCRM)—Australia 2019, http://www.jag.navy.mil/organization/code_10_mcrm.htm.

¹²⁰⁷ DoD MCRM—China 2017 (full cite above).

¹²⁰⁸ DoD MCRM—Costa Rica 2017 (full cite above).

¹²⁰⁹ DoD MCRM—Ecuador 2017 (full cite above); U.S. Dept. of State, U.S. Dept. of State, Bureau of Oceans and Int'l. Environmental and Scientific Affairs, Policy Issues, The Ocean and Polar Affairs, Key Topics, Limits in the Seas No. 147, https://www.state.gov/limits-in-the-seas/.

¹²¹⁰ DoD MCRM—Guyana 2014 (full cite above).

¹²¹¹ DoD MCRM—Haiti 2017 (full cite above). *See generally* William J. Aceves, *The Freedom of Navigation Program: A Study of the Relationship between Law and Politics*, 19 HASTINGS INT'L & COMP. L. REV. 259, 291-293 (1996), https://repository.uchastings.edu/hastings_international_comparative_law_revi ew/vol19/iss2/2/ (providing a detailed example of a U.S. FON diplomatic protest to Haiti).

¹²¹² DoD MCRM—India 2016 (full cite above).

¹²¹³ DoD MCRM—Maldives 2017 (full cite above); U.S. Dept. of State, Limits in the Seas No. 126 (full cite above).

¹²¹⁴ DoD MCRM—North Korea 2016 (full cite above).

¹²¹⁵ DoD MCRM—Pakistan 2014 (full cite above).

¹²¹⁶ DoD MCRM—Seychelles 2014 (full cite above).

¹²¹⁷ United Nations Convention on the Law of the Sea (UNCLOS) art. 76(1), Dec. 10, 1982, 1833 U.N.T.S. 397, https://www.un.org/Depts/los/convention_agreements/convention_overview_co nvention.htm.

¹²¹⁸ UNCLOS. art. 77 (full cite above).

¹²¹⁹ UNCLOS. art. 58(1) (full cite above).

¹²²⁰ UNCLOS, art. 79(1) (full cite above).

¹²²¹ UNCLOS, arts. 79(3) & (5) (full cite above); DONALD R. ROTHWELL & TIM STEPHENS, THE INT'L. LAW OF THE SEA 125 (2ⁿᵈ ed. 2016).

¹²²² DoD MCRM—Angola 2017 (full cite above).

¹²²³ DoD MCRM—Cabo Verde 2017 (full cite above); U.S. Dept. of State, Limits in the Seas No. 129 (full cite above).

¹²²⁴ DoD MCRM—Cambodia 2016 (full cite above).

¹²²⁵ DoD MCRM—China 2017 (full cite above); U.S. Dept. of State, Limits in the Seas No. 127 (full cite above)

¹²²⁶ DoD MCRM—Syria 2017 (full cite above).

¹²²⁷ DoD MCRM—Uruguay 2017 (full cite above); U.S. Dept. of State, Limits in the Seas No. 123 (full cite above).

1228 DoD MCRM—Vietnam 2016 (full cite above).
1229 DoD MCRM—Australia 2019 (full cite above).
1230 DoD MCRM—China 2017 (full cite above).
1231 United Nations, Division for Ocean Affairs and the Law of the Sea, Commission on the Limits of the Continental Shelf (CLCS), https://www.un.org/Depts/los/clcs_new/clcs_home.htm.
1232 DoD MCRM—Chile 2013 (full cite above).
1233 DoD MCRM—Ecuador 2017 (full cite above); U.S. Dept. of State, Limits in the Seas No. 147 (full cite above).
1234 DoD MCRM—India 2016 (full cite above).
1235 DoD MCRM—Iran 2014 (full cite above).
1236 DoD MCRM—Nicaragua 2016 (full cite above).
1237 Aceves, The FON Program, pp. 264-265 (full cite above), quoting Scott Truver, The Law of the Sea and the Military Use of the Ocean in 2010, 45 LA. L. REV. 1221, 1227 (1985), ALFRED T. MAHAN, THE INFLUENCE OF SEAPOWER UPON HISTORY 1660-1783 (1965), and U.S. DEP'T OF DEFENSE, NATIONAL SECURITY AND CONVENTION ON THE LAW OF THE SEA 8 (1994).
1238 John Norton Moore, Navigational Freedom: The Most Critical Common Heritage, 93 INT'L. L. STUD. 251, 259 & 261 (2017), https://digital-commons.usnwc.edu/ils/vol93/iss1/8/.
1239 "Adding a gloss" to a text (such as the U.S. Constitution, or an international treaty) means adding an interpretation of the text, which can avoid conflicts with related language and/or put the text in a certain context.
1240 U.S. NAVY, MARINE CORPS & COAST GUARD, THE COMMANDER'S HANDBOOK ON THE LAW OF NAVAL OPERATIONS, NWP 1-14M/MCTP 11-10B/COMDTPUB P5800.7A, ¶ 2.8 (p. 2-15) (2017), www.jag.navy.mil/distrib/instructions/CDRs_HB_on_Law_of_Naval_Operations_AUG17.pdf.
1241 Vienna Convention on the Law of Treaties (VCLT) art. 31(3)(b), May 23, 1969, 1155 U.N.T.S. 331. See also Dept. of Defense Law of War Manual § 1.7.4, p. 29 (June 2015, updated Dec. 2016), https://www.hsdl.org/?view&did=797480. Although the United States is not a party to the VCLT, it considers the VCLT to represent customary international law. Sean D. Murphy, The George Wash. Univ. Law Sch.: "Should the U.S. Join the International Criminal Court?" A Moderated Panel Discussion, Feb. 13, 2006. See also Letter Of Transmittal Forwarding The 1982 UN Law Of The Sea Convention To The United States Senate, DOS Commentary p. 17 (William J. Clinton, Oct. 7, 1994) (S. Treaty Doc. 103–39), https://www.foreign.senate.gov/imo/media/doc/treaty_103-39.pdf (noting that "[u]nder customary international law, as reflected in ... the Vienna Convention on the Law of Treaties (92nd Congress; 1st Session, Senate Executive 'L')"); Brookings Institution, Center for East Asia Policy Studies, East Asia Policy Paper 9, The U.S. FON Program in the South China Sea—A lawful and necessary response to China's strategic ambiguity, p. iii (Lynn Kuok, June 2016), https://www.brookings.edu/research/the-u-s-fon-program-in-the-south-china-sea/; Permanent Court of Arbitration, Cases, Past Cases, [2013-19] The South China Sea Arbitration (The Republic of Philippines v. The People's Republic of China), Documents, Award (July 12, 2016) ¶¶ 274, 476, 552-553 (pp. 115-116, 205, 231-232), https://pcacases.com/web/sendAttach/2086; Aceves, The FON Program, pp. 311-313 (full cite above).

1242 U.S. Dept. of Defense, Under Secretary of Defense for Policy, OUSDP Offices, FON, DoD Annual Freedom of Navigation (FON) Reports, *Freedom of Navigation: FY 2020 Operational Assertions*, p. 2, https://policy.defense.gov/OUSDP-Offices/FON/.

1243 Permanent Court of Arbitration, Cases, Past Cases, [2013-19] The South China Sea Arbitration (*The Republic of Philippines v. The People's Republic of China*), Documents, Award (July 12, 2016) ¶ 274 (pp. 115-116), https://pcacases.com/web/sendAttach/2086.

1244 U.S. NAVY, MARINE CORPS & COAST GUARD, THE COMMANDER'S HANDBOOK ON THE LAW OF NAVAL OPERATIONS, NWP 1-14M/MCTP 11-10B/COMDTPUB P5800.7A, ¶ 2.8 (p. 2-15) (2017), www.jag.navy.mil/distrib/instructions/CDRs_HB_on_Law_of_Naval_Operations_AUG17.pdf.

1245 Brookings Institution, Center for East Asia Policy Studies, East Asia Policy Paper 9, *The U.S. FON Program in the South China Sea—A lawful and necessary response to China's strategic ambiguity*, p. 5 (Lynn Kuok, June 2016), https://www.brookings.edu/research/the-u-s-fon-program-in-the-south-china-sea/.

1246 Helmut Türk, *Questions Relating to the Continental Shelf Beyond 200 Nautical Miles: Delimitation, Delineation, and Revenue Sharing*, 97 INT'L. L. STUD. 231, 247 (2021), https://digital-commons.usnwc.edu/ils/vol97/iss1/18/.

1247 U.S. Embassy & Consulate in Vietnam, News & Events, *Secretary of Defense Mark T. Esper Remarks at Diplomatic Academy of Vietnam* (Nov. 20, 2019), https://vn.usembassy.gov/secretary-of-defense-mark-t-esper-remarks-at-diplomatic-academy-of-vietnam/.

1248 COMMANDER'S HANDBOOK, ¶ 2.8 (p. 2-15) (full cite above). *See also* Elliot L. Richardson, Power, Mobility and the Law of the Sea, J. FOREIGN AFF., 902, 902 (1980). *See also* William J. Aceves, *The Freedom of Navigation Program: A Study of the Relationship between Law and Politics*, 19 HASTINGS INT'L & COMP. L. REV. 259, 287 (1996), https://repository.uchastings.edu/hastings_international_comparative_law_review/vol19/iss2/2/ (providing a detailed account of the origins of the U.S. FON program, and noting that "[t]he exercise of rights—the freedom to navigate on the world's oceans—is not meant to be a provocative act. Rather, in the framework of customary international law, it is a legitimate, peaceful assertion of a legal position and nothing more. If the United States and other maritime states do not assert international rights in the face of claims by others that do not conform with the present status of the law, they will be said to acquiesce in those claims to their disadvantage. What is particularly difficult in this situation is to understand that the more aggressive and unreasonable and provocative and threatening a claim may be, the more important it is to exercise one's rights in the face of the claim. The world community can't allow itself to be coerced-coerced into lethargy in the protection of the freedom of the seas.").

1249 *See generally* Aceves, *The FON Program*, pp. 279-284 (full cite above) (discussing how the U.S. "Defense Department had not conducted naval and air maneuvers in disputed waters in deference to the ongoing law of the sea negotiations. However, naval officials began arguing that the United States should no longer refrain from exercising its perceived maritime rights," especially as UNCLOS negotiations started to depart from U.S. interests, as well as the international community's "surprise and concern" when they learned of the U.S. FON "show the flag" program).

¹²⁵⁰ DoD Annual FON Reports, *FY 2020 Operational Assertions*, p. 2 (full cite above) ("Formally established in 1979, the FON Program consists of complementary diplomatic and operational efforts to safeguard lawful commerce and the global mobility of U.S. forces. The Department of State protests excessive maritime claims, advocating for adherence to international law, while the Department of Defense (DoD) exercises the United States' maritime rights and freedoms by conducting operational challenges against excessive maritime claims. In combination, these efforts help preserve for all States the legal balance of interests established in customary international law as reflected in the Law of the Sea Convention.").

¹²⁵¹ Stephen Rose, *Naval activity in the EEZ—Troubled waters ahead?*, 39 NAVAL L. REV. 67, 84 (1990).

¹²⁵² U.S. Dept. of State Foreign Affairs Manual (FAM) and Handbook (FAH), 7 FAM 034, *"Demarches"* (2005), https://fam.state.gov/FAM/07FAM/07FAM0030.html. *See generally* U.S. Dept. of State FAM/FAH Search, https://fam.state.gov/search.

¹²⁵³ DoD Annual FON Reports, *FY 2020 Operational Assertions*, p. 2 (full cite above); COMMANDER'S HANDBOOK, ¶ 2.8 (p. 2-15) (full cite above); U.S. Dept. of State, Bureau of Oceans and Int'l. Environmental and Scientific Affairs, Policy Issues, The Ocean and Polar Affairs, Key Topics, Limits in the Seas No. 112, https://www.state.gov/limits-in-the-seas/. *See also* Brookings Institution, *U.S. FON Program in the South China Sea*, p. 9 (full cite above). *See also* Aceves, *The FON Program*, pp. 287-288 (full cite above) (noting that "[t]he Freedom of Navigation program combines diplomatic and operational challenges to contest objectionable claims. The Departments of State and Defense are jointly responsible for the program and operations are conducted pursuant to careful interagency review.").

¹²⁵⁴ DoD Annual FON Reports, *FY 2020 Operational Assertions*, p. 3 (full cite above).

¹²⁵⁵ DoD Annual FON Reports, *FY 2020 Operational Assertion* (full cite above). *See also* Brookings Institution, *U.S. FON Program in the South China Sea*, p. iii (full cite above) (making a number of helpful suggestions to strengthen the U.S. FON program, including having the U.S. State Department publicize their diplomatic protests as well as the U.S. DoD).

¹²⁵⁶ Aceves, *The FON Program*, pp. 293-294 (full cite above).

¹²⁵⁷ *But see* Aceves, *The FON Program*, pp. 316-324 (full cite above) (critiquing the U.S. FONOPs program on both legal and normative grounds, including the inherent risk of them resulting in violent confrontations, and thus "FON operational challenges are inherently confrontational precisely because they challenge disputed claims.").

¹²⁵⁸ *See, e.g.*, Aceves, *The FON Program*, p. 293 & note 191 (full cite above) (providing detailed responses for U.S. ships and aircraft if challenged during FONOPs conducted in 1985).

¹²⁵⁹ *See generally* United Nations Convention on the Law of the Sea (UNCLOS) Introduction at p. 5, Dec. 10, 1982, 1833 U.N.T.S. 397, https://www.un.org/Depts/los/convention_agreements/convention_overview_convention.htm (noting that the "[a]nother of the peculiarities of the law of the sea treaty is that it is a major instrument which has equally authentic Arabic, Chinese, English, French, Russian and Spanish texts."); Aceves, *The FON Program*, pp. 314-315 (full cite above) (providing a detailed example of how U.S. FONOPs in the Black Sea led to the "the signing of two bilateral agreements [between Russia and the U.S.] in 1989: the Agreement on the Prevention of Dangerous Military Activities and the Uniform Interpretation of Rules of International Law Governing Innocent Passage,"

and explaining how differences in the Russian and English texts of UNCLOS Article 22 led to the disagreement between Russia and the U.S.).

[1260] U.S. Dept. of Defense, Under Secretary of Defense for Policy, OUSDP Offices, FON, DoD Annual Freedom of Navigation (FON) Reports, *DoD Freedom of Navigation Program – Fact Sheet 2* (Feb. 28, 2017), https://policy.defense.gov/OUSDP-Offices/FON/. *But see* William J. Aceves, *The Freedom of Navigation Program: A Study of the Relationship between Law and Politics*, 19 HASTINGS INT'L & COMP. L. REV. 259, 281-282 (1996), https://repository.uchastings.edu/hastings_international_comparative_law_revi ew/vol19/iss2/2/ (noting that the original "Commander in Chief, U.S. Atlantic Command (CINCLANT) ... memorandum on the Freedom of Navigation program ... added that in certain instances, U.S. forces must consider going out of their way to contest a maritime claim. However, the CINCLANT memorandum noted that while the United States must ensure that it is seen as unequivocally exercising its rights, it must avoid any irrational disposition of force and not challenge claims in an aggressive manner."); Aceves, *The FON Program*, p. 324 (full cite above) (noting that since U.S. FONOPs are inherently provocative, the U.S. "should not engage in maritime operations merely to assert U.S. navigational rights in disputed waters. If other foreign policy interests require maritime operations in disputed waters, these operations should then be conducted.").

[1261] U.S. Dept. of Defense, Under Secretary of Defense for Policy, OUSDP Offices, FON, DoD Annual Freedom of Navigation (FON) Reports, https://policy.defense.gov/OUSDP-Offices/FON/; U.S. NAVY, MARINE CORPS & COAST GUARD, THE COMMANDER'S HANDBOOK ON THE LAW OF NAVAL OPERATIONS, NWP 1-14M/MCTP 11-10B/COMDTPUB P5800.7A, ¶ 2.8 (p. 2-15) (2017), www.jag.navy.mil/distrib/instructions/CDRs_HB_on_Law_of_Naval_Operations _AUG17.pdf.

[1262] U.S. Dept. of Defense, Under Secretary of Defense for Policy, OUSDP Offices, FON, DoD Annual Freedom of Navigation (FON) Reports, *Freedom of Navigation: FY 2020 Operational Assertions*, p. 3, https://policy.defense.gov/OUSDP-Offices/FON/.

[1263] Brookings Institution, Center for East Asia Policy Studies, East Asia Policy Paper 9, *The U.S. FON Program in the South China Sea—A lawful and necessary response to China's strategic ambiguity*, p. iii (Lynn Kuok, June 2016), https://www.brookings.edu/research/the-u-s-fon-program-in-the-south-china-sea/.

[1264] One U.S. Navy author has opined that President Trump encouraged our allies to begin FONOPs in the South China Sea. Jonathan G. Odom, *The Value and Viability of the South China Sea Arbitration Ruling: The U.S. Perspective 2016–2020*, 97 INT'L. L. STUD. 122, 167-168 (2021), https://digital-commons.usnwc.edu/ils/vol97/iss1/16/.

[1265] Brookings Institution, *U.S. FON Program in the South China Sea*, p. 5 (full cite above).

[1266] Brookings Institution, *U.S. FON Program in the South China Sea*, p. 8 (full cite above). *See also* John Norton Moore, *Navigational Freedom: The Most Critical Common Heritage*, 93 INT'L. L. STUD. 251, 259 (2017), https://digital-commons.usnwc.edu/ils/vol93/iss1/8/ (arguing that "[n]ations should work together to jointly coordinate the sending of protest notes to countries that are not complying with UNCLOS. This compliance obligation should not be left to a few maritime powers. More nations should copy the U.S. practice of conducting freedom of navigation activities in relation to illegal claims.").

¹²⁶⁷ Lawfare blog, South China Sea, *The British are Coming to the South China Sea, and It's About Time* (Julian Ku, Feb. 28, 2018), https://www.lawfareblog.com/british-are-coming-south-china-sea-and-its-about-time. *See also* South China Morning Post, This Week in Asia, Politics, *America's message: time to pick sides in the South China Sea* (Bhavan Jaipragas, Oct. 6, 2018), https://www.scmp.com/week-asia/politics/article/2167247/americas-message-time-pick-sides-south-china-sea.

¹²⁶⁸ Defense News, Naval, *In challenging China's claims in the South China Sea, the US Navy is getting more assertive* (David B. Larter, Feb. 5, 2020), https://www.defensenews.com/naval/2020/02/05/in-challenging-chinas-claims-in-the-south-china-sea-the-us-navy-is-getting-more-assertive/.

¹²⁶⁹ United Nations, Division for Ocean Affairs and the Law of the Sea, Commission on the Limits of the Continental Shelf (CLCS), Submissions, through the Secretary-General of the United Nations, to the Commission on the Limits of the Continental Shelf, pursuant to article 76, paragraph 8, of the United Nations Convention on the Law of the Sea of 10 December 1982, Submission No. 33, https://www.un.org/Depts/los/clcs_new/commission_submissions.htm; DONALD R. ROTHWELL & TIM STEPHENS, THE INT'L. LAW OF THE SEA 103 (2ⁿᵈ ed. 2016).

¹²⁷⁰ Maritime Issues, International Law, *Extended Continental Shelf: A Renewed South China Sea Competition* (Nguyen Hong Thao, Apr. 19, 2020), http://www.maritimeissues.com/law/extended-continental-shelf-a-renewed-south-china-sea-competition.html.

¹²⁷¹ "China ... has not clarified the meaning of the dashed line, which may be a claim to all the waters within the dashed line or (merely) to the land features contained therein and maritime zones made from them in accordance with UNCLOS. If the former, it is also unclear whether the claim is one of historic title or 'historic rights'—whatever any such claim may mean for navigation rights—and whether historical claims survive the Convention." Brookings Institution, *U.S. FON Program in the South China Sea*, p. 20 (full cite above). *See also* Brookings Institution, Global China, *How China's Actions in the South China Sea Undermine the Rule of Law*, p. 2 (Lynn Kuok, November 2019), https://www.brookings.edu/research/how-chinas-actions-in-the-south-china-sea-undermine-the-rule-of-law/; Permanent Court of Arbitration, Cases, Past Cases, [2013-19] The South China Sea Arbitration (*The Republic of Philippines v. The People's Republic of China*), Documents, The Philippines' Memorial – Volume I (Mar. 30, 2014) ¶ 4.34 (p. 82), https://files.pca-cpa.org/pcadocs/Memorial%20of%20the%20Philippines%20Volume%20I.pdf; Permanent Court of Arbitration, Cases, Past Cases, [2013-19] The South China Sea Arbitration (*The Republic of Philippines v. The People's Republic of China*), Documents, Award on Jurisdiction and Admissibility (Oct. 29, 2015) ¶¶ 160 & n.121, 167 (pp. 62-63, 65), https://pcacases.com/web/sendAttach/2579; Shicun Wu, *A Legal Critique of the Award of the Arbitral Tribunal in the Matter of the South China Sea Arbitration, in* 24 ASIAN YEARBOOK OF INT'L. LAW 151, 177 (2020), https://brill.com/view/book/edcoll/9789004437784/BP000019.xml ("Nor is it clear that China ever claimed exclusive sovereignty over the natural resources of the South China Sea. Rather, it has stated that it respects freedom of navigation in and overflight over the waters in (at least part of) the maritime areas encompassed by the 'nine dash line'. The 'nine dash line' has been, for 50 years, a consistent point of reference for China. But there is no particular international obligation incumbent upon China to specify what exactly is meant by this historic line and its related historic rights."). *But see* universitätbonn institute for public int'l. law, Bonn

Research Papers on Public Int'l. Law, Paper No 14/2018, *The South China Sea Arbitration: Observations on the Award of 12 July 2016*, pp. 10-14 (Stefan A. G. Talmon, May 17, 2018), https://papers.ssrn.com/sol3/papers.cfm?abstract_id=3180037 (noting that "[t]he Chinese Government has repeatedly pointed out that 'China's sovereignty over the South China Sea and its claims to the relevant rights have been formed over a long course of history', or that 'China's sovereignty and relevant rights in the South China Sea [were] formed in the long historical course'. These statements prima facie show that China puts forward a claim to territorial sovereignty derived from historical circumstances and that this claim is not limited to insular land territory, i.e. to individual features in the Nansha Islands, but that it extends to the Nansha Islands as a whole, i.e. the group of islands including their interconnecting and adjacent waters.").

[1272] Mark E. Rosen, *U.S. International Oceans Law and Policy Interests in the South China Sea Arbitration: Implications for the U.S. Administration in the South China Sea and Elsewhere*, 22 J. OF CHINESE POLIT. SCI. 251, online unnumbered p. 4 (2017), https://www.readcube.com/articles/10.1007/s11366-017-9468-9. The Chinese State-run South China Sea "think tank" suggests that China views the South China Sea as a "semi-enclosed sea." Shicun Wu, *A Legal Critique of the Award of the Arbitral Tribunal in the Matter of the South China Sea Arbitration*, *in* 24 ASIAN YEARBOOK OF INT'L. LAW 151, 205 (2020), https://brill.com/view/book/edcoll/9789004437784/BP000019.xml. However, "[t]he Convention calls upon States bordering an enclosed or semi-enclosed sea to cooperate in carrying out their duties under the Convention, but gives such States no greater or lesser rights vis-a-vis third States. ... These provisions do not place or authorize any additional restrictions or limitations on navigation and overflight with respect to enclosed or semi-enclosed seas beyond those that appear elsewhere in the Convention." Letter Of Transmittal Forwarding The 1982 UN Law Of The Sea Convention To The United States Senate, DOS Commentary p. 90 (William J. Clinton, Oct. 7, 1994) (S. Treaty Doc. 103-39), https://www.foreign.senate.gov/imo/media/doc/treaty_103-39.pdf.

[1273] Raul (Pete) Pedrozo, *China's Revised Maritime Traffic Safety Law*, 97 INT'L. L. STUD. 956, 957 (2021), https://digital-commons.usnwc.edu/ils/vol97/iss1/39/.

[1274] American Historical Association, Pamphlets, *The Oldest Living Civilization*, https://www.historians.org/about-aha-and-membership/aha-history-and-archives/gi-roundtable-series/pamphlets/em-42-our-chinese-ally-(1944)/the-oldest-living-civilization.

[1275] Permanent Court of Arbitration, Cases, Past Cases, [2013-19] The South China Sea Arbitration (*The Republic of Philippines v. The People's Republic of China*), Documents, Award on Jurisdiction and Admissibility (Oct. 29, 2015) n.121 (p. 62), https://pcacases.com/web/sendAttach/2579; Permanent Court of Arbitration, Cases, Past Cases, [2013-19] The South China Sea Arbitration (*The Republic of Philippines v. The People's Republic of China*), Documents, Award (July 12, 2016) ¶¶ 180-181 & n.149 (pp. 71-72), https://pcacases.com/web/sendAttach/2086; Talmon, *Observations on the Award*, p. 18 (full cite above) (noting that "the Chinese Government internally circulated an atlas in 1947, drawing an eleven-dash line to indicate the geographical scope of its authority over the South China Sea. In the same year, the Ministry of the Interior published a list of 172 geographical names, in both Chinese and English, for the islands in the South China Sea.... [A] ten-dash line was shown on a map, published in Beijing in 1965 and reproduced in Western publications."); Jiangyu Wang, *Legitimacy, Jurisdiction and Merits in the South China Sea Arbitration: Chinese*

Perspectives and International Law, 22 J. OF CHINESE POLIT. SCI. 185, online p. 19 (2017), https://papers.ssrn.com/sol3/papers.cfm?abstract_id=2967254 ("Known also as the "dashed line" in Chinese literature, it first appeared as an eleven-dash line on an official map published by the Republic of China government in 1948. Two dashes were removed in 1953, reportedly thanks to Chairman Mao Zedong's decision to hand over the Gulf of Tonkin to Vietnam in 1952, resulting in today's nine-dash line.").

1276 Permanent Court of Arbitration, Cases, Past Cases, [2013-19] The South China Sea Arbitration (*The Republic of Philippines v. The People's Republic of China*), Documents, The Philippines' Memorial – Volume I (Mar. 30, 2014) ¶¶ 3.44 & n. 215, 4.32 (pp. 54, 81-82), https://files.pca-cpa.org/pcadocs/Memorial%20of%20the%20Philippines%20Volume%20I.pdf; National Public Radio (NPR), WAMU 88.5, American University Radio, Parallels— Many Stories, One World, Conflict Zones, *A Primer on the Complicated Battle for the South China Sea* (Rami Ayyub, Apr. 13, 2016), https://www.npr.org/sections/parallels/2016/04/13/472711435/a-primer-on-the-complicated-battle-for-the-south-china-sea. (noting that the initial claim was made by the then-Republic of China, now Taiwan); Rosen, *South China Sea Arbitration*, p. 4 (full cite above); Wu, *A Legal Critique*, pp. 171, 175 (full cite above). *But see* Talmon, *Observations on the Award*, pp. 33-39 (full cite above) (noting that China claims "[a]ncient title[dating back over 2,000 years, which] is an *original title* ... based on a State's discovery and occupation of territory. The State, by way of discovery and occupation, becomes the lawful original owner of the territory. The doctrine of ancient title can apply only to the acquisition of territory which international law, at the time of acquisition, considered *terra nullius*, i.e. territory unclaimed by any other State.158 A claim to ancient title must be judged upon the law prevailing during the period the discovery and occupation took place.").

1277 Wu, *A Legal Critique*, p. 175 (full cite above).

1278 Brookings Institution, Global China, *How China's Actions in the South China Sea Undermine the Rule of Law*, p. 1 (Lynn Kuok, November 2019), https://www.brookings.edu/research/how-chinas-actions-in-the-south-china-sea-undermine-the-rule-of-law/.

1279 Jonathan G. Odom, *The Value and Viability of the South China Sea Arbitration Ruling: The U.S. Perspective 2016–2020*, 97 INT'L. L. STUD. 122, 126 (2021), https://digital-commons.usnwc.edu/ils/vol97/iss1/16/.

1280 A U.S. Assistant Secretary of State estimated the value at "$2.5 trillion in recoverable energy reserves" in the South China Sea. Asia Reassurance Initiative Act (ARIA) in Action, Part 3: Implementation and the Indo-Pacific Strategy, Hearing Before the Subcomm. on East Asia, the Pacific and International Cybersecurity Policy of the S. Comm. on Foreign Relations, 116th Cong 114 (2019) (statement of David R. Stilwell, Assistant Secretary Bureau of East Asian and Pacific Affairs, U.S. Department of State), https://www.foreign.senate.gov/imo/media/doc/10%2016%2019%20--%20ARIA%20in%20Action%20-%20Implementation%20and%20the%20Indo-Pacific%20Strategy.pdf.

1281 U.S. Dept. of Defense, Office of the Secretary of Defense, *Annual Report To Congress: Military and Security Developments Involving the People's Republic of China 2020*, pp. 9, 133, https://media.defense.gov/2020/Sep/01/2002488689/-1/-1/1/2020-DOD-CHINA-MILITARY-POWER-REPORT-FINAL.PDF.

¹²⁸² For example, "Malaysia's state-owned [company] Petronas is exploring [for oil] on the extended continental shelf claimed by both [Malaysia] and [Vietnam]," and within China's 9-dash line. China has sent military vessels near the exploration/drilling ship to observe and/or harass. Asia Maritime Transparency Initiative, Malaysia Picks a Three-way Fight in the South China Sea (Feb. 21, 2020), https://amti.csis.org/malaysia-picks-a-three-way-fight-in-the-south-china-sea/. In response, the U.S. sent 2 Navy ships near the exploration/drilling ship as a show of support. America's Navy, Forged by the Sea, News, *Montgomery, Cesar Chavez operate near West Capella* (May 7, 2020), https://www.navy.mil/submit/display.asp?story_id=112891&utm_source=phplist5 649&utm_medium=email&utm_content=HTML&utm_campaign=U.S.+Navy+Top +Stories. *See also* America's Navy, Forged by the Sea, News, *U.S. Navy Maintains Persistent Presence Near West Capella* (Lauren Chatmas, May 12, 2020), https://www.navy.mil/submit/display.asp?story_id=112941&utm_source=phplist5 694&utm_medium=email&utm_content=HTML&utm_campaign=U.S.+Navy+Top +Stories; The Heritage Foundation, Event, Asia, David Stilwell, *VIRTUAL EVENT: Lessons from the West Capella Incident: Successful Naval Presence in the South China Sea* (Mar. 10, 2021), https://www.heritage.org/asia/event/virtual-event-lessons-the-west-capella-incident-successful-naval-presence-the-south?mkt_tok=ODIoLU1IVCozMDQAAAF76ubq82sGAxbUdDJQLRDU9aO_Z82_vci ySdmo7OO6sN-FZQdGYuzepo_oo_9VFtm-6SghOgPivIhX4rw1ad1YvOJ5ONqPG3_IOA3YynBckabD1G1M.

¹²⁸³ Stephen Rose, *Naval activity in the EEZ—Troubled waters ahead?*, 39 NAVAL L. REV. 67, 84 (1990).

¹²⁸⁴ U.S. Dept. of State, Bureau of Oceans and Int'l. Environmental and Scientific Affairs, Policy Issues, The Ocean and Polar Affairs, Key Topics, Limits in the Seas No. 112, https://www.state.gov/limits-in-the-seas/. *See also* Brookings Institution, Center for East Asia Policy Studies, East Asia Policy Paper 9, *The U.S. FON Program in the South China Sea—A lawful and necessary response to China's strategic ambiguity*, p. iii (Lynn Kuok, June 2016), https://www.brookings.edu/research/the-u-s-fon-program-in-the-south-china-sea/.

¹²⁸⁵ Brookings Institution, *U.S. FON Program in the South China Sea*, p. 7 (full cite above).

¹²⁸⁶ Brookings Institution, *U.S. FON Program in the South China Sea*, pp. 8-9 (full cite above).

¹²⁸⁷ Brookings Institution, *U.S. FON Program in the South China Sea*, pp. 11-12 (full cite above).

¹²⁸⁸ South China Morning Post, This Week in Asia, Politics, *America's message: time to pick sides in the South China Sea* (Bhavan Jaipragas, Oct. 6, 2018), https://www.scmp.com/week-asia/politics/article/2167247/americas-message-time-pick-sides-south-china-sea.

¹²⁸⁹ For example, "Chinese diplomats and visiting officials have been telling their Australian counterparts for two years now that if they conduct a FONOP in the South China Sea, there will be consequences for the bilateral relationship." South China Morning Post, *America's message: time to pick sides* (full cite above). *See generally* United Nations Convention on the Law of the Sea (UNCLOS) Introduction at p. 2, Dec. 10, 1982, 1833 U.N.T.S. 397, https://www.un.org/Depts/los/convention_agreements/convention_overview_co nvention.htm (noting that the genesis for UNCLOS negotiations originated in "the First Committee of the [UN] General Assembly, as the item was perceived from the

very beginning as being of primarily political significance, and not limited to strictly legal or economic concern"); THE FLETCHER SCHOOL OF LAW AND DIPLOMACY—TUFTS UNIVERSITY, LAW OF THE SEA, A POLICY PRIMER 6 (2017), https://sites.tufts.edu/lawofthesea/introduction/ (noting that "[p]olitical, strategic, and economic issues are reflected in the historical tension between the exercise of state sovereignty over the sea and the idea of 'the free sea.'"); William J. Aceves, *The Freedom of Navigation Program: A Study of the Relationship between Law and Politics*, 19 HASTINGS INT'L & COMP. L. REV. 259, 259 (1996), https://repository.uchastings.edu/hastings_international_comparative_law_revi ew/vol19/iss2/2/ (noting that there is a "persistent interaction between law and politics" throughout the history of the development of the Law of the Sea, as exemplified by the U.S. FONOPs program); Military.com, News, Headlines, *'Elephant Walk' on Guam Serves as Timely US Airpower Demonstration, Defense Expert Says* (Seth Robson, Apr. 15, 2020), https://www.military.com/daily-news/2020/04/15/elephant-walk-guam-serves-timely-us-airpower-demonstration-defense-expert-says.html?ESRC=eb_200416.nl (reporting that in order to counter the perception that U.S. military projection power was degraded due to the sidelining of the aircraft carrier USS THEODORE ROOSEVELT (CVN 71) in Guam due to its crew being infected with Coronavirus 2019 (COVID-19), the U.S. Air Force conducted an "elephant walk" of 11 of its largest airplanes in Guam; this caught the attention of North Korea, which fired shore-based cruise missiles and air-to-surface missiles into the Sea of Japan off its eastern coast the following day in response).

[1290] *See, e.g.*, Military.com, Military News, *China Sends Aircraft Carrier Strike Group Near Okinawa in Message to US and Japan* (Jesse Johnson, Apr. 5, 2021), https://www.military.com/daily-news/2021/04/05/china-sends-aircraft-carrier-strike-group-near-okinawa-message-us-and-japan.html?ESRC=eb_210406.nl; Military.com, Military News, *Philippine Presidential Aide Warns of 'Unwanted Hostilities' in South China Sea* (Apr. 5, 2021), https://www.military.com/daily-news/2021/04/05/philippines-accuses-china-of-plans-occupy-more-south-china-sea-features.html?ESRC=eb_210406.nl (reporting that 200 Chinese fishing/Maritime Militia vessels harbored at Whitsun Reef, which lies in the contested Spratly Islands).

[1291] TUFTS, LAW OF THE SEA, p. 6 (full cite above).

[1292] "President Obama's administration was reportedly reluctant to approve FONOPs in the South China Sea, or at least certain categories of those operations." Jonathan G. Odom, *The Value and Viability of the South China Sea Arbitration Ruling: The U.S. Perspective 2016–2020*, 97 INT'L. L. STUD. 122, 163-164 (2021), https://digital-commons.usnwc.edu/ils/vol97/iss1/16/.

[1293] The White House, President Barack Obama, Briefing Room, Speeches & Remarks, The White House, Office of the Press Secretary, *Remarks by President Obama in Address to the People of Vietnam* (May 24, 2016), https://obamawhitehouse.archives.gov/the-press-office/2016/05/24/remarks-president-obama-address-people-vietnam ("As we go forward, the United States will continue to fly, sail and operate wherever international law allows, and we will support the right of all countries to do the same."). President Obama expressly referred to FONOPs in his U.S. Ocean Policy: "exercise rights and jurisdiction and perform duties in accordance with applicable international law, including respect for and preservation of navigational rights and freedoms, which are essential for the global economy and international peace and security". Executive Order 13547:

431

Stewardship of the Ocean, Our Coasts, and the Great Lakes ¶ 2(vii) (Pres. Barack Obama, July 19, 2010), 75 Fed. Reg. 43,021, https://www.federalregister.gov/documents/2010/07/22/2010-18169/stewardship-of-the-ocean-our-coasts-and-the-great-lakes. President Trump revoked President Obama's U.S. Ocean Policy, and replaced it with a more U.S.-centric policy that does not even reference freedom of navigation: "exercise rights and jurisdiction and perform duties in accordance with applicable domestic law and — if consistent with applicable domestic law — international law, including customary international law". Executive Order 13840: Ocean Policy To Advance the Economic, Security, and Environmental Interests of the United States ¶ 2(c) (Pres. Donald Trump, June 19, 2018), 83 Fed. Reg. 29,431, https://www.federalregister.gov/documents/2018/06/22/2018-13640/ocean-policy-to-advance-the-economic-security-and-environmental-interests-of-the-united-states.

[1294] Jonathan G. Odom, *The Value and Viability of the South China Sea Arbitration Ruling: The U.S. Perspective 2016–2020*, 97 INT'L. L. STUD. 122, 162, 165 (2021), https://digital-commons.usnwc.edu/ils/vol97/iss1/16/.

[1295] Defense News, Naval, *In challenging China's claims in the South China Sea, the US Navy is getting more assertive* (David B. Larter, Feb. 5, 2020), https://www.defensenews.com/naval/2020/02/05/in-challenging-chinas-claims-in-the-south-china-sea-the-us-navy-is-getting-more-assertive/. *See also* South China Morning Post, This Week in Asia, Politics, *America's message: time to pick sides in the South China Sea* (Bhavan Jaipragas, Oct. 6, 2018), https://www.scmp.com/week-asia/politics/article/2167247/americas-message-time-pick-sides-south-china-sea. The author would note that calculating the number of FONOPs is not possible based solely upon reviewing the annual DoD FON Reports. Before 2017, the annual DoD FON Reports merely listed the *types* of FON assertions against a particular State. Thus, for Fiscal Years 2015 through 2017, the DoD FON Report listed the following FONOPs against Chinese excessive maritime claims (multiple FON assertions are marked with an asterisk):

2015: China*	Excessive straight baselines; jurisdiction over airspace above the EEZ; restriction on foreign aircraft flying through an Air Defense Identification Zone (ADIZ) without the intent to enter national airspace; domestic law criminalizing survey activity by foreign entities in the EEZ; prior permission required for innocent passage of foreign military ships through the TTS.
2016: China*	Excessive straight baselines; jurisdiction over airspace above the EEZ; restriction on foreign aircraft flying through an ADIZ without the intent to enter national airspace; domestic law criminalizing survey activity by foreign entities in the EEZ; prior permission required for innocent passage of foreign military ships through the TTS.

	Excessive straight baselines	Paracel Islands
	* Jurisdiction over airspace above the exclusive economic zone (EEZ)	South & East China Seas
	* Restriction on foreign aircraft flying through an Air Defense Identification Zone (ADIZ) without the intent to enter national airspace	East China Sea
2017: China	* Domestic law criminalizing survey activity by foreign entities in the EEZ	South China Sea
	Prior permission required for innocent passage of foreign military ships through the TTS	Paracel Islands
	* Actions/statements that indicate a claim to a TTS around features not so entitled	Spratly Islands

U.S. Dept. of Defense, Under Secretary of Defense for Policy, OUSDP Offices, FON, DoD Annual Freedom of Navigation (FON) Reports, https://policy.defense.gov/OUSDP-Offices/FON/. *See also* Brookings Institution, Center for East Asia Policy Studies, East Asia Policy Paper 9, *The U.S. FON Program in the South China Sea—A lawful and necessary response to China's strategic ambiguity*, pp. 22-29 (Lynn Kuok, June 2016), https://www.brookings.edu/research/the-u-s-fon-program-in-the-south-china-sea/ (suggesting that the U.S. FON program be more obvious as to what the U.S. is asserting (both operationally and diplomatically) and more specifically where it is doing so); Odom, *The Value and Viability of the South China Sea Arbitration Ruling*, pp. 162, 165 (full cite above) (noting that in response to a new requirement in the National Defense Authorization Act, the 2017 DoD FON Report started including "a third element of information: '[t]he nature of each claim, including the geographic location or area covered by such claim (including the body of water and island grouping, when applicable).' But this additional information still does not provide the full clarity necessary to perform external analysis about whether the frequency of FONOPs are increasing or decreasing, particularly in the South China Sea.").

[1296] Defense News, *In challenging China's claims*, (full cite above).

[1297] China implemented a Maritime Police (MPL) on February 1, 2021, which purports to give broad authority to Chinese coastal police agencies (CCG). "The CCG could also rely on the MPL to justify increased interference with U.S. ships engaged in freedom of navigation operations (FONOPS), military surveys, and presence operations in the [South China Sea]. China has repeatedly protested U.S. FONOPS in the Spratlys and Paracels as an infringement of Chinese sovereignty. Article 21 illegally authorizes the CCG to use force, including 'forced eviction and forced towing,' against foreign warships and other sovereign immune vessels that refuse to leave waters under PRC jurisdiction for purported violations of China's laws and regulations. Except in situations where a foreign warship has demonstrated hostile intent or committed a hostile act, the sole remedy for noncompliance with coastal State laws and regulations in the territorial sea is an order to leave the territorial sea and a diplomatic protest. Seaward of the territorial sea, foreign warships and other sovereign immune vessels have complete immunity from the jurisdiction of any State other than the flag State. A threat or use of force by the CCG against a U.S. warship would certainly generate a response in self-defense by the warship consistent with the U.S. Standing Rules of Engagement." Raul (Pete) Pedrozo, *Maritime Police Law of the People's Republic of China*, 97 INT'L. L. STUD. 465, 470 (2021), https://digital-commons.usnwc.edu/ils/vol97/iss1/24/.

[1298] Reuters, World News, *U.S. warships sail in disputed South China Sea, angering China* (Idrees Ali, Nov. 21, 2019), https://www.reuters.com/article/us-usa-china-southchinasea-military-idUSKBN1XV2NS. Part of the issue is that China not only claims sovereignty over artificial "islands" in the South China Sea, but also that these artificial islands possess the same maritime zones (including the lucrative 200 nm EEZ) as natural islands. Although artificial islands may be constructed in a Coastal State's Exclusive Economic Zone, they are not entitled to any maritime zones. United Nations Convention on the Law of the Sea (UNCLOS) arts. 56, 60 & 121, Dec. 10, 1982, 1833 U.N.T.S. 397, https://www.un.org/Depts/los/convention_agreements/convention_overview_convention.htm. *See also* Imogen Saunders, *Artificial Islands and Territory in International Law*, 52 VANDERBILT J. OF TRANSNATIONAL LAW 643 (2019); THE FLETCHER SCHOOL OF LAW AND DIPLOMACY—TUFTS UNIVERSITY, LAW OF THE SEA, A POLICY PRIMER 16 (2017), https://sites.tufts.edu/lawofthesea/introduction/. Chapter 12 discusses the requirements for claiming the status of an island in more depth in the context of the Permanent Court of Arbitration Tribunal's decision in the South China Sea arbitration.

[1299] Brookings Institution, Center for East Asia Policy Studies, East Asia Policy Paper 9, *The U.S. FON Program in the South China Sea—A lawful and necessary response to China's strategic ambiguity*, p. iii (Lynn Kuok, June 2016), https://www.brookings.edu/research/the-u-s-fon-program-in-the-south-china-sea/.

[1300] *But see* U.S. Dept. of Defense, Under Secretary of Defense for Policy, OUSDP Offices, FON, DoD Annual Freedom of Navigation (FON) Reports, *Freedom of Navigation: FY 2020 Operational Assertions*, p. 3, https://policy.defense.gov/OUSDP-Offices/FON/ (noting that "To maintain the operational security of U.S. military forces, the DoD Annual FON Report includes only general geographic information on the location of operational challenges.").

[1301] Brookings Institution, *U.S. FON Program in the South China Sea*, pp. 22-29 (full cite above). *See generally* William J. Aceves, *The Freedom of Navigation Program: A Study of the Relationship between Law and Politics*, 19 HASTINGS INT'L & COMP. L. REV. 259, 288-293 (1996), https://repository.uchastings.edu/hastings_international_comparative_law_review/vol19/iss2/2/ (providing detailed examples of U.S. FON diplomatic protests to Romania, Finland and Haiti).

[1302] Brookings Institution, *U.S. FON Program in the South China Sea*, p. 30 (full cite above).

CHAPTER 12: MANDATORY DISPUTE SETTLEMENT

"[T]he Spratly Islands, a constellation of small islands and coral reefs, existing just above or below water, that comprise the peaks of undersea mountains rising from the deep ocean floor. Long known principally as a hazard to navigation and identified on nautical charts as the 'dangerous ground', the Spratly Islands are the site of longstanding territorial disputes among some of the littoral States of the South China Sea."
—Permanent Court of Arbitration (The South China Sea Arbitration Award of 12 July 2016, ¶ 3)

"A PERENNIAL ISSUE OF PUBLIC INTERNATIONAL LAW IS ITS ENFORCEABILITY. Given that the international rules-based order is primarily an anarchical system, there are limited ways in which the rules underlying the international order can be enforced against individual States. This is especially true for decisions rendered by international courts and tribunals, including those of the International Court of Justice, the International Tribunal for the Law of the Sea, and arbitral tribunals such as those constituted under UNCLOS."[1303] This Chapter will discuss UNCLOS' enforcement mechanism, and use the South China Sea arbitration as an illustrative example.

As discussed in Chapter 9, States recognized after World War II that they had been unable to prevent that incredibly devastating conflict. As American President John F. Kennedy said when he addressed the UN General Assembly in 1961: "Mankind must put an end to war, or war will put an end to mankind."[1304] Thus, in 1945 States signed the United Nations (UN) Charter to promote international peace and security. In order to include an effective enforcement mechanism to prevent war, States "confer[red] on the [UN] Security Council primary responsibility for the maintenance of international peace and security, and agree[d] that in carrying out its duties under this responsibility the Security Council acts on their behalf."[1305] Once a dispute between States has escalated to the level of a "threat to the peace, breach of the peace, or act of aggression," the UN Security Council (UNSC) may take action pursuant to Chapter VII of the UN Charter in order to maintain or enforce international peace and security.[1306] Thus, the key to the continued vitality of the UN Charter 75 years later has been its enforcement mechanism in Chapter VII.

Similarly, State representatives attending the Third UN Conference on the Law of the Sea from 1973 to 1982 (which culminated in UNCLOS) sought to include an effective enforcement mechanism to peacefully resolve maritime disputes that would inevitably arise. Nevertheless, dispute settlement was another contentious issue during UNCLOS negotiations.[1307] The U.S. had negotiated many treaties and had found it difficult, if not impossible, to enforce their provisions. Therefore, the U.S. favored a system of mandatory dispute settlement in UNCLOS, which was ultimately adopted. "Part XV of the Convention, which establishes an elaborate system for the settlement of maritime disputes, became one of the main achievements of the Third United Nations Conference on the Law of the Sea."[1308]

> The Convention establishes a dispute settlement system to promote compliance with its provisions and the peaceful settlement of disputes. These procedures are flexible, in providing options as to the appropriate means and fora for resolution of disputes, and comprehensive, in subjecting the bulk of the Convention's provisions to enforcement through binding mechanisms. The system also provides Parties the means of excluding from binding dispute settlement certain sensitive political and defense matters.[1309]

The mandatory dispute settlement framework in UNCLOS begins with the proposition that disputes between States (in interpreting or applying UNCLOS provisions) shall be settled peacefully in general, and specifically "by any peaceful means of their own choice."[1310] Although this would seem to beg for creative methods between State leaders ("Wouldn't you prefer a good game of chess?"[1311]), it is actually an implicit reference to Article 33(1) of the UN Charter:

> The parties to any dispute, the continuance of which is likely to endanger the maintenance of international peace and security, shall, first of all, seek a solution by negotiation, enquiry, mediation, conciliation, arbitration, judicial settlement, resort to regional agencies or arrangements, or other peaceful means of their own choice.[1312]

The process envisioned was that if there was a dispute under UNCLOS, the States involved would first seek to agree upon resolving their dispute by using any one of a number of "peaceful means of their own choice."

At any point in time, the parties may resolve the issue by independently agreeing on a peaceful resolution of the dispute. They should follow a series of efforts to reach a resolution.

First, they should have an exchange of views. If a resolution of the dispute, independent of the [UNCLOS] procedures, is not pursued or ach[ie]ved, then the parties have an obligation to "exchange views" as to whether a "settlement by negotiation or other peaceful means" is possible in their view.

Second, in accordance with Article 284, a party to a dispute may "invite the other party or parties to submit the dispute to conciliation." If the parties agree to submit the dispute to conciliation, they are bound to comply with the rules set out by the conciliatory process of [UNCLOS] and cannot prematurely terminate the conciliation. If the invitation is declined or the parties fail to agree on the conciliation procedure, then the conciliation is considered to have ended. Conciliation is a process by which the dispute is submitted for consideration by an independent party, but the parties are not obligated to accept the independent party's conclusions.

If the parties agree to conciliation, then a conciliation commission is formed, composed of five members. The two parties each propose two members, forming a group of four, which selects the fifth member of the commission. Once the commission is established, it determines its own procedures (unless the parties agree to an alternative procedures), and decisions are made by majority votes. The commission "shall hear the parties, examine their claims and objections, and make proposals to the parties with a view to reaching an amicable settlement." Within 12 months, the commission will issue a non-binding report on the proposals regarding the "questions of fact or law relevant to the matter in dispute" and will make recommendations "as appropriate" for an "amicable settlement." The first conciliation case under [UNCLOS] began in 2016, relating to a dispute between Timor-Leste and Australia regarding the maritime boundary between the two States.[1313]

Only if the parties were unable to resolve their dispute peacefully within a reasonable period of time, would the mandatory dispute settlement provisions of UNCLOS apply.[1314] Thus, UNCLOS' mandatory dispute settlement provisions are a backup, "com[ing] into operation only when no settlement can be reached by the parties by recourse to such means of their own choice."[1315]

UNCLOS provides 3 methods of mandatory dispute settlement, with a State being able to declare its preferred method for settling disputes upon ratifying or acceding to UNCLOS, or at any time thereafter. The 3 methods of mandatory dispute settlement are:

1) the International Tribunal for the Law of the Sea (ITLOS),
2) the International Court of Justice (ICJ), or
3) "an arbitral tribunal constituted in accordance with Annex VII,"[1316] or a special arbitral tribunal under Annex VIII.[1317]

If two States involved in a dispute have selected the same method, then they would use that method to resolve their dispute. If the States have chosen different methods, or if either State has not made an election, then an arbitral tribunal would be used as the default (unless they agree on another method).[1318]

Of the 3 methods of mandatory dispute settlement under UNCLOS, the International Tribunal for the Law of the Sea (ITLOS) is the newest, having been specifically created by UNCLOS in 1982 to resolve maritime disputes. Representatives from States which are party to UNCLOS elect 21 members[1319] (recognized as Law of the Sea experts) to serve on the Tribunal for 9-year-terms, with an equitable geographical distribution of members. ITLOS is based in Hamburg, Germany,[1320] and ITLOS judges are also frequently used in UNCLOS arbitrations, as will be discussed below in the context of the South China Sea arbitration.

The International Court of Justice (ICJ) is the 2nd newest/oldest of the 3 methods of mandatory dispute settlement under UNCLOS, having been formed by the UN Charter in 1945 to resolve disputes between States. The UN General Assembly and UN Security Council elect 15 members to serve on the court for 9-year-terms, with an equitable geographical distribution of members. The ICJ is based in the historic Peace Palace in The Hague, Netherlands.[1321]

The default method of mandatory dispute settlement under UNCLOS is to use "an arbitral tribunal constituted in accordance with Annex VII."[1322] Annex VII of UNCLOS established the following process:

> State Parties to the 1899 and 1907 Hague Conventions each nominate up to 4 arbitrators to a list of arbitrators maintained by the UN Secretary General.[1323]

> "[T]he arbitral tribunal shall, unless the parties [to the dispute] otherwise agree, be constituted" of 5 members, with 1 member appointed by each party and the 3 other members "appointed by agreement between the parties," all members "preferably [coming] from the list" mentioned above.[1324]

> If the parties to the conflict cannot agree on 1 or more additional members, they can either agree to have a 3rd State make the appointment(s), or "the President of [ITLOS] shall make the necessary appointments" from the list mentioned above.[1325]

> "Unless the parties to the dispute otherwise agree, the arbitral tribunal shall determine its own procedure, assuring to each party a full opportunity to be heard and to present its case."[1326]

Although not required by the Annex VII process, "[a]ll but one of the Annex VII arbitrations so far has been conducted using the services of the Permanent Court of Arbitration (PCA)."[1327] The PCA serves as the "registry" (or administrative secretariat) for the arbitral tribunal, and was created by the 1st Hague Peace Conference in 1899 as a forum for the peaceful resolution of disputes between States. The historic Peace Palace in The Hague, Netherlands (which, as discussed, also houses the ICJ) was originally built to provide a home for the PCA, where it still resides.[1328]

However, although State representatives attending the Third UN Conference on the Law of the Sea sought to include an effective enforcement mechanism in UNCLOS, they also wanted to permit States some flexibility in exercising their maritime sovereignty. So, for example, States are free to regulate Marine Scientific Research (MSR) in their Exclusive Economic Zone (EEZ) and on their Continental Shelf without being subject to mandatory dispute settlement to consider the reasonableness of their regulations.[1329] Similarly, States are free to conserve the living resources (e.g., fisheries) in their EEZs without being subject to mandatory dispute settlement to consider the reasonableness of their conservation measures.[1330] In addition, States may elect to "opt out" of mandatory dispute settlement for "certain sensitive political and defense matters."[1331] Article 298 permits State Parties to "opt out" of mandatory dispute settlement in 3 situations:

1) Delimiting their *maritime borders* (which may still be subject to compulsory but non-binding conciliation, such as between Australia and Timor-Leste, mentioned above);
2) Disputes concerning *military activities*; and
3) Disputes in which the *UN Security Council* is exercising its functions (e.g., in maintaining international peace and security).[1332]

SOUTH CHINA SEA DISPUTE

The South China Sea situation is a complex security problem, which involves several interwoven dynamics. These include not only international law but also geopolitical power, economic competition, transnational security threats, food insecurity and frictional nationalism. International law alone is not a solution, but a "rules-based approach" can help frame many security challenges, manage the territorial and maritime disputes between the claimant States and ultimately resolve those disputes. The South China Sea arbitration and the arbitral tribunal's resulting award were a positive step in applying a rules-based approach to framing, managing and resolving some of the international disputes.[1333]

This Chapter's second sub-topic (and the final topic in this book) is the South China Sea dispute as an illustrative example of mandatory dispute settlement under UNCLOS. The South China Sea dispute has been a recurring theme throughout this book, from serving as an example of a maritime "hot spot" in Chapter 1, to serving as benchmark for what constitutes an "island" in Chapter 4, to serving as an example of a potential conflict that may require the use of U.S. military force (especially naval force) in Chapter 10, to serving as an example of excessive maritime claims and an area ripe for Freedom of Navigation Operations (FONOPs) in Chapter 11.

As a memory refresher, Vietnam, Malaysia, Brunei, the Philippines and China have overlapping claims to the islands and waters in the South China Sea, as shown best on the following detailed chart. The following chart suggests a number of potential overlapping Exclusive Economic Zone (EEZ) and Continental Shelf claims. As discussed in Chapter 8, the delimitation of both EEZ and Continental Shelf claims involves a 3-step process:

1) States shall seek to reach an "agreement on the basis of international law … in order to achieve an equitable solution."

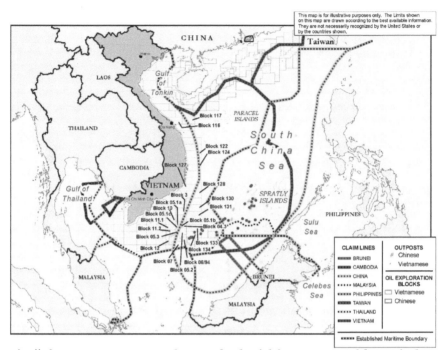

2) "If no agreement can be reached within a reasonable period of time, the States concerned shall resort to the procedures provided for in Part XV" (Settlement of Disputes).[1334]

3) However, if one or both States have "opted out" of mandatory dispute settlement for the delimitation of their maritime borders, then the States can only return to step #1, and seek to reach an equitable agreement. Without a possible 3rd step, there is no way to force resolving the dispute "within a reasonable period of time."

The delimitation of EEZ and Continental Shelf claims harken back to the 1969 decision in the North Sea Continental Shelf case, where the ICJ held that delimitation of maritime borders must be by agreement between States, who have an obligation to negotiate in good faith, taking into account all relevant circumstances, in order to arrive at an equitable solution.

Two of the States with overlapping EEZ and Continental Shelf claims in the South China Sea are the Philippines and China, both of whom are parties to UNCLOS, and neither of which has made a declaration selecting a method for mandatory dispute settlement.[1335] Therefore, if the Philippines and China are unable to resolve their dispute within a reasonable period of time, then "an arbitral tribunal constituted in accordance with Annex VII" would serve as their default election for mandatory dispute settlement.[1336] Recognizing this fact, the Philippines initiated an arbitration with China related to their South China Sea dispute:[1337]

> On 22 January 2013, the Republic of the Philippines instituted arbitral proceedings against the People's Republic of China under Annex VII to the United Nations Convention on the Law of the Sea (the "Convention"). The arbitration concerned the role of historic rights and the source of maritime entitlements in the South China Sea, the status of certain maritime features in the South China Sea, and the lawfulness of certain actions by China in the South China Sea that the Philippines alleged to be in violation of the Convention. China adopted a position of non-acceptance and non-participation in the proceedings. The Permanent Court of Arbitration served as Registry in this arbitration.
>
> * * *
>
> In a Note Verbale to the PCA on 1 August 2013, and throughout the arbitration proceedings, China reiterated "its position that it does not accept the arbitration initiated by the Philippines."[1338]

The Philippines appointed ITLOS Judge Rüdiger Wolfrum (Germany 1996-2017) as an arbitrator to serve on the 5-member arbitral tribunal.[1339] China would prefer to resolve the South China Sea dispute via bilateral negotiations with each State involved.[1340] Since China questioned the jurisdiction of the tribunal, China decided not to participate in the arbitration.[1341] In the absence of China's participation, the President of ITLOS[1342] appointed 3 other

Judge Cot | Judge Pawlak | Judge Mensah (Presiding Arbitrator) | Judge Wolfrum | Professor Soons

ITLOS Judges to serve as arbitrators: former Judge Thomas A. Mensah (Ghana 1996-2005) as Presiding Arbitrator, Judge Jeanne-Pierre Cot (France 2002-present), and Judge Stanislaw Pawlak (Poland 2005-present). The President of ITLOS appointed Professor Alfred "Fred" H.A. Soons as the 5th and final arbitrator. Professor Soons (Netherlands) also has specialized Law of the Sea expertise, as he wrote his doctoral thesis on the international legal regime of marine scientific research.[1343] Thus, the tribunal was comprised entirely of independent experts from regions completely unconnected with the South China Sea dispute.[1344]

The arbitral tribunal recognized that the South China Sea dispute between the Philippines and China was multifaceted (i.e., had many layers), only some of which fell with the tribunal's jurisdiction to resolve.[1345] The Philippines specifically asked the tribunal to resolve a series of 15 submitted disputes,[1346] which the tribunal grouped into 4 categories:

1) Whether the source for maritime rights and entitlements in the South China Sea is solely UNCLOS, or whether it also includes China's claim to historic rights within its claimed "9-dash line."
2) The status of various maritime features in the South China Sea as either Islands[1347] (each with its own EEZ and Continental Shelf), Rocks (which only generate Territorial Seas), or Low Tide Elevations (LTEs) "incapable of generating such entitlements."
3) The lawfulness of China's actions in the South China Sea, and whether they interfered with the Philippines' rights in its EEZ and on its Continental Shelf under UNCLOS (e.g., fishing, oil exploration, navigation, and the construction of artificial islands), failed to protect and preserve the marine environment, and inflicted severe harm on the marine environment (e.g., by constructing artificial islands and engaging in extensive land reclamation).
4) Whether China has aggravated and extended its disputes with the Philippines during the course of the arbitration.[1348]

The Philippines was careful to ask the arbitral tribunal to avoid opining "as to any question of sovereignty over islands, rocks or any other maritime features" (i.e., which State "owns" which maritime features), as such questions would be beyond the purview of UNCLOS.[1349] In addition, the Philippines had to address the fact that China had "opted out" of mandatory dispute settlement (under Article 298) for delimiting its maritime borders and resolving other issues, and thus the arbitral tribunal would lack jurisdiction to do so.[1350] Thus, the Philippines narrowly framed its request: "To the contrary, only issues of entitlement to – not the delimitation of – maritime space are presented. The case law from both ITLOS and the ICJ make it emphatically clear that issues of entitlement and delimitation are distinct and may not be conflated."[1351]

Thus, the Philippines was careful to cabin its request for a declaration on the general issue of the *status* of various maritime features in the South China Sea (as either Islands, Rocks, or LTEs), *not which State owns which maritime features*. In other words, a Rock is a Rock (and has no entitlement to either an EEZ or Continental Shelf, as discussed in Chapter 2), regardless of who owns it.[1352] As the tribunal noted:

While all sea boundary delimitations will concern entitlements, the converse is not the case: all disputes over entitlements do not concern delimitation. Where, as here, a party denies the existence of an entitlement, a possible outcome may well be the absence of any overlap and any possibility of delimitation.[1353]

The Philippines also recognized that article 283 of UNCLOS admonishes States to give peaceful negotiations a reasonable opportunity to work before submitting their dispute to mandatory dispute settlement. The Philippines explained that tensions were rising with China, and "all possibility of bilateral negotiation had been exhausted, as had multilateral efforts under the auspices of the Association of Southeast Asian Nations ('ASEAN')."[1354] The arbitral tribunal recognized that the Philippines had met its burden to exchange views and attempt to negotiate with China before resorting to mandatory dispute settlement.[1355] "[R]epeated insistence by one party on negotiating indefinitely until an eventual resolution cannot dislodge the 'backstop of compulsory, binding procedures' provided by Section 2 of Part XV [of UNCLOS]."[1356]

After 3 years of closed proceedings[1357] before the arbitral tribunal (sitting at the Permanent Court of Arbitration), the tribunal took another 6 months before issuing its landmark 501-page "award" (i.e., decision, which is about as long as this book!).[1358] Although "China [had] declined to participate in the establishment of the Tribunal, or to appear before it, ... [China] issued a very detailed position paper regarding the matters before the Tribunal which, in the end, the Tribunal heavily relied upon."[1359] Besides its detailed position paper, China also wrote 6 letters, and numerous diplomatic *notes verbale* to the members of the arbitral tribunal (despite their admonition against *ex parte* communications from the parties), as well as made "regular public statements of Chinese officials that touch[ed] on the arbitration."[1360] This represented a significant level of vociferous "participation" for a State which refused to officially participate! The tribunal had little difficulty discerning China's position on the South China Sea dispute,[1361] although the Philippines had to pay China's portion of the costs of arbitration.[1362]

The first decision facing the arbitral tribunal was whether it had jurisdiction over the various specific disputes.[1363] The tribunal carefully analyzed the question from all possible angles, and unanimously concluded that it had jurisdiction over the majority of the specific questions.[1364] While China's non-participation made the tribunal's work more challenging, it did not prevent the tribunal from hearing or deciding the case.[1365] Moreover, "[t]he Tribunal [took] a number of measures to safeguard the procedural rights of China."[1366] Since UNCLOS is a comprehensive agreement (aka a "package deal"),[1367] "State[] Parties to the Convention are accordingly not free to pick and choose the portions of the Convention they wish to accept or reject."[1368] Moreover, China is still bound by the tribunal's decision, in accordance with article 296(1) of UNCLOS, and article 11 of Annex VII to UNCLOS.[1369]

The first category of specific disputes which the Philippines submitted to the arbitral tribunal was whether the source for maritime rights and entitlements in the South China Sea is solely UNCLOS, or whether it also includes China's claim to historic rights within its claimed "9-dash line." The tribunal reviewed the *travaux préparatoires* (i.e., negotiating record) of the Third UN Conference on the Law of the Sea (which culminated in UNCLOS) and noted:

For all of the reasons discussed above, the Tribunal concludes that China's claim to historic rights to the living and non-living resources within the 'nine-dash line' is incompatible with the Convention to the extent that it exceeds the limits of China's maritime zones as provided for by the Convention. This is apparent in the text of the Convention which comprehensively addresses the rights of other States within the areas of the exclusive economic zone and continental shelf and leaves no space for an assertion of historic rights. It is also reinforced by the negotiating record of the Convention where the importance of adopting a comprehensive instrument was manifest and where the cause of securing the rights of developing States over their exclusive economic zone and continental shelf was championed, in particular, by China.

Accordingly, upon China's accession to the Convention and its entry into force, any historic rights that China may have had to the living and non-living resources within the 'nine-dash line' were superseded, as a matter of law and as between the Philippines and China, by the limits of the maritime zones provided for by the Convention. ... The Convention was a package that did not, and could not, fully reflect any State's prior understanding of its maritime rights. Accession to the Convention reflects a commitment to bring incompatible claims into alignment with its provisions, and its continued operation necessarily calls for compromise by those States with prior claims in excess of the Convention's limits.[1370]

The arbitral tribunal explained that China's ratification of UNCLOS did not extinguish its historic rights in the waters of the South China Sea. Rather, China relinquished the High Seas freedoms that it had previously enjoyed in certain areas now assigned as the EEZs of other States. In exchange, China received a greater degree of control of the maritime zones adjacent to its extensive coastline. China's High Seas freedom to navigate the South China Sea remained unaffected.[1371] The tribunal's rejection of China's "9-dash line" and historic rights claim "vindicated the analytic framework that the [U.S.] Department of State, and other respectable international legal scholars, have separately used to denounce the ["9-dash line"] claim."[1372]

The second category of specific disputes which the Philippines submitted to the arbitral tribunal was the status of various maritime features in the South China Sea as either Islands, Rocks, or Low Tide Elevations (LTEs). The tribunal noted that UNCLOS distinguishes between "naturally formed" Islands in article 121 (which generate all maritime zones), and artificial islands in articles 56, 60 and 80 (which do not generate any maritime zones, and instead constitute a resource subject to Coastal State control if the artificial islands are created within a Coastal State's EEZ or on its Continental Shelf). Thus, the status of features is based upon the "natural condition" of a maritime feature, and not any manmade improvements:

As a matter of law, human modification cannot change the seabed into a low-tide elevation or a low-tide elevation into an island. A low-tide elevation will remain a low-tide elevation under the Convention, regardless of the scale of the island or installation built atop it.[1373]

Even the Chinese State-run South China Sea "think tank" agrees that "[t]he significance of the Tribunal's observation, that 'human modification cannot change [...] a low-tide elevation into an island', is uncontroversial."[1374] Thus, LTEs are not considered land, and no measure of control or occupation can establish sovereignty over them, unless the LTEs fall within a Coastal State's Territorial Seas or Continental Shelf.[1375] In contrast, "high-tide features" (i.e., either Islands or Rocks, which are always above water) are entitled to Territorial Seas and can be appropriated (i.e., sovereignty over them can be claimed). Islands also possess the other maritime zones provided by UNCLOS.

Reviewing in detail the "natural condition" of various maritime features in the South China Sea as reflected in historical records,[1376] nautical charts, surveys, and sailing directions (and ignoring any manmade improvements thereon), the arbitral tribunal found that 6 features in the South China Sea are "high-tide features" (i.e., either Islands or Rocks that are naturally always above water), and 5 are LTEs: Hughes Reef, Gaven Reef (South), Subi Reef, Mischief Reef, and Second Thomas Shoal.[1377] Even the Chinese State-run South China Sea "think tank" agrees with almost all of these conclusions, except that Mischief Reef is an LTE.[1378]

Subi Reef is in the middle of the South China Sea (almost 232 nm from the Philippines and 502 nm[1379] from China).[1380] Yet China has turned it into an artificial island with multiple buildings and a runway, and stationed military and government personnel there. As an LTE, Subi Reef is not land, and no degree of control or occupation can establish sovereignty over it.[1381] Since Subi Reef lies within 12 nm of Thitu, which is a Rock occupied by the Philippines,[1382] the Philippines has sovereignty over Subi Reef as well. Thus, the arbitral tribunal implicitly concluded that China is essentially "squatting" on a maritime feature that belongs to the Philippines![1383]

Mischief Reef and Second Thomas Shoal lie in the EEZ and on the Continental Shelf of the Philippines, and thus the Philippines has sovereignty over them as well.[1384] This is despite the fact that China has also turned Mischief Reef into an artificial island with

multiple buildings and a runway, and stationed military and government personnel there.[1385] Thus, the arbitral tribunal implicitly concluded that China is essentially "squatting" on another maritime feature that belongs to the Philippines![1386] China has also prevented the Philippines from resupplying Filipino forces stationed on Second Thomas Shoal.[1387]

Thus far, the tribunal's interpretation of UNCLOS was consistent with how most Law of the Sea commentators viewed maritime features in general, and particularly in the South China Sea. However, the tribunal applied a much more rigorous test in analyzing which of the "high-tide features" qualified as Islands in their "natural condition" under article 121(1), and which were only Rocks incapable of sustaining either "human habitation or economic life of their own [and thus] shall have no exclusive economic zone or continental shelf"[1388] under article 121(3).

The arbitral tribunal began its analysis of the "high-tide features" by noting that:

Article 121 has not previously been the subject of significant consideration by courts or arbitral tribunals and has been accorded a wide range of different interpretations in scholarly literature. As has been apparent in the course of these proceedings, the scope of application of its paragraph (3) is not clearly established.[1389]

The tribunal recalled that a treaty "shall be interpreted in good faith in accordance with the ordinary meaning to be given to the terms of the treaty in their context and in the light of its object and purpose," and taking into account "any subsequent practice in the application of the treaty which establishes the agreement of the parties regarding its interpretation."[1390] "[A]s supplementary means of interpretation, recourse may be had to the preparatory work of the treaty to confirm its meaning, or determine the meaning when it is otherwise ambiguous, obscure, or leads to a manifestly absurd or unreasonable result." Thus, the tribunal "review[ed] the text [of UNCLOS], its context, the object and purpose of the Convention, and the *travaux préparatoires* [i.e., negotiating record]."[1391]

The tribunal first considered the text of article 121, and found that the critical distinction was between Islands and "Rocks which cannot sustain human habitation or economic life of their own."[1392] The test is not whether any particular "high-tide feature" currently sustains human habitation or economic life, but whether it has the capacity to do so in its natural condition.[1393] Although not dispositive:

[H]istorical evidence of human habitation and economic life in the past may be relevant for establishing a feature's capacity. If a known feature proximate to a populated land mass was never inhabited and never sustained an economic life, this may be consistent with an explanation that it is uninhabitable. Conversely, positive evidence that humans historically lived on a feature or that the feature was the site of economic activity could constitute relevant evidence of a feature's capacity.[1394]

Use of the word "sustain" in Article 121 "means to provide that which is necessary to keep humans alive and healthy over a continuous period of time, ... in a way that remains viable on an ongoing basis."[1395] However, "[a] feature that is only capable of sustaining habitation through the continued delivery of supplies from outside does not meet the requirements of [an Island]."[1396] The arbitral tribunal considered that:

The mere presence of a small number of persons on a feature does not constitute permanent or habitual residence there and does not equate to habitation. Rather, the term habitation implies a non-transient presence of persons who have chosen to stay and reside on the feature in a settled manner. Human habitation would thus require all of the elements necessary to keep people alive on the feature, but would also require conditions sufficiently conducive to human life and livelihood for people to inhabit, rather than merely survive on, the feature. ... At a minimum, sustained human habitation would require that a feature be able to support, maintain, and provide food, drink, and shelter to some

---

humans to enable them to reside there permanently or habitually over an extended period of time ... by a group or community of persons.[1397]

Use of the phrase "of their own" in Article 121 means:

that a feature itself (or group of related features) must have the ability to support an independent economic life, without relying predominantly on the infusion of outside resources or serving purely as an object for extractive activities, without the involvement of a local population. ... [F]or economic activity to constitute the economic life of a feature, the resources around which the economic activity revolves must be local, not imported, as must be the benefit of such activity. Economic activity that can be carried on only through the continued injection of external resources is not within the meaning of "an economic life of their own." Such activity would not be the economic life of the feature as "of its own", but an economic life ultimately dependent on support from the outside. Similarly, purely extractive economic activities, which accrue no benefit for the feature or its population, would not amount to an economic life of the feature as "of its own".[1398]

The arbitral tribunal next considered the context of article 121, as well as the object and purpose of UNCLOS. The tribunal explained why the status of features must be based upon their "natural condition," and not any manmade improvements:

If States were allowed to convert any rock incapable of sustaining human habitation or an economic life into a fully entitled island simply by the introduction of technology and extraneous materials, then the purpose of Article 121(3) as a provision of limitation would be frustrated. It could no longer be used as a practical restraint to prevent States from claiming for themselves potentially immense maritime space. In this regard, the Tribunal agrees with the Philippines that "[a] contrary rule would create perverse incentives for States to undertake such actions to

> extend their maritime zones to the detriment of other coastal States and/or the common heritage of mankind." Were a feature's capacity to sustain allowed to be established by technological enhancements, then "every high-tide feature, no matter . . . its natural conditions, could be converted into an island generating a 200-mile entitlement if the State that claims it is willing to devote and regularly supply the resources necessary to sustain a human settlement."[1399]

Thus, the object and purpose of UNCLOS would be subverted if States could convert Rocks (eligible only to a 12 nm Territorial Sea) into Islands (which generate a 200 nm EEZ and Continental Shelf). Otherwise, it would be a "race to build and bolster presence"[1400] in the South China Sea and throughout the world's oceans, which surely goes against everything for which UNCLOS stands.

The arbitral tribunal finally considered the *travaux préparatoires* [i.e., negotiating record] of article 121. Beginning in the 1970s, States began discussing the possibility of expanding maritime entitlements beyond the Territorial Seas.[1401] The UN General Assembly convened the Third UN Conference on the Law of the Sea specifically to consider not only the breadth of the territorial sea and fishery limits, but also ownership of resources on the Continental Shelf and other matters.[1402] The delegates "linked the regime of islands and the need for restrictions on the features that would generate an exclusive economic zone with development and the common heritage of mankind."[1403] They recognized that allowing the smallest uninhabited high-tide feature to generate a 200 nm EEZ and Continental Shelf would detract from the availability of the High Seas and Deep Seabed as "the common heritage of mankind."[1404] Therefore, they realized that a reasonable balance needed to be achieved.[1405] Unable to resolve the issue in general session at the Third UN Conference on the Law of the Sea:

However, the delegates eventually realized that it would be virtually impossible to develop a bright-line rule between Islands and Rocks based upon other criteria (e.g., size/surface area of the high-tide feature, availability of resources, proximity to a Coastal State, population size and density, etc.). "Against such attempts at precision, the drafters clearly favoured the language of the compromise reflected in Article 121(3)."[1407]

Applying this comprehensive interpretation of Article 121, and what constitutes a Rock versus an Island, the arbitral tribunal first disposed of remote and "miniscule" high-tide features in the South China Sea that lack fresh water, vegetation and living space in their natural condition, and thus clearly constitute Rocks entitled to only a Territorial Sea: Scarborough Shoal, Johnson Reef, Cuarteron Reef, Fiery Cross Reef, Gaven Reef (North), and McKennan Reef.[1408]

Turning to the larger high-tide features in the Spratly Islands:

There is no question that all of the significant high-tide features in the Spratly Islands are presently controlled by one or another of the littoral States, which have constructed installations and installed personnel. This presence, however, is predominantly military or governmental in nature and involves significant outside supply. Moreover, many of the high-tide features have been significantly modified from their natural condition. Additionally, accounts of current conditions and human habitation on the features may reflect deliberate attempts to colour the description in such a way as to enhance or reduce the likelihood of the feature being considered to generate an exclusive economic zone, depending on the interests of the State in question. Accordingly, the Tribunal considers historical evidence of conditions on the features—prior to the advent of the exclusive economic zone as a concept or the beginning of significant human modification—to represent a more reliable guide to the capacity of the features to sustain human habitation or economic life.[1409]

Two of the most significant high-tide features in the Spratly Islands (Itu Aba and South-West Cay) had small water wells that tapped into "small freshwater lenses ... [although t]he quality of this water will not necessarily match the standards of modern drinking water and may vary over time, with rainfall, usage, and even tidal conditions affecting salinity levels. ... the Tribunal notes that the freshwater resources of these features, combined presumably with rainwater collection, evidently have supported small numbers of people in the past ... and concludes that they are therefore able to do so in their natural condition, whether or not that remains the case today."[1410]

Similarly, "the larger features in the Spratly Islands have historically been vegetated." Japan intentionally introduced fruit trees on Itu Aba in the early 1900's, and apparently inadvertently introduced mice as well, with "almost all the ripe bananas ... becom[ing] food for the mice."[1411] Although Itu Aba apparently has arable land capable of supporting cultivation, "[a]t the same time, the Tribunal accepts the point that the capacity for such cultivation would be limited and that agriculture on Itu Aba would not suffice, on its own, to support a sizable population. The Tribunal also considers that the capacity of other features in the Spratly Islands would be even more limited and that significant cultivation would be difficult beyond the larger and more vegetated features of Itu Aba and Thitu."[1412]

The arbitral tribunal also found that "small numbers of fishermen" were consistently present on the main features in the Spratly Islands, at least seasonally.[1413] "There is, however, no evidence of any commercial fishing operation having been established in the Spratly Islands since 1945. Nor, in light of the advances in shipbuilding and fishing technology since that date, does the Tribunal see that a base of operations on a small, isolated feature such as Itu Aba would be economically necessary, or even beneficial."[1414] In addition, Japan attempted to establish commercial activities in the Spratly Islands in the early 1900s, primarily to mine "sea bird guano" for use as fertilizer. "By 1933, however, mining operations had apparently ceased" as no longer being commercially viable.[1415] During World War II, Japan used Itu Aba as a military base until U.S. Navy aircraft bombed it in 1945.[1416]

The physical characteristics of the principal features of the Spratly Islands are neither obviously habitable nor obviously uninhabitable. Thus, "with features that fall close to the line in terms of their capacity to sustain human habitation, ... the Tribunal [was] called upon to consider the historical evidence of human habitation and economic life on the Spratly Islands and the implications of such evidence for the natural capacity of the features."[1417] "For the Tribunal, the criterion of human habitation is not met by the temporary inhabitation of the Spratly Islands by fishermen, even for extended periods." None of the fishermen claimed to be from the Spratlys, "nor is there any suggestion that the fishermen were accompanied by their families," or built permanent shelters. "Rather, the record indicates a pattern of temporary residence on the features for economic purposes, with the fishermen remitting their profits, and ultimately returning, to the mainland."[1418] The tribunal reached the same conclusion for laborers working at Japanese commercial activities on Itu Aba and South-West Cay. The tribunal likewise did not consider the stationing of military or other government personnel, supported "by a continuous lifeline of supply" in order to support the various claims to sovereignty, as constituting "human habitation" for the purposes of article 121 of UNCLOS.[1419]

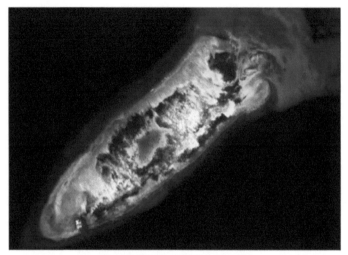

Figure 20: Fiery Cross Reef, 17 January 2012
(Annex 788)

Figure 21: Fiery Cross Reef, 19 October 2015
(Annex 788)

In conclusion:

The Tribunal sees no indication that anything fairly resembling a stable human community has ever formed on the Spratly Islands. Rather, the islands have been a temporary refuge and base of operations for fishermen and a transient residence for labourers engaged in mining and fishing. The introduction of the exclusive economic zone was not intended to grant extensive maritime entitlements to small features whose historical contribution to human settlement is as slight as that. Nor was the exclusive economic zone intended to encourage States to establish artificial populations in the hope of making expansive claims, precisely what has now occurred in the South China Sea. On the contrary, Article 121(3) was intended to prevent such developments and to forestall a provocative and counterproductive effort to manufacture entitlements.

The Tribunal sees no evidence that would suggest that the historical absence of human habitation on the Spratly Islands is the product of intervening forces or otherwise does not reflect the limited capacity of the features themselves. Accordingly, the Tribunal concludes that Itu Aba, Thitu, West York, Spratly Island, South-West Cay, and North-East Cay are not capable of sustaining human habitation within the meaning of Article 121(3). The Tribunal has also considered, and reaches the same conclusion with respect to, the other, less significant high-tide features in the Spratly Islands, which are even less capable of sustaining human habitation, but does not consider it necessary to list them individually.[1420]

This unanimous conclusion, that none of the Spratlys was actually an Island, was a surprise to the international community,[1421] especially because it established a high standard for what constitutes an Island.[1422] The vast majority of Law of the Sea scholars believed that at least the largest feature in the Spratlys, Itu Aba (which the Chinese called Taiping Dao or 太平岛, and the Filipinos called Ligaw Island) was an Island.[1423] It is 1.4 km long by .4 km wide (.9 x .25 miles), with multiple buildings, a lighthouse, a runway and port facilities. Itu Aba is currently under Taiwan's

control, which stations approximately "600 military and technical personnel" there.[1424] It has somewhat brackish, but potable water (although the tribunal found that it was not potable by modern standards).[1425] Itu Aba has vegetation and soil suitable for cultivation, although the tribunal found the vegetation was neither sufficient nor sufficiently diverse to permit even a small population to survive long-term.[1426] Itu Aba had a history of small groups of fishermen and laborers living on it, although not indefinitely, and they neither built permanent shelters nor brought their families to form a stable local community.[1427] The Taiwanese military and government personnel currently stationed there likewise do not form a stable local community. No one ever claimed to be "from"

Itu Aba. Nor was the slight and sporadic extractive fishing and mining evidence of an economic life of its own.

As a Rock, Itu Aba can be appropriated (i.e., a State can assert its sovereignty and claim the resources thereon), but the economic benefit is whatever resources can be extracted from the land and its 12 nm Territorial Sea—it does not "generat[e] a further entitlement to a 200-nautical-mile exclusive economic zone and continental shelf that would infringe on the entitlements generated by inhabited territory or on the area reserved for the common heritage of mankind."[1428] After dropping its bombshell that none of the Spratlys constituted an Island, the arbitral tribunal went on to consider the rest of the Philippines' claims.

The third category of specific disputes which the Philippines submitted to the arbitral tribunal was the lawfulness of China's actions in the South China Sea, and whether they interfered with the Philippines' rights in its EEZ and on its Continental Shelf under UNCLOS (e.g., fishing, oil exploration, navigation, and the construction of artificial islands), failed to protect and preserve the marine environment, and inflicted severe harm on the marine environment (e.g., by constructing artificial islands and engaging in extensive land reclamation). The tribunal held that China breached UNCLOS when it:

> - interfered with gas exploration on the Philippines' Continental Shelf in the area of Reed Bank,[1429]
> - deterred Filipino fishermen from fishing in the Philippines' EEZ,[1430]
> - failed to "prevent fishing by Chinese flagged vessels at Mischief Reef and Second Thomas Shoal" in the Philippines' EEZ,[1431]
> - "prevented Filipino fishermen from engaging in traditional fishing at Scarborough Shoal,"[1432]

- failed "to protect and preserve the marine environment in respect of its toleration and protection of the harvesting of giant clams by the propeller chopping method,"[1433]
- "caused devastating and long-lasting damage to the marine environment" by its "artificial island-building activities on the seven reefs in the Spratly Islands,"[1434]
- constructed an artificial island at Mischief Reef within the Philippines EEZ and on its Continental Shelf not only without permission from the Philippines, but "in the face of the Philippines' protests,"[1435] and
- repeatedly violated the International Regulations for Preventing Collisions at Sea (COLREGs),[1436] which are incorporated into UNCLOS by article 94, by having "Chinese law enforcement vessels in the vicinity of Scarborough Shoal, create[] serious risk of collision and danger to Philippine vessels and personnel."[1437]

The fourth and final category of specific disputes which the Philippines submitted to the arbitral tribunal was whether China has aggravated and extended its disputes with the Philippines during the course of the arbitration. The first few specific issues dealt with Philippines' armed forces stationed on Second Thomas Shoal engaged in a stand-off with Chinese Navy and Coast Guard vessels that "have attempted to prevent the resupply and rotation of the Philippine troops."[1438] The Tribunal determined "this represents a quintessentially military situation," and therefore that it lacked jurisdiction to resolve this particular dispute because China has "opted out" of mandatory dispute settlement for military activities (under article 298).[1439]

However, the arbitral tribunal found that "China's intensified construction of artificial islands on seven features in the Spratly

Islands during the course of the[] proceedings has unequivocally aggravated the disputes between the Parties" in 3 respects:

> "First, China has effectively created a *fait accompli* at Mischief Reef by constructing a large artificial island on a low-tide elevation located within the Philippines' exclusive economic zone and continental shelf, an area in which only the Philippines has sovereign rights ... and where only the Philippines may construct or authorise artificial islands. In practical terms, the implementation of the Tribunal's decision will be significantly more difficult for the Parties, and Mischief Reef cannot be returned to its original state, before China's construction work was begun."[1440]

> "Second, China has ... caus[ed] irreparable harm to the coral reef habitat at Cuarteron Reef, Fiery Cross Reef, Gaven Reef (North), Johnson Reef, Hughes Reef, Subi Reef, and Mischief Reef. ... China has seriously violated its obligation to preserve and protect the marine environment in the South China Sea .... Whatever other States have done within the South China Sea, it pales in comparison to China's recent construction. In practical terms, neither this decision nor any action that either Party may take in response can undo the permanent damage that has been done to the coral reef habitats of the South China Sea."[1441]

> Third and "[f]inally, China has undermined the integrity of these proceedings and rendered the task before the Tribunal more difficult. At the same time that the Tribunal was called upon to determine the status of features in the Spratly Islands and the entitlements that such features were capable of generating, China has permanently destroyed evidence of the natural status of

those same features .... The small rocks and sand cays that determine whether a feature constitutes a low-tide elevation or a high-tide feature capable of generating an entitlement to a territorial sea are now literally buried under millions of tons of sand and concrete."[1442] The arbitral tribunal concluded its lengthy unanimous opinion by declining the Philippines' request for it to issue a declaration that China shall abide by its duties under UNCLOS. The tribunal considered that this request fell "within the basic rule of '*pacta sunt servanda*',[1443] expressed in Article 26 of the Vienna Convention on the Law of Treaties as: 'Every treaty in force is binding upon the parties to it and must be performed by them in good faith.' In essence, what the Philippines is requesting is a declaration from the Tribunal that China shall do what it is already obliged by the Convention to do."[1444] "It goes without saying that both Parties are obliged to resolve their disputes peacefully and to comply with the Convention and this Award in good faith."[1445] As discussed in Chapter 2, "States comply with international law because it is in their interest to do so."[1446]

China's position on the arbitration is clear. We do not recognize or implement the award. It is just a piece of waste paper. You may just chuck it in the bin, leave it on the shelf, or put it in archives. In the end, the parties concerned will be back to the track of negotiation.[1447]

Ironically, for mandatory dispute settlement that purports to be UNCLOS' "enforcement" mechanism, "while the decision is considered legally binding [on China and the Philippines], there is no mechanism for enforcing it."[1448] This is particularly true since China has a permanent seat on the UN Security Council (UNSC), and thus could "veto" any UNSC Resolution (UNSCR) with which it disagrees, as discussed in Chapter 9. For example, China would veto an UNSCR that directed China to turnover its artificial island on Mischief Reef, which sits within the Philippines' EEZ and on its Continental Shelf, to the Philippines.[1449] At least one commentator argues that despite the U.S. and China's views on UNCLOS, it would be in both of their interests to abide by UNCLOS in general, and the arbitral tribunal's decision in the South China Sea dispute in particular:

> UNCLOS[] is supposed to be the constitution of the oceans .... The negotiators of [] UNCLOS never anticipated, however, that two of the five permanent members of the UN Security Council would, in the case of the United States, not ratify the treaty, or would, in the case of China, disregard many of the most important features of the Convention, including its dispute settlement procedures.
> * * *
> China's continuing rejection of the [arbitral tribunal's] decision will, in the long run, cause the decline of international law and cast doubt on whether the U.S., and other developed countries, can expect to have a rules-based order to govern their security and economic affairs if the decision is not respected by [the] world's second most powerful country. For this reason, it is in the United States interest to make China's compliance with the Arbitration decision a central [tenet] of U.S.[/]China Policy and, in doing so, persuade China that it has much to gain from a rules-based order at sea.[1450]

One bright light in the South China Sea dispute, is that "[t]he Philippines, one of the United States' two treaty allies in Southeast Asia (the other being Thailand), has adopted a conciliatory approach towards China .... It has shelved the South China Sea tribunal ruling and focused efforts on concluding the agreement to cooperate on oil and gas development."[1451] China and the Philippines are discussing joint development of the potentially significant hydrocarbon resources found at Reed Bank,[1452] which may be a pragmatic result. Both States want and need to exploit the oil and gas resources found in the Spratlys, and should be able to reach a reasonable, bilateral agreement.

"Although Beijing decried the ruling as 'null and void' and of 'no binding force,'[1453] it broadly kept to its letter if not its spirit in the first year after the award."[1454] However, soon after the 1-year anniversary of the arbitral tribunal's decisions, China renewed its efforts to "militarize" its artificial islands in the South China Sea:

By the end of 2017, China effectively had operational naval and air facilities in the South China Sea. Beijing's militarization of features escalated in 2018: in April, it deployed anti-ship and anti-aircraft missiles and electronic jammers to Fiery Cross Reef, Subi Reef, and Mischief Reef in the Spratlys; in May, it landed long-range bombers on Woody Island in the Paracels; and in November, it built a platform on Bombay Reef, also in the Paracels, later outfitting it with radar and communications interception capabilities.
* * *
The perception in the region is that while Washington was asleep at the wheel, China built huge fortresses in the sea and presented the world with a fait accompli.
* * *
The view by many ... in the Philippines is that Beijing is likely to attempt building on Scarborough Shoal before [2022]. The Obama administration had privately warned China that building on Scarborough Shoal was a red line; there are no indications that the Trump administration has issued similar warnings. ... a failure by the United States to act to stop China from building on Scarborough Shoal would nonetheless give the impression that the United States is a paper tiger and an unreliable ally.[1455]

China directed its State-run South China Sea "think tank" to commission "A Legal Critique of the Award of the Arbitral Tribunal in the Matter of the South China Sea Arbitration,"[1456] which was published in the 2020 Asian Yearbook of International Law.[1457] China has also enacted maritime laws that would permit it "to engage in grey zone operations below the threshold of armed conflict to intimidate its neighbors and further erode the rule of law at sea in the Indo-Pacific region ... [and] allow China to illegally and unilaterally assert maritime law enforcement jurisdiction throughout the waters of the First Island Chain to the detriment of its neighbors and other user States."[1458]

So who "won" in the South China Sea dispute? Some commentators have claimed that the arbitral tribunal's award "was a major victory for the Philippines. ... [especially vis-à-vis] clarify[ing] resource rights."[1459] Arguably, both States won. The Philippines' claims were vindicated and it gained some negotiating leverage over a much more powerful State. China is still able to resolve specific disputes using bilateral negotiations,[1460] which favors its stronger bargaining position. Moreover, "a review of the case history of many real-world disputes shows that the claimant States often bounce among international courts and tribunals, arbitration, mediation, and direct negotiations for a single or set of disputes, before they eventually resolve them."[1461]

Although non-parties to the South China Sea arbitration are not bound by its decision,[1462] the arbitral tribunal's decision is already starting to have ripple effects throughout the international community.[1463]

[E]ach of the tribunal's legal conclusions about which geographic features have maritime entitlements and which do not could, if applied universally among all the South China Sea claimants, significantly reduce the actual geographic ar-eas of dispute. ... the tribunal's review of specific features with objective evidence provides a useful methodology for claimant States in their international negotiations or other tribunals in

future cases to effectively assess the legal and factual status of specific South China Sea features. In short, not only were the tribunal's legal determinations rooted in a thorough application of UNCLOS, but they have a practical value in offering a possible way ahead for addressing several of the unresolved issues in the South China Sea.[1464]

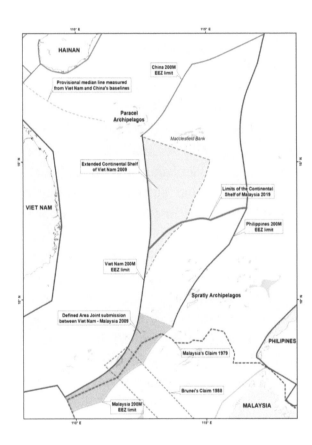

Seizing the "opportunity to benefit from the ruling,"[1465] Malaysia submitted an updated claim for an extended (aka Outer) Continental Shelf in the South China Sea[1466] to the Commission on the Limits of the Continental Shelf (CLCS).[1467] As discussed in Chapter 6, the CLCS only makes recommendations based upon their independent scientific analysis of the data provided—it is up to States to resolve their Continental Shelf disputes through delimitation[1468] (discussed in Chapter 8). However, Malaysia's submission "implicitly shows support for the 2016 Tribunal Award [in the South China Sea arbitration] that qualified all insular features of the Spratlys archipelago as having only 12 nm territorial sea and no claim to generating their own exclusive economic zones and continental shelves.[1469] Malaysia's submission also "indirectly rejects the validity of China's nine-dash line claim".[1470] Although China opposed Malaysia's updated claim to an Outer Continental Shelf, it wisely chose not to cite to its "9-dash line" claim,[1471] opting instead to base its opposition on its purported ownership of the "Four Shas" islands.[1472] The CLCS is not scheduled to review Malaysia's claim until the summer of 2021.[1473]

The decision also established clear standards for what constitutes an Island, albeit a fairly high bar. Besides the South China Sea dispute between China and the Philippines, there is an East China Sea dispute between China and Japan. If China and Japan were to agree with the arbitral tribunal's decision and accept the fact that the maritime features in the Senkakus are Rocks (since they lack potable water and arable land sufficient to support agriculture), they could delimit their maritime borders in the East China Sea, which would further reduce tensions and support development.[1474] The same could also be true for the Liancourt Rocks dispute between South Korea and Japan in the Sea of Japan.[1475] The tribunal's decision therefore has the potential to add to the "legal certainty over the legal status of [maritime] features and their associated water space claims[, which] has been a longstanding goal [of the U.S.]"[1476] Both "the United States and China ... have an interest in ensuring stability and keeping competition, however fierce, within the parameters of the law to minimize the risk of conflict."[1477] As Law of the Sea expert John Norton Moore once again puts so succinctly and so eloquently:

[O]f even greater importance, the rule of law serves as a check on power. An oceans space driven by out-of-control national claims and a "might makes right" credo can neither serve community common interests nor restrain conflict. The Law of the Sea Convention is a

remarkable achievement in the rule of law—providing both stability and
a check on power.[1478]

States are also chastened that their claims to sovereignty over certain maritime features as Islands (each with its own EEZ and Continental Shelf) may not be on as firm a legal footing within international law after the arbitral tribunal set such a high bar for what constitutes an Island. For example, the U.S. "went quiet on the [arbitral tribunal's] ruling partly because of [the Philippines'] reticence, but also because of the ruling's implications for U.S. claims to EEZs from small, uninhabited features in the Pacific (these would not generate EEZs)."[1479]

Almost exactly 4 years after the tribunal's decision, U.S. Secretary of State Mike Pompeo unequivocally renounced the former U.S. neutrality with regards to the South China Sea dispute, and aligned the U.S. position with the tribunal's decision:

The United States champions a free and open Indo-Pacific. Today we are strengthening U.S. policy in a vital, contentious part of that region — the South China Sea. We are making clear: Beijing's claims to offshore resources across most of the South China Sea are completely unlawful, as is its campaign of bullying to control them.

In the South China Sea, we seek to preserve peace and stability, uphold freedom of the seas in a manner consistent with international law, maintain the unimpeded flow of commerce, and oppose any attempt to use coercion or force to settle disputes. We share these deep and abiding interests with our many allies and partners who have long endorsed a rules-based international order.

These shared interests have come under unprecedented threat from the People's Republic of China (PRC). Beijing uses intimidation to undermine the sovereign rights of Southeast Asian coastal states in the South China Sea, bully them out of offshore resources, assert unilateral dominion, and replace international law with "might makes right." Beijing's approach has been clear for years. In 2010, then-PRC Foreign Minister Yang Jiechi told his ASEAN counterparts that "China is a big country and other countries are small countries and that is just a fact." The PRC's predatory world view has no place in the 21st century.

The PRC has no legal grounds to unilaterally impose its will on the region. Beijing has offered no coherent legal basis for its "Nine-Dashed Line" claim in the South China Sea since formally announcing it in 2009. In a unanimous decision on July 12, 2016, an Arbitral Tribunal constituted under the 1982 Law of the Sea Convention – to which the PRC is a state party – rejected the PRC's maritime claims as having no basis in international law. The Tribunal sided squarely with the Philippines, which brought the arbitration case, on almost all claims.

As the United States has previously stated, and as specifically provided in the Convention, the Arbitral Tribunal's decision is final and legally binding on both parties. Today we are aligning the U.S. position on the PRC's maritime claims in the SCS with the Tribunal's decision.

* * *

The world will not allow Beijing to treat the South China Sea as its maritime empire. America stands with our Southeast Asian allies and partners in protecting their sovereign rights to offshore resources, consistent with their rights and obligations under international law. We stand with the international community in defense of freedom of the seas and respect for sovereignty and reject any push to impose "might makes right" in the South China Sea or the wider region.[1480]

Secretary Pompeo's statement put down a marker vis-à-vis China: China's maritime claims and "bullying" actions are unlawful, and the U.S. is prepared to support its allies in the region in defending against them. "What the US basically said is that we are going to remain neutral on questions of who owns what island or rock in the South China Sea, but we're no longer going to keep quiet on China's illegal claims to the waters."[1481] Most importantly, the U.S. appears prepared to back up its new stance, having deployed 2 U.S. aircraft carriers to the South China Sea on July 4, 2020 and again on February 9, 2021 (which had only happened twice previously in the past 20 years: in 2001, and in 2014).[1482] "Having two or more carriers operating alongside each other at once is a major expenditure of resources that makes these kinds of shows of force uncommon".[1483]

The tribunal's decision also validates U.S. Freedom of Navigation Operations (FONOPs) against excessive maritime claims[1484] (discussed in Chapter 11). "As a matter of law, regular assertions of maritime rights and freedoms [through FONOPs] ensure that rights are not lost through acquiescence to excessive maritime claims; as a matter of practice, they guard against the South China Sea becoming a Chinese lake."[1485] Thus, the decision may also serve to focus FONOPs:

The ... tribunal decision in the Philippines case against China will facilitate the planning, execution and messaging of FON operations by clarifying the status of features. Insofar as the conduct of FON operations is consistent with the tribunal's award, it will bolster the United States' ability to argue that its actions are in accordance with international law. Regular assertions of maritime rights in respect of features that are the subject of the tribunal's decision will give the award teeth and render it more difficult for China to ignore the ruling.[1486]

The U.S. could also use the tribunal's decision as a shield against potential Chinese incursions into the EEZs off the coast of American Islands, such as Guam, Midway and Hawaii.[1487]

While President Biden is not expected to "spend the political capital needed to secure US accession to UNCLOS,"[1488] the Biden administration continues to actively support U.S. allies in the South China Sea in defending against China's excessive maritime claims and "bullying" actions.[1489] Within a month of President Biden's inauguration, the U.S. Navy conducted 2 FONOPs within 12 nm of the Spratly and Paracel Islands, and (as previously mentioned) deployed 2 aircraft carriers to the South China Sea.[1490]

[T]he Biden administration should continue to speak directly about the tribunal ruling and its international significance, insist that the two parties comply with their obligations under the ruling, and encourage non-party States to voluntary adhere to the elements of the ruling. Words are important, but words alone are insufficient. More can and should be done.

***

President Biden and his administration should continue to utilize the U.S. military to conduct such operations [within 12 nm of Chinese-occupied features in the South China Sea] and should consider whether there are other elements of the tribunal's ruling that could be directly effectuated by FONOPs and other military presence activities.[1491]

Recognizing China as "our most serious competitor," President Biden also announced the creation of a new U.S. Department of

Defense (DoD) China Task Force to "chart a strong path forward on China related matters."[1492] The U.S. Secretary of Defense (SECDEF), retired Army General Lloyd J. Austin III, directed the DoD China Task Force "to look at the pacing challenge that China poses to [DoD] from our perspective, and what we need to do to make sure we're ready to meet that challenge".[1493]

This book has now come full circle as it concludes. States drafting the United Nations Convention on the Law of the Sea (UNCLOS) sought to "establish[] ... a legal order for the seas and oceans which will facilitate international communication, and will promote the peaceful uses of the seas and oceans, the equitable and efficient utilization of their resources, the conservation of their living resources, and the study, protection and preservation of the marine environment".[1494] After digesting this lengthy book, the (hopefully) more fully informed reader[1495] is left to decide whether UNCLOS has achieved this lofty goal.

[1303] Jonathan G. Odom, *The Value and Viability of the South China Sea Arbitration Ruling: The U.S. Perspective 2016–2020*, 97 INT'L. L. STUD. 122, 162, 177-178 (2021), https://digital-commons.usnwc.edu/ils/vol97/iss1/16/.

[1304] American Rhetoric Online Speech Bank, John F. Kennedy Address to the United Nations General Assembly (delivered Sep. 25, 1961), https://www.americanrhetoric.com/speeches/jfkunitednations.htm.

[1305] United Nations, Charter of the United Nations, art. 24(1), https://www.un.org/en/charter-united-nations/.

[1306] UN Charter, arts. 39-51 (full cite above).

[1307] Jiangyu Wang, *Legitimacy, Jurisdiction and Merits in the South China Sea Arbitration: Chinese Perspectives and International Law*, 22 J. OF CHINESE POLIT. SCI. 185, online p. 5 (2017), https://papers.ssrn.com/sol3/papers.cfm?abstract_id=2967254.

[1308] Wang, *Legitimacy, Jurisdiction and Merits in the South China Sea Arbitration*, pp. 5-6 (full cite above).

[1309] Letter Of Transmittal Forwarding The 1982 UN Law Of The Sea Convention To The United States Senate VII (William J. Clinton, Oct. 7, 1994) (S. Treaty Doc. 103–39), https://www.foreign.senate.gov/imo/media/doc/treaty_103-39.pdf. *See generally* United Nations Convention on the Law of the Sea (UNCLOS) Part XV (arts. 279-299), Dec. 10, 1982, 1833 U.N.T.S. 397, https://www.un.org/Depts/los/convention_agreements/convention_overview_convention.htm.

[1310] UNCLOS, arts. 279-280 (full cite above).

[1311] WarGames (1983), https://www.imdb.com/title/tt0086567/.

[1312] UN Charter, art. 33(1) (full cite above).

477

1313 THE FLETCHER SCHOOL OF LAW AND DIPLOMACY—TUFTS UNIVERSITY, LAW OF THE SEA, A POLICY PRIMER 67-68 (2017), https://sites.tufts.edu/lawofthesea/introduction/. *See also* Permanent Court of Arbitration, Cases, Past Cases, [2016-10] Timor Sea Conciliation (*Timor-Leste v. Australia*), https://pca-cpa.org/en/cases/132/.

1314 United Nations Convention on the Law of the Sea (UNCLOS) Part XV (arts. 279-285), Dec. 10, 1982, 1833 U.N.T.S. 397, https://www.un.org/Depts/los/convention_agreements/convention_overview_co nvention.htm; Permanent Court of Arbitration, Cases, Past Cases, [2013-19] The South China Sea Arbitration (*The Republic of Philippines v. The People's Republic of China*), Documents, Award on Jurisdiction and Admissibility (Oct. 29, 2015) ¶ 195 (p. 76), https://pcacases.com/web/sendAttach/2579 (noting that "The next question under Article 281 is whether the Parties 'have agreed to seek settlement of the dispute by a peaceful means of their own choice.' If there is no such agreement, then Article 281 poses no obstacle to jurisdiction.").

1315 Jiangyu Wang, *Legitimacy, Jurisdiction and Merits in the South China Sea Arbitration: Chinese Perspectives and International Law*, 22 J. OF CHINESE POLIT. SCI. 185, online p. 6 (2017), https://papers.ssrn.com/sol3/papers.cfm?abstract_id=2967254.

1316 UNCLOS, art. 287(1) & Annex VII (Arbitration) (full cite above).

1317 Special arbitration under Annex VIII is available to resolve "disputes concerning the interpretation or application of articles of the Convention relating to (1) fisheries; (2) protection and preservation of the marine environment; (3) marine scientific research; and (4) navigation, including pollution from vessels and by dumping". Letter Of Transmittal Forwarding The 1982 UN Law Of The Sea Convention To The United States Senate, DOS Commentary p. 88 (William J. Clinton, Oct. 7, 1994) (S. Treaty Doc. 103–39), https://www.foreign.senate.gov/imo/media/doc/treaty_103-39.pdf. However, "State parties to UNCLOS can indicate their preferred method of dispute settlement under Article 287 of the Convention. But so far, only 11 states have selected Annex VIII arbitration as one of their preferred means of settlement. So the chances of a dispute being referred to special arbitration are rather small. In contrast, Annex VII arbitration is a lot more common because it is the default choice of procedure. This means that when the parties to a dispute have chosen different procedures as their preferred method of settlement or have not made a choice at all, the dispute will be dealt with by an Annex VII arbitral tribunal." Universiteit Leiden, *International Law in Action: the Arbitration of International Disputes*, Video Transcript, https://www.coursera.org/lecture/arbitration-international-disputes/arbitrating-law-of-the-sea-disputes-ZZR3e. Were the U.S. to ever accede to UNCLOS, it may have a preference for selecting a special arbitral tribunal for mandatory dispute settlement. *See*, e.g., Letter Of Transmittal Forwarding The 1982 UN Law Of The Sea Convention To The United States Senate VII, pp. IX-X, 84-85 (William J. Clinton, Oct. 7, 1994) (S. Treaty Doc. 103–39), https://www.foreign.senate.gov/imo/media/doc/treaty_103-39.pdf.

1318 UNCLOS, art. 287 (full cite above); DOS Commentary, p. 84 (full cite above).

1319 ITLOS members are elected based upon merit, and not nationality (other than ensuring an equitable geographic distribution, with no more than 1 member from any particular State). Thus, even if the U.S. were party to UNCLOS, it would not be guaranteed a seat on ITLOS. J.G. MERRILLS, INT'L. DISPUTE SETTLEMENT 185 (3rd ed. 1998). This is another reason for conservative U.S. opposition to acceding to UNCLOS.

[1320] Int'l. Tribunal for the Law of the Sea, https://www.itlos.org/en/top/home.
[1321] Int'l. Court of Justice, https://www.icj-cij.org/en.
[1322] UNCLOS, art. 287(1) & Annex VII (Arbitration) (full cite above); TUFTS, LAW OF THE SEA, p. 69 (full cite above).
[1323] UNCLOS, Annex VII (Arbitration) art. 2 (full cite above).
[1324] UNCLOS, Annex VII (Arbitration) art. 3 (full cite above).
[1325] UNCLOS, Annex VII (Arbitration) art. 3(e) (full cite above).
[1326] UNCLOS, Annex VII (Arbitration) art. 5 (full cite above).
[1327] universitätbonn institute for public int'l. law, Bonn Research Papers on Public Int'l. Law, Paper No 2/2014, *The South China Sea Arbitration: Is There a Case to Answer?*, p. 10 (Stefan A. G. Talmon, Feb. 9, 2014), https://papers.ssrn.com/sol3/papers.cfm?abstract_id=2393025 (noting that "[o]nly the Southern Bluefin Tuna Case was arbitrated using the services of the Secretariat of the International Centre for the Settlement of Investment Disputes (ICSID)"). *See* Southern Bluefin Tuna Case (*Australia and New Zealand v. Japan*) (Award on Jurisdiction and Admissibility) (2000) 119 ILR 508.
[1328] Permanent Court of Arbitration, https://pca-cpa.org/en/home/.
[1329] UNCLOS, arts. 246, 253 & 297(2) (full cite above). This is sometimes referred to as the "MSR Carve Out" from UNCLOS' Mandatory Dispute Settlement provisions.
[1330] UNCLOS, art. 297(3) (full cite above). This is sometimes referred to as the "Fisheries Carve Out" from UNCLOS' Mandatory Dispute Settlement provisions. Thus, "[a] coastal State need not submit to binding arbitration or adjudication any dispute relating to the exploration, exploitation, conservation, or management of living resources in the EEZ, including, for example, its discretionary powers for determining the allowable catch. However, such disputes may, in limited circumstances, be referred to compulsory but non-binding conciliation. Fishing beyond the EEZ is subject to compulsory, binding arbitration or adjudication. ... Neither the Convention's dispute settlement provisions nor any of its other provisions, however, limit the ability of the United States to use other means, including trade measures, provided under U.S. law to promote compliance with environmental and conservation norms and objectives." DOS Commentary, p. 51 (full cite above).
[1331] Letter Of Transmittal Forwarding UNCLOS To The Senate (full cite above).
[1332] UNCLOS, art. 298 (full cite above).
[1333] Jonathan G. Odom, *The Value and Viability of the South China Sea Arbitration Ruling: The U.S. Perspective 2016–2020*, 97 INT'L. L. STUD. 122, 123 (2021), https://digital-commons.usnwc.edu/ils/vol97/iss1/16/.
[1334] UNCLOS, arts. 74 & 83 (full cite above).
[1335] DoD Maritime Claims Reference Manual (MCRM)—China 2017 & Philippines 2016, http://www.jag.navy.mil/organization/code_10_mcrm.htm; South China Sea Arbitration, Award on Jurisdiction and Admissibility, ¶ 109 (p. 38) (full cite above).
[1336] UNCLOS, art. 287(3) & Annex VII (Arbitration) (full cite above); South China Sea Arbitration, Award on Jurisdiction and Admissibility, ¶ 109 (p. 38) (full cite above).
[1337] Permanent Court of Arbitration, Cases, Past Cases, [2013-19] The South China Sea Arbitration (*The Republic of Philippines v. The People's Republic of China*), Documents, The Philippines' Memorial – Volume I (Mar. 30, 2014) ¶ 3.75 (pp. 67-68), https://files.pca-cpa.org/pcadocs/Memorial%20of%20the%20Philippines%20Volume%20I.pdf.

¹³³⁸ Permanent Court of Arbitration, Cases, Past Cases, [2013-19] The South China Sea Arbitration (*The Republic of Philippines v. The People's Republic of China*), https://pca-cpa.org/en/cases/7/.
¹³³⁹ Permanent Court of Arbitration, Cases, Past Cases, [2013-19] The South China Sea Arbitration (*The Republic of Philippines v. The People's Republic of China*), Documents, Award on Jurisdiction and Admissibility (Oct. 29, 2015) ¶ 28 (p. 16), https://pcacases.com/web/sendAttach/2579.
¹³⁴⁰ South China Sea Arbitration, Award on Jurisdiction and Admissibility, ¶¶ 83, 190, 196, 230, 234, 247, 342 (pp. 27, 75-77, 89, 91, 95, 119) (full cite above); Permanent Court of Arbitration, Cases, Past Cases, [2013-19] The South China Sea Arbitration (*The Republic of Philippines v. The People's Republic of China*), Documents, Award (July 12, 2016) ¶ 160 (pp. 61-62), https://pcacases.com/web/sendAttach/2086; National Public Radio (NPR), WAMU 88.5, American University Radio, Parallels—Many Stories, One World, Conflict Zones, *A Primer on the Complicated Battle for the South China Sea* (Rami Ayyub, Apr. 13, 2016), https://www.npr.org/sections/parallels/2016/04/13/472711435/a-primer-on-the-complicated-battle-for-the-south-china-sea (noting that China "is unlikely to get behind a multiparty deal where its influence is diminished," and that China "took a page from the U.S. playbook in this case — you're better off cutting smaller deals where you wield a lot more influence.").
¹³⁴¹ South China Sea Arbitration, Award on Jurisdiction and Admissibility, ¶¶ 10-12, 37, 50, 56, 58, 64, 75, 89, 96, 105, 130, 112-123, 114, 116, 133, 159, 323, 358, 413 (pp. 2, 11, 17, 19, 21-23, 26, 30-32, 35-36, 39-42, 45-46, 62, 112, 127, 149) (full cite above). Russia took a similar tack when it "contested the arbitral tribunal's jurisdiction on the grounds that the dispute, in essence, concerned Ukraine's claim to sovereignty over Crimea and was therefore not a dispute concerning the interpretation or application of UNCLOS. Russia also asserted that UNCLOS did not regulate internal waters, such as the Sea of Azov and the Kerch Strait. In addition, Russia invoked the military activities and law enforcement exceptions under UNCLOS Article 298(1)(b) ... ." Nilüfer Oral, Ukraine v. The Russian Federation: *Navigating Conflict over Sovereignty under UNCLOS*, 97 INT'L. L. STUD. 478, 479, 481 (2021), https://digital-commons.usnwc.edu/ils/vol97/iss1/25/ (discussing the 3 cases that Ukraine initiated against Russia under UNCLOS; "The common thread in these three cases is the conflict between Ukraine and Russia over sovereignty in Crimea. ... The real issue in these cases is whether Ukraine or Russia has sovereignty over Crimea, but the legal analysis is skillfully couched within the language of UNCLOS.").
¹³⁴² China questioned the impartiality of the 3 other ITLOS judges selected by the ITLOS President, since the ITLOS President at the time was Japanese, and was the former Japanese Ambassador to the U.S. China also claimed that the arbitrators were "Euro-centric," since 4 of them came from Europe, and the Presiding Arbitrator from Ghana "lived in Europe permanently." Jiangyu Wang, *Legitimacy, Jurisdiction and Merits in the South China Sea Arbitration: Chinese Perspectives and International Law*, 22 J. OF CHINESE POLIT. SCI. 185, online p. 11 (2017), https://papers.ssrn.com/sol3/papers.cfm?abstract_id=2967254. *See also* South China Morning Post, China, Diplomacy, *Questions of neutrality: China takes aim at judges in South China Sea case* (Liu Zhen, July 11, 2016), https://www.scmp.com/news/china/diplomacy-defence/article/1988119/questions-neutrality-china-takes-aim-judges-south-china.

480

1343 South China Sea Arbitration, Award on Jurisdiction and Admissibility, ¶¶ 29-31 (p. 16) (full cite above). *See generally* Int'l. Tribunal for the Law of the Sea, Members of the Tribunal since 1996, https://www.itlos.org/en/the-tribunal/members-of-the-tribunal-since-1996/; United Nations, Legal, Audiovisual Library of Int'l. Law, Faculty Directory, https://legal.un.org/avl/faculty.html.

1344 Mark E. Rosen, *U.S. International Oceans Law and Policy Interests in the South China Sea Arbitration: Implications for the U.S. Administration in the South China Sea and Elsewhere*, 22 J. OF CHINESE POLIT. SCI. 251, online unnumbered p. 12 (2017), https://www.readcube.com/articles/10.1007/s11366-017-9468-9.

1345 South China Sea Arbitration, Award on Jurisdiction and Admissibility, ¶¶ 141-142, 152 (pp. 48-49, 59) (full cite above).

1346 South China Sea Arbitration, Award on Jurisdiction and Admissibility, ¶¶ 99, 101 (pp. 33-35) (full cite above).

1347 *See generally* THE FLETCHER SCHOOL OF LAW AND DIPLOMACY—TUFTS UNIVERSITY, LAW OF THE SEA, A POLICY PRIMER 73-74 (2017), https://sites.tufts.edu/lawofthesea/introduction/ (providing a brief history of the possession of islands in the South China Sea by neighboring littoral States since World War II).

1348 South China Sea Arbitration, Award, ¶¶ 7-10, 34, 112 (pp. 2-3, 13, 41-42) (full cite above).

1349 South China Sea Arbitration, Award on Jurisdiction and Admissibility, ¶¶ 8, 142-144, 153, 398-411 (pp. 2, 49-50, 59-60, 140-147) (full cite above); South China Sea Arbitration, Award, ¶¶ 5, 28, 153-154, 170, 264, 266-267, 283, 392-393, 545, 690, 750, 759, 792-793, 926-927, 932, 940, 1024, 1045, 1108, 1153, 1203 (pp. 1-2, 11-12, 58-59, 67-68, 112-113, 120, 176-178, 228-229, 277, 295-296, 299, 310-311, 369-371, 373, 411, 417, 435, 453, 471-477) (full cite above).

1350 South China Sea Arbitration, Award on Jurisdiction and Admissibility, ¶¶ 107 & n.16, 138, 364-378 (pp. 37, 47, 129-134) (full cite above); South China Sea Arbitration, Award, ¶¶ 6, 28, 153, 155, 170, 204, 283, 392-393, 420, 628, 633, 691-694, 759, 926-927, 932, 1024-1025, 1045, 1153, 1203 (pp. 2, 11-12, 58-59, 67-68, 85, 120, 176-178, 185, 255-256, 278, 299, 369-371, 411-412, 417, 453, 471-477) (full cite above).

1351 Permanent Court of Arbitration, Cases, Past Cases, [2013-19] The South China Sea Arbitration (*The Republic of Philippines v. The People's Republic of China*), Documents, The Philippines' Memorial – Volume I (Mar. 30, 2014) ¶¶ 1.53, 5.117, 7.15, 7.112-7.157 (pp. 14, 151, 222, 254-270), https://files.pca-cpa.org/pcadocs/Memorial%20of%20the%20Philippines%20Volume%20I.pdf; South China Sea Arbitration, Award on Jurisdiction and Admissibility, ¶¶ 8, 26, 146, 155-157, 398-411 (pp. 2, 15, 53, 60-61, 140-147) (full cite above).

1352 South China Sea Arbitration, Award on Jurisdiction and Admissibility, ¶ 144 (p. 50) (full cite above).

1353 South China Sea Arbitration, Award, ¶ 204 (p. 85) (full cite above). *See also* South China Sea Arbitration, Award on Jurisdiction and Admissibility, ¶¶ 144, 146, 156, 398-411 (pp. 50, 53, 61, 140-147) (full cite above).

1354 South China Sea Arbitration, The Philippines' Memorial – Volume I, ¶¶ 1.30-1.33, 1.40, 3.22-3.74 (pp. 8-9, 11, 45-67) (full cite above).

1355 South China Sea Arbitration, Award on Jurisdiction and Admissibility, ¶¶ 322-352, 416 (pp. 112-123, 149) (full cite above).

1356 Permanent Court of Arbitration, Cases, Past Cases, [2013-19] The South China Sea Arbitration (*The Republic of Philippines v. The People's Republic of China*), Documents, Award on Jurisdiction and Admissibility (Oct. 29, 2015) ¶ 247 (p. 95), https://pcacases.com/web/sendAttach/2579.

1357 The other littoral States bordering the South China Sea were permitted to observe the proceedings. The PCA Secretary General also attended part of the hearings as an observer, which were otherwise not open to the public. The arbitral tribunal rejected the U.S. request to observe the hearings, since the U.S. is not Party to UNCLOS. The UK received permission to observe the proceedings, but elected not to attend. Australia, Indonesia, Japan, Malaysia, Singapore, Thailand and Vietnam all sent observers. South China Sea Arbitration, Award on Jurisdiction and Admissibility, ¶¶ 69, 84, 86-87 (pp. 24-25, 27-29, 30) (full cite above); Permanent Court of Arbitration, Cases, Past Cases, [2013-19] The South China Sea Arbitration (*The Republic of Philippines v. The People's Republic of China*), Documents, Award (July 12, 2016) ¶¶ 15, 65-68, 70 (pp. 5, 22-24), https://pcacases.com/web/sendAttach/2086. The Philippines was represented by the venerable Washington, DC law firm "Foley Hoag LLP," as well as English Law Professors Philippe Sands and Alan Boyle, and Professor Bernie Oxman (U.S. Ambassador to Third UN Conference on the Law of the Sea, and the only American to serve on both the ICJ and ITLOS). South China Sea Arbitration, Award on Jurisdiction and Admissibility, ¶ 88 (pp. i, 29) (full cite above); South China Sea Arbitration, Award, ¶¶ 70-71 (pp. 23-26) (full cite above); University of Miami School of Law, Faculty Directory, Bernard H. Oxman, https://www.law.miami.edu/faculty/bernard-h-oxman.

1358 South China Sea Arbitration, Award, (full cite above). *See also* Jiangyu Wang, *Legitimacy, Jurisdiction and Merits in the South China Sea Arbitration: Chinese Perspectives and International Law*, 22 J. OF CHINESE POLIT. SCI. 185, online p. 2 (2017), https://papers.ssrn.com/sol3/papers.cfm?abstract_id=2967254 (noting that "[t]he *South China Sea Arbitration* ... is deemed a landmark case in the history of both international law and international relations because of not only the geopolitical significance of the dispute but also the determination of the relevant arbitral tribunal in rendering a ruling to boldly define the rights, entitlements, and obligations of the parties based on [UNCLOS].").

1359 Mark E. Rosen, *U.S. International Oceans Law and Policy Interests in the South China Sea Arbitration: Implications for the U.S. Administration in the South China Sea and Elsewhere*, 22 J. OF CHINESE POLIT. SCI. 251, online unnumbered p. 5 (2017), https://www.readcube.com/articles/10.1007/s11366-017-9468-9. *See also* Ministry of Foreign Affairs of the People's Republic of China. 2014. Position Paper of the Government of the People's Republic of China on the Matter of Jurisdiction in the South China Sea Arbitration Initiated by the Republic of the Philippines (Dec. 7, 2014), https://www.fmprc.gov.cn/mfa_eng/zxxx_662805/t1217147.shtml; South China Sea Arbitration, Award on Jurisdiction and Admissibility, ¶¶ 14-15, 55-57 (pp. 11-12, 20-21) (full cite above); South China Sea Arbitration, Award, ¶¶ 11, 19, 29, 31, 37, 42, 48, 53, 59, 65, 82, 87, 114, 116, 166, 1180 (pp. 3, 6, 12-19, 22, 28, 30, 42, 45, 64-65, 463-464) (full cite above).

1360 South China Sea Arbitration, Award on Jurisdiction and Admissibility, ¶ 121 (p. 41) (full cite above).

1361 South China Sea Arbitration, Award on Jurisdiction and Admissibility, ¶¶ 10, 14-15, 19, 40, 56-57, 64, 83, 91, 96, 98, 103 & n.9, 105 & n.12, 119, 121, 124 & n.26, 132-139, 151-152, 155, 157, 166, 190, 192 & n.169, 185, 190, 192, 194, 196, 202-206,

213, 216-217, 223, 228, 230-231, 234-237, 247, 256, 275, 292, 303, 311, 323-325, 330, 344, 357, 366-373, 385, 387, 391 (pp. 2, 11-13, 18, 21, 22-23, 27, 31-32, 35-36, 41-42, 45-48, 58-61, 65, 73, 75-79, 82-84, 86-92, 95, 98, 102, 106, 108-109, 112-114, 120, 126-127, 130-132, 137-139) (full cite above); South China Sea Arbitration, Award, ¶¶ 13, 18, 29, 37, 42, 51, 53, 61, 82, 89, 96-97, 100, 102-103, 115, 126-127, 130, 137, 144, 146, 152-153, 180-187, 200-201, 298-302, 446-472, 687-689, 729-732, 786-791, 912-924, 935-937, 1019-1023, 1027-1028, 1076-1080, 1116, 1119-1120, 1122, 1125, 1141-1149, 1189-1190 (pp. 4, 6, 12-18, 20-21, 28, 30-37, 42-43, 48-50, 52-53, 55-58, 71-74, 84, 130-131, 195-204, 276-277, 290, 309-310, 363-369, 372, 409-413, 426-428, 439-441, 444, 450-452, 466-467) (full cite above).

[1362] South China Sea Arbitration, Award on Jurisdiction and Admissibility, ¶ 98 (p. 32) (full cite above); South China Sea Arbitration, Award, ¶ 110 (pp. 38-39) (full cite above).

[1363] United Nations Convention on the Law of the Sea (UNCLOS) art. 288(4), Dec. 10, 1982, 1833 U.N.T.S. 397, https://www.un.org/Depts/los/convention_agreements/convention_overview_co nvention.htm (noting that a court or tribunal has jurisdiction to decide whether it has jurisdiction to resolve a dispute under UNCLOS' mandatory dispute settlement provisions). This is known as the "*Kompetenz-Kompetenz-Doktrin*" in German, and "*principe de compétence-compétence*" in French.

[1364] South China Sea Arbitration, Award on Jurisdiction and Admissibility, ¶¶ 397-413 (pp. 140-149) (full cite above); South China Sea Arbitration, Award, ¶ 1203.A (pp. 471-473) (full cite above). *See also* Wang, *Legitimacy, Jurisdiction and Merits in the South China Sea Arbitration*, p. 9 (full cite above) (noting that "[i]t would not be imprecise to describe China's response to the above award [on jurisdiction] as a furious one.").

[1365] South China Sea Arbitration, Award, ¶¶ 12, 117-118, 143, 150, 165 (pp. 3-4, 45, 55, 57, 64) (full cite above).

[1366] South China Sea Arbitration, Award on Jurisdiction and Admissibility, ¶¶ 11-12, 113, 117, 413 (pp. 11, 39-40) (full cite above); South China Sea Arbitration, Award, ¶¶ 15, 58, 85, 88, 90, 121, 131, 133, 136, 138, 144, 821 (pp. 5, 19, 30-31, 46-47, 50-53, 55, 320-321) (full cite above). For example, the arbitral tribunal hired independent experts on technical matters, such as an expert hydrographer from Australia, an expert on navigational safety issues from the UK, and 3 coral reef experts from Germany, UK and Australia. *But see* universitätbonn institute for public int'l. law, Bonn Research Papers on Public Int'l. Law, Paper No 14/2018, *The South China Sea Arbitration: Observations on the Award of 12 July 2016*, pp. 97-98 (Stefan A. G. Talmon, May 17, 2018), https://papers.ssrn.com/sol3/papers.cfm?abstract_id=3180037 (concluding that the arbitral tribunal failed to adequately safeguard China's interests).

[1367] UNCLOS, Introduction at p. 2 (full cite above) (noting that the "package deal" concept became a *leitmotif* (accompanying melody) that permeates throughout UNCLOS); THE FLETCHER SCHOOL OF LAW AND DIPLOMACY—TUFTS UNIVERSITY, LAW OF THE SEA, A POLICY PRIMER 9 (2017), https://sites.tufts.edu/lawofthesea/introduction/; DONALD R. ROTHWELL & TIM STEPHENS, THE INT'L. LAW OF THE SEA 13, 79 (2nd ed. 2016). *See also* G.A. Res. 2750 (XXV), ¶ C, U.N. Doc A/AC.138/58 (Dec. 17, 1970), https://research.un.org/en/docs/ga/quick/regular/25 (noting "that the problems of ocean space are closely interrelated and need to be considered as a whole" when the United Nations General Assembly convened the Third United Nations Conference on the Law of the Sea); Permanent Court of Arbitration, Cases, Past Cases, [2013-19]

The South China Sea Arbitration (*The Republic of Philippines v. The People's Republic of China*), Documents, Award on Jurisdiction and Admissibility (Oct. 29, 2015) ¶¶ 107, 225 (pp. 37, 87-88), https://pcacases.com/web/sendAttach/2579.

¹³⁶⁸ South China Sea Arbitration, Award on Jurisdiction and Admissibility, ¶¶ 107, 225 (pp. 37, 87-88) (full cite above); Permanent Court of Arbitration, Cases, Past Cases, [2013-19] The South China Sea Arbitration (*The Republic of Philippines v. The People's Republic of China*), Documents, Award (July 12, 2016) ¶ 253 (p. 107) (pp. 5, 22-24), https://pcacases.com/web/sendAttach/2086. *See also* DONALD R. ROTHWELL & TIM STEPHENS, THE INT'L. LAW OF THE SEA 13, 79 (2ⁿᵈ ed. 2016); G.A. Res. 2750 (XXV), ¶ C, U.N. Doc A/AC.138/58 (Dec. 17, 1970), https://research.un.org/en/docs/ga/quick/regular/25 (noting "that the problems of ocean space are closely interrelated and need to be considered as a whole" when the United Nations General Assembly convened the Third United Nations Conference on the Law of the Sea).

¹³⁶⁹ South China Sea Arbitration, Award on Jurisdiction and Admissibility, ¶ 114 (pp. 39-40) (full cite above); South China Sea Arbitration, Award, ¶¶ 12, 117-118, 143, 150, 165 (pp. 3-4, 45, 55, 57, 64) (full cite above).

¹³⁷⁰ South China Sea Arbitration, Award, ¶¶ 261-262 (pp. 111-112) (full cite above). *See generally* South China Sea Arbitration, Award, ¶¶ 169-278 & 1203 (pp. 67-117 & 471-477) (full cite above).

¹³⁷¹ South China Sea Arbitration, Award, ¶ 271 (p. 115) (full cite above). *But see* universitätbonn institute for public int'l. law, Bonn Research Papers on Public Int'l. Law, Paper No 14/2018, *The South China Sea Arbitration: Observations on the Award of 12 July 2016*, pp. 51-57, 60 (Stefan A. G. Talmon, May 17, 2018), https://papers.ssrn.com/sol3/papers.cfm?abstract_id=3180037 (positing that "the question of historic waters is not regulated by the Convention," and that "China's claim to territorial sovereignty over the Nansha Islands as a whole constitutes a plausible claim to ancient title over land and maritime areas in the South China Sea. Such a claim is in conformity with international law and is not precluded by the UNCLOS.").

¹³⁷² Mark E. Rosen, *U.S. International Oceans Law and Policy Interests in the South China Sea Arbitration: Implications for the U.S. Administration in the South China Sea and Elsewhere*, 22 J. OF CHINESE POLIT. SCI. 251, online unnumbered p. 10 (2017), https://www.readcube.com/articles/10.1007/s11366-017-9468-9. *But see* Shicun Wu, *A Legal Critique of the Award of the Arbitral Tribunal in the* Matter of the South China Sea Arbitration, *in* 24 ASIAN YEARBOOK OF INT'L. LAW 151, 170 (2020), https://brill.com/view/book/edcoll/9789004437784/BP000019.xml ("The finding of the Tribunal that UNCLOS 'leaves no space for an assertion of historic rights' is highly questionable. The concepts of 'historic titles' and 'historic right' are not as clearly and consistently distinguished as the Tribunal asserts in its Award. Rather, the two terms are often used interchangeably. Historic rights can and do continue to exist next to and independent from UNCLOS, as confirmed by the award in the *Eritrea/Yemen* case. ... Therefore, the conclusion of the Tribunal in paragraph 278 of the Award that 'the Convention superseded any historic rights or other sovereign rights or jurisdiction in excess of the limits imposed therein' is probably wrong.").

¹³⁷³ South China Sea Arbitration, Award, ¶ 305 (p. 131) (full cite above). *See generally* South China Sea Arbitration, Award, ¶¶ 89, 140-142, 305, 508, 511, 541, 559, 562, 565, 568 (pp. 30-31, 54-55, 131, 214-215, 227, 233-235) (full cite above).

¹³⁷⁴ Wu, *A Legal Critique*, p. 178 (full cite above).

[1375] South China Sea Arbitration, Award, ¶ 309 (p. 132) (full cite above); Wu, *A Legal Critique*, p. 178 (full cite above).

[1376] South China Sea Arbitration, Award, ¶¶ 548-549 (p. 230) (full cite above) (noting that "evidence of physical conditions will ordinarily suffice only to classify features that clearly fall within one category or the other [i.e., a Rock or an Island]. ... The Tribunal considers, however, that evidence of physical conditions is insufficient for features that fall close to the line. It will be difficult, if not impossible, to determine from the physical characteristics of a feature alone where the capacity merely to keep people alive ends and the capacity to sustain settled habitation by a human community begins. This will particularly be the case as the relevant threshold may differ from one feature to another. In such circumstances, the Tribunal considers that the most reliable evidence of the capacity of a feature will usually be the historical use to which it has been put. ... the Tribunal can reasonably conclude that a feature that has never historically sustained a human community lacks the capacity to sustain human habitation."). *See also* Jonathan G. Odom, *The Value and Viability of the South China Sea Arbitration Ruling: The U.S. Perspective 2016–2020*, 97 INT'L. L. STUD. 122, 127 (2021), https://digital-commons.usnwc.edu/ils/vol97/iss1/16/ (noting that these historical records "predated the South China Sea disputes and the filing of the arbitration case, so their veracity could be trusted. More specifically, they were intended to inform mariners of the accurate status of geographic features rather than serve as manufactured evidence to skew the legal status of those features for some future litigation."); Wu, *A Legal Critique*, p. 207 (full cite above) (agreeing that "the most reliable evidence of the capacity of a feature will usually be the historical use to which it has been put").

[1377] South China Sea Arbitration, Award, ¶¶ 382-384 & para. 1203.B(3) (pp. 174 & 473-474) (full cite above).

[1378] Wu, *A Legal Critique*, pp. 182-183 (full cite above).

[1379] The Straits Times, Asia, East Asia, *China to expand land reclamation activities in South China Sea, say experts* (Feb. 6, 2018), https://www.straitstimes.com/asia/east-asia/china-to-expand-land-reclamation-activities-in-south-china-sea-say-experts. Photo: Philippine Daily Inquirer And Inquirer.Net: "A picture showing alleged Chinese military construction work going on at Subi Reef (also known as Zamora Reef), on Oct 10, 2017."

[1380] South China Sea Arbitration, Award, ¶ 289 (p. 122) (full cite above).

[1381] South China Sea Arbitration, Award, ¶ 309 (p. 132) (full cite above).

[1382] Bloomberg Opinion, Politics & Policy, *The Tiny Island That's Key to China's Maritime Ambitions* (Tobin Harshaw, Mar. 1, 2020), https://www.bloomberg.com/opinion/articles/2020-03-01/china-s-naval-power-may-hinge-on-thitu-island.

[1383] Rosen, *South China Sea Arbitration*, p. 8 (full cite above).

[1384] South China Sea Arbitration, Award, ¶¶ 627-633 & 1030 (pp. 254-256 & 413) (full cite above).

[1385] The Straits Times, Asia, East Asia, *China's air and naval facilities on contested islands in South China Sea 'almost ready'* (Feb. 5, 2018), https://www.straitstimes.com/asia/se-asia/new-photos-show-china-is-nearly-done-with-its-militarisation-of-south-china-sea. Photo: Philippine Daily Inquirer/Asia News Network, Inquirer.Net: "Most of the photos, taken between June and December 2017, showed the reefs that had been transformed into artificial islands in the final stages of development as air and naval bases". Although not

485

noted by the arbitral tribunal, apparently China pays stipends to fishermen who agree to live on Mischief Reef and other "islands" for at least half the year. Center for International Maritime Security (CIMSEC), Asia-Pacific Capability Analysis, *Riding A New Wave of Professionalization and Militarization: Sansha City's Maritime Militia* (Conor Kennedy, Sep. 1, 2016), https://cimsec.org/riding-new-wave-professionalization-militarization-sansha-citys-maritime-militia/27689.

[1386] Mark E. Rosen, *U.S. International Oceans Law and Policy Interests in the South China Sea Arbitration: Implications for the U.S. Administration in the South China Sea and Elsewhere*, 22 J. OF CHINESE POLIT. SCI. 251, online unnumbered p. 8 (2017), https://www.readcube.com/articles/10.1007/s11366-017-9468-9. *See also* Duncan French, *In the Matter of the South China Sea Arbitration: Republic of Philippines*, 19(1) ENV. L. REV. 48, 52 (2017) (noting that "by not finding any feature to be an island, the result was that two of the most contested features – Mischief Reef and Second Thomas Shoal ... remain part of the maritime entitlement of the Philippines. It is worthwhile pausing here to reflect what the Tribunal has done. It has not ruled on sovereignty but, in effect, it has. By finding that something is a low-tide elevation (the first order question), incapable of being possessed by means of territoriality, the Tribunal has in essence ruled out the question of sovereignty [over Mischief Reef and Second Thomas Shoal] (a second-order question).").

[1387] "Philippine marines maintain an outpost on the BRP Sierra Madre, a Philippine Navy warship intentionally grounded on Second Thomas Shoal in 1999. The presence of these marines has, in effect, been validated by the arbitral tribunal award, which concluded that the Shoal is a low-tide elevation that is part of the Philippine EEZ and continental shelf and therefore not subject to appropriation by China. On occasion, the [Chinese coastal police agencies (CCG)] and Chinese Navy have attempted to interfere with the resupply of the marines but have not yet tried to expel them from the Shoal. The [Maritime Police Law of the People's Republic of China (MPL), which took effect on February 1, 2021] could prompt a CCG attack on the marines, which would clearly invoke U.S. defense obligations." Raul (Pete) Pedrozo, *Maritime Police Law of the People's Republic of China*, 97 INT'L. L. STUD. 465, 469 (2021), https://digital-commons.usnwc.edu/ils/vol97/iss1/24/. Even the Chinese State-run South China Sea "think tank" agrees that "the Tribunal's conclusion that Second Thomas Shoal is also a low-tide elevation, and is thus incapable of appropriation and cannot generate any maritime entitlements ... appears to accord with the evidence before it. ... We see no basis on which to challenge this conclusion."). Shicun Wu, *A Legal Critique of the Award of the Arbitral Tribunal in the Matter of the South China Sea Arbitration*, *in* 24 ASIAN YEARBOOK OF INT'L. LAW 151, 182-183 (2020), https://brill.com/view/book/edcoll/9789004437784/BP000019.xml.

[1388] United Nations Convention on the Law of the Sea (UNCLOS) art. 121(3), Dec. 10, 1982, 1833 U.N.T.S. 397, https://www.un.org/Depts/los/convention_agreements/convention_overview_convention.htm.

[1389] Permanent Court of Arbitration, Cases, Past Cases, [2013-19] The South China Sea Arbitration (*The Republic of Philippines v. The People's Republic of China*), Documents, Award (July 12, 2016) ¶ 474 (p. 204), https://pcacases.com/web/sendAttach/2086.

[1390] Vienna Convention on the Law of Treaties (VCLT) art. 31(3)(b), May 23, 1969, 1155 U.N.T.S. 331. *See also* Dept. of Defense Law of War Manual § 1.7.4, p. 29 (June 2015, updated Dec. 2016), https://www.hsdl.org/?view&did=797480.

[1391] South China Sea Arbitration, Award, ¶¶ 476-477 (p. 205) (full cite above), *citing* Vienna Convention on the Law of Treaties (VCLT) arts. 31-32, May 23, 1969, 1155 U.N.T.S. 331.

[1392] South China Sea Arbitration, Award, ¶ 475 (p. 204) (full cite above).

[1393] South China Sea Arbitration, Award, ¶¶ 483, 541, 545-547 (pp. 206-207, 227-229) (full cite above).

[1394] South China Sea Arbitration, Award, ¶ 484 (p. 207) (full cite above).

[1395] South China Sea Arbitration, Award, ¶ 487 (pp. 207-208) (full cite above).

[1396] South China Sea Arbitration, Award, ¶¶ 547, 550 (pp. 229-231) (full cite above).

[1397] South China Sea Arbitration, Award, ¶¶ 489-491, 542 (pp. 208, 227-228) (full cite above).

[1398] South China Sea Arbitration, Award, ¶¶ 500, 543, 547 (pp. 211-212, 228-229) (full cite above). Even the Chinese State-run South China Sea "think tank" agrees with the arbitral tribunal that a feature's economic life must be independent in order to qualify as an Island. Wu, *A Legal Critique*, p. 199 (full cite above).

[1399] South China Sea Arbitration, Award, ¶ 509 (p. 214) (full cite above).

[1400] National Public Radio (NPR), WAMU 88.5, American University Radio, Parallels—Many Stories, One World, Conflict Zones, *A Primer on the Complicated Battle for the South China Sea* (Rami Ayyub, Apr. 13, 2016), https://www.npr.org/sections/parallels/2016/04/13/472711435/a-primer-on-the-complicated-battle-for-the-south-china-sea.

[1401] South China Sea Arbitration, Award, ¶ 526 (p. 220) (full cite above).

[1402] G.A. Res. 2750 (XXV), ¶ C.2, U.N. Doc A/AC.138/58 (Dec. 17, 1970), https://research.un.org/en/docs/ga/quick/regular/25.

[1403] South China Sea Arbitration, Award, ¶ 529 (p. 221) (full cite above).

[1404] UNCLOS, Preamble unnumbered ¶ 7 & arts. 125(1), 136, 137(2), 140(1), 143(1), 149, 150(i), 153(1), 155(1)(a), 155(2), 246(3), 311(6) & 1994 Implementing Agreement Preamble ¶ 2 (full cite above); THE FLETCHER SCHOOL OF LAW AND DIPLOMACY—TUFTS UNIVERSITY, LAW OF THE SEA, A POLICY PRIMER 8 (2017), https://sites.tufts.edu/lawofthesea/introduction/.

[1405] South China Sea Arbitration, Award, ¶¶ 518-519 & 527-529 (pp. 217 & 220-221) (full cite above); TUFTS, LAW OF THE SEA, p. 2 (full cite above).

[1406] South China Sea Arbitration, Award, ¶¶ 531-532 (p. 222) (full cite above).

[1407] South China Sea Arbitration, Award, ¶¶ 537, 546 (pp. 225, 229) (full cite above).

[1408] South China Sea Arbitration, Award, ¶¶ 554-570 (pp. 232-235) (full cite above). Even the Chinese State-run South China Sea "think tank" agrees with this conclusion, and "that recent construction activities on these features, however extensive, cannot elevate their status from a rock to a fully-entitled island under Article 121." Wu, *A Legal Critique*, p. 207 (full cite above).

[1409] South China Sea Arbitration, Award, ¶ 578 (p. 238) (full cite above).

[1410] South China Sea Arbitration, Award, ¶ 584 (p. 240) (full cite above).

[1411] South China Sea Arbitration, Award, ¶¶ 585-586 (pp. 240-241) (full cite above).

[1412] South China Sea Arbitration, Award, ¶ 596 (p. 245) (full cite above).

[1413] South China Sea Arbitration, Award, ¶¶ 597-601 (pp. 245-246) (full cite above).

[1414] South China Sea Arbitration, Award, ¶ 614 (p. 250) (full cite above).

[1415] Permanent Court of Arbitration, Cases, Past Cases, [2013-19] The South China Sea Arbitration (*The Republic of Philippines v. The People's Republic of China*), Documents, Award (July 12, 2016) ¶¶ 602-609 (pp. 246-249), https://pcacases.com/web/sendAttach/2086.

[1416] South China Sea Arbitration, Award, ¶¶ 361, 612 (pp. 157, 249-250) (full cite above).

[1417] South China Sea Arbitration, Award, ¶ 616 (p. 251) (full cite above).

[1418] South China Sea Arbitration, Award, ¶ 618 (p. 252) (full cite above).

[1419] South China Sea Arbitration, Award, ¶¶ 619-620 (pp. 252-253) (full cite above).

[1420] South China Sea Arbitration, Award, ¶¶ 621-622 (p. 253) (full cite above). *But see* Shicun Wu, *A Legal Critique of the Award of the Arbitral Tribunal in the* Matter of the South China Sea Arbitration, *in* 24 ASIAN YEARBOOK OF INT'L. LAW 151, 214-221 (2020), https://brill.com/view/book/edcoll/9789004437784/BP000019.xml (criticizing the arbitral tribunal for "ignor[ing] some of the evidence before it ... [such as] the 39 evidentiary exhibits that had been provided by the Chinese (Taiwan) Society of International Law in its Amicus Curiae submission of 23 March 2016, which primarily related to human habitation and economic life on Itu Aba.").

[1421] Jiangyu Wang, *Legitimacy, Jurisdiction and Merits in the South China Sea Arbitration: Chinese Perspectives and International Law*, 22 J. OF CHINESE POLIT. SCI. 185, online p. 4 (2017), https://papers.ssrn.com/sol3/papers.cfm?abstract_id=2967254; Mark E. Rosen, *U.S. International Oceans Law and Policy Interests in the South China Sea Arbitration: Implications for the U.S. Administration in the South China Sea and Elsewhere*, 22 J. OF CHINESE POLIT. SCI. 251, online unnumbered p. 13 (2017), https://www.readcube.com/articles/10.1007/s11366-017-9468-9; Wu, *A Legal Critique*, pp. 191-192 (full cite above). *See also* SEAN D. MURPHY, INT'L. LAW RELATING TO ISLANDS 94 (2017) (noting that "[t]he [arbitral] tribunal's approach in deciding the case almost seems to impose a burden of proving that an island does not fall within Article 121, paragraph 3, rather than the other way around. Such a burden seems inconsistent with the structure of Article 121, which presents paragraph 3 as an exception to a general rule that all islands are entitled to full maritime zones."); universitätbonn institute for public int'l. law, Bonn Research Papers on Public Int'l. Law, Paper No 14/2018, *The South China Sea Arbitration: Observations on the Award of 12 July 2016*, pp. 87-91 (Stefan A. G. Talmon, May 17, 2018), https://papers.ssrn.com/sol3/papers.cfm?abstract_id=3180037 (positing that the arbitral tribunal's ruling exceeded what the Philippines had requested, and thus was *ultra petita* (i.e., beyond what was requested, or beyond the pleadings of the parties, and thus a question of law that the arbitral tribunal should not have made)).

[1422] *See, e.g.*, THE FLETCHER SCHOOL OF LAW AND DIPLOMACY—TUFTS UNIVERSITY, LAW OF THE SEA, A POLICY PRIMER 77 (2017), https://sites.tufts.edu/lawofthesea/introduction/ (noting that the U.S. Howland Island might not qualify as an Island under this rigorous standard). Howland Island is located in the Pacific, half-way between Hawaii and Australia, and consists entirely of the Howland Island National Wildlife Refuge. U.S. Fish and Wildlife Service, Howland Island National Wildlife Refuge | US Minor Outlying Islands, https://www.fws.gov/refuge/howland_island/. *See also* Jonathan G. Odom, *The Value and Viability of the South China Sea Arbitration Ruling: The U.S. Perspective 2016-2020*, 97 INT'L. L. STUD. 122, 169-177 (2021), https://digital-commons.usnwc.edu/ils/vol97/iss1/16/ (noting that the U.S. has neither made any official statements nor taken any official actions regarding the arbitral tribunal's determination that none of the disputed land features actually qualified as an Island, and opining that "[p]art of the reason for this noticeable silence might be the potential legal ramifications of this element of the tribunal's ruling if it were applied universally, including to [8 smaller and mostly uninhabited] U.S. islands remotely located in the Pacific Ocean. ... if one reviews ... publicly-available photographic images for each of the islands, they could reasonably conclude that, with the possible exception of Midway Atoll, none of these remote islands appear to be 'capable of human habitation or economic life.' ... The question is whether each of these islands is legally entitled to an EEZ. When considered together, the available evidence regarding the historical use, geographic size, remote nature, and physical conditions of these islands strongly suggest that the U.S. claim to an EEZ for some or all of them is questionable."); Wu, *A Legal Critique*, pp. 284-293 (full cite above) (providing 2 tables comparing Itu Aba to other "[s\mall features mutually recognized" or "unilaterally claimed as fully-entitled islands under Article 121(2) of UNCLOS"); Gerhard Hafner, *Some Remarks on the South China Sea Award: Itu Aba Versus Clipperton*, 34 CHINESE (TAIWAN) YEARBOOK OF INT'L. LAW & AFFAIRS 1, 10 (2016) (noting that "if applied universally, [the arbitral tribunal's reasoning] would imply that a large number of such high-tide elevations in the oceans should be stripped of their present EEZ and continental shelf entitlements."); Talmon, *Observations on the Award*, pp. 82-86 (full cite above) (providing tables of rocks and islets that would not satisfy the arbitral tribunal's requirements for an Island, and yet claim EEZs and continental shelves); Wang, *Legitimacy, Jurisdiction and Merits in the South China Sea Arbitration*, p. 24 (full cite above) (observing that "[a]s a matter of fact, there are indeed many islands in the world which support an independent economic life through 'relying predominantly on the infusion of outside resources,' Singapore and Hong Kong being such examples. The Jan Mayen conciliation offers another example.").

[1423] Rosen, *South China Sea Arbitration*, p. 8 (full cite above). *See also* Wang, *Legitimacy, Jurisdiction and Merits in the South China Sea Arbitration*, p. 25 (full cite above) (observing that the arbitral tribunal failed "to analyze contrary evidence, like the ample documentary and other evidence submitted in the *Amicus Curiae* [i.e., 'friend of the court' brief] by the Chinese (Taiwan) Society of International Law. Taiwan's *Amicus Curiae*, citing numerous books, reports, and other forms of empirical or scientific research, aimed to prove that the Taiping Island not only had a 'longstanding history of human habitation,' but also 'currently sustains the habitation of hundreds of people'.").

[1424] South China Sea Arbitration, Award, ¶ 401 (p. 179) (full cite above). *See also* Wu, *A Legal Critique*, pp. 284, 286 (full cite above).

[1425] South China Sea Arbitration, Award, ¶ 584 (p. 240) (full cite above). *But see* Wu, *A Legal Critique*, pp. 215-216 (full cite above), *citing* Myron H. Nordquist, *UNCLOS Article 121 and Itu Aba in the South China Sea Final Award: a correct interpretation?*, in THE SOUTH CHINA SEA ARBITRATION: THE LEGAL DIMENSION 176, 177-190 (S. Jayakumar, Tommy Koh, Robert Beckman, Tara Davenport & Hao D. Phan, eds., 2018), https://www.e-elgar.com/shop/usd/the-south-china-sea-arbitration-9781788116268.html (noting that "as Professor Nordquist has observed, no reference is made to water at all in the text of Article 121(3), nor was any meaningful discussion held about the presence (or not) of water as a relevant during its negotiation. Also, ... it is clear that many fully-entitled island features generating EEZ entitlements do not host potable freshwater, still less sufficient freshwater up to 'modern standards' to support a human population. ... the Tribunal's assessment of the evidence of potable freshwater on Itu Aba was also lacking. For example, it did not even address the evidence before it as to the substantial volume of drinkable water available on Itu Aba, and the hundreds of people that were reliant on it during certain periods. In particular, the Tribunal ignored the evidence submitted by the Chinese (Taiwan) Society of International Law with its Amicus Curiae submission, including evidence from the Water Quality On-site Survey stating that the quality of the groundwater drawn from the four wells has been proved to be suitable for daily human use, and in particular, the quality of the water drawn from Well No. 5 is suitable for drinking."); *Amicus Curiae* Submission by the Chinese (Taiwan) Society of International Law on the Issue of the Feature of Taiping Island (Itu Aba) Pursuant to Articles 121(1) and (3) of UNCLOS, South China Sea Arbitration, pp. 13-15 (Mar. 23, 2016), http://www.assidmer.net/doc/SCSTF-Amicus-Curiae-Brief-final.pdf (noting that "Taiping Island has an abundant supply of groundwater. Scientific studies of the Holocene geology of Taiping Island ('Geological On-site Survey') indicate that due to the porous nature of bioclastic sands and the coral reef underneath, Taiping Island has a permanent freshwater lens. The Geological On-site Survey notes that for decades, more than 100 marines or coast guard personnel have lived on the island, relying on groundwater because the fresh water is easily replenished by precipitation, which averages 1800-2200 mm per year. It is estimated that 0.9-1.1 million cubic meters of rainwater fall on the island per year. Currently, there are four groundwater wells operating on Taiping Island (Well Nos. 5, 9, 10, and 11), with Well No. 5 being the main groundwater well supplying drinking water. According to a field scientific survey conducted on 22 and 23 January 2016 ('Water Quality On-site Survey'), based on the observation of rainwater infiltration to the aquifer storage, it is estimated that the total quantity of groundwater supplied by the aforementioned four wells could reach 237,000 tons per year. Among those wells, one well is used for cultivating tilapia, and Well No. 5 alone supplies 2 to 3 tons of drinking water per day, while Well No.7 can supply 42 tons, and Well No. 10 supplies 20 tons of water per day. That means the wells can supply a total of 65 tons of water, including drinking water, per day. Based on the average amount of drinking water required per person per day (i.e. 2,000 c.c.), Well No. 5 alone could supply drinking water to as many as 1,000 to 1,500 persons every day. According to the Water Quality On-site Survey, the quality of the groundwater drawn from the four wells has been proved to be suitable for daily human use, and in particular, the quality of the water drawn from Well No. 5 is suitable for drinking. The temperature of the groundwater from the four wells ranges from 26.9 °C to 29.3 °C, and the pH is fairly stable at 7.3 to 7.7. The salinity of the water from Well No. 5 was lower than 1‰, while the other three wells measured between 1‰ and 3‰, far below the average salinity of 33‰ to 35‰ of sea water, making the water from all four (4) groundwater wells usable for cleaning, sanitation, and cultivation. For Well No. 5 in particular, the total dissolved solids content (results obtained from two samplings are at 427 mg/L and 418 mg/L, respectively, close to the quality of Evian, brand bottled water, one of the most well-known brands of natural mineral water in the world, at 330 mg/L.50) meet the ROC's Drinking Water Quality Standards and Standard of the Drinking Water Source. Such results also pass various standards/definitions of fresh water provided by different renowned institutions, such as Practical Fishkeeping (which defines freshwater as water which contains total dissolved solids of less than 3,000 mg/L), the American Meteorological Society and the US Geological Survey (1,000 mg/L), and the Groundwater Foundation (USA) (500 mg/L). Therefore, the fresh water supplied by Well No. 5 is indisputably

490

suitable for drinking. In comparison, the Water Quality On-site Survey results show that the quality of water supplied by Well No. 5 on Taiping Island is even better than that of Penghu Island (Pescadores, 澎湖), another island appertaining to the ROC (Taiwan), which is currently home to approximately 100,000 residents. In fact, quality freshwater on Taiping Island has been recorded and attested to by a great deal of historical documentary evidence, including the China Sea Directory in 1879 and Asiatic Pilot in 1925, all evidencing that the water found in the wells on Taiping Island is suitable for drinking, and that its quality is superior to water in other locations. In 1937, a Japanese government official, Hitoshi Hiratsuka (平塚均), was sent to Taiping Island and recorded that out of the four wells on the Island, one well can supply about 10 tons of drinking water per day. Osaka Asahi Newspapers in 1939 also reported that drinking water was available a long time ago on Taiping Island, and fishermen used to visit the Island to obtain drinking water during sailing trips. Historical documentary evidence also shows that Taiping Island had a freshwater supply when the ROC government took over, and thereby recovered Taiping Island in 1946.).

    [1426] *But see* Shicun Wu, *A Legal Critique of the Award of the Arbitral Tribunal in the Matter of the South China Sea Arbitration, in* 24 ASIAN YEARBOOK OF INT'L. LAW 151, 217-218 (2020), https://brill.com/view/book/edcoll/9789004437784/BP000019.xml, *citing Amicus Curiae* Submission by the Chinese (Taiwan) Society of International Law, pp. 13-15 (full cite above) (noting that "the Tribunal had before it (but made no reference to) evidence presented of livestock being raised in modern times on Itu Aba, showing that locally raised 'goats, chickens, and eggs are a source of food for people on the island' ... [and that] "Personnel stationed on the island have long utilized all types of resources on the island and cultivated various tropical vegetables and fruits, including staple foods such as corn and sweet potato as well as 10 other types such as okra, pumpkin, loofah gourd, bitter melon, and cabbage.").

    [1427] *But see* Wu, *A Legal Critique*, pp. 220-221 (full cite above) (noting that "the Tribunal ignored the fact that the most substantial historical population appears to have abandoned Itu Aba as a result of an "intervening force", in the form of World War II").

    [1428] Permanent Court of Arbitration, Cases, Past Cases, [2013-19] The South China Sea Arbitration (*The Republic of Philippines v. The People's Republic of China*), Documents, Award (July 12, 2016) ¶¶ 624 & 1203.B(7) (pp. 254 & 474), https://pcacases.com/web/sendAttach/2086.

    [1429] South China Sea Arbitration, Award, ¶¶ 708 & 1203.B(8) (pp. 282 & 474) (full cite above). *See also* Raul (Pete) Pedrozo, *Maritime Police Law of the People's Republic of China*, 97 INT'L. L. STUD. 465, 466-468 (2021), https://digital-commons.usnwc.edu/ils/vol97/iss1/24/ (noting that "the Maritime Police Law of the People's Republic of China (MPL), which took effect on February 1, 2021 ... authorize[s] the use of the [Chinese coastal police agencies (CCG)] to protect survey vessels (e.g., *Haiyang Dizhi* 8) or oil rigs (e.g., *Hai Yang Shi You* 981) engaged in hydrocarbon exploration in foreign EEZs and continental shelves ... [which] would interfere with the sovereign resource rights of other nations and would directly violate UNCLOS.").

    [1430] South China Sea Arbitration, Award, ¶ 712 (p. 284) (full cite above). *See also* Pedrozo, *Maritime Police Law of the People's Republic of China*, pp. 476-477 (full cite above) (noting that "China does not have a good track record when it comes to observing the rules-based international legal order when conducting maritime law enforcement activities. The CCG has repeatedly harassed and engaged in excessive use of force against Vietnamese, Japanese, and Filipino fishermen to advance China's illegal claims in the [East China Sea] and [South China Sea] and unlawfully deny access to offshore resources in coastal State EEZs.").

[1431] Permanent Court of Arbitration, Cases, Past Cases, [2013-19] The South China Sea Arbitration (*The Republic of Philippines v. The People's Republic of China*), Documents, Award (July 12, 2016) ¶¶ 757 & 1203.B(10) (pp. 297 & 475), https://pcacases.com/web/sendAttach/2086. China specifically builds and mans its fishing boats for military confrontation: "The Hainan provincial government, adjacent to the South China Sea, ordered the building of 84 large militia fishing vessels with reinforced hulls and ammunition storage, which the militia received by the end of 2016, along with extensive subsidies to encourage frequent operations in the Spratly Islands. This particular [People's Armed Forces Maritime Militia] unit is also China's most professional. Its forces are paid salaries independent of any clear commercial fishing responsibilities and recruited from recently separated veterans." U.S. Dept. of Defense, Office of the Secretary of Defense, *Annual Report To Congress: Military and Security Developments Involving the People's Republic of China 2020*, p. 72, https://media.defense.gov/2020/Sep/01/2002488689/-1/-1/1/2020-DOD-CHINA-MILITARY-POWER-REPORT-FINAL.PDF. *See also* Center for International Maritime Security (CIMSEC), Asia-Pacific Capability Analysis, *Riding A New Wave of Professionalization and Militarization: Sansha City's Maritime Militia* (Conor Kennedy, Sep. 1, 2016), https://cimsec.org/riding-new-wave-professionalization-militarization-sansha-citys-maritime-militia/27689 (noting the Chinese "introduction of new classes of vessels with dedicated weapons and ammunition storage rooms, reinforced [steel] hulls, and water cannons. Significantly, the Sansha Maritime Militia is being created from scratch using personnel that receive extremely generous guaranteed salaries—seemingly independent of any fishing or marine industrial activity on their part, a dedicated arrangement that we have not seen elsewhere."). These large, reinforced steel-hulled militia fishing vessels are most accurately classified as "government ships operated for non-commercial purposes." United Nations Convention on the Law of the Sea (UNCLOS) art. 32, Dec. 10, 1982, 1833 U.N.T.S. 397, https://www.un.org/Depts/los/convention_agreements/convention_overview_co nvention.htm; U.S. NAVY, MARINE CORPS & COAST GUARD, THE COMMANDER'S HANDBOOK ON THE LAW OF NAVAL OPERATIONS, NWP 1-14M/MCTP 11-10B/COMDTPUB P5800.7A, ¶ 2.3.1 (p. 2-3) (2017), www.jag.navy.mil/distrib/instructions/CDRs_HB_on_Law_of_Naval_Operations _AUG17.pdf; Rob McLaughlin, *An Incident in the South China Sea*, 96 INT'L. L. STUD. 505, 516-518 (2020), https://digital-commons.usnwc.edu/ils/vol96/iss1/16/.

[1432] South China Sea Arbitration, Award, ¶¶ 814 & 1203.B(11) (pp. 318 & 475) (full cite above). *See also* THE FLETCHER SCHOOL OF LAW AND DIPLOMACY—TUFTS UNIVERSITY, LAW OF THE SEA, A POLICY PRIMER 75 (2017), https://sites.tufts.edu/lawofthesea/introduction/ (describing the 2012 standoff on Scarborough Shoal between the Philippines and China).

[1433] South China Sea Arbitration, Award, ¶ 966 (p. 384) (full cite above). *See also* Raul (Pete) Pedrozo, *Maritime Police Law of the People's Republic of China*, 97 INT'L. L. STUD. 465, 466-468 (2021), https://digital-commons.usnwc.edu/ils/vol97/iss1/24/ (noting that "the Maritime Police Law of the People's Republic of China (MPL), which took effect on February 1, 2021 ... authorize[s] the use of the [Chinese coastal police agencies (CCG)] to ... protect Chinese fishing vessels engaged in illegal, unreported, and unregulated fishing in the [South China Sea] ... [which] would interfere with the sovereign resource rights of other nations and would directly violate UNCLOS.").

1434 South China Sea Arbitration, Award, ¶ 983 (p. 394) (full cite above).

1435 South China Sea Arbitration, Award, ¶ 1037 (pp. 414-415) (full cite above).

1436 Int'l. Maritime Organization (IMO), English, About IMO, Conventions, List of Conventions, Convention on the Int'l. Regulations for Preventing Collisions at Sea, 1972 (COLREGs), http://www.imo.org/en/About/Conventions/ListOfConventions/Pages/COLREG.aspx.

1437 South China Sea Arbitration, Award, ¶¶ 1109 & 1203.B(15) (pp. 435 & 476) (full cite above).

1438 "An attack by the [Chinese coastal police agencies (CCG)] on Philippine military forces in the SCS at Second Thomas Shoal or Scarborough Shoal would ... invoke U.S. defense obligations under Articles IV and V of the U.S.-Philippines Mutual Defense Treaty (MDT)." Pedrozo, *Maritime Police Law of the People's Republic of China*, p. 469 (full cite above).

1439 South China Sea Arbitration, Award, ¶¶ 1161-1162 (p. 456) (full cite above).

1440 South China Sea Arbitration, Award, ¶ 1177 (p. 462) (full cite above).

1441 South China Sea Arbitration, Award, ¶ 1178 (pp. 462-463) (full cite above).

1442 South China Sea Arbitration, Award, ¶ 1179 (p. 463) (full cite above).

1443 Vienna Convention on the Law of Treaties (VCLT) art. 26, May 23, 1969, 1155 U.N.T.S. 331 (providing the treaty maxim *pacta sunt servanda*: "Every treaty in force is binding upon the parties to it and must be performed by them in good faith."). Put simply: agreements must be kept. *See also* Dept. of Defense Law of War Manual § 1.10.1.1, p. 36 (June 2015, updated Dec. 2016), https://www.hsdl.org/?view&did=797480. Although the United States is not a party to the VCLT, it considers the VCLT to represent customary international law. Sean D. Murphy, The George Wash. Univ. Law Sch.: "Should the U.S. Join the International Criminal Court?" A Moderated Panel Discussion, Feb. 13, 2006. *See also* Letter Of Transmittal Forwarding The 1982 UN Law Of The Sea Convention To The United States Senate, DOS Commentary p. 17 (William J. Clinton, Oct. 7, 1994) (S. Treaty Doc. 103-39), https://www.foreign.senate.gov/imo/media/doc/treaty_103-39.pdf (noting that "[u]nder customary international law, as reflected in ... the Vienna Convention on the Law of Treaties (92nd Congress; 1st Session, Senate Executive 'L')"). The treaty maxim *pacta sunt servanda* is implicit in UNCLOS Article 300: "States Parties shall fulfil in good faith the obligations assumed under this Convention...." DOS Commentary, p. 93 (full cite above).

1444 South China Sea Arbitration, Award, ¶ 1195 (p. 467) (full cite above).

1445 South China Sea Arbitration, Award, ¶ 1200 (p. 468) (full cite above).

1446 COMMANDER'S HANDBOOK, Preface (p. 17) (full cite above).

1447 Foreign Minister for the People's Republic of China, the South China Sea Issue, *Vice Foreign Minister Liu Zhenmin at the Press Conference on the White Paper Titled China Adheres to the Position of Settling Through Negotiation the Relevant Disputes Between China and the Philippines in the South China Sea*, https://www.fmprc.gov.cn/nanhai/eng/wjbxw_1/t1381980.htm.

1448 National Public Radio (NPR), WAMU 88.5, American University Radio, Parallels—Many Stories, One World, Conflict Zones, *A Primer on the Complicated Battle for the South China Sea* (Rami Ayyub, Apr. 13, 2016), https://www.npr.org/sections/parallels/2016/04/13/472711435/a-primer-on-the-complicated-battle-for-the-south-china-sea. *See also* THE FLETCHER SCHOOL OF LAW AND DIPLOMACY—TUFTS UNIVERSITY, LAW OF THE SEA, A POLICY PRIMER 71 (2017), https://sites.tufts.edu/lawofthesea/introduction/ (noting that "[h]istory has taught that despite having a "binding" effect between the parties, enforcing these rulings can be difficult. China has refused to comply with rulings against it in the SCS case, and there are no easy ways to enforce compliance. When a great power loses in an international dispute, ... there is no effective enforcement mechanism. Other powerful countries are usually reluctant to intervene."); The Diplomat, The Debate, *Of Course China, Like All Great Powers, Will Ignore an International Legal Verdict* (Graham Allison, July 11, 2016), https://thediplomat.com/2016/07/of-course-china-like-all-great-powers-will-ignore-an-international-legal-verdict/ (noting that "no permanent member of the UN Security Council has ever complied with a ruling by the PCA on an issue involving the Law of the Sea. In fact, none of the five permanent members of the UN Security Council have ever accepted any international court's ruling when (in their view) it infringed their sovereignty or national security interests. Thus, when China rejects the Court's decision in this case, it will be doing just what the other great powers have repeatedly done for decades. ... In the Nicaragua case, when the [ICJ] found in favor of Nicaragua and ordered the United States to pay reparations, the U.S. refused, and vetoed six UN Security Council resolutions ordering it to comply with the court's ruling. U.S. Ambassador to the UN Jeane Kirkpatrick aptly summed up Washington's view of the matter when she dismissed the court as a 'semi-legal, semi-juridical, semi-political body, which nations sometimes accept and sometimes don't.' Observing what permanent members of the Security Council do, as opposed to what they say, it is hard to disagree with realist's claim that the PCA and its siblings in The Hague – the International Courts of Justice and the International Criminal Court – are only for small powers. Great powers do not recognize the jurisdiction of these courts – except in particular cases where they believe it is in their interest to do so. Thucydides' summary of the Melian mantra – 'the strong do as they will; the weak suffer as they must' – may exaggerate. But this week, when the Court finds against China, expect Beijing to do as great powers have traditionally done.").

[1449] Jonathan G. Odom, *The Value and Viability of the South China Sea Arbitration Ruling: The U.S. Perspective 2016–2020*, 97 INT'L. L. STUD. 122, 178-179 (2021), https://digital-commons.usnwc.edu/ils/vol97/iss1/16/.

[1450] Mark E. Rosen, *U.S. International Oceans Law and Policy Interests in the South China Sea Arbitration: Implications for the U.S. Administration in the South China Sea and Elsewhere*, 22 J. OF CHINESE POLIT. SCI. 251, online unnumbered pp. 1-2 & 15 (2017), https://www.readcube.com/articles/10.1007/s11366-017-9468-9. *See* *also* Brookings Institution, Global China, *How China's Actions in the South China Sea Undermine the Rule of Law*, p. 9 (Lynn Kuok, November 2019), https://www.brookings.edu/research/how-chinas-actions-in-the-south-china-sea-undermine-the-rule-of-law/.

[1451] Brookings Institution, *How China's Actions ... Undermine the Rule of Law*, p. 7 (full cite above). However, the Philippines "did not give up the arbitration ruling, and it continues to bring it up when it sees fit in dealing with neighboring countries." Maritime Issues, International Law, *Extended Continental Shelf: A Renewed South China Sea Competition* (Nguyen Hong Thao, Apr. 19, 2020), http://www.maritimeissues.com/law/extended-continental-shelf-a-renewed-south-china-sea-competition.html. *See also* CNN, World, Asia, *Philippine foreign minister tells China to 'Get the F**k Out' over South China Sea dispute* (May 3, 2021), https://www.cnn.com/2021/05/03/asia/philippines-locsin-profanity-south-china-sea-intl-hnk/index.html?utm_term=16201234757502df0f657850a&utm_source=cnn_Five+Things+for+Tuesday%2C+May+4%2C+2021&utm_medium=email&bt_ee=S%2BSHFotu2rPWafvZxkBDS9oH6Yfqf3AR7P5k56gUhPZYzUOx%2FwTyW4xlxpIV3mDp&bt_ts=1620123475752 (reporting that the Philippine foreign minister tweeted "China, my friend, how politely can I put it? Let me see... O...GET THE F**K OUT".).

[1452] Rosen, *South China Sea Arbitration*, p. 10 (full cite above); Brookings Institution, *How China's Actions ... Undermine the Rule of Law*, p. 4 (full cite above); Asia Maritime Transparency Initiative, *A Philippine-China Deal on Joint Development in the Making?* (Renato Cruz de Castro, Nov. 3, 2020), https://amti.csis.org/a-philippine-china-deal-on-joint-development-in-the-making/.

[1453] Maritime Issues, *Extended Continental Shelf: A Renewed South China Sea Competition* (full cite above) (noting that China "continues the position of three no(s), namely: do not participate; do not accept the jurisdiction of the Tribunal; and do not recognize the arbitration award"). The arbitral tribunal's decision may "have also helped fan nationalism in China, strengthening the belief of realism and power politics in international relations. From the very beginning, the SCS arbitration has been depicted in China as a U.S.-led conspiracy to contain China. It is not difficult for conspiracy theories like this to find audience in China, as the public in China has a very strong victim mentality with respect to China's relations with the international society, especially the Western world.... [T]he 'counterproductive effect of the award is to stir up Chinese nationalism while undermining moderate voices represented by professional diplomats.'" Jiangyu Wang, *Legitimacy, Jurisdiction and Merits in the South China Sea Arbitration: Chinese Perspectives and International Law*, 22 J. OF CHINESE POLIT. SCI. 185, online p. 27 (2017), https://papers.ssrn.com/sol3/papers.cfm?abstract_id=2967254.

[1454] Brookings Institution, *How China's Actions ... Undermine the Rule of Law*, p. 2 (full cite above). *See also* Wang, *Legitimacy, Jurisdiction and Merits in the South China Sea Arbitration*, p. 4 (full cite above) (noting that "China has portrayed the arbitral institution as a 'law-abusing tribunal' who has issued an 'ill-founded' award that 'abuses international law [and] threatens world order'.").

[1455] Brookings Institution, *How China's Actions ... Undermine the Rule of Law*, pp. 5-6 & 9 (full cite above).

[1456] Unsurprisingly, the "independent" legal critique concluded that "our analysis indicates that there are substantial grounds to question the validity of most of the [arbitral] Tribunal's central findings of jurisdiction and merits in the Award." Shicun Wu, *A Legal Critique of the Award of the Arbitral Tribunal in the Matter of the South China Sea Arbitration*, *in* 24 ASIAN YEARBOOK OF INT'L. LAW 151 (2020), https://brill.com/view/book/edcoll/9789004437784/BP000019.xml. *See also* Nat'l. Institute for South China Sea Studies (NISCSS), About Us, Introduction, http://en.nanhai.org.cn/index/survey/index.html.

[1457] ASIAN YEARBOOK OF INT'L. LAW (Seokwoo Lee & Hee Eun Lee, eds., 2020), https://brill.com/view/serial/AYIL.

[1458] Raul (Pete) Pedrozo, *China's Revised Maritime Traffic Safety Law*, 97 INT'L. L. STUD. 956, 967-968 (2021), https://digital-commons.usnwc.edu/ils/vol97/iss1/39/.

[1459] Brookings Institution, *How China's Actions ... Undermine the Rule of Law*, p. 2 (full cite above). *See also* Wang, *Legitimacy, Jurisdiction and Merits in the South China Sea Arbitration*, pp. 1, 3 (full cite above) (noting that "[o]ne of the most significant events in China's history of engaging international law was its legal defeat in the

South China Sea Arbitration case," and the arbitral tribunal's ruling "deal[t] China a complete defeat in the case.").

[1460] Maritime Issues, International Law, *Extended Continental Shelf: A Renewed South China Sea Competition* (Nguyen Hong Thao, Apr. 19, 2020), http://www.maritimeissues.com/law/extended-continental-shelf-a-renewed-south-china-sea-competition.html (citing a 2020 Chinese *note verbale* as saying: "China and the Philippines have reached consensus on properly addressing issues on the South China Sea arbitration and have returned to the right track of settling maritime issues through bilateral friendly negotiation and consultation.").

[1461] Jonathan G. Odom, *The Value and Viability of the South China Sea Arbitration Ruling: The U.S. Perspective 2016–2020*, 97 INT'L. L. STUD. 122, 152 (2021), https://digital-commons.usnwc.edu/ils/vol97/iss1/16/.

[1462] United Nations Convention on the Law of the Sea (UNCLOS) art. 296(2), Dec. 10, 1982, 1833 U.N.T.S. 397, https://www.un.org/Depts/los/convention_agreements/convention_overview_convention.htm; Permanent Court of Arbitration, Cases, Past Cases, [2013-19] The South China Sea Arbitration (*The Republic of Philippines v. The People's Republic of China*), Documents, Award (July 12, 2016) ¶ 637 (p. 257), https://pcacases.com/web/sendAttach/2086; THE FLETCHER SCHOOL OF LAW AND DIPLOMACY—TUFTS UNIVERSITY, LAW OF THE SEA, A POLICY PRIMER 71 (2017), https://sites.tufts.edu/lawofthesea/introduction/.

[1463] Then-President Trump even offered to help resolve the South China Sea dispute between Vietnam and China: "South China Sea, as you know, we're looking at; we're looking at it together. If I could help mediate or arbitrate, please let me know. And you've had a dispute for quite a while with China. If I can help in any way, I'm a very good mediator and a very good arbitrator. I have done plenty of it from both sides. So if I can help you, let me know." UC Santa Barbara, The American Presidency Project, Documents, *Remarks Prior to a Meeting With President Tran Dai Quang of Vietnam in Hanoi, Vietnam* (Nov. 12, 2017), https://www.presidency.ucsb.edu/documents/remarks-prior-meeting-with-president-tran-dai-quang-vietnam-hanoi-vietnam.

[1464] Odom, *The Value and Viability of the South China Sea Arbitration Ruling*, p. 129 (full cite above).

[1465] Maritime Issues, *Extended Continental Shelf: A Renewed South China Sea Competition* (full cite above).

[1466] United Nations, Division for Ocean Affairs and the Law of the Sea, Commission on the Limits of the Continental Shelf (CLCS), Submissions, through the Secretary-General of the United Nations, to the Commission on the Limits of the Continental Shelf, pursuant to article 76, paragraph 8, of the United Nations Convention on the Law of the Sea of 10 December 1982, https://www.un.org/Depts/los/clcs_new/commission_submissions.htm; DONALD R. ROTHWELL & TIM STEPHENS, THE INT'L. LAW OF THE SEA 103 (2nd ed. 2016).

[1467] United Nations, Division for Ocean Affairs and the Law of the Sea, Commission on the Limits of the Continental Shelf (CLCS), https://www.un.org/Depts/los/clcs_new/clcs_home.htm.

[1468] TUFTS, LAW OF THE SEA, pp. 61-62 (full cite above).

[1469] The Diplomat, Flashpoints, Security, Southeast Asia, *Malaysia's New Game in the South China Sea* (Nguyen Hong Thao, Dec. 21, 2019), https://thediplomat.com/2019/12/malaysias-new-game-in-the-south-china-sea/.

[1470] The Diplomat, *Malaysia's New Game in the South China Sea* (full cite above). Vietnam also implicitly rejects China's "9-dash line" claim. In fact, "[m]ost of the claimants, except China and Brunei, through their statements and actions, expressed acceptance and support for the 2016 Tribunal Award." Maritime Issues, *Extended Continental Shelf: A Renewed South China Sea Competition* (full cite above).

[1471] "Since the arbitration ruling, China has downplayed its rhetoric on the nine-dash line in official media. ... China rejected the ruling and, immediately after it, issued a Government Statement, a Foreign Ministry Statement, and a White Paper to state its position on maritime disputes with the Philippines. In these documents, China deemphasized the nine-dash line but, for the first time, expressly and unambiguously claimed 'historic rights in the South China Sea.' ... China has adjusted talking points to exclude references to the claimed 'nine-dash line,' probably to avoid taking a position that directly opposes the ruling and risks additional regional backlash." U.S. Dept. of Defense, Office of the Secretary of Defense, *Annual Report To Congress: Military and Security Developments Involving the People's Republic of China 2017*, pp. 8-9, 41, https://dod.defense.gov/Portals/1/Documents/pubs/2017_China_Military_Power_Report.PDF.

[1472] Maritime Issues, *Extended Continental Shelf: A Renewed South China Sea Competition* (full cite above); South China Morning Post, China, Diplomacy, *Beijing urges UN commission not to consider Malaysian claim in South China Sea* (Laura Zhou, Dec. 17, 2019), https://www.scmp.com/news/china/diplomacy/article/3042333/beijing-urges-un-commission-not-consider-malaysian-claim-south. The U.S. responded to China's *note verbale* by "urg[ing] China to conform its maritime claims to international law as reflected in the [LOS] Convention; to comply with the Tribunal's July 12, 2016 decision; and to cease its provocative activities in the South China Sea." United States Mission to the United Nations, *Protesting China's Unlawful Maritime Claims at the UN* (June 1, 2020), https://usun.usmission.gov/protesting-chinas-unlawful-maritime-claims-at-the-un/.

[1473] United Nations, Division for Ocean Affairs and the Law of the Sea, Commission on the Limits of the Continental Shelf (CLCS), Partial Submission by Malaysia in the South China Sea, https://www.un.org/Depts/los/clcs_new/submissions_files/submission_mys_12_12_2019.html.

[1474] Mark E. Rosen, *U.S. International Oceans Law and Policy Interests in the South China Sea Arbitration: Implications for the U.S. Administration in the South China Sea and Elsewhere*, 22 J. OF CHINESE POLIT. SCI. 251, online unnumbered p. 14 (2017), https://www.readcube.com/articles/10.1007/s11366-017-9468-9.

[1475] Rosen, *South China Sea Arbitration*, p. 14 (full cite above).

[1476] Rosen, *South China Sea Arbitration*, p. 13 (full cite above).

[1477] Brookings Institution, Global China, *How China's Actions in the South China Sea Undermine the Rule of Law*, p. 1 (Lynn Kuok, November 2019), https://www.brookings.edu/research/how-chinas-actions-in-the-south-china-sea-undermine-the-rule-of-law/.

[1478] John Norton Moore, *Navigational Freedom: The Most Critical Common Heritage*, 93 INT'L. L. STUD. 251, 253 (2017), https://digital-commons.usnwc.edu/ils/vol93/iss1/8/.

[1479] Brookings Institution, *How China's Actions ... Undermine the Rule of Law*, p. 9 (full cite above).

[1480] U.S. Department of State, Press Statement, Secretary of State, *U.S. Position on Maritime Claims in the South China Sea* (Michael R. Pompeo, July 13, 2020), https://www.state.gov/u-s-position-on-maritime-claims-in-the-south-china-sea/.

[1481] CNN Politics, *US declares 'most' of China's maritime claims in South China Sea illegal* (Jennifer Hansler, July 14, 2020), https://www.cnn.com/2020/07/13/politics/south-china-sea-pompeo-announcement/index.html. *See also* The Diplomat, Flashpoints, Risk Intelligence, Security, Southeast Asia, *The US Announces a New Position on Maritime Claims in the South China Sea: First Takeaways* (Ankit Panda, July 14, 2020), https://thediplomat.com/2020/07/the-us-announces-a-new-position-on-maritime-claims-in-the-south-china-sea-first-takeaways/ (same).

[1482] CNN, *US declares 'most' of China's maritime claims in South China Sea illegal* (full cite above); CNN, *Tensions heat up in South China Sea as US makes significant show of force* (Brad Lendon, July 6, 2020), https://edition.cnn.com/2020/07/06/asia/south-china-sea-aircraft-carriers-intl-hnk-scli/index.html; The Drive, The War Zone, *Here Are Photos Of Two U.S. Navy Carriers In The South China Sea For First Time In Six Years* (Joseph Trevithick, July 6, 2020), https://www.thedrive.com/the-war-zone/34598/here-are-photos-of-two-u-s-navy-carriers-in-the-south-china-sea-for-first-time-in-six-years; Military.com, Military News, *Navy Admirals Reject Beijing's Claim that Dual-Carrier Drills in South China Sea Were 'Symbolic'* (Caitlin Doornbos, Feb. 11, 2021), https://www.military.com/daily-news/2021/02/11/navy-admirals-reject-beijings-claim-dual-carrier-drills-south-china-sea-were-symbolic.html?ESRC=eb_210212.nl.

[1483] The Drive, *Here Are Photos Of Two U.S. Navy Carriers In The South China Sea For First Time In Six Years* (full cite above).

[1484] Mark E. Rosen, *U.S. International Oceans Law and Policy Interests in the South China Sea Arbitration: Implications for the U.S. Administration in the South China Sea and Elsewhere*, 22 J. OF CHINESE POLIT. SCI. 251, online unnumbered p. 10 (2017), https://www.readcube.com/articles/10.1007/s11366-017-9468-9.

[1485] Brookings Institution, Global China, *How China's Actions in the South China Sea Undermine the Rule of Law*, p. 8 (Lynn Kuok, November 2019), https://www.brookings.edu/research/how-chinas-actions-in-the-south-china-sea-undermine-the-rule-of-law/. *See also* Ronald Reagan Presidential Library & Museum, Statement on United States Ocean Policy (Mar. 10, 1983), https://www.reaganlibrary.gov/research/speeches/31083c; U.S. NAVY, MARINE CORPS & COAST GUARD, THE COMMANDER'S HANDBOOK ON THE LAW OF NAVAL OPERATIONS, NWP 1-14M/MCTP 11-10B/COMDTPUB P5800.7A, ¶ 2.8 (p. 2-15) (2017), www.jag.navy.mil/distrib/instructions/CDRs_HB_on_Law_of_Naval_Operations_AUG17.pdf.

[1486] Brookings Institution, Center for East Asia Policy Studies, East Asia Policy Paper 9, *The U.S. FON Program in the South China Sea—A lawful and necessary response to China's strategic ambiguity*, p. iii (Lynn Kuok, June 2016), https://www.brookings.edu/research/the-u-s-fon-program-in-the-south-china-sea/.

[1487] Rosen, *South China Sea Arbitration*, p. 11 (full cite above).

[1488] New York University School of Law, Institute for International Law and Justice, *International Law in a Biden Administration*, p. 6 (José Alvarez, Nov. 2020), https://www.iilj.org/publications/international-law-in-a-biden-administration/.

1489 *Cf.* This Week in Asia, Opinion, *On South China Sea, expect more of the same from US President Joe Biden* (Ding Duo, Dec. 8, 2020), https://www.scmp.com/week-asia/opinion/article/3112866/south-china-sea-expect-more-same-us-president-joe-biden; VN Express International, News, *Biden's US to remain active in South China Sea, but confront China less: analysts* (Viet Anh, Nov. 21, 2020), https://e.vnexpress.net/news/news/biden-s-us-to-remain-active-in-south-china-sea-but-confront-china-less-analysts-4193381.html; National Review, World, *Why Beijing Hopes for a Biden Win* (Helen Raleigh, Nov. 2, 2020), https://www.nationalreview.com/2020/11/why-beijing-hopes-for-a-biden-win/#slide-1; Medium, Frame of Reference, *Weighing the South China Sea Dispute Under Trump or Biden Leadership* (Jhemmylrut Teng, Oct 30, 2020), https://medium.com/frame-of-reference/weighing-the-south-china-sea-dispute-under-trump-or-biden-leadership-107fa1fb735d.

1490 CNN, Asia, *US steps up challenges to Chinese-claimed islands in South China Sea* (Brad Lendon, Feb. 17, 2021), https://www.cnn.com/2021/02/17/asia/us-navy-south-china-sea-freedom-of-navigation-intl-hnk/index.html. Although these Naval operations were undoubtedly planned well in advance of President Biden's term, he could have stopped them from occurring.

1491 Jonathan G. Odom, *The Value and Viability of the South China Sea Arbitration Ruling: The U.S. Perspective 2016–2020*, 97 INT'L. L. STUD. 122, 182-183 (2021), https://digital-commons.usnwc.edu/ils/vol97/iss1/16/.

1492 American Military News, China, *Biden announces new DOD 'China Task Force' – here are the details and who's leading it* (Laura Widener, Feb. 10, 2021), https://americanmilitarynews.com/2021/02/biden-announces-new-dod-china-task-force-here-are-the-details-and-whos-leading-it/.

1493 U.S. Department of Defense, News, Defense News, *China Task Force Begins Work; DOD Makes Progress on COVID-19* (Jim Garamone, Mar. 1, 2021), https://www.defense.gov/Explore/News/Article/Article/2519254/china-task-force-begins-work-dod-makes-progress-on-covid-19/.

1494 United Nations Convention on the Law of the Sea (UNCLOS) Preamble, Dec. 10, 1982, 1833 U.N.T.S. 397, https://www.un.org/Depts/los/convention_agreements/convention_overview_convention.htm.

1495 Any reader interested in learning more about the Law of the Sea may wish to consider attending courses at the following institutions:
1) International Maritime Law Institute, Malta: https://imli.org/;
2) University of New Hampshire, School of Marine Science and Ocean Engineering, Rhodes Academy of Oceans Law and Policy, https://marine.unh.edu/academics/rhodes-academy; and
3) World Maritime University, Malmo, Sweden: https://www.wmu.se/.

CPSIA information can be obtained
at www.ICGtesting.com
Printed in the USA
LVHW071638020822
725001LV00001B/1